# MARSHALLING
## THE FAITHFUL

*Berkley Caliber Books by Charles W. Henderson*

SILENT WARRIOR

MARINE SNIPER

MARSHALLING THE FAITHFUL

GOODNIGHT SAIGON

# MARSHALLING
## THE FAITHFUL

The Marines' First Year in Vietnam

# CHARLES W. HENDERSON

A BERKLEY CALIBER BOOK
NEW YORK

**THE BERKLEY PUBLISHING GROUP**
**Published by the Penguin Group**
**Penguin Group (USA) Inc.**
**375 Hudson Street, New York, New York 10014, USA**
Penguin Group (Canada), 90 Eglinton Avenue East, Suite 700, Toronto, Ontario M4P 2Y3, Canada
(a division of Pearson Penguin Canada Inc.)
Penguin Books Ltd., 80 Strand, London WC2R 0RL, England
Penguin Group Ireland, 25 St. Stephen's Green, Dublin 2, Ireland (a division of Penguin Books Ltd.)
Penguin Group (Australia), 250 Camberwell Road, Camberwell, Victoria 3124, Australia
(a division of Pearson Australia Group Pty. Ltd.)
Penguin Books India Pvt. Ltd., 11 Community Centre, Panchsheel Park, New Delhi—110 017, India
Penguin Group (NZ), cnr. Airborne and Rosedale Roads, Albany, Auckland 1310, New Zealand
(a division of Pearson New Zealand Ltd.)
Penguin Books (South Africa) (Pty.) Ltd., 24 Sturdee Avenue, Rosebank, Johannesburg 2196, South Africa

Penguin Books Ltd., Registered Offices: 80 Strand, London WC2R 0RL, England

MARSHALLING THE FAITHFUL

PRINTING HISTORY
Berkley mass-market edition / December 1993
Berkley Caliber trade paperback edition / July 2006

Berkley Caliber trade paperback ISBN: 0-425-20997-0

Caliber is a registered trademark of Penguin Group (USA) Inc.
The "C" design is a trademark belonging to Penguin Group (USA) Inc.

An application to register this book for cataloging has been submitted to the Library of Congress.

PRINTED IN THE UNITED STATES OF AMERICA

10  9  8  7  6  5  4  3  2  1

This book is for Lillian,
who stayed home and waited for me.

# · CONTENTS ·

# PREFACE

FOR ME, 1965 REMAINS ONE OF THE MOST SIGNIFICANT YEARS OF my life. It was the year that I fell in love with a very special girl, a condition from which I have never recovered. It was also the year that I became a man. Many of us did that year, especially the boys who went to South Vietnam. The world took a drastic turn that year because Beaver Cleaver went to war.

America watched the burning priests and the protesting students in Saigon on the nightly news, but it had meant little until 1965. That year, when we saw boys we knew from school now gaunt and leather-faced treading the battlefront on television, wearing faded helmets and looking frighteningly more realistic as soldiers at war than Vic Morrow and his platoon ever did on *Combat*, South Vietnam became significantly real. As the war continued and more sun-scorched faces that belonged to more sons and brothers and lovers flashed on the TV screens, South Vietnam became important. Yet, South Vietnam became most real and most important to those men and women who were there.

1965 was the year we believed that we could clear up that conflict, that dirty little brush war, in short order and then come home. After all, what did the French know? Most of the boys saw it as another deploy-ment, one more expedition, an adventure. Our wise war veterans who had survived their baptism on Bloody Ridge and Chosen Reservoir knew better. In a few months the boys had become men and they knew better too.

When they wept as men for fallen brothers who looked like boys but were men, when they hurt as men and cried out for justice and support from home and got little notice, then they knew better. The truth spoke to them, and it said this will be a long, tough war.

My hope for this book is to give readers a taste of life at that time. A look within a band of Marines who went to South Vietnam during those days and weeks when President Johnson made the historic decision to in-vest our country's most precious asset, the blood of our future, to combat there.

Much of this book is drawn from personal conversations with the various characters within its pages. The remainder is based on published works and the official records and data that I obtained from the Marine Corps Historical Center in Washington, D.C.

Although this book is a nonfiction work, I have taken the liberty to disguise certain characters with fictional names and backgrounds. These persons include Wesley Burkehart, the Marine who mistakenly killed two of his comrades when they approached his position one night on Hill 327; Staff Sergeant Eddie Mayes, the Marine who was as brave as a lion patrolling in daylight but at night his fears of what he couldn't see over-whelmed him; and Thomas Jones, the lieutenant whose fear of patrolling with Captain Pat Collins led him to the day when he fell on the ground crying, hugging his captain's legs and begging not to go on patrol. Also the names Slyde Slydell and Robbie Katz are fictional. All other names of characters are real. All persons in this book, including those I have as-signed fictional names, are real.

Many may argue that I should have used the names and backgrounds of the actual persons from the events described above, but in my opinion, it was their actions that should be of interest. I believe that these men have paid for their misfortunes, again and again, all of their lives follow-ing the events. I am certain that feelings of regret haunt them today. It serves nothing to bring them further pain by disclosing their identities.

As far as Captain Slyde Slydell, a crazy helicopter pilot, and his crew chief, Sergeant Robbie Katz, are concerned, they are real people, except that their names are fictional. Neither Pat Collins nor any of the others who served with him could remember the names of the Marines on that helicopter.

I have never claimed to be an historian, nor do I wish to be considered one. I am a storyteller. I am most interested in the enjoyment of my readers, therefore, I write with a novelist's style. Because I choose this style of storytelling, I have taken certain literary liberties in setting scenes and developing the characters' dialogue.

I have taken the recollections told to me by the various people in this book, developed them into mental images of the events, and described them to you in my own writing style. Where the characters have not been able to recall full details of events, I have drawn conclusions regarding these missing elements based on historical information and the experiences of others who were there at the time. I have done this to give you, the reader, a taste of what life at that time and at that place was most probably like.

In many cases, the dialogue is exactly as the persons interviewed recalled it. In other cases, however, I have had to develop the characters' dialogue from their recollections, which were often foggy, and from their styles of speaking and mannerisms I observed in them today. Hardly anyone can remember word for word what anyone said more than twenty years prior unless it was recorded in some fashion. Therefore, the dialogue, as with the scene setting, is what I believe to be a reasonably accurate portrayal of what happened then. Again, the objective was not to preserve the exact words of the characters, an absolute impossibility, but to tell their story.

As in any writing, I have a personal perspective. I believe it is impossible for anyone to write about any subject without involving his own attitudes regarding it. Human beings are emotional and base beliefs on what we know to be the truth. Various perspectives provide various truths, and no person knows the absolute truth about anything, not even themselves. That insight, I believe, rests only with God.

Because I subscribe to the belief that all writing is biased, I offer you the tilt of my thinking on South Vietnam so that you can adjust your understanding of this book:

America was right in the decision to aid and defend the people of

South Vietnam. The North Vietnamese invaded South Vietnam with four Regular Army regiments in support of the Communist insurgent operation carried on by terrorist guerrillas in their final mobilization effort *before* we ever landed our Marines in March of 1965. South Vietnam would have fallen to North Vietnam in a matter of months without our direct military support.

Militarily, we were successful in South Vietnam, despite the fact that selfish political concerns at home by our elected leaders tied our combatants' hands and prevented them from pursuing the enemy on his home ground, North Vietnam, and thereby ending the war many years and tens of thousands of lives sooner, and with a different outcome.

The two weeks in 1972 when President Nixon ordered daily B-52 strikes on Hanoi proved this to be true. While the bombs fell on Hanoi, the previously stubborn and uncooperative North Vietnamese representatives at the Paris Peace Talks quickly became very cooperative because their country was crumbling by the day.

My fellow service members who shouldered their responsibilities and courageously served in South Vietnam, whether or not they agreed with the leadership, wisdom or lack of it that put them there, won the war. We never lost a battle, and when we left in 1971, North Vietnam and the Communist effort were nearly finished.

The Vietnam conflict is not the war that the United States lost. It is the war that our nation's leaders quit. The people of South Vietnam are the people that our nation's leaders and many of its silent majority cowardly deserted. Deserted at such a dark hour that since that time no other small and struggling country has risked putting their faith in us again, until the action in Kuwait. I thank God that President George Bush did the job right this time and did not fall into the pit of betrayal as all his predecessors since Vietnam had.

When our troops left Vietnam, we told the people of that nation that they could hold it on their own. "We will support your efforts," we told them. "We will keep the arms and money coming to aid you while your army fights your war." But first Congress cut off the arms, then cut off the money, and finally we turned our backs.

By deserting the people of South Vietnam, our leaders violated a principle stated by Thomas Jefferson in the Declaration of Independence, ". . . when a long train of abuses and usurpations pursuing invariably the same Object evinces a design to reduce them under absolute Despotism, it is their right, *it is their duty*, to throw off such government, and to provide new Guards for their future security."

Nothing is more threatening to a people than an invader who would rob them of their lives and their liberty, and their pursuit of happiness (having food, home, security, and a reasonable expectation for a positive future), as the North Vietnamese Communists have robbed from not just the South Vietnamese people but from the entire region that we once knew as Indochina. Today that region is one of the great shames of our planet.

The shame with our involvement in South Vietnam, however, does not rest with the men and women who fought and won there. It lies in the halls of Congress and in the White House and in the indifference of thousands of Americans who did not give a damn. They placed themselves at the center of the universe and turned their backs on the inherent responsibility of all free people toward those who desire freedom.

For the first time, we went back on our word. We deserted an entire society and left them to an overpowering invader who placed these people under a yoke of absolute tyranny and despotism. The truth of this is evidenced in the blood baths and genocides and purges of the late 1970s suffered by the Southeast Asian people at the hands of the Communists in both Vietnam and Cambodia. The holocaust that they committed there compares to that of Hitler's Nazis or under Stalin's iron fist, yet it has gone virtually without comment. The truth is further evidenced by the conditions suffered by these poor people today.

Because of my perspective, some people will call me a hawk or warmonger. They will see me as a person who admires battle and would seek to go to war. Anyone who knows me knows better.

I believe that I am little different from most other Marines or soldiers who have seen war. You will find that we detest it more than anyone else can. Men and women who have survived war's ugliness, who have seen their brothers and sisters brutally cut down in their youth, and who have seen the innocent victims caught under combat's grinding treads know too well the price war exacts.

Although I hate war and have heartbroken memories of its cost, I hate tyranny and despotism more. Their horrors cannot lie still in my conscience. The mountains of bleached human bones on the killing fields of Indochina ignite my anger. I will gladly risk my life to save my people from such unthinkable cruelty. It is the ethic of Thomas Jefferson's closing words in our Declaration of Independence, ". . . we mutually pledge to each other our lives, our Fortunes and our sacred Honor."

I count fellow Marines such as Colonel Pat Collins, Colonel Carmine J. "Sean" DelGrosso, First Lieutenant Frank Reasoner, Gunnery Sergeant B. C. Collins, and others in this book as Americans who share these ideals. They are men with great honor and courage, and they risked their lives in South Vietnam because it was their duty. A duty to a people who wished to remain free.

—Charles W. Henderson
August 1992

Since this book was first published in 1993, much has changed in Vietnam. During the later 1990s that nation stepped away from despotic Communism and embraced a more liberal, free-market system of government. I observed the beginning of these changes when I returned there in the fall of 1994, when I began my research for *Goodnight Saigon*. By subscribing to a free society with open markets and free trade, international commerce has returned to Vietnam. The nation's economy is rapidly improving, its people now enjoy a better quality of life, and America has reestablished diplomatic ties with Vietnam, opening an embassy in Hanoi. However, the words I wrote in 1992, in the Preface above, remain valid for that time, and my beliefs have not changed.

—Charles W. Henderson
March 2006

"Everything in war is simple, but the simplest thing is difficult. The difficulties accumulate and end by producing a kind of friction that is inconceivable unless one has experienced war."

—Karl von Clausewitz

# MARSHALLING THE FAITHFUL

# VIETNAM'S WAR:
## WHY AMERICA JOINED THE FIGHT

EVEN THOUGH THE SECOND WEEK OF AUGUST 1964 HAD BARELY begun, the hangouts on Marshal Street were already crowded with early-arriving students, preparing for another year at Syracuse University, one block away. Many students arrived early for some final good times before the grind, while others came to hear the President of the United States speak, in person.

Most college girls that year wore pleated and dressy skirts, and pastel blouses, and fixed their hair in a ratted-thick, neatly combed-in-a-flip, heavily hair spray–coated bouffant style. Black mascara, blue eye shadow, and frosted lipstick colors dressed their faces.

The boys wore narrow ties and belts, pastel-colored Oxford cloth or madras plaid shirts with buttoned-down collars, and sharkskin slacks with the legs sharply creased above oxblood or black loafers with tassels, and always white socks. Even though Beatles hits blared from every juke-box on Marshal Street, only the "radical and unclean sleaze" had adopted the Liverpool group's shaggy look. Long hair on this affluent campus was not yet "in." The boys here kept their hair short. Crew cuts remained fashionable on this hot August, upstate New York noon.

President Lyndon B. Johnson stood behind a lectern with an octopus of microphones anchored on its front. His silver wire-framed glasses slid slightly down his nose, slick with a glow of sweat, as he raised his eyes from the speech he had prepared for this day. He gazed across the massive crowd gathered below him on the steps of the newly constructed S. I. Newhouse School of Public Communications. It represented one of the best journalism colleges money could buy, and Johnson was about to dedicate it as the newest block in the foundation of the "Fourth Estate."

Johnson looked at the young men wearing their pastel or plaid shirts and their crew cuts, and the young women with their hair ratted and stacked and sprayed stiff. He quietly cleared his throat by swallowing, and began his speech.

One irony to emerge from this day was so many of this crowd of future leaders, journalists, and politicians who applauded his statements and cheered at his resolve would come to curse it. On this hot August day in 1964, a sweltering President Johnson stood on the steps of the newly finished Newhouse School, dedicating the ten-million-dollar complex as Syracuse University's new home for journalism and photography, and announced his acceptance of the Tonkin Gulf Resolution.

While a crowd of enthusiastic citizens applauded and cheered the President before an approving national press, more than 6,000 Marines of the 9th Marine Expeditionary Brigade, who left Okinawa on August 6 aboard Seventh Fleet ships, already sailed in the South China Sea, off the coast of Vietnam.

In his speech at Syracuse University, the President told America of the "Tonkin Gulf Incident," and how that act of aggression had made the congressional resolution necessary in order to preserve freedom. He told of the growing war and political instability in Southeast Asia, and how little more than a week earlier the Communist enemy had struck directly at the United States when North Vietnamese torpedo boats attacked two U.S. Navy destroyers, the USS *Turner Joy* (DD 951) and the USS *Maddox* (DD 731), while sailing in international waters within the Gulf of Tonkin.

The Joint Chiefs of Staff recommended retaliatory air strikes against several North Vietnamese patrol boat bases and fuel storage areas. The President approved the reprisal attacks on August 4, and Seventh Fleet carrier-based aircraft carried out the bombing missions the following day.

Congress passed the Tonkin Gulf Resolution with only two dissenting

votes on August 7, 1964. It authorized the President ". . . to use all measures, including the commitment of armed forces to assist the Republic of
Vietnam in the defense of its independence and territorial integrity. . . ."
The resolution approved and supported ". . . the determination of the
President, as Commander in Chief, to take all necessary measures to re-
pel any armed attack against the forces of the United States, and to prevent further aggression." Now, five days later, he signed the resolution,
and told America of it on the steps of a journalism school.

During later years, a critical press looked back at the Tonkin Gulf
skirmish as the key element for direct U.S. intervention in the Vietnam
War. Some went so far to say that the attack never really happened, while
others blame the incident on American support of aggressive South Vietnamese naval patrols off the coast of North Vietnam. Although the Tonkin
Gulf Resolution's significance cannot be overlooked—it did give the President unquestionable power to commit armed forces to combat—other
events and policy decisions had greater bearing on the United States's involvement in South Vietnam: an escalating commitment to war that was
inevitable.

U.S. policy had been consistent since 1946 when the Viet Minh rebellion first opposed France in then Indochina. When the Japanese signed
the instrument of surrender aboard the battleship USS *Missouri* on September 2, 1945, they also released a five-year grip on French Indochina.
Ten days later a 150-man detachment from the French Expeditionary
Corps arrived in Saigon to assist the British in accepting the Japanese surrender there. France had not been included in the surrender, therefore, this
was a gesture of courtesy extended to the French by the Allied powers.

France seized upon the opportunity and quickly reclaimed those
areas known as Cochinchina and Annam (central and southern Vietnam).
By the end of February 1946, France had struck an agreement with Na-
tionalist China to replace the Chinese occupation forces above the six-
teenth parallel—the remainder of Indochina that was predominantly the
state of Tonkin (North Vietnam).

During the World War II years, Ho Chi Minh, a member of the Com-
intern and a graduate of the Lenin Institute, managed to organize his
feeble Communist political party into a major power. The Communist
guerrilla organization, called Viet Minh, was organized, trained, and led
by Ho's close confidant Vo Nguyen Giap (previously a history teacher in

the south [Annam], and who in 1968 would lead the siege on the Marines at Khe Sanh).

While World War II engulfed Southeast Asia, the United States provided Ho and the Viet Minh with advisers, arms, and supplies. In return, the Viet Minh assisted downed U.S. pilots and fought minor skirmishes with the Japanese. However, rather than using the bulk of their assets in major confrontations with the Japanese, Ho and the Viet Minh concentrated on organizing and building the Communist strength until it extended throughout the Red River Delta and Annam.

At war's end, the Viet Minh held Tonkin's capital city, Hanoi, and proclaimed the Democratic Republic of Vietnam. On March 6, 1946, with the Viet Minh poised now to directly confront them, France proclaimed the Democratic Republic of Vietnam a "free state within the French Union." In response, Ho welcomed the French Army with "open arms."

By September 1946, French troops controlled every major strategic point from the Chinese border to the tip of the Ca Mau Peninsula (Vietnam's most northern and southern points). Meanwhile, the French and Viet Minh tried to come to agreement on actual political control of those areas called the Democratic Republic of Vietnam. When diplomatic talks failed in December, fighting erupted.

Because of the Chinese Communist influence in Korea during 1949 and 1950, the United States took a strong stand against any action that would bring Asia entirely under Communist domination. This included the Viet Minh rebellion, and ushered in limited U.S. support of the French in their fight with Ho Chi Minh.

The so-called *Sale Guerre*—dirty war—finally came to an end, however, on May 7, 1954, at a French garrison called Dien Bien Phu. The French Union Army's Expeditionary Corps had accomplished few successes of note and had become worn in its fight with the Viet Minh. Most important, popular support in France grew extremely low as the numbers of French casualties mounted. With the loss of the 13,000-man garrison under the command of General Henri Navarre, and the news that 2,000 French soldiers had died defending the fortress, the French people demanded an end to the fighting.

At the time of Dien Bien Phu, both the French Army and the Viet Minh were at their breaking points. France called on the United States for air support in holding the fortress at Dien Bien Phu. The U.S. denied the request and the French fell.

Decades later, President Richard M. Nixon cited this denial of air support to the French at Dien Bien Phu as the single most critical mistake in U.S. foreign policy that led to the loss of South Vietnam to the Communists. Nixon held that had the U.S. provided the air support, not only would Dien Bien Phu have been held by the French but that the Viet Minh would have fallen in defeat and would have dissolved because they had expended everything in this battle.

As it was, the Viet Minh's victory at Dien Bien Phu won them new life and the war.

The French and Viet Minh signed a cease-fire agreement in Geneva on July 20, 1954. This agreement substantially altered the map of Southeast Asia. Laos, Cambodia, and Vietnam all gained full independence. But most significantly, the agreement divided Vietnam at the seventeenth parallel, along the Ben Hai River, and created a demilitarized zone—the Cease-fire and Demarcation Line American servicemen would come to know as the DMZ.

With South Vietnam in a political shambles, unable to begin governing itself, the French-sponsored emperor, Bao Dai, who resided in France and chose not to return to power in South Vietnam, appointed a pro-western premier—the product of a prosperous family, a man who now resided at a Catholic seminary in the United States—Ngo Dinh Diem.

From his appointment in 1954 until 1960, Diem's government fared well. The United States formed the Military Assistance Advisory Group in Saigon and began training and supporting the South Vietnamese Armed Forces in conjunction with the French. After the last French advisers departed South Vietnam in 1957, the U.S. continued the entire advisory and assistance effort alone.

Through the years of the Diem government, the Communist influence in the south was limited mostly to an effort of developing cells and of building a guerrilla force, in line with the three-phase model of the Communist Insurgent Doctrine: the Passive, Active, and Final or Counter-Offensive phases.

This Communist doctrine subscribes to waging a "protracted revolution" developed from "within the masses of struggling peoples." The beginning of the "struggle," or insurgency, is based on spreading the "ideals" of communism and gaining support of a revolution—the Passive Phase. Once cells stand in place and enough strength exists to support guerrilla activities, sporadic warfare begins in the forms of ambushes, sabotage, and assassinations of political leaders—the Active Phase. After the guerrilla armies have gained enough control and strength en masse to wage all-out war, the final mobilization effort commences—the Final or Counter-Offensive Phase. Supporters of this doctrine assume victory as an inevitable end, no matter how long it takes.

During 1960 the National Liberation Front's army, which the Diem government named "Viet Cong" (a derogatory term for Vietnamese Communist), began the Active Phase of the so-called revolution with their 10,000-man force committing an average of 650 violent incidents per month by 1961. The National Intelligence Estimate, released by the Kennedy administration in March of 1961, claimed that nearly 58 percent of South Vietnam was under some sort of Communist domination.

In the first year of his administration, President John F. Kennedy sent General Maxwell D. Taylor, former Chief of Staff of the U.S. Army, to Saigon with one question to resolve: "What action would the United States require itself to commit to prevent a Communist takeover in South Vietnam?"

Kennedy had little more than walked into the Oval Office when he was confronted with the Vietnam issue, in terms of the Counter-Insurgency Plan of January 28, 1961, (which he approved) that called for a 20,000-man increase in the regular South Vietnamese Army and a 32,000-man buildup of the South Vietnamese Civil Guard, along with increased U.S. military aid to support this increase in South Vietnamese military strength.

When General Taylor conducted his mission to Saigon in mid-October 1961 he became deeply concerned. South Vietnam was in "grave danger." In his November report, he told President Kennedy that South Vietnam would be lost unless the United States abandoned its policy of strictly military advice (which had prohibited U.S. advisers of accompanying Vietnamese units into combat) and began cooperating with the South Vietnamese in a "limited partnership." This would involve "working" advisers and "working" U.S. military units to aid South Vietnam's forces.

Taylor called for an aggressive buildup of Republic of Vietnam forces, coupled with a greatly increased U.S. advisory staff. Most significantly, he called for the introduction of three U.S. Army helicopter companies and 6,000 to 8,000 regular U.S. ground troops "to be deployed immediately to Vietnam." Kennedy approved all but the deployment of U.S. military ground units.

During 1961, for the first time U.S. advisers accompanied Vietnamese units into combat, and the first U.S. helicopter units arrived in South Vietnam where they would fly support missions for the Army of the Republic of Vietnam.

These new efforts grew month by month, and on Palm Sunday, 1962, the first Marine helicopter squadron to operate in Vietnam, Marine Medium Helicopter Squadron 362 (HMM-362), commanded by Marine Lieutenant Colonel Archie J. Clapp, arrived for duty. The mission was code-named Operation Shufly.

During those same months, the political situation grew worse for Diem and his principal adviser, Ngo Dinh Nhu, Diem's brother. A Buddhist uprising began in opposition to Diem's Catholic government. By 1962 monks were setting themselves afire in the streets of South Vietnam's major cities. In August 1963 Diem sparked open rebellion when he arrested the Buddhist movement's leaders.

At the same time, Diem's brother, Nhu, directed a program, begun in 1959, which now grew more and more unpopular with the people it was supposed to serve. Called the Agroville Program, and later renamed the Strategic Hamlet Program, the effort was to bring about improved economic and social conditions for the rural areas. However, the most these programs could ever accomplish was to resettle the rural peasants—which made up more than 80 percent of South Vietnam's population—into resettlement camps. These peasants were called "Agrovilles," and were frequently victimized by the Viet Cong. They found themselves more or less "wards of the state."

Further aggravating political matters, Diem put an end to free elections of village chiefs and began appointing those leaders instead. This action greatly served to enhance popular sympathy toward the Communists.

By the fall of 1963 U.S. advisers were in a "wait-and-see" posture with the political unrest and the massive Buddhist protests. Then on November 1, 1963, the Diem government fell to a junta of South Vietnamese generals led by Major General Duong Van Minh—"Big Minh" (who was to be the last President of South Vietnam on April 28, 1975, and who surrendered to the North Vietnamese two days later). On the day following the coup, an ARVN officer murdered Diem and his brother Nhu.

With the murder of Diem and twenty days later the assassination of President Kennedy, a new and more volatile era began in Southeast Asia.

All those supporting the Diem regime were ousted, including 31 military officers. A new military junta emerged on January 6, 1964, consisting of Minh as chief of state, and Major General Tran Van Don and Major General Le Van Kim, both of whom would run the government and the armed forces respectively.

Twenty-three days later Major General Nguyen Khanh assumed power from the junta, leaving Minh as chief of state. However, on September 26, 1964, because of Buddhist opposition to Khanh, the Vietnamese Revolutionary Council elected civilians Phan Khac Suu as the chief of state and Tran Van Huong as premier. But the real power remained with the military forces, which dissolved the Civilian High National Council on December 20.

When Operation Shufly began, the increased numbers of American servicemen put a strain on the U.S. Military Assistance Advisory Group. On February 8, 1962, an umbrella command, under which both the air operation and the advisory/assistance operations would come, began. It was the U.S. Military Assistance Command, Vietnam, and was under the leadership of General Paul D. Harkins, U.S. Army.

By year's end more than 12,000 U.S. military servicemen were under MACV's command in Vietnam. After the rocky year that 1963 had been—and with the promise of further conflict—by 1964's end MACV swelled to more than 20,000 American military men.

While an escalating war ushered in 1965, two battalions of Marines continued to sail through the South China Sea. After the Tonkin Gulf Incident cooled, and the 9th MEB returned to garrison, the Special Landing Force, normally a single Battalion Landing Team of Marines sent on "float" to Southeast Asian ports, was increased from one BLT to two. While one BLT sailed to and from port in the Philippines, the other would stand ready off the shore of Vietnam. This would allow a landing force to come ashore while a BLT remained available as the Special Landing Force to fulfill SEATO commitments or answer emergencies.

The fall of 1964 had been active with growing confrontations between ARVN forces and Viet Cong. On November 1, four American soldiers died when Viet Cong forces launched a mortar attack on U.S. facilities at Bien Hoa Air Base. Besides killing the four Americans, the Viet Cong destroyed five B-57 medium bombers and heavily damaged eight others.

While 100,000 people jammed into New York City's Times Square to welcome the New Year, 1965, South Vietnam's Marines suffered their most decisive defeat of the war.

On December 28, 1964, near a hamlet called Binh Gia, on an abandoned rubber plantation, a column of Vietnamese Marines, three U.S. Marine advisers, and a fourth U.S. Marine, "in country" on a two-week On-the-Job Training tour to observe combat "firsthand," were assaulted by a force of between 1,200 and 1,800 guerrillas. After five days of fighting the Vietnamese Marines suffered 112 men killed in action, 71 wounded, and 13 missing. All three U.S. Marine advisers were wounded and the fourth Marine, there on two-weeks' OJT, Captain Donald G. Cook, was taken prisoner by the Viet Cong. Cook reportedly died in captivity in 1967.

On the heels of Binh Gia, President Johnson completed a month-long review of U.S. policy regarding North Vietnam, triggered by the Bien Hoa attack. He implemented a two-phase plan that paralleled escalation of North Vietnam's participation in the war.

Phase I centered on stepped-up bombing of infiltration routes used by the North Vietnamese into South Vietnam, while Phase II focused on bombing attacks on North Vietnam, with increasing severity, that were directly parallel to NVA future actions.

First phase of the plan commenced in January 1965, with news that four North Vietnamese Army regiments now operated in South Vietnam. Two new North Vietnamese Army regiments—the 32nd and the 101st—entered South Vietnam in January and were now carrying out combat operations. A third NVA regiment was reported in the first stages of formation in Quang Tri Province. These three NVA regiments, added to the one known to have begun operating in the Kontum Province in the closing days of 1964, forced U.S. military leaders to take a grave look at the South Vietnamese government's status and the Communist threat.

During the first week of February President Johnson sent a delegation to South Vietnam, headed by his special assistant McGeorge Bundy. General Maxwell Taylor had replaced Henry Cabot Lodge as ambassador to South Vietnam, and General William C. Westmoreland had replaced General Harkins as commander, MACV. The mission was to discuss the feasibility of air strikes against North Vietnam.

Bundy reported to the President that the situation in Vietnam was deteriorating, and "without new U.S. action, defeat appears inevitable . . . within the next year. There is still time to turn it around," Bundy said, "but not much."

Westmoreland pointed to Binh Gia as the point where the insurgency had moved into the Final or "Mobilization" Phase. He said of the increase of activities and the presence of North Vietnamese forces in the south, "These are numbers of a new order of magnitude, but we must face the stark fact that the war has escalated."

During the next six weeks the 9th Marine Expeditionary Brigade finished preparations to land its force of 9,000 men in South Vietnam to defend the air base and antiaircraft missile battalion at Da Nang. Before the end of 1965, more than 42,000 Marines would be conducting offensive combat missions throughout I Corps.

America now took its last long step into war.

# NOISES IN THE WIRE

•1•

D ON'T BOTHER GOING TO THE VILLE, JOHN," A BOYISH-LOOKING Marine lieutenant standing in the doorway said to another boyish-looking lieutenant who was six inches taller. "You can't afford it anymore. None of us can."

The taller lieutenant stepped past the other Marine without breaking stride and unbuttoned his khaki shirt as he walked inside the painted white with green trim, concrete-block, single-story barracks at Camp Schwab, Okinawa, after standing watch the last 24 hours as 3rd Reconnaissance Battalion's officer of the day. It was Saturday morning and John DelGrosso looked forward to spending some time in Hinoko, where he could buy cold beer and try to make up for the Friday night liberty that he had missed.

"What?" John DelGrosso said, dropping his shirt into a white laundry bag.

The shorter Marine followed John DelGrosso as he walked next to the desk in his room, sat on a straight-backed chair, and began unlacing his shoes.

"That bunch from Bravo Company. You know, they mounted out

from Hawaii this week with 1st Brigade, supposed to be headed to South Vietnam," the shorter lieutenant said, exerting as much seriousness as he could muster into his youthful voice. "In just a couple of nights they have all but ruined the liberty here, throwing their money around like fools back on Hotel Street in Honolulu. They lay down a dollar for a beer and leave the change. A quarter is bad enough, but a dollar! Oh, and the *naisans*, I don't have to tell you what kind of impact they've had with them. Why, the bar girls see a Marine in a Hawaii-print shirt and their eyes roll watermelons straight across. A two-dollar short-time now costs five bucks!"

"Isn't that first lieutenant with the flat-top Bravo Company's commanding officer or XO?" John DelGrosso said as he laid his trousers on the bed and took a towel from the metal shelf inside his wall locker.

"Right, Reasoner's his name. Frank Reasoner."

John DelGrosso smiled as he dropped his T-shirt and undershorts into the laundry bag, tied the bag by its draw cord to the foot of his bed's steel-pipe frame, and then wrapped the towel around his waist. "I'm hitting the ville anyway. A shower, a nap, and I'm gone. Maybe I will run into this Lieutenant Reasoner and have a talk. See if he has any ideas of what to do about these big spenders."

· 2 ·

THE SWEET SMELL OF OLD SPICE COLOGNE CAUGHT THE WOMAN'S attention first, then she looked up to see the smiling, fresh-shaved face of John DelGrosso. He dressed much the same as other Marine officers and staff noncommissioned officers stationed on Okinawa. He wore a tailor-made madras shirt with a buttoned-down collar and a center pleat in the back. The same tailor had made his tan slacks. Everything fit perfectly and was much finer than he could have afforded on his Marine Corps salary had he tried to purchase them at home in New York.

"Hey, how's the slop-chute life, Sach?" John DelGrosso said with a smile as he leaned across the bar on his forearms. "Make it a bottle of your stinking Irish beer."

The woman behind the bar was forty years old and for three years had owned this tavern that Marines from 3rd Reconnaissance Battalion dominated as their bar of choice. After the war she had worked as a *naisan*, a bar girl, until she had managed to save enough money to open her own establishment.

After she had left her family home in Ishikawa, she assumed a fictitious name, Sachiko, as did most other girls who made their living being pleasant company for the men who sought to lift their spirits with some drink and a *naisan*'s trivial companionship in the Okinawan nightclubs. Taking the alias protected her family from the embarrassment that her work might cause, and it had been nearly twenty years now since anyone had called her by her real name, Yuki, which is Okinawan for "snow."

To make enough money to pay her rent, eat, and still save for her future, she had frequently sold her sex to the soldiers and Marines that she entertained. They always paid well, and rarely bought more than a short-time.

Like many other girls who had begun this flesh trade as young hostesses in Naminoui, the fashionable nightclub district of Naha, as she grew older and less marketable, she moved northward to villages outside the military camps. Hinoko was the northernmost camp town, and it was at this end-of-the-line community of bars and brothels next to Camp Schwab that she managed to open her bar, which had its proper name, but among the Marines who drank there, it was known only as "Sach's."

There was nothing that any of these young Americans could show or tell to Sachiko that she had not already heard or seen. But to keep the atmosphere gay and these young men returning to spend their money at her bar, she willingly played the patsy. She had lost count of the times she had heard the Irish beer joke, but once again she acted out her sucker's role.

"We no have-uh Irish beer-ru, John-san," the round-faced woman said.

"Sure you do, Sach," the young lieutenant said, pointing to a score of Orion beer bottle necks jutting out of the long ice-filled cooler behind the bar. "Right there. That O-Ryan beer."

"John-san," she said, laughing at the twist to the name of the popular Okinawan beer. "Not O-Ryan beer-ru, Orion. Or-eee-onn. You GI all alike. Always make joke. Number ten, John-san."

"You Irish are all alike, Sach. How about that beer. It tastes like you soaked your papa-san's dirty socks in it, but at least it's cold."

"You like *takusan* Orion or *chisai*, John-san?"

"*Takusan*, Sach. Biggest you've got. I stood duty all night; I don't want any dinky *chisai* bottles."

The woman hooked her finger down a cotton cord turned dark from being handled hundreds of times daily and nimbly snatched a silvery beer opener tied to the string's end. In the same motion she snapped off the large beer bottle's cap with a pop, trying to mimic the sound made by a champagne cork.

"*Hi dozo,*" she said as she slid the icy brown bottle into John Del-Grosso's hand, and then smiled when he laid down a dollar bill. "*Ichi* George Washington, *nay*."

"Don't forget my change, Sachiko," he said, turning the bottle straight up while pushing away the water-spotted glass that she tried to hand to him.

"You make tip, John-san?" the woman asked hopefully but knew that he would not let her keep the change.

"I'll tip when I'm finished. Like always."

"Hawaii Marines, they tip each drink. Sachiko like that way best."

"I'll bet they drink out of your dirty glasses too," John DelGrosso said. Then in a serious tone, "Sach, you seen any of those bums around?"

"No, John-san. Not today. They be here *most-skoshi*, you wait. Drink more Orion, *desho*," the woman said and dropped two quarters on the bar for the lieutenant.

He was about to make fun of the Okinawan word of affirmation, *desho*, with his usual, "the show? What show?" and then follow with, "oh, the show *desho*!" but then he saw his change. "What's this? Fifty cents? What happened to a quarter for a beer? That's a 100 percent price hike, you old thief."

"Big Orion half dollar all over Hinoko now," the woman said quickly. "You go Kin Village, Koza, even Taragawa, every GI bar *takusan* Orion now fifty cents. All go up when Hawaii brigade land Okinawa."

"And you wanted a tip too?" John DelGrosso said. "Jesus, Joseph, and Mary, I can get a little Orion for a nickel and the big ones for a dime at the Kadena officers' club."

"Then you go, you drink at Habu Pit, John-san; Hinoko *nisan*, Sachiko no miss you. *Takusan* GI pay *dijobu*, tip *dijobu*, no complain. No need-oh John-san. Hawaii GI be here *most-skoshi*," the woman said. "You *takusan* number ten, John-san. Hawaii Marine number one."

"Hawaii Marine number ten, Mama-san," John DelGrosso said lightly. "Hawaii Marine *oki sukana*."

The woman grumbled incoherently in Okinawan and walked to the other end of the bar where two early-arriving bar hostesses sat. The two women, even though they called themselves *naisans*, had not seen girlhood for ten years. Their mature age showed despite their attempts to hide it behind layers of makeup. The three women spoke in rapid chains of Okinawan, looked back at John DelGrosso, and then laughed.

The lieutenant lifted his bottle and tilted it toward them in response and then drank. They laughed more and he smiled back.

He had finished two beers when the first three Hawaii-based Marines entered the bar. They crowded into one booth, and seeing them, the two *naisans* sitting at the bar gathered their cigarettes and small clutch purses and walked to where the three Marines now sat.

The two bar girls each immediately cuddled next to a Marine, and like a well-rehearsed play, they began reciting words they knew young men out for a good time, with money in their pockets, like to hear.

"Hey, boys," the Marine without a girl said in a loud voice, "I want you to meet the Ko sisters. Mitchiko and Fumiko."

The Marines laughed and the two women pretended to enjoy the joke too. The men each took out a cigarette, and before they could attempt to light them, the two women had struck matches and provided the service.

"You Hawaii GI," the first woman said. "You have *takusan okani, desho*!"

The second followed, "Hawaii Marine rich GI, *nay*?"

The Marine sitting with the first woman put his arm around her and laid his hand squarely over her breast and squeezed. "Fuck an A, honey. I got *takusan* everything that'll make a girl like you happy. You be nice and I let you ride the baloney pony."

The woman squealed and pulled the Marine's hand away and giggled with the other *naisan* while the three Marines guffawed and bellowed.

Seeing that the two hostesses had confirmed themselves with the party, Sachiko hurried to the table.

"Whiskey-water, mama-san," the Marine who sat next to the first hostess called out. "Whiskey-water all around. Old GrandDad, mama-san."

The woman hurried back behind the bar where she poured overflowing shots of whiskey in three glasses, and in two, she carefully dripped only enough whiskey to give the water a hint of color and smell.

John DelGrosso watched and nursed his beer. What a bunch of

boneheads, he thought. Too bad they can't see how stupid they look, and with the over-the-hill bunch too.

With the five drinks on her brown plastic tray, the woman hurried back to the table and collected a five-dollar bill from the Marine who again squeezed the hostess's breast. She laid a small blue ticket each by the two *naisans*'s drinks, and as the two hostesses collected the paper tokens and tucked them safely inside their clutch purses, Sachiko purposefully fumbled for the change in her apron, hoping to hear a now familiar phrase.

"Keep the change, mama-san," the Marine who was buying said, and John DelGrosso swiveled on his chair and looked toward the booth where he saw Sachiko bowing and backing away from the table, holding the five-dollar bill in her hand.

A week ago they could have bought twenty drinks in here for that price, the lieutenant thought to himself. He turned back to the bar and looked across it at the woman who now showed him a triumphant smile that was accented by her two gold-capped front teeth. She held the bill tight between her hands and shook it at the lieutenant.

"Abraham Lincoln, *dijobu*! Hawaii GI, number one, John-san," she said, and John DelGrosso had to agree with her. There was no greater catch in the sea than these from Hawaii who had swum into the nets of the hungry Okinawan saloon keepers.

"*Honto!* Sach. *Honto!*" the lieutenant said, laughing, and he lifted his bottle of beer in salute to her. "Another beer, *kudesai ichi-ban, mama-san!*"

As the three Marines in the booth happily sipped their drinks and the two women quickly drank theirs and begged for refills, another Marine walked through the door. He stood no more than five feet six inches tall, and had his golden-brown hair cleanly cut close to his scalp in a flat-top. He wore sandals and white socks, white Bermuda shorts, and a bright blue Hawaiian shirt with large red flowers printed on it.

What caught John DelGrosso's eye was not the shirt, nor the Marine's short yet extremely muscular stature. It was the pipe. A pipe that nearly hid the man from sight. Not since Sherlock Holmes had he seen such a pipe. It began with a small black stem that the man clenched in his teeth, tapered out and bent down to the base of a huge yellow bowl that curved upward four inches. Had it been made of brass, he would have sworn that the man held a saxophone.

This has got to be the guy, John DelGrosso told himself, and turned toward the door where the man still stood. He motioned for him to come inside and pointed to the stool next to him at the bar.

"That Cherry Blend? Sure smells good," John DelGrosso said and put out his hand. "You're Frank Reasoner, right?"

The Marine took the huge pipe from his mouth and shook hands. He looked at this friendly man who invited him to share company at the bar and then spoke with great seriousness. "It smells a bit like Cherry Blend, but it is a custom mix. I stumbled upon it at West Point. I didn't catch your name?"

"Lieutenant John DelGrosso, but please call me John. I'm in Company D."

Frank Reasoner sat on the stool next to John and ordered a large beer. When the woman set the beer in front of the new customer, he laid out two quarters and then turned toward John. The woman raked the two quarters across the bar and grumbled, trying not to see the wide smile that now spread over John DelGrosso's face.

"I'm sorry I hadn't met you earlier," Frank Reasoner said, trying to keep the conversation professionally solid. "Since the brigade landed, I've been kept busy settling in. I'm afraid I haven't really gotten to know too many people in the battalion yet."

"There's lots of time for that," John DelGrosso said. "Don't worry. In a couple of weeks you'll be just another salt on the rock."

"Well, I am certainly glad to meet you, Lieutenant DelGrosso."

"John, John."

"Right, John."

"My christian name is Carmine. Dad's Italian and Mom's Irish. New York Irish. She named me Sean, that's my middle name. It's Gaelic for John. When I joined the Corps, Mom said I should use John so that I could be sure to get paid. Carmine is too much of a mouthful, and Sean, well. I get my pay by the name John DelGrosso. Everybody here calls me John."

"New York," Frank Reasoner said. "That's not hard to miss with that Brooklyn brogue of yours. You sound like you just stepped off the BMT subway."

"You don't sound like you're from anywhere I can spot, Midwest maybe?" John DelGrosso said.

"Idaho. A town called Kellogg; it's in the mountains east of Coeur d'Alene, which is just across the border from Spokane. My wife and son are there now."

"Idaho, eh," John said and then took a drink of beer.

"You ever hear of Pappy Boyington?" Frank Reasoner said.

"Sure. Marine Corps ace, Medal of Honor from World War II," John said.

"He's from Coeur d'Alene," Frank said, offering that fact to lend significance to his home.

John DelGrosso took a drink of his beer and then in a serious voice said, "You mind if we talk a little shop?"

"No."

"Good," John said. "I know that you guys came here with a lot of new gear, and I think that's terrific. You must have impressed the shit out of brigade to get outfitted like that. Guess they figure you'll go into Vietnam first."

"I think we will go first, and that is why we have the new equipment," Reasoner said. "I've also been where you are, lacking nearly everything and trying to patch up what you have. It's no fun."

"Don't get me wrong, I think it's great you guys have so much good gear. That's not what we need to talk about, though. It's morale. My guys' morale, which is in the shitter," John DelGrosso said and now felt a little awkward since he had said it.

Frank Reasoner drew hard on his pipe and then looked at John DelGrosso and waited to hear more as the cloud from his mouth filled the air between the two men.

"You notice that the beer is fifty cents?"

"Yeah, not bad considering it was a dollar in Hawaii."

"That's it. A week ago that beer in every Okinawan bar cost a quarter. It's only a dime at the club."

Reasoner looked over his shoulder at the three Marines sitting at the booth who now quietly sipped their drinks since he had come inside the bar. He looked back and said, "We raised prices here?"

"Let's say you had a significant impact on an economy that is generally based on greed," John DelGrosso said and smiled. "The locals call guys like those sitting at that booth, flashing that GI bankroll—a stack of singles wrapped in a ten-dollar bill—*Oki Sukana*. That's Okinawan for

'Big Fish.' Those two broads and this mama-san will clean those boys out before the night is over, and it hasn't even started."

Frank Reasoner smiled and glanced back at his three men. "They're throwing it around, feeling pretty big right now. They must believe that those two hogs think they're real special."

John DelGrosso smiled and looked at Frank Reasoner. "You got it, Lieutenant. They'll love these guys until they're broke. Then it's 'Don't worry, GI, payday come *most-skoshi*.' The sooner you guys get the word that the price of beer is a quarter and a whore costs two dollars for a short-time, and that throwing money around is a sucker's game, the sooner life in the ville will return to normal. That's when my guys will smile again."

"Give them a couple of weeks," Frank Reasoner said. "Some will smarten up. The others, well, they'll get theirs the hard way. They'll end up completely broke and get wise. But these guys here, did you get a good look at the two bimbos they've got cornered?"

"Who's got who cornered?" John DelGrosso said and laughed. "Those two old hookers have been working this corner since before we were born. Once you're here awhile, you'll see that when the bar girl hits Hinoko, she's at the last stop."

Frank Reasoner looked at the two women. "I think that I would pass out before I could drink enough to make those two look good."

John DelGrosso laughed. "You're a married man, so I won't worry about you facing that test. But Marines up here get lonesome and that makes any woman start to look good fast, especially after a dollar's worth of this water-bull piss. I usually pack up and head south for serious liberty. That's where they keep the young ones. Kin Village, down by Camp Hansen, is fair, Koza outside Kadena Air Base is better, and the best of all is at Naha. A district called Naminoui. It means on the waves in Okinawan, and down there you almost have to speak the language."

• 3 •

**H**E HELD HIS BREATH AND GENTLY HOOKED THE OPENER'S BLADE over the top of the can, and gripping its key with his two fingers he twisted it hard, breaking the seal on the olive-green container of C-ration crackers. As the blade knifed through the lid, releasing the vacuum, the sudden, purposefully made loud pop caused the soldier looking out the bunker, over the top of his machine gun, to jerk as the sound drop-kicked his concentration on the night.

"Motherfucker! Goddamnit! Don't do that shit," the soldier manning the machine gun said, swearing in a strained whisper. "Fuck me to tears! I damned near cranked off a round, you scaring me like that. Goddamn, that would've had every cocksucker on the line shooting."

"Flinches," the one with the can said, and he stood and socked the startled man on the shoulder.

"Fuck you and your flinches," the machine gunner said, taking a half-hearted swipe at his partner. Then he sighed and cracked a smile at his buddy who shared the bunker with him. "Asshole."

Both soldiers laughed, and the man with the crackers then took a white plastic spoon and dug into a flat can of peanut butter, left from an earlier meal, and spread it on one of the round John Waynes.

"Want some peanut butter and crackers?" he said, stuffing it in his mouth. "Guaranteed to stop up your shit for a week."

"Yeah, what the fuck. I'm so constipated now, that can't make it any worse. We gotta get some real chow, this shit's enough to make you go sterile," the soldier manning the machine gun said.

Below the bunker stretched 200 yards of "no man's-land" filled with barbwire, coiled above a maze of fences that zigzagged over more wire that crisscrossed in a flat, tangle-foot pattern a few inches above the ground, blanketing every square foot of this open area that surrounded the U.S. Army Special Forces compound and airfield at Pleiku, South Vietnam.

Pleiku was an outpost buried deep in the central highlands, eighty miles due west from the coast and too close for comfort to the Cambodian/Laotian borders, a haven for the Communist forces. This stretch of rolling hills and mountainous backcountry had never been a popular tourist spot, and among U.S. advisers it was even less popular, being so close to the enemy and so far from everyone else. To them, it seemed a good place to get entrapped and overrun.

Added to the layers of barbwire encircling the compound, thousands of punji stakes tilted out of the ground, sharpened and waiting for an unfortunate soul to step on or fall over. Every few feet a spent C-ration can with a pebble resting inside dangled on the barbwire, waiting to rattle its alarm should someone disturb it.

Beyond the wire, where the soldiers manning the machine gun again trained their attention, listening for the clink of metal or the thud of footsteps and looking for the spiritlike shadows of Viet Cong sappers, another hundred yards of cleared land met a line of thick brush and tall grass. In the darkness the brush and grass looked rough and black next to the light shade of this apron of open land that was their shooting gallery. If anything moved in that cleared space, they had orders to open fire.

Behind the two men, small lights twinkled in a string of clusters. There, other soldiers worked through the night, patching bullet holes and mending oil lines and fixing what was broken on an acre of helicopters and other small airplanes that would fly new missions in a new day's first light.

Although Vietnam's climate is primarily tropical, the elevations of the central highlands are cool at night, especially winter nights. Pleiku this February night on the "graveyard shift" was uncomfortably cool.

A breeze added to the 2:00 A.M. chill, and Specialist Jesse Pyle pulled his jacket closed at his neck as he looked out at the no-man's-land where he stood watch, waiting for the dawn of February 7, 1965, when he could leave this post and get some sleep. The sound of the generators droned through the darkness in a hypnotic din that made the soldier wish for morning and his turn to sleep.

Through the hum of the generator engines, a soldier's lone voice carried into the night and those men standing watch listened as the man sang while he worked. It was a country song and he sang it properly through his nose and his voice's lonely trill made other soldiers standing watch in the trenches and bunkers that surrounded the Pleiku compound think of dirt-road summertime and creeks with willows and wish very much that they were home.

"What's that?" Pyle said, coming alert to a sound that was neither generator nor singing.

"What?" another soldier said.

"That. A sound. Like running!" Pyle said, searching the no-man's-land, muscling his eyelids wide, straining to see anything in the blackness.

"Yeah!" another now tense soldier exclaimed as he heard it too.

Pyle climbed out of his trench and when he did he saw several figures silhouetted against the cleared ground, running along the edge of the wire.

"Sappers!" he shouted and jumped back in the trench.

A machine gun opened fire that second and immediately the entire world lit afire with tracers. In another second, behind the line where the soldiers stood firing their rifles into the blackness past the edge of the wire, mortar shells exploded. Pleiku was under attack.

"We're gonna die . . . !" a soldier cried out near Pyle while others held to the butts of their rifles and machine guns and chopped away at the sappers running toward their positions despite the barbwire and punji stakes.

The barrage of Communist mortars found its mark in the sleeping quarters of the Special Forces advisers. The soldiers inside never had a chance.

· 4 ·

**M**ORE COFFEE, SIR?" THE ORIENTAL STEWARDESS ASKED, LEANING toward the window of the plane where Eddie Adams sat half sleeping and half watching the water below, trying to see ships or islands or whales, anything to break the boredom of the long flight.

"Okay," he said, turning to see the stewardess already filling his cup that sat on the small tray on the seat back. Adams, a New York–based photographer with the Associated Press, was on his way to Saigon where he would join AP bureau chief Malcolm Browne and writer Peter Arnett in covering the rapidly developing Vietnam conflict.

The stewardess continued her in-flight waitressing and Eddie picked up the newspaper that he had earlier folded and stuffed down the side of his seat. He again looked at the front page where the headline story told about nine U.S. advisers being killed and 128 others being wounded in a Viet Cong mortar attack at Pleiku that also damaged 122 aircraft, totally destroying at least 10 of them.

The article went on to say that because of this escalation of hostilities, President Johnson had ordered the families of all U.S. personnel to depart South Vietnam for safer regions, and that the United States had retaliated with air strikes against North Vietnam. The Pentagon called the air raids Operation Flaming Dart.

The February 8, 1965, newspaper story said that Johnson had gone on television after hearing news of the attack on Pleiku and ordered the retaliatory air raids, and in addition had said, "I have ordered the deployment to South Vietnam of a Hawk air defense battalion. Other reinforcements, in units and individuals, may follow."

Eddie, now barely thirty years old—a man destined to photograph a South Vietnamese general blowing a Viet Cong assassin's brains out and for snapping that picture receive the Pulitzer Prize—read the last sentence quoting the President. He folded the paper and again looked out the window, searching for small islands or flotsam or ships. As his vision glazed to soft focus and drifted with the world's deep blue and scattered white, he wondered whether this trip was such a good idea after all.

· 5 ·

THE FEBRUARY RAIN FELL COLD ON THE BACK OF JIM SHOCKLEY AS he ran from the taxicab to the high chain-link fence that surrounded Camp Schwab. The Marine lance corporal kept in the shadows, despite the cover that the rain provided him, so that he stayed far from the view of the Marines standing guard in the gate shack a quarter mile farther up the road.

Jim Shockley had never stayed out late before. The young Company A radio operator, who enjoyed reading a good book in the barracks more than dogging himself out in Hinoko's bars and skivvy houses, had always made it a point to be in bed by ten o'clock. He was always the Marine who gathered the others' liberty cards and returned with them to the barracks early, where he would check in the still-absent Marines. The NCO standing duty never asked questions, since he too enjoyed the same no-questions-asked service whenever he wanted to remain in Hinoko, drinking and enjoying the girls after liberty had secured.

By standing orders, Marines could only check out for liberty before 10:00 P.M., and they had to return to base by midnight. They had come to call the practice of having a friend check in liberty cards while the cards' owners remained out "Cinderella Liberty" since the stroke of midnight was their magic hour. Because they had no liberty cards to get them past the front gate, they would climb the fence or crawl under it, and sneak to the barracks before morning muster.

Tonight, Jim Shockley had especially enjoyed himself. He and his re-con buddies were in good form with the bar girls, and he considered that he might go home with one of the new *naisan*s they had met this evening. So instead of him collecting his friends' liberty cards and going to the bar-racks early, as usual, another Marine, who had spent his last dollar, vol-unteered to check in everyone.

However, Jim had begun to change his mind about the girl when he saw the *naisan* in the bright light that came on inside the tavern when Sachiko, the owner, began to close. The girl smiled at him in this sober-ing light, and all the young Marine could see was her eyes shaded by long, black false lashes caked with clods of mascara and her face heavily masked with thick makeup. Shockley then knew that he could not stay, and decided to chance getting back on base alone instead of waiting to follow his more experienced friends over the fence.

"Lindy, you and Freddy have fun," he said as he got in the backseat of the small red taxi. The driver knew the routine, one that he repeated many times during the late-night hours on the weekends following mili-tary payday. He would drive near the top of the hill, shut off the car's headlights, and quietly drive off the shoulder to let the Marine out near the Camp Schwab fence.

"Shockley," the one called Lindy shouted through the rain. "You sure you know the spot?"

"No sweat, GI," Jim Shockley shouted back through the downpour. As the cab sped away in the heavy rain, Shockley felt the knot tighten in his stomach. He groped in his pocket for his still-warm pipe, and the feel of it seemed to give him a sense of security. If I get caught, I'll tell them I was out for a smoke, he thought to himself. I hope I can find the right spot to climb over.

Liberty had secured more than two hours earlier, and if he was caught outside the base, after midnight and with no liberty card, he knew that he would pay dearly in the morning for the transgression. The thought of facing 3rd Reconnaissance Battalion's commanding officer, Lieutenant Colonel Don H. "Doc" Blanchard, gave him extra motivation to avoid capture.

This has got to be the right spot, he thought as he pulled himself up the crisscrossed wire and cautiously worked his way over the barbed wire that tilted outward from the top of the fence. The rain frustrated him as he reached for the edge of the roof of the building that stood next to the fence, and as he balanced himself on the top strands and leaned toward the building, he nearly fell, and his heart choked in his throat.

This isn't worth it, he told himself as he now dangled from the roof's edge while the rain blinded him. As he pulled one elbow onto the roof and then the other, and then pushed the rest of his body up onto the roof, he saw the headlights of a jeep swing past on the street inside the fence that ran past the corner of the building. His heart pounded in his chest as he lay still on the roof and waited until he could no longer hear the jeep's engine nor see the reflection of its lights.

Now, I'll just drop to the ground and trot down to the barracks, he told himself, filled with fresh confidence and a sense of triumph as he hung from the other side of the roof and let go.

The Marine standing guard duty in the parking lot of 3rd Amtrack Battalion heard the thud, even though the rain pounded on his helmet and the rubber poncho that he wore. The sound could not have come from more than twenty feet away.

"Halt!" he called into the darkness and downpour. "Who is there?"

"Shit!" Shockley said, picking himself up from the ankle-deep mud that covered the amtrack parking area. He looked at his khaki uniform and saw the great circles of mud and oil that now stained them despite the driving rain that soaked him. "It's only me, Lance Corporal Shockley. Where am I?"

"Third track's parking lot. What the hell are you doing out here?" the private standing guard duty asked. "Everybody else comes in over the warehouses back yonder or under the fence along the ditch over there, out of sight."

"I've never done this before," Shockley said. "I got mixed up."

"Well, you shit in it too," the sentry said. "The corporal of the guard is coming right now, that's his headlights, and if I let you go, he'll see you. You better come up with something good, fast."

Jim Shockley shoved his hand in his pocket and felt his pipe. He had been smoking it earlier and it still held a load of tobacco. "Let me get under your poncho for a second," he asked the sentry.

"Why?"

"I need to light my pipe," Shockley said as he knelt to one knee and leaned under the poncho while the sentry spread it for better shelter.

"Private," the corporal of the guard shouted from the jeep as it stopped and he saw Jim Shockley kneeling under the sentry's poncho. "What's going on?"

"Corporal," the sentry said, letting down his poncho and walking toward the jeep. Jim Shockley stood and pulled hard on his pipe while he sheltered the bowl with his hand. "I found Lance Corporal Shockley wandering around in the parking lot."

"Shockley," the corporal shouted, "get your ass over here!"

Jim Shockley walked casually to the jeep, still pulling smoke from his pipe. "I'm just out for a walk, Corporal. Any law against that?"

"You're out here in your khakis, in this fucking typhoon, and you expect me to believe you're out for a walk?" the corporal bellowed. "Who the fuck do you think I am? You're gonna tell your story to the sergeant of the guard, I don't have time for this horse shit. Get in."

"Honest," Shockley said as he climbed inside the jeep and sat next to the radio.

The sergeant of the guard was a thin man who looked battle-hard. He wore four rows of ribbons on his khaki shirt and Jim Shockley recognized the red-white-and-blue ribbon that represented the Silver Star medal at the top of the rows. Obviously this sergeant has seen action in Korea and probably in World War II as well. He would be wise to any lies, but the young lance corporal had already committed himself.

"Check with the duty NCO," Jim Shockley suggested before the sergeant had time to consider what to do about the young Marine who claimed to be out for a walk and a smoke in the rain and mud.

"Good idea," the sergeant said. "Let's see if you were legally in or out."

"I'm checked in," Shockley said with confidence. "It's like I've been saying. I checked in from liberty at ten o'clock, and I couldn't sleep. I got up, put on the dirty uniform. What could the rain hurt with a dirty uniform? I went out to smoke my pipe. I can't smoke it in the barracks after lights out."

"That's the biggest crock of shit I've ever heard," the sergeant said.

In a moment, the corporal of the guard returned to the guard shack and reported to the sergeant that Lance Corporal Shockley was registered in the Duty Log as having returned from liberty at 10:00 P.M.

The sergeant glared at Jim Shockley and pointed to the door. "Get the fuck out of here."

The lance corporal snapped an about-face and marched quickly to the door, and just as he pushed the screen door open, the sergeant shouted, "Shockley, don't think for a minute that you got away with anything. I was a snuffy too, and I know all about checking in buddies from liberty and this fence-climbing crap. You can't snow the snowman! We'll all be over in South Vietnam sooner than you think, and you pull this kind of bullshit over there and your buddy standing guard might just shoot first. I'm making a point to talk to your first sergeant, John Henry. We're old partners. Don't think this is over, lad. Not by a long shot."

Jim Shockley shoved his right hand into his pocket and clutched his pipe tightly as he let the screen door slam behind him. He never looked back.

### • 6 •

SMOKE STILL ROSE FROM THE RUBBLE. IT HAD GOTTEN HIS ATTENTION first. Eddie Adams turned the focusing ring on his camera lens and sharpened the image of the smoke and the American soldiers in it, poking through the debris that was once their home, looking for what few personal possessions they might still recover. Sadness and anger gripped his soul as he watched these soldiers, mostly boys who were away from home for the first time. He snapped their pictures and thought of the Viet Cong who did this, and in his heart he felt a need for justice. Why did they have to bomb the enlisted men's barracks? he asked himself.

He thought of the article that he had read about Pleiku only two days earlier, and he wondered if the same guerrillas had done this work too. Pleiku was eighty miles due west, but he reasoned that the Viet Cong could have easily hit Pleiku and then marched eastward to the coast and struck Qui Nhon.

Eddie listened to the other reporters, who had come to Qui Nhon to see the damage, as they questioned the Army information officer while they walked in a group back to the flight line and their waiting helicopter that would shuttle them back to Saigon. The information officer spoke in step with choppy phrases that told facts of the tragedy in sanitary terms that Eddie considered gave little justice to those young boys who had slept in the now shambled structure and had died in it only a few hours ago.

Like Pleiku, the compound at Qui Nhon housed a number of U.S. Army Special Forces advisers and helicopter support crews. The enclave consisted of administrative and barracks buildings and an airfield. On the night of February 10, the Viet Cong sappers did not reach the airfield, but they did manage to get through the wire and bomb the enlisted men's barracks. This time twenty-three American soldiers had died and twenty-two others had survived with wounds.

It had taken only a matter of minutes for the press to get its story today, and each reporter hurriedly jotted notes and numbers on his pad and recorded last-minute thoughts that would lead the news articles, once they had returned to Saigon. Eddie simply sat, strapped to his seat, and watched the smoke and the boys and the rubble.

He thought to himself how deceptive the word "soldier" seemed, so grown adult, ready to die, and that these soldiers were really forty-five boys who fell. Boys who less than a year ago had played sandlot baseball and had worried about school grades and the girls next door, and now twenty-three of them would never again see the sun rise. No, he thought, "soldier" was a word devised to separate the human child who died and his sick-to-the-soul family who mourned him from the faceless, nameless pawn that the rest of America would envision after reading the news accounts of Qui Nhon, and would hardly care. After all, these casualties were just soldiers.

While Eddie and the other reporters flew back to Saigon, more than one hundred U.S. Navy aircraft launched from a carrier and flew a second Flaming Dart reprisal attack on North Vietnam.

After the Qui Nhon incident, defense advisers told President Johnson that the retaliatory raids of Operation Flaming Dart had not achieved the intended effect, and they recommended that he approve a "sustained pressure" campaign to include continuing air strikes against targets in North Vietnam, naval bombardment, covert operations, intelligence patrols, and cross-border operations in Laos, and, most significantly, the landing of American troops in South Vietnam.

## • 7 •

"YOU SEE THIS?" MALCOLM BROWNE SAID, TEARING OFF A PIECE OF teletype copy from the AP machine in the Saigon bureau.

"What's that?" Eddie Adams said, walking through the door.

"McGeorge Bundy told President Johnson that South Vietnam will fall within the year unless the United States does something to turn it around," Browne said. "He says there's still time, but not much."

Eddie took the camera bag from his shoulder and set it on the table where other camera equipment and stacks of photographs cluttered most of its area, leaving only a small cleared space where he did his office work. He took a package of Pall Mall cigarettes from a small pocket on his sleeve and stuck one in his mouth as he walked to the machine where Browne stood reading the copy.

"I think we're going to see American troops land soon," Eddie said, and walked back to the table and sat down. He reached toward a butt-filled ashtray and tapped his cigarette on its edge.

Already the whole thing seemed obvious to him and he knew it was just a matter of time. He had come to South Vietnam to work for two weeks and then go home. He had been here less than a week, and in that time he had seen the war nearly double in escalation. He knew that, so far, Bundy was right, South Vietnam was very quickly going down the tubes. Eddie felt certain that American ground forces would be coming before that happened, and he made his decision to be there when they came ashore.

"I want to telex New York," Eddie said. "I'm going to stay a few more weeks."

"Fine," Browne said, walking away from the machine, "you can stay a year, if you want."

"I have an idea that Johnson will send in the Marines anytime," Eddie said. "That will be the story."

## • 8 •

JOHN DELGROSSO LAID DOWN TWO DOLLARS AND LOOKED AT THE retired U.S. Air Force master sergeant who tended bar at the Kadena

Air Force Base officers' club, and said, "Set 'em up for the house, and keep the change."

The bartender poured six drinks and handed out eleven bottles of beer. Then he laid the two dollars in the cash drawer and took out three dimes that he then dropped into a glass near the center of the bar that held a dollar bill and several coins.

As he sold a beer or a mixed drink, the customer would frequently drop a nickel or a dime into the glass. The bartender had put in the dollar bill, hoping that its presence might encourage a customer to feel that it was alright to tip a bill. Rarely did anyone, however, and usually the dollar tip would come at the end of a drinking session where the customer had not tipped earlier.

Although the tips were small, traffic was heavy in the club that had somehow picked up the unofficial name "Habu Pit," which is the Okinawan word for snake. In a week he usually cleared nearly a hundred dollars in tips. Added to his retirement pay, the money that he earned at the o'club made him a wealthy man by local standards. He and his Okinawan wife lived well.

John DelGrosso tilted his beer toward Frank Reasoner, gesturing a toast, and said, "Drinks for the house at less than two bucks. You can't beat these prices."

Frank Reasoner was busy stuffing a load of tobacco into his calabash pipe and didn't look up. He said, "No, John, but this won't last forever either. Sooner or later you've got to go home, and a GI's pay doesn't buy shit these days. When I was a sergeant, I got about thirty dollars a payday; now I get over twice that, thank God, but ask my wife, even in Idaho she and my boy still have to get by on bare bones."

John looked at his friend. "Forgive me, Frank, but I don't subscribe to young Marines getting married. You know all too well why. I'm not taking that stumble down the aisle until I make lieutenant colonel."

"You may never then, John. You'll be lucky to see captain," Frank Reasoner said and winked at his friend. "Speaking of colonels, what the hell is Colonel Blanchard doing? Every now and then I see him lean over and squirt some liquid down the bar."

"Lighter fluid," John DelGrosso said. "When I bought the drinks, he shot me across the arm. I thought he had a water pistol until I smelled the stuff. He's got a giant can, see, under the bar there," and he pointed to where the lieutenant colonel stood at the bar and had laid a yellow-and-blue can on the empty seat next to him.

"Yeah, I see it," Frank said.

"He's been squirting that shit all over the bar," John said.

"Don't suppose it can hurt anything, can it?" Reasoner said, lighting his pipe.

"Naw. The bar has a copper top. The stuff is just mixing in the water and booze. Probably evaporates in a heartbeat," John said.

"He's up to something," Reasoner said and looked back at his friend.

John DelGrosso shrugged. "Whatever it is, it doesn't seem to be working. Nobody's paying attention. Bet he's just trying to get a rise out of one of those Air Force Phantom jocks, but they aren't biting."

"They know better," Frank said and both men chuckled.

"I can't help it, but I get a real kick watching our guys fuck with these zoomies' minds week after week," Frank Reasoner said. "It's like a ritual. The Marines show up here at three o'clock when the bar opens, do their best to soak up five dollars' worth of booze, and at six o'clock, when the airedales show up with their round-eyed old ladies, these turds pull the same old shit."

John DelGrosso laughed. "All they want to do is dance with their wives, not fuck 'em."

"No, John," Frank Reasoner said, "they want to fuck 'em."

"Yeah, Frank, and those women, you can't tell me that it isn't a turn-on for these Marines to go sniffing up their legs. Even the ugly ones," John DelGrosso said, almost sounding serious.

"It sure pisses their old men, though," Frank Reasoner said. "That's the only thing that makes the trip down from Schwab worth it."

Doc Blanchard leaned on the bar and took out an eight-inch-long, half-inch-thick, hand-rolled cigar that he had bought in the Philippines. He bit off its tip, spit it toward Frank Reasoner and John DelGrosso, and smiled at them. Then he struck a wooden match, put it to the cigar as he took several steps from the bar, and then dropped the match in an ashtray on a table where two Air Force lieutenants sat.

"Doc's in rare form," Frank Reasoner said, watching 3rd Recon's commanding officer swagger back to the bar, pick up the blue-and-yellow can, and launch a stream of fluid that nearly reached halfway down the thirty-foot-long bar.

"Hey, watch that shit!" someone at the bar shouted.

"That's our CO!" John DelGrosso said and laughed.

"Maybe somebody will take a swing at him," Frank said.

"Yeah, and we'll end up like that kid Shockley and those other wise guys who got in that donnybrook over at the Hill Top Club last Friday night," John DelGrosso said.

"Just remember to fill out your statement with a pencil," Frank Reasoner said and laughed.

Another lieutenant sat at the table. "Hey, Del, Reasoner, those two Air Force fucks told me that I couldn't fart in the officers' club."

Frank Reasoner looked at the lieutenant and grinned behind his pipe. "So you showed them, huh?"

"Right," the lieutenant said, "I cut one, just to test their theory. You can too fart in here, just fine. I told them they must have asshole problems. What's this pencil bullshit?"

"This kid from Alpha Company, Lance Corporal Shockley, he's a radio operator," John DelGrosso said. "He and some other snuffies damn never leveled the enlisted club, and Shockley walked on account he filled out his statement in pencil."

"You gotta be shitting me. A fucking pencil is all that stood between him and the wrath of Genghis Blanchard?" the lieutenant said.

"No shit," John DelGrosso said. "Shockley comes by to ask my advice since I'm in dirty Delta Company, out of his chain of command, and he and I get along anyway because he's a real scholar. Anyways, Shockley comes by my office on Tuesday and he's all shook. Now I had already heard about the brawl, but Shockley filled me in on the details.

"He said that some guys from 3rd Motor T were in there raising hell and got out of line with a corporal from Recon. Well, Shockley's standing next to him when these two assholes start. One of the Motor T guys is supposed to be a karate black belt, and he starts breaking heads and furniture. Shockley said he took a pretty good shot, got knocked to the floor, and was trying to crawl out when this bum grabs the bottom of his blouse and rips our boy a vent right up to his collar. Jim Shockley is on the small side but a very solid kid, slow to burn, but very solid. And this got him.

"Shockley knows that he can't take this guy straight out, so he grabs a chair. Then someone else grabs a chair. Then the whole place is a wreck.

"Just then the camp guard reaction force invades the Hill Top Club and starts cracking heads. They drag Shockley and his partners down to the guard shack where this pissed-off sergeant doesn't give two shits about their Article 32 rights,[1] and he makes them write out confessions. They all use black ink, except Shockley. He said he didn't like the idea of making a statement, so he used a pencil. He said he didn't know why, but it just seemed that since the Marine Corps prefers everything that is official to be signed in black ink, he thought writing in pencil might give him an edge.

"That kid is smart. He doesn't know it, but he is. Maybe someday he'll be a lawyer because he's got good instincts. The pencil bit paid off.

"The legal officer is reading the statements and comes across Shockley's. He has the young lance corporal down there, standing tall, and tells him to rewrite the thing in ink. Shockley looks at this lieutenant and asks him if he can think about it. The lieutenant says no. So Shockley says he doesn't think he wants to rewrite it, that the pencil statement will have to do.

"Tuesday, I'm in my office and Shockley raps on the window. I meet him on the stoop and he fills me in on all this. He asks me what I think.

"I tell him that it really doesn't make any difference, pen or pencil, but apparently the legal officer thinks so, and based on that, I tell him that he'll probably walk if he sticks to his guns.

"None of the other guys had mentioned his name in their statements, so they don't have a thing on him except his own confession, in pencil."

Frank Reasoner laughed. He looked at both lieutenants and said, "Doc Blanchard gave 'em all EPD[2] and the corporal a suspended bust. Shockley slid right out of that and got picked up on the next quota to scuba school in the Philippines. So now Shockley's down in the PI pulling the best liberty on earth while those other poor bastards are spending their weekends cutting grass."

The lieutenant looked at John DelGrosso. "You think Blanchard knows?"

"I wouldn't bet against it," John DelGrosso said. "He probably gave

---

[1]Article 32 under the Uniform Code of Military Justice is the rights of an accused. They prevent him from being questioned without legal counsel and guarantee him that he may not be forced to make any statements of self-incrimination.
[2]Extra Punishment Duty.

Shockley the PI quota as a reward for using his noodle. Anyway, Shockley's a good egg. He never makes trouble."

One of the Okinawan waitresses delivered a fresh order of beers to the table where the three Marines sat and pointed toward Doc Blanchard. He held the cigar in his teeth and sent another stream of lighter fluid down the bar. This time he failed to get the full thrust of fluid so he up-ended the can and sent several Marines who stood at the bar rushing backward.

"Looks like that bullshit has finally come to an end," Frank Reasoner said. "Probably a good thing too. The place is really filling up with the zoomies and their wives."

John DelGrosso looked over his shoulder and saw that several Air Force officers and their wives had gathered at tables away from the bar, but now since those tables were filled, the newcomers were forced to sit nearer to the bar where more than twenty Marine officers sat or stood drinking.

Several Marines had already begun flirting with some of the American women, and one officer walked to the jukebox, reached behind it, and turned up the machine's volume.

"On your feet!" he then shouted in speech slurred by several hours of drinking. "Don't let this good music go to waste. If these flutter-tails won't dance with you ladies, we got a dozen Marines who will!"

Frank Reasoner looked at John DelGrosso and dumped his pipe in the ashtray. "Looks like the evening is showing lots of promise. We may get in a little PT after all. These guys don't look real happy."

"Oh, shit," John DelGrosso said. "I've got a bad feeling. Look at Doc!"

Frank Reasoner turned to the bar just in time to see a dozen Marines crash backward, rushing away from the bar, and Doc Blanchard drawing hard, again and again on the cigar that was now down to a three-inch-long butt with an inch-long brightly glowing coal.

"Jesus!" John shouted just as the dimly lit club suddenly ignited broad-daylight orange as the bar became a sudden wall of flame. Behind him he could hear the screams of both men and women and the crash of furniture upended, accompanied by the sound of glass shattering across the floor. "He threw his fucking cigar on the bar!"

There was little smoke, and the flash of fire that had licked the ceiling in a thirty-foot-long line died to a few flickers in a matter of seconds, but its horrifying effect cleared the club.

The Air Force officers, with their wives crying and pleading, crowded outside the club's front door and shouted obscenities at Doc Blanchard and a dozen half-drunk and howling Marines that he led away. The bartender never left his post next to the cash register, and now he could only manage to scream streams of profanity at the only two people he could see—John DelGrosso and Frank Reasoner who just sat at their table, struggling breathlessly in a fit of laughter.

None of Blanchard's Marines returned to the Kadena Air Force Base officers' club after that. In a matter of three weeks, they had all shipped out to South Vietnam.

John DelGrosso claimed that Doc Blanchard must have known that his Marines would not be coming back to the o'club, that they were all headed to South Vietnam. He believed it was the lieutenant colonel's way of saying good-bye to the Air Force officers and their wives that his Marines had harassed weekend after weekend.

·9·

CAPTAIN PATRICK G. COLLINS SAT AT ONE OF THE LONG, FORMICA-topped tables on the mess deck of the attack transport ship USS *Bayfield* (APA 33), drinking a second cup of orange juice with his breakfast. Next to him sat a young-looking second lieutenant, one of Collins's platoon commanders, and at another table across the mess deck from where the officers sat, a cluster of his Marines from 3rd Reconnaissance Battalion chatted and ate. The captain and what was left of his reconnaissance company were supporting the 2nd Battalion, 3rd Marine Regiment, en route to participate in a SEATO training exercise in Thailand called Jungle Drum III.

At thirty-two, Captain Pat Collins, square-jawed and tan, was tough as a bulldog and built like a small tank. He had enlisted in the Marine Corps in 1952, made corporal, and saw his first combat in Korea as a scout/observer. He got out of the Corps in 1955 and headed home to Grosse Isle, Michigan. While he went to college in Detroit, Collins joined the Marine Corps Reserve and returned to active duty as a sergeant in

1958. That same year, as a meritorious NCO, he went to Officer Candidates School and was commissioned a second lieutenant.

He had become what enlisted Marines call a "Mustang"—an officer usually worthy of their greatest trust because he had worn stripes, walked in their shoes, and, therefore, was kin. To a man, Collins's Marines were devoted to him. His Marines saw Pat Collins as the guy up front who feared nothing and knew everything, and they knew with certainty if a Marine stuck close enough to Collins, the "Mad Man" would sooner or later scare the hell out of him.

While plates and cups clanked and his Marines talked, Collins sat, sipping his juice and listening to the latest radio news, broadcast over the ship's public address system. The day was March 7, 1965, and the newscaster's top story headline was "Vietnam, the Marines are landing," but it was no surprise to Pat Collins. He and his men had spent the past six months preparing to land in South Vietnam, and strongly suspected that it would happen any day since Jungle Drum III had shrunk from brigade size to battalion and since their whittled-down Navy Task Group 76.6 had gone to Thailand while the flagship USS *Mount McKinley* (AGC 7) and the muscle of Navy Task Force 76 set sail for the South China Sea.

The newscaster led the story with the revelation that President Johnson announced that in addition to the Operation Flaming Dart retaliatory air strikes presently flown against North Vietnam, he had approved a "limited and measured" air campaign called Operation Rolling Thunder.

The newscaster then told that because of the political instability in the past weeks—the takeover of the government by the Vietnamese Armed Forces Council, the ousting of General Nguyen Khanh as Commander in Chief of the armed forces, and the coming to power of Major General Nguyen Van Thieu and Air Vice Marshal Nguyen Cao Ky—"General William C. Westmoreland, Commander, U.S. Military Assistance Command, Vietnam, has asked President Johnson to land two battalions of Marines to guard the air facility at Da Nang because of its vital importance in supporting the air campaign against North Vietnam."

The reporter then said that President Johnson had just announced his approval of Westmoreland's request and that the Marines would soon land.

Collins sipped his juice without a word while others sitting at the mess deck's long tables had hushed to listen to the news and now talked excitedly about the prospects of how it might affect them.

Nudging the lieutenant sitting to his left, Collins said, "Let's go up on deck and get some air. We need to talk."

The two men said nothing to any of the other Marines and sailors, and they hardly noticed Collins and his lieutenant leaving, except an excited, square-faced Marine who shouted to the two officers, "Hey, Skipper. Just our luck. We're here and we oughta be over there."

Looking back and seeing the Marine who spoke, one of his corporals, beaming a confident smile, Collins said, "We'll be there soon enough."

"You think so, sir?" the corporal said with a voice that rose sharply.

"Take my word for it, lad," Collins said quickly, "your honey-wah back at Hinoko will just have to forget about her cherry-boy."

The corporal laughed. "Skipper, that hog? Piss on her. She's probably giving some limp-dick squid the clap right now anyway."

"Fuck you, jarhead!" a voice grumbled.

The corporal looked down the table to a boatswains mate—a red-haired man with a ruddy, round face and a thick red mustache—and cawed, "You squids. The only reason you have Marines aboard is so you's can have some men to dance with."

Collins and the lieutenant ducked through the hatchway and could hear the jeering and laughing that erupted behind them.

Gray sky and stormy seas greeted the two Marines as they climbed the ladder that led them up to the bridge. Leaning over the railing and looking at the waves spraying over the ship's gunwales, Collins motioned for the lieutenant to come close. The wind blew steady and strong from the southwest and the heavy seas heaved the ship as it cut through them, heading westerly.

"This isn't good," Collins shouted above the wind's roar as the lieutenant came close and looked below at the rough water. "By tonight this storm system will be hitting the task force landing the 9th MEB."[3]

"They'll have a tough time getting into the boats if it's anything like this," the lieutenant shouted back.

"Dick Gesswein and Bill Vankat are landing their platoons in that shit," Collins said. "Thank God Dave Whittingham and his subunit[4] did

[3] 9th Marine Expeditionary Brigade.
[4] Subunit 1, 1st Force Reconnaissance Company.

the underwater surveys in February; they would have had problems with this weather had they not seen this landing coming."

The lieutenant looked at the captain and said, "You didn't want to come out here to talk about Captain Whittingham and the weather, sir."

"No," Collins said. "I thought you might like to know how we fit in."

"Me and the troops," the lieutenant said.

"We'll talk to them. I want them thinking about two-three[5] and this exercise, though. You know we have that to do first," Collins said.

"You think like my old football coach," the lieutenant said.

"I am, in a way. Only the stakes in this game are a lot higher," Collins said.

"So what's the score?" the lieutenant asked.

Collins looked at the rough sea and said, "We'll support two-three until the close of the exercise, but we're not hanging around for the critique." Then he looked at the lieutenant and said, "We're going in behind the 9th MEB with the rest of 3rd Marines. Don't count on seeing Okinawa anytime soon, and plan on missing your rotation date home. I've got a hunch that a lot of guys are going to spend a little more time West-Pac[6] than they planned on."

The lieutenant said nothing and looked out to the stormy sea while the wind whipped his face. After a moment of thought he looked at Collins and said, "I thought it was a mission to beef up the defense around Da Nang Air Base and the 1st LAAM Battalion[7] Hawk sites."

Collins looked at the lieutenant and said, "That's the excuse. But if you believe that, I've got a bridge on New York's Lower East Side I'll sell you for a hundred bucks. You don't have to be any great brain to put two and two together. There are a lot of guys who want us in there kicking Communist ass because those goofy South Vietnamese can't do shit. We aren't going to win this war unless we go in and do the fighting."

"Sure, you're right, sir," the lieutenant said. "Just listen to those guys back there on the mess deck. No way would they be satisfied just sitting behind sandbags and walking guard duty."

[5]2nd Battalion, 3rd Marine Regiment.
[6]Western Pacific.
[7]1st Light Anti-Aircraft Missile (LAAM) Battalion was the Hawk air defense battalion that President Johnson had deployed to Da Nang on February 7, 1965, following the attack on Pleiku.

Collins clapped the young officer on the back and started to walk away, but looked back and said, "Oh, yeah. I don't need to tell you not to write your wife or anybody else about all this until after we are ashore in South Vietnam."

The lieutenant nodded and smiled understandingly at the captain. Then once Collins had stepped through the hatchway that led back down the ladder to the mess deck with its PA-system music and the loud talk and laughter from the mixture of Marines and Navy men, he looked again at the stormy sea and the spray curling over the ship's gunwales and enjoyed the coolness of the wet wind as he thought of his future.

## • 10 •

FREDDY!" REAR ADMIRAL DON W. WULZEN SAID AS HE KNOCKED ON the bulkhead outside the hatchway that led into Brigadier General Frederick J. Karch's stateroom. It was midnight but a light was still on and the admiral could see the Marine's stocking feet cross-ankle at the chair where Karch was sitting, still awake. "Here's a dispatch."

Karch, the deputy commander of the 3rd Marine Division, had assumed command of the 9th Marine Expeditionary Brigade on January 22, 1965. His two Battalion Landing Teams, the 1st and the 3rd Battalions of the 9th Marine Regiment, were on alert at sea, standing at a point thirty miles off Cap St. Jacques, seventy miles southeast of Saigon.

The U.S. was not yet committed to sending in ground units and all seemed stable enough in South Vietnam, so the day after he assumed command, Karch received orders to relax his brigade's alert status. Battalion Landing Team 3/9[8] sailed off on normal sea operations and a planned liberty stop in Hong Kong while BLT 1/9 moved out to a limit that would allow them a ninety-six-hour reaction time to land in South Vietnam.

The same day that the 9th MEB split up, the floor fell from beneath the current South Vietnamese government with Buddhist-inspired riots in Saigon and Hue, and then the ouster of Premier Tran Van Huong a few days later. The 9th MEB sailed back to Cap St. Jacques and waited.

Things again cooled, but in the meantime General Westmoreland had

[8]3rd Battalion, 9th Marine Regiment.

asked that the Seventh Fleet position one amphibious group off Cape Varella, within twenty-four-hour strike time from either Saigon or Da Nang, Admiral Ulysses S. Grant Sharp, Commander in Chief, Pacific, denied Westmoreland's request but did approve a seventy-two-hour alert status for one amphibious group—General Karch and his 9th MEB.

Karch and his Marines sailed for Subic Bay, the Philippines, where one of the two battalions would alternate the watch, remaining on seventy-two-hour alert. Karch had participated in the planning of Jungle Drum III when the attacks on Pleiku and later Qui Nhon took place, changing everything. The Thai government had to settle on a Marine battalion landing team rather than a brigade for the Jungle Drum III exercise; meanwhile, 1/9 and 3/9 shipped out again for Cap St. Jacques and Da Nang.

By the end of February the future had become obvious and President Johnson approved sending in two battalions of Marines. The 9th MEB would soon land, and Karch briefed all his staff, and they planned the landing. While 2/3 sailed for Thailand, Karch and his Marines made ready to land at either Da Nang or Saigon, once the order came.

While Karch and his Marines made ready to land, Ambassador Maxwell Taylor met with Vietnamese Prime Minister Phan Huy Quat and received permission to bring ashore the United States ground combat forces.

Taylor also met with the minister of the Vietnamese Armed Forces, General Nguyen Van Thieu, and the chairman of the Vietnamese Joint General Staff, General Tran Van Minh ("Little Minh"), and discussed with them the details of the 9th MEB landing. Neither offered objections to landing U.S. ground combat troops; however, they did say that they were concerned about how the Vietnamese populace might react, and they asked that the forces come into Da Nang "in the most inconspicuous way feasible."

Hearing of the Vietnamese generals' concern, Assistant Secretary of Defense John T. McNaughton said that it would be best to bring in the 173rd Airborne Brigade by air from Okinawa rather than landing the Marines. Both General Westmoreland and Ambassador Taylor immediately objected and sent messages of the same to Admiral Sharp. The admiral cabled the Joint Chiefs of Staff:

Since the origination of OPLAN 32 in 1959, the Marines have been scheduled for deployment to Da Nang . . . contingency plans and a myriad of supporting plans at lower echelons reflect this same deployment. As a result, there has been extensive planning, reconnaissance, and logistics preparation over the years. The CG, 9th MEB, is presently in Da Nang finalizing the details for landing the MEB forces in such a way as to cause minimum impact on the civilian populace . . . I recommend that the MEB be landed at Da Nang as previously planned.

With the new questions of who should go ashore and the political red tape still tangled, Karch wondered while he drilled his staff in their busy preparations to land if this would be another false alarm or would they actually go ashore.

On February 26 he and his staff completed Operation Plan 37D-65 for the amphibious landing of one BLT and the airlift of another from Okinawa to Da Nang. Karch's G-1, Major Ruel T. Scyphers, got his instructions from the general at 8:00 P.M. the next day, and by 3 A.M. on February 28 he had the operation order finished and boxed for distribution.

Then on March 2, Karch received orders to proceed with his staff in Okinawa directly to Da Nang, where his Marines had waited offshore since February 8. Karch issued a warning order to the 3/9 commander, Lieutenant Colonel Charles E. McPartlin, Jr., to be prepared to "administratively land the landing force."

While General Karch and his staff departed for Subic Bay, McPartlin and his battalion landing team began their wait. Hour by hour. Day by day. The bored Marines stood ten miles off the shore of Da Nang, knowing yet not really knowing what the next hour might bring nor what their futures might contain.

On March 6 General Karch and his 9th MEB staff returned to Da Nang and then joined the wait aboard the Task Force 76 flagship, USS *Mount McKinley* (AGC 7), standing by, as his orders had said, "for further instructions."

Seeing the general, the Marines' hopes immediately rose, but after the first day and into the second, with no word, their enthusiasm quickly soured.

Karch, a small man with a pencil-thin mustache, looked up as Admiral Wulzen, the Task Force 76 commander, stepped through the hatchway to the general's stateroom. Karch had been sitting, wondering how long it would take before the politicians would make up their minds on whether to send in the Army Airborne from Okinawa or his Marines.

"Freddy, here. Look!" Wulzen said, handing the sheet of paper to the general and knowing what the dispatch he held in his hand meant, but saying nothing.

"Close Da Nang. Land the landing force," Karch read aloud. He looked at the admiral who now sat across from him. "Don, do you think in Washington they know what time it is in Da Nang? This means a night landing if we close Da Nang at this point."

As they spoke, both men listened to the storm that had rocked Pat Collins and his Marines and now tossed about the amphibious task force off the shores of South Vietnam.

The admiral said nothing but nodded in agreement and shared wonder.

"That storm outside is the worst I've seen here, ever," Karch said; he stood and began pacing. "What's the visibility?"

"A hundred fifty, maybe two hundred yards, and heavy seas," Wulzen responded.

"It's midnight now," Karch went on, "and we're going to take between four and five hours to get into position in Da Nang harbor."

"That's the way I see it," Wulzen said.

"H hour will be at zero-eight-hundred. We're not going to make a night landing when it's an administrative move. With these conditions, it's just too dangerous. I don't think Washington will care one way or the other," Karch said.

"I don't think they'll notice," Wulzen said. "We had better turn to."

General Karch hurried up to the ship's Combat Operations Center and radioed General Nguyen Chanh Thi, the South Vietnamese I Corps commander, who was regarded by many as the virtual warlord of South Vietnam's five northern provinces.

"I apologize for getting you up, General Thi," Karch said, "but we're coming ashore in the morning."

"I know," Thi responded, "your State Department made the announcement this evening so that the Vietnamese people could be told at about the same time you came ashore. They did not want to surprise the people or frighten them."

"I understand," Karch said. "We'll start at eight and be finished by sixteen-hundred on the ninth."

"Very good," Thi said.

"General Thi," Karch said, "I would like your assurance that Route One will be closed to civilians for those thirty-six hours that we are making our movement to the airfield."

"Consider it done," Thi said. "I will have my forces regulate traffic from the beach to the air base, and I will leave the beachhead to you."

"Excellent," Karch responded and signed off.

The Marine general then radioed Lieutenant Colonel McPartlin and told him that he would be responsible for the beachhead traffic while the Vietnamese Army would take care of the rest. Karch assured him that civilians would not be a problem with their movement.

"I've got Thi's word on that," Karch said, and then after he signed off with the BLT commander, the general recalled his first meeting with Thi.

That had been on February 27 and he had traveled up from Saigon to meet Thi and discuss the landing plan. As Karch and Army Brigadier General William E. DePuy, General Westmoreland's operations chief (J-3), approached General Thi's headquarters, a jeep rolled up with a *New York Times* reporter in it.

Recognizing the reporter, DePuy turned to Karch and said, "That is bad news."

When the two generals got inside the Vietnamese general's headquarters, a call had already come in for General DePuy from Saigon. "Get Karch and his staff out of the country as quickly as possible."

As General Karch walked back to his quarters to try for a couple of hours' rest before dawn, he felt troubled about General Thi's cooperation. That was not in the warlord's nature.

· 11 ·

EDDIE ADAMS HAD PACKED HIS EQUIPMENT AND CLOTHES AND hauled it and himself to Da Nang as quickly as he could, once he saw the "Flash" story ticker over the wire on the morning of March 7, 1965. He and Peter Arnett along with *Life* magazine photographer Larry Burrows caught the first helicopter north and set up shop at a Da Nang hotel as close to the air base as they could find.

A reporter showed up at the hotel bar that night and said, "They're landing in the morning. I got the word from an inside source. They'll land

in the morning on a stretch they've named Red Beach 2. That's along the
north end of the bay."

"What time?" Eddie asked.

"My guess is daylight," the reporter said.

"Makes sense," Eddie said to Larry Burrows, and finished his beer and
walked away from the bar, heading for his room. "I'll see you on the beach."

At 5:00 A.M. Eddie Adams sat on the sand and huddled against one
of the trees that lined Red Beach, trying to shelter himself from the damp
air and drizzle. In the darkness, he pulled a cigarette from the pack in his
sleeve and lit it.

"That you, Eddie," a voice in the darkness spoke from somewhere
behind him.

"Right, Larry," Eddie said.

"I don't see anything on the horizon, but did you catch a look at
those banners and garland along Route One and at the beach entry?" another voice in the darkness said.

"I smell General Thi," Eddie said. Then he closed his eyes and waited
in the darkness, sitting under the trees, trying to keep dry with the other
reporters and photographers who got there early too.

At 6:00 A.M. the sky brightened enough to show its thick gray clouds.

"Flat light," Eddie said, "and there's the ships."

Less than 4,000 meters away from the beach, four ships dropped
their anchors and over their loudspeaker systems came the voice of Admiral Wulzen: "Land the landing force."

Eddie could not clearly hear the words said, but he knew what the announcement had been. He had served in the Marine Corps during the
Korean War and had made the rank of staff sergeant. It was there that
Eddie Adams began working as a news photographer, taking pictures and
writing stories for his command newspaper and hoping that some of his
work might get published in the magazine of the Marine Corps; *Leather-
neck*.

During those years in the Marine Corps as a combat correspondent,
Eddie had learned about the commands "Close the beach" and "Land the
landing force."

Quietly Eddie got to his feet and walked to the water's edge, put up
his longest telephoto lens, knelt to the steadiness of one knee, and looked
at the four ships, one by one. During the early morning the weather had

improved to only an intermittent drizzle, with a moderate wind coming from the northwest and visibility easily five miles. Eddie could see the dark shapes of men at the edges of the ships and the black webs of cargo netting hanging from the ships' sides. He looked at his watch: 6:15 A.M.

"It will be an hour at least before the first wave comes ashore," he said.

"You think so?" a voice responded to his left.

"Shit, I didn't see you standing there," Eddie said.

"An hour?" the reporter said and knelt next to Eddie, where he looked through binoculars at the ships.

"At least," Eddie said as he stood. Then with the back of his hand, he knocked the wet sand from the knee of his khaki trousers and started back to the drier shelter of the trees.

### • 12 •

LIEUTENANT!" A STAFF SERGEANT SHOUTED TO A MARINE WHOSE face still hinted at manhood. "Lieutenant Gesswein!" he again yelled.

The youthful Marine looked up to the bridge where the staff sergeant stood. Second Lieutenant Dick Gesswein raised his hand and motioned for the Marine to come down to where he stood on the deck of the amphibious transport ship USS *Vancouver* (LPD 2).

"We're not going to make it before this weather craps out," the lieutenant said to the staff sergeant once the Marine had come to his side. It was after 7:00 A.M. and already the waves had risen to ten feet and slammed against the hull of the ship. The wind whipped across the decks and a constant spray of seawater and rain splashed over the ponchos that the two Marines wore.

"Right, sir," the staff sergeant responded, "looks really shitty. I'm just glad we don't have to fight those cargo nets like those guys out there."

"There's Vankat and his platoon on the landing nets, see," Gesswein said, pointing to a ship pitching in the heavy seas near them.

An LCVP bobbed in the churning water alongside the ship, and four men tried to hold fast the landing net but they kept falling and losing hold. Several times the Marines tried to climb down the side of the pitching ship only to climb back up because the landing net lost its anchor. On one of the last occasions, a Marine fell to the water twenty-five feet below.

Gesswein and the staff sergeant watched as his head popped up at the surface and the sailors in the landing craft fished him out. He still had his rifle, but his pack and helmet were gone.

"That's one way down. Good thing he knew enough to have his helmet unsnapped and his pack on loose," the staff sergeant said. "Practicing landings off Hawaii a couple of years ago, I saw a kid break his neck because he had his chin strap hooked. It was just like he hit the end of the hangman's rope when he went in the water. Snapped his neck.

"Then the silly shit sunk like a rock. He did everything wrong. He had his pack straps tight and his rifle slung over that and across his chest. He was dead from the start."

"Didn't his squad leader inspect him before he went down the net?" the lieutenant asked.

"No, sir. At least I wouldn't think any experienced Marine would let another climb down the net with his shit all fucked up," the staff sergeant said. "If someone had inspected him before he got on that net, and then let him go all fucked up, I'd say the son of a bitch ought to be stood against a wall and shot."

Only a few of the small boats with Marines and equipment aboard (LCMs and LCVPs)[9] motored about their mother ships at 7:30 A.M., still waiting for the first wave to finish loading when word came down that Admiral Wulzen postponed H hour from 8:00 A.M. until 9:00 A.M.

Dick Gesswein and his staff sergeant waited and watched for the storm to die enough to get the men and machines started ashore. The sailors aboard the LCVPs pulled them away from the ship and a few minutes later one of the large LCMs motored alongside.

"There's Vankat." Gesswein pointed, watching the Marines again start down the landing nets. This time, the heavier landing crafts rode

[9]The LCM—Landing Craft, Mechanized—a steel-hulled boat, was made in two sizes, LCM-6, which carried 80 troops or 24 tons of cargo, and the LCM-8, which carried 200 troops or 60 tons of cargo. The LCVP is the classic wooden-hulled Personnel and Vehicle Landing Craft. It carries thirty-six troops or four tons of cargo. In films of Marines "splashing ashore" it is what is commonly seen. The "Amtrack" or LVTP-5 (today Marines use the AAV7A1) was a steel amphibian-tracked vehicle capable of carrying thirty-four troops or six tons of cargo. The LCM and LCVP were organic to the Navy while the LVTP-5 was organic to the Marine Corps.

more steadily in the crashing sea and the Marines were able to make it down the nets.

"There go the amtracks," the staff sergeant said and pointed to the stern of their own ship. "I count eleven of them."

"Looks like we're finally under way," Gesswein said, looking at his watch. "They'll be close on the nine o'clock landing."

• 13 •

A T 9:03 A.M., EDDIE ADAMS STOOD WITH HIS TROUSER LEGS WET TO his knees, snapping photographs as the first Marines stepped ashore at Red Beach 2. It was like a carnival, and the shocked Marines who expected to only walk ashore, climb on trucks, and ride to Da Nang Air Base faced a thousand or more well-wishing Vietnamese people waving American flags and shouting an incomprehensible volley of words that apparently meant welcome.

Second Lieutenant Bill Vankat raced from the landing craft, leading his reconnaissance platoon, once the vehicle's gate splashed down, and ran headlong into a crowd of laughing schoolgirls with armloads of flower garlands.

An old man took Vankat's hand and started shaking it while one of the girls draped the ring of cup-sized, red and yellow blossoms around his neck. He looked behind to see two of his men, flowers draped around their necks too, holding their rifles and smiling for a photographer.

General Karch had flown to Da Nang Air Base by helicopter when he saw that the landing would not go on time. He wanted to take the opportunity that the delay presented to see what General Thi had laid on. He wasn't happy with what he saw.

All along Route One between Red Beach 2 and the airport, thousands of Vietnamese civilians crowded the shoulders of the roadway waving and cheering and celebrating the U.S. Marines' arrival. Once he reached Red Beach, he saw the whole stretch of oceanfront lined with more civilians and then came the girls with the flowers.

"Brigadier General Karch," General Thi said, extending his hand to the brigade commander. "Welcome to Vietnam."

At Thi's side stood the mayor of Da Nang, and ceremonially a young girl, at the mayor's signal, stepped forward, in front of a line of news cameras and reporters, and hung a flower garland around the Marine general's neck.

"Welcome, U.S. Marines," she said and stepped away, smiling yet covering her mouth with her hand and ducking her head in humility.

Karch, completely frustrated by Thi's play for press and politics, clasped his hands behind his back and watched while his Marines carried out the landing.

"Can you smile, General Karch?" Eddie Adams said, snapping a photograph of the Marine looking solemnly toward the sea, hands clasped behind his back and large yellow and red flowers hiding his shoulder-holstered pistol.

He shifted his eyes away from Eddie and never smiled. Eddie snapped two more frames and walked away.

## •14•

PAT COLLINS SAT AT HIS TABLE ON THE MESS DECK OF THE USS *Bayfield* and opened a day-old edition of *Pacific Stars and Stripes* that a logistics helicopter had dropped off with that week's mail. Collins laughed out loud and shoved the newspaper across the table to his lieutenant who looked at him with a questioning expression.

"Bet Freddy's fit to be tied," Collins said gruffly. "Look at that puss. That's a look that would sour milk."

"Poor guy," the lieutenant said. "That had to be humiliating. The flowers and all."

Pat Collins nodded but said nothing.

"Sir, look," the lieutenant said and he pointed at the page. "The story tells about the beach being crowded with civilians, like it was the Fourth of July."

"God, he sure looks pissed,"[10] Collins said and laughed more.

---

[10]Regarding this photograph, General Karch later said: "That picture has been a source of a lot of trouble for me. People say, 'Why couldn't you have been smiling?' But you know, if I had it to do over, that picture would be the same. When you have a son in Vietnam, and he gets killed, you don't want a smiling general with flowers around his neck as the leader at that point."

# . . . THEN TURN LEFT

## •1•

HEAT. IT SEEMED EVERY MARINE HAD THAT SAME FIRST IMPRESSION of South Vietnam. But its torturous blast was more than just an impression, it was an inescapable hell.

John DelGrosso gasped as he stepped down the Air Force C-130's ramp and walked onto the tarmac at the Da Nang airfield. Okinawa had been hot, but nothing like this Vietnamese March afternoon that engulfed John and left him feeling as though his lungs could never fill completely full no matter how hard he breathed. He had barely taken three paces from the shade cast under the airplane's tail when he felt his whole body soak wet. It was immediate, as though he had walked into a steamy shower room.

He looked across the tarmac, and in the distance he saw the buildings and shanties of Da Nang dancing in the heat waves, appearing as almost liquid apparitions. Nearer to him the green tents and sandbags and dirt looked even hotter. He thought, Nothing can look as hot as green canvas under full sun, and he imagined that those poor souls who had to sit beneath that hot, dirty green canvas and work truly must be a miserable lot.

Near the tents, several green trucks sat silent, waiting. The dusty green canvas draped over the great ribs that arched above the trucks' beds, rigged for troop transport, drew in the sun's heat and made their interiors broiling, breathless holes. Inside the trucks' canvas-topped cabs, the hot drivers sat sweating and waiting. They swigged piss-warm water from their canteens, sucked dry-lipped on cigarettes, and looked out at the hot tents and the hot dirt and the hot sandbags and concrete. They watched as two platoons of Marines walked across that hot concrete, hot and feeling their hot feet get hotter, and their hot heads and their hot brains get even still hotter.

The two platoons followed John DelGrosso and Frank Reasoner as they walked across the flight line and found the trucks waiting to take them to their new home, a community of dusty, green canvas tents staked down on the bare-dirt crest of Hill 327, just west of Da Nang. John was happy that they would at least get to live on a hill where the breeze might make life a little better there than at this stifling hole.

The two new platoons added to Dick Gesswein's and Bill Vankat's made up the 9th Marine Expeditionary Brigade Reconnaissance Company. It was a composite of platoons from all the companies of 3rd Reconnaissance Battalion and would be formally organized into a company once Captain Pat Collins arrived from Thailand and took command.

Black smoke poured from the exhaust stack as the first truck lurched from its parking spot and led the second truck through the airfield's gate and onto a dirt road flanked by shacks and people and water-filled ditches and diked-in paddies full of deep mud, murky water, and green rice stalks.

The dust billowing from under the heavy tandem of duel wheels drifted onto the fields and settled into a film on the water with other dust from earlier trips by countless other trucks. The green blades of the rice plants that rose from the dirty water suffered from a gray cast caused by the dust, and even though they grew deep rooted in water-colored mud, they too looked dry and tired.

"Goddamned place is a misery," a corporal called out. He sat on the steel floor of the truck bed with his back against the tailgate and choked on the dirt that billowed inside. It settled on his sweaty face and turned muddy. He wiped a smear across his forehead and down his cheek with his green utility cap and then looked at the mess that his sweat left on the cap's crown. "Fuck this! How much longer we got of this bullshit?"

Nobody answered him. A few men glanced at him but they returned their stares back out at the cab and hood of the truck that followed in the choke of dust that mixed with the black diesel exhaust that poured out the tall pipe clamped to the back corner of the truck's cab. Each man held his M-14 rifle with its butt on the floor and its muzzle pointed up.

They thought about the four magazines full of ammunition that they each had loaded while at the airfield. Except for the rifle range, this was the first time most of them had loaded up with anything other than blanks.

Many of the men had talked tough about going to war. They had bragged of mounting out to South Vietnam to kick Communist ass and turn back this red invasion from North Vietnam, but that had frequently been in the cool comfort of an air-conditioned bar with the wisdom and courage that comes from beer. Yet in their private thoughts at night, when the lights went out and they lay quietly in their barracks beds, they tried to imagine going on patrol, meeting the Communists in battle, and killing them. That yet unknown challenge had worried some. But today this was no dream. Now they had live ammunition.

For several of the Marines, the seriousness of what they were about to embark on had now begun to become real in their minds. They began to realize that life and death rested at their fingers, and as their eyes wandered from the rice fields to the dirty canvas to the wet faces of their brother Marines, sweating in the back of that truck, they wondered who among them might soon die.

• 2 •

THE NEWLY STACKED SANDBAGS FELT COOL TO THE TOUCH AS THE moisture from the freshly dug soil that filled them evaporated through the green mesh. Brigadier General Frederick J. Karch laid his hand on the top row of the growing wall and looked to where several shirtless Marines dug into the orange earth with picks and long-handled shovels. They filled other sandbags with the damp soil and hoisted them up to other shirtless Marines who hefted them to the wall.

He looked down the slope to the southeast where the South Vietnamese Army trained new soldiers, and then he spoke to the Marine who stood quietly as his side, Lieutenant Colonel Charles E. McPartlin, Jr., commanding officer of the 3rd Battalion, 9th Marine Regiment. "Those ARVN recruits still giving you trouble with their stray rounds impacting in your positions?"

"Not as often as when we first moved up here," McPartlin said. "But any is too much."

"I'll mention it again to General Thi," Karch said. "He's having a difficult time with this whole thing. An old warlord like that doesn't give up ground easily. He told me that he preferred that we remain out here, out of the way. He said that otherwise the Americans might provoke incidents in the villages and antagonize the local populace."

"Any change in those Rules of Engagement?" McPartlin asked in an almost sarcastic tone, hoping to get an insight on what progress had been made. As it stood, the Marine brigade was bound to the confines of the two mountains southwest of Da Nang, Hill 327 and Hill 268, and the area surrounding Da Nang Air Base. It was a total of eight square miles, and if anyone fired into the 9th MEB's Tactical Area of Responsibility, the hills and the airfield, the Marines could not fire back. Instead, the Rules of Engagement instructed them to "report those persons to the Combined Coordination Center."

The general frowned. "No, nothing yet." He rested his foot on sandbags and looked down the slope at the low grass and bushes. "I've let it be known, though, that I don't like these conditions. As a practical matter, there is no doubt that the brigade commander will be held responsible for any successful assault on the airfield. They have to at least give us the flexibility to properly defend our positions."

"They're well dug here, sir," McPartlin said. "The way we have the Hawk missile battalion emplacements, it would take one hell of an assault to get at them."

The general smiled. "I know. I expect the enemy knows too. They're obviously keeping away from this high ground or else your patrols would have made contact along your wire. I guess that is some consolation." He looked over the sandbags again and spit. "It's the airfield that worries me."

## • 3 •

THE UNCHANGING DRONE OF THE GASOLINE-POWERED GENERATORS and the steady hum of electricity spinning through coils and windings and capacitors and driving servos and motors had an hypnotic effect on the Marines who manned the graveyard watch inside the large green metal compartment that housed the target acquisition radar control consoles on Hill 327.

Every Marine who manned a scope at this hour when most humans sleep fought that urge as his eyes followed the bright line that swept round and round the circular cathode ray tube, revealing echoes and shadows and clutter that appeared on the screen as green blotches and blips.

In the darkness of the van, the dim light glowing from each scope illuminated its operator's face with a radium-green cast that fell to blackness just past his ears and shoulders. The operator held up his increasingly heavy eyelids with the concern that should he close them for only a moment, something might move and he would not see it. It was hard-edged tension that kept those men nervously awake.

The Marines based on Hill 327 had just erected the TPQ radar antennae on the compound's west slope, and now they anxiously watched the round, green screens for blips that would tell them that the enemy was coming through the wire, under the cover of darkness but still seen by the radar's invisible eye.

In the darkness that surrounded the van that held the radar night watch, listening posts and machine-gun positions ringed the lower edge of the compound and spread down the fingers of Hills 327 and 268. In those sandbagged fighting holes and low-set bunkers, nervous hands gripped machine guns and rifles and awaited the signal to open fire.

The Marines manning the defense knew that night was when things happened in this strange land. They knew that suicidal attackers called sappers, carrying explosive charges, might hurl themselves into the wire, blowing holes for their comrades to follow in a great horde. It was the kind of thing that anyone sitting in a hole, looking out into unknown blackness, would dread to see. That thought put every Marine standing watch on edge.

Inside the humming metal box that housed the radar operators and their scopes, a lieutenant leaned over a small desktop that folded out from a cabinet built into the wall. In the small fluorescent light that shone inside the white-walled desk compartment, he nervously scratched comments into a logbook. He looked at his watch, made a note, and then stood, hooking his right finger into the handle of a coffee mug that he had smuggled from the ship.

"Any coffee left?" he asked.

A green-painted urn sat on a stool just inside the doorway where passersby could hook a cup too. A corporal who sat nearby leaned out of his chair and gave the jug a shake.

"Still half full, sir," he said.

The lieutenant walked to the jug and filled his small milk-glass mug, which had two blue rings and an anchor painted near the lip.

The corporal looked at him and said, "You know, a canteen cup holds twice that much coffee."

"I know," the lieutenant said, "but it just tastes better coming off glass."

"It all tastes pretty bad to me, sir," the corporal said. "I don't think metal or glass would make much difference. And it's strong enough to float a boot. I figure between the bad taste and hard kick that this coffee has, I should have no problem staying awake."

The lieutenant clamped his hand on the corporal's shoulder just below his neck and gave him a good-hearted squeeze. "Anything moving?"

"Nothing, except for a big bat or bird, and now and again a small animal. Mostly ground clutter," the corporal said.

"Sir, wait a minute," a lance corporal who sat eyes fixed on one scope called out. "I've got movement. Looks like people. See. Look. Got arms and legs. See? There."

"I've got them too," another now excited radar operator called out. "They're people, all right. Moving right up toward our positions. They're in the edge of the brush, moving parallel to the wire."

The lieutenant looked at one screen and then another. He hurried to the telephone that sat in the white-painted desk compartment and called to the Marines standing watch in the operations tent. "We've got movement on the west slope. Looks to be a company-size force approaching our positions, crossing through our wire."

He listened and waited, and then the call came back. "Are they within our TAOR?"

The lieutenant shouted back, "Sir, they will be in our tents in a minute." He paused and then said, "Yes, sir. That does mean they are within our TAOR."

The sergeant sitting next to the field telephone in the command bunker that oversaw the several listening posts and machine-gun nests that guarded the west side of the hill answered the phone immediately when it sounded its croaking ring.

"Sir, we hear 'em, but we can't see a thing," he said. He had just finished doing his best to calm several very excited and inexperienced Marine privates and lance corporals who manned the positions under his charge and who called because they heard noises.

"My boys are real antsy," he said. "They say there must be a lot of people, or something, coming up the hill. They can hear 'em crashing through the brush."

There was a pause and then the sergeant answered back, *"You're damned right, sir. It's a damn good possibility we're gettin' overrun."*

Next to the sergeant another Marine strained his eyes through binoculars, searching the shadows in the dim moonlight. A flash caught his attention as a shot cracked from a fighting hole, and then another from the hole next to it.

The Marine who fired looked hard at the night, trying to see if the figure he saw run bent next to the ground had fallen.

"I missed that son of a bitch!" he told the Marine who stood in the hole next to him, his fingers wrapped tight on his rifle as his excited eyes focused through the rear sight.

"I saw the cocksucker run," the other Marine said, breathing hard from the sudden excitement. "Little fuckers, ain't they."

Suddenly above the Marines' heads, the sky filled with flares suspended by parachutes and among them green-star-cluster pyrotechnics that arched upward and then disappeared in blackness as they burned out and fell. Then from both flanks, streams of hundreds of red tracers, marking every fourth round fired from the machine guns, raked across the land below them and once striking ground or rocks or trees skipped up into the night sky in great red arcs.

"Final Protective Fire, man! They've called for the fucking FPF!" the excited Marine shouted to his partner who had already begun to shoot his rifle rapid fire along a sector that he had marked with two stakes at each side of his rifle.

"They must be coming up through the brush at us! Gotta be sappers!" the other Marine cried out in a desperate wail while both rifles cracked shot after shot at the still unseen enemy.

"Nothing, sir," the corporal said to the lieutenant as they both leaned over a third Marine and the green light shone on their faces as all three men's eyes searched the radar scope for moving blips.

Two red-star-clusters raced skyward above the war that raged onto the brushland that hugged the lower western slopes of Hill 327, signaling cease-fire. In a moment the booming roar settled to a crackle, then a few bangs, and then silence.

Through the remainder of the darkness, orange flares danced under parachutes as they drifted to earth, one after another, lighting the western slopes while nervous Marines sweated behind their rifles and waited for the attack's second wave.

Dawn came slowly, and the sergeant who had manned the command bunker above the slope that night watched as a string of Marines spaced thirty paces apart slowly worked their way toward the bullet-chewed bushes and small trees that lived on Hill 327's western side.

"You see any blood?" the sergeant asked over the handset of the radio.

It crackled back, "Roger. Lots of it. Have located the KIAs too."

"Any kind of count?" another voice broke from another radio.

"Roger that," the patrol leader answered. "Looks like about fifty. Repeat fifty."

"Fifty Viet Cong or NVA?" the voice called again.

The patrol leader said, "Negative on Victor Charlie or November Victor Alpha. We have fifty dead apes."

"Apes?"

"Roger that. Monkeys."

• 4 •

JIM SHOCKLEY SHOULDERED HIS SEABAG AND THEN LOOKED AHEAD of him at the Marine staff sergeant gripping his brand-new green valet pack. The lance corporal admired the look of the suitcase with its green rubberized nylon pockets bulging on the sides, heavy brass zippers with leather pulls tied to the brass tabs, double-stitched seams. It was a work of art, a bag that would last a lifetime.

"Man makes staff sergeant or becomes an officer, and they automatically issue you a val-pack just like that," Shockley said to the lance corporal to his rear, also standing in line at the Cubi Point airfield in the

Philippines. Both men had completed scuba diving training and now waited their turn at the counter to have their names checked on the manifest for the next flight back to Okinawa.

"They just give you that?" the Marine asked.

"Sure," Shockley said and then qualified the remark. "They actually issue it to you, and you keep it until you retire. They don't ask for it back, 'cause it's like getting issued glasses or gym gear down at special services. It's one of the freebies that comes with making grade."

"I'd sure like one of them instead of this damned seabag," the Marine said. "My uniforms and shit get all fucked up every time I go anywhere."

"No shit," Shockley said. "I'll spend a good ten dollars getting my trash unfucked when I get back to Schwab. If I had a val-pack, hell, that'd save me a bundle."

The line dragged and Jim Shockley took hold of the handle sewn to the side of his seabag and eased it off of his shoulder and then let it swing down to the floor. "Son of a bitch, that's getting heavy, waiting here. What's the holdup?" he said.

The staff sergeant looked over his shoulder at Shockley and said, "They got a plane going into Da Nang, and they're asking people what unit they're in so that they can join 'em in South Vietnam, if their unit's already shipped over there."

"Shit," Shockley said, looking at the other lance corporal who had also dropped his seabag to the floor. "What'd ya think? Reckon the battalion's shipped out?"

"Maybe we oughta call First Sergeant Henry," the Marine said.

"You know his number?" Shockley said. "If he's in Okinawa, then we probably oughta go there."

"Bet it'd cost ten bucks to call anyway," the Marine said.

"I know we have Recon in Da Nang," Shockley said. "If we flew to Da Nang, we could report to a 3rd Recon unit. Want to try it?"

"Hell yes, why not," the Marine said. "What the fuck can they do?"

"Run us UA," Shockley said, smiling but serious.

"I don't care," the Marine said. "We go to Okinawa, we'd miss out on the action. We'd be in the rear with the gear, reading about it."

"We hop over to Vietnam, and we could also wind up doing the jailhouse rock," Shockley said.

"I'll go if you will," the Marine said.

"Let's see what the guy says," Shockley said, not agreeing but still not showing weakness either since he left the possibility open.

The staff sergeant moved forward, and took his place at the counter behind which a Marine sergeant wearing starched but wrinkled khakis stood. He pulled a cigarette from behind his ear, lit it, and let loose a lungful of smoke directly in the staff sergeant's face.

"Name and unit," the sergeant said to the staff sergeant.

"I'm on the plane to Da Nang," the staff sergeant said, handing over his identification card and a letter with the Defense Department seal in the upper-left-hand corner and United States Marine Corps printed at the top center.

"You don't need to show me shit," the sergeant said. He looked at the staff sergeant's identification card, and copied his name and service number onto a list that he had fastened to a clipboard. "They'll announce the flight in a couple of hours. Don't go running off for a last-minute shot of pussy from that LBFM you left in the ville, you could miss your flight. Sometimes they leave early."

The sergeant cracked a wry smile filled with coffee- and tobacco-stained teeth, but the staff sergeant said nothing. He picked up his valet pack and turned back toward Shockley. "Obviously this turd thinks we're all like him, too fucking lazy to jack off."

Shockley thought he understood, and did agree somewhat. The whores in Olongopo did live up to the reputations of Little Brown Fucking Machines, and he had heard the remark, "Anybody fuck one of them whores is too lazy to jack off." But then nearly every Marine he knew had been very lazy in that regard since they seemed to spend every free hour searching for that fresh, young LBFM that had not yet been spoiled by too many hard nights.

The sergeant behind the counter looked at Jim Shockley and flipped the ashes off his cigarette into a butt-filled cup. As he spoke, Shockley could smell the man's heavy breath, bitter from too many cigarettes and too much coffee. The scent of body odor mixed with the smoker's breath and Shockley had to turn away his face as he reached in his back pocket for his identification card.

"We going to Da Nang?" the lance corporal asked Shockley.

Jim Shockley turned and looked toward a crowd of Marines lounging on the floor, in chairs and leaning against the wall, all waiting for the flight to Da Nang. Then he looked at the relaxed group across the way who waited for their flight to Okinawa.

"First Sergeant Henry would kick our asses," he said to the lance corporal. Then he turned to the sergeant. "We're both with 3rd Recon Battalion. We'd better get on to Okinawa."

· 5 ·

THE RED FELT HAT HAD A POINTED CROWN AND JOHN DELGROSSO laughed when he first put it on his head and looked in the mirror that hung from a nail driven into his tent's center post. It reminded him of the hat that Chico Marx had worn in the many Marx Brothers movies that he had watched and loved as a boy. The pointed hat with its turned-up brim exaggerated the narrowness of John's face, and when Captain Pat Collins saw him standing inside the tent, looking at himself wearing it, he laughed too.

"Hey, Skipper," John said, "how's she look?"

"Like shit," Collins said. "Just don't get caught dead wearing it."

Frank Reasoner looked at John DelGrosso and said, "You really don't plan to wear that in the bush?"

"Yeah, why not?" John said. "Just along the wire, on the candy patrols."

"But it's not tactically sound," Frank said. "You'll give away our position. You'll draw fire."

"What fire?" John said. "From the PFs[1] who report to man the checkpoints and then go home? Or from the ARVN recruits down the hill? And as far as giving away our position, I don't think we are any kind of secret here, and certainly not out on these walks we take along the wire. I'll wear the hat to give my guys a little laugh. Besides, they'll see me better."

"So will the VC," Frank said.

John admired the hat in the mirror once again and then looked at Frank Reasoner, who sat on the cot nearest to the door and puffed heavily on his yellow calabash pipe, and John saw that Frank did not see any humor.

"Look, Frank," John said, "don't be so damned serious. It's just along the wire. What can it hurt?"

[1]Popular Force. Local militia recruited for service in their own village areas.

"It looks bad," Frank said. "Sets a bad example."

"It's not such a big deal. The guys need a mental break now and then. This will cut the tension," John said. "I pull this out of my pack, and they lighten up. Besides, the only thing they laugh about right now is the other people on this hill fucking up. After they killed all those monkeys the other night, I think we can get too much on edge."

## • 6 •

H E COULD CLOSE HIS EYES AND IMAGINE THAT HE WAS AT HOME IN East Texas. A warm night a year ago seemed almost like this one. Frogs chirped in the nearby darkness and in the farther darkness he imagined an overgrown stream where as a boy he had caught catfish and as a young man a year ago he had lain in the cool, damp grass, hidden from the road by the willows but open to the night sky, and had made love for the first time.

The wet smell of earth and water brought back that vision and how in the moonlight he saw her small but well-shaped breasts with her still-maturing nipples, rounded and puffy. He admired her long legs and slim body and felt the smallness of her waist and hips, so tight and so smooth. In the darkness of that East Texas night, he kissed her and held her close to him and she cried because she felt she would lose him if he went away.

She begged him to get a college deferment. "Go to Lamar Tech or Sam Houston State," she said. They were nearby colleges, and he and she could be together. If he laid out of school and worked until he got drafted, like many of the boys who graduated a year ahead of him had already done, she might lose him to one of the more exciting girls who lived near the Army bases. She loved him and wanted to marry him and he loved her. But Rita was only sixteen years old.

She had never needed makeup. Rita had naturally long lashes, heavy and black, that surrounded her wide blue eyes. She had narrow, naturally red lips and coal-black hair with a slight natural curl. Her skin so milk-white had turned slightly gold by August, and that was the last time he had seen her. That day the Greyhound pulled out of the bus station and carried him, on a ticket bought by the county Selective Service Board, to Houston where he took an induction physical and met the Marine Corps recruiter.

"Mr. Burkehart," the recruiter said to him, "the Marine Corps promises you nothing. On most days you will get food in your belly, but no guarantees on quality, and you'll get a place to sleep and a rifle. The place to sleep might be a mud hole, but your rifle will be the best money can buy. We're not like the Army and the Navy, promising you the world so that you'll join us. We don't want you. You have to want to be one of us. If you're good enough, and you make it through our rites of passage, then we will allow you to call yourself a Marine. Nobody joins the Marines. You become one. So what do you say?"

Wesley Burkehart thought of Rita, how she wanted him to go to college so he could avoid the draft and be near to her. He had not listened and now he was classified 1-A and was taking that infamous physical. He knew that in a matter of weeks, he would be on a bus headed to Fort Polk, Louisiana, or Fort Leonard Wood, Missouri. He thought about his pal Johnny Black who was drafted last year. He went to Fort Polk skinny and came home after six months, thick and solid.

He looked at his own skinny arm resting on the corner of the Marine sergeant's desk. He looked down at his twenty-nine-inch waist and then looked at the sergeant, who was thick and solid like Johnny.

"Will I beef up?" Wesley asked hopefully. He had always felt inadequate because he was so skinny. He had gone out for football and baseball, but because of his thinness, he rarely got to play.

"Son, you got a good frame. What are you, six feet?" the sergeant asked.

"Five eleven," Wesley answered. "I'm just under 150 pounds too."

"When you finish infantry training, six months from now, you'll gross out a good twenty pounds heavier, and not an ounce of fat," the sergeant said.

Rita cried a lot. Every time he called. When he didn't come home from the induction physical, but chose instead to go on to San Diego and basic training, it had broken her heart and she did not get over it.

When he did come home on his ten days' leave before shipping out to Okinawa, she refused to see him. He went to the place along that overgrown creek where she and he had lain, and there he cried for her.

He still wrote to her, several times a week, and occasionally he would get a letter from her. Nice but not filled with love. He could tell that she had changed and wanted to move on. But as he leaned against the wall of his fighting hole, next to a Marine who held an M-60 gun against his shoulder, and he smelled the humid air and listened to the millions of frogs and looked down in the darkness at black bushes and brush and weeds and grass, and imagined an overgrown stream with a grassy bank, he could only think of that night in East Texas and how much he missed Rita.

"Wake up, asshole," a voice commanded and broke into his dream. "You get caught sleeping on watch and you'll be burning shitters for a month."

"Wasn't asleep," Wesley Burkehart said crossly to the Marine who shouldered the machine gun. "I'as daydreamin'. Thinkin' 'bout how at home the night was a whole lot like this. The way the air smells like muddy water."

"Smells like shit to me," the third Marine said in an Upper Michigan accent.

"Listen, Burkehart," the first Marine said, "you were too asleep. Your snoring woke me up."

The three Marines laughed when the other man admitted to dozing off too.

Behind them, a radio softly spewed static except that once in a while a voice would crackle and report a listening post all clear or a guard position still secure or call for a radio check just to make sure that the rest of the free world had not disappeared. At 2:00 A.M. life and time dragged as the strain of trying to see in darkness lit only by a quarter moon wore deeply on the minds of the men standing watch.

Because it was so dark, every man listened with pointed ears. He searched for the sound of human approach, and dreaded to hear a foot crunching dry grass or a leg breaking brush or the thud of someone slipping in the dark. The buzzing chirp of the frogs and occasional squawk of a night bird kept the Marines from hearing too many sounds that were not there, but when a small animal might jump or a branch might fall it sent blood rushing and hearts pounding.

As the night dragged on, and the Marines stood watch with frightened boyish faces peering from behind sandbagged protection into the unknown darkness, something or someone stepped into the barbed fencing and shook several cans tied to the wire with rocks inside them for rattles.

Wesley Burkehart now stood his turn at watch behind the .30-caliber machine gun. He heard the metal clink and as his heart jumped in his chest, he looked wild-eyed at the man to his right, a lance corporal from Upper Michigan who was in command of this position.

"That's no fucking bird," Burkehart said.

"Pig. Bet it's another goddamned pig," the lance corporal said.

A crack followed by a thud stopped the lance corporal; it sounded as though a branch from a tree had broken and whatever had climbed on it had fallen with the limb to earth. It had been a deep, hard crack and heavy thud.

The three men listened, but heard nothing more.

"Goddamned ape. Bet it's a fucking ape," the lance corporal said.

"What if it's a VC?" Burkehart asked.

"Then you hose 'em down with that gat," the other Marine said, trying to hide the quiver in his voice with the confidence in his remark. "Send 'em straight to hell. Don't pass go. Don't collect two hundred dollars."

Burkehart toughened up some, but still felt the icy grip on his heart and lungs as he struggled for courage.

The lance corporal put up a pair of binoculars and scanned the brush line but saw nothing. "Too fucking dark. Can't see a thing. Bet it's a rock ape," he said.

He looked at the two privates first class who depended on him for leadership since he had the crossed rifles under his stripe and then looked back out again at the dark hillside below their position. "Burkehart, you stay on the gun. Me and shit for brains here are gonna go check out the noise. You hear shooting, call for help."

"Wait," Burkehart said. "There's nothing in our orders that says we gotta go out and check out the sounds. We're supposed to call in and wait for orders."

"And what if it's a fucking monkey or something? Which it most likely is," the lance corporal said contemptuously. "We're just gonna walk out a few meters, take a look, and walk back. You scared to be alone? You got the fucking M-60!"

"Fuck no, I'm not scared," Wesley Burkehart lied. "I just think it's foolish for you two to go out there and go pokin' around. There might be a whole company of VC out there and they'll cut your heads off without a sound."

"Burkehart, stay put," the lance corporal said, and then he looked at the other Marine. "Grab your rifle and let's go."

Alone. He had never felt so damned alone in his life. Only one other time had fear gripped him so hard.

A lantern had fallen to the floor of his house during a rainstorm that had knocked out the electricity. He remembered how panic and fear had seized him when the flames rose from the spilled lantern fuel, and how he had bolted outside and run through the downpour, splashing through the mud and ankle-deep water that ran like a river down the road in front of his house. He recalled how in his stampede through the screen door he had looked back and had seen his mother and baby sister huddled in the corner and his father alone battling the blaze.

He ran to a neighbor's house a half mile up the road and begged for help, but the people could not understand him because he was crying so hard, and then he ran away. He remembered how when he came home again that the fire was out and how his father had laughed about it all and how the neighbors had thought someone had died. He remembered how he felt so ashamed.

As he gripped the machine gun and swore to himself that he would not lose control, he listened to the now faint footsteps of his comrades as they moved farther and farther away. The sound of their movement had kept him assured that all was well, but now those sounds disappeared into the quiet blackness. No frogs. No birds. Not even a breeze. Only the soft crackle of radio static.

Now he felt alone. He looked at the radio's handset and thought of his father laughing. I can't call. I'd never live it down. They would suspect I was a coward, he told himself.

Wesley Burkehart tried not to think, but his mind went wild. He could not hear a sound, and it began to worry him. Have they been captured and now will they come after me? he asked himself. He remembered his buddy's parting comments, "Hose 'em down with that gat . . . send 'em straight to hell."

It's been half an hour, he told himself as he looked at his watch. No, they left at a quarter after, that makes it forty-five minutes. Forty-five minutes! he screamed in his mind. Hell, Wes, they could have gone three maybe four miles. Something's happened to them. They're fucking dead and now the VC will be coming at me next. I gotta call in.

He looked at the radio, but he couldn't call. *What can I say?* Fifteen minutes, he told himself. *After a full hour and they're gone, I'll call for help. That's reasonable and not cowardly. It's smart,* he told himself.

Five minutes more passed and Wesley Burkehart had soaked his shirt and cap with sweat as he held tightly to the M-60 machine gun and prayed for the sight of his two comrades, safe. He wished hard but another crack and the louder pop of a branch clearly breaking from the weight of a man's foot sent Wesley Burkehart's self-control reeling. He hoped that the noise might just pass, but again the sounds of people moving came, and their crunching footsteps along his flank sent his heart into overdrive.

*They're circling around. They're going to try to take me from the rear,* he told himself as cold sweat drained down his face and splashed on his hands that were locked white on the stock and pistol grip of the machine gun that he hoped would not jam.

"Listen, jughead!" the lance corporal whispered hoarsely. "You just pick up your goddamned feet and follow me. You see up there? You see that hump sticking up? That's our fucking bunker!"

"Hey," the other Marine said, "don't get sore at me, I'm not the asshole who said let's go take a walk in the dark and check out that sound. Not a fucking thing out here, and we lose our butts off chasing fucking ghosts, and you're sore at me? Fuck you, Jack!"

"You're the asshole who said he knew a shortcut back to the position, Jack!" the lance corporal said.

"So fucking court-martial me," the Marine said.

Both men crouched low and looked down the hill at their bunker where PFC Wesley Burkehart stood behind the machine gun, praying but ready to kill anything that moved.

"Think we ought to warn him before we come in?" the Marine asked the lance corporal.

"Yeah and what? We throw rocks and really get him going?" the lance corporal said. "He ain't gonna shoot with us approaching from the rear. Besides, when we get close, I'll yell at him that we're coming in."

"You lead the way, Cisco," the other Marine said.

Wesley Burkehart waited quietly, praying hard and holding to life by his sweaty grip of a machine gun. He gasped for a sudden gulp of air and blinked through a river of sweat as he strained to hear over the deafening noise made by his thundering heart and panicked breathing.

He clenched his jaw tight and his chest ached as he held his breath and listened. What was it? Footsteps? Then a crash in the brush behind the bunker sent his heart pounding so hard that his vision blurred from the rush of blood that came coursing from his excitement. He screamed as his breath exploded, and without hesitation, the frantic Marine pushed the barrel of his machine gun out the bunker's rear port and let go.

He fired blindly, totally filled with the same kind of panic that had sent him running through an East Texas thunderstorm when a lantern had fallen. But now, he could only think of life. Of repelling this attack and surviving.

After it was done. After help had arrived. After they had found the riddled bodies of the two Marines who had walked out to investigate a sound in the night, had become disoriented, had walked past the listening post before realizing their mistake, and had then casually approached it from the rear. After they had died in their tracks. After a Navy hospital corpsman and a chaplain had tended to these two men who were also boys. After that was done. After it all, a shattered Wesley Burkehart tried desperately to understand why but never could.

# LEARNING GUERRILLA

# 1

THE WESTERN SLOPE OF HILL 327 HAS SEVERAL FINGERS THAT spread down and across a green farm country that rises upward to mountains and ridges and deep canyons that are the eastern face of the Annamite Cordillera, a range of mountains that reach up from the swampy, tropical lowlands and touch the foot of the Himalayas. This range of jungle-covered granite extends through North and South Vietnam like the spine of a gargantuan dragon with two great heads.

At the Chinese border Mount Fan Si Pan forms one of this Annamite Dragon's great heads, the north's highest peak, nestled between the Red and the Black rivers that flow past Hanoi, the Red on the north and the Black on the south, to Haiphong and Nam Dinh on the coast. Fan Si Pan stands 10,308 feet high.

From the tidal marshes and waterways of the Mekong Delta where Saigon overlooks the northern shore, the Annamite Dragon curls its huge tail forming mountains that rise upward dividing the coastal lowlands of South Vietnam from the jungle highlands of Laos and then extend on into the north. As though resting upon its curled tail, the great dragon's second head, Mount Quang Ngai, stands as Vietnam's highest point, 10,761 feet above the sea.

All along the Annamite mountains, thick jungles with double and triple canopies cover the dragon and appear almost like rich green velvet from the distance. Misty white clouds shroud the high peaks like thin chiffon and their fog flows down the dark canyons in wisps and curls, leaving a wetness that has never dried.

Throughout these green velvet mountains, tigers, cobras, jade-green vipers, large apes, and beautiful birds populate the dense forests, and with them communities of primitive mountain people who know little of politics, money, or modern thinking live as they have done for 10,000 years.

As John DelGrosso squatted near a tree on the lower slopes of Hill 327 and looked to the southwest, watching the last orange light of an April day dwindle behind the prominence of Mount Quang Ngai, he marveled at the greatness and beauty, and thought too of the many enemy who lurked there—regiments and battalions of North Vietnamese Army regulars and companies of South Vietnamese Communist guerrillas. He thought of the day when he might stand atop one of the high mountains and look back toward the sea, and wondered how long before that time might come.

"Weird, isn't it, sir," First Sergeant Harry Rogers said to John Del-Grosso. Rogers was a stocky-built man with a pug nose and flat face. He looked as though he had gone many rounds as a boxer, and no man dared argue with him. Rogers was the classic Marine in every respect. Rock hard and quick to discipline.

As if awakening from a dream, John DelGrosso looked over his shoulder at the top enlisted Marine in Company D and asked, "What's weird?"

"This. Look at it. It's about the most beautiful country I've ever seen," Rogers said. "Did you see that water and the beaches when we landed? Crystal clear, and palm trees and sand right out of a picture book. But to think about what's going on in the middle of all this—you know, the Communist invasion and the fighting—it just don't make sense."

"Does it ever?" John DelGrosso asked.

Harry Rogers shrugged and then looked back at the platoon that had patrolled the lower, western contours of Hill 327, just outside the wire. They had spent the day walking above the farmland and examining the hedgerows, looking for a yet-to-be-seen enemy: exercising their bodies to become accustomed to the hot climate, and training their minds to think in terms of the land, the cover, and the best ways to fight.

"We'll set up in a V-shaped ambush for the night," John DelGrosso told the first sergeant. "On either side of this trail. See how it comes off the rice fields? How all those dike paths run into this one and then runs along that hedgerow?"

"Yes, sir," Rogers said. "Seems to be the main footpath leading up this hill."

"Set up the automatic weapons at the apex and at the end of each leg, and make sure everybody has his sector of fire pegged so that they interlock down there, where this trail runs at the base of this draw," the lieutenant said, pointing to a clear and flat area of ground that was a textbook-perfect killing zone. He looked at his first sergeant and waited for a comment that might correct any error he might have made in his tactics.

"I'll position myself with the automatic weapon on the right leg," Rogers said. "That way I'll be close to our lookouts."

"We will open fire from this position, here, at the apex, and the legs will close the back door," DelGrosso said. "Make sure that every man knows to wait until I open fire. We don't want to kill some innocent farmer carrying a hoe or something that one of our guys might mistake for a rifle."

"Got you covered, sir," Rogers said and started to exit, but stopped. "That Marine shooting his foxhole buddies got you spooked, doesn't it?"

"I was spooked before that. He just confirmed what I was spooked about," DelGrosso said, and took off the red Chico Marx hat that was now showing dark sweat stains all around the pointed crown. He rolled the hat along its brim and then stuffed it in his pack.

Rogers smiled as he watched the lieutenant take out his green cap and put it on. John DelGrosso looked at Rogers and winked. "I feel safer waiting out here until daylight. Nervous as they are, I think they'd kill half the platoon if we tried to come through the wire after dark. I just don't want to take that risk. Those guys are too tight."

"We think alike on that, sir," Harry Rogers said and started down the hillside. He looked back again. "Once it's good and dark, we'll move down to our ambush positions. Gooks probably watching, ya know."

John DelGrosso nodded and then took out his canteen and sipped some of the warm water from it. "Have the platoon eat chow now. Once we get in place, I don't want any movement. They don't eat now, they wait until daylight."

As Harry Rogers disappeared, John DelGrosso looked back to the dark mountains and red sky. He thought of the lessons he and his men had already learned in a matter of weeks. How they discovered that underwear bound up and caused heat rashes, so they dispensed with wearing any.

He sipped more water even though he didn't feel that thirsty. He knew that if he waited until he felt really thirsty before he took a drink he could already be sick from the heat, and he dreaded that lesson. Heat exhaustion, the upset stomach, the cold sweat, cramps; or heat stroke, the splitting headache, hot and dry and very sick. It could kill a man. Better take a little more salt, he told himself as he thought of the symptoms, and he looked at the Marine who sat by the radio and ate his can of beef stew cold.

"You better grab some more water," he told the Marine. "Call down to the first shirt and tell him to pass the word, everybody drink up too."

· 2 ·

BEADS OF WATER DRIPPED DOWN THE SIDES OF THE COORS BEER can and Captain Pat Collins watched as the circle of water grew under it. As he watched, he tried to time the quickness at which the moisture gathered on the cold metal and puddled on the Formica tabletop, and by that estimate the humidity in the heavy, warm air. He picked up the can, watched the water run and drip, and then he took a slow sip of beer.

The American beer was especially a treat here where the common brew came from unknown sources in the Philippines, Thailand, Korea, and South Vietnam and contained a variety of chemicals, including formaldehyde as a preservative. These beers, San Miguel, Obe, all had one thing in common: to the American pallet, they tasted terrible.

The smooth sweetness of the ice-cold Coors tasted especially good to Collins and several other Marines sitting inside a sandbagged tent in the main compound on Hill 327 that they called "The Club." To them, it tasted so good mostly because the beer was American. Rocky Mountain spring water, the choicest barley and hops. All-American from Golden, Colorado.

"I grew up with this stuff," Frank Reasoner said. "You can get it only in the Rocky Mountain states. The best beer in the world."

Pat Collins watched the lieutenant draw a deep breath of smoke from his pipe. "Frank, maybe where you come from, but not in Detroit."

"Every man to his own taste," Reasoner said and looked out at the black night that had come. "No moon. Guess John will have to feel his way around out there."

"Even with no moon, there's a lot of light from the stars," Pat Collins said. "You can see more than you think, once you've got your eyes adjusted to it. We need to start spending more time patrolling at night. Our Marines have to learn that the night is their friend. Especially if you're in the offensive."

Frank Reasoner looked at the captain and then again out at the night. "People are naturally afraid of the night. All their superstitions come alive in the dark. Ghosts and stuff like that."

"Nothing in the night that isn't in the daylight," Collins said. "And you're right, people are naturally afraid of the dark, just like they're naturally afraid to jump out of an airplane, but we train and soon enough, we learn that it's all in knowing what you're doing. These gooks are spooky as shit, they don't like the dark at all. Hell, they're scared of all sorts of supernatural mumbo jumbo floating around in the bush. They'll see a ghost behind every tree. I believe we'll get the upper hand on them if we get good at night work."

"I saw you and Colonel Wheeler with those MCI courses,[1] is that what this is all about?" Frank Reasoner asked.

"Partly," Collins said and took another sip of his beer. "This little brush war is a brand-new bag of tricks for just about everybody. We have only a handful of combat veterans, some damn good ones, but not enough. And none of them has ever gone up against anything like this. Not even

---

[1] Marine Corps Institute correspondence courses.

a guy like Colonel Ed Wheeler, who fought the Japs at Bloody Ridge on Guadalcanal with Edson's Raiders. He's probably seen more combat than anybody around here, in both World War II and Korea, but this is like trying to kill ants with a pointed stick.

"We haven't had contact with the enemy, haven't even seen him, even if we could recognize him, but we know he's watching us. When he's ready to fight us, he'll pick the place, unless we do something to take the initiative.

"Another fact we have to face, most of these Marines here aren't even ready to go to war, at least not this kind of war. They have to relearn a lot of basic infantry tactics, conduct of fire and patrolling procedures.

"Meanwhile, we're digging into MCI courses, field manuals, you name it. We gotta get our act together. I think that might work, once we master it, might give us the advantage."

Frank Reasoner bit on his pipe and sucked hard, and when he got no smoke, he struck a match and pulled the flame down into the bowl as he drew for smoke. He watched the red glow deep inside his pipe and thought for another moment. Then he looked back out at the night. "You know I'm taking my platoon up to the Hue/Phu Bai area with 2nd Battalion, 3rd Marines, in a few days?"

"Sure," Collins said and drank the last of his beer. He looked at the lieutenant. "Let me get us two more."

In a minute Pat Collins was back with two full cans and handed one to Frank Reasoner. Both men drank and then Collins said, "That's thick country up there, you'll have plenty to do. But you'll be pissing in the wind unless you establish a good concept of operations and you have your men trained."

"Every day we patrol, we train. Train hard," Reasoner said. "We may be moving north, but we won't stop training. I think that we have patrolling down fairly well, but I am not letting up on immediate action drills. That's where men can get killed. Walk into an ambush, you have to depend on immediately doing the right thing instead of following survival impulses."

Collins smiled. "I've seen where a whole squad got killed in an ambush because they dove for cover instead of turning into the fire and shooting their way out. That's a hard lesson to learn, but if you lay down in the killing zone, you're dead. I don't think that a unit can work too hard on immediate action drills. I can tell you this, we sure won't cut any slack there."

Reasoner took another drink of beer and then looked at Collins. "After one-nine[2] registered their mortars right on top of 3rd Marines' headquarters, Colonel Wheeler made no secret of what he thought about the general state of readiness. I think everybody took that hint and has gone to work."

"Wheeler's got a whole elaborate scheme of training 3rd Marines in all sorts of counterguerrilla operations, cordon and search, interdicting insurgent forces, a whole variety of countermeasures," Collins said. "I know you and the other platoon leaders have been doing a lot, learning a lot, but we need to take a look at what Wheeler's talking about and get down to dealing with the enemy on terms he can appreciate."

Both men drank more beer and looked outside at the night. They thought about the patrol led by John DelGrosso and wondered if he would make first contact with the Viet Cong. They also thought about how it would feel to go patrolling far outside the wire, probing and searching for this elusive enemy in earnest for the first time.

· 3 ·

WHEN THE MARINES HAD LANDED IN SOUTH VIETNAM, GENERAL William C. Westmoreland envisioned them quickly taking the offensive, going out after the enemy where he lived and turning the initiative from the Communists.

However, in the original landing order, the Joint Chiefs of Staff directed that the "U.S. Marine Force will not, repeat, will not, engage in day-to-day actions against the Viet Cong." This was in support of the policy that provided the South Vietnamese government with helicopter support of its combat operations, and the support of Operation Rolling Thunder, the strategic bombing of North Vietnam, which was carried out in large part from Da Nang.

General Westmoreland was disappointed in 1964 when he took charge of the U.S. Military Assistance Command, Vietnam, and found that the South Vietnamese, ARVN, forces patrolled only around their

[2]1st Battalion, 9th Marine Regiment.

bases of operations and did little to pursue the Viet Cong in the bush. He made it his immediate task to get them out of the camps and after the Communists.

When he saw that the ARVN forces were not effective in turning back the Communists, he knew then that the only realistic choices were to either give up South Vietnam to the Communists and go home, or bring in American forces to do the bulk of fighting for the South Vietnamese.

Now that he saw the Marines confined in and around their compounds and not probing the surrounding countryside to find the enemy, he quickly became frustrated. He said, "If you wait for the enemy, he will hit you, and he will hit you without warning."

During his years as a cadet and throughout his career as a regular Army officer, William Westmoreland had studied the American Civil War in great detail. With its 500,000 soldiers killed in action, the Civil War had been one of the bloodiest and most frustrating conflicts that Americans had ever faced, primarily because it was a war of movement.

Occupying terrain was not meaningful in the prosecution of the Civil War because of the vastness of the country. If a force held a territory, their enemy skirted around them, carried out assaults on their flanks, and controlled the fight. Thus the objective was not to control the geography, but to break the enemy's ability and will to fight by interdicting him.

South Vietnam, General Westmoreland contended, fit this same perspective. Most ominous to him was the 800-mile-long hostile front that extended along the Cambodian and Laotian borders. Unless the United States mobilized its full forces, as it had done during World War II, it would be impossible to control this line, and this was without consideration of what it would take to eliminate the enemy within the extensive Vietnamese interior with its rugged mountains and ample jungle cover.

Ideally, if the hostile front could be closed to the influx of enemy troops and supplies, then the remainder of the war would be a war of attrition within the contained South Vietnamese battle theater.

General Westmoreland knew that the task at hand presented almost impossible odds, given the amount of muscle and dedication that the United States was willing to commit. He told his superiors of the odds and the probable costs that he knew all too well from his Civil War studies. He then accepted his mission and began developing plans.

While the Marines sat atop Hill 327 and surrounded Da Nang Air

Base, Army troops began arriving in the southern regions of the country. This was the result of Westmoreland's recommendations and landmark decisions made by President Johnson, based upon the general's recommendations.

In late March 1965, Westmoreland had taken what he termed "a classical commander's Estimate of the Situation to think through in a logical and precise manner, strategy, objectives, enemy capabilities, and our own courses of action before making what may prove to be in the light of history, a momentous recommendation."

His recommendations greatly broadened the mission of the U.S. forces from simple air base security to a three-fold initiative: "Protection of vital U.S. installations, defeat of the Communist efforts to control Kontum and Pleiku Provinces, and the establishment of enclaves in the coastal region."

At a special meeting of the National Security Council on April 1, 1965, after reading Westmoreland's "Estimate of the Situation," hand-carried to Washington by Ambassador Maxwell Taylor and Brigadier General William E. DePuy, MACV Operations chief, President Johnson made several far-reaching decisions. Most significantly, he approved an 18,000- to 20,000-man increase in U.S. forces committed to Vietnam, including the deployment of an additional brigade of Marines. Furthermore, President Johnson permitted a change in the 9th MEB mission, which would allow the use of American forces in "active combat under conditions to be established and approved by the Secretary of Defense in consultation with the Secretary of State."

This buildup of force and approval to allow U.S. ground forces to engage in active combat initiated General Westmoreland's tactical strategy: a war of movement in South Vietnam. A plan where American forces would interdict the enemy, wipe out his numbers, destroy his infrastructure, break his will to fight, eliminate his supplies and support, and thereby end the South Vietnamese Communists' insurgence and the North Vietnamese Communists' incursion of South Vietnam.

All along the 800-mile western front, U.S. Army Special Forces camps quietly began building strength and number. According to General Westmoreland's plan, these troops would engage the enemy whenever they learned of NVA or guerrilla movement. The general envisioned that the soldiers would fight, win, and return to their bases, leaving the terrain.

Tying down his limited number of troops to hold terrain was a luxury Westmoreland considered not affordable. The terrain was not important, and the troops had to be kept mobile to meet the enemy wherever he arose.

One problem, however, would come to haunt the soldiers tasked with guarding Westmoreland's 800-mile-long hostile front: the nature of the terrain, steep mountains covered with thick jungle, and the insufferable heat and wetness made troop mobility extremely difficult at best. It was not unreasonable for a patrol to take three days to cover an eight-kilometer stretch of the border. Because of this slow movement, it was not difficult for the enemy to skirt these patrols.

In the south, Westmoreland considered General Ulysses S. Grant's control of the Cumberland, Mississippi, and Tennessee rivers during the Civil War to be his guide and he copied that philosophy to gain the initiative in the riverous world of III Corps, the Mekong Delta region, and the Camau Peninsula.

For thousands of years the Vietnamese had used these, as well as major rivers that flowed in the more northern regions near Da Nang and Hue, as roadways. General Westmoreland knew that the North Vietnamese and the South Vietnamese Communists used these vast waterway networks as supply lanes and means of moving large numbers of troops. Thus in the tradition of Grant in the Civil War, he challenged naval planners to develop a riverine force to patrol South Vietnam's waterways.

When General Westmoreland settled on the war of movement strategy, he knew that the Vietnam conflict would be only the second time in history that American soldiers would fight such a war. At that time, however, no one foresaw that just as the Civil War had split the nation a hundred years earlier, this Third World brush fire would also violently divide America, issuing such a deep wound to the nation's soul that even decades after the war's end, the soreness would remain.

• 4 •

H E HAD HIS BOOTS OFF AND THE ELASTIC BLOUSING GARTERS THAT held his dungarees tight around his shins made his trousers resemble knickers the way they ballooned above his green wool stockings. Brigadier General Frederick J. Karch scratched the top of his left foot with his right heel and across his lap spread open the copy of *Pacific Stars and Stripes* that told of the "buildup" in South Vietnam. He looked at the picture of Marine Corps Commandant General Wallace M. Greene, Jr., walking along a line of Marines, formed for his inspection in front of hangars at Da Nang Air Base.

In little more than a month, the entire mission had changed, and General Karch wondered where it would all end. Even in the newspaper, the signs were obvious, the mission to defend Da Nang Air Base had been a ruse, it was really the first step into a full-scale war and he knew it.

General Greene obviously knew it too, and had gone so far as to comment that the Marines pinned behind a fence in Da Nang would be outside that fence searching for and destroying the enemy. All the newspapers quoted him when he said, "You don't defend a place by sitting on your ditty box."

Karch took a pair of scissors from his desk and began cutting out the page opposite the photograph of General Greene. It was a photograph of him welcoming Lieutenant Colonel William C. McGraw, commanding officer of Marine Fighter Attack Squadron (VMFA) 531, who had just arrived in Da Nang with his squadron of F-4B Phantom II jet fighters, the first Marine Corps fixed-wing tactical aircraft to deploy to Vietnam in 1965. They had arrived as part of the air element of the 3rd Marine Expeditionary Brigade, which had landed its fighting elements to reinforce Karch's 9th MFB.

"General Karch," a voice called to him. The general looked up and saw his aide standing in the doorway. "General Krulak's aide called. They're on their way over."

"Thanks," Karch said and reached behind his chair and found his boots. He began lacing them and glanced up at his aide. "He's heading back to Hawaii today, and they say that he's not very happy with Westmoreland's plans."

"I thought those plans were pretty well established," the aide said.

"They are, now," Karch said. "Westmoreland has asked for 33,000 troops. Part here and part down in the central highlands of II Corps. But the burr under old Brute Krulak's saddle is that communications facility and airfield up at Phu Bai."

The aide interjected, "That's an Army communications outfit isn't it, the 8th Radio Research Unit?"

"Right," the general said as he pulled his boot laces tight and tied them. "Westmoreland's worried that they'll be overrun, and he wants a reinforced infantry battalion up there for protection. That's got old Brute's nose out of joint."

"It's our only outpost north of the Hai Van Pass," the aide offered.

"Sure it is, but why do we need to be up there until we can afford it," the general said with a smile.

He stood, hooked his finger in the handle of his coffee cup, put his hand on his aide's shoulder, and walked with him to his outer office where a coffeepot perked. He pulled down the black handle on the container and filled his cup. "General Westmoreland has not been happy with our mission from the start. Now he's got the edge with President Johnson's approval of those recommendations that he sent to Washington with Bill DePuy. Westmoreland's pushing to get on the offensive fast. So for starters, he's issued us a revised mission statement or to use his words, 'concept of operations.'"

The aide filled his cup too and blew over the hot coffee as he lightly sipped. "I saw that, but isn't that what we want?"

"I don't know if we really want that specifically, but it is in our nature as Marines to want to go out after the enemy," the general said, sipping his coffee. "Did you see the paper? General Greene's comment about getting off our ditty boxes?"

"Yes, sir," the aide said.

"In most Marines' books, General Krulak is the number-one expert on counterinsurgency. When he says something, I pay attention. Brute Krulak isn't totally sold on this thing, especially the idea of putting troops up at Phu Bai, and I tend to agree. But Westmoreland has operational control, General Krulak doesn't, and so we're going to Phu Bai. We don't have to like it, though."

"What about the revised concept of operations?" the aide asked.

"It's what we knew would come, that's no surprise. A lot of people are happy about that, but I think that Marines prefer to establish priorities for Marines. We accept the mission, but we prefer to choose our means. But then it's never been a perfect world. No, I guess Westmoreland's revision is in tune with our thinking. It does give us the flexibility to really protect ourselves and go out and do a job."

Westmoreland's revised concept of operations read simply and to the point: "1) Establishment of defensive bases, 2) Deep reconnaissance patrols of the enemy's avenues of approach, 3) Offensive action as a reaction force in coordination with the Vietnamese, and 4) Undertake in coordination with Republic of Vietnam I Corps, an intensifying program of offensive operations to fix and destroy the Viet Cong in the general Da Nang area."

The screen door at the front of the building slammed and General Karch and his aide heard voices in the hallway. Karch immediately handed his coffee cup to his aide and walked into the hallway to meet General Krulak.

Lieutenant General Victor H. Krulak, a 1934 Naval Academy graduate and recipient of the Navy Cross for valor in World War II, stood a mere five feet five inches tall. Yet Marines who knew him affectionately called him "The Brute." They described him as being small in stature but very large in character.

As commanding general of the Fleet Marine Force, Pacific, headquartered in Hawaii, Krulak was responsible for the combat readiness and logistical support of all Marines in the Pacific, but he had no operational control over those assigned to duty in Vietnam. Nonetheless, his influence was strong.

Before his assignment at Fleet Marine Force, Pacific, he had been the special assistant for Counterinsurgency and Special Activities for the Joint Chiefs of Staff. While at that post, he had designed the Enclave Plan that established friendly held territories and coastal enclaves from which U.S. military forces could operate in pursuit of the Communist insurgent guerrillas and North Vietnamese regulars.

After the plan was accepted, he was asked what to call it. He had thought for a moment and then responded, "Chu Lai." The general was fluent in Mandarin Chinese and Chu Lai was the Chinese characters that represented his name and coincidentally meant "coming and going." The first enclave established from this plan was fifty-seven miles south of Da Nang and also bore Krulak's name, Chu Lai.

"I guess we win some and lose some," Karch said to the general as they walked to his office and sat down.

Krulak looked at the subordinate general and nodded. "We'll do all right. That General Thi is another story. Difficult man. We went over the revised concept of operations issued by General Westmoreland, and I suggested that probing south of the air base and across the Da Nang River would put us into quick contact with the enemy. He agreed that it would, but he said, "That's enemy country. You are not ready to operate there."

Both men laughed and Karch said, "Maybe he doesn't realize that's why we give our Marines rifles and go on patrol. We want to destroy the enemy. We can't do that unless we go where he lives."

"I have a hunch that when we do go south," Krulak said, "we will find the honey pot. The sooner we get to operating down there, the sooner we'll hit those Communists where they'll hurt."

"What about up north?" Karch said.

General Krulak shook his head, "We have no business putting that Battalion Landing Team up there. It just isn't good. Here is an example of dollar economics wagging the tail of the military deployment. Phu Bai is tactically indefensible, period. But General Westmoreland is determined that we go there anyway because he has the 8th RRU with about five million dollars invested in them there, and because they are locked in place, he is determined not to move the unit."

"I don't like the idea of having a thousand or more Marines cut off over the Hai Van Pass," Karch said, agreeing with Krulak.

"I don't either," Krulak said. "He's got his experts saying that Phu Bai is an excellent location from a technical point of view, and whether or not this is true is open to conjecture because we have people who question it. Yet he is insisting that we go there despite the tremendous land barrier between Da Nang and Phu Bai and the logistical problems that it presents. Besides, there are many better uses that I can see for that Battalion Landing Team."

"Looks like we could make better use out of moving the 8th RRU," Karch said.

"Certainly, and we would be better off by keeping our forces more closely linked," Krulak responded, "but we've walked this cat as far as it will go and Admiral Sharp[3] is not prepared to override General Westmoreland, so I wanted to personally let you know that is that."

[3]Admiral Ulysses S. Grant Sharp was the Commander-in-Chief, Pacific.

General Krulak stood and picked up his green utility cap and walked toward the door, "With the addition of Ed Wheeler's[4] RLT 3, you've got a little company. Ed's very sharp and should do a lot of good here."

"With nearly 9,000 Marines under my command, we can handle anything the enemy may try. I'm satisfied. When you land the division, I'll be ready for that too," Karch said as they walked to his door.

General Krulak smiled as he shook Karch's hand. He stepped into the hallway and said, "The way things are moving here, Freddy, another month and you won't recognize this place."

## • 5 •

I T WAS THE FLASH OF RED THAT STARTLED THE MARINE STANDING watch and he almost shot at the movement in the distance, but then he saw the man. The sudden rush of adrenaline left him feeling dizzy. He had to sit down, and as he sat, he quaked at the thought of nearly opening fire on the Marine patrol that approached in his sector of fire.

John DelGrosso grasped the red hat on its pointed crown, and with the back of his wrist, he wiped the sweat from his forehead.

"First Sergeant," he called to his rear and waited for Harry Rogers to respond.

"Sir," Rogers called forward as he walked from his position near the rear of the platoon to the point where the lieutenant waited.

"Have we been cleared to come in?" DelGrosso asked as he snugged the red hat back on his head.

"Yes, sir," Rogers said, "but I still think that we should approach with caution. Maybe we should hoist a white flag so they won't shoot. I don't trust those guys."

John DelGrosso pushed up one of the three canteens that he wore on his web belt and reached inside his hip pocket, where he found his handkerchief. He looked at Harry Rogers, stood and stepped from the cluster

---

[4]Colonel Edwin B. Wheeler, USMC, was commanding officer of the 3rd Marine Regiment and Regimental Landing Team 3, which consisted of RLT headquarters; Battalion Landing Team 2nd Battalion, 3rd Marine Regiment; Battalion Landing Team 3rd Battalion, 4th Marine Regiment; and an air element consisting of Marine Air Support Squadron (MASS) 2 and Marine Fighter Attack Squadron (VMFA) 531.

of low trees and bushes where the platoon had taken cover, and began wading through the high grass and weeds that covered the lower slopes of the hill, all the while waving the handkerchief above his head.

A low profile of sandbags stood out from the upper slope and John DelGrosso watched it as he carefully walked several paces into the clearing to a place where he knew that whoever stood the watch inside the small bunker could see him. In a moment a hand raised above the hump of sandbags and waved back at him, and the lieutenant looked over his shoulder and motioned for the platoon to follow.

It seemed almost neurotic to him to resort to such tactics, avoiding coming inside their lines after dark and waving white flags on top of radioing their position and telling that they were coming through the wire. But then he didn't want to die in this war nor did he want to lose any of his men, especially not by the hands of his own people. Better to be a little overcautious and spend the night out on a fruitless ambush, he told himself as he now trudged upward along the slope of the hill, leading his men back to where they could get a hot meal and some well-deserved rest.

He had hardly entered the compound where dozens of tents and sandbags stood like a community of green canvas and dirt when he saw Pat Collins, Frank Reasoner, and a stranger walking toward him.

"How'd they hold up?" Collins asked.

"I think we're in shape, Skipper," DelGrosso responded. "Not one heat casualty, and the feet are no worse for wear. I think we're broken in pretty well."

Collins looked at the stranger, an average-sized man of about thirty years of age with a small, black mustache and black hair combed straight back, exposing a quickly receding hairline. "Eddie, this is John Del-Grosso, my executive officer."

"Eddie Adams," the stranger said as he put out his hand.

John DelGrosso immediately noticed the cameras that hung from Eddie Adams's neck and the green canvas bag slung across his shoulder. He glanced at Collins and when he saw the look of approval, he shook Adams's hand.

"You a reporter?" DelGrosso asked.

"I'm a photographer," Eddie said, correcting the lieutenant. "I've set up shop in Da Nang outside the press center. You know Colonel Tom Fields?"

"No," the lieutenant said and looked at his captain. When Pat Collins shrugged, John DelGrosso looked back at Adams. "He must have come in with the new arrivals."

"He's in charge of the press center in Da Nang, opened it," Eddie said. "Set it up next to a slaughterhouse. I was there at daybreak and they were killing pigs. Sounded like they were clubbing them to death. I had to get out of there, so he gave me a sergeant and a jeep, and we came here."

Collins put his hand on Eddie's shoulder. "Adams here is a Marine. Served in Korea as a combat correspondent. Made staff sergeant."

John DelGrosso smiled and looked again at the photographer. "You're one of us then, Semper Fi."

"Once a Marine, always a Marine," Eddie said.

"Let's get your pack off and talk," Collins said to John DelGrosso, and the four men walked to the general purpose tent that served as head-quarters for the reconnaissance Marines.

The Marines who worked inside the large tent had rolled up its sides to let in the light breeze that drifted across the hill. The tent offered shade from the blistering sun that now stood straight overhead and baked the orange-colored earth pale.

Frank Reasoner ducked under the tent's low roof and motioned for the Marines inside to set up some folding chairs. Reasoner located a chair for himself and found his pipe and lit it as Collins, Adams, and Del-Grosso sat.

"We have anything cold?" Collins asked a Marine who sat on a foot locker and was sharpening his K-bar knife.

"Nothing, sir," he said. "I made coffee. They say a hot drink will cool you off too."

"Bullshit," Collins said, "and I don't drink coffee anyway. See if you can get us a jug of Kool-Aid down at the mess tent."

The Marine slipped his knife back in its scabbard, then he ducked un-der the side of the tent and disappeared behind a rusted green conex box,[5] which served as the reconnaissance unit's storage shed.

Collins put his feet up and looked at John DelGrosso, who had al-ready taken off his boots and was busy unbuttoning his shirt. His pack

---

[5]A container built of heavy steel and used to transport equipment aboard ships and from ship to shore. Most stand five feet tall by eight feet wide by ten feet deep.

and suspender straps, which held up his web belt, canteens, rifle magazine pouches, and first-aid kit, lay in a heap next to his rifle, a 5.56-mm carbine with a metal peg with a foot on the end for a stock.

Marine and Army researchers had issued the experimental rifle, called AR-15 carbine, to Special Forces and Marine Reconnaissance officers and staff noncommissioned officers. It looked futuristic with its molded alloy body, magazine well that extended down like a submachine gun's and pistol grip, but John DelGrosso was not sure of such a light firearm that shot a mere .223-caliber bullet. He liked the 180-grain, .308-caliber bullet that the M-14 fired, even though the rifle was much heavier, and he was glad that his men still had their M-14 rifles.

"Stop with your trousers, unless you're wearing underwear," Collins said as he watched DelGrosso getting cool and comfortable.

"No skivvies, Skipper, sorry," DelGrosso said as he relaxed, shirtless and barefooted. He unbuckled his belt and ran his thumbs around his trousers' waistband to massage his skin, which had wrinkled red under his belt's tightness. "Now we can talk."

Reasoner looked at his fellow lieutenant and said, "You want some chow, I'll grab you a plate. I've already talked through this anyway."

"You don't mind?" DelGrosso said. "I can grab some in a little while. No sweat."

"No. You relax," Reasoner said. "I'll be back in a minute."

Frank Reasoner walked toward the mess tent and Collins began to talk to both the photographer and the lieutenant.

"John," Collins began, "Frank is headed to up over the Hai Van Pass to a place called Phu Bai, outside Hue. He'll be patrolling along the Perfume River with 2nd Battalion, 3rd Marines. They've got the responsibility of keeping the Viet Cong away from that air strip and the Army radio unit up there."

"Too bad we're losing him," John said.

"He'll be around," Collins said. "Doc Blanchard and the rest of the battalion will be landing in a few days anyway, so it's not like we're breaking up the family or anything. We'll still work together. We've got heavy-duty plans in the works."

John DelGrosso looked at Eddie Adams, who sat puffing on a cigarette and listening quietly. Collins saw the glance and looked too at Eddie.

"In a few days, we're going on a company-size patrol. The first of many to come," Collins said. "I've already gotten it cleared for Adams to go along too. I think it would be good for you two to get to know each other since he will be either with you or with me."

Eddie looked at John DelGrosso and felt uncomfortable with the captain's suggestion; he thought that it would be better if he got to know the officers and enlisted of the company on his own. Having the commanding officer put him on the men seemed to establish him in a superior position with them, and Eddie never liked being treated as being superior to anyone. Eddie thought too and considered also that he never liked having people superior to him either.

"To tell you the truth," Eddie said, trying to place himself in a most positive light with the lieutenant, "me being a former staff sergeant, I feel a little out of place in officers' country."

"Hey, Mr. Adams," DelGrosso began, "you—"

"Wait a minute," Eddie interrupted. "What's this mister stuff. I was a staff sergeant. Come on, Lieutenant, call me Eddie."

DelGrosso smiled and saw the discomfort that his formality left with Eddie. "Sure, Eddie," he said. "Captain Collins says you're all right, that's good enough for me. You're welcome to come along with us anyplace too."

Collins said, "You'll get to know everyone once we've gone on a few patrols together. That's the quickest way to get to know anyone. And speaking of patrols, here's the lowdown."

The captain unbuttoned his shirt pocket and took out a green notebook and began flipping through pages. He found where he had made notes from his meeting at Da Nang. "First item," he said, "in four days we will launch out on extended patrols, fifteen or twenty miles beyond the wire, and like I said, they will be company size, reconnaissance in force. Besides our three platoons, we'll have a reinforcement of a platoon of South Vietnamese whatever, ARVN if we're lucky but more likely Regional or Popular Force volunteers." He looked at Eddie. "Like our reservists back home, but these guys aren't trained."

Eddie looked at Pat Collins. "I know. I've seen them."

Pat Collins raised his eyebrows. "They've relaxed the Rules of Engagement so that we can pursue the enemy, but everyone is still restricted primarily to this area, Da Nang Air Base, and Hue/Phu Bai, where Reasoner is going. Units still have to get permission to fire and the rest of that bull-shit. And every patrol outside the wire has to have South Vietnamese forces with them."

John DelGrosso looked at the two men and said, "So we're the candidates for all the extracurricular activity."

"That's it," Collins said. "We're damn lucky. The rest of these guys will be bored crazy sitting back here, and we will be out there, making history. These will be the first real patrols of this deployment, not like those candy jobs we've been training on. I expect we will see the enemy and we will see some action, finally."

"So what's the plan?" DelGrosso asked. "We don't just march out at dawn, do we?"

"You might be kidding, but it's a lot more like the French Foreign Legion movies than you think," Collins said. "The plan is based on a hammer and anvil tactic successfully used by the French in Algiers and fits our current doctrine and the situation very well. In fact it's right in the M1428 tactics manual that you had at The Basic School."[6]

"We called it Sparrow Hawk or something," DelGrosso said.

"When we go out," Collins said, "a Sparrow Hawk battalion will stand by at Da Nang Air Base. A squadron of helicopters will be on the line, ready to fly when we call for help. We get into a scrap, we make the call, and this battalion chops out. We've also got a squadron of Fox-4 Phantoms ready to launch with them, for whatever good that will do."

Eddie Adams smiled intently until he heard the closing phrase from Pat Collins. "What do you mean, 'whatever good that will do'?" he asked.

"We don't have any UHF radios," DelGrosso offered, already knowing exactly what Collins meant. He looked at Eddie Adams. "The Phantoms all have UHF radios, and we can't talk to them. We have to call someone who has both a UHF and VHF capability, like a helicopter. They relay our call for an air strike to the jet."

"If we're in a fight," Collins added, "chances are more likely that

---

[6]The Basic School is twenty-six weeks of basic infantry training conducted at Quantico, Virginia. Every Marine Corps officer attends this school before going on to his or her specialty school. During the Vietnam War, only pilots did not attend The Basic School, or TBS, as it is commonly called by Marines. After 1976, all officers including pilots were required to attend TBS.

we'll be at close quarters. If I can't talk to the pilot dropping the load my-self, I don't want any close air support."

"Why don't they have radios?" Eddie asked.

John DelGrosso shrugged and Pat Collins shook his head, showing his frustration. "I'm not sure why. I could guess, something to do with space or weight, but it would only be a guess. Hopefully, we'll get our hands on some of these transistorized UHF radios before too much longer."

"Here's brunch," John DelGrosso said, taking a box and setting it in front of where he sat. In the distance he could see Frank Reasoner carry-ing a stack of plates, one for each of the men, and behind him the Marine who went after Kool-Aid carried a green vacuum jug under one arm and a stack of food-filled paper plates in his free hand.

"Got plastic forks and napkins in my cargo pocket," Frank Reasoner said as he ducked inside the tent. Eddie took three plates from him and passed two to Pat Collins and John DelGrosso. The other Marines who had been working quietly at the other end of the tent stopped their work and grabbed plates from the Marine with the jug. He had propped the jug in the back of an empty folding chair and allowed the spout to protrude out the opening in the back of the chair. The officers watched as the en-listed Marines poured canteen cups full of the red-colored juice before they took some for themselves.

· 6 ·

IN THE DARKNESS THE SILHOUETTES OF THE TREES LOOKED ALMOST like home, when he had lain in his front yard and looked down the hill to where the trees grew along the creek and he had fished there as a boy. He liked dreaming of home this way, and as the sun dropped farther and farther behind the mountains, it looked more and more like home.

As he lazily gazed past the front sight of his rifle, footsteps tromping outside the small, two-man bunker woke him from his daydream.

"Come on outta there," the corporal called down to the two Marines manning the post. "Your relief has arrived."

"Shit, I'm glad you guys got here," the one Marine said, crawling out of the hole. "I gotta go see a man about a dog, real bad. I think it was that cocktail of coffee and chocolate that did it."

His partner laughed. "My café o-lay gave you the trots? Sure it wasn't that bog water you drank on patrol? I told you the stuff would give you the screamers, so don't lay it off on my café o-lay."

"I gotta get to the head, man," the Marine said, and walked away with the cheeks of his buttocks clenched tightly together.

"Look at him, walkin' like a bitch," his partner said to the corporal. "Fixin' to drop a load right now."

The corporal and the two men who were the relief laughed with the other Marine as they watched the distressed man hurry up the hill, following a now well-worn trail that led past a row of screen-covered six-inch diameter pipes jutting out from the ground, built as field urinals, and two plywood privies, built for the other.

Kenneth H. White and Charles D. Lagle were both privates first class, and they were both Pat Collins's boys. They had drawn the night watch at the listening post most distant from the main compound. Both men, even though they joked on their way down, worried about being so far from the protection that the defensive positions that protected the central compound offered.

They both had heard the stories told during boot camp about how the listening post Marines always died. They were expendable. On listening post duty, if you're gonna be overrun, you're dead, their drill instructors had even said. They thought about this as they stared out into the increasing blackness of the night.

"Nothing's gonna happen," White said to himself, trying to build confidence so that he could really believe, really feel that nothing was actually going to happen. That he would survive this so-called suicide duty.

"What are you babbling about," Lagle mumbled as he too stared out into the darkness.

"Nothing. Not a damn thing."

"No use in both of us wearing ourselves out," Lagle said. "We'll take shifts. Want to flip for first watch?"

"No," White said, "I've got it. You sit down and relax."

Lagle lay back in the dark hole but he could not rest. He closed his eyes and listened to the night birds, the frogs, the crickets. In the distance he heard the bark of a dog. And in the farther distance, he could hear the whine of truck engines and generators where Marines continued to work through the night, depending upon Privates First Class Charles Lagle and Kenneth White to sound the alarm should the enemy decide to attack.

"Lagle," White said, looking out at the shadows and silhouettes of bushes and mountains. "So tell mc about what's going on down at the air base."

Lagle looked up and said, "All I know is what that combat correspondent sergeant told me. That these guys down at Da Nang get liberty in the ville, and that they got this regular boys' town they're a callin' Dog Patch."[7]

"Every place Marines have ever been's got a Dog Patch," White said.

"I don't know about messing around with any gook whore," Lagle said, and stood again, looking outside too. "Hell, they could be VC and cut your balls off. I mean, can you imagine one of them VC hookers sloppin' on your Johnson and takin' a bite out of it. Jesus Christ, I'd kill her, but I'd still be in one hell of a fix."

"I heard of a guy in Okinawa, down at Kin Ville, outside Camp Hansen," White said, "he was shakin' up with this bar hog, and she found out he was rotating back to the World early. So he's getting his flute tooted by this bitch, and just when he's about to blow his wad, she clamps down on that bad boy. Shit, she bit all the way through, and when he yanked it out of her mouth, it was hanging by a sliver of skin. Well, that poor bastard pulls on his britches and goes runnin' for the main gate with no shoes, no shirt, and blood running down his crotch. The MP at the gate sees this guy and asks what happened. This stupid asshole says, 'I got my dick hung in my zipper.'"

Both Marines laughed aloud.

"They get him to the battalion aid station and sew his dick back on," White finished, "and that's when he told the doctor the truth about it."

"I heard stories about shit like that," Lagle said. "Reckon they're true?"

"I know for a fact this one is," White said. "I got a buddy works at the Public Information Office down at Camp Hansen and he showed a bunch of us the copy of the Serious Incident Report. I read it. Man, Lagle, it's true. No shit."

"Jesus!" Lagle said. "That poor son of a bitch. Reckon he can get his dick hard?"

---

[7]Taken from the Al Capp comic strip *Li'l Abner*, the Yokem family's hometown. Marines adopted the name to describe Third World villages that were nearest to their camps. In later years the name would change to Hooterville, taken from the popular television series *Petticoat Junction*.

"Shit no," White said. "He'll be lucky it don't fall off after them sewin' it back on. I bet if it don't fall off, all he'll be able to do is pee with it. Sure as hell can't fuck with it. Can't get no pussy with a dead dick."

Lagle laughed at the play on words, and White sniggered because he hadn't seen it coming either.

"We better cool the bullshit," White said. "Captain Collins'll have our asses, we get put on report for bullshitting on LP duty."

"What'll they do," Lagle mused, "shave our heads, send us to South Vietnam, and put us on LP duty?"

"I don't fuck around with Captain Collins," White said. "He's a good guy, but I sure don't want him pissed at me."

Both Marines stood silently in the night, and watched and listened. Lagle checked the selector switch on the side of his M-14 rifle and pressed it to the full automatic position. He glanced at Kenneth White and smiled, and then laid his cheek against the rifle and looked out over its sights.

Quietness grew, and Charles Lagle began to wonder. He looked at Kenneth White and whispered, "I don't hear anything."

"Good," White said. "I don't wanta hear anything."

"No," Lagle said, "I wanta hear something. I wanta hear the frogs and those birds. They're not doing anything. I think there's something out there."

"You're full of shit," White said. "You'll be seeing ghosts next."

"Listen," Lagle said, "if there was nothing out there the frogs and whatever else is out there would be croaking or chirping. There's nothing. Only sound I can hear is the generator back at camp."

White said nothing and thought about what Lagle was saying; he thought more and became troubled too.

"Maybe I better call in a sitrep," White said and knelt down in the hole and found the radio. He was about to call when suddenly the crack of a bullet exploding into one of the small listening post's sandbags sent his heart reeling. Before he could stand and see what had happened, several other bullets slammed into the ground and sandbags.

Charles Lagle opened fire with his automatic rifle, sending a stream of 7.62-mm bullets chopping into the weeds and dense brush on the lower slope of Hill 327.

"We're under fire! We're under fire!" White shouted on the radio, then he dropped it next to his pack and grabbed his rifle. He shoved its muzzle outside the listening post and began shooting at dark figures running in the distance.

"Jesus Christ," Lagle cried out, and fell into the hole, holding his hands over his face. "I'm hit! I'm hit in the face!"

White fired his rifle and shouted over his shoulder. "How bad?"

"I don't know, but I think it got my eye," Lagle sobbed.

White dropped his head below the parapet and put his face close to Lagle's. "I don't see a bullet hole, but your eye is fucked up and bleeding. Think a bullet might have blown trash up into your eye?"

"It's possible," Lagle said. "Sure hurts, though."

White was back on his feet looking out, trying to find the running silhouettes when a voice from the rear of the listening post called to them, "Corporal of the guard coming up."

"Come ahead," White called and saw the figure of the corporal who had posted them scramble across the ground in a fast low-crawl. The Marine dropped in the hole.

"Got a reactionary force coming down now," the corporal said. "You all right?"

Lagle, now reasonably sure that he would not soon die, said, "I need to see the doc. Took a shot in the eye. I think one of their rounds hit some debris and I caught some rocks or wood in my eye and cheek."

"We'll have you outta here in a shake," the corporal said. "What happened?"

"It got real quiet," White tried to explain, "then when I was about to make a sitrep, all hell broke loose. They opened fire, and we returned it. Then they took off."

"I knew it would happen sooner or later," the corporal said. "I guess they finally got the word."

"Is Lagle gonna get a Purple Heart?" White asked.

"Sure," the corporal said, "he took enemy fire and got a wound that requires medical attention."

"That makes you the first," White told Lagle with a sense of pride. "That'll make you somebody."

5

# FIRST FIREFIGHT

**P**IG SHIT. NOTHING ELSE MORE ADEQUATELY DESCRIBED THE SMELL of the air most mornings in Vietnam. The stink seemed to dwindle as the days wore on, but it never completely burned off. On Thursday, April 22, 1965, near the foot of Hill 327, about six miles west of Da Nang, the awful smell hung heavy in the morning's dank air.

Eddie Adams climbed down the tailgate of the Marine Corps truck—"six-bys" they call them—and stepped onto the dusty roadway where he caught a full, double-nostril blast of the stench. Two cameras dangled from black straps looped around the photographer's neck while a small, green canvas bag hung from his right shoulder.

The sun cresting the hill and burning the morning dampness from the air gave him a sense of hope that today would be *the* day. After the other patrols with Pat Collins and his men, Eddie felt depressed that all they could find were a few signs—matted grass and broken twigs—that let them know the VC was there, watching them. However, he knew that sooner or later Collins and his Marines would connect with the Viet Cong, making them the first American ground combat unit to go on an offensive patrol and engage the Vietnamese Communists in a fight. This sense of history in the making struck Eddie, and he believed it was important for him to be there, recording the moment with photographs, when this first fight began.[1]

Although Eddie felt its significance, he knew that today's operation would probably receive little public attention; it was merely one more bit of historical trivia lost in an increasing backwash of copy that ticked out from the AP's Saigon teletypes daily, most of which wound up on back pages near grocery or tire advertisements. These days of 1965, most Americans really didn't know that much nor care about this *Sale Guerre*—"Dirty War," as the French continued to call it in their criticism

---

[1]The first American ground unit to actually conduct independent operations in Vietnam had landed nearly a year earlier. It was a composite force designated Marine Detachment, Advisory Team One. The world took little note of them—they were hardly the stuff of headlines. These Marines, however, were under strict orders that explicitly prohibited them from patrolling or engaging in any activity that might be construed as "offensive in nature." More or less a safeguard to ensure no unwanted headlines did come of it.

Team One arrived in Da Nang on May 20, 1964, under the command of Major Alfred M. Gray, Jr., USMC (a Marine who would rise through the ranks from private to general and on July 1, 1987, become commandant of the Marine Corps).

A radio detachment designated the Signal Engineering Survey Unit was the force's primary element, and consisted of three officers and twenty-seven enlisted Marines from 1st Radio Company, Fleet Marine Force, Pacific, and from Headquarters Marine Corps. They were supported by a seventy-six-man infantry detachment from Company G, 2d Battalion, 3rd Marine Regiment, reinforced with an 81-mm mortar section (two mortars).

During the final days of May, U.S. Air Force C-123 transports airlifted Team One to the Civilian Irregular Defense Group camp at Khe Sanh. Once there, the composite force built a solid supply base and began communications operations. By June 21, Major Gray had managed to move 73 Marines, 100 Vietnamese troops, and tons of communications equipment to a 5,000-foot peak on nearby Tiger Tooth Mountain. There they conducted communications operations in extremely primitive conditions (so primitive that the men were limited to two canteens of water daily, and they could neither bathe nor shave).

In mid-July a storm all but destroyed the Tiger Tooth Mountain base, and then on July 17 Viet Cong attacked the position. Since the Marines were under strict orders prohibiting them from any "offensive" activities, and with their position devastated by the storm and its location now known by the enemy, Major Gray withdrew his force and returned to Da Nang on July 22, 1964.

of increased U.S. involvement. Most Americans—including the Marines in Vietnam on this stinking morning—really didn't care about that either.

The diesel exhaust, which blew in the trucks' beds during the short and very bumpy ride, had masked the morning air's odor en route. Now, as the passengers piled out, the stink struck full force with most of the eighty Marines from Pat Collins's reconnaissance company.

"Shit!" several men said, following the exclamation with lowly mumbled strings of profanity while they fanned the air in front of their faces. Everything in this backward and mostly rural country seemed to keep a coating of orange dirt, and either smelled like rotting fish or pig shit. This morning smelled like both.

"Hey, Pat!" Eddie shouted to Collins, who stood ten yards away, directing his men out of the trucks. "If we're lucky, we'll get ambushed!"

Both men laughed.

These days it was easy to laugh at such a comment. Few Americans had yet died in this war. No American ground units had taken on the enemy. There were no ambushes . . . yet. A year later, the same remark, at very least, would receive in response a cold look and a raised middle finger.

But today, Eddie's sarcasm seemed good humor as the thirty-four-year-old captain stood at the road's edge organizing his men for their mission: patrolling on a deep probe west of Hill 327, gathering intelligence on the lay of the land, nature of the countryside, and habits of the people, and demonstrating to the local peasants (who made up more than 80 percent of the Vietnamese population) that the United States was now here—"presenting a presence," as politicians put it. The button pushers and memo writers far from the battlefront—people who slept safely in warm beds every night and viewed the conflict with the sanitized perspective of pins in a map—hoped this "presence" would discourage further insurgency.

Collins knew better. He had studied revolution and insurgency much of his career. The captain clearly understood the Communist doctrine's philosophy of "Protracted Revolution"—war with no deadlines and, from the Communist's perspective, only one possible outcome. He also knew very well the nature in which this war should be fought.

The best tactics, he believed, relied on the use of small units, spread far into the hills and jungles—beneath the thick canopy that covered most infiltration routes. There these small units could ambush and effectively interdict the enemy as they moved along the lacework of trails.[2]

"You're getting to be a regular Ricky Recon," Collins said to Eddie Adams as he watched his men climbing off the trucks and pulling down their backpacks and rifles.

"This is where it's at," Eddie said, aiming his camera at Collins and turning the focusing ring. "Smile."

Collins cracked a wide grin and shot Eddie the finger. "Print that, asshole," the captain dared.

With each patrol, Eddie Adams and Pat Collins grew closer and friendlier. Eddie felt safe with Pat, and Pat liked having Eddie along.

"You're a good Marine," Collins said sincerely, but then cracked, "fucked up in every other way, but a good Marine."

"Listen," Eddie shot back, "I made staff sergeant in less than six years. How many fuck-ups you know make staff sergeant in less than six years."

"That's because you were kissing the general's ass," Collins said. "Everybody knows where you combat correspondents got that dark brown stain on your noses. You were a fuck-up because it took you six years instead of three like the rest of those typewriter terrorists."

"I guess I learned to hump your fucking ammo and paddle your fucking rubber boats from kissing ass too," Eddie fired back.

"I don't know. I never had my nose stuck up anybody's ass before. No telling what you might learn back there. Could be that's where they come up with all these great ideas, tattooed on asses," Collins said, trying hard to push Eddie's button.

"What it was," Eddie said with a wide smile, "while I was standing in line behind all you lizard-fucking snake eaters, trying to get a shot at the old man's ass, I picked up a few fine points of fieldwork."

"In your fucking dreams," Collins said. "You're okay, Adams, but

---

[2]Years later, as a colonel and an author of Marine Corps "Low-Intensity Conflict" and "Special Operations" doctrine, Pat Collins commented about the tactics of trying to bomb the infiltration routes in Vietnam. He said, "All that the B-52 strikes ever did was piss off the monkeys."

Pentagon reports confirm his position. They note that at the war's close the United States had dropped in Vietnam two and one half times the tonnage of bombs dropped in World War II, and proved to be of little to no result.

don't let that go to your head. Just remember, the day you stop pulling your weight and covering the guy's ass next to you, that's when you lose your ticket to this party: just like any other grunt on this parade."

Collins knew that he didn't have to remind the photographer of a Marine's first responsibility—that to the men at his side—but he did it anyway, just to dig a bit at Eddie's thin skin. No one had ever asked Eddie to pick up a box, or help paddle, or share his water with a Marine down with the heat. He just did it. Eddie Adams still had a lot of Marine left in him, and Pat Collins liked that.

"That's the smell of money," one country boy drawled as the gaggle behind the trucks took shape and two lines of Marines route-stepped westward along each side of the roadway.

"Bet they don't rob many banks where you live," a gruff voice retorted, sending a ripple of yuks down the extending line of Marines.

A sense of adventure stirred among these young men despite the already intensifying morning heat. Less than six weeks ago they had been part of the first (official) American ground combat force to land in Vietnam—green and full of mistakes. Now, they felt confident, well oiled. Today they looked and acted like veterans.

"Keep your intervals," First Sergeant Harry Rogers called back to his men, reminding them to maintain several meters distance between each other. This first month in Vietnam had taught many lessons, and reminded leaders of other lessons from other wars that seemed to have lost their importance, until now. A wide space between Marines meant fewer casualties, should a man trip a mine or the patrol fall into an ambush.

Today marked Company D's third patrol beyond the Hill 327 contours. The two previous days' patrols ended with little more than frustration from the heat, sore feet, and a boring intelligence debrief. As they walked along the roadway and Hill 327 lay farther and farther behind them, a certain uneasy excitement seemed to generate with each step.

"Hey, John," Eddie called as he jogged up the center of the roadway toward the head of the three-platoon column, one hand clutching his cameras against his chest while the other hand held fast to the strap of his camera bag as it bounced against his hip.

John DelGrosso looked over his left shoulder and said, "Ed, my man. So tell me, any news from New York?"

"I haven't talked with anyone back there in a week," Eddie said, trying to catch his breath as he changed step to a walk. "You need anything passed on to your family?"

"No, just small talk," DelGrosso said. "I guess everybody's kinda tight, going out again. Third time's a charm, maybe."

"As long as we don't get fucked up," Eddie said cautiously.

"Right," the lieutenant said. "These kids are ready though. We've got our immediate action procedures down pretty solid, at least in the drills. I keep telling these guys, What you do in practice, you'll do in the race."

"I hope you're right," Eddie said. Then he stopped in the roadway and pointed his camera toward the rear of the column and began shooting photographs of the Marines walking toward him—their faces now aglow with sweat. He dropped to one knee, snapped a shot, stood, snapped a shot, and then waited for Pat Collins to arrive at the point where he stood.

"You better save your film," Collins said. "You'll be out of ammo before the battle."

"I've got plenty," Eddie said, stepping off again with the captain. "I guess we're all a little nervous."

"They'll settle down," Collins said. "A few miles and these guys will forget about jitters."

While Company D marched westward in the rising heat, Bravo Company, 1st Battalion, 3rd Marine Regiment, stood watch as the Sparrow Hawk Company at Da Nang, waiting near several UH-34D helicopters and a flight of F-4B Phantoms that would race into action with them, should Collins call.

Second Lieutenant Bill Vankat led his Marines at the point of the three-platoon column. Barely twenty years old but the senior second lieutenant in the company, John DelGrosso followed with his men. Collins and Adams walked ahead of the third platoon, along with its commander, Lieutenant Dick Gesswein, and a South Vietnamese Marine who served as an adviser and liaison.

Eddie wore ankle-high boondocker boots, similar to those issued to him in 1954, as a Marine, but since then, the Corps had changed its footwear and Eddie had bought this pair at a sporting goods outlet in New York. As he walked, he wished that he had worn thicker socks; he could feel the heat from the roadway already cooking up through his soles after only little more than a mile of walking.

The morning sky was dark blue and scattered with thin, nearly transparent clouds. It looked cool compared to the baked-hard clay and gravel rocks that covered the roadway and caked dust over Eddie's shoes.

As the lead column disappeared around a curve in the road where a tree line jutted along a ditch, hiding where a second road converged with this main route, the radio operator, walking behind Collins, spoke up, "Sir, first platoon is at checkpoint alpha. They report the Vietnamese troops are there, waiting to rendezvous."

"Right," Collins said. "Tell Lieutenant Vankat to keep moving, but slow his pace until I contact him again, and tell him to advise the Vietnamese platoon leader to wait for me there with his men. We'll pick them up behind third platoon."

Making the turn at the tree line, Eddie saw the crowd of Vietnamese men armed with an array of old rifles sitting at the side of the road. He jogged ahead of Collins's platoon and began snapping photos of the ununiformed and undisciplined group waiting for the Marine patrol.

"These guys are different than the ones we had yesterday," Eddie said to Collins when his platoon reached the fork in the roadway where the Vietnamese men wearing an odd assortment of web gear and equipment waited.

"We had RFs yesterday—Regional Forces. These guys are the bottom of the barrel—Popular Forces. PFs," Collins said, looking at the rabble gang of so-called local militia that would represent the Vietnamese armed forces support of this day's patrol.

Current policy required that these Vietnamese troops would act as the U.S. patrol's guides, advisers, and translators, as well as assist them in a fight. However, the usefulness of the Vietnamese support in a fight was questionable.

ARVN recruits periodically fired their rifles, inadvertently, into the Marine positions atop Hill 327. This lack of fire discipline left many Marines leery of having those same soldiers following in trace of their column. And, though the Vietnamese Marines and ARVN fought well, the Regional Forces and Popular Forces were completely unreliable. In fact, the "PFs" had a reputation of being quick to leave a post and, in a fight, even quicker to run.

"Which one of you guys is in charge?" Collins said gruffly.

One man wearing brown shorts and a white shirt leapt to attention, snapping his rifle to the order-arms position with his right hand, next to his tire-tread-sandaled feet. He cracked his open palm skyward and clipped it sharply above his left eyebrow in a British-fashioned salute, and said, "Captain, sir! We await your orders."

Collins returned the salute, and said, "At ease, soldier. Next time, try it with the other hand. Salute with your right, not your left."

"Oh, sorry sir," the man said with embarrassment. Then he quickly shuffled his rifle to his left side, slammed its butt into the dirt, and then snapped his right hand into a more appropriate salute, still in the finest British form.

"That's better," Collins said, "but don't salute out here. VC might be watching. You don't want to get me shot, do you?"

"No, sir! Sorry, sir," the man said, jerking his arm back to his side, now more nervous than ever, and offering the captain his friendliest smile, chock-full of gold teeth.

Collins looked at the South Vietnamese Marine liaison officer who had accompanied them and said, "Captain. Will you get these guys in position at the rear?"

The captain smiled and said, "My pleasure, Captain." Then he turned to the little man with the gold-tooth smile, still at attention, and began shouting commands in Vietnamese. The man bolted stiff, his eyes widened, and the friendly expression flew from his face. In its place came a mask of shocked silence.

While the Vietnamese captain shouted in the face of the PF leader, his thirty-seven men scrambled for their equipment and ran to the rear of Collins's column.

Pat looked at Eddie and said, "Guess it's all in how you put it. This guy's definitely got their attention."

Throughout much of the patrol's route, curiosity-filled children intercepted and followed the three platoons of Marines and thirty-eight PF troops. American soldiers were something new, but even now the youngsters had already learned that there was booty to be gained from the GIs. Marines carried candy that they saved from their C-rations, and word of it spread.

"Chocolate?" the children asked again and again. Although they spoke little or no English, the small brown kids with wide, white-toothy smiles who had learned this magic word "chocolate" reaped a sweet reward.

The nearly naked and bone-skinny youngsters learned fast. So did the Marines. It was fun to toss a foil-covered disk and watch the ensuing scramble for the prize. Pitching out several boxes of chewing gum had an even wilder result.

Hot dust boiled in orange clouds around the Marines' feet as they pushed westward along the road. While the Marines' backs and brains cooked in the increasingly cruel heat, the sun rose higher toward ten o'clock, pushing the temperature toward three digits.

Almost as quickly as they had descended on the patrol near the foot of Hill 327, the children disappeared. It was as though the school bell rang, and a once bustling playground suddenly stood silent.

Sounds from the world quieted too, leaving only the buzz of insects that swarmed undaunted by the rising temperature. The baked dry earth and dull green weeds, cooked to a dead-looking gray by the tropical sun, loudly crackled under each man's footsteps, adding a psychological accent to this day's tormenting heat. And as the men walked on, wilting and bored, the quietness caught Collins's attention.

"Something's up," the captain said to his radio operator, Adams, and the Vietnamese Marine adviser who walked a few paces behind. The men stopped and the Marine with the radio strapped to his back put the handset to his ear and called forward for the column to "take five."

"I haven't heard a sound for nearly half an hour," Collins said in a voice that rose in concern. "No radios, no kids, no farmers. Nothing. Not even a bird. I think we're walking into something."

"Sir. Sir. Something's up," the radio operator said, interrupting the captain who now sat while he talked, like the other Marines, resting along the roadside. "Sir, Lieutenant Vankat reports that his platoon hears drums or something. He thinks it's coming from the village up ahead."

Collins looked at the Vietnamese Marine officer who now stood, dusting off his tiger-stripe camouflage uniform. "Captain, what's up?"

"I think maybe alarm at Binh Thai," the Vietnamese officer said. "Villagers know we coming."

"You think they're VC? Maybe they're gonna hit us."

"Don't know. Maybe they just scared."

"Maybe they just VC too," Collins said in a grunting voice while scrambling to his feet. "Let's move up."

Glancing back at his radioman, Collins said, "Tell Lieutenant Vankat to move up and reconnoiter the village. Second and third platoons will follow in column at ten-minute intervals."

He looked at Eddie, who was grabbing up his camera bag and cameras and was rushing to snug his bootlace tight. Then he looked back to see his Marines again on their feet, their rifles now in their hands and very serious expressions on their faces. At the rear, Collins could see the PF leader waving his arms and scolding one of his men who still sat.

"What's up?" Collins asked the Vietnamese captain, pointing to the PFs with his thumb.

The captain just smiled and walked to the rear.

"Okay," Collins said, glancing at Eddie and seeing he was set, "move out and let's keep a good safe interval between every man."

Eddie jogged to the front of the platoon and turned, looking back at the column as the men marched toward him. They looked different now that danger pressed near, and as they passed by him, he imprinted their boyish yet stern expressions on his film and into his mind.

The drums grew louder as the three platoons snaked cautiously forward along the road's edge. The Marines had walked nearly nine miles, and for the past four miles, the road had followed parallel to a river called Tuy Loan. It then turned northwest and continued along the Binh Thai River.

On the column's left, low trees and brush grew along the river's bank while farther, across the water, a bluff that ranged from thirty to fifty feet high extended into the distance. Trees and thick undergrowth flanked the right side of the column.

"Sounds like someone hammering steel," Collins said, tilting his ear toward the north. "Definitely an alarm of some sort."

Eddie Adams jogged ahead of Collins's platoon, trying to get closer to the front; then the first volley of gunfire cracked through the air in an echoing cascade.

"Get down," someone shouted, and before he could think beyond the split second that surrounded his consciousness, Eddie suddenly found himself belly-down in the dirt, holding his cameras to his side and craning his neck, trying to see who was shooting. He slid to the side of the road, and seeing the Marines crouched but not under fire, he again got to his feet and jogged forward a few yards at a time, stopping to survey the situation and then moving ahead.

At the point of the column, Bill Vankat and his platoon had broken out of the tree line that flanked the roadway and moved through an expanse of semidry rice paddies 300 meters wide by 400 meters long, cutting diagonally across them, heading directly toward Binh Thai proper, which stood at the far right-hand corner of this huge clearing.

Vankat's platoon had shifted from their column formation to on line, and were halfway across the paddies when the first volleys of gunfire erupted from the village, directly ahead.

"Hit and roll! Hit and roll!" Vankat shouted to his men, reminding them of their first immediate action step. "Set up a base of fire, then attack! Immediate action! Immediate action!"

Lying belly-down, the lieutenant low-crawled to a low dike and looked ahead, trying to see the enemy. Machine-gun fire from the trees on the platoon's left front began chewing through the field around them, sending black clods and debris flying skyward.

"Fire on the tree line to the left," a sergeant shouted to his automatic rifleman.

Before the Marine could return fire, more small-arms and sniper fire chopped into the paddies from the knolls that stood across the river to their rear and left flank.

"Where's it coming from," Vankat shouted, seeing the turf behind him exploding from the bullets' impact as well as on the forward side of the low dike in front of him.

"We're caught in their cross fire," the sergeant shouted at the lieutenant.

"No shit!" Vankat shouted. "Move up. Remember immediate action. Attack! Turn into the ambush. Fire and movement. Fire and movement!" The lieutenant then stood and began directing his men forward. They were caught squarely in the three-way cross fire—the killing zone—of a well-executed L-shaped ambush.

The Viet Cong had massed an organized, reinforced company into Binh Thai. There, they sent out a platoon with a machine-gun section to set up a position right of the main force, between 150 and 200 meters southwest of the village. Establishing the long axis of the L, another rifle platoon, consisting of small arms, automatic rifles, and snipers, dug in across the river on the crest of the knolls 300 meters south-southwest of the village proper. This left the remaining VC company to operate from a series of trenches, tunnels, and fortified positions within the village.

When the first shots echoed through the trees, John DelGrosso and his platoon rushed up the road and rapidly moved on line along the southern edge of the fields, just outside the tree line. Once there, second platoon knelt in the knee-high grass that bordered the rice fields.

DelGrosso looked back and saw Pat Collins, Dick Gesswein, and the third platoon running to positions among the trees to his rear. The lieutenant turned toward Harry Rogers and said, "Hold the men here. I'm gonna check with the captain."

Keeping low, John DelGrosso zigzagged his way back to the roadway and then ran along its edge until he passed the point man of third platoon. "How far back's the captain?" he said, gulping for air.

"About fifty meters, just in the trees," the Marine said.

DelGrosso sprang to his feet and again ran to where Collins and his radio operator were crouched.

"Sir, what now?" DelGrosso asked.

Collins, calm yet in his typical rapid-fire manner of speaking, had already assessed the situation, and in a matter of moments decided on his company's battle plan.

"Normally," Collins said, looking at his lieutenant, "the best move to counter an L-shaped ambush is to take out the long axis and turn on the enemy flank. But with them set up across the river that pretty well scrubs that idea. The only other reasonable option is an envelopment from the strong side."

DelGrosso nodded approvingly and said, "I'll buy that."

"Vankat's gonna assault from the front and give us a base of fire," Collins said. "You sweep to his right and establish a frontal attack. Gesswein and I will take third platoon and envelop around the end of your line."

DelGrosso rushed back to his men. He felt the excitement flooding his head and pounding in his ears as he ran. Eddie Adams hurried at his side, camera up, stopping a second to snap photos, then running again. For the Marines waiting in the tall grass at the edge of the rice field while their lieutenant was away, the few moments seemed an eternity. Their hearts strained as they watched their brothers in first platoon fight slowly forward in a scattered line, fire team by fire team, progressing toward the village in a methodical and disciplined fire and movement: resisting the deadly temptation of trying to cover up and wait for help.

"Okay, men!" Lieutenant DelGrosso shouted breathlessly as his Marines, seeing him return, scrambled to their feet. "Fix bayonets!"

When Eddie heard that order—fix bayonets—he couldn't believe it. He had never been in a fix-bayonets situation, ever. Now, as each Marine quickly snapped the long blade on his M-14, beneath the rifle's muzzle, a shudder quivered through the photographer's body. This is it! he told himself. Action! Better than any John Wayne movie. But it is no movie. This is real!

In a matter of seconds, DelGrosso and his Marines were on line and shooting toward the village as they rushed forward, an echelon at a time.

As the reality of the fight struck Eddie's consciousness, so did the gunfire's chatter. Bullets cracked overhead and snapped through the knee-high grass. He felt suddenly vulnerable. And somewhere in the midst of feeling extremely mortal, like a tattoo on his soul, that proud part of him that still called itself "Marine" left his heart swelling as he photographed these kids—his blood brothers—led by a skinny, twenty-year-old lieutenant, leaning at the fire, moving fearlessly forward: bayonets fixed.

"I'm hit!" a nearby voice cried out.

Eddie let down his camera and looked to see a sprawled Marine with blood spreading across his face. Without a thought, Eddie fell to his knees and huddled over the youngster. A bullet had creased the side of the Marine's head and left a long cut cascading blood down his face. The sight of it proved much worse than the actual wound.

"Corpsman!" Eddie shouted. "Damn it! Corpsman, get over here! This guy's hit!"

A few yards away a hospital corpsman huddled next to a tree that shielded him from the direct line of fire. He looked at the photographer kneeling beside the downed Marine, and felt fear lock every muscle in his body.

Eddie saw the young Navy doc huddled beside the tree, and felt a surge of anger fill his chest. "You! Corpsman!" Eddie shouted. "I'm really getting pissed! Get over here. Now!"

The last syllables no more than left the photographer's lips when the corpsman bolted from the tree's protecting cover, ran through the gunfire, and squatted at the side of the bleeding Marine. Eddie patted the doc on his shoulder, stood, and then ran to DelGrosso's advancing platoon.

"Where are the PFs?" the Vietnamese Marine captain asked Collins, who now waited with a radio handset pressed to his ear. He had moved up with DelGrosso's platoon and had made a quick survey of the situation while Collins and Gesswein were angling third platoon toward the Viet Cong company's flank.

"You're not going to like it," Collins said in a low voice.

"What?" the Vietnamese captain said.

"The second after you took off, we started taking rounds," Collins said. "I'm making a report on them right now. Listen."

Collins then turned to the handset and began talking: "That's right. As soon as the first shots cracked overhead, I called for a hasty advance forward. All thirty-eight of those Vietnamese Popular Force troops took off.

"They were at high port—running like hell—headed the other way, last time I saw them," the exasperated captain shouted over the radio as he reported his position to 3rd Marine Regiment's operations section.

"Those PFs were out of here like a shot!" Collins exclaimed. "They'll probably still be running come nightfall."

Collins glanced at the Vietnamese Marine who had buried his face in his hands. He could not tell if the man was laughing or crying.

"You can land the Sparrow Hawk Company right in the rice paddies," Collins said, again talking to headquarters. "We'll be working our way into the village. Also, see what you can work up on the other side of the river to try and neutralize that bunch."

The captain signed off the radio and moments later the Bravo 1/3 Sparrow Hawk Marines jammed aboard the UH-34D helicopters, and in a swirl of churning dirt and chopping rotors launched skyward, each man excited and scared as he rushed toward the unknown finality of his first battle.

As the Bravo Company Marines lifted away from the airfield, a half-dozen strapped and saddled, wide-eyed pilots—like jockeys in a derby—raced their flight of VMFA-531 Phantom jets—two by two, seething their blue-flame thunder in twin pairs of 30-foot-long, 44,000-pounds-of-thrust after-burner tails—down Da Nang Air Base's runway, bristling for a first fight too.

"Corpsman! Corpsman!" Bill Vankat's platoon sergeant shouted seeing the lieutenant suddenly go down. "The lieutenant's hit."

"I'm all right!" Vankat shouted back. "Just clipped my arm. Corpsman, keep your position."

Looking to the right of his platoon, Vankat could see John Del-Grosso's men now linked on line with his right flank. He saw the Marines opening a concentrated stream of fire into the village, establishing a solid base of cover so that he could charge his platoon forward.

His arm gashed near his shoulder and blood streaming down his fingers, Vankat again stood. The chattering cross fire chewed through the grass and dirt all around him as he shouted to his men, "Move out! Move out! Let's go get 'em."

The words had barely cleared his throat when the whole line of Vankat's men surged forward, the young Marines shouting and shooting with their taste of first blood.

When the combat began, the battle seemed nearly metaphysical for many of these slick-faced Marines who had never before felt war's numbing first jolt: that split-second, dreamlike mind-cloud that requires a brain-clearing blink or two before the virgin warrior can grasp the mortal reality of a first fight. Yet the crack and pop of bullets clipping past their ears quickly shattered any sense of dream. Their awakening was a rattling one, punctuated by sudden terror and amplified reactions. For these Marines, the heat and excitement of first battle came at its fullest.

"Slow your fire," John DelGrosso shouted to his men, who in the blur of excitement—or awakening as newly baptized combat veterans—sent their volleys into the ground, trees, and air. "Take aim! Don't waste your ammo!"

DelGrosso, himself still shaking from the reality of first combat, continued to scold his Marines until their fire settled into the bodies of several VC who stood in the open. This sight further steadied the Marines with feelings of added confidence.

While DelGrosso's and Vankat's platoons found marks with their rifles and advanced on the village from the front, Collins and Dick Gesswein's platoon now moved quickly through the cover that the trees offered them, in hopes of closing on the VC's exposed flank.

More than twenty minutes had now passed since the first shots had sounded in this firefight, and already the Viet Cong were showing signs of second thoughts.

In nearly every instance until now, when the VC ambushed a South Vietnamese patrol, the government force would either withdraw under fire or squat like sitting ducks while Victor Charlie picked them off. However, the tactics that the Marines displayed caught Charlie by surprise. Rather than squat and be picked off, the Marines attacked.

By the time DelGrosso's platoon had linked on line with Vankat's, and closed toward the village, the VC had already begun their withdrawal. Several Viet Cong lay wounded between huts after jumping from two long trenches that paralleled the line of Marines a hundred meters away. One guerrilla lay sprawled, hacked, and bloody—clearly dead.

High in the blue, 90-degree-warm sky a hollow, coursing roar cascaded to earth and echoed off the bluffs across the river and through the trees and across the rice paddies where the battle still raged. It seemed, at first, distant and unassuming. Few men even noticed. But in a second, the thunder and horrifying squall of two diving F-4 jets—slingshotting over the village at treetop height—sent shudders booming through the earth and adrenaline spiking the heartbeats of every man on the ground, including the Marines.

There are few things so immediately frightening as an F-4 Phantom jet suddenly, and without warning, screaming past at more than 500 knots and a few feet above the trees. At one moment, all is quiet. And in a second, the world quakes with the sudden shake and boom as the gray flash thunders past, literally bending trees in its wake.

Several Marines cheered. Captain Collins only watched with increased frustration. With no UHF radios he could not talk directly to the fighter pilots and guide them in so that they could bomb and strafe the now retreating VC.

Collins looked at his radioman and said, laughing about this display of close air support, "All those jets can do is fly through the treetops, knock down branches, and try to scare the hell out of Charlie. Maybe some of the VC'll die of heart attacks!"

The sound of the clanking iron, followed by several sharp whistle blasts, rang through the village and surrounding trees and hills. As this similar signal had alerted the ambush a good thirty to forty minutes earlier, it now signaled retreat.

At the sight of Charlie's withdrawal, several squads of Marines leapt to their feet and charged forward, yelling and firing at the fleeing enemy.

While the two platoons intensified their assault from the front, Collins and the Marines from third platoon closed on the right flank, provoking the VC to scatter and run. When the Marines were not moving forward, they lay prone to present the smallest target and have the steadiest of aiming positions.

A distant and familiar beat of helicopter blades chopping through the late morning's heat caught the attention of several dozen Marines who now lay in the open field and fired with careful aim at the retreating enemy.

The VC who manned the machine guns at the Marines' left had long since withdrawn, as did the rifle platoon located on the knolls across the river. The company-sized ambush—approximately ninety to one hundred guerrillas—had in effect carried out its mission of making contact and now wisely bugged out before it was too late.

As he too lay on his belly, Pat Collins looked over his shoulder and watched several helicopters swooping in low over the trees. He was about to stand and wave the choppers into the rice field when they turned nose up and banked hard right, climbing up and away to the rear.

"What in hell's going on!" the captain shouted to no one in particular. He jumped to his feet and yelled, "Where in hell they goin'?"

Only a few rifle shots cracked and chattered, and they were mostly friendly. The confused captain took a moment before he realized that the appearance of his Marines, all lying flat throughout the rice paddy, must have given the helicopter pilots the impression that the Marines on the ground were pinned down—that this was an LZ under fire.

Collins turned to see Eddie now back at his side. The frustrated Marine pulled off his cap and slapped it against his leg, raising a cloud of dust.

"Goddamn those fucking airedales!" he swore. "I don't care if there's a solid wall of lead pouring in, I'm never again going to let incoming helicopters see my Marines on their bellies. No matter how heavy the fire, we're gonna be up, walking around."

Seeing what they believed were Marines under fire, the helicopters turned away and landed at alternate landing sites hundreds of meters away from the fight. There they unloaded Bravo Company.

By the time that the point Marines of the Sparrow Hawk unit had found their way to the complex of grass huts and rice fields, the fight had completely died away. The only remaining sound of war was the squall of several Phantom jets still circling high overhead, hoping for an enemy target far enough away so that an air strike would not threaten the friendly forces.

"Where's the war?" one of their officers called to Collins as he stepped through the bush at the edge of the rice paddies.

"Scattered west, south, and southwest," the captain replied. "Several of my squads are trying to chase down the bastards and catch a final shot or two at them, but so far no luck."

While Bravo Company fanned out along the tree line and established security around the village, Collins and his Marines entered Binh Thai.

Eddie Adams took out a gray handkerchief and wiped his brow and the top of his head where thinning wet strands of black hair covered an otherwise bald scalp. He felt the distinctive soreness of a working sunburn and now looked for his hat.

Pat Collins also wiped sweat from the stubble of hair on his balding head. As he tucked on his soft cap, he saw John DelGrosso inspecting the line of trenches and punji pits just behind the thorn-branch and stick fence that surrounded Binh Thai.

Several tunnels opened at the ends of the trenches and under the huts. And between the tunnel entrances and trenches were splatters of blood and scars in the dirt where wounded Viet Cong fell and their fellows had dragged them away in retreat.

"See any bodies?" Collins asked.

"No, sir," DelGrosso said, "but I'm sure we killed one of 'em. Look here."

The two Marines examined a large, smeared puddle of blood and bowels where obviously one man had died.

"They were good," Collins said.

"Yes, sir. You have to give them good marks. They knew what they were doing," DelGrosso said as he took a quick survey of the village.

"They must have set up here and just expected that sooner or later we'd be coming through," Collins said.

"That, or someone back in the rear tipped them off about our plans," DelGrosso said.

Collins eyed his lieutenant and frowned as he considered the idea and said nothing. It was a disturbing thought and, considering the layers of Vietnamese red tape involved in this patrol, a real possibility.

"I have fire teams checking out these tunnels," DelGrosso said, pointing to a hole that opened near a hut. "They have all sorts of underground earthworks here. Maybe some wounded hiding down there."

"What about arms?" Collins asked.

"Yes, sir. Come and look."

The two officers walked to a hut where four Marines stabbed its mud walls with their bayonets.

"Look here, Skipper," DelGrosso said, pointing to several packages of ammunition, covered in plastic. "They wrap it in this, and pack it in the mud walls. We found all sorts of explosives and rounds like this. And look in here," the lieutenant said, stepping inside the hut and picking up a rifle. "We find these stuffed up in roofs and down in the floor mats."

Collins looked at the several dozen huts and looked back at DelGrosso. "Regular little ammo dump."

The captain knew they could not pick the huts apart and collect all that the Viet Cong had stored in this cache. That would take the rest of the day, and he did not want to spend the night here . . . alone.

"Think we could blow 'em in place?" Collins said, watching the Marines pull another book-size package of ammunition out of the hut wall.

"Only explosives we have are the grenades for the M-79. They'll blow right through the walls and out the other side," DelGrosso responded. "We'd do better to burn 'em."

The captain walked to the side of the hut, put his cigarette lighter under the banana-leaf and rice-straw thatched roof, and tried to set it afire. Nothing happened.

"We're gonna have to use toilet paper," DelGrosso said. "Stuff it in the rafters and set it off. I don't think that these roofs will burn by themselves."

An hour later half a dozen helicopters lifted away the last of Bravo Company. Pat Collins, John DelGrosso, Dick Gesswein, Bill Vankat, a Vietnamese Marine captain, Eddie Adams, and all the Marines of Company D, 3rd Reconnaissance Battalion, walked southeastward along the roadway that had led them into this first American firefight of the Vietnam War.

Several Marines looked over their shoulders as they walked, and watched the village of Binh Thai burn in the fire storm they set—explosions in the flames confirming why.

"Hey, Doc!" Eddie Adams called to a familiar-looking corpsman walking in line across from him.

He looked at the photographer and smiled. "You wanna take my picture?"

"Sure," Eddie said, and raised his camera and exposed one frame, catching the Navy hospital man's dirty face and wide smile. "Hey, I'm sorry for yelling at you back there, but I guess I was really excited and you didn't seem to be moving."

The corpsman wrinkled his mouth and studied his inner thoughts for a moment and then spoke: "I was really scared back there when the shooting started. I couldn't move! But then I saw you out there trying to help that guy . . . in the open . . . no weapon . . . just your cameras. I thought, if you could be out there. Like that. So could I."

"What's your name?" Eddie said. "For the picture caption."

"Arilious," the corpsman said, "Marcus Antonius Arilious." Then he smiled. "It's Irish."

Later that year, the same corpsman would earn the Silver Star medal for valor in another battle.

As they walked away from the scene of this fight—two Americans slightly wounded and one VC believed killed—black smoke billowed into the sky.

That night, Eddie Adams would write of U.S. Marines ambushed by more than one hundred Viet Cong this day, marking the first action of American ground forces in Vietnam.

George MacArthur, at the AP's Saigon bureau, would send the story and Eddie's photographs throughout the planet where headlines would herald "U.S. Marines Engage Viet Cong for the First Time."

But as the Marines left this village that once had only housed farmers, who for generations only grew rice along the edges of the Binh Thai River, and now fell to ashes beneath swirling flames and exploding ammunition—a farm community turned VC fortress—not a single man, except Eddie Adams, even considered that they had made history this day.

They did not consider the fact that they were the first American unit to fight in this war. Nor did they care.

As they looked in the sky at the smoke's black signature boiling up from Binh Thai, these grimy, sweat-soaked Marines—who again stirred the roadway's hot, orange dust in nasty clouds around their feet as they strode the long walk toward home and now smelled smoke instead of pigshit—thought only of being finished with this day. They wished only to rest.

# GOING AFTER CHARLIE

· 1 ·

NORTH OF DA NANG THE GROUND RISES SHARPLY ONCE HIGHWAY One crosses the Song Ca De, which American soldiers and Marines who hunted Viet Cong there came to call the Cade River. There at the Nam O Bridge, where the national railway and Highway One crosses to the west of a battery of oil tanks owned by Esso, the land spreads out flat on the right of the bridge and narrows sharply into the mountains on the left. Across the bridge the road winds upward past Le My, upward more through a triple-thick canopy forest and finally over the Hai Van Pass.

Beyond the Hai Van, the city of Hue has existed on the banks of the Perfume River for a thousand years and more. The ancient citadel had seen generations of wars, but now the pocks and erosion had begun to show not just on the walls of its buildings, it also had become clearly visible on the grim faces of its people. A people whose population expanded daily as refugees fled from the nearby hills to the relative safety of the city where American forces now provided protection from the invading North Vietnamese Communists and their South Vietnamese guerrilla counterparts.

Near Hue, the enclave called Phu Bai also grew daily with more U.S.

soldiers and Marines to man and defend the airfield and Army communications facility located there. General Westmoreland had envisioned Phu Bai as an auxiliary airfield that would lighten the traffic load on the increasingly congested Da Nang Air Base. With more and more aircraft inbound to South Vietnam's I Corps, Da Nang would quickly become impossible without the relief that the new airfields at Chu Lai, to the south, and at Phu Bai, to the north, could provide.

Every day, without fail, Frank Reasoner led his Marines through the Phu Bai enclave's defensive wire on excursions into the mountainous jungles that towered over the Perfume River, patrolling in search of Viet Cong. Reasoner remained in contact with Pat Collins, keeping him updated on the Bravo Company platoon's activities, and routinely, the savvy captain would travel to Phu Bai and accompany the lieutenant and his men on patrol.

Commanding this composite reconnaissance company that supported the quickly growing Marine brigade kept Pat Collins on the move, first with one platoon, then another, and occasionally with two or three platoons on a hammer-and-anvil reconnaissance in force. And as the tactical area of responsibility for the brigade expanded, Collins found himself traveling farther and farther from his home base at Da Nang.

What had begun as a composite reconnaissance company had grown to nearly battalion strength. Now as May wore toward June and Pat Collins again joined Frank Reasoner and his platoon on patrol, he knew that it would be only a matter of days before Lieutenant Colonel Don H. "Doc" Blanchard and the remaining platoons of 3rd Reconnaissance Battalion would be in country, and would finally operate in South Vietnam as a complete organization.

Pat Collins would again take Delta Company, and the men with whom he had become close in the platoons from Alpha, Bravo, and Charlie companies would go to their separate assignments, under other captains' commands. Of course he would see the men from time to time, but it wouldn't be as it had been these past few weeks when they had learned together how to live in this sweat-filled hothouse of a country. The thought of it saddened him some, but too, he looked forward to having his Marines in what he affectionately called "Dingin' Deadly Delta" back together.

He looked straight up, and high above him, above the layers of broad leaves and long limbs that stretched and spindled like vines, seeking to find a spot of sunlight, one small glimmer of blue shone through. The column of light shimmered on the forest's wet floor where a carpet of small plants bathed themselves in the rare and drifting shaft. To one side of this new carpet of green lay the quickly rotting hulk of a once great tree that Pat Collins assumed had previously filled that hole in the jungle's canopy.

It was amazing to him how the thick growth seemed to cling to everything: vines draping and reaching and tangling the forest structure as though some great weaver were twining together an enormous green blanket. Twisting into this blanket, layers upon layers of plants sank their roots into rotting debris collected into the forks of trees and sprouted emerald life even higher than their hosts. He had seen a palm tree growing from the crotch of a thick-trunked tree with a smooth bark like a beech or birch. The palm tree's roots clung to the host tree more than thirty feet above the ground, yet there was enough nourishment in that high fork to send the palm jutting up another thirty feet, spreading its top into the sky.

Several Marines had walked past the captain as he examined the forest floor, taking note of the swath of new greenery stimulated by the sweeping light. He stood gazing, fascinated by the beauty that this rain forest offered, when a soft voice near him brought him back, the way a hypnotist might awaken a subject by the snap of his fingers.

"What are you looking at, Skipper?" Frank Reasoner said as he walked to the side of Pat Collins.

"Oh, uh, nothing," the captain said and began walking again with the patrol.

They had begun their patrol from the Phu Bai enclave before dawn and had made their way along the ridges beneath the heavy jungle canopy through most of the day, scouting for Viet Cong but with little luck. They had seen signs of encampments where small groups had spent a recent night or day, three or four men at most, and the patrol had followed the dim trails, marked by cleverly laid stones or by broken bits of red or blue plastic, all left as signals to Viet Cong comrades who might follow after the inhabitants of the camps had moved on. Yet the Marines had seen no one.

As the patrol had located each encampment and trail, Pat Collins marked its location on his map and wrote a comment of it in his notebook. For each camp he drew a small red circle, and for the trails he made a cross with an arrow pointing its direction. Perhaps the clusters of circles and crosses might tell a story over time, but for now it was simply something to do as the platoon pushed farther and farther along.

"You know," Pat Collins said to the lieutenant as he shoved his map back inside his shirt where he had the top two buttons opened, "we would do better with four-man patrols. We're too visible like this."

"Too bad we can't," Reasoner said. "Maybe if we ever get some dependable radios."

When the reconnaissance Marines first began patrolling away from Hill 327 and remaining out for more than a day, they discovered that their radios' batteries might last an hour, four hours, or a day. But there was no way of establishing exactly how long. They began carrying extra batteries and backup radios. This required more men for the added weight.

Additionally, South Vietnam's jungle environment was something new to most of Pat Collins's Marines. With the unknown number of enemy units operating in the hills that surrounded them, a four-man patrol could easily get into serious trouble should they get caught. One man being wounded or killed could spell disaster for the other three.

Although Pat Collins subscribed to the effectiveness of a well-trained, fast-moving, silent and deadly four-man reconnaissance patrol, he knew that he had to compromise for the safety of his men.

Considering the doubtful reliability of their radio batteries and the little-known threat, he chose to develop strategy using a series of eight-man patrols that would work together. The patrols would work in sweeps of areas, close enough to each other's flanks so that should one team get into a fight the others at its sides could rapidly reinforce them, turning the eight-man squad into sixteen or twenty-four or even more. But with so many men in one area, the probability of being seen first by an evasive enemy was great, and was probably what was happening today.

As the patrol pushed forward in a wide fan across a hill and then began to sweep down to a rare opening where for some unknown reason no trees grew but high grass in its place, Pat Collins could see the thickness of the dark jungle clearly. Collins looked at Reasoner and motioned for him to stop.

"You could move a division through this and no one would ever see them, unless someone was on the ground, at the right place, watching," Pat Collins said.

Frank Reasoner knelt next to the captain. "With the whole Laotian and Cambodian borders like this, it's no wonder that they can move tons of weapons and troops in and out at will."

"The way to fight these guys is going to be by direct interdiction," Collins said. "You have to blanket these mountains with small units, operating under cover, and then ding the shit out of the enemy. Artillery, air, all this other, it won't work. I know damn good and well that as soon as you start setting up H-and-I fires,[1] they'll move between the artillery fans and never get hit. There's just too much country and too much cover for them. Small units patrolling will be the most effective measure."

"We haven't been that effective today," Reasoner said and raised to a crouch. He looked to his flank and caught the attention of the platoon sergeant. When Frank Reasoner pointed across the clearing and then made a sweeping half circle with his hand, the sergeant understood that he meant to skirt around the clearing and remain under cover.

Both Reasoner and Collins stood and began walking along the edge of the clearing, looking across it, and as they walked, Frank Reasoner caught something moving out of the corner of his eye, perhaps a man or perhaps a shadow. He snapped his head and froze in his steps.

"What?" Collins whispered.

"Something, maybe nothing. But I could swear something moved across the way," Reasoner said. "See the dead tree, then the outcropping of rock just below it?"

"Sure," Collins said.

"There," Reasoner said, pointing with his left index finger. "It may have been a bird or something falling. Since we're on the left flank, I know it's none of our people."

"Let's set up here and send a team around to flush him out," Collins said. "If it's nothing, they'll find nothing. But the way we're finding VC

---

[1]Harassment-and-Interdiction fire. Conducted usually by artillery or aerial bombardment. It is designed to inhibit enemy movement and suppress their efforts during periods when patrolling is not practical, such as during hours of darkness and foul weather. It is also used to cover wide areas where personnel strength limits patrolling.

signs, I'd bet if something did move over there it's some of our little brown friends."

Frank Reasoner raised his arm and motioned for the sergeant to come close when suddenly the branches cracked with a loud pop above his head and sent a shower of leaves floating down. He looked at Pat Collins and saw the expression on the captain's face that confirmed his instincts that it had been a bullet fired at him. In that split second of thought, Frank Reasoner was already dropping to his knees and reaching for the AR-15 carbine slung behind his shoulder.

"Son of a bitch!" he said as he wrapped his fingers around the short rifle's pistol grip and jammed the metal foot of the stock against his shoulder. Just as he put his cheek down to the tubular stock post, he again rose to his feet, sighted at a black clump on the edge of the stone outcropping, and fired.

Sharp splinters of rock ripped his neck and cheek, and the lone Vietnamese guerrilla recoiled backward, grabbing his face where the tiny stone flakes sent blood oozing from a hundred pepper-size holes. He lay on his back and struggled forward, reaching for his rifle when across the clearing he saw the Marine whom he had missed with his shot now taking aim at him again.

Just as Frank Reasoner fired his second shot, he shouted to several of his men who had rushed to the clearing's edge, ready to join in the shooting, "Don't anybody pop him, he's mine!"

The bullet exploded into the roots of the tree that grew behind where the Viet Cong had fallen. He rolled just as the Marine fired, but had he remained on his back, he still would have been alive. The Marine's second shot was far from its intended mark.

"Goddamn that lucky bastard!" Reasoner exclaimed as he again fired and saw his bullet strike close, but again clear of the lone enemy.

"You better let these other people fire, or he'll get away," Pat Collins said, still crouching and watching the Viet Cong guerrilla roll and dodge while at the same time try to get to his feet and grab his rifle, and not succeed in any of those endeavors.

"Anybody shoot him, and they have me to deal with," Frank Reasoner shouted to his men. He tried to remain calm and aim without emotion, but the frustration of the short rifle with its unsteady stock and odd sights set his anger to boil. He fired again and then again, and when he missed with those shots, he looked at Pat Collins, took a deep breath, fired again, and missed.

"Try rocks, Frank," Collins said. "You could pelt him to death with rocks and do better."

Behind him, both officers heard the muffled chuckles of several of the men as they watched their lieutenant rapidly losing his control.

The shooting seemed to have stopped for a breath or two, and the shaken guerrilla found his legs and leapt for his rifle. He rolled again and then stood to take aim, uphill, over the waist-high grass, at the enraged Marine who shouted words that the Vietnamese man could not understand. Yet even though he did not know the words, the tone told him that a rapid retreat would be wise. This enemy American was clearly out of his head.

"You better get him, Frank," Pat Collins said, "he's bugging out for sure. He'll be gone in a second."

Another shot clanged from the .223-caliber carbine and this time the bullet hit so close to the Viet Cong that he took a diving roll when it struck. When he dove, it had been with such energy that he sent his rifle hurtling twenty feet above his head and the Chinese SKS came crashing down in the tall grass, far from his sight and reach.

"You see that!" Pat Collins said, and just as he said it, he saw the Viet Cong guerrilla leap to his feet and run.

"Fuck it!" Frank Reasoner said as he took his rifle from his shoulder, glanced at it for a split second with absolute contempt, and then dropped it in the hands of Pat Collins who still crouched at his side.

"Wait, goddamnit!" Collins shouted, and tried to grab the lieutenant, all too late.

Frank Reasoner had seen the man bolt, and rather than let him get away, the lieutenant launched himself into the clearing, running after the fleeing enemy. Reasoner only heard an unintelligible call from his captain as he charged after the escaping guerrilla.

As the lieutenant leapt and ran, ripping his way through the grass, chasing his quarry, he yelled a war cry that echoed through the jungle and sent birds winging from the trees. The cry also halted the Vietnamese man for a second, but when he turned and saw the charging Marine, he again bolted.

Ahead of Frank Reasoner, the guerrilla's black head bobbed up and down in the tall grass as he ran against the green saw-blade sea that ripped cut after cut on his bare legs. Yet he felt nothing. The adrenaline that coursed through his body, rattling his heart the way a boxer might pummel a speed bag, also numbed him against any pain that might accompany his retreat.

Pat Collins looked at Frank Reasoner's sergeant and laughed. "Now I know he's nuts. You'd better take a couple of men and sweep around that side of the clearing. I'll take the rest of the patrol on around this side and we'll meet up down there."

Once the Viet Cong had broken from the grass and had again entered the jungle, he thought that he was safe. Perhaps that is what caused him to slow his gait. It was just enough, however, to give Frank Reasoner a new surge of confidence when he saw that he was now gaining on the man who wore black shorts, a tan shirt, and had lost one of his sandals in the grass, nearly tripping the lieutenant, and now discarded the other as he entered the jungle.

Both men dodged around trees and leapt over bushes, sometimes tumbling, sliding, falling, but always scrambling, always running. They turned and twisted and ran toward exhaustion.

By the time the guerrilla stopped to catch his breath and took a glance over his shoulder to see if the American was still chasing, Frank Reasoner was on top of him. The Vietnamese man never quite realized what hit him until he was on the ground and the American had clamped his legs into a figure-four wrestling hold and laid a hard left fist directly on his cheekbone.

Frank Reasoner had been a champion wrestler and boxer at West Point, and during his career as an enlisted Marine he had been an avid cross-country runner. For him the chase was made to order, and its ending fit well too.

"Take that, you son of a bitch!" Frank Reasoner coughed breathlessly, and hit the guerrilla again and again.

The brown man tried to fight back, but without a chance for a breath and with both his legs feeling as though they might break at any instant, he could only cry, *"Chu hoi! Chu hoi!"* and pray that the American could understand his plea for mercy.

Frank Reasoner took the man by the front of his shirt and yanked him to his feet, and then for good measure, he belted him on the jaw so hard that his lower lip blossomed into an immediate bloody swell.

"I'll teach you to shoot at me and miss, you little bastard!" Reasoner growled, and then he dragged the exhausted man by his shirt back to the edge of the clearing where they both dropped, breathless, finished and glad of it.

It had taken only minutes for the platoon to skirt down to where Frank Reasoner sat on his prisoner. Pat Collins was still laughing after two of Reasoner's Marines had tied the prisoner's hands to a short pole and began leading him back toward Phu Bai.

Frank Reasoner felt a bit self-conscious once it had all ended, but for his men, and for Pat Collins too, they saw another side of the short and stocky West Point athlete that they all liked. They saw that Frank Reasoner was more like them than the high-brow "Ring Bearers" from that gray stone academy on the Hudson River where the mustang lieutenant had earned his bars. Frank Reasoner was "Hard Corps. Truly Recon."

· 2 ·

ARE YOU ABOUT READY, SIR?" THE AIDE DE CAMP ASKED BRIGADIER General Frederick Karch as he took one last look at his quarters at Da Nang Air Base and then walked toward the opened screen door where the lieutenant and all the baggage waited.

"Let's get going," Karch said and grabbed two of the canvas satchels.

"I got a clip from the paper back home," the lieutenant said as he helped the driver lift the bags into the back of the general's jeep.

"Yes?" the general said, stopping to take a look at the newspaper article.

"My wife sent it," the lieutenant said. "It's about Captain Collins and his reconnaissance company engaging the Viet Cong at Binh Thai last month."

The general smiled as he read the story and looked at the lieutenant. "Doesn't look like as important a story as we thought it would be."

"All the civil rights protests back home are really taking priorities, I think," the lieutenant said.

"It's just as good," Karch responded as he settled into the front passenger seat, and the lieutenant climbed in the back among the baggage. "There are too many unsettled questions here just yet. We can well do without all the attention in the press."

A slim corporal with a sunburned neck and ears ground the gears as he pushed the jeep's shifter and found low. The vehicle lurched forward as he slipped the clutch and the lieutenant bounded backward, grabbing hold of the baggage.

The lone jeep droned as it wound its way through a grid of narrow roads that led between Quonset huts and concrete-block buildings, and in five minutes it had reached the flight line where a lone Marine Corps C-130 transport plane waited.

When the crowd of Marines lying in the shade of the airplane's huge wing saw the jeep approach, a gunnery sergeant shouted and the lounging men scrambled to their feet and fell in formation with their seabags at their sides, ready to file aboard when the gunny got the high-sign from the general's aide.

Like the general, they were flying back to Okinawa. Most of them would be there only a day or two before they boarded a commercial jet that they came to call "The Freedom Bird" and would fly back to the United States, bound for other assignments or release from active duty. General Karch was resuming his duties as assistant commander of the 3rd Marine Division, taking charge of the few units that still remained in Okinawa.

"Just think, sir. A few hours from now we'll be able to get in a game of tennis at Camp Courtney, golf at Kadena, or take a swim at Tiger Beach," the lieutenant said as he waved to the gunnery sergeant under the plane's wing. Then he looked at the general. "The troops will be aboard in a couple of minutes. If you want to grab a cup of coffee or a Coke, I'll get our gear aboard and make sure that all is locked and cocked with the pilots."

General Karch said nothing. He just nodded his approval to the lieutenant and then walked to the operations building where the airplane's pilots busily studied their weather briefing and amended their instrument flight plan, and where his boss, Major General William R. "Rip" Collins, waited.

With the expansion of their mission, the combat task organization that began as the 9th Marine Expeditionary Brigade rapidly grew to involve seven of the nine infantry battalions of the 3rd Marine Division, most of the 12th Marine Regiment,[2] and a large portion of the 1st Marine Aircraft Wing.

On May 5, 1965, as the bulk of the expanded ground forces offloaded from Naval Task Force 76 ships and landed ashore at Chu Lai, President Johnson approved the establishment of a Marine Force/Division/Aircraft Wing headquarters to include the commanding generals of the 3rd Marine Division and the 1st Marine Aircraft Wing. That day, the 9th MEB became history and relinquished control of the Marine Corps units in South Vietnam to the III Marine Expeditionary Force.

"We were hardly in operation long enough for the ink to dry on our letterhead before General Westmoreland asked that we change it," Major General Collins said as he shook hands with Brigadier General Karch. Collins had just taken command of the Naval Component Command, retained command of the 3rd Marine Division, and established command of the III MEF in South Vietnam.

General Karch saw the smile on his commander's face and knew that the name changing was little more than another small bump in the road. It was simply a friendly way to begin a casual conversation with a friend.

When the III MEF was authorized by President Johnson, General Westmoreland suggested to the Joint Chiefs of Staff that the Marine Corps ought to select a different name for their newly established command in South Vietnam. The general cited that the Vietnamese disliked the French and the word "Expeditionary" in the new command's name had an unpleasant connotation for them. He said that the South Vietnamese related it to the French Expeditionary Corps, and already the Communists had launched a propaganda campaign that compared the United States forces with the French, keying on the word "Expeditionary."

Agreeing with Westmoreland, the Joint Chiefs of Staff referred the renaming to General Wallace M. Greene, commandant of the Marine Corps. On May 7, 1965, the Marine Corps replaced "Expeditionary"

---

[2]12th Marines is the artillery arm of the 3rd Marine Division.

with "Amphibious" in all its combat task organizations. The III Marine Expeditionary Force became the III Marine Amphibious Force.[3]

"General Greene wanted to call it the III Marine Amphibious Corps, because we had that name in World War II, but hell, he figured that the Vietnamese probably wouldn't like Corps either so he opted to keep Force," Collins said.

"I wonder if they'll ask us to drop Corps from Marine Corps?" Karch said, joking.

Collins laughed. "Westmoreland knows better. He knows that we draw the line long before that, good local relations or not. I'll tell you, though, this name changing is nothing. The hot gossip now is about this little power struggle we've got going on here."

"I had heard some rumblings," Karch said as the two generals walked outside and stood in the shade that the eaves of the operations building cast, away from the prying ears of the Marines who manned the weather and flight planning desks.

"You now Keith B. McCutcheon?" Collins said.

"Yes, sir," Karch remarked. "Wasn't he an ace in World War II and Korea?"

"I'm not sure if he was an ace, probably so, but he is one outstanding pilot," Collins said. "He holds the Distinguished Flying Cross and the Silver Star. He pioneered the development of close air support and helicopter tactics. The perfect mind for this kind of war. Well, of course you know he's a major general selectee, and he is set to relieve Paul Fontana as commanding general of the 1st Wing."

"Major General Fontana just got here," Karch said.

"Right, but he's like me, ready to rotate because of his time on watch when we were based on Okinawa. However, he's not at all anxious to get out of here," Collins said. "I'm due out. Paul knows this, and he sees the III MAF boss job as his ticket to stay."

---

[3]The use of the word "Amphibious" within the names of Marine Corps combat task organizations would remain until 1987 when Commandant General Alfred M. Gray reverted back to the classical use of "Expeditionary" within the names of Marine task units. The Marine Corps retained the use of the Force/Division/Aircraft Wing combat task organization. Today the III MEF continues to exist, headquartered at Okinawa, as well as the more recently organized II MEF at Norfolk, Virginia, and I MEF at Camp H. M. Smith, Hawaii.

"I see the problem," Karch said. "Lew Walt,[4] as I understand it, has the III MAF slot."

"Right you are," Collins said. "Now Lew is a real hero type, as you know. General Greene knows this too. Even though Chesty Puller is chomping at the bit to come out of retirement and plow his way into this fight, we know that will never happen and Lew Walt is as close to Chesty as you can come. Hell, Walt's got two Navy Crosses and the Silver Star, and there isn't an enlisted Marine in the Corps who wouldn't cut off his right arm for the guy. That and Lew's combat record with Edson's Raiders at Guadalcanal and his command of 5th Marines in Korea, he's like Keith McCutcheon, a very logical choice."

"So where's the punchline?" Karch asked, looking toward the flight line where he could see the pilots standing by the transport's door.

Both Marines began walking toward the waiting aircraft and General Collins said, "Paul Fontana has sent a letter to the commandant and has laid it on the line. He cited that he is the senior major general here, and that Lewis W. Walt is the junior major general, once he's promoted, dead last list in the entire Marine Corps, and Paul has said that he will remain in command of the 1st Marine Aircraft Wing until, quote-unquote, forced to leave!"

"Can you really blame General Fontana?" Karch said as they stopped by the aircraft's door.

"Yes and no. I can't blame him for wanting the job and for feeling hurt that the most junior man got it," Collins said. "But that's the way the dealer shuffled the deck. Hell, in a year Lew Walt will pin on a third star, and Paul Fontana will probably get promoted to a rocking chair. They did it to Chesty Puller and they'll do it to you and me. That's life."

The two men shook hands. Then Fred Karch raised his right hand and saluted his commander.

"We'll talk, soon as Walt gets in," Collins said, returning the salute.

[4]Lewis W. Walt served as III MAF commanding general from June 4, 1965, until June 1, 1967, when he departed Vietnam as a lieutenant general. Shortly after leaving Vietnam, he attained the rank of general, the first Marine in history to rise to the four-star rank in an assignment other than that of commandant of the Marine Corps, and served as assistant commandant of the Marine Corps until he retired from active service on February 1, 1971.

"I'll buy you a Kobe steak dinner down at Naha. You did a damn fine job here, Freddy."

General Karch smiled at Collins. Then he climbed the steps that folded out of the airplane's front door and walked to the seat next to his aide who sat reading a Louis L'Amour western. General Collins leaned inside and shouted, "Have a good trip back to the rock, all you guys. There's a little bit of work for you there, not much, but enough to keep you out of jail."

• 3 •

T HE SEABAG FELT AS THOUGH SOMEONE HAD ADDED A HUNDRED pounds of rocks to it and Corporal Byrant C. Collins grunted as he heaved the bulging green canvas sack over his shoulder and followed the lance corporal sent to meet him and several other Marines who had just landed on the beach at Chu Lai, South Vietnam. There, U.S. Navy Seabees and Marine engineers busily dumped firm red earth onto the powdery white beach sand and laid aluminum runway matting on it, building the new SATS[5] airfield, scheduled to land the first plane by June. The May heat and humidity had sent a flood of sweat soaking through each of the newly arriving Marines' uniforms as they followed the lance corporal.

"Jesus God," Collins growled in his naturally gravel-throated voice, "is it always this hot?" Then he hurried his step and walked at the side of the lance corporal as they made their way to the waiting truck.

"I don't know, I hope not," the lance corporal said, glancing over to the burly new corporal. "I've only been here a couple of weeks myself."

"This damn heat's got my strength," Collins said, wiping sweat off his forehead with the back of his wrist. "I'm zapped."

"They told me that after a few weeks you'll get used to it," the lance corporal said.

[5]Short Airfield for Tactical Support. A rapidly constructed expeditionary airfield with arresting gear and catapults and runways made of heavy aluminum matting. The Chu Lai airfield used 1,400,000 square feet of matting, all that the Marine Corps had in the Pacific. It was planned and built in approximately one month's time with the first aircraft, a Douglas A-4 Skyhawk from Marine Attack Squadron (VMA)-225 and piloted by Colonel John D. Noble, commanding officer of Marine Aircraft Group (MAG)-12, landed at Chu Lai at 8:10 A.M. on June 1, 1965.

"I sure as hell hope so," Collins said in a huff of breath. "All these guys going to Recon?"

"As a matter of fact," the lance corporal said, "we're not just going to Recon, we're all going to Alpha Company."

"Must be one hell of a turnover in troops for this many replacements to be going to the same company," Collins said.

"Something's sure happening," the lance corporal said. "I think there's more leaving than coming in, though. I heard that they're gonna involuntarily extend everyone because here they are, trying to build up units and so many guys are rotating home."

Collins tilted his head up and looked at the bright blue sky with the high cirrus, mares'-tail clouds and then he looked back at the lance corporal and said, "This time of year. Ever notice that's when most people get transferred?"

The lance corporal turned his head to see Collins's heat-reddened face and said, "Now that you mention it, I guess so, but they still say that they're gonna involuntarily extend everybody at least through October."

"Well, lad," Collins said, "I'm no old salt in the Crotch, but I know that summer is transfer time for most Marines. I've got a hunch that once we hit midsummer, that wave will have reached its crest. I figure replacements will come pouring in during June and peak in July."

"I hope they get enough so that I can go home on my rotation date," the lance corporal said. "I've already got nine months on the rock in Okinawa. I'm supposed to go home around Labor Day."

"Don't count on it," Collins said. "Like I said, I'm no old salt, but I've been around the Crotch long enough to know that if anything can go wrong, it will. Never count on anything. Plan on the worst and hope for the best. If scuttlebutt says that they're extending everybody, I'd plan on staying. That way in the worst case you won't be disappointed."

"That's kinda the way I see it too," the lance corporal said, and then he thrust out his hand for the corporal to shake. "Jim Shockley."

Collins took Shockley's hand, shook it once, and then let it go. "Glad to know you, Shockley. Byrant C. Collins, but everybody calls me B.C."

"We get up to camp, I'll take you over to First Sergeant Henry. He'll get you squared away in one of the NCO tents," Shockley said. "I'll be moving in there too, soon as I put on my stripe. I'm due. A guy told me that during war, you make rank faster too."

B. C. Collins laughed. "I'm not looking for sergeant anytime soon. When you know me a little better, you'll understand. When I make it, I make it, and it won't be because I kissed any ass to get it."

Jim Shockley swung himself over the tailgate of the truck and reached down to give B. C. Collins a hand, but Collins had already climbed up.

"Save your strength, lad," he said and then flopped down on his seabag. "Sure is hot. I never saw a place so damn hot."

## • 4 •

ALTHOUGH THE WEATHER IN DA NANG ON JUNE 4, 1965, OFFERED CLEAR skies, the change of command ceremony for the III Marine Amphibious Force commanding general took place indoors: cloaked from public view, alien to the traditional Marine change of command ceremony—normally a full parade filled with pomp and pageantry.

It was an historic ceremony, nonetheless. The press was there, so were officials from both the government of South Vietnam and the United States Embassy. It was a very festive event, plenty of food and drink and happy talk, but for Major Generals Rip Collins and Lew Walt they held it with some consternation.

Political restrictions prohibited the displaying of the United States flag outdoors in South Vietnam. Because the presentation of colors and the exchange of those colors from the outgoing commanding general to the incoming commanding general was the focal point of the change of command ceremony, General Collins and Walt exchanged flags indoors.

June was a month of change of the III MAF, not just with the commanding general but throughout the force. Many of the men, including commanding officers, reached the end of their overseas tours of duty and prepared to rotate home. Among them, the commanding officer of Company A, 3rd Reconnaissance Battalion.

Reliefs, however, were slow coming. For the commanding officer of Company A, his replacement, a captain who had been sent to South Vietnam from the Philippines, was not able to take command. He had suffered a wound in the leg during action against Communist guerrillas near Manila, and he had not fully healed. Doc Blanchard had to find a new man. He had to find a captain when there were no excess captains in country or soon inbound.

As June wore on, more and more of the III MAF command headquarters moved to Hill 327, including 3rd Reconnaissance Battalion's. Doc Blanchard sat inside his makeshift office, a hard-backed tent with large screen windows and a chest-high ring of sandbags surrounding it, and chewed the end of a Filipino cigar a friend had bought for him in Olongopo. He watched a swirl of rust-colored dust rise with the heat and thought about his choices of whom he could assign to command Alpha Company.

"Colonel," Pat Collins said as he stepped inside the tent and distracted Blanchard from his thoughtful stare.

"What do you have, Pat?" Doc Blanchard asked.

"Have you decided who you're going to send down to run Alpha Company?" Pat Collins said.

"Funny you should ask," he said. "I thought my problems were solved when I got that captain from the PI, but nobody counted on him pulling up lame. Now I'm back to square one, and III MAF is fresh out of captains qualified to lead a reconnaissance company."

"You have a lieutenant up at Phu Bai who could do it," Collins said.

"Reasoner?" Blanchard said.

"Yes, sir," Collins said. "He was a sergeant, and he had reconnaissance experience before he went to West Point. Frank's a natural leader and he has balls as big as an elephant's. I've never known a more gutsy Marine."

"Grab a chair, Pat," Blanchard said, smiling at the captain. "I don't detect a bit of partiality, do I? I can think of another salty Marine mustang who has balls as big as an elephant's. It wouldn't be that Paddy Collins sees a lot of himself in Lieutenant Reasoner?"

"Sir," Collins said, "that has nothing to do with the fact that Frank Reasoner has command capability and leadership experience. More experience than many captains. You need a commanding officer for Alpha Company, and Frank is your best choice."

"If that's the case, why are you here?" Blanchard said.

"I wanted to make sure you knew you could trust your decision. That's why I offered you my opinion about Reasoner," Pat Collins said. "I knew that you were going to have to make that assignment today, and I just wanted you to feel confident so I threw in my two-bits. Reasoner's your man."

"Why do I have to make the decision right now?" Blanchard asked and leaned toward Collins, looking at his eyes.

Pat Collins felt his throat slightly tighten and then he spoke. "You don't know?"

"What?"

"There's a Freedom Bird that's about to launch down at Da Nang, and it's going to have the outgoing Alpha Company commanding officer aboard," Collins said. "I thought you knew."

Doc Blanchard stood and walked to the door of the tent and looked back at Pat Collins. "I ought to get in my jeep and go down to Da Nang and yank him. He has no right to leave without his replacement in command."

"He's got his orders, his XO has the company," Collins said. "He hung around, but he wasn't going to hang forever. He wants to go home too."

"Frank Reasoner, huh," Blanchard said, spitting tobacco that he had chewed off the end of his cigar outside the tent. "That's a big move for a lieutenant. Even if he is a hotshot Ring Bearer."

"In twenty years, that hotshot Ring Bearer will wear stars," Collins said. "You give him command and he'll do well by you."

"You want to tell him?" Blanchard said.

"No, sir," Pat Collins said. "It will mean more coming from you. You were already thinking about him anyway, I just made up your mind."

"I'll send Frank down to see you once he moves out of Bravo Company," Blanchard said. "When you get back from the Dong Den mission, I want you to run him through the Paddy Collins advanced course in command strategy. I've got my doubts about a lieutenant, any lieutenant, and we have several really good ones. No matter how much experience he had as a sergeant, it's not the same. Once you're in command, it's different."

As he spoke, Doc Blanchard caught the questioning expression on Pat Collins's face and said, "But then I'm not telling you anything that you don't already know."

Pat Collins smiled. He knew that he was right, and so did Doc Blanchard.

## • 5 •

EDDIE MAYES HAD GROWN UP IN THE MOUNTAINS OF NEW MEXICO and he was proud of the fact that his great-grandfather had stood alongside Geronimo in Arizona when the Cherokawa Apaches refused to leave their land. His great-grandfather had died at Fort Sill, Oklahoma, while his children and their children moved to a reservation in New Mexico and now called themselves Mescalero. In his heart he knew that he was Cherokawa and that is what he called himself.

He was a brave man. He had proved it by taking some special two-man missions off the flanking fingers of Hill 327 and had lain out in the bush and had grabbed passing Viet Cong and killed them with his knife. He and another Native American had done this together several times. It had impressed all the men in the platoon, and in Eddie's mind it had gained him great respect.

Now, as the night crowded out the last gray whisper of confident daylight and the blind black jungle lay over him like a heavy blanket, fear stung his heart. This fear made him feel ashamed so he hid it, but what it did to his senses, he could not hide.

When he had made his first night patrol with Captain Pat Collins, Eddie had seen a bear. He had called it a bear because it was dark with a humped-back shape, shaggy-looking, and it smelled. It was the smell that first made him see it on a night with no moon. For him a haunted night.

Captain Collins had told him there were no bears in Vietnam, and Eddie accepted it, but he still insisted that it was something. Something that could hurt a man if it ever got hold of him.

As a staff sergeant, Eddie had responsibilities to his platoon and to his lieutenant, but the night work had become more and more difficult with each mission.

When Eddie said that he saw the bear, Captain Collins had laughed. But for Eddie, it had been a bear, it was black and shaggy, like the bear.

"Listen, Chief," Pat Collins had said that night. "You're gonna have to get a grip on yourself. You're hearing ghosts and seeing bears, it's starting to work on the men. You may have seen a pig or a water buffalo, or it might have been one of these damned apes, but you can't go to general quarters when you hear a spider fart."

One trouble with Eddie Mayes, though, he could hear a spider fart, when he was scared. When he was scared he could see and hear and smell and taste and feel everything.

Eddie never understood why darkness haunted him so, but it did. He needed to see, and when he could not see, he felt vulnerable. It was one thing walking in the mountains where he had grown to manhood. There were bears there, especially in Sixteen Springs Canyon. He had even spent nights there. But here, he felt bad omens. Evilness in the bush.

He heard movement. He felt the presence of something. He smelled it and tasted it, and when it had consumed him, it became whatever might be reasonable to startle any man, even the bravest.

The black communications wire that Eddie had looped over his wrist began to feel sharp and he worked his finger under it to loosen its grip. He lay in the blackness, concentrating on the feel of the wire, waiting for the Marine several yards to the left of him to pull the wire once and signal that the enemy had entered the ambush's killing zone.

Captain Collins lay thirty feet to Eddie's right and as he felt the signal from his left, he would pass it to his right. When he felt two tugs from the left and one from the right, that meant all of the enemy patrol was within the killing zone and to open fire. Pat Collins had devised this system to ensure that the enemy would not have part of its force outside the killing zone where it could turn on his flanks and counter the ambush.

The wisdom of such a tactic had impressed Eddie. Such a tactic could only come from a great warrior, and for Eddie, Captain Pat Collins was one of the greatest warriors he had ever known. Because Collins was this great warrior, Eddie felt doubly ashamed that he could only wish for daylight to hurry.

Eddie lay still and felt the lines of sweat roll down his cheeks, and as they dropped onto the leaf-matted floor of the forest, he could hear each drip's signature as it splashed against the ground. His heart beat hard in his chest and he felt it flex his eardrums as blood rushed through, and this made him more uncomfortable. How can I hear the enemy if my body is making so much noise? he asked himself.

The air smelled damp and rotten with decay and mildew, yet something else was there. A smell of fish or sour milk. Eddie stretched his eyes wide to see, but without a moon, there were only the shadows of the trees against the patches of sky.

When a twig snapped in the distance, Eddie's heart almost stopped. He felt a tug on the wire on his right wrist and he passed it to his left. Something was coming.

Pat Collins lay quietly and waited to see the first of the enemy patrol when the small shape of a pig came clearer and clearer in the deep blackness. When he saw that it was only a pig, he did nothing. A false alarm.

The pig kept rooting and moving, and as it came closer to Eddie Mayes, it began grunting and pushing against a rotted limb. Where's the tug? Eddie asked himself. Why don't they open fire? They're here.

Eddie pulled hard on both wires and put his rifle into his shoulder. The noise now seemed deafening and Eddie could not understand why they had not opened fire, unless this thing had come from another direction. But the skipper pulled the wire, Eddie told himself. Maybe he only heard it and still waited for the thing, the enemy, whatever it might be to cross his path.

As Eddie strained his eyes behind the sights of his M-14 rifle, he saw movement. He saw a shape near the ground, but it was big, round, and black. It smelled. He could smell its strong, pungent odor.

Somebody fire! Eddie screamed in his mind. And just as he hooked his finger around his rifle's trigger, about to open fire, a hand clamped his right shoulder and a soft voice whispered in his ear. "Staff Sergeant Mayes, don't."

"A gorilla," Eddie said as he jerked his head to his shoulder to see Pat Collins's face near his. "I saw it, there. A gorilla. It's a gorilla!"

"A pig," Pat Collins said, holding tightly to the shaking Marine. "It's a pig. Just a pig."

• 6 •

WHEN LIEUTENANT THOMAS JONES SAW STAFF SERGEANT EDDIE Mayes load his seabag into the back of the waiting jeep and then shake hands with a dozen Marines from his platoon, Jones could only think, Why him? Why not me?

As Pat Collins shook the staff sergeant's hand and reassured him that he would be more productive in the division operations section, he glanced toward the tent where Lieutenant Jones stood and saw the young officer looking. Jones quickly looked away, feeling guilty and knowing in his heart that the captain had read his face well. Jones ducked inside the tent to hide from Pat Collins's knowing eyes.

For the last week, Collins and Eddie Mayes's platoon had been in the field. They had climbed the big mountain that overlooked Elephant Valley, a peak called Dong Den, and they had cleared its top and emplaced on it a radio relay site and built an observation post.

Pat Collins had liked the idea of the relay site. Now he and his men could patrol deep beyond the artillery fan, well into the mountains that touched the Laotian border, and still maintain radio contact. But the idea of an observation post on Dong Den seemed to him hardly worth manning.

When he had seen the view from the mountaintop, he agreed that it was magnificent. A world of high peaks footed by fluffy clouds and thick haze. As far as anyone seeing anything below the clouds that covered the lower slopes of the mountain like a cotton blanket, unless they had infrared vision that could penetrate the fog, observation of the valley would be impossible on most days. Yet as the dominant high ground, Dong Den offered the Marines an excellent radio relay signal to the northwest.

Pat Collins had joked with Eddie Mayes when they had finished blowing off the mountaintop and clearing an area to build a camp, "This is great for watching angels." Then he said more seriously, "One good thing, though, when we want to cool off, this is the place to come. It's got to be 104 degrees down below and barely 70 up here."

That had been a good day, but Pat Collins had already decided that even though Eddie Mayes was uncommonly brave and was an excellent warrior and leader who was smart and knew tactics, Eddie would not last with his anxiety of darkness. With more and more emphasis on night work, Pat Collins knew that Eddie Mayes would eventually crumble under the stress.

When they had returned from the mission, Pat Collins bought Eddie Mayes a beer and talked to him with great care. In spite of it, Eddie had taken Collins's decision to send him to the rear tough. Yet Eddie's frustration with the news reaffirmed for the captain that his opinion of Eddie was right. He still was a good Marine.

That was Eddie Mayes, and Pat Collins respected him. Thomas Jones, however, evoked a growing feeling of anger within the captain. Respect had long ago dwindled to a just-passing professional courtesy.

Thomas Jones was supposed to go on the Dong Den mission, but again the lieutenant had unexpectedly drawn watch to stand. Before that, he had been on limited duty because he had sprained his knee. Before that he had managed to get selected to an intelligence detail that kept him at division headquarters. Then he was sick again.

The lieutenant had made few patrols, and seemed to be more and more in demand for administrative details or at sick bay. When Pat Collins saw him duck inside his tent, he knew it was to hide from him.

"Listen, Ed," Pat Collins said. "You stay in touch. I need guys like you at operations to make sure we don't get hung out to dry."

"Sir, thanks," Eddie said, "I know. I'll keep you guys on the front burner. Don't worry. I'm your man."

"Better get along," Collins said and slapped Eddie Mayes across his shoulder. Then the captain walked toward the tent where Lieutenant Thomas Jones sulked inside.

The hot smell of the canvas baking in the afternoon had always made Jones's stomach turn so he usually kept busy away from the tent during the day. However, that seemed small as he watched Pat Collins come his way and he knew that the captain had a mission. Thomas had heard from John DelGrosso that a rugged and thickly jungle-covered mountain due west called Ban Nha was Collins's next target for a long and exciting patrol to establish another radio relay site.

As soon as General Walt had taken command of the Marines in South Vietnam, 3rd Reconnaissance Battalion divided four ways. Bravo Company became the reconnaissance arm of the 4th Marine Regiment, Alpha Company joined with 9th Marines, Charlie Company became reconnaissance for 3rd Marines, and Pat Collins's Company D became the Division Reconnaissance Company.

As the Division Reconnaissance Company, some believed that Pat Collins had drawn the short straw. In World War II, General Walt had commanded Charlie Company, 1st Raider Battalion. He had led them on Guadalcanal at the Battle of Bloody Ridge. Ironically, three of his platoon commanders in the Raider days were three of his regimental commanders now: Colonel Edwin B. Wheeler had 3rd Marines, Colonel Edward P. Dupras had 4th Marines, and Colonel Oscar F. Peatross commanded 7th Marines. Colonel Peatross had also commanded a battalion under Walt when the general had the 5th Marine Regiment in the Korean War.

General Walt and the three colonels had reputations for having a so-called Raider mentality, and Delta became the predominant company that carried out their exotic experiments. Collins and his Marines tested many of the theories and with them ran the risks.

Even though June had been mostly a building month for the Marine Corps organizations ashore, Delta Company had been busy. General Walt wanted them to go deep, like British Special Air Service troops, and stay under the canopy for a week, a month, or even two. But to do this the patrolling units needed the ability to talk to division.

Pat Collins had successfully established the relay on Dong Den and now to complete the program he needed another relay to the west. Ban Nha stood as the highest peak and became the next logical choice.

An abandoned French fortress stood atop the mountain, and Collins had heard that there was a road leading to it hidden somewhere in Ban Nha's thick jungle. Since the mountain was too high for the CH-34 helicopters to reach and since its slopes were too steep to allow for any type of landing zone, Pat Collins's only choice to reaching the fort was a very long and rugged walk, unless a reconnaissance patrol could find the road.

Thomas Jones sat at the end of his cot and waited. He heard the crush of gravel stop near the tent flap, and when he heard the rustle of the canvas as Pat Collins began rolling up the wall, he walked outside and took hold of the roll of canvas.

"Let me get that, sir," Jones said in a voice clogged by nervousness.

"Thanks," Pat Collins said and handed over the task. "It's goddamned hot. Why's the flap down, you worried somebody might see you on your ass?"

"No, sir," Jones said. "I just wanted a little privacy while I worked out a few things. I've got problems and I know it."

"You're right there, coach," Collins said. "If I didn't know better, I'd swear you were malingering. You haven't made patrol in a couple of weeks."

"I've always had a legitimate reason, sir," Jones said in a stronger voice. "I've pulled guard officer, then there was my knee, and then I landed duty. I've been sick."

Collins glared at him. "Yeah, and it's getting old. You've got the duty here, or over there, or you've volunteered to write some memo. Bottom line, sports fan, you've played it pretty thin and now you've got to pull your share. Hell, I've got Vankat, DelGrosso, and Gesswein reeling up your slack and it isn't fair to them."

"But I don't have anything to do with duty rosters or any of that," Jones said, now pleading his innocence.

"Then you'd better have a talk with the adjutant or staff secretary or whomever, and when your name pops up on another to-the-rear-march detail, you let them know that you've already paid dues there," Pat Collins said. "They give you any problems about it, tell me, I'll take care of it."

The lieutenant looked blankly at Pat Collins and swallowed hard. He knew it was now or never, and if he didn't do something, he would surely dig his own grave.

"Sir," the lieutenant said and almost mumbled but caught himself. "I can't go. That's the problem I've been trying to work out. I can't go on that mission up Ban Nha."

Pat Collins had stood almost ready to leave, but the lieutenant's statement caught him wrong-footed and he had to sit. Collins studied Jones for a moment and then said, "You're serious. You're telling me that you'll refuse orders to go on patrol?"

"No, sir. I won't refuse orders," Jones said. "I'm respectfully requesting a transfer to a less adventurous unit. I'll go to motor transport, supply, anything that will get me out of here. I can't take it. The stress. Some men can do it, but do you know how much courage I have to muster each time we cross the wire? A lot. One hell of a lot. And I can't take it anymore."

"I don't believe this," Collins said. "A goddamned Marine officer. Don't you know that every man in this company gets scared. That's human. But I'll tell you what, coach, there's a big difference between you and these Marines. They get scared, but they get brave too. Brave as shit. They go and they don't turn tits up and run like a goddamn coward. Listen to this, lad, and hear me clear. Your life isn't worth one speck more than any other man's here. You'll go on patrol and be brave, or I'll pack you out with a goddamned yellow stripe painted down the backside of your utilities. Got that?"

"Yes, sir," Jones said. He sat on the end of his cot and fixed his eyes between the toes of his boots. His shame cut deeply. He couldn't raise his face at all.

"I'm getting out of here," Pat Collins said and walked to the door. He looked back at the sulking man and said, "We're briefing for the operation tomorrow morning and then we'll launch out at dark. You've got between now and then to get your act together."

Pat Collins kicked dirt as he walked away from the tent, feeling a need to vent the anger that boiled inside him. He knew that he could not keep the lieutenant; a man that shaky would get men killed. I'll can him when we get back, Pat told himself. He's got to go on patrol first. Then he can leave. On my terms.

## • 7 •

HEY, TOM, YOU READY?" JOHN DELGROSSO CALLED TO THOMAS Jones, who had walked to the back of the tent, loaded with his pack, rifle, and map case. Jones stood next to a stack of sandbags and watched the late afternoon sun grow large and orange against the horizon. He did not answer.

"Listen, pal," John DelGrosso said as he walked to where Thomas Jones stood, and he clapped his hand over Jones's shoulder. "We've got to shove off. The skipper's ready to haul ass down to the LZ. We want to get to our departure point before total darkness. Come on, put it in gear."

Thomas Jones wheeled toward the lieutenant, startling John Del-Grosso so that he bounded backward to avoid a surprise swing that never came.

"I'm not going. I've got to get home alive and if I go out there tonight, I'm not coming back. I know it. I just know it," Thomas Jones said in hard, choppy breaths.

"Shit, Tom," John said. "You were at the briefing. We're only going to climb a mountain and set up a radio relay. We're not going out to assault anybody. We'll just spend a leisurely week or so swatting bugs and busting our humps struggling up that mountain. I'm more concerned about the heat and the jungle and the steep slopes. No VC in his right mind will chase us up there."

"You know that Captain Collins draws trouble every time we go out," Jones said. "The man is bent on self-destruction. We make contact every time. Every time. And it's always a wild, running gun battle. That's his style. That man is crazy and I'm going to die if I go with him again. I know it. I just know it."

"You fade out now, they'll shoot you for cowardice," John said. "Tell the skipper that you're no good to him and he'll move you out. He won't keep anyone who isn't solid. You saw how fast he got rid of Eddie Mayes. And he liked him."

"I asked him to transfer me," Jones said. "I told him yesterday. I said I couldn't face another patrol. He bit my ass and told me I was going."

"You gotta pull your weight until they replace you," John said.

"I can't," Jones said and looked back toward the setting sun.

"We gotta go," John DelGrosso said and looked down the hill toward the company assembly area where Pat Collins had already begun his prepatrol inspection. "We gotta get down there with our men or he'll come up here after us, and you know how he can get."

"I'm cashing it in," Jones said. "You tell him. I'll stand trial, but I can't go."

"I don't think you know how serious a step you're taking," John said. "Nothing's going to happen except a lot of hard climbing and we blow down a bunch of trees and set up radios. Take a walk. Once we get going, it'll get easier. It always does."

Thomas Jones looked at John DelGrosso and thought. Then he took a step and John took his shoulder and pulled him another step, and the two lieutenants walked down to where Delta Company had already assembled in formation and First Sergeant Harry Rogers was talking to Captain Collins.

"Let me take a look at your gear," Pat Collins called to the two lieutenants as they came close.

Pat Collins walked around the two men and ran through a mental checklist as he inspected them. "Where you guys been? Gunny Holt and Dutch Miller had to inspect your Marines." Then he looked at Jones. "You men get over to your platoons and haul up the slack. We've got to move."

John DelGrosso took advantage of the opportunity to clear away from the captain and avoid a further scolding for being late, but Thomas Jones stood and looked directly at Collins. When John saw the lieutenant frozen in place, he hesitated but realized he had accomplished a great deal just getting Lieutenant Jones to this point. It was up to the captain now, and what would happen was completely up to Jones.

"There's not a man here who hasn't been scared shitless," Collins began and worked hard to suppress his temper. He knew that it would be short if Jones put up any argument, but he nonetheless tried to help the man overcome the anxiety that self-preservation produces in men in combat.

"Sir," Jones began and then hesitated for a second but then spoke. "I've had dreams. Like premonitions. I die."

"You're no gypsy," Collins aid gruffly. "Forget the dreams. You have a job. You have men who depend on you. I don't want to hear this crap anymore. Now join your platoon, Lieutenant."

"Sir, please," Jones said and his voice began to quiver as he held back sobs that shoved up his windpipe and twisted in his throat. His chest began to heave. "Sir, I'm, I'm not worth a damn to you or to those men." He swept his arm toward the platoon and then dropped it as his side. "Yes, they depend on me. I owe it to them not to go."

"You might have something there, coach, but you're not going to be worth shit to anybody unless you find the balls you were born with and saddle up," Collins said, fighting to hold control of his temper. He didn't like the confrontation, not in front of the company. "I don't want you to embarrass either of us by continuing this little production. Go with your men, Lieutenant. Now!"

Jones began to shake and his legs began to bow. "Please, sir," he sobbed and dropped to his knees.

"Get up!" Collins said through clenched teeth, straining to keep his voice down. "The goddamned men are watching!"

"If I have to get on my knees and beg, I will," Jones cried, and now tears streamed down his face. Then he reached his arms forward and grasped hold of Pat Collins's legs. "I can't take another patrol. If I don't get killed, I'll lose my mind."

Thomas Jones now sobbed violently and fell to his belly and held hard to Pat Collins's legs, leaving the captain teetering off balance and speechless.

Harry Rogers and John DelGrosso hurried to where Pat Collins stood and knelt to take away the distraught lieutenant.

"Get the bastard out of here!" Collins growled. "Send him down to medical and get him looked at. Tell them he cracked up going out, but make sure they know I don't want him back. We'll hold up for you down at the LZ, so hurry."

• 8 •

H OT WIND BLEW INSIDE THE UH-34 HELICOPTER'S OPEN DOOR AND rumbled in Pat Collins's ears. The frustration he felt from losing the battle of nerves with Thomas Jones kept the heat of anger burning within him for a long time after Harry Rogers and John DelGrosso had returned. Now he kept to himself to let it pass.

It had been dark when the helicopters lifted off and now as they flew low over the jungle toward a black and purple western sky and the jagged mountains of the Annamite Cordillera, Pat Collins wished that they had been able to start early enough to at least have a glimmer of twilight on this moonless June night by which the helicopter pilots could better see to land.

The helicopters flew without position lights, the pilots hoping that Charlie would not see the lumbering aircraft, even though the settled night air would carry the engine noises miles farther than in the daytime and would signal patrolling enemy units to draw near the sounds of the beating blades as the choppers settled to land.

Pat Collins had already briefed his staff and officers to move the platoons out quickly once they had landed. However, he had made those plans based on landing with just a smattering of light and still-rustling daytime atmospheric conditions. With the sun now well down and the surface winds dead calm, the captain knew that the sound would carry farther. It was now more important than ever for the company to hastily move away from the landing zone and regroup at a clandestine assembly area that he had selected during his planning and had located on a map for his men during their briefing.

As the night rushed under his feet, Pat Collins tried to rid his mind of thoughts about Lieutenant Jones and how his emotional breakdown had set the mission off late. He hoped that the dark landing would be the only problem that his company encountered tonight.

At first the sound of the helicopters did not draw their attention. Helicopters flying over the countryside had become more and more common with each day that the Americans had begun operating in South Vietnam. But when the hard thumping of the blades seemed to remain fixed, then grow louder and then drop to a steady hum, the guerrillas took up their rifles. They had hardly begun moving toward the direction of the engine sounds when again they heard the beating of rotor blades and knew that the first chopper had gone.

The Communist soldiers hurried their steps as the third and fourth helicopters landed, and then slowed their progress as the fifth and sixth followed. With this many helicopters, they knew that the force was much larger than they could handle on their own. If they had a chance to snipe any of the patrolling soldiers they would, but for now, instead of ambush, they would attempt to locate the landing zone, track the men who had gotten off, and report their numbers.

D OC THOMAS PULLED HIS MEDICAL BAG AROUND FROM BEHIND HIS back and checked to be sure that nothing had broken when he had rolled off the helicopter. The ground had seemed closer, but as he stepped off, he too quickly discovered that what he thought was earth turned out to be the tops of the rice plants growing in the field that was their landing zone. He hit hard but rolled, saving himself a possible sprain or fracture. He wasn't so sure about his medical kit since he felt it crunch under his weight as he rolled over it.

"Come on, Doc," Gunnery Sergeant Bob Holt told the Navy hospital corpsman who had his hand inside the green, rubberized canvas bag, feeling for broken articles. "You can play in your purse later. Victor Charlie's probably burning his heels to get over to greet us. We gotta get scarce, fast."

"Coming right now, Gunny," Thomas said. "Just making sure that everything is still in one piece."

"It don't mean a thing, Doc. If something's gone, it's gone," the Hawaiian gunnery sergeant told the corpsman. "We're not going back to restock, so there's no use worrying over what you may have lost or broken now."

"I think it's all intact," Thomas said as he jogged through the field in trace of Holt. "I didn't find anything broken. I hit pretty hard, but everything seems to have survived it."

"The trick now is to make sure you don't need to use is," Holt said and looked over his shoulder at Thomas. "We have some yardage to make up. I think that we're tail-end Charlie, so watch your six o'clock. These little monkeys like to pot shoot your backside."

With that warning, Doc Thomas remembered the patrols through the coastal villages on the southern outskirts of Da Nang and how the snipers seemed to wait until the last man had cleared town when they opened fire. He had patched several Marines in those instances, and the thought of being the last man out of the landing zone sent a chill up his back. He closed his gap with Holt and stepped quickly, but now he had the uncomfortable feeling that he truly was not the last man in this line of march.

A HAND REACHED OUT IN THE DARKNESS AND GENTLY TOOK HOLD OF the tiger-striped camouflage uniform that the South Vietnamese Marine wore. The Marine did not show the alarm that sent his heart pounding, and he coolly turned to face whatever it was that took hold of his clothes. Hguyen Duc was a fatalist. He believed that if it was his time, it was his time. He had grown to accept fate as he accepted life, and he always made the best of the moment.

Duc was assigned as one of the Vietnamese Marine Corps liaison officers with 3rd Reconnaissance Battalion, and for the past two months he had made each of the company-sized patrols that Pat Collins had led, including the American forces' first firefight at Binh Thai.

"Duc," a voice in the darkness whispered, and the South Vietnamese Marine captain relaxed at its sound.

"Captain," Duc said, "you scare holy cow from me."

"You walked right over the top of me, pal. I think you're losing your touch," Pat Collins said. "Any sign of Vankat's or DelGrosso's bunch?"

"Yes, sir," Duc said. "They move this way hubba hubba. Be here no time. Me and Kit Carson scouts make big circle after landing, I see Gunny Holt and Doc Thomas coming last. They get here, we all accounted for."

"That knoll is our assembly point. We'll take a head count and a breather up there, once we get regrouped," Collins said. "You and the Kit Carson scouts can go ahead and establish our position. The sooner we get out of this farm country and move up under the canopy, the happier I'll be."

"Also me, sir," Duc said. "I think VC coming. This country stay beaucoup VC. Wait here, we make contact I think."

"I think so too," Pat Collins said and looked at his watch. "I don't plan to wait around, though. I want to be on the slopes before morning."

The knoll was the nearest high ground to the rice fields, and stood at the base of several higher hills that led to the steep slopes of the mountain called Ban Nha. Just beyond the knoll, where several higher hills stood, the thick jungle spread down Ban Nha's slopes and into the flatlands where generations ago farmers had cleared away the trees and brush, leaving only hedgerows, and there they built dikes and planted rice. Feeding the canals that bordered the fields, small, hand-dug streams branched from the river that flowed from the deep canyons between the mountains and emptied into the sea several miles south of Da Nang, where another abandoned French outpost stood near an iron railway bridge.

Pat Collins looked at his watch. At 11:00 P.M. he pushed himself up and signaled to John DelGrosso and Bill Vankat to start the patrols moving into the hills and on toward the mountaintop. They had waited for an hour in a security circle atop the knoll, hoping to see any enemy patrols that might have pursued them. They saw no one.

When the helicopters had landed in the rice fields and dropped Company D, they had made a circle and landed again in another set of rice fields three kilometers east. Then they circled again and hovered over a wide field of salt grass six kilometers south.

The Viet Cong had tracked east, believing that the Marines had begun a patrol through a series of villages that lay nearby and discounted the first and third landings as decoys since they were not near anything of importance. They searched until dawn but found nothing.

John DelGrosso reached for another low-hanging branch with which he could steady himself as he struggled another step upward. Wet moss and algae mixed into a green slime that covered every rock, tree, and root that clung to Ban Nha's sharply tilted mountainside. The huge trees' heavy roots crisscrossed into a gnarled, grease-slick lacework that hid the ground and kept the Marines' feet slipping and so unsecured that their principal means of climbing the mountain was by hand over hand, grasping for low branches and stalks. Their feet were nearly useless.

The men had climbed since the night before and now as the sun lay low and again turned the jungle dark, the exhausted Marines looked for the mountaintop where they could finally make camp and rest.

John DelGrosso looked over his shoulder and then looked up, and for the past three hours it had seemed that the mountain's top was just ahead. But he knew better. He had climbed other steep mountains and realized that as the slope tilted ever toward the peak, all a climber could see above him was the outer edge of the slope. He knew the top would come almost as a surprise. A very sweet surprise.

## • 9 •

THEY HAD BEEN ON BAN NHA NEARLY TEN DAYS AND HAD COMPLETED clearing away the overgrowth from the abandoned French fort that at an earlier time had stood as a sentinel overlooking the colonial farmland that French plantation owners had then controlled. Now the peasants who once kowtowed to the French kowtowed to the Viet Cong in this region flanked by mountains on one side and sea on the other.

As John DelGrosso stood behind a wall of freshly stacked sandbags at the ledge that overlooked the steep side of Ban Nha and pulled the flap shut on his haversack and looped it over one shoulder, he stared down a thousand feet and dreaded the climb on which this patrol would take him and his men for a day and a night.

He thought of the journey and stretched his muscles in his shoulders and upper back in slow punching motions like a boxer might. His arms still ached from the last journey down and back to the top, two days earlier, and the thought of traversing halfway down and a quarter of the way around and then back up the slope made the idea of patrols near Da Nang seem inviting.

"You have the helium bottle?" John asked as he turned and saw Staff Sergeant Dutch Miller leading eight Marines, all loaded with packs and rifles.

"Yes, sir," Miller said. "Got a dozen red balloons and two rolls of fishing line too."

"Let's run through the inspection and then get going," the lieutenant said. "Maybe we'll get lucky and find that road. It's bad enough patrolling on this terrain, but playing packhorse, that's the pits."

"I don't think there is any damned road left, sir. We've been searching for days and I can't see how we could miss running across something
as big as a road," Miller said as he began pulling straps and checking
packs and rifles on his men.

"I think the skipper is beginning to doubt it too," John DelGrosso
said as his eyes followed the staff sergeant's check of each man. "Maybe
it just grew back over. The French quit using this fort more than ten years
ago. Up here, lots of vegetation can grow pretty thick in that much time."

"Everybody have a radio battery?" Miller asked. When the men answered yes, he looked at the lieutenant. "Ready and loaded. Any questions, sir?"

"Dutch, you take the point and I'll stick close to the radio," John Del-
Grosso said. "We'll make the sweep and see if we can find a sign of that
road. After fourteen-hundred, we'll move to the resupply point and send
up the first balloon, then we'll go to the two alternate points and finish
the triangle. Hopefully the planes will be on time and on target with their
drops, and Charles will be too far below to find us."

It was after ten o'clock that morning before the patrol managed to let
themselves down through the jungle to a slight ridge that allowed them
better footing to make a four-hour sweep along the face of the mountain
in search of a road that to them at this point was only a faint red line on
an old French map.

Pat Collins had wanted to find the road on the reconnaissance flights,
but the jungle canopy had completely obscured all that existed on the
mountain, including the French fort. Captain Collins knew that once he
had located the road, truck convoys could bring up the loads of supplies
and equipment to establish the radio relay rather than doing it piecemeal
on the shoulders of his men as they picked up the regular resupply drops.

Late each night and before dawn each morning, a Company D radio
operator transmitted messages to Da Nang. Sometimes the information
was pointless double-talk designed to confuse the enemy who most surely
was listening to the signals. Other times the messages coded times and coordinates for aerial resupply.

Pat Collins had kept reconnaissance teams working around the
mountain both day and night. When he had scheduled a resupply drop,
one of the squads would move down the mountain, patrol an arch around

its face, and set out a triangle of helium balloons that the team would let up through the thick canopy and fasten in place with fishing line.

When they reached the primary resupply point, John DelGrosso's patrol was already an hour behind their schedule. The mountain's rough face had seemed to work against them as they pushed through the thick undergrowth. Between the point where they let up the second balloon and the third, the patrol found a place where a rocky ledge cropped out flat from the face of the mountain and offered a clear field of view of the vast countryside below.

From that spot the Marines could see the village that dotted the riverside with huts and behind them opened a patchwork of rice fields that spread north and south. With his binoculars, John DelGrosso followed the river eastward, twisting and turning and branching into farmlands, feeding the rice crops. At its end, the earth turned white and changed to a land that looked almost desert with white dunes and pastel-colored salt marshes edged with sprigs of gnarled brush topped with green and mixed with thin stands of tall grass and reeds.

Beyond the white sand, the pale blue sea turned ink dark near the horizon, and there tall cumulus clouds grew and boiled in the late afternoon sun. At this height, the world seemed to rest peacefully as the shadow of Ban Nha and the other peaks of the Annamite stretched eastward.

After they had set the third balloon, John DelGrosso and his men returned to the ledge and observed the countryside while they waited for the first plane. By the time they had returned, the sun lay only a few degrees above the horizon and the shadow of Ban Nha covered the lower hills and much of the rice land where the helicopters had let them out.

When he scanned the countryside with his binoculars, John DelGrosso noticed a dozen or more farmers working in one rice field. Two days earlier he had watched the same fields from a vantage point more north than this but nearly as clear. That day only three people worked in the field: a man and two women. Today they were all men.

"Something's strange," John DelGrosso said to Dutch Miller. "Look at these guys in that rice field." And he handed the binoculars to Miller.

"Bet they're VC, Lieutenant," Miller said. "They don't seem to be accomplishing too much. They're pretty much in the same spot. They bend over, stick their hands down in among the rice plants, and then raise up again. That many men working in a field like that, they ought to get something accomplished pretty fast. They just don't seem to be moving."

After watching for a while, Staff Sergeant Miller handed back the binoculars to the lieutenant. John DelGrosso continued watching the men far below.

"That is the very spot where we landed," John DelGrosso said. "I'll bet that they chased one of the decoy landings and have now figured out where we got off."

"Yes, sir," Miller said. "Want to get a real chill?"

"Not really, but what?" John DelGrosso said.

"With us having three bright red balloons flying above these pretty green treetops, how long will it take them to notice them and want to take a look?" Miller said.

John DelGrosso frowned as he looked through the binoculars. "If they haven't noticed already, they sure as hell will when the planes start flying their patterns."

"You're right there, sir," Miller said. "It won't take them as long to get here as it will take for us to get up topside either. If we're gonna get back in one piece, we're gonna have to run like hell or ambush the bastards."

"Any ambush sites come to mind?" John DelGrosso asked.

"Nothing very good," Miller said. "We could watch how they deploy once they see the planes. Dollar to a donut that they come up on line. We spread along a line space fairly wide, and we can catch 'em face-on when they come to see where the gear dropped in."

"They have us outnumbered nearly two to one," John DelGrosso said.

"Skipper says three to one is even odds against Charlie," Miller said. "Guess we've got the advantage."

"What if we went down and nailed them?" DelGrosso asked.

"Go the distance down there, come back up here, then haul that trash back up topside?" Miller said. "Jesus!"

"We'd never make it down there before they'd be coming our way," John DelGrosso said, canceling his own idea much to the relief of Dutch Miller.

"Lieutenant, we can clear a good killing zone and use the supplies as bait," Miller said.

John DelGrosso smiled and said, "We'll make a fight of it. Then again, they may not come this way at all."

Three planes came in one flight, and then three more. They broke off high and came in low over the rice fields first, and then swept up and flew along the contour of the mountain. The planes flew to the next mountain and flew patterns, as though they were searching for enemy patrols or targets of opportunity. Then as they crisscrossed and again swept low over the trees where the balloons drifted just above the upper boughs, the planes dropped their supplies.

At first, when the planes came, the Viet Cong patrol ducked for cover. They dropped in the field of knee-high rice and grabbed their rifles and ran toward a hedgerow that bordered a narrow canal that had flooded the fields a month earlier but was now blocked off to allow the paddies to dry and the rice to turn and ripen. Once under cover they watched the planes dive and turn, and they knew that it was a ruse. They had no guerrilla patrols on the mountain. Then they saw the three tiny red specks contrasted by the jungle's several shades of green.

When John DelGrosso saw the Viet Cong run for the hedgerow and then move in column to the foot of the mountain, he knew he had guessed correctly. He knew that in a matter of hours they would meet these men face-to-face.

Pat Collins lay sleeping in the evening coolness that Ban Nha's high altitude gave. He slept well in the thin, crisp atmosphere. He had been on patrol with Dick Gesswein and had waited until the late afternoon before he took time to rest. After nearly two days with little to no sleep, the cool air and soft mat of leaves and boughs gave him a sense of comfort and he rested well.

The captain had been asleep only three hours when the first radio message came through from Lieutenant DelGrosso. Harry Rogers and Bill Vankat listened to the brief report, which sounded like routine traffic except that inserted within the double-talk a signal came that made the radio operator sit up and suddenly take out his notebook and pencil. It gave grid coordinates and told the Marines who listened to the transmission that Lieutenant DelGrosso's platoon was waiting in ambush for a pursuing enemy.

"Think we'd better wake the captain?" Rogers said, looking at the lieutenant.

"Let him sleep awhile," the lieutenant said. "He can't do any good for DelGrosso right now, so why disturb him?"

The first sergeant shrugged in agreement and leaned back and waited to hear the scheduled radio traffic from 3rd Division headquarters in Da Nang. The transmission began as most evening's messages, a great deal of numbers and names and meaningless garble. But the code words again made the radio operator sit up quickly and again open his notebook and start writing.

"What the hell now?" Harry Rogers said.

"We'd better wake the captain," Lieutenant Vankat said.

When Pat Collins read the message he crumpled the paper into a tight ball. He looked at Bill Vankat and then opened his hand and unwadded the paper.

"Did you read this?" he asked Vankat.

"Yes, sir," Vankat said. "You want my platoon to take the mission?"

"Not much choice," Pat Collins said. "You're supposed to be next out. You're rested and this mission looks like a good deal of work. Frankly, I'd rather stay in the mountains. You'll kill just as many gooks up here and you've got a better chance of dodging bullets. Down there, you can look for yourself, there isn't much cover."

"We can operate at night," Vankat said. "We actually prefer night work these days."

"Night is your friend, Bill," Pat Collins said, "but I don't think you can do it all at night. You'll need the daylight to find the river crossings for the heavy stuff, especially the tanks. Tanks can only clear so much water, and that river is wide and deep in places."

When Bill Vankat issued the warning order to his platoon, John Del-Grosso and his men had lain in ambush for nearly four hours. He was beginning to have doubts whether or not the Viet Cong would discover the drop zone. John DelGrosso didn't like the idea of trying to haul the two litters loaded with everything from C-rations to fresh radio batteries up the mountain with an enemy patrol working in the neighborhood. He would wait another hour, he knew that by then the enemy would have either found them or missed them completely. Then they would have to risk everything.

He had looped communications wire from each man's wrist and when he felt the sudden tug, it came as almost a relief. John DelGrosso looked along the swath they had cut through the jungle, opening a killing zone just below the two piles of supplies that his men had hidden behind the thick jungle foliage. He knew that the Viet Cong could not help but notice the hacking that his men had done, but he hoped they would believe that it was to clear a landing zone for the supply drop. He also hoped that the Viet Cong would see the deep scars that the litters had left and that they would believe that his men had made a run for it.

When the single guerrilla scout crawled out from the cover of the undergrowth downhill from where John DelGrosso's men lay waiting, that was when Doc Thomas pulled the communications wire, signaling both to his right and left that he had the enemy in sight. The Navy corpsman snuggled into his M-14 rifle and followed the small man who wore a black shirt and black shorts. He knew that the moment of ambush was near.

John DelGrosso did not see the guerrilla at first, but when the man stood and casually walked downhill, back to his comrades, John knew that they had swallowed the hook. The remainder of the enemy squad was not so cavalier; they came into the clearing one at a time and gathered looking at the deep scars in the earth where the supply sleds had struck ground and slid, digging foot-deep gouges. John watched intently as they traced the twin scars left by his men pulling the litters forward, and as the men neared the uphill side of the clearing, a rifle shot directly in front of the enemy squad cracked through the night and lit the jungle to life with squawking as birds and other creatures fled from the sudden report.

One of the Viet Cong reeled backward and fell, rolling several yards before stopping in a dead heap. At the same time, the other half-dozen soldiers immediately fell to the earth, rolled, and began firing into the bushes ahead of them. As they fell, John DelGrosso and the other eight men of his patrol opened fire on the guerrillas.

"Watch the flanks!" John DelGrosso shouted. He heard several voices repeat his command, but he still felt no better. He knew that he had less than half the enemy patrol in the killing zone when the battle began. He dreaded the next moments when the remainder of their squad would pick the flank to strike.

Doc Thomas lay second from the end of the left flank and heard the crashing in the undergrowth to his left. He had emptied one magazine and had just jammed another into his rifle when the first bullet stung him across the back. He felt his flesh tear and knew that the bullet had actually grazed him, laying open the flesh just below his shoulder blades.

"Left flank!" the corpsman shouted. "They're turning on the left flank!" Then he swung his body around and fired at the muzzle flashes in the jungle.

The Marine who had the flanking position on the left fell back to his alternate position behind Doc Thomas and opened the field of fire. Seeing the attack coming from the left flank, Dutch Miller and John DelGrosso closed their line toward the left and opened fire into the woods. Several men shouted and cried as the Marines' bullets struck, and the remainder of their group broke away from the fight. In a matter of minutes the night was again quiet except for the moans of several wounded men.

When John DelGrosso managed to reach the men on his left flank, he found both of them wounded. His heart sank as he saw that the worst hurt was his corpsman, a man who with other units would not have had to even pick up a rifle.

"How bad, Doc?" John DelGrosso asked as he knelt beside the wounded corpsman. He could see that the man was in great pain from the wound that appeared to have broken two ribs as the bullet passed through the side of his chest.

"I think my lungs are intact, but I don't think I can climb with these broken ribs," the corpsman said. "My back's cut from another round, but when they clipped my side, I went down hard. I thought I was dead."

"If it's any consolation, Doc," the lieutenant said, "the bleeding doesn't look that bad."

"I'm still in a little shock, I'm gonna need to get to a hospital," he said with professional coolness.

Doc Thomas was very professional and had a knack for keeping a clear head even at the worst of times. Pat Collins had liked him when they first met, and after their first combat patrol, he liked him even more. Thomas was one of the few corpsmen who stayed on after the captain had issued his Rules of Engagement.

Collins had said, "If you're not willing to sling lead, I can't use you. This is too small an outfit to have people along who can't help in a fight. I need lead slingers first and corpsmen second. Got it?"

They all had gotten it, and several of the corpsmen had left. Pat Collins respected those who left; he understood the men's pacifism but he had no room for them. Doc Thomas and Doc Arilious had stayed and agreed to become gunslingers as well as corpsmen. When they went on patrol, they carried rifles. When the patrol lay in ambush, they were on line as riflemen, shooting but also ready to save the lives of their brothers in arms. That was the way Pat Collins wanted it, and that was fine by them.

After his earlier briefing, Pat Collins had lain down again, and he awakened with a jolt when he heard the shooting start. "What the hell's going on," he growled to Lieutenant Vankat.

"Sir, that's DelGrosso's ambush," Vankat said.

Collins frowned. "What's the situation?"

"Nothing since you went back to sleep," Vankat began. "We've been standing by for a sitrep."

As he spoke the chattering firefight had died to an intermittent pop of a Soviet AK answered by the hollow crack of an American M-14. Then the radio crackled to life and John DelGrosso issued the situation report himself: "Four enemy confirmed killed, suspect two killed or wounded, no prisoners. No friendly killed, two wounded. Request medical evacuation."

"We can't get a chopper down there," Collins said.

"I can pick him up on my way out," Vankat said.

"Tell DelGrosso to beat feet with the wounded to Thrust-Point Echo and wait for Vankat. They'll be there by daylight," Collins said to the radio operator. "Remind him to hide those supplies. We'll send down six extra men to help DelGrosso drag the stuff back here."

It took a full day for Bill Vankat and his platoon to reach John Del-Grosso's patrol and take the two Marines down to the flatlands below Ban Nha where UH-34 helicopters picked them up and flew eastward. John DelGrosso had reached the natural observation post of the flat ledge of rocks where he had rested and watched the enemy in the field a day earlier when he heard the helicopters lift off and watched their dramatic departure through his binoculars.

Several Viet Cong had closed on the landing zone, a waist-high field of rice, but Vankat and his men scrambled aboard the choppers just seconds after the enemy had begun shooting. The tracers from the machine guns mounted in the doors of the helicopters mixed in an arch with the tracers fired at them by the Communist guerrillas as the slow-flying aircraft banked away, hugging close to the treetops to quickly escape the effectiveness of the Commnists' gunfire.

The gooks are mad as ants, he told himself as the helicopters faded into the gray distance of the darkening evening sky. John DelGrosso felt tiredness embrace his whole body, yet he knew that the worst was yet ahead. Shouldering the heavy load of supplies 1,000 feet upward on a mountain face whose grade was at least a 50-degree incline would take all the drive and push he and his men could muster.

He looked at Staff Sergeant Miller whose long face and lanky build accented the fatigue that possessed the man. "They'll be coming back after us," he said to the staff sergeant.

"We gonna ambush them again?" the staff sergeant asked in a voice that dragged the words out slowly.

"We ought to," John DelGrosso said. "They sure wouldn't expect it. But the skipper wants us to get moving. The four extra bodies will make the uphill climb faster."

A thick layer of clouds hid the moon and stars that night and rain soaked the dozen struggling men who felt they now knew the suffering that the Hebrew slaves must have endured under their Egyptian yokes in the times of Moses. Building pyramids could be no tougher than this. The radio batteries and boxes of ammunition weighed most and required two men, whose backs were also loaded, pulling each large box uphill together, slipping on the slimy tangle of roots and rain-soaked jungle floor that seemed to tilt more and more steeply as they neared Ban Nha's summit.

Dutch Miller took the column's point. He had a huge sack of equipment slung low on his back and with both his gangling arms free he pulled himself like a great ape, hand over hand, while his toes pushed easily against the twisting roots and undergrowth. He scouted forward and then waited for the Marines lugging the boxes to climb in his trace. He watched them as they scrambled upward, grappling for branches and stalks, anything for a handhold, with their one free hand while gripping tightly to the ropes tied around the boxes and jerry cans.

The heavy downpours had come early in the night while the patrol was low on the slope and left the men bone-soaked. The rain had slacked to a thin drizzle and then stopped when the patrol crawled over the last ridges that finally angled directly toward the mountain's top. They pushed higher and higher over the ridge and up the final slope, and found themselves surrounded in the fog of the clouds. Higher still the fog too thinned and then rested behind them, leaving the cold night sky, filled with stars and a bright moon shining above them, lighting up the jungle in eerie shades of silver, black, and gray. And as the cool air of altitude began to set in on the men, leaving them shivering with aching bellies and bones, John DelGrosso's heart sank with the sound of crashing brush just ahead of Staff Sergeant Miller.

His first thought was that the Viet Cong had guessed correctly on their route and destination, and now moved along their flank in the rain, searching for the opportunity to assault them. The lieutenant quietly dropped to his knees and motioned for the men to get down and prepare to fight.

Staff Sergeant Miller had pushed hard at the point once they had cleared the rain. He hurried to keep warm and had stopped to wait for the gap behind him to close when the crash came once from beside him and then in front of him. He looked over his shoulder toward the patrol and saw the men crouch down and slide to cover, and he began to kneel when the crash came again, directly above his head.

He felt as though his heart could explode at any second. Nothing would move. His knees locked and his shoulders froze under its 150-pound load. The staff sergeant's hands dangled at his sides with his fingers curled level at his bent knees. When he heard a muffled chuckle from one of the hiding Marines, he slowly turned his face forward to see what had confronted him. What had crashed from the tree above his head and landed with a hard thud two feet in front of him.

The giant ape screamed when Staff Sergeant Miller looked at him eye to eye, their noses nearly touching. Miller yelled too, but after the ape had leapt backwards and shot up the tree, crashing through the branches and screaming his shrill, high-pitched call of alarm to the rest of his pack.

For John DelGrosso and the rest of the platoon, it appeared almost as a planned comedy. The one thing that made them relax and feel as though they could make it to the top. To see the dumbfounded staff sergeant, looking almost like an ape himself because of his load and his long arms and bent back, staring eye to eye with an equally startled creature of the trees, left the men teary-eyed from laughter.

Dutch Miller didn't laugh, however, not at first, not until he had sat under the tree and looked back at the platoon trying to stand and pick up their loads and then fall down from laughing. Then he began to laugh too.

# GOING SOUTH

• 1 •

FIRST SERGEANT JOHN O. HENRY SAT QUIETLY ON THE CAMP STOOL outside the doorway of the tent that he shared with three other staff noncommissioned officers from Company A, 3rd Reconnaissance Battalion. He watched as an older woman and a younger woman dressed in black silk pants and shirts that fit like baggy pajamas walked with four half-naked children along the side of the gravel-covered road near John Henry's tent.

The two women carried straw baskets hung on the ends of long poles, which they balanced on their shoulders. The women teetered right and left as they walked, following the rhythm of their loads with their footsteps.

Behind the women, the children played in the dirt, and as the women's distance lengthened between them and the children, the youngsters stopped their play, ran ahead and found a new spot of dirt, squatted and played again, never stopping their jabbering and laughing. Such was life outside the compound south of Da Nang where First Sergeant Henry and his Marines of Company A waited, staged to go when the word to move came from III MAF headquarters.

John Henry spit on the sharpening stone that he cradled in the palm of his left hand and carefully drew his Ka-Bar across it, grinding its edge into the wet spot. He counted the strokes on the one side and when he had scraped it a dozen times, he turned the blade over and ran the blued steel twelve times on its other side. He liked having a good sharp knife.

The day had been a quiet one, groups of South Vietnamese farmers, women, and children and occasionally a vehicle passed along the all-weather roadway that ran past the tent compound. Beyond the gravel road, a ditch and hedgerow partially hid a camp where Seabees from the U.S. Navy Construction Battalion had established a base of operations. Rumors among the Marines reported that these Seabees had ice cream machines and an air-conditioned Quonset hut, inside which they had a refrigerator filled with cold beer and steaks, and that they showed movies every night. Rumors, John Henry thought. Perhaps the one about the ice cream machine was true.

Since the former commanding officer had left, First Lieutenant William T. "Bill" Henderson had taken charge of the unit, and many of the men had hoped that he or another of the lieutenants to whom they had become close would pick up the command. However, another rumor reported that the Ring Bearer who smoked the great calabash pipe had gotten the nod from Doc Blanchard.

John Henry believed this rumor because he had heard it told by too many of the officers who he knew to usually get the lowdown fairly straight and who were not led to conclusion jumping. This rumor did not disturb him, though. He liked Frank Reasoner when he first met him on Okinawa some months before and knew that the former sergeant would be good for the men. However, he was an unknown factor to many of the Company A Marines and John Henry knew well that the unknown nearly always made men nervous.

The first few days would tell much, and John Henry knew that if Frank Reasoner performed half as well as he believed that the lieutenant could, any prejudice that the men might hold, because their better known Company A lieutenants had not gotten the commanding officer's job, would quickly disappear. He knew Doc Blanchard well, and knew that this man, even though prone to be a bit stiff at times, was a good judge of Marines. For John Henry, the idea of the Ring Bearer with the great calabash pipe taking command left him with a good feeling.

The first sergeant had spent the previous day cleaning his rifle and inspecting its parts for wear. He did it in the open where the company's staff sergeants could see him, and the power of suggestion had prompted those Marines to suggest that men in the company who were not patrolling should do the same.

Once John Henry had reassembled his rifle, he visited each platoon and casually inspected the men's rifles. This kind of leadership meant much to him: setting an example rather than issuing orders. When he could promote initiative, such as rifle cleaning, without saying a word, he considered it a significant indication of organizational unity. This meant that they were together in action and thought, something that his men called "tight." Something that John Henry called "gung ho," an old Chinese term that meant "pulling together." To John Henry, the company was becoming a real team.

He believed in the idea of the team. Teamwork. Unity. That is how battles are won. No man can do anything alone; John Henry had learned that in Korea. Many of his team had gone home packed in boxes. A grateful nation had awarded him the Silver Star medal for his heroism, but he felt that the tribute belonged to his team, especially to those who had died. It had been tough for him, losing those guys. The war had been tough, but he had been tougher. He learned that too. A good Marine had to be tougher.

His Ka-Bar was the last item that he had to finish. Once he had oiled and sharpened the knife to his satisfaction, all of his combat equipment would then be back in first-class order. Ready for another operation.

John Henry planned to inspect the men at their afternoon formation to ensure that their equipment was in first-class condition too, before the new commander arrived. That first impression of the company, he believed, reflected directly on him and his professionalism as a Marine leader. He also believed that it would have a great impact on the quality of life that the men enjoyed from the new CO.

As he raked his thumb over the blade and felt its fine edge draw into the first layer of skin with the slightest touch, he smiled. Then he closed his left eye and brought the blue-finished steel a few inches from his opened right eye and examined the edge with great detail. The bared metal shone and appeared almost perfect, no nicks nor breaks from hilt to tip.

John Henry licked his left thumb and index finger and squeezed the Ka-Bar's bright edge, slowly drawing it down to the tip. When he wiped away the black residue that had collected on his fingers, a shout from behind his tent startled him and he nearly cut his hand.

"First Sergeant Henry?" the unfamiliar voice called again, and John Henry slipped the knife into its scabbard, which hung on his web belt that he had looped over the corner of an upended ammunition crate that he used as a table. He stood and followed the direction from where the voice came, and there he saw the squat Marine, pack and war belt loaded and a seabag on his shoulder and the great calabash pipe in his mouth.

Sweat ran down Frank Reasoner's face as he trudged toward the tent, and when John Henry saw the heavily loaded Marine, he jogged to his side and grabbed the seabag from his shoulder.

"Sir" John Henry said, "why didn't you call ahead? We could have had some of the troops help you. There's no need for you to break your back."

"It's my gear," Frank Reasoner said, releasing the seabag to the first sergeant. "If I can't carry it myself, I probably don't need it."

John Henry began walking toward a General Purpose tent staked far to the left of the GP tent where he lived and Frank Reasoner said, "That where you live?"

"No, sir," John Henry said. "I live in that GP tent behind us. Me and the other staff NCOs."

"Who lives in that tent?" Frank Reasoner said, pointing to the tent that John Henry had started toward.

"That's the officers' tent," John Henry said. "Your tent, I believe."

"That'll do for the moment," Frank Reasoner said. "Let's just drop this inside and I'll square away a few things while you call the company to formation. I want to introduce myself and take a look at the men."

John Henry remembered that he had planned to inspect the company before the new commanding officer arrived. Now he had to change those plans and trust his staff to ensure that all was in order. As he set the seabag on the floor made of plywood laid over supply pallets, the first sergeant said, "I'll get the company together. They'll be in formation in half an hour. Can you manage?"

Frank Reasoner looked slyly at the first sergeant and then said, "I think so. You look as if you're in a hurry to get started. I won't hold you up."

John Henry fought to keep from running, and when he saw one of the staff sergeants he did run to catch the Marine.

"Jimmy, get your platoon inspected and then fall them out for company formation in half an hour," John Henry said.

Staff Sergeant Jimmy Knee looked blankly at the senior Marine. "What's up, First Sergeant? I thought—"

"The new CO's already here," John Henry said. "I have to pass the word and get the company in formation. He wants to meet everyone. I'll talk to you some more later, but now I want to make sure that everyone is up to snuff before he can inspect anyone. We've got to make sure he knows that he's picked up a top-drawer outfit. No second chances to make a first impression, so this has got to be good. Now get going. I'll see you in thirty minutes."

The staff sergeant jogged toward his platoon area and as he passed a second staff sergeant he spoke to him and then pointed back to the tent where John Henry had gone.

Nearly eighty Marines stood in three groups, packs and rifles ready for inspection, as Frank Reasoner laid down his pipe in a makeshift ashtray made from a cut-down coffee can and walked from the tent to where his new company stood in formation. He glanced at each lieutenant who stood centered in front of his platoon and then at the platoon sergeants who stood at the end of each group. He walked smartly to the first officer and then to the first Marine on the first row as that officer followed him.

The first man's rifle smelled of Hoppe's gun-cleaning solvent and Frank Reasoner immediately knew that in the half hour that it took to fall out the company, First Sergeant Henry had managed to ensure that every man had given his rifle one last, quick cleaning. He handed back the rifle and looked at the pack and web belt on the next man. It was clean and straight too.

Frank Reasoner walked back to the center of the platoon where the officer had returned and again stood at attention. "Your platoon looks squared away," Reasoner said, "I guess I don't need to look any further."

"No, sir," the platoon commander told Frank Reasoner. "The company is in good order, and ready for inspection."

When Frank Reasoner walked to his post at the center of the company, he saw First Sergeant Henry standing at one side, smiling. Then he cast his look to each platoon.

"First Sergeant's got a right to smile," Frank Reasoner said, "you men look good. I'm pleased." Then he relaxed his stance and called out, "Platoon commanders, have your men stand at ease."

The three officers spun about-face and issued the first order directed from their new commanding officer. As they turned back to the front and stood with their legs slightly spread and their hands clasped behind their backs, Frank Reasoner began to speak.

"I want you to know that I am very proud at this moment, assuming this command," he began. "I intend to see this company stand out as one of the most productive in the 3rd Marine Division, so plan on plenty of work.

"I believe in platoon commanders taking care of their platoons, so I will stay out of your way. The only time I will get involved is when we have a large operation or special mission that requires my being with you. Each platoon commander will find work for his platoon and you will be busy with that while I work on the matters that involve the entire company or a great portion of it.

"That's about it. If there are no questions, I'd like a word with the first sergeant. The rest of you are dismissed."

John Henry jogged to where Frank Reasoner stood shaking hands with the three platoon commanders and exchanging friendly words. When the lieutenant saw the first sergeant, he excused himself from the other officers and began walking toward the tent where he had left his belongings. He looked at John Henry and motioned for him to come too.

"I've got a command post tent, cots, and a desk coming down this afternoon and I want you to move into it with me," Frank Reasoner said as he walked.

"Excuse me, sir?" John Henry said.

"That's right," Frank Reasoner said, cracking his broad smile that made John Henry immediately know that a great deal of goodness lived in this Marine's soul. "It's too big for me by myself."

"The XO will be glad to move in with you and get out of the officers' tent," John Henry said.

"I would rather have him there, it's good for the other officers," Frank Reasoner said and looked directly at the first sergeant. "To be honest, I don't plan on assigning an executive officer. I figure that you and I can do a fine job of running the company. I need to know how the troops feel. You understand, don't you? I need to know what goes on in their heads. You're closer to the source. That's why I want to have you close to me. I want you to grab up your trash and move in this afternoon."

"That's really an XO's place, sir," John Henry said. "Isn't it traditional?"

"The others will understand, and I'm sure agree," Frank Reasoner said. "I was a sergeant before I was a lieutenant, and I haven't forgotten that much. Besides, we'll get along. You had a battlefield commission in Korea, so living like an officer isn't exactly new to you. We can work up our plans for company operations while day to day the platoon commanders take care of the platoons."

Frank Reasoner then put his arm over the first sergeant's shoulder before the two men had shaken hands. "Relax, John. I know what I'm doing."

Later that evening two Marines in a truck delivered the command post tent, and John Henry, Frank Reasoner, and four other Marines took less than an hour to get it up. Frank Reasoner had finished rolling out his sleeping bag on the cot at the end of the tent when John Henry pushed open the tent flap and plopped down his seabag and pack.

"Got anything more that you need a hand with?" Frank Reasoner said.

"Sir," John Henry said with a grunting laugh that came from his belly, "if I can't carry it, I probably don't need it." Then he looked at Frank Reasoner and bared a wide smile. "I've got a couple of other things, but they're small. Ammo crates and stools, they'll make this place a little more livable."

"Need a hand?" Frank Reasoner said.

"I'll get them," John Henry said. "I've got to talk to the staff NCOs and get some things straight. You go ahead and clean house here, I'll only take a few minutes."

When John Henry returned, he held a box with books and stools and other scavenged items that he would pass on to other Marines when he left this place. He noticed the second cot that Frank Reasoner had erected while he was away, and he set the box of goods on it. He began setting up the makeshift bookshelves next to the cot when Frank Reasoner lit his pipe and motioned for the first sergeant to stop and sit.

"Don't get too comfortable, First Sergeant," Frank Reasoner said. "We're not going to spend that much time here."

"I expected that," John Henry said. "The company's ready to go, just give the word."

"I saw Doc Blanchard yesterday and he said that General Walt wants to open up the TAOR south of the Cau Do River," the lieutenant said.

John Henry leaned forward and rested his elbows on his knees and clasped his hands together and looked at Frank Reasoner. "We've heard that too," the first sergeant said. "Word is they're expanding Chu Lai and Phu Bai TAORs to run up the contours of the mountains as the western limit and then north and south to link up those enclaves with Da Nang."

"You've got a good source of information, First Sergeant," Frank Reasoner said. "Bill Vankat is supposed to start river surveys as soon as he gets off that mountain with Pat Collins. Once General Walt gets the nod, 9th Marines will set up operations from the old French fort called Dai Loc, near that big iron bridge that crosses the Cau Do River. We can use that as our patrol base. From there our teams will probe three to four miles south and eight or ten miles west. In the meantime, we'll keep working with Colonel Wheeler and 3rd Marines up here."

"That's a lot of Indian country," John Henry said.

"We'll have the 9th Marine Regiment backing us up," Frank Reasoner said.

"Still," John Henry said, "we get hung out there and clipped pretty hard, it might get a little scary waiting for the cavalry to ride over the mountaintop."

"Nobody said that it wouldn't be exciting," Frank Reasoner said and again offered his wide, friendly smile.

• 2 •

HE KNELT TO MEDITATE AND NO ONE NOTICED HIM WATCHING THE men digging the tunnel. Beads of sweat glistening in the noonday light clung to the gray stubble on his scalp that now pricked through his skin since he had not shaved his head today. The sun bore down hot as he quietly chanted to himself, his eyes following the men who worked near the huts.

He wore the yellow robes of a Buddhist priest, and this was his village. When, as a boy, he first shaved his head and put on the yellow robes as a new monk, he had watched the French soldiers and then the Japanese come, then the French again and now the Americans. In all those years, he had never gotten involved in politics or war. Now, he could not help himself.

He watched a generation of families change from peaceful farmers and rural peasants to guerrillas and killers. He saw his world evolve from a quiet countryside of three small hamlets to an enclave harboring Communist fanatics who recognized no faith, neither Catholic nor the ancient beliefs of the Vietnamese.

When these Communists, calling themselves the National Liberation Front, came to him demanding 270 piasters, he told them no.

The leader, a man whom he had watched grow from a boy right here in his home village of Duong Son, looked at him and said: "Old man, you are no better than any other citizen. Each of them happily pays this tax of 270 piasters."

"But I have no money. I own nothing," he told the young man.

"Then you must work and pay your obligation in that way," he said.

"I will not. You would use what came from me to support your war, to buy weapons so that you can destroy people, and I will not contribute to the death of anyone," the old priest told the young man.

"You will be made to leave the village then," the young man said.

"This is my home. I have nowhere else," the priest said and pointed to the temple that he and his monks maintained for the village. "Our place is here; we harm no one."

"It is the wish of the people that every person pay a tax to support our people's struggle for liberation," the young man said.

"I have no struggle for liberation," the priest said.

"But you will benefit from our struggle, therefore, you must pay," the young man said. "If you do not pay, someone must pay for you, or we will burn this temple and you with it."

The old man did not ask for help, but those in the village who worried about the fate of this priest and the monks and their temple collected enough among themselves to satisfy the tax. Nevertheless, the men who called themselves liberators and fought the puppet government of the south mistrusted the priest and his monks, and watched them.

When the Marines landed at Da Nang, the forty-man guerrilla force from the Army of the National Liberation Front, who called themselves the People's Liberation Army but who the government of the south called Viet Cong, began reinforcing huts and digging trenches and tunnels. They constructed bunkers and foxholes and punji pits, and set in booby traps along the trails and in the fields that surrounded this complex of three hamlets that lay along the south bank of the Song Cau Do called Duong Son village.

The priest could see that these men who called themselves liberators were fashioning the village into a site for battle, and by his teachings, he could be no part of this. He could be no part of war.

He worried and meditated and finally concluded that by his silence he supported their regime and contributed to the potential deaths of those that these liberators sought to destroy.

When he finished his meditation, he rose to his feet and glanced a look at the men still working on the tunnel. They did not notice him as he slowly walked along the path that led past the last hut and beyond the rice fields. When he crossed the iron bridge that spanned the wide river, he rested in the shade beneath, and fought back the fear that now crept within his heart. He prayed that no one had noticed him leave.

"I must see the commander of the Marines," the priest tried to tell the guard. He risked much when he slipped past the Viet Cong roadblocks and walked from Duong Son to the airfield at Da Nang, wanting to tell the American leaders, to warn them of the growing danger. But the guard could not appreciate, nor even know that about him.

"I have much to tell your commandant," the old man said. "The guerrillas now keep a four-man roadblock at the railroad tracks near my village of Duong Son. There is a garrison there of forty men and they have made my village into a fortress. They have dug tunnels and trenches and set traps and made punji pits. They let no one leave nor enter unless they are friendly to the Communists."

The young man wearing the green uniform did not speak Vietnamese nor French, and he shook his head and said, "I don't understand. *Je ne comprends pas*," and he waved at the priest to go away. "Go find someone to speak English for you, then come back."

The old man, frustrated but refusing to go, sat by the gate and waited.

The day wore into the afternoon, and as the sun drifted low over the westward mountains, a jeep with four men, also wearing the green uniforms of the American Marines, approached the sentry post where now another guard stood watch and where the old priest sat quietly waiting.

Seeing the silver eagle painted on the red plate fastened to the front of the jeep, the priest stood and held his right hand up, showing his open palm to the driver.

"Sir," a captain riding in the backseat said, tapping the shoulder of the colonel who sat in the jeep's front seat. "I think this Buddhist monk wants us."

The colonel motioned for the driver to stop and he called to the sentry, "Corporal, what's with the monk?"

"Sir, he's been here all day. He doesn't speak English, but he keeps saying things to me that sounds like French," the Marine sentry told the officer.

"I speak French, sir," the captain in the backseat said, and climbed out of the jeep.

## • 3 •

THE BANKS OF THE SONG CAU DO MATCHED THE COLOR OF THE RUST that encrusted the girders on the iron bridge named Phong Le that crossed the river under the bloodred sun. It had just crested the South China Sea and spread its tint of warm orange over the rice fields and thatched huts that sprawled from the tamarack that was thick at the water's edge. The long shadows of the Marines crossing the bridge flickered down between those of the thick girders and stretched up the river toward the mountains where these men had patrolled two days ago.

Today, Bill Vankat led his platoon across the great iron bridge in search of fords for the main battle tanks of the 3rd Marine Division so that they could cross through the water and support operations south of the river.

Before dawn, the platoon had ridden trucks from the Marine compound at Da Nang to the group of thick-walled, concrete bunkers, marked on the map as Dai Loc, but known to the men as the old French fort. The outpost stood on the north side of the river and overlooked the Phong Le Bridge where a gravel-covered all-weather road called Highway One and the national railway tracks, which paralleled the highway, crossed.

Behind the fort's crumbling walls Bill Vankat and his platoon finalized their plans in the morning darkness.

The job sounded routine to the men of the reconnaissance platoon and they felt glad to be out of the rough terrain of the high mountains. Their recent patrols in search of the road to the top of Ban Nha and their lugging of fresh supplies back to the mountain's summit had left them tired. This mission, although an embark into a little-known and reportedly dangerous territory, seemed to them a deserved respite and a good turn of luck in the face of where they had been and where their brothers remained this morning.

When the first four Marines had crossed the bridge, they walked to the right of the railroad tracks and followed the edge of the roadbed to a covered spot where a large fallen tree lay clogged with debris and growing brush. There they took up a defensive stand as protection against a possible unseen aggressor while the remaining members of their platoon followed across the bridge.

The low dunes and weeds to the east of them blended into a landscape of canals, dikes, lines of trees, and straw-roofed huts. The flatness of the countryside contrasted the red hills that rose to the west and the high green mountains where Ban Nha towered farther west. The view resembled the pictures one might see on a postcard, which might have printed on it in yellow and brown bamboo-style lettering, "South Vietnam, Rice Bowl of the Orient."

Two unseen men watched as the first four Marines patrolled along the railroad bed and then scrambled behind the stand of scrub bushes growing along the thick body of the fallen tree. The two men had lain quietly at the place where the People's Liberation Army had established a four-man roadblock, and when they had seen the first men on the bridge, two of the guerrillas had sneaked away to the village to make a report while the remaining two men hid to keep watch on the incurring enemy patrol.

The Marines in the patrol did not speak. They had learned that to talk while patrolling distracted concentration, which in this country kept a man alive. When the second team from the platoon crossed the bridge, the first team picked up their weapons and moved farther along the railroad bed. When the third team crossed, the first two hustled farther down. After the last man had crossed the bridge, the whole patrol column cautiously snaked forward.

Bill Vankat had planned to probe with his platoon one kilometer south of the bridge and then sweep on line to the river, hopefully clearing away any guerrillas that might lurk there. Once the platoon had reached the edge of the water, he planned to probe westwardly along the river, in search of suitable fords.

The Marine walking at the patrol's point hadn't quite set his knee against the ground, kneeling to retie his boot laces, when he saw the fresh scrape marks and handprints in the dirt. He stood and then waved to the lieutenant.

"Sir," he whispered as Bill Vankat came close, "Charles appears to be watching. Look," and the corporal pointed to the ground.

The lieutenant knelt and raked his fingers through the dirt and saw that the corporal was correct. Whoever had been here had just left. The handprints were not distorted by wind or morning moisture.

Bill Vankat looked at the Marine with his eyes narrowed and spoke in his quietest whisper, "I want you to lead the patrol forward, slowly, and be ready to fire. I'll sit tight and pass the word as the men move past me and then pick up at the end."

Then the lieutenant stood and put his hand on the Marine's upper arm and gripped it hard. "Immediate action, Ace! Don't forget what to do. If it's an ambush, charge at them, guns blazing, and watch for my signal. Either you or tail-end Charlie will have to lead the action to close around their flank. Be ready. And above all: think!"

A cluster of huts that overlooked rice fields that stretched to the river stood in quietness as the sun turned from red to yellow and began to cook dry the salt grass that grew from the dunes on the east side of the railroad tracks. In a trench dug at the foot of one of the huts, the two Viet Cong guerrillas who had manned the roadblock earlier now watched the man stand after the patrol had passed him and then as he jogged back to his place at the center of the column. They agreed that he was obviously the leader, and they chose him as their primary target.

Six other guerrillas hid in a trench to their right and ten more Viet Cong hid behind a dike that bordered the rice field that butted into the cluster of huts and followed the edge of the railroad tracks that gently curved toward the southwest. Each man held a Chinese-built SKS rifle and sweated as they watched the Marines grow larger in their sights.

The corporal walking point felt sweat run under his green utility uniform, dripping down his chest and down his legs in worm-crawling rivulets as he took each step farther along the tracks. At first he thought something had gotten inside his clothes, but realized when he shoved his hand under his shirt that it was sweat. It made him more nervous to have so much on edge that even normal body functions that he had hardly noticed before now distracted him.

Each step that he took crunched in the gravel, and to him sounded incredibly loud. The breeze that drifted from the nearby sea roared in his ears. His eyes searched every bush, hump, clump of grass, dike, and knoll. He knew that out there, somewhere, death lurked.

Ahead of him, he could see the light brown straw matting that covered the sides of the huts and the dark brown thatched roofs. He could see the rails of a fence, lashed by twine and at one corner a rusted trough made from a steel barrel cut in half. However, life there had disappeared. Nothing moved around the huts. Not a chicken. Not a pig or a goat. No birds flew nor did he hear their sounds. They are there, he told himself, and he suddenly dropped to his knees.

When he looked to his right, he saw the first man rise behind his rifle. Then he saw another one's head and rifle, pricking up from behind the dike that ran along his flank and led to the village. The corporal felt his right hand grip the small of his rifle stock and as the butt jammed into his shoulder, he heard the crack of his first shot. As that bullet struck and lifted a sudden cloud of dirt on the dike, he glanced to his right and saw the Marines behind him scrambling off the railroad bed, their rifles raised to fight.

They had not expected the Marines to shoot first so when the corporal opened fire, the surprise had stunned many of the Viet Cong who laid in ambush. When they saw that the enemy patrol had not yet entered into their killing zone, but now swept toward their flank, the guerrillas who had lain along the dike began to run toward the village.

Seeing their comrades running to the safety of the trenches that lay at the edge of the village, the Viet Cong who waited there opened fire on the Marines. Their bullets skipped and sang off the rails and gravel, ricocheting and splitting rocks and spraying dirt.

When the first bullet struck behind the corporal, he wheeled and took aim at the village and fired three shots before he leapt to the side of the roadbed. Behind him he could hear the shouts of his brothers and the cracks of their rifles. He saw one of the Viet Cong fall and when a comrade turned to help the wounded man, he fell too.

Once he had found a place where the enemy bullets seemed unable to strike, he felt the first rush of fear slam into his consciousness. The chill that raced down his spine made him shudder. He knew that but for the grace of God he might easily have died. The idea that he had just rolled the dice in a high-stakes crap shoot and by luck had held on to his life for now turned rapidly in his mind and he spit angrily in the dirt.

"I don't need this shit!" he said to no one but it still felt good to say it. He felt as though someone had just pushed him in front of a speeding train, and by some miracle the deadly wheels had missed. Outrage swelled in him as his mind searched for who or what to blame for such a situation that shoved him so close to disaster. The lieutenant? The Marine Corps? Himself?

He spit in the dirt again. "Jesus H. and Mother Mary," he said to himself and pulled his rifle into his shoulder and was about to rise above the cover of the embankment when a body landed in the dirt next to him and slid through the roadbed's gravel.

"You alive?" the Marine asked and when the corporal saw his face, he smiled.

"Lieutenant!" the corporal said. "We coulda been wiped out!"

"Thanks to you we weren't," Bill Vankat said. "You going down hard like that, I thought you got hit. You didn't hear anyone yell?"

"I only heard lead splattering, sir," the corporal said.

"Okay, tiger," the lieutenant said, "let's get back to friendlier ground."

"We going to San Diego?" the corporal said and laughed. It felt good to laugh. The tension seemed to slacken within him.

Bill Vankat looked at the corporal. "You got it, hero," he said. "All of us. Soon as we can." Then the lieutenant crouched with his knees drawn down as though he were preparing to go long for the Hail Mary touchdown pass.

"Shoot the gap, Lieutenant," the corporal said. "I'm on your six."

Suddenly, from the other end of the village, the side of a hut swung up and inside it a machine gun chopped across the rice field toward the right flank of where the Marine platoon had come on line and now faced the entrenched enemy head-on. As he and the corporal dashed for their lives, Bill Vankat quickly realized that the quiet-looking hamlet that he had chosen as a pivot point in his sweep plan was a Viet Cong fortress where any number of an entrenched enemy might hold up.

The machine-gun fire chopped along the roadbed, and as the two Marines dashed along the side of the tracks, the fire seemed to intensify in its concentration on them. It had only taken a matter of seconds to close the thirty-yard gap, but in that time, the corporal felt as though he just survived a lifetime. Each of his steps had been punctuated by the shattering lead. The bullets had struck in front of him and behind him and to the side of him, and the corporal had felt the sharp zip and zing of the air as they ripped past his body.

When he saw the lieutenant dive, his feet left the ground too. They both crashed hard into the gravel and dirt at the side of the tracks, and the small rocks left them skinned and sore. The two men slid close to another Marine who had a radio strapped to his back, and without stopping for a breath Bill Vankat shouted to the radio operator who busily chased a running Viet Cong with shots from his M-14, "Call the Sparrow Hawk."

The Marine took the rifle from his shoulder and laid it against the dike behind which he had taken cover. He pulled out the handset from the backpack and listened for the crackle that told him that his battery still held its charge.

In less than twenty minutes, a skyful of helicopters landed behind the dunes that blocked a clear shot from the village to the beach. When Bill Vankat saw the first wave of riflemen from 2nd Battalion, 9th Marine Regiment, come on line behind the roadbed, he signaled his men to charge.

Seeing the horizon lined with helicopters and then an overwhelming force of Marines come pouring over the sand dunes, up the railroad tracks, and across the rice fields, the comparatively small band of Viet Cong entrenched at the edge of the village stopped their fire and fled.

When the first squad of Marines had reached the village, the Viet Cong had taken up their dead and wounded and had vanished. The

Marines searched for an hour and then moved to the old fort that stood on the north side of the Song Cau Do above where the gravel road and the railway tracks crossed over the river on the rusted iron bridge.

That afternoon, 2nd Battalion, 9th Marines, and Bill Vankat's reconnaissance platoon began a sweep across the flat rice land and randomly scattered hamlets. Again they found the Viet Cong waiting, entrenched. And this time, the Marines pulled back.

The next morning two more battalions joined the fight and pushed what they estimated to be a reinforced Viet Cong regiment out of the hamlets and into the red hills to the west.

In that push, a bullet had creased Bill Vankat's head. Although it had left his face and hair covered in blood, the headache caused by the concussion had been the worst of it. Bill Vankat needed only a day of rest before he was back with his men, but the Red Cross had taken the initiative to notify his mother, who had a dangerous heart condition. Her trouble was so serious that the lieutenant had left special instructions on his record of emergency data that she was not to be notified in the case of his injury or death.

The message that Mrs. Vankat received from the Red Cross was short. It simply said that her son had been shot in the head.

• 4 •

A LARGE, BLACK CEILING FAN TURNED SLOWLY ABOVE THE DESK AND sofa chairs in Major General Nguyen Chanh Thi's office. Major General Lew Walt sat on one of the chairs and sipped a glass of iced tea that the South Vietnamese general's aide handed to him a moment earlier.

"Your Marines are not ready to go south of the Song Cau Do, General Walt," Thi said, standing with his arms folded as his aide set a second glass of tea on a coaster at the corner of the general's desk. Thi took the glass, sipped a small swallow, and continued his lecture to the III MAF commander. "It is a very bad country down there. For more than a generation, those people have been Viet Cong. We know this."

Walt rubbed his crew-cut head with his open hand and said, "General Thi. We cannot win a war by avoiding the enemy. Your government has agreed to expand 9th Marines' TAOR to include that area three miles south of the Cau Do River. It is now our responsibility to close with and destroy any enemy in that area. I've had the intelligence briefs. I know that my Marines are not accustomed to unfriendly villagers. Hell, except for that skirmish down there the other day, all they've seen are the mama-sans and papa-sans that work around the compounds and that bunch of your compatriots up at Le My, but we'll never learn to swim unless we go off into the deep water."

"I am saying," General Thi said, "I agree. Your Marines must learn to swim. I am warning you, however, to not teach them to swim in waters filled with sharks."

"We will follow your warning and move cautiously into the area," Walt said, "but we must establish our patrols south of the Cau Do. Sharks or no sharks."

"I accept your decision," Thi said, "and agree for you to patrol south of Song Cau Do," pausing, "reluctantly."

## • 5 •

WHAT'S THE GOOD WORD, SIR," CAPTAIN PAT COLLINS SAID AS Lieutenant Colonel Don H. "Doc" Blanchard stepped inside the Company D headquarters, a plywood and canvas structure that the Seabees who built it called a sea hut.

"We're going south, Paddy," he said, walking back to a folding chair and then sitting down. "9th Marines has picked up all the land from the beach west to the Yen River, and from Da Nang Air Base to three and a half miles south of the Cau Do River."

"And?" the captain asked.

"And you are going down there to scout the territory," Blanchard said, pausing to relight his cigar. "Company D and Company A."

"What's to scout?" Collins replied. "I hear there's just hedgerows, huts, and rice paddies. Open country and farmers. About 100,000 gooks who are mostly VC, according to Vankat."

"Closer to 50,000, but they are probably all VC or VC sympathizers, according to III MAF G-2," Blanchard said. "They've talked to some old Buddhist priest who says that's where a lot of the VC are concentrated. He said that his village, Duong Son, is crawling with Charlie and that they have turned it into a regular little fortress. The old man walked all the way to Da Nang to warn us so that we would know not to go there."

"Too bad he didn't run into Vankat first," Collins said. "I heard about the foul-up with his mother. That's totally unsat. I thought she was out of the loop. What happened?"

"Red Cross. Guess they didn't trust our casualty officers," Blanchard said and frowned.

"Vankat's pissed as hell, as usual," Collins said. "As a matter of fact, so am I." Then he looked at Blanchard. "So about this big intramural, what are we going to do?"

"We're heading south as soon as possible," Blanchard said. "Damn near all of us. Reasoner will patrol west and south with Company A while you work south and along the river in the eastern area, around those villages where Vankat caught hell."

"Plenty for everyone, huh," Collins said as Blanchard walked toward the door. "That all?"

"Yeah," Blanchard said and then looked at Pat Collins. "One other thing. That goofy red hat."

"DelGrosso?" Pat Collins said.

"Yeah," Blanchard said. "Tell him to lose it. The damned thing isn't tactical. Bad for discipline."

"It's gone," Collins said.

"Oh, Paddy," Blanchard said as he walked away from the sea hut. "I almost forgot."

"What's that, sir?" Pat Collins said, now walking toward the lieutenant colonel.

"That phantom road," Blanchard said. "Up on Ban Nha."

Pat Collins frowned. "That goddamned thing, don't tell me."

Blanchard bit ragged tobacco off the end of his cigar and spit. "A patrol found it."

"Bullshit. I can't believe it. We covered every inch of that mountain," Pat Collins said.

"Apparently not every inch," Doc Blanchard said and laughed. "A patrol stumbled across it on the south side of the mountain. Division's got trucks going up there now."

Pat Collins smiled. "We were convinced that it had completely grown over."

"Somebody noticed a straight line cutting through the canopy, and they realized that it was the road," Blanchard said. "Nothing on the ground. Tracks completely gone, but the gap in the forest still there. I guess you just had to see it the right way."

"Funny how you can look at something like that and not see it," Pat Collins said. "I know we had to have walked right across it."

"I'm headed Reasoner's way, need me to pass anything to him?" Blanchard said.

"No," Collins said. "I hear him on the radio net, jockeying his teams around. He's getting to be a regular little general with that bunch."

"I've heard him too," Blanchard said and spit shredded cigar on the ground. "He's got a mouth."

"What, the dirty words burning your ears?" Pat Collins said and laughed.

"No," Doc Blanchard said, "but he ought to watch it on the net. Sounds bad. No telling who might hear."

"Sounds like a problem for the chaplain," Pat Collins said.

When Doc Blanchard reached the Company A compound, he found Corporal B. C. Collins and Lance Corporals Lindy Hall and Jim Shockley shirtless in a hole where they worked filling sandbags under the blistering afternoon sun. He approached the hole and B. C. Collins stopped, clicked the dirty heels of his boots.

"Afternoon, sir," B. C. Collins said.

"Where's Lieutenant Reasoner?" Doc Blanchard said, chewing on the stub of his cigar.

"In the field, sir," the corporal said.

"Is First Sergeant Henry here?" Blanchard said.

"Should be back in a few minutes," Collins said. "He's up in your area picking up some papers."

"You see him, tell him to come to my tent. I need to talk to him," Doc Blanchard said.

An hour later John Henry stood outside 3rd Reconnaissance Battalion's command hut. He rapped his knuckles on the plywood cover that stood out as a shade over the wide screen window next to the door.

"First Sergeant Henry," Doc Blanchard called, "come on in."

John Henry presented himself to the lieutenant colonel and Doc Blanchard motioned for him to sit while he finished lighting a fresh cigar.

"You need to see me?" John Henry asked as he sat on a steel chair next to a four-foot-by-eight-foot series of maps and overlays mounted to a plywood backing and propped on red two-by-four legs.

"You know this young commanding officer you've got?" Blanchard began.

"Yes, sir," John Henry said.

"Well, he's a little bit wild on the radio," Blanchard said. "He gets to using vulgarity and cussing. We can't have that. We've got to have radio procedure."

John Henry blinked a moment and then he narrowed his eyes and tilted his head. "Colonel Blanchard," he said, "I'm gonna tell you what, and lock me up, but this man is getting the job done, he gets it over to those boys in the field and they understand what he's talking about, and personally, I don't give a damn."

Blanchard looked at the first sergeant but did not speak.

John Henry tried to smile but could not find it in himself. Then he locked his eyes on Doc Blanchard's. "This isn't going to hurt anybody. I mean, we don't have anybody listening like back stateside. Although there is good radio discipline. But come on, Colonel."

"Now don't get upset," Doc Blanchard said in a voice broken by a laugh.

"Well, I'm not," John Henry said, "but it just makes me mad that the man's doing a fine job, and somebody's gonna jump on him for using a couple of cuss words."

When John Henry saw Frank Reasoner that night, he mentioned that Doc Blanchard had noticed his profanity on the radio net, and suggested that he might watch the talk. Although the suggestion made Frank Reasoner a bit angry, he did improve his radio procedure after that, but he never completely stopped. Doc Blanchard, however, never mentioned it again.

· 6 ·

A CHILD RAN PAST HIM, AND AS HE FOLLOWED HIM WITH HIS EYES, he noticed that the men digging the tunnel also stopped to watch. The old priest knew he must leave this afternoon and walk to the Phong

Le Bridge where he would meet the Marine captain who had been kind to him and listened. The captain had asked the old man to meet him there after ten days and to tell him more of what he saw being done in his village.

As the old man pulled himself to his feet and brushed the dirt from his yellow robes, he again looked at the children. His heart ached for them and for the times of a generation past when the village men and women worked in the fields and not in tunnels beneath the houses. He slowly walked from the village as the men continued to dig and the children played. No one paid attention to him except for two of the workers who laid down their picks and stepped behind the hut.

## • 7 •

S IR, I WAS HOPING THAT WE WOULD HAVE AN UPDATED BRIEF FROM our contact in the village," the captain who worked in the intelligence section said, apologizing to Lieutenant Colonel George R. Scharnberg, commanding officer of 2nd Battalion, 9th Marine Regiment. "He was supposed to meet me at the bridge this afternoon. I guess he had second thoughts. I have nothing newer than our reconnaissance observations of the villages."

"I think, based on your earlier information, we will assume the worst and prepare for it," the colonel told the captain. Then he addressed the other officers who had gathered in his headquarters tent for the final briefing on the evening of July 11. "We'll move forward at daylight. I have two of my companies flanking Duong Son(1)[1] and Captain Collins will have Company D set up a blocking force on the southwest side and cover any attempted egress while Company B, one-nine, will enter the village."

Collins left the tent with Frank Reasoner.

"You're on patrol with one-nine?" Collins said.

"Sort of, sir," Reasoner said. "They're our support in the rear. We will be a bit farther south and to the west of you. I'll take Bill Henderson

---

[1] The number in parentheses represents one of what may be several villages that make up a single hamlet. All the villages bear the hamlet's name, in this case Duong Son, but are differentiated by the numbers.

and his platoon and chop in to Dai Loc Fort, leave John Henry and a radio relay and then take a reinforced platoon down that road that branches southwest through all those hamlets south of Cam Ne. They're called An My or some such. It's hard to tell one from the next."

"Whose brilliant idea is this plan, running a reconnaissance up a road?" Pat Collins asked, considering that patrolling up a road was not the best of maneuvers.

"I'm not sure. From on high is all I know. They want to open up that south country," Reasoner said. "We have help standing by, and I'll be on the net with John Henry the whole way."

"Meat on a stick," Collins said.

"We've got some new people and I thought it best if I led this one," Reasoner said. "Mostly because it is, like you say, meat on a stick."

Pat Collins looked at Frank Reasoner and started to speak, but then waited a moment and thought. "You sure about this?"

"Second thoughts?" Reasoner said.

"Always. But nothing's perfect. I think you could have had more experience before you took on a company," Collins said seriously to the lieutenant. "Although that last patrol south where you cleaned out that village and brought back two VC prisoners, that was impressive. You're doing an outstanding job, just as I knew you would, but hell, Frank, you're still a kid."

"Pat. Look around. Most of us here are kids. We regard you as an old man, and what are you, thirty? Thirty-two?" Reasoner said. Pat Collins put up both of his hands as if to surrender, but Frank Reasoner kept talking. "If you're worried about me, you're crazy. I think I'm safer now that I'm away from Mad Man Paddy Collins than I ever was before."

"No you're not," Collins said. "Now, you're the boss. Your guys will live or die because of what you do. I scared shit out of you guys, plenty. You scared shit out of me too." Then Collins put his arm over Frank Reasoner. "But command is tough, and we're so short on help."

"That's right," Reasoner said. "And we're short on experience. You tell me. If I had not taken Company A, who would Doc Blanchard have gotten? He had you running all over the country looking for a CO, and did you find anyone? No. Colonel Blanchard had to look inside. I was the officer wanting the challenge, and I had the leadership experience. I've lived my life to command. It was all that I worked for at West Point."

"You're right, and that's why you've got the job," Collins said. "Don't forget, I recommended you for it."

"Thanks," Reasoner said as they walked. "Just relax, I'll be okay. I'm not about to go pulling any of your stunts. But I'm not going to be timid either."

• 8 •

I 'LL TELL YOU THIS," B. C. COLLINS SAID AS HE PULLED AGAINST A rope that held the side of the General Purpose tent while Jim Shockley looped the end over a stake they had driven into the ground and then slid the wooden grip up the rope to hold it fast. "It's time for a Falstaff."

Jim Shockley grunted as he pulled hard on the next rope and looked at Collins. "So why don't you just jump on over to the club and pick up a few cases?"

"Why not?" B. C. Collins said, taking hold of the rope and pulling enough slack in it so that Jim Shockley easily dropped the loop over the tent stake. "But two beers doesn't cut it. We ought to rat-hole a couple of cases."

"Shit, B.C.," Shockley said, "Doc Blanchard would have your ass. All he needs is one more excuse to burn you. Besides, looks like you would have had your fill after taking that ride with Staff Sergeant Knee."

"You sure as hell didn't turn down any of that beer," B. C. Collins said. "Anyway, Colonel Blanchard let it slide because I thought we were on the regular afternoon supply run."

Jim Shockley laughed. "Sure, to the club and back."

"Hell, Staff Sergeant Knee had to have someone ride shotgun," B.C. said. "Besides, I never asked any questions and he never offered any answers. I never doubted it wasn't an authorized run."

"It's a good thing Knee did it," Shockley said, "otherwise you would have burned. I mean, he is the luckiest man I know. He can pull something, and nobody figures out that he was the one who did it until weeks later, and then they don't care anymore. I'll swear, and you tell me if I'm wrong, but you or I steal Doc Blanchard's jeep and trailer, and make a beer run into the ville. We'd be in jail!"

"That's a no shitter, lad," B.C. said and laughed. "That crazy asshole Knee, he's the luckiest bastard around."

Another two Marines working from the other side of the tent finished tying down their ropes and walked to where B. C. Collins and Jim Shockley were finishing.

"You think we could get some cold beers?" one of the Marines said.

His partner on the working party brushed dust from his trousers and looked at B. C. Collins. "I'll take my ration right now. Let's get over to the club before we get grabbed for another working party."

The four Marines walked toward the area of the compound where the battalion had opened an enlisted men's club of sorts. The establishment, located inside a doublewide sea hut, sold warm beer that was restricted to two cans a day per man, warm soda that the men could drink without limit, and the poorest imitation of a hamburger; the meat varied in texture and color, and no one dared ask what was its contents. Although none of the Marines would have settled for such sorry fare even at Okinawa, the men bought the warm beer and ate the lousy burgers as though they were the best.

First Sergeant John Henry noticed the four men walking toward the club and he checked his watch. It was not quite 3:00 P.M.

"A little early for the water hole," John Henry said to Frank Reasoner. The first sergeant stood at the door of their tent, leaning against the pole while the lieutenant sat inside, carefully putting the finishing touches on a map overlay for the next day's mission.

"Let 'em go," Frank Reasoner said. "We'll hold our briefing after dinner so they can't go tonight, and with us launching tomorrow they probably won't have another chance for several days."

"Oh, I'm not worried, unless they figure a way to get extra beers and get drunk, which is a good bet for a couple of them," John Henry said.

"You're as bad as an old mother hen, John. Don't fret about those boys. You can check them tonight, if you're worried they're going to bootleg beer and get drunk," Frank Reasoner said without shifting his eyes from his work. When he had laid down the last mark with the red grease pencil, he looked up. "John, take a look at this and tell me what you think."

"You fishing for compliments, sir?" John Henry said, taking the map from the lieutenant. "I have never seen anyone so careful with everything. This is absolutely classroom perfect. Just like you do everything. You have to be about the most thorough and conscientious young officer I've

ever known. This map overlay is a good example. Most guys just slap it
down and leave it at that, but your overlays are always neat and picture
perfect. Just like your briefings and frag orders, warning orders and five-
paragraph orders. Perfect. If I didn't know better—"

"Okay, John," Frank Reasoner said, standing and laughing and waving both hands above his head in retreat, "I get the message. I won't
pester you anymore for faint praise. I promise!"

Every few days, John Henry made it his business to get a case of
C-rations from the supply tent for him and the commanding officer. He
kept the meals wrapped under a piece of tent material to make it more
difficult for rats to invade the food supply and eat the candy and various
other items that were not sealed inside the tin cans. Frank Reasoner lifted
the canvas and took out a box labeled "Ham and Lima Beans," which
many Marines liked to call "ham and motherfuckers," walked out of the
tent to the ammo boxes that he and John Henry had arranged as an eating area. He sat down and began opening his evening meal.

"If you'll put my can of ham and mothers on the heat tab," John
Henry told him, "I'll go get the mail. That way we can read letters while
we eat."

Frank Reasoner waved him off and set up a second can to heat John
Henry's meal. When the first sergeant returned carrying several letters,
the lieutenant had already begun eating.

"Here's a couple from Idaho," John Henry said. "I've got a letter too."

They sat quietly and ate and read. Both men loved their families and
home, so letters served as an uplift for them as the beer and burgers did
for the young, single Marines in their company. Both John Henry and
Frank Reasoner had children born on almost the same date, so this gave
them a great deal of common ground about which to talk. Their closeness
had grown to the point in the six weeks that they had lived together that
after they read their letters from home, they would trade and let the other
read his letters. They had done this so much that they felt as though each
knew the other's family even though they had never met. For John Henry,
a Marine veteran nearing forty years of age, and for Frank Reasoner, a
marine early in his twenties, neither could have a better friend.

"Smile," a voice said, and as the two men looked up a Marine with a
camera snapped their photograph.

"What the hell is that for?" Frank Reasoner said. He had finished his food, but John Henry was still eating ham and lima beans from his mess kit plate.

"For you, if you want it," the Marine said. "I had some film to burn on this roll. I thought instead of wasting the frames I'd grab some snaps and give 'em out as freebies."

"Shoot another one," John Henry said, "only let us be really smiling."

"Okay," the Marine said and pointed the camera at them again.

"Now laugh, sir," John Henry said, and Frank Reasoner gouged the first sergeant in the ribs and caused him to spill food off of his spoon. John Henry laughed and Frank Reasoner laughed and the Marine snapped the picture.

"That was the last one," the Marine said. "I'll leave it off when I get them developed."

"If we're not here, just put it inside the logbook on my desk," Frank Reasoner said. "The first sergeant or I will be sure to get it there."

When the Marine left, John Henry finished his plate of food and the two men sat, waiting while the sun moved lower on the horizon. Frank Reasoner looked at his watch and ran his finger under its expansion bracelet.

"Damn thing is getting beat up," Frank Reasoner said, rubbing the watch crystal with his thumb.

"Rolex, isn't it?" John Henry said.

"Yeah. It's really a valuable watch, but they're damn near indestructible," Frank Reasoner said.

"Like my Timex," John Henry said. "Except I could buy a used pickup truck for the difference in what my watch and that one cost."

"I never thought of it, but you're right," Frank Reasoner said, admiring the watch. "But not a very good pickup."

"I can get a pretty good one for two or three hundred dollars," John Henry said.

"I figure that if this watch gets through the punishment that I put it through over here, I'll pass it down as an heirloom," Frank Reasoner said.

"Good watch like that will last," John Henry said. "Lot longer than most of us."

"Maybe," Frank Reasoner said.

"You mind if I get a little critical, sir?" John Henry asked.

"Probably," Frank Reasoner said, "but you're gonna tell me anyway, aren't you."

"I find it pretty incredible that anyone would plan a reconnaissance patrol of a reinforced platoon to go up a road through some pretty hostile villages," John Henry said. "And they don't have any prep fire or artillery or anything ahead of it. Why I think that's—"

"Downright stupid!" Frank Reasoner said, finishing the sentence for the first sergeant. "I've heard it already. It's not my plan. We've gotta carry out the mission."

"Right," John Henry said. "Go up that road and get ambushed sure as hell."

"You said yourself that we can have the cavalry over the mountaintop in a matter of seconds," Frank Reasoner said. "This will work like a hammer and anvil. We're the anvil and 9th Marines has the big hammer to drop."

"I could just as easily call it a pork and frying pan maneuver too," John Henry said sarcastically. "We're the pork, 9th Marines is holding the frying pan, and those villages are the fire. Trick is to keep the pork out of the fire. Especially when the frying pan is back in the rear with the gear."

"I look at it as a challenge," Frank Reasoner said. "This will be the deepest probe that any of our ground forces have made down there. We're going to be the first. This is something significant for Alpha Company."

An hour later Frank Reasoner stood at the center of a circle of Marines from first platoon. Lieutenant Bill Henderson stood at one side and scratched notes in a green memo book that he carried in his breast pocket. John Henry stood next to him.

The men sat on the dirt, and each one had a notebook similar to Lieutenant Henderson's. B. C. Collins, Freddy Murray, and Jim Shockley sat near the front and listened as Frank Reasoner told them what he had told Pat Collins that morning and John Henry an hour ago.

"We will chop out at daylight, so that means that you will be getting your gear on in the dark," Frank Reasoner said. "When we launch out, we can't come back to get what you forgot, so, team leaders, make sure that your men have it all when we leave.

"Once we set down at Dai Loc, First Sergeant Henry and a radio team will set up comm at the old fort. Chances are they will be able to observe us most of the way from that position. We will stay in contact with the first sergeant, and if we get hit, we will immediately call for support.

"This represents the farthest patrol south that any unit has gone on. We will be invading unknown hamlets and they are considered hostile, so we must be on our toes at all times. We must be aggressive and decisive. This patrol will be looked at with significance. I don't intend to take any unnecessary risks, but mark my words, we will be tough out there. We will be aggressive.

"I will lead this patrol along with Lieutenant Henderson, not because he isn't an able leader, but because the opportunity for significant action is great.

"I want you to think about that so that you will know what kind of fighting spirit I expect. We will show everyone that Alpha Company is the hardest outfit over here."

When Frank Reasoner finished, Bill Henderson's platoon clapped and cheered with true football locker room spirit. They believed in themselves too, and it felt good to know that they were going out to fight with no holds barred. Yet somewhere in the back of each man's head, he wondered.

"This guy is fucking crazy," B. C. Collins growled under his breath as the men stood dusting off their trousers and preparing to make final checks of their gear while they still had some of the quickly fading daylight left.

A Marine looked at Collins. "You call him nuts? I've seen you in action, and then nobody is as wild as your daddy, Mad Man Collins. Shit, this guy's just another lunatic like the rest of us. That shouldn't scare you."

"I don't mean to rob him of any gunsmoke," B.C. said. "He just sounded a little spooky."

"Yeah," the Marine said, "that's something he must have picked up at West Point. I hear that all those Ring Bearers are nutty about medals and shit like that up there."

"Fuck it," B. C. Collins said. "As long as he's in front, he can get all the medals he wants. Our team is in the rear, pulling tail-end Charlie."

"The way they snipe our asses," the Marine said as they walked to their tent, "I think I'd rather walk point."

"Yeah," B. C. Collins said, "point in a hooker patrol in Da Nang, I bet."

## • 9 •

FOG LAY ACROSS THE RICE FIELDS AND THE SHALLOW SLOPES AND low bluffs along the Cau Do River as Pat Collins and his men paddled their small, black rubber boats upriver to a dense thicket of rushes and low bushes where they quietly stepped ashore in gray silence an hour before dawn.

Each man had covered his face with dark and light green camouflage paint from a hard stick that nearly took off their skin as they rubbed it on their cheeks and necks, hiding their human glow.

Several of the men wore broad-brimmed bush hats. Pat Collins had taken a large, black metal Marine Corps emblem and had fastened it to the front of his. Many of them also had exchanged their green sateen utility uniforms for those designed by the Army for jungle wear: a lighter variety of garb made of thin, ripstop material; they featured large patch-pockets sewn at a slant on the chests of the baggy jackets and even larger pockets that ballooned out on the legs of the trousers.

Once Pat Collins's Marines had hidden the small boats, a team at a time moved silently along the patchwork of hedgerows and grass-covered dikes that bordered the rice fields that surrounded Duong Son (1), the first hamlet southwest of the Phong Le Bridge.

As they walked, the captain could hear dogs barking and roosters crowing and other sounds of the new day already awakening in the small hamlet that he and his company swiftly but silently maneuvered around. And while they crept, they kept a careful watch for those who might see them and sound the alarm.

## • 10 •

NO ONE COULD RECALL WHETHER THE OLD MAN HAD RETURNED TO the village, nor did they take notice that he had not. The monks at the temple worried, but the old priest had left on other occasions and had always returned safely one or two days later from his journey.

As they rang the temple bell and its deep-bellied voice cascaded across the rice fields and drifted over the low bluffs of the Song Cau Do and echoed into the hills that rose from the lowlands north and west of the two great bridges that crossed the river, the young men with their heads shaved smooth and their bodies wrapped in yellow cloth thought of the priest but believed that he would return; if not today, tomorrow.

The sound of the bell fell silent against the drone of Marine UH-34 helicopters that replaced its melodic base tone. One by one the aircraft hovered down near the Dai Loc fort like gigantic green locusts, blowing sand and leaves and branches out from their whirling wings. As each helicopter settled on its wheels, a squad of Frank Reasoner's Marines scrambled from the beast's belly and then, one by one, the roaring machines shuddered and lifted away, bound to Da Nang where hot coffee waited for the crews.

"Looking good this morning," Frank Reasoner said, slapping John Henry across the shoulders. "We'll have a final coordinating session here, and then we're off, down that yellow brick road to see the wizard."

"You know, you ought to let Lieutenant Henderson take this patrol, they really don't need you," John Henry said to the lieutenant, hoping this one last plea might catch him with a fresh and more conservative perspective. "I honestly don't like anything about the setup of this patrol, no prep fire, no nothing."

"Too many operations out here, I guess," Reasoner said quickly. "We have two battalions over to our right, including Pat Collins and Dingin' Deadly Delta. Lots of activity. Besides, there're supposed to be Popular Forces coming up from the south to rendezvous with us. Artillery fire might get them, although for a lot of people that would be a major improvement."

"I have a great idea, sir," John Henry said. "We have comm right here with the patrol. Why, if they got into action, we could jump on a helicopter and be there in seconds. We can see damn near the whole patrol route from here."

"John, I wish you could hear how you sound," Frank Reasoner said. "Like some old mother hen. I need to be out there with this patrol. It's too much for one officer because of all the extra bodies we have in tow.

There's that dog team and the PF people and a group of Regional forces. I can't dump it all on Bill Henderson and then jockey the unit from up here. I've made up my mind, John. I've got to go." Then he took hold of his collar with his fingers and shook the silver bar pinned on it at John Henry. "Okay?"

"I'm gonna stay on the net the whole time," John Henry said, now that Frank Reasoner had set his mind to going. "You get the slightest hint of trouble, you call me. Remember, you'll be way off with no flanking support and your only hope is in the reaction time of a Sparrow Hawk unit."

"I'm depending on you to do that," Frank Reasoner said, and he hugged John Henry over his shoulders with one arm. "We're eating up too much daylight as it is," and he checked his Rolex watch. "With us launching out at fifteen-thirty, it'll be late afternoon before we hit. An My (1) and that's just the start of the hamlets that we're supposed to explore."

"Watch your ass and don't break your son's watch," John Henry said. "I'll be up on the net, just shout for help and I'll get it there."

## •11•

THE WHINING SOUND OF SERVO MOTORS CLOSING THE GREAT BACK door of the Air Force C-141 cargo jet awoke Doc Thomas, and he banged his head against the corner of the wooden crate next to which he had fallen asleep. He still limped from his wounds, but the news that III MAF had opened the TAOR south of Da Nang had disturbed him so much that he sneaked out of the military hospital on Guam at four o'clock that morning. He had to get back to his company.

In Guam, life focused on B-52 pilots flying missions over Vietnam and worried little about Marines or corpsmen in the hospital, recovering from wounds they had received while the bombers flew overhead.

No one noticed Doc Thomas when he slipped behind the shrubs wearing blue bedroom slippers and a matching blue hospital gown with the back opened to his naked butt. No one noticed either when he slipped behind cases of supplies stacked on the flight line and ran to the waiting Air Force C-141 that sat with its tailgate down while airmen operating yellow forklifts and carts busily pushed pallets of supplies inside the aircraft. No one noticed because they paid little attention to anything except the chores at hand. After all, no enemy had lurked here in twenty years and Vietnam was a long way away.

Even though the Navy designated him a corpsman, a noncombatant, Doc Thomas still regarded himself as a lead slinger from Delta Company, a Recon Warrior. He had believed from the day he had landed in South Vietnam that the enemy made his camp much closer than most people thought. He believed that the Viet Cong no doubt had stood on the beach at Da Nang, tossing flower wreaths, when the Marines landed. He believed that Charlie bided his time, watching his new enemy and would pick his place and time to fight. He also believed that Charlie anticipated and planned for the worst too.

Doc Thomas felt certain that Charlie lived in the flatland south of Da Nang where the palms and rice and thousands upon thousands of huts spread across the countryside from mountainside to shore. He felt certain too that Charlie, anticipating the worst, would prepare to face the Marines on that home turf, and he would fight hard from dug-in and fortified positions. In such a fight, the corpsman knew that his Marines would need him.

The heavy boxes shook and pulled against the nylon straps that kept them tied to the floor. He had picked a spot where a crewman would have to look straight down between the loads to see him, but that spot also seemed threatening when the big engines turned and the body shook and twisted as the airplane rolled faster and faster and then sprang back as the giant craft leapt into the air, roaring westward to Da Nang.

Once airborne, the threat ended. The straps had held the load in place. Now he knew that fate was with him, and as his confidence grew, Doc Thomas relaxed and fell asleep.

· 12 ·

S IR!" A LANCE CORPORAL CALLED OUT FROM THE BRUSH WHERE HE patrolled forward from the Phong Le Bridge. "We've got a dead gook over here."

The lieutenant rushed to the side of the young Marine who had shouted and looked to see what his men had found.

"Contact the rear and tell them that the Vietnamese liaison should come forward and take charge of this guy. Tell them we have found what looks like a murder victim," he said. The lieutenant looked at the lance corporal. "Move on out. I'll leave a handkerchief up here on the bushes so they can find him."

The lance corporal shuddered as he stepped from the bushes that flanked the roadside near the bridge. "They really hacked the shit out of that guy," he said, and then looked at his lieutenant. "Sir, why would they want to kill an old guy like that?"

"I don't know," he said. "You never know about these cats. Life doesn't mean much to them. Apparently not even a holy man's."

"Yeah," the lance corporal said as he walked on, in line with the rest of the company as they now stepped in a tightening arch that stretched around the northeast side of Duong Son (1). "Fucking gooks."

· 13 ·

THE OLD FRENCH FORT NAMED DAI LOC GREW SMALLER AND SMALLER in the distance on the far side of the Cau Do River, near the end of the Phong Le Bridge, as the two companies from 2nd Battalion and the one company from 1st Battalion pressed south-southwest toward the now awake hamlet.

A breeze drifted from the hills to the west and swept over the village and carried smoke from the cooking fires and the smells of pork and spice on the morning air. And while the three companies of Marines closed to their objective and faintly caught scent of breakfast, Pat Collins and his Marines sat quietly along a hedgerow that followed the railroad tracks north and separated Duong Son from a nearby complex of four other hamlets clustered to the northwest called Cam Ne.

At just before ten o'clock the first shots cracked across a rice field at the edge of Duong Son (1) and killed the Marine walking point for Bravo Company's lead platoon. In that instant, as the man whose life spread in a puddle beneath him and bled into the soil, a thousand shots recoiled back into the huts and lean-tos and the mud walls and haystacks and chicken coops, and they riddled the earth and pocked the walls of the temple and chipped notches from the brass bell and killed several of the National Liberation Front guerrillas who had seen the Marines approaching and quietly waited and killed the first man to venture into the open.

Seeing the result of the first shots and the size of the force that now approached their village, the nearly forty Viet Cong who had initiated the ambush rushed to the southwest side of the village and were about to escape across the rice fields, and join their comrades in Cam Ne, when Pat Collins shouted to his men, "Open fire!"

"Shit," one Marine cried out, "look at 'em run. There must be a hundred of them!"

Pat Collins's Marines chopped through the retreating Viet Cong, sending them back into their village to face the advancing platoons of Bravo Company that now stood poised at their final coordination line, less than 300 yards from the brushwood and mud fences that ringed the hamlet. Two Viet Cong bodies lay sprawled below a dike on the edge of a rice paddy while their comrades now opened fire on Company D.

"Control your fire," Pat Collins shouted to the men near him who jammed fresh magazines into their rifles and in a matter of seconds had them empty and were looking to reload. "Let them think about what to do next, don't just dump your ammo on them. They're not going anywhere."

The sudden excitement of the initial battle settled into a slower rhythm after the Viet Cong retreated back into the earthworks of their village. Collins's Marines now watched and fired sporadically as the Viet Cong tested the perimeter, hoping for a weak spot where they could break out and escape.

Suddenly from the left flank of Pat Collins's line a Marine shouted, "Corpsman! Corpsman! Man down!"

"What the hell?" Collins said, looking at Lieutenant John DelGrosso, who had his platoon nearest to the captain. "How could he get hit over there? He's behind solid cover!"

Smoke puffed from the brass shell casing after it tumbled to the mud behind the low rice paddy dike where the Viet Cong sniper lay. He pushed the bolt forward on his Mosin-Nagant and then turned the handle down, locking another 7.62-mm round into the rifle's chamber. But before he put his eye back to the short scope sight and fired the round, he picked up the spent shell casing and dropped it into the ragged canvas shoulder bag that lay at his elbow.

The enemy sniper with the Russian-made rifle and a dozen other Viet Cong guerrillas who lay in covered positions behind Pat Collins's company, pot-shooting the recon Marines, had low-crawled there from the hamlet called Cam Ne (1), less than 2,000 meters northwest of Duong Son (1) where the three companies of Marines now pushed on its northeast side. The reinforced Viet Cong company operating from Cam Ne had heard the shooting and began a counteroffensive against the flanks of the attacking Marine battalion and sent the sniper and rifle squad behind Company D.

John DelGrosso knelt next to Pat Collins and was about to ask what was going on when he saw more bullets slam into the dike and send several clods sailing into the sky. Then another Marine cried out for help.

"Goddamnit!" Pat Collins shouted at the lieutenant. "We've got fucking gooks behind us!"

Mud, dirt, chucks of wood, straw matting from huts, exploded sporadically through the air as the hundreds of bullets fired by the attacking Marine companies from the northeast side of Duong Son village number one struck in the hamlet, chasing the confused and darting Viet Cong. The forty men who had waited to ambush the Marines in the village that morning had planned to escape out the opposite side of the hamlet and join their compatriots in Cam Ne village number one until Delta Company surprised them. Now they rushed frantically from hut to hut searching for tunnels where they could hide and perhaps escape underground.

When the shooting began behind Duong Son, cutting off the guerrilla platoon there, the sniper had looked at his commander in Cam Ne and without saying a word understood what he had to do. He motioned to his squad and hurried to the edge of the village where they could see the Marines lined behind the dike nearly 2,000 yards away.

At first they ran along the main rice paddy dike, crouched with their rifles held near their ankles, skirting around a rice paddy recently filled with water and deep in mud. Then as they narrowed the distance between them and the Marines who blocked their comrades' retreat, they dropped to their knees and crawled to the line of bushes and small trees that grew beside the dry dike that drew parallel along the Marines' rear.

He had seen Pat Collins first, but lost his shot when the captain had rolled behind his radio operator, unknowing that the move had just saved him. The sniper swung the PU, 3.5-power scope sight along the dike where the Marines lay, shooting at the Viet Cong guerrillas pinned down in Duong Son, and found the back of a large man who seemed to be directing others. When he set the pointed sight post inside the scope directly on the center of the man's back, he nodded to his squad to open fire and then he fired, striking the Marine.

"John," Pat Collins told Lieutenant DelGrosso, "your platoon will set up a suppression fire on that hedgerow and try to keep Charlie busy while Vankat sweeps around and clears out that rats' nest. Third platoon will hold this blocking position so that those assholes over in the ville don't get any bright ideas."

John DelGrosso pointed to the hedgerow and his platoon took the direction immediately, lying down and opening fire into the low bushes, spraying debris, leaves, and dirt into the sniper's face.

He spit dirt from his mouth and sat up to see his men. He looked down the low dike where he and his platoon had hidden and raised his hand to signal that he was unhurt, but suddenly he fell backward, the side of his head spraying shreds of skin, bone, and blood onto the leaves that surrounded him.

None of John DelGrosso's Marines knew that they had just killed a man; all they could see were the leaves and bushes that hid the enemy. They kept firing and Bill Vankat raised his arm and pointed to the flank of the Viet Cong. He had no more than pointed when his platoon dashed, a man at a time, from the cover along the rice paddy dike and ran to the place where the hedgerow butted into the side of a dike that bordered another rice field. The position allowed them a perfect angle on the Viet Cong who now scrambled down the dike to the place where their leader had fallen.

Two of the men slung their SKS rifles across their backs and took the dead man by his arms and dragged him as they ran. The others began shooting back at John DelGrosso's men and at the advancing platoon of Bill Vankat.

"They're running back to that village," John DelGrosso shouted to Pat Collins. Then he cried out to his men, "Keep on them, don't let up."

Bill Vankat saw the men run too. "Open up on them," he shouted before his men had gotten to position. They fired as they ran and their bullets cut at an angle across those fired by John DelGrosso's men and forced the two men dragging their dead leader to drop him.

"Look!" an anxious guerrilla who was more a boy than a man shouted to several other young Vietnamese who watched as the main body of their reinforced company moved toward the Marines attacking from the northeast side of Duong Son. Their group had remained in Cam Ne as reserves to reinforce whoever needed help in their attack. As the boy pointed, the other guerrillas looked and saw their comrades now dashing, zigzagging across the open rice field.

The eight men still running for their lives saw the others in the village standing and waving them on. The village looked so close, yet the flooded rice field that they skirted going out stood between them and survival.

The two men who faced the water first turned and ran along its edge, along the low dike. The other six were about to follow when a bullet struck the second man and he splashed into the muddy water. His sudden death turned their panic into terror and the six men leapt into the knee-deep muck, flailing in the bog, struggling to cross the hundred yards of mud.

When the hail of gunfire opened from the village, Bill Vankat sent his men for cover. The sudden shower of lead from Cam Ne gave the men in the rice paddy the edge necessary to make it out and to the cover that the fortified village offered.

"John, get a head count," Pat Collins shouted as he saw Bill Vankat and his platoon running back to Delta Company's position.

"None killed, eight wounded," John DelGrosso called back.

"Get them together and chopped out of here while we have a chance," Collins said. It felt good to have no one killed in such a cross fire. It felt good too that the platoons had performed so well, pushing out the enemy that otherwise might have broken their blocking position and let out the trapped Viet Cong in Duong Son (1).

As the medevac helicopter lifted away his wounded Marines, Pat Collins could hear a heavier and more distant concentration of fire beyond the hedgerows and fields to his north where 2nd Battalion's western flank company now took hard licks from the reinforced Viet Cong company that had swept out of Cam Ne after them.

"Sounds like World War III over there," Pat Collins said to his radioman, who sat next to him with his face streaked with camouflage paint and dirt and sweat.

## • 14 •

AFTER A C-RATION LUNCH IN THE SHADE OF THE IRON BRIDGE, AT 3:30 P.M., July 12, 1965, Frank Reasoner motioned for Lieutenant Henderson to start the patrol of fifteen Marines and one corpsman across the bridge and down the road that would take them several kilometers south and several more west before they would reach their first objective hamlet.

According to his operation order, Frank Reasoner planned for his first and second platoons to spend the days of July 13 and 14 observing and the nights of the twelfth and thirteenth patrolling. Meanwhile First Sergeant Henry and the company headquarters section split duty manning the relay radios at Dai Loc and work as monitorial station and liaison group at 3rd Marine Regiment's command post.

Second platoon had chopped directly to LZ Pelican, where they would patrol and observe in a clover-shaped pattern during the next two days and nights. They would spend the first evening moving below and left of the landing zone to their patrol base, a center point where their left and right patrol circles converged. From the patrol base they covered the left circle the first night and the right circle the second night, and finished the third back to the landing zone on the third day. There they would wait until five o'clock for their afternoon choppers home.

First platoon, however, had the task of following a narrow roadway to a helicopter landing zone that they had designated LZ Parrot. Between Dai Loc and the landing zone lay three checkpoints, around which the platoon would progressively patrol during darkness and observe during light from now until the morning of July 14.

Then first platoon would spend the last day observing the area near LZ Parrot, moving into the landing zone at five o'clock that afternoon and catching their helicopters back to the company's base of operations near Da Nang.

John Henry felt a tightness build in his chest as the line of Marines stretched down the roadway under the afternoon sun. He watched as his friend and commander, Frank Reasoner, walked at the center of the column with the AR-15, which the Air Force had issued him to test, strapped loose over one shoulder.

## • 15 •

THE FIRST FIRE TEAM FROM BRAVO COMPANY, 9TH MARINES, TO reach the fence that ringed Duong Son (1) scrambled next to it for cover. The lance corporal who led the three other Marines waved to his squad leader to send the second team forward. Bravo Company had managed to push its way to a hedgerow that stood as the last cover between them and the village, and used it as their final coordination line for their attack. When the lieutenant saw his first squad now squatted at the fence, he waved his arm to the captain who then signaled the remaining company to attack.

"Fire in among the hooches," the lance corporal cried out and began shooting his M-14 across a sector of fire that interlocked with the Marines to his right and left. "Keep their heads down!" he shouted, knowing that the first squad now provided the covering fire that allowed the company to invade the village.

Seeing that the enemy had apparently abandoned their original emplacements, the lance corporal stood and dashed into the village, leading his fire team to the right where they would begin the sweep. It had gone so easily, but when the side of the hut sprang up and revealed the two Viet Cong who opened fire with their automatic rifles, all the lance corporal could think was that it had been too easy.

"Corpsman up!" he heard a voice cry. It sounded different somehow and when he tried to raise his head to see who had called for help, he found that he could not move. He could hear the intense fire cutting above him and the shouts of other Marines, apparently hit too, but he could do nothing but watch the clouds building to thunderheads above him.

As he lay, he could feel himself growing very tired; a rapidly growing need to sleep invaded him and he struggled to stay awake. He knew that he was dying. He had seen it. His blood loss made him feel tired and he cried out, trying to keep his eyes open. He felt the tears streaming down his face and no one came. Only more shooting. And the sky began to grow dark, and then he could only see red as his eyelids fell.

The lance corporal may have heard the explosion that killed the Viet Cong who manned the hut bunker. However, he never felt the two sets of hands that took hold of his shoulders and dragged him away from the front of the hut and laid him next to two other Marines who had died in the fight, not far from four Bravo Company Marines who lay wounded.

Bravo Company swept the village but found few of the Viet Cong who had fought them. When they blew the entrances to the tunnels and underground bunkers shut, they hoped that whoever had escaped into them had fallen victim to the collapsing earthworks. But no one would ever know for sure that they had killed the Viet Cong or if they had found a tunnel that led out of the village and opened into a hedgerow where they may have escaped to join their comrades in any of the several villages of the Cam Ne complex or in Duong Son (2) or Duong Son (3).

Grazing fire swept across the battlefront as the two companies from 9th Marines held the line that they had formed around the north and east side of Duong Son. With the reinforced company pushing closer to the flank of the Marines, they began to shift away from their support role of Bravo Company and now began concentrating their force against the Viet Cong who attacked them from the west.

"Pull them back," Lieutenant Colonel Scharnberg snarled over the radio to company commanders. "No point in walking into that meat grinder." He looked at his air liaison officer who sat at a small table inside the concrete bunker at Dai Loc fort where the battalion had established its operation headquarters and where First Sergeant John Henry now spoke on a radio in short phrases to Frank Reasoner and the platoon from Alpha Company as they pushed on southward. Scharnberg snapped at the ALO, "Get MAG-11 on the horn. Tell them I have a village that needs some heavy work."

"Sir," Pat Collins's radioman called out, "I just got word that the first objective is secure."

"Contact the platoon commanders and tell them to rally on my position in ten minutes," the captain shot back. A little more than three kilometers to his north, above the village of Cam Ne, a familiar, hollow coursing sound drew his attention. He turned back to his radioman and smiled. "Phantoms. Good-bye Charlie!"

The sounds grew louder and the hollow sounds rose to rumbles and then to thunder and then the earth shook and the shock wave of wave after wave of 500-pound bombs exploding slammed across the countryside.

"Damn!" John DelGrosso called out to Pat Collins. "I guess they got tired of screwing around. That's some big stuff."

"Noise never killed anyone," Pat Collins said. "That'll flatten the area, but you can count on Charlie to still be around there after the dust settles. Just like a fucking ant bed. You can burn 'em, stomp on 'em, and dig 'em up, but they still come back."

"I can't take this," someone behind Pat Collins mumbled, "I got used to the noise, now it's too quiet."

"You better enjoy it," Pat Collins said without turning his head.

Above them, a single propeller–driven plane tottered in the unstable air as it made a wide circle around the column of black smoke that rose from what remained of Cam Ne. Inside the O-1B spotter plane, the pilot looked to his left as he tilted down the wing and spiraled lower through the smoke, assessing the damage.

"Roger," he said, "confirm six enemy dead and secondary explosions in areas encircling the village, apparently the bombs cooked off Charlie's mine field."

Shading his eyes from the westward-moving sun, Pat Collins looked up, watching the spotter plane make several more circles and then it dipped its wing right and climbed away toward the northeast. The sun made him sneeze and he heard the Marine behind him say, "God bless you, sir."

It struck him, as he trudged on the slow march back to the Dai Loc fort and the Phong Le Bridge, that despite the ugliness and death they had encountered it had not erased this man's good nature. "Thank you," Pat Collins said.

· **16** ·

THE RUMBLE OF BOMBS EXPLODING AND THE SQUALL OF THE DIVING Phantom jets at Cam Ne caught Corporal Bryant C. Collins's ear as he walked with his reconnaissance team near the rear of the column. He turned to Lance Corporal Freddy Murray, who walked a few paces to his right, and smiled. "Charlie's catchin' hell somewhere," he whispered.

Frank Reasoner looked ahead where his two point men had stopped. He guessed that they were listening to the sound of the faraway battle too. The rumble made him feel uneasy. It confirmed his belief that this was where Charlie lived. That the Viet Cong had to be dug in deep and solidly to warrant such a heavy air strike.

His days at West Point taught him to press on, however, and the worry of who might be hurt or possibly even killed was something that he had to keep out of his mind. Right now, even though the heavy fighting was several kilometers northeast of his position, he knew that his two small patrols, farther south from friendly lines than any other American units had gone until now, risked perhaps even greater danger.

"Indian country," the intelligence officer had said. "Bet there's nothing but bad guys down there."

Frank Reasoner had found it amusing that they should label enemy territory "Indian country." And at the same time, nothing seemed more appropriate—men from the civilized west fighting savage natives. It was, in many respects, like cowboys and Indians.

The sunlight shone down in smoky shafts through the canopy of trees that lined the roadway along which the patrol walked while the oven-hot air teamed with insects and smelled of earth and decay. The narrow road, which at times was no more than a cow trail, wound through the flat farm country and now led the platoon toward the series of An My villages that was their first objective. They had seen no enemy, but his sign was everywhere.

Any minute, Frank Reasoner told himself as he watched the two Marines at the point. A fight is near. He felt its certainty—that tension across his stomach and down his back that came when that little voice within his soul told him that the enemy was watching. He hoped that when the skirmish came, however, that he could be the one to pick the place and plan its execution. He wanted to see the enemy first.

When the bombing stopped, Frank Reasoner looked at his Rolex wristwatch. Its stainless-steel frame, square and polished around the black, round watch face set in its center, shone in the late afternoon sun. Five-thirty, he told himself as he rubbed the crystal with his thumb, wiping away a film of dirt and sweat that had gathered on it. He wanted to clear this objective and get set before nightfall.

Until now, at each hour, he had radioed John Henry, "Bravo Report. Alpha, Sierra, Sierra, Romeo, Sierra." All secure, situation remains the same. But as the patrol pushed along a bend in the road the lieutenant and most of his Marines knew this was probably about to change.

As the road turned, Frank Reasoner could see the first village. A deep ditch curved from along the roadway around the left side of the village and out toward a tree line and rice field beyond. On the right, the line of trees that surrounded the road curved next to the village and followed in a curve around a rice field beyond the village to a stand of trees that connected them with the trees on the left.

Staff Sergeant Jimmy Knee and First Lieutenant Bill Henderson lay close to Frank Reasoner and watched the village from behind the cover that the bend in the tree-lined roadway offered them. As the road turned toward the village, all cover fell away, however. The twenty to thirty meters of open roadway that led straight into the village gave the enemy a small but adequate killing zone.

"There!" Jimmy Knee said and pointed to a hut that sat to the left of where the road entered the village. "See? The stack of sandbags behind the brush fence. A VC just crawled behind there."

Frank Reasoner watched and saw nothing, but when one of the two Marines who lay ahead of them at the roadside got to his knees and began to crawl back to cover and a sniper's bullet slammed into the embankment at the Marine's feet, the lieutenant realized that Jimmy Knee was right. "Pass the word back to sit tight," Reasoner said. "We've got VC up front."

By the time the message reached the rear of the platoon where B. C. Collins and Freddy Murray sat, just ahead of the squad of South Vietnamese Popular Force soldiers that also reinforced the platoon, per the Rules of Engagement, the word had become, "VC up front."

"Come on Freddy," B. C. Collins said to Lance Corporal Murray, who had correctly heard the comment from ahead, "VC up front." But B. C. Collins had heard, "B.C. up front."

Freddy Murray did not realize the mistake and waited until Corporal Collins had moved ten paces ahead of him before he stood to go forward.

As B. C. Collins made the turn that opened to the village, he saw Lieutenant Reasoner, Lance Corporals Jim Shockley and Lindy Hall, Staff Sergeant Knee, and Lieutenant Henderson hugging the ground at the embankment on the side of the road.

"You want me, sir?" B. C. Collins called ahead as he and Freddy Murray walked close to where the lead element of the patrol lay, hugging the ground.

"What the fuck you two doing here?" Reasoner growled at Collins and glanced at Murray who squatted behind the corporal. "Get down, B.C.! You want your fucking head blown off? We've got VC up front."

When Frank Reasoner said that, B. C. Collins realized his error and squatted just as a volley of gunfire raked the brush and branches above him. "I thought you said B.C. up front, sir," he said, trying to explain himself. Then a second spray of gunfire struck closer to the corporal.

"Shit!" Collins said as he scrambled next to Reasoner. "That sniper is just behind that clump of trees up there."

"I see him," Jimmy Knee said.

"Well," Frank Reasoner said, looking at B. C. Collins, "since you're so fucking bright, why don't you go with Staff Sergeant Knee and get him."

"You got it, sir," Collins said, snatching up his rifle.

Jimmy Knee picked up his rifle too and as B. C. Collins moved toward the huts along the left side of the road, Knee walked at the corporal's right.

"I think he slipped back into the ville," Knew said, holding his M-14 pointed ahead of him, his finger resting on the trigger and the rifle's selector switch turned to the automatic position.

"No. Look there!" Collins said and opened fire as the Viet Cong raised above the grassy clump at the base of the trees.

Jimmy Knee immediately pulled his trigger and released a volley into the clump with Collins's shots. The combination of their fire sent the guerrilla tumbling backward.

As he fired, B. C. Collins saw flashes of green-clad figures running behind the trees and started to turn his fire on them, but then he thought, Shit, those must be the PFs coming on our flank. I could have killed one of them.

"Let's go ahead into the ville and check it out," Jimmy Knee said, walking to where the dead guerrilla lay. He looked back at Frank Reasoner and motioned to the village. When the lieutenant put his thumb in the air, both men stepped past the brush and pole fence that encircled the hamlet.

Nothing moved in the village, no chickens, no dogs, no living creature. Not even birds sang near and this put both Marines on edge. They had cleared the first two huts and started around the third when sudden gunfire cracked the silence and Jimmy Knee let out a yell from the pain that knifed through his upper thigh.

"Get out!" he shouted to Collins, who had dropped to one knee and began firing at the side of the hut where several baskets filled with rice stood and served as cover for their assailant.

Collins saw the staff sergeant limp and immediately ran to the Marine and held him on his injured side. "Can you run?" he asked.

"Yeah, let's didi on outta here," Knee said, putting his weight on B. C. Collins and starting to hobble in a run. The bullets struck above them and behind them but did not hit either man again.

"Another sniper in the ville, but I didn't see anything else except our PFs running on the flank," B. C. Collins said to Frank Reasoner.

"You sure?" Frank Reasoner asked. "I didn't send them around there."

"Well, somebody in uniforms or ponchos were dashing around our flank," Collins said as Jimmy Knee lay in the undergrowth and watched as the corpsman cut his trouser leg at the wound and began work to stop the bleeding.

"Henderson," Reasoner said, "you take half the platoon and Staff Sergeant Knee, and get in that ditch to the left and follow it around the flank." Then Reasoner looked at Collins. "You and Murray take the point. The rest of us will clear the village and Lieutenant Henderson and his section can catch 'em as they run out."

B. C. Collins and Freddy Murray cautiously walked on each side of the road and entered the village. Behind them, Frank Reasoner and his grenadier, Lance Corporal Lindy Hall, walked, and behind them Lance Corporal Jim Shockley and Privates First Class Thorace L. Pannell, Kenneth R. Hahn, and Thomas Gatlin. Both Hall and Shockley carried radios strapped to packboards.

Frank Reasoner took the handset from the radio that Hall carried and put it to his ear. "Roger, received twenty rounds sniper fire at niner-two-two-six-zero-two. Returned fire and pursued with no success," Reasoner said to John Henry who sat close to his radio at Dai Loc, feeling tension build as he heard the lieutenant report his situation.

As John Henry waited for further developments to squawk over the radio, Frank Reasoner followed Collins and Murray at the point with

Lindy Hall and Jim Shockley at his sides and the three others at his rear. The eight Marines followed their patrol route along the road, leaving the village in the distance, and through a series of dry rice fields.

While moving well into the openness of the road stretching through the rice fields and then bending into a distant line of trees, Collins and Murray began to study the cover that it could provide an enemy ambush. Something was unnatural. The lack of birds, perhaps? The strangeness of the way the bushes seemed to bunch together at the base of the trees, slightly on a rise and almost forming a wall, blocking off any avenue over the higher ground.

"I don't like it," Reasoner said and looked at Lindy Hall. "Go ahead and move about ten more meters over to my right. I want to get everyone spread as far apart as possible."

As the lieutenant moved ahead, he looked back to catch a glimpse of the three Marines who were spread in an echelon, far behind him. He looked to his left and saw the sweat running off Jim Shockley's face and noticed the concern in his eyes. Frank Reasoner knew that if any sizable enemy force lay waiting anywhere near, his patrol would confront them at any moment.

As the eight men drew closer to the tree line, he thought again about the sniper in the village. How he could have served only as a lure. A piece of bait to draw the patrol into a trap.

He was angry that he did not see any enemy in the village. He remembered his first tactics classes at West Point and an early lesson taught about Hannibal's legion in the Pyrenees. How Hannibal was outnumbered and faced a better-armed enemy, but that he took advantage of the high ground, placing his bowmen on the mountainsides that surrounded a valley. He sent out a small force to engage the great army and then retreated into the valley, drawing the great army behind them in close pursuit. Once the massive force had entered the valley, Hannibal's legion closed the valley entrance and from above his bowmen slaughtered the enemy to the last man.

Frank Reasoner looked far to his left and saw Bill Henderson and his men moving at his flank. Surely if he had been lured into such a trap, the flanking force would offset it and allow them an escape.

It had been forty-five minutes since they had encountered the sniper. Even at 6:15 the afternoon heat of July 12, 1965, baked B. C. Collins's head beneath his bush hat as he drew nearer and nearer to the place where the roadway made a bend through the trees on the far side of the clearing. He glanced over his shoulder to see Frank Reasoner twenty meters behind him and the five other Marines.

Hard clods baked together by the summer sun twisted under B. C. Collins's feet and he guessed that in the past several years of conflict, the farmers here had obviously quit trying to grow crops in this field. Now only weeds wilting in the 100-degree temperatures grew on this uncomfortable land and regenerated their annual crops of bristling sharp spines, thorns, and stickers.

"Heads up!" he heard the lieutenant say in a low voice. He saw Frank Reasoner's face and followed his glance to the bend in the road where three men, each wearing ponchos and helmets, dashed for cover behind the trees.

B. C. Collins looked to his right and saw Freddy Murray had raised his hand to point toward something in the trees, but before he even spoke, the surprise written on his face told B. C. Collins the message that this young Marine's voice would never carry. Just as he opened his mouth to shout and warn off the patrol, a bullet cracked out from the trees and sent the Marine crashing into the scorched-dry weeds.

"Say something!" Collins shouted to him after he too had hit the ground, diving for cover and then rolling hard to his right, trying to position himself closer to his downed brother. "You still alive?"

"I'm fine!" Murray shouted back. "Damn near caught me, but I'm fine."

"Stay cool," Collins yelled and raised to his knees, trying to see where the Viet Cong were hiding.

Directly ahead, three men with rifles at their shoulders fired at the other Marines diving for cover, and now stood behind the brush that hid their ambush.

B. C. Collins, in quick succession, put his sights on the first man and sent a 7.62-mm bullet smashing into his skull, followed through with a shot to the second man's chest, and then caught the third man in the back as he dove for cover.

Frank Reasoner had seen both point men drop. He reacted with a diving roll himself and was on his knees when he saw Corporal Collins raise and fire and drop the three VC.

"Collins," Reasoner yelled, "I'll get help. You two keep the road open."

"Right, sir!" Collins shouted. "You hear that, Freddy?"

"Yeah," Murray said.

"How you feel?" B. C. Collins asked, concerned that Freddy Murray's wound might be worse than his partner had told him. "You need to get to the rear or can you help here?"

"I'm fine, I ain't hit," Murray shouted, "but this is all fucked up, look!" He pointed to their right flank where a line of enemy soldiers began shooting a grazing fire across the field.

"We're in the middle of a horseshoe ambush!" Collins shouted back, and began firing into the enemy positions that also opened fire to the Marines' left, concentrating most of their work into the ditch where Bill Henderson and the rest of the platoon had scrambled.

Frank Reasoner and Lindy Hall and PFC Kenneth Hahn had dived to a low paddy dike that bordered the road. Before they could get to the cover, however, Hall, who carried an M-79 grenade launcher along with his backpacked radio, had caught a bullet in his arm and now bled badly.

As they lay tight against the dirt bank, Frank Reasoner shouted on the radio, "Fuck it, John. We're in some real shit! We've gotta have helicopters and help now. We've got wounded and oppose a force of about one hundred uniformed enemy!"

"I'll call for the Sparrow Hawk. Confirm grid coordinates niner-two-seven-six-zero-eight," John Henry said, but there was no answer. He waited and heard only the crackle of dead air. He looked at the South Vietnamese Marine who waited with him at the radio relay station at Dai Loc. "Looks bad, Dai We."

Jim Shockley also dove to the low dike that ran near the road when the shooting started. He could see Hahn beyond the lieutenant, defending the small patrol's left flank. When Shockley saw Lindy Hall lying behind the dike several meters ahead of him, bleeding badly, and Frank Reasoner trying to jam the broken antenna back into his radio where a bullet had sheared it off, the lance corporal decided that he had to get to the lieutenant so that he could make radio contact with First Sergeant Henry and get help.

He ran hard and then dove headlong into the hard earth beside Reasoner. Automatic rifles chattered from nests all along two sides of the clearing while at least two machine-gun crews laid down a grazing fire that swept across the field, snapping the thorny brush and weeds and kicking up small spouts of earth and hitting every foot of ground around Reasoner's position.

The lieutenant raised to his knees and again opened fire with his rifle, this time killing two Viet Cong and silencing one of the machine guns.

"You hit?" Reasoner asked Shockley.

"No, sir," Shockley said. "I thought you could use the backup radio."

"Good man," Reasoner said, reaching for the handset.

Just as Jim Shockley leaned his back toward Frank Reasoner, to allow him to get to the handset, he pushed his elbow above the top of the dike.

Suddenly a bullet snapped the lance corporal's arm back, shattering the bone. It didn't really hurt at first, and Jim Shockley was not sure if the bullet had actually hit him until he saw his twisted and bloody arm.

"We've gotta get outta here," Reasoner said. "There's at least a company of VC up here. No way our little patrol can tangle with them. There's just too many. How do you feel?"

"I'll get by sir," Shockley said with clenched teeth, now beginning to feel the pain of his wound.

"Let's get that radio off, and you've got to make a run for that ditch where Lieutenant Henderson has the rest of the platoon under cover," Frank Reasoner said, pulling the radio off Jim Shockley's back.

Once he was clear of the radio, Jim Shockley looked across the thirty yards of open ground where he could see Bill Henderson and the remainder of the patrol, firing into a line of uniformed enemy soldiers who were closing on their position.

Shockley looked ahead and saw the grazing fire sweeping across the open ground. If I stand up to run, they'll hit me. If I crawl that's too slow, he told himself.

Once he had gathered his nerve, he pushed his injured arm snugly inside his shirt and began rolling as fast as he could across the open land.

B. C. Collins turned to look back at Frank Reasoner and saw the lieutenant with the handset of Shockley's radio at his ear. He watched as Jim Shockley began rolling across the open land and was about to open fire on the enemy machine-gun nest that began firing at the rolling Marine when Shockley screamed in pain as another bullet struck him.

Jim Shockley could not move. The heavy bullet had devastated him and when he tried to move, he nearly passed out.

Frank Reasoner saw the wounded man and watched the dirt exploding into the air all around him as the enemy machine gunners fired at him as though he was their aiming point.

"I've got more wounded!" he shouted at John Henry on the radio. "Get the helicopters in here now!"

"Roger that, sir," John Henry said. "I've got the choppers fragged."

As he spoke, John Henry looked south, below the fort and the Phong Le Bridge, and in the dimming light of late afternoon, he could see the streams of opposing tracers beyond the village.

"I can see your position," John Henry said in a voice strained by the tension of the battle. He felt helpless as he watched. "The choppers should be coming at any minute. Try to hold on."

"Collins!" Frank Reasoner shouted to the corporal who now fired through his third full magazine of ammunition. "How many men over there?"

"Two, sir!" Collins answered.

"Move on back here to Hall and Hahn and give the wounded some cover fire!" Reasoner told Collins and Murray. "I've got to get to Shockley!"

"Yes, sir," B. C. Collins shouted back.

"I'm going to need some cover fire so that the wounded can get back to the rear," Reasoner said. "I'll take care of Shockley if you can cover me."

B. C. Collins laid down a cover fire and Freddy Murray dashed for the low dike where Frank Reasoner, Kenneth Hahn, and Lindy Hall waited. In a moment, Collins followed, diving behind the dike. When the two Marines reached their commander's position, Freddy Murray pulled out his field dressing and began wrapping it around Lindy Hall's arm.

"Shockley!" Reasoner shouted.

"Sir!" Jim Shockley cried back.

"Hold your ground!" Reasoner shouted. "I'm coming over."

"Don't do it, sir!" Shockley cried out. "I'm never gonna make it! I'm hit too bad! Take care of the others!"

Freddy Murray heard the lance corporal's cries. His heart sank with the thought that Shockley might be dead. Then he watched the lieutenant, ignoring his radioman's plea.

Frank Reasoner felt his head and noticed that he had lost his bush hat. Sweat streamed in his eyes and he rubbed his close-cut hair, sending a spray of water into the air and showering onto his face.

It was just like a place they called Dragons' Teeth back at The Basic School at Quantico: open terrain and an enemy hidden in the trees. Back then they had been enlisted Marines working as aggressors, and they had tanks, but he and his company had still won the fight there. Only the bullets weren't real, and there were no Marines lying in the dirt, bleeding and near death.

He said a short prayer and then sprang from behind the dike. The green and the brown and the sky blurred as he leapt in his typical all-American athletic fashion. He heard the machine gun still chopping and the rattling chatter of the automatic rifles chewing through the air, and he heard what sounded like someone shouting to him.

"Sir!" B. C. Collins screamed as he saw his lieutenant spring from the dike, run several steps, and then suddenly leap backward.

"Sir! Goddamnit, sir! Say something!" Collins cried out desperately, but there was no response. There was no motion where his lieutenant fell. There was only the sounds of the enemy automatic rifles and machine gun chewing through the clearing.

Jim Shockley still lay needing help, but cried out to his comrades, "The lieutenant's down. He's hit real bad! You guys don't worry about me!"

Collins looked at the three Marines and said, "I'm going out after the skipper and Shockley. If I don't get back here in a couple of minutes, lads, that means I'm dead. You guys go ahead and drag your asses out with what you have or you're gonna die."

"We're not doing any good out here," Freddy Murray said and looked at Lindy Hall, who now had his arm wrapped tightly and could do little more than offer moral support to his fellows. "Go ahead and start for that ditch. Hahn and I will follow you and try to give you some cover."

Hall pushed his way from the small dike that ran along the roadway, and Freddy Murray followed him with PFC Hahn bringing up the rear, shooting and running.

Between them and the ditch, the trio of Marines saw a grave and took cover behind the headstone and raised earth.

"Take off, B.C.," Murray shouted to Collins. "We'll cover you from here!"

Satisfied that his three buddies now had better cover and could direct their fire in his assistance, B. C. Collins scrambled to where Jim Shockley lay. "Jesus H," he said, seeing the several wounds on Shockley's body, "you really took some hits, lad. Can you move on your own?"

Shockley could only groan, but began trying to roll.

"I gotta check on the skipper," Collins said and then bolted away.

"Sir!" Collins shouted again, thinking of Frank Reasoner and that just by chance he might still be alive, only badly wounded and unable to make a sound.

While Freddy Murray and Kenneth Hahn directed their covering fire, B. C. Collins fought his way to the spot in the field where Frank Reasoner lay. He saw that the lieutenant had died almost at the instant that the bullet had struck his neck.

"Collins!" Freddy Murray shouted. "While you're out there, get the radio! We'll cover you!"

Hoping to call in air or artillery, he scrambled for the radio that lay on the packboard a few meters away from the lieutenant's feet. But when the corporal rolled it over, he saw the riddling that it had taken from the machine gun.

"Motherfuckers!" Collins roared and shot into the tree line, bringing back another volley of fire. With that burst, he spent the last of his M-14's ammunition.

"Fuck it," he growled and field-stripped the M-14, throwing its parts in several directions and shoving its bolt in his pocket. The AR-15 that Frank Reasoner had been testing for the Air Force lay next to his body and B. C. Collins took it along with the ammunition pouches and map case that had belonged to his dead commander.

"We've got a radio and we're up on the net!" a Marine shouted to Freddy Murray from the ditch where the remaining platoon now waited and offered what supporting fire they could while at the same time protecting themselves.

"Forget the radio, B.C.!" Murray shouted to Collins. "What about the skipper?"

"Skipper's dead!" Collins shouted.

"Get on back to our position," Murray called back. "We gotta take out that machine gun or Shockley's had it too!"

B. C. Collins could only think, Where's the damn grenade launcher?

He shouted to Lindy Hall, "The M-79! Can you see it?"

"Yeah!" the Marine answered. "Hahn's got it."

"Keep what you've got, I'm coming over," Collins shouted, and then he ran, dodging through the hail of gunfire.

"Come on," Collins growled at Kenneth Hahn and tossed him Lindy Hall's pack filled with 40-mm grenades for the M-79. "Let's go blow away that gun."

He didn't wait for an answer but leapt to his feet and ran toward the place in the tree line where the machine gun continued to pour its fire into the field, trying to finish off Jim Shockley, hitting him a third and a fourth time.

With the grenade launcher in hand, Kenneth Hahn instinctively ran close to Collins as the corporal fired the small rifle at the tree line.

As he ran, B. C. Collins could see the two men behind the big gun pulling on its butt, swinging the stream of tracers toward him and Hahn.

"You better fucking hurry, Charlie!" Collins shouted at them as Hahn aimed the grenade launcher straight at the machine gunners and sent the projectile into them.

The two Marines dove and rolled again just as the grenade exploded.

"Freddy!" B. C. Collins shouted to his partner, who had continued to fire and cover the two Marines as best he could.

"Yeah," Murray called back.

"Coming in!" Collins cried back and then he and Hahn scrambled to the grave where Murray and Lindy Hall waited.

"Hall," Murray said, tightening the bandage on the Marine's arm, "go ahead and make a run for the ditch." Then he looked at Collins. "We gotta get the skipper and Shockley, and all of us get out of here."

Breathless, Collins nodded and began to crawl to where Frank Reasoner lay dead, and beyond him where Jim Shockley lay motionless and bleeding badly from several serious wounds.

"We're going after the casualties!" Murray shouted toward the ditch. "We're gonna need a little help up front!"

In the fading light, Privates First Class Thorace L. Pannell and Thomas Gatlin scrambled from the ditch as Lindy Hall rolled into its cover. In a moment they had joined Freddy Murray and began crawling to where Frank Reasoner lay.

B. C. Collins had already reached the lieutenant's body and began pulling him. Freddy Murray scrambled to his side and helped drag their dead commander thirty yards before Pannell reached them. Then the three Marines ran to the ditch, carrying the lieutenant.

As the Marines reached the ditch, Collins released his hold on the fallen commander, and dashed to where Jim Shockley lay.

"I want you to just lay still," Collins told Shockley. "You're gonna hurt like a motherfucker when I roll you over, but I've got to do it to get you out."

B. C. Collins took Jim Shockley's shirt collar in his hand and rolled him onto his back. The wounded Marine cried out as the corporal pulled him snug against his back and began to low-crawl toward the ditch.

It was not long before Murray, Pannell, and Gatlin reached Collins and Shockley, and then carried the wounded Marine toward the road where they met Hahn and a radioman.

As the group of Marines reached the ditch, B. C. Collins watched as several more hands grabbed Jim Shockley and pulled him down where the corpsman began his work on the wounds.

"Doc, once you get him ready," he said, "we're all vacating this little garden spot."

Collins could see that Lieutenant Henderson, who had now maneuvered to the rear with the remainder of the platoon, was holding their ground, waiting for the helicopters.

With the Marines behind the relative cover offered by the ditch, the enemy firing had stopped. Cautiously, the men began moving along the road, back to the rear where Lieutenant Henderson waited.

"Freddy," B. C. Collins said, "you think you can get these lads back to Lieutenant Henderson's position?"

"Yeah," Freddy Murray said. "I think we're out of the fight now."

"Then you get these lads back and I'll worry about Lieutenant Reasoner," B. C. Collins said.

"Sure, but don't you want help?" Murray asked.

"I've got this little toy rifle and the blooper," the corporal said. "You just get these lads back to safety. I'll probably catch you before you get there anyway."

While the Marines hurried along the road, carrying Jim Shockley, the enemy soldiers opened fire on them again.

The orange sky made silhouettes of the advancing line of soldiers that now closed in pursuit of the retreating Marines. When B. C. Collins saw them as he emerged from the ditch and back into the killing field once again, he snarled at them, and fired the AR-15 into the enemy line, dropping several of the surprised soldiers who thought that the fight had ended moments ago.

In the seconds that it took for the enemy to again open fire across the field, B. C. Collins lifted the dead Marine. "We never leave our own," he said softly, cradling Reasoner.

Then he heaved the limp body of his commander across his shoulders and turned toward where his comrades had retreated and now waited. As he ran, he reached around his waist with the AR-15 and fired the small rifle with one hand at the attacking Communists. Shooting and scrambling those final steps out of that killing field, bullets clipped through the weeds and snapped through the air around him, but none struck him.

When the helicopter lifted off, bound for Da Nang Air Base, carrying the body of Frank Reasoner, B. C. Collins sat next to him. He had refused to put down his commander until he was safely back to the landing zone where Bill Henderson had retreated with the platoon, well away from the cluster of villages. The helicopters had arrived just after dark, four hours after Jim Shockley had been wounded.

Bill Henderson sent Shockley and the other wounded out on the first bird and he sent Frank Reasoner and B. C. Collins out on the last.

Seeing the lieutenant's body rocking under the poncho with the motion of the helicopter, a great sadness grew in the young corporal's heart. Even though he was a Ring Bearer and B. C. Collins had only known him for six weeks, there was something that kept him at Frank Reasoner's side. Maybe it was because the lieutenant had been a snuffie like him, or that in that few minutes of intense tragedy, they had become brothers. Whatever it was, B. C. Collins felt bad.

The helicopter crew chief looked at the corporal sitting cross-legged next to the dead lieutenant, and felt a bolt of anger and grief cut through him too. He turned his face out toward the setting sun and watched the iron bridge and old French fort pass under their wheels. In the past two months he had taken many Marines wrapped in ponchos out of the field, and most had a sad-faced buddy sitting near them. He guessed that it would always be that way. It always hurts to see your brother die.

## • 17 •

I T FELT STRANGE TO HIM, LYING NEARLY NAKED, WRAPPED ONLY IN THE blue hospital gown with the back open. The cold air in the Air Force C-141 chilling him for the past several hours had left his muscles tight and aching, so when the sound of the engines dropped and he heard the servo motors driving down the flaps, a feeling of triumph gripped Doc Thomas. Oh, God! Finally, he said in his mind, as he shivered in the sheet-thin gown that he had tucked down tight around his ankles and drew his knees under his chin, trying to get warm.

When the weight of the wheels dropping down shook through the body of the plane, the wounded corpsman got to his feet and pushed himself back between the boxes strapped to the pallet. He looked at the webbed nylon straps shaking from their tension against the weight of the boxes and mumbled a quick prayer, just in case.

He could feel the plane squirm and sway as it settled toward the runway, slower and slower, bumping and tilting from a thermal rising in the hot afternoon and his heart raced, slamming against his chest and in his ears. "Oh, God. Please don't let these boxes break loose," he prayed aloud, knowing that his voice fell silent under the noises that the engines now made, crying their way to the ground.

The blast of hot air that invaded the cargo bay of the huge aircraft when the rear gate finally opened let him know that he was back in South Vietnam. No one looked between the boxes when the forklift drew out the pallet and carried it to the side of the runway where other inbound cargo sat still strapped and baking in the hot afternoon sun. No one noticed him when he slipped out either, or as he ran to a nearby hut, one hand behind him gripping shut the hospital gown.

Once he had gotten past the first line of buildings, he let go of the gown and jogged down the roadway that led to the compound where he knew 3rd Reconnaissance Battalion had several tents. As he ran, airmen of Marines working, digging bunkers, hauling supplies, driving trucks, busy, saw him. Live and let live, they all believed because their work was more important than worrying about some nut running in a powder-blue gown and slippers. He was someone else's problem.

The supply tent stood near the water buffalo and generator, and Doc Thomas did not stop running until he ducked inside the door. His back and legs hurt badly, and he looked at the dressing on his wound. It had colored dark yellow and brown in the center and he knew that he had to change it soon or fight infection.

"You got a corpsman kit?" he asked, breathing hard. His face dripped and his hair lay plastered flat on top where he had let it grow.

"Aren't you supposed to be laid up in Guam, Doc?" the corporal in the supply tent said. "If you're looking for Dirty Delta, they're all down south, where that iron bridge crosses the river at the old French fort."

"You didn't answer me," Thomas said. "I need to put a new dressing on and antiseptic. Don't you have a corpsman bag, or at least a first-aid kit?"

"You want to sign for a resupply?" the corporal said. "I've got some stuff for resupply, but you have to get drugs and stuff from the battalion aid station. You know that."

"Damnit!" Doc Thomas said. "I just want some bandage and iodine, monkey blood, anything antiseptic."

"Sure," the corporal said, walking back to a bin. He came back with a first-aid pouch, snapped it open, and handed the corpsman a field dressing and a bottle of antiseptic. "You want more, they'll outfit you down at that battalion aid station, but I wouldn't walk in there in your nightie. They might lock you up."

Doc Thomas glared back at the corporal as he untaped his wound's dressing and then poured the entire bottle of Merthiolate on the injury.

"Fuck me to tears, Doc!" the corporal said, watching the corpsman pant and weave with the sudden pain that the antiseptic generated as it dried. "That's gotta hurt like a motherfucker!"

"Not as bad as infection," Thomas said, gasping and regaining his legs. He unfolded the bandage and looked at the corporal. "Tape. The wider the better."

"Got some of this stuff that we ripped off to wrap bats and ankles when we play ball," the corporal said, pulling a dirty roll of two-inch-wide medical tape. "I guess you don't care what it looks like."

"That's fine," Thomas said, pulling off strips and ripping them with his teeth. "I need duce gear. Can you give me some? I'll sign a custody card, but I gotta have at least a war belt, helmet, and boots."

"As long as you sign the chit," the corporal said, dragging out a set already rigged together. "One of your guys got clipped pretty good up at

Ban Nha the other day. I haven't had a chance to square it away but it's all there and in good condition.

"Thanks," the corpsman said, slipping the suspender straps over his shoulders and adjusting the belt for his waist. He unlaced the boots and was about to slip them on his bare feet when he looked at the corporal. "Socks, got any?"

"I got some of mine I'll loan ya, but don't forget where you got them," the corporal said and tossed them to the corpsman. "You look pretty goofy, you know."

"Yeah," Thomas said, "you got some utilities?"

"Afraid not," the corporal said and laughed. "You're stuck with what you've got, unless some of your pards want to divvy up some of theirs."

"I'll get them," Thomas said. "You think I can get a chopper out there?"

"Like that?" the corporal said and laughed again.

"What the fuck else am I gonna do?" Thomas said.

"We got choppers going back and forth," the corporal said, "they'll either throw you in the can or take you. I'd just get on a chopper and hope that they don't give a shit."

"What about my rifle and magazines?" Thomas said.

"Check the armorer's bunker, but unless you got your rifle card, you ain't gonna get shit outta those boys," the corporal said.

"I ain't got shit," he said and then smiled. "I got taken out of the field, and they got my rifle. If they turned in my rifle, they gotta still have my rifle card too."

"Maybe," the corporal said. "I don't know about that shit. They might just help you out, but you know how they are with weapons. No ticket, no ride."

The sergeant in the bunker where they had stored the rifles hardly asked any questions. He recognized Doc Thomas and went to a steel box where he thumbed through alphabetic dividers and pulled out the card.

"Got you covered, Doc," he said, pulling the corpsman's rifle from the rack and handing it to him. "No charge for the cleaning, you can buy me a beer for it later. Got any magazines?"

"No," the corpsman said.

The sergeant reached into a wooden ammo box and pulled out four.

"That's a start. You really ought to get into some kind of uniform, though. You go walking out there without Captain Collins around and they're liable to lock you up."

"I've been told that," Thomas said.

When he ran back through the lane of buildings and cut across the tarmac apron, the Marines and airmen working saw him again, but this time wearing his war belt and carrying his rifle. They noticed but kept working. So did the air crews who busily inspected their UH-34 helicopters as they prepared to fly south.

"I need a lift to Delta Company, 3rd Recon," Thomas said, panting from his run.

The pilot, a huge captain, slightly overweight and wearing a grease-smeared flight suit, looked at him and laughed. "That your Summer Service Zulu uniform, stick horse?"

Doc Thomas glared at the pilot. "I'm doing a wear test for a new flight suit," he said and then cracked a smile.

"No pockets, but it does look cool," the captain said, laughing again. "That back-door air-conditioning standard or is that a special order option?"

The two other Marine airmen wheezed and howled at that and Doc Thomas joined them. He knew he had made a lucky choice. These men were not the kind to get tight-jawed and run him up for being out of uniform.

"I need to get south, someplace where an iron bridge is by an old French fort," Thomas said, reminding the men of his request.

"Yeah, get on," the sergeant who was the crew chief said. "We're headed your way. Everybody is. Lots of shooting down there."

The helicopter flew along the coast, near the water, and the cool air coming off the sea felt refreshing after breathing the hot air on the tarmac. He watched the setting sun and a line of helicopters flying from the south. He could see the Marines jammed inside through the aircraft's open doors and he waved at them, but no one waved back.

When he landed just above the Phong Le Bridge, near the old French fort, he could see a line of Marines headed up the hill from the bridge, carrying several black rubber boats and led by a familiar stocky figure crowned with a bush hat.

For Pat Collins the walk back had seemed much longer than the trip out. After paddling the rubber boats back to the bridge and then dragging them up the hill to the Dai Loc fort, he could only think of finding a soft spot where he could curl for a while and sleep. His back and shoulders ached and he wondered if old age had already begun to set in. He felt very low and worried about the eight men he had sent out on helicopters. Anytime he had men wounded it depressed him, and lately he felt depressed more and more of the time. Purple Heart medals among his company seemed the standard. He had even adopted a rest and recreation plan where three Purple Hearts and a man won a two-week ticket. He had to make it three Hearts just to be fair.

When he looked up the hill, he had to blink a few times. It seemed his vision had blurred because he could swear that a Marine stood there, silhouetted against the gray evening sky wearing a dress and battle gear.

"Captain!" Doc Thomas shouted and jogged with a limp to where Pat Collins stood amazed at what he saw.

"Holy shit!" the captain said. "Where in hell did you come from?"

"Guam," Thomas said. "I didn't have time to change."

"You bailed out of the hospital, huh?" Pat Collins said, twisting his mouth as he sized up the corpsman's wardrobe. "I guess I'm gonna catch a ration of shit from Blanchard. You know how he gets about regulations."

"I'll face him, sir," Thomas said. "I'm fine, though. Healed up well enough to go back to the field. I just gotta stay out of the water for another week or two."

"Any other asshole and you would be executing an about-face and shagging your ass back up that hill," Pat Collins said. "I'll let Doc Blanchard know you're here. Just fall in under one of those boats." Then the captain laughed. "You're a goddamned lunatic, you know that, don't you?"

"This whole fucking company is a bunch of lunatics, sir," the corpsman said, stepping under the boat where he became just another set of legs in the darkness. "I fit right in."

## • 18 •

JOHN, MIND IF I COME IN?" PAT COLLINS CALLED OUTSIDE THE TENT where John Henry and Frank Reasoner had lived.

"Sure, Skipper," the first sergeant's muffled voice answered from inside. "I'm just packing up the lieutenant's gear. Not much to send back, but I imagine that his wife and son will want it. I know I would."

Pat Collins pushed the tent flap up and hooked it to a corner post, letting in the daylight. "I hear you ripped some reporter a new ass the other day."

"Yes, sir," John Henry said. "I mean, I had just gotten the word about Lieutenant Reasoner, and to be honest with you, Skipper, I just broke down and cried like a little baby. It was only six weeks, but we got to be real close. You know we have children born on the same day. I just took it real hard."

"I don't think Colonel Blanchard realized," Pat Collins said.

"No, sir," John Henry said, "and I'm real sorry if I disappointed the colonel, but sending that reporter down here to interview me about Lieutenant Reasoner was bad timing."

"I know how you feel," Pat Collins said. "I had heard that Alpha Company had a few wounded and one killed, but I never thought it would have been Frank. When I got up to the headquarters the next morning, I saw the bodies of the Marines killed down there. They had them laid on stretchers and covered with ponchos. But I noticed an arm lying out, and I saw the wristwatch. Nobody else has one like that, so I knew it was Frank. I didn't even have to look under the poncho. I knew."

"And you know what, sir!" John Henry said, fighting back tears. "Some lowlife son of a bitch stole that watch!"

Pat Collins locked his jaw and his expression told John Henry what he felt.

"Sir," John Henry said, "I never thought anybody, I mean any American serviceman, could be so low as to rob the dead. That watch meant everything to the lieutenant."

"It had to be one of the gooks we've got buzzing around this place," Pat Collins said. "I can't see any of our guys dong something like that. It had to be one of the locals."

"I hope you're right, sir," John Henry said, wiping the wetness from beneath eyes. "Losing that boy was tough. It'll take me a while to get over this."

The captain picked up the calabash pipe that lay on the field desk where Frank Reasoner had left it, and he looked at John Henry. "Me too," he said. "And we're going to lose others, and we'll feel bad for them too, but we've got a job, like it or not." Then he laid down the pipe and stood, ready to leave. "Colonel Wheeler said that he would like you to work with some of his people at 3rd Marines and go back to the Dai Loc fort. They've got that radio relay there and we need a good recon Marine to keep his eye open for targets. You up for that?"

"Hell, I'm always up, sir," John Henry said. "That'll be fine. There's that little Dai We over there, and he and I got to be pretty good friends. He cooked up some interesting food. I never asked if it was dogs or rats, but it tasted fairly edible. I'll catch a hop out tomorrow, if that'll do."

"I'll let Colonel Blanchard know," Pat Collins said and left the tent. He had walked past the battalion command post when a familiar voice called from a tent where the sounds of working radios and several other voices mumbling gave it a sense of clutter and ongoing busyness.

"Hey, Pat!" the voice called.

"Colonel Blanchard," Collins answered, seeing that the voice was that of his commanding officer. "What a day. First Sergeant Henry's set to go back to Dai Loc. Tomorrow, if that's okay."

"Tomorrow's fine," Blanchard said. "General Walt wants Reasoner put in for a Medal of Honor."[2]

"Frank wouldn't take it," Collins said gruffly. "Frank would go pin it on that goddamned Smedley Collins. Hell, what's he getting?"

"Bronze Star, maybe Silver Star," Blanchard said.

"Like hell!" Pat Collins said in a voice raised by sudden anger. "God-damned Medal of Honor! That corporal saved their asses. You know damned well. Frank was brave as ten men, and God knows he deserves more than a chunk of brass on a ribbon and an extra hundred dollars a month. But for Collins, for Christ sake, the Bronze Star is ridiculous."

"We'll push it, but you know how these things can go," Blanchard said, reminding the captain of the political process that sometimes seemed to overpower proper tribute.

---

[2]First Lieutenant Frank S. Reasoner was posthumously awarded the Medal of Honor while Corporal Bryant C. Collins received the Navy Cross and Freddy Murray received the Silver Star. Besides 3rd Reconnaissance Battalion's headquarters compound bearing Reasoner's name, today the main auditorium at The Basic School, Marine Corps Combat Development Command, Quantico, Virginia, is named Reasoner Hall. Gunnery Sergeant Bryant C. Collins retired from the Marine Corps at Camp Lejeune, North Carolina, after twenty years' service; so did Sergeant Major Freddy Murray.

"Yes, sir," Collins said. "Why the hell am I arguing with you, anyway?"

"You're right, Pat," Blanchard said. "It'll all get ironed out."

"Here's a news flash for you, sir. I'll make it my business," Pat Collins said. "I know how the rear-echelon politicians work, they want to get a Medal of Honor awarded and Reasoner fits the mold. That goddamned Smedley Collins has some barnyard habits and a goddamned page 11 history,[3] but he still deserves credit for what he did."

"No argument, Pat, they both deserve a great deal of credit, and while we're at it, don't forget Lance Corporal Murray's contribution either," Blanchard said with tactful sharpness. Then he said with a slight smile, "One other thing. Recon Battalion Headquarters. We've already cleared it with General Walt. In a couple of weeks we'll put up a sign on Hill 327. Camp Reasoner."

"That'll sure make up for a lot," Pat Collins said sarcastically.

"No, Pat, it makes up for nothing," Blanchard said in a voice punctuated by his own grief for Frank Reasoner, "but it lets people know what we thought of him. You sure as hell won't find a man who will argue that Frank Reasoner's name does not belong on our camp headquarters."

---

[3]Page 11 of the enlisted Marine's Service Record Book contains records of disciplinary actions and punishments.

# BACK TO CAM NE:
## Zippos and CBS News

• 1 •

TWO F-4 PHANTOMS FROM MARINE FIGHTER ATTACK SQUADRON (VMFA) 531 streaked down the runway at Da Nang, black smoke swirling in their wakes. In seconds they lifted their noses skyward and banked right, pivoting on their wing tips, and then rocketed straight up as the South China Sea turned beneath them. John Henry could hardly see the airplanes with his naked eyes, but when he looked through the powerful binoculars that Doc Blanchard had given him, to use in his mission of watching for enemy movement from the promontory where the French had many years ago built the Dai Loc fort, he could see the two jets clearly.

He watched the Phantoms as they turned and climbed past the peak named Monkey Mountain. It stood at the northern tip of a narrow strip of land that jutted into Da Nang Bay, and the Americans had come to know its easterly facing stretch of sand as China Beach. A huge rock called Marble Mountain overlooked the gently curving, easterly facing strand's other end. With the Da Nang River running behind the beach, limiting it from access except by boat or by foot up the narrow swath of land, and in either instance always under the watchful eyes of sentries posted at Marble Mountain, China Beach presented itself as an inviting spot.

John Henry could just make out the bathers lying there, basking peacefully in the sun, and he imagined that for those fortunate souls this little brush war seemed distant at this moment. With the clean sand and restful palms leaning in the gentle breezes, those lucky sons enjoying the tropical sun, crystal-blue sea, and sugar-white sand could easily imagine themselves at Palm Beach or Miami.

As he held the binoculars' nearly foot-long scopes against his eyes and tilted their darkly coated lenses downward toward the stream that ran behind the fort and led to a larger river that flowed to Da Nang, he smiled. The sampans still were there.

John Henry let the heavy glasses hang on the leather strap that he had looped around his neck and he walked back to the trench that led around the old bunker complex to the other side where the South Vietnamese soldiers had made a breakfast of boiled rice topped with beans, cabbage, scallions, and shreds of meat. He never asked which kind. John Henry knew that any creature, including an occasional cockroach, fell as fair game for a Vietnamese cooking pot.

"Hey, Dai We," John Henry called to the South Vietnamese soldier who served as his liaison with the platoon of government regulars who had taken residence of the Dai Loc fort with him and two other Marines who operated the radios. The South Vietnamese had two 105-mm howitzers and a section of machine guns to protect the bunker where John Henry and the two other Marines had installed several large radios. With them they communicated with patrols working nearby, with aircraft flying support missions, and with ships that could supply naval gunfire when they were on station. The radios also linked John Henry to III MAF headquarters and Doc Blanchard, who would walk through the camp daily, a cigar clenched in his teeth, and proudly show the other staff officers the situation reports sent to him by John Henry.

"Big problem she come," the Vietnamese soldier answered, seeing John Henry. He ran to the first sergeant and breathlessly said, "I look for you everywhere!"

"I walked around to see if those boats were still tied along that little stream on the north side," John Henry said. "We got to have an escape and evasion route out of here, just in case."

"Maybe we need soon. Beaucoup Charlie coming," the small man said rapidly. "Kit Carson scouts come. They see maybe two companies. They say many, many VC wearing black, and other soldiers—beaucoup others—wearing green uniforms."

"North Vietnamese?" John Henry said.

"Yes, yes. Absolutely so," the soldier said. "They moving past fields, on low hills. They coming this way soon I think."

"We'll know soon enough," John Henry said. "I want to take a look for myself."

Both men walked to the bunker. There, John Henry took a gray spotting scope, two feet long with a front optic six inches across, dropped it in a pack, and hung it over his shoulder. He picked up his Air Force–issue AR-15 rifle with one hand and with the other he grabbed a tripod for the scope. The two men then started to leave the deeply dug safety of the reinforced concrete bunker for the shallow place on the hillside where the South Vietnamese solders kept watch from a hole behind a waist-high stack of sandbags when a burst of heavy machine-gun fire raked across the fort's upper structure, blowing out several chunks of the wall.

"I think they're coming," John Henry said, ducking his head low between his shoulders and being careful to stay behind cover. "I want to get a good look at them. Maybe we can get some help from Uncle Sam and take care of those guys."

Bullets chewed across the hill, splitting and splattering rocks and dirt, chasing the two men as they ran to the lower earthworks where the South Vietnamese soldiers jerked and cocked and recocked their bolt-action Springfields and automatic rifles and machine guns, and sprayed pounds of lead by the second into the distant forest and clusters of huts where the enemy hid.

"Where's the injuns," John Henry said as he slid behind the sandbags that ringed the emplacement where the South Vietnamese had set in their howitzers. None of the men could speak English, they could only point.

In the midst of the distant village, a concrete-block building towered three stories about the huts. John Henry set the wide lens of the Unertl[1]

---

[1]Unertl scopes are manufactured in Pennsylvania by a company founded by Mr. John Unertl, a World War I German sniper. The John Unertl Company produces match-grade rifle scopes and spotting scopes, popular in marksmanship competitions and in the Marine Corps Scout/Sniper program.

40-power spotting scope just above the layer of sandbags and peered
through the eyepiece. As he slowly turned the rear optic carrier, bringing
in focus the distant enemy, he saw the men hustling from trenches and
bunkers to huts and the building. Many of them wore the black uniforms
typical of the Viet Cong, but many more wore green uniforms. Uniforms
that John Henry recognized as North Vietnamese.

"We're under attack by a concentration of enemy south of our position, outside our TAOR," John Henry shouted through the handset to
the radio operator at III MAF headquarters.

"What kind of enemy, Hank," Doc Blanchard returned on the radio
from III MAF, ignoring any codes or call signs.

"I count about fifty or more Viet Cong in black pajamas," John
Henry said, "and two companies of men in dark green uniforms."

"Are they North Vietnamese?" Doc Blanchard asked John Henry.

"Yes, sir," John Henry said. "I have no doubt. They are NVA." John
Henry paused a moment and then said, "Sir, I think I need some air
support."

The radio was silent for several minutes and then it crackled back
with Doc Blanchard again. "Will you put that in the form of a message—
that you need air support, and that there is no doubt in your mind that
you're under attack by NVA?"

John Henry knew what his colonel was asking him. He knew that by
the Rules of Engagement that they were not allowed to fire outside their
TAOR and that this greatly concerned the staff officers who sat listening
at the other end of the radio conversation. He knew that it all had to be
formal in case some bureaucrat somewhere questioned what had happened. The same politically motivated bureaucrats who prohibited them
from flying the United States flag outdoors.

"Sir, you can write that down," John Henry said. "I have absolutely
no doubts."

The radio was silent once more as rifle fire chattered from above and
below. Then Doc Blanchard's voice crackled through the small green
speaker box. "Henry?" he said.

"Yes, sir," John Henry answered.

"We've just checked and there are no friendly troops in that area
whatsoever," Doc Blanchard said. "We'll have a flight of Phantoms on
station at your position in about ten mikes."

While John Henry wrote down the various coded frequencies over which he could talk to the Phantoms, a lone O-1B spotter plane tilted and turned a zigzag pattern overhead.

"Looks like the bird dog's already here," John Henry said and turned the knob of the radio to the observation plane's frequency. "Tallyho, bird dog," John Henry then spoke into the radio's handset.

In a second the speaker crackled back, "Roger, beach boy, can you mark the target? Over."

"That's affirmative," John Henry called back. "I'll lay down some Willy-Peter on it. Over."

The two howitzers fired white phosphorus projectiles that struck in the cluster of huts at each side of the brick building, exploding in fountains of fire and smoke that appeared from above as two great white lilies suddenly blooming on velvet green.

"Tallyho your target, beach boy," the pilot spoke. "I'm gonna get out of your way now, your Phantoms are on station."

John Henry listened and could hear the distant coursing howl of the jets' engines, and then the radio's speaker crackled again, "Beach boy, beach boy, snake one, over."

"Roger, snake one," John Henry replied.

"What kind of targets you got?" the flight leader said.

John Henry keyed the microphone and said, "I've got a mass of troops, probably two companies. That white phosphorus we just fired is the center of it. We'll put one more round right there. If you'll go three-to-five hundred meters north and three-to-five hundred meters south and about a hundred meters wide, that's wide-open space. Do what you can."

"Roger, beach boy," the flight leader said. "What do you want me to use first?"

"Man, I'll leave that up to you," John Henry replied. "You come on in and just mow 'em down."

"Well, buddy," the flight leader answered, "we'll come on in with 20-mm."

The phosphorus shell's white plume still drifted in the air when the first F-4 Phantom screamed full throttle just above the cluster of huts and the single brick structure. Both of the jet's 20-mm cannons banged busily, chopping the trees, ground, huts, and several unlucky Viet Cong and NVA who fell in the twin trails chewed by the heavy guns.

When the first plane tilted its nose up and turned away toward the sea to climb back to his attack altitude, the second jet attacked, and then the third.

John Henry watched through the 40-power spotting scope while his South Vietnamese liaison officer watched through the powerful binoculars. After the last plane had obliterated a path through the enemy position, leaving ragged debris hanging from the trees and huts, the South Vietnamese soldier pointed. "Look! Look! John Henry. See?"

As he tilted the long scope to the right where the soldier pointed, John Henry saw the first group of NVA soldiers running toward the brick building. Then from the left came another group, and then another.

"I think they're coming out of their holes," John Henry said. "Looks like a bunch of 'em are going to hold up in that building."

"Beach boy, snake one, over," the flight leader called to John Henry.

"Roger, snake one, beach boy right here," John Henry said. "You got at least a platoon or better down there in that building. That lone brick building by itself."

"Gotcha," the flight leader said and steered his Phantom jet down again, attacking the path that John Henry had laid out for them. As the jet leveled off above the trees, several streams of fire and smoke poured from under his wings behind six rockets that he sent exploding into the lone brick structure where the enemy soldiers hid. The second plane followed with more rockets and the third with even more rockets until nothing of the building stood.

After a second run where the planes finished off their arsenal of rockets, they made their final pass. One by one, each plane dived over the debris that once was a brick building and a community of huts and they each let fly with two bullet-shaped silver barrels, tapered round at its ends, and as each canister tumbled down and struck the broken bricks and chopped trees, an arching, hundred-yard-long stream of boiling orange fire and black smoke exploded over everything.

In a matter of seconds the entire village and forest and the pile of concrete rubble that once stood three stories high lay under a seething napalm inferno. No living thing moved after that.

"Looks like the war's over," John Henry spoke into the radio to the flight leader. "There is nothing moving, no shooting, flat nothing left down there."

"Roger that, beach boy," the flight leader said. "We'll take her home. You ever get to Da Nang, look us up. We'll buy you some beers. You got our call sign."

"I'll sure do that, if I get the chance," John Henry said as he watched the jets disappear back over the South China Sea.

"Say, Dai We," John Henry said to his South Vietnamese partner. "You reckon we could get some volunteers and make a patrol down there to assess the damage?"

The soldier looked doubtfully at the Marine and then said, "We wait. See what big boss want."

John Henry smiled. "Sure. I mean if we can get permission."

"We see," Dai We said.

It was as though the soldier already knew. John Henry barely finished his request when the answer came back an emphatic no. "No dice. It's outside the TAOR," Doc Blanchard told him. They would send an O-1B and rely on the reports returned by South Vietnamese forces who would later enter the area on patrol.

When the patrol finally did, however, they found no bodies. They found dried blood and gore and the rotting black debris of burned human remains. They talked to the local villagers and learned that a large number of NVA had died there but they could never account for any numbers. They only said many.

Even though the Phantoms had killed "many" that day, many more Viet Cong remained in the clusters of villages below the Dai Loc fort, and each day John Henry, behind his powerful spotting scope, watched men and women whom he suspected were Viet Cong and counted them as they came and went from the nine villages of the Cam Ne hamlet and six villages of Duong Son.

John Henry, perched on an upended ammo crate behind the spotting scope, concentrated his attention on a group of suspicious-looking men when the sound of a Huey helicopter landing in the clearing behind the fort distracted him. He jotted a comment of the observation in a green notebook that he kept in his shirt pocket and then walked toward the back of the hill where the helicopter had landed.

In a moment he saw two Marines run up the hill from the square of red earth that the Marine engineers had cleared weeks earlier as a helicopter landing site and he recognized the one man that he knew, Lieutenant William T. "Bill" Henderson.

"First Sergeant Henry," Henderson began, "you ready to take a break from this molehill?"

"Not particularly, unless you have a better offer," he said.

"This is Captain Hunter, the new company commander," Henderson said, and saw the hesitant smile come across the first sergeant's face.

"I'm sorry about Lieutenant Reasoner," Captain Hunter said, offering John Henry his hand.

"We all are," John Henry said as he shook it.

"Doc Blanchard asked us to take a look down here and give you a little relief," Hunter said. "You could do with some time off."

"Aw, I'm an old warrior, sir," John Henry said. "I'll stand on my head and stack BBs if I have to."

"No need of stacking BBs, First Sergeant. You rate a break," the captain said. "I've brought you a relief, so as soon as you're packed, we'll chop back to Da Nang."

"Anything you say, sir," John Henry said. He tried to sound positive because he did look forward to taking a hot shower and eating a warm American meal, but seeing the new captain and remembering Frank Reasoner, his death so fresh and the pain still sharp within him, he found it difficult to muster his usual enthusiasm.

"I'll show the skipper the lay of the land here while you get your gear, First Sergeant," Lieutenant Henderson said, seeing that John Henry needed to be alone.

In an hour the three Marines sat inside the Huey, watching the tarmac at Da Nang Air Base draw close to the aircraft's green skids. In another moment they settled to the ground and John Henry could see Doc Blanchard standing next to his jeep, a fresh cigar clamped in his teeth.

"Come on, Hank. I want you to have breakfast with me in my tent," Doc Blanchard said. "We've got a lot to talk about and more work ahead of us. You did an outstanding job out there, directing that air attack. Took out a lot of enemy"

"Thank you, sir, but I just pointed them out. Those Phantom drivers deserve the credit. They flat did a job on those boys," John Henry said. "But about breakfast, could we put that off and make it lunch? I'd sure like to see my Marines. The ones that got hit at An My with Lieutenant Reasoner."

Doc Blanchard put his arm around John Henry's shoulder and then he said, "Several of them are locked on for medevac to the Philippines, but as of now, I think they're all still down at Charlie Med. Take my jeep. Those boys will be glad to see you."

•2•

H E TURNED AND THE PAIN FROM THE WOUNDS AWOKE HIM. WHEN HE opened his eyes, he first saw the globe covering the light hanging from the white ceiling. When Jim Shockley looked down, he saw his father sitting in a chair next to the bed, looking at him. He smiled.

"Dad!" Jim Shockley said and then realized that he was not in South Vietnam but in Illinois. Jim Shockley's father, a lieutenant colonel in the Air Force, had arranged for his son to recuperate at Scott Air Force Base where he was stationed and where Jim could be close to family.

"I was just watching you sleep," his father said.

"I was dreaming—I think," Jim Shockley said. "I remember bits and pieces of things, or maybe I just dream them. It's quite confusing, but I think it really happened."

He paused and his father waited without speaking.

"My first sergeant, John Henry. He came into the hospital tent and I saw him stop at the door. Then Staff Sergeant Knee said, 'Hey, Top! How ya doing?' I saw First Sergeant Henry look at us and begin crying. I tried to hug him and tell him that we looked a lot worse than we really were, but I don't remember if I said it or if I just thought it," Jim Shockley said.

It had been several days after he was wounded before Jim Shockley really knew where he was and then he wrote to his mother and father at Scott Air Force Base and told them that he was in the Philippines recovering from the wounds in his legs and back. Much to the lance corporal's surprise, no one, neither the Marine Corps nor the Red Cross, had notified his parents that their son was wounded in action. His father called him in the Philippines and then again once he had arrived at Travis Air Force Base, California.

Lieutenant Colonel Shockley lived next door to the executive officer of the hospital at Scott Air Force Base, and because he was on staff at Military Airlift Command headquarters, he arranged for a general there to call an admiral and very quickly a MAC flight from Travis brought Jim Shockley to the Illinois base. There he would recover for the next four months and continue physical therapy as an outpatient, living at his parents' home for several more months.

"Your first sergeant sounds like a Marine who cared quite a bit about you fellows," his father said.

"He's outstanding," Jim Shockley said. "He used to be an officer during the Korean War and won the Silver Star. A lot of us felt bad that he got reverted back to being an enlisted man."

"That happens," his father said. "Old war-horses like him, they understand. It's difficult for them, emotionally, but they understand."

"I want to stay in the Marine Corps," Jim Shockley said.

"That's fine, as long as you can fully recover, son," his father said. "You're pretty badly hurt. I don't know about that leg. Doctors think you'll always have trouble with that. You think the Marines will accept those physical problems?"

"I'll overcome them," Jim Shockley said. "I want to be an officer, like Lieutenant Reasoner. He was enlisted and then went to West Point. I think Marines like him, former enlisted, make the best officers."

"He also had four years of college, Jim," Lieutenant Colonel Shockley told his son. "You're smart and I would not be surprised if, with this mess in South Vietnam, the Marine Corps offered you a ticket to OCS."

"I hear that they're needing more officers," Jim Shockley said.

"You say you boys felt badly for First Sergeant Henry," his father said. "Many enlisted men who get those kinds of commissions don't have a college degree. If they manage to keep their commissions, they rarely make it very high up the ladder. Take my advice. Go to college. Then go to OCS. You'll do much better for yourself. You won't be limited."

Jim Shockley thought for a moment and then gave his father a reassuring smile. "I'll remember that," he said. "Thanks."

• 3 •

IT WAS A FRENCH VILLA IN CLASSIC STYLE: SHRUBS, FLOWERS, IRON-work around the windows, and inlaid tile flooring. For American officers, especially senior officers, life in Saigon could be lived in a grand style for a very modest price. Thus it was not unusual for Colonel Barry Zorthian to enjoy the luxurious accommodations of this French villa on a fraction of his Marine Corps salary.

He stood quietly near the door and sipped an icy cocktail as he waited for the remaining guests to arrive for what he hoped would be a friendly and productive evening "bull session."

As spokesman for the U.S. Military Assistance Command, Vietnam, he had come to enjoy his work, which involved being the middleman between the press covering the war and MACV. He worked on a first-name basis with most of the leading journalists there, and though he maintained a professional separation between himself and them, in many cases these relationships had grown quite friendly. The reporters and photographers liked him.

Because he had always treated them with fairness and integrity, they trusted him and relied on his good nature to get them where they needed to go in order to cover the war. It was this trust that had convinced several of the more influential journalists to agree to come to his villa and talk this evening.

Life in and around Saigon had become, in his words, "a zoo," lately. Three days ago, on July 16, Secretary of Defense Robert S. McNamara had landed in South Vietnam with outgoing Ambassador Maxwell D. Taylor and his successor, Henry Cabot Lodge, now assuming the post as ambassador to the Republic of South Vietnam for a second time. While Taylor and Cabot Lodge kept a large segment of the press busy, mostly grandstanding, many other reporters kept on the heels of McNamara and his spokesman, Assistant Secretary of Defense Arthur Sylvester. President Johnson had already announced that he was prepared to step up manpower in South Vietnam based on McNamara's review of the military situation.

Rumor had already spread among the press that McNamara planned to ask President Johnson to vastly increase troop strength in South Vietnam and to commit more American units to the direct fight with the North Vietnamese and Viet Cong. General Westmoreland told McNamara that the Army of the Republic of Vietnam was no longer able to cope with the Viet Cong and were losing critical rural areas to the enemy. He believed that it was obvious that unless United States and Allied strength was increased there was "little chance for arresting the trend."

Barry Zorthian had little word that he could share with the reporters about this, and because Arthur Sylvester tended to carry a superior attitude regarding himself in relation to the reporters in the field, the Marine colonel found himself tap dancing in a mine field as far as press relations were concerned. A week later President Johnson would announce that he was increasing the manpower level of American forces in South Vietnam to 125,000, and that General Westmoreland would receive reinforcements as needed.

With only a day left before Sylvester would return to Washington with Secretary McNamara, Barry Zorthian looked forward to the end of this visit, and hoped that this evening's friendly gathering between himself, Sylvester, and the small but influential group of reporters would patch up wounds and perhaps open new avenues of improved press relations.

Barry Zorthian glanced at his watch as he looked outside, hearing a car door slam and voices echo behind the shrubs, hidden in the darkness of the tropical summer evening. He pushed open the door and swatted away mosquitoes as the two men stepped inside.

"Go on in and make yourselves a drink if you want," he said. "Secretary Sylvester is already here."

As the two men entered the living room, Zorthian looked at the assistant secretary of Defense, who sat in a rattan easy chair, sipping from an icy glass, and said, "Mr. Sylvester, this is Morley Safer and Murray Fromson of CBS News. You've met Edward White from the AP and Jack Langguth of *The New York Times*. And, of course, you know Keyes Beech from the *Chicago Daily News*."

Barry Zorthian was a handsome man whose ancestry benefited him with a classic Grecian profile, accented by his olive skin and jet-black hair that he oiled and combed neatly back. He was polished and sophisticated, and well acquainted with the customs of the New York–based press. His uniform fit him well and projected him with the same sense of importance that a dark, three-piece suit might otherwise. Some even said of him that he would look important even in a pair of coveralls. Yet his casual nature relaxed nearly anyone who met him, and they always left with a feeling that there was much more to this man than met the eye.[2] He truly had been a good choice as MACV's man with the press.

When Barry Zorthian introduced Arthur Sylvester to the several journalists that evening, the tension between the assistant secretary of Defense and the reporters struck him. Sylvester offered the men a cool hello, and at once Zorthian knew he could have serious trouble here tonight.

There had been talk in the Pentagon of exercising censorship in Vietnam, but the Johnson administration saw that move as a greatly drastic tactic to take regarding the negative stories that the press seemed to be airing increasingly.

Censorship had become a hot topic in the hack watering holes around Saigon, and the rumor that it was coming to South Vietnam was nothing new. The reporters had heard from various sources that a censorship plan was already being written.

In a way around censorship, Zorthian had issued ground rules that laid out what both the military and the media would do in relation to press coverage of the war. Both sides agreed that if a reporter violated the rules he could lose his credentials. That meant he would have no access to stories, transportation to combat zones, and could not attend the afternoon press briefings that Zorthian initiated, which later became sarcastically known as "the Five O'Clock Follies."

Arthur Sylvester was among those who believed that the press in World War II had been more patriotic toward the military effort and that censorship worked well with them. By his tone when introduced to the reporters this evening, it became very clear that he held a contemptuous regard of them.

Now as conversations began, Zorthian could see that Arthur Sylvester was not there to make peace with the reporters and gain some ground as far as their coverage of the war was concerned.

The assistant secretary's chilly greeting followed with cutting remarks that regarded the way some reporters covered the war from a hotel roof in Saigon rather than from the vantage point of the front lines. He let the men know that there was a lot going on in the war that they were not reporting.

[2]When Colonel Zorthian retired from the Marine Corps, he joined Time Incorporated and rose to the position of president and chairman of the board, and would be succeeded at Time Inc. by another Marine, J. Richard Munro.

Terrorism had for years been common in Vietnam. Almost daily there was incident after incident of Viet Cong atrocities committed against uncooperative villages. The VC regularly used women and children as cover for booby traps and bombs aimed at government workers, officials, or the Americans. Yet these rarely if ever amounted to a story as far as the press was concerned. Many of the American command in South Vietnam as well as Pentagon officials in Washington, D.C., regarded this lack of coverage of enemy abuses against the peasants of South Vietnam as onesided journalism. They wondered why the only news that seemed to make headlines was how American involvement in South Vietnam was growing, or how innocent victims fell in the midst of battles carried out by South Vietnamese and American forces.

"I don't know how you guys can write what you do while American boys are dying out there," Sylvester said.

"What do you want? A fight? You'll lose," Zorthian heard one man say.

"Wait a minute," Zorthian said, trying to stop the exchange, but before he could cool anyone Sylvester opened up.

"Listen, I don't even have to talk to you people. You deal with him," he said, pointing to Barry Zorthian, who felt his heart sinking deeper than he had ever felt it plunge before. "I know how to deal with you, with your editors and publishers back in the States."

"Hold it a minute. Please," the colonel said, finally stopping the exchange. "We can call each other names all night, and we will just wind up ruining relations. The press needs to get better and faster communications regarding military activities. We need to improve the transportation capabilities we can afford for the press. These are serious matters. Without improvements in these areas, your understanding of what we are doing here will continue to suffer. Can't we get down to business?"

White, Beech, Safer, and the others agreed. They lived and worked there, and needed to improve their capabilities of covering the war. They and Zorthian agreed that faster and more frequent reports from the field and rapid transportation to the site of an event would greatly enhance the reportage coming from Vietnam. This was something that someone in Sylvester's position could bring them.

"What do you think, sir," Zorthian said to Sylvester. "Can you push for an improvement here? I think that the more information that we can get to the press the better their understanding will be of what's going on. If they understand the situation better, their stories will be better."

"What does this mean?" Sylvester said. "We go do the reporting for you? Do you guys want to be spoon-fed?" He watched as Zorthian closed his eyes, and then he turned toward Jack Langguth. "Why don't you guys get out and cover the war?"

"We do," Langguth said. "I take your remark to mean that you don't have any faith in what people like Colonel Zorthian tell us. Is that the case?"

"Look," Sylvester said, "if you think any American official is going to tell you the truth, you're stupid! The way you guys cover this war, I wouldn't trust telling you the time of day. You ought to be working with us instead of against us. In time of war, the press has the obligation to be the handmaiden of government."

Barry Zorthian could not believe what he was hearing from the senior Defense Department spokesman, the man who should be the smoothest and best liaison with the press, but who this evening seemed intent upon burning what few bridges now existed between them.

Morley Safer stood and looked at Zorthian; clearly the frustration had taken him beyond the edge and now his bloodred face showed the colonel that if he did not leave now he would certainly lose his temper. Safer looked at his CBS colleague, Murray Fromson, who also appeared on the verge of bursting, and both men stormed straight out of the house.

*Wham!* The door slammed hard behind Safer and Fromson and shook the windowpanes as the two men left.

"Hell!" Zorthian said, looking at Sylvester, who smiled. "You really didn't have to say that. The press has the obligation to be the handmaiden of government? Handmaiden of government? Really, sir!"

"Listen, I didn't mean it quite that way," Sylvester said, seeing that he had pushed too hard. "I was being sarcastic, you know. Anyone knows the fourth estate and all. That handmaiden comment was more a joke. Sarcasm."

"Barry," Edward White said, "we'll talk, but I think it's time we called it a night."

As the frustrated colonel ushered the remaining reporters out, he tried to smooth their feelings, but he knew that a deep trench now gaped wider than ever between the press and the Defense Department, and that with these hostile battle lines drawn, his effort to get good press would be tougher than ever.

"Sir, how could you take these guys on like that?" Barry Zorthian said after closing the door and pouring drinks for himself and Arthur Sylvester. "What the hell's going on? This will really make things tough for me."

"Relax, Barry," Sylvester said. "I'm not going to sit down and take bunk from these guys. They don't run things here. Now and again they've got to be put in their places. They needed it. It was good for them."

Arthur Sylvester had little more than returned to the United States when American bombers struck targets in the heart of North Vietnam, destroying missile sites. The Johnson administration decided that the event should be played low-key since after Johnson's announcement of increasing the numbers of troops in South Vietnam to 125,000 it would appear to be another move to escalate U.S. involvement in the war. When Zorthian learned of the raid and then received orders not to release any information regarding the air strike, he knew that the reporters in Vietnam would take it as another move to freeze them out.

When the announcement finally came first in Washington, D.C., and not in South Vietnam, and the Saigon bureau chiefs learned of the event by way of New York telex, the credibility gap between the military and the press grew deeper than ever. Zorthian and nearly every other military information officer knew that the wrath of the press would soon come, and that it would be ugly.

• 4 •

THE JEEP BOUNCED AS IT CROSSED THE RATTLETRAP BRIDGE THAT spanned the little canal, one of dozens that crisscrossed the area south of Da Nang where the Marines had camped around the air base. The sun had already dropped behind the high mountains to the west and the air now felt good after such a hot afternoon. Morley Safer had just come to the Da Nang area from Saigon and knew hardly anyone. He had heard of General Walt, but never met him.

"Who is in charge here?" Safer asked the Marine who accompanied him in the jeep. The young man worked in the Da Nang Press Center and in a matter of a few weeks had come to know the names and positions of most of the key Marine Corps officers. Much of his job simply involved introductions and getting the reporter safely inside a particular compound.

"First Battalion, 9th Marines, sir," the Marine said, "that would be Lieutenant Colonel Verle Ludwig."

"Can we meet him?" Safer asked.

"We can try," the Marine said.

It took little effort before the men were inside the compound and shaking hands with Ludwig.

"What do you have going on?" Safer asked the commander.

"We've got a company going out tomorrow on a sweep of a village complex called Cam Ne, about 400 huts in a cluster of a half-dozen hamlets," Ludwig said. "Pretty much routine. You're more than welcome to come along, you might see a little action."

"What time you leave?" Safer asked.

"Come on down at about zero-five or so," Ludwig said. "We'll launch in the amtracks from the Phong Le Bride. You can meet us there."

Pat Collins could feel his heart beating solidly against the warm mud as he pulled himself up the riverbank. He lay there watching the faint silhouettes of the village huts while he waited. The sun still hid far below the horizon on this morning of August 3, 1965, when the captain and reinforced platoon of his reconnaissance Marines from Delta Company had arrived at this spot along the Song Yen, some 1,200 yards down from the junction where the Yen River converged with the Song Cau Do.

Pat Collins and John DelGrosso's platoon had paddled rubber boats upstream from where the iron railroad bridge, named Phong Le, crossed the Cau Do River below the Dai Loc fort. When Collins and his men reached the fork where the Yen turned southward and the Cau Do continued eastward, they caught the Yen's flow and quietly slid downstream, riding with the current, until they came abeam of the dim, distant lights of the village called Cam Ne (2). The journey had gone quietly and well under the cover that the darkness had given them.

Once they had landed, the reconnaissance Marines hid their boats and spread out their ranks along the front of the river, watching to see any movement of the enemy that they could report to the forces that would soon advance behind them. In less than a minute after the last man had slid into his position on the bank, the frogs and other voices of the night resumed their songs. The line of departure was set. Now they waited.

More than two weeks earlier, when Lieutenant Colonel George R. Scharnberg's 2nd Battalion, 9th Marine Regiment, had clashed with the Viet Cong at the cluster of hamlets called Cam Ne, the Communist forces had resisted but had not shown their real strength. It seemed that the enemy, especially the North Vietnamese, was not yet willing to fully engage the American forces and used hit-and-run tactics to keep the Marines off balance until the NVA and Viet Cong had more adequately developed their fighting muscle in this region.

In the July 12 combat, the Marines had won a toehold at Duong Son (1) and managed to keep that village relatively secure. Scharnberg detailed his executive officer, Major John A. Buck, to establish a forward command post in the concrete bunkers built by the French northwest of the Phong Le Bridge, and there Buck controlled two companies of Marines who remained in and around the Duong Son (1) hamlet. The Marines maintained regular contact with the Duong Son village chief and the hamlet's elders, yet they continued to receive fire daily from Duong Son (2) and Cam Ne (2).

After nearly two weeks of unyielding attacks from two hamlets and from the fields and hedgerows surrounding them, and after John Henry's confrontation with the substantial forces of NVA and Viet Cong to the east, General Walt ordered a clearing operation of the hamlets.

Upriver from where Pat Collins and his men lay, farther back down the Cau Do, near the Phong Le Bridge, just below the Dai Loc fort, several amtracks sat quietly in the sandy mud at the water's edge, shrouded by brush and willows that the Marines who operated them had laid over the hulking armored machines. They waited for Captain Herman B. West, Jr., and his Company D, 1st Battalion, 9th Marines, to issue the order to launch.

One day earlier, on August 2, at Da Nang Air Base the 1,062 Marines and 56 Navy medical corpsmen who composed the 1st Battalion, 3rd Marine Regiment, stood final inspection in the morning darkness before they boarded the UH-34 helicopters that waited in row after row on the flight line. Within the hour, this battalion departed Da Nang and joined with an ARVN battalion, and together began to establish a line south of the Cam Ne and Duong Son complexes from the Yen River eastward. The two battalions would block any retreat by the enemy that hid this night in those several villages along their northern front.

While that force of more than 2,000 Marines and South Vietnamese soldiers stood the picket on the southern flank, ten miles south of Da Nang, on the morning of August 3, Captain West and his 300 Marines prepared to march into the potential meat grinder and perform their dangerous work of clearing and destroying the Communist strongholds in and around these hamlets.

Now as the sun still lay well below the edge of the sea, Morley Safer and his cameraman, Ha Tue Can, wound their way along the narrow roadways that crossed the webwork of canals north of the Song Cau Do, south of Da Nang, and led to the great iron bridge that crossed the wide river.

As he approached the bridge, he could see the deep ruts left by the amphibian personnel carriers as they left the roadway and cut through the brush to the river's edge. He could hear the quiet rushing of the water as it washed against the concrete bridge piers. It was the same batch of concrete that the South Vietnamese government had years earlier given to the villagers in these hamlets. Then, these villages were part of the Agrovilles Program and later became part of the Strategic Hamlet Program. The villagers were given concrete so that they could construct shelters and other fortifications against any guerrilla attack.

Morley Safer knew this and he had also heard through his Vietnamese sources that the warlords in Da Nang were not getting along with the people in this southland, and because these villagers had not paid taxes to the local government, they were to be punished in some fashion. He wondered if somehow the Marines had unwittingly been drawn into a plan by the South Vietnamese administrators of this region? Were the Marines this morning going to unknowingly perform that punishment?

"Recon launched out hours ago, but we got to hold here until after daybreak," Lieutenant Colonel Ludwig said to Safer and his cameraman as they shook hands. "You two can stow your gear on that tractor right there. You might as well get comfortable."

The men huddled together in the dark cover of the brush that grew along the bank, above the Cau Do River. They drank coffee and made friends while they waited for dawn.

It seemed as though the lights never went out at III MAF headquarters on the night of August 2 and the very early morning of August 3. Major General Lew Walt brushed his bristled, crew-cut hair with his hand as he walked to the front of the briefing room where a six-foot-high map stood, tilted on a waist-level stand, depicting five northern provinces of South Vietnam, an area that people there commonly called I Corps. A pattern of red and black grease-pencil lines, drawn on a clear-plastic overlay, arched around Da Nang and represented the III MAF Tactical Area of Responsibility. This was a quickly growing section of countryside spreading from Da Nang in all directions.

Now, as the sun still lay a half hour before dawn, the general concentrated his attention to the area that followed the coastline eight miles south of the Song Cau Do and was bordered by the Yen River on the west.

A slight-built Marine, who combed his receding, graying hair straight back, flat against his head, and whose sharp features offered a distinguished, gentlemanly face with a friendly smile, stood next to a man who wore a tan bush jacket and khaki pants. Next to them a burly, square-faced Marine, whose bristling crew cut rivaled General Walt's, stood quietly and watched with several other newsmen who carried notebooks and small camera bags.

"Tom," General Walt said when he saw the slight-built Marine.

"Sir," the colonel said, "I believe you know our reporters."

The men put out their hands and in a jumble of words they managed to each greet General Walt.

"Could I interest you boys in a cup of coffee?" the general said as he shook the newsmen's hands and then nodded in acknowledgment to the Marines who accompanied them. "It's not the best in the world, but it will sure get the sleep out of your eyes."

The square-faced Marine sergeant major who had remained quietly at the rear turned to a sergeant who came into the room. He motioned the sergeant toward a three-gallon vacuum can filled with coffee set on a long table next to a brown tray stacked with white mugs. The colonel nodded when the sergeant major held up six fingers, meaning that he should fetch each of the reporters a cup of coffee and the colonel too.

General Walt, seeing the sergeant major and the sergeant bringing coffee to the newsmen, led the group to chairs near the front of the briefing room.

"If you have any questions about today's operations, please feel free to ask," the general said as a lieutenant handed him a cup of coffee.

Already several other officers had entered the room; most of them had already heard much of what was to be repeated, partly for the benefit of the reporters who would cover the day's activities. A major took his post next to the map and General Walt sat on his chair at the front row, to the right of the colonel and the newsmen.

"Gentlemen," the major began, "as I speak, 1st Battalion, 3rd Marine Regiment, begins their second day of Operation Blastout and actively sweeping the areas south of the village complexes of Duong Son and Cam Ne. Those are helicopters flying their support missions that you hear now. One item of interest today, one-three will provide a blocking force for Company D, 1st Battalion, 9th Marine Regiment, who will sweep the villages of Duong Son (2) and Cam Ne (2). As you may have been told, we have received concentrated fire from these two complexes for several weeks.

"Company D will embark at daylight aboard a platoon of LVTP-5 amtracks and motor upstream to the junction of the Yen River, turn there and land approximately 1,200 meters south of the rivers' merge at approximately ten o'clock this morning. A detachment from Company D, 3rd Reconnaissance Battalion, is already on station at that point and has established the operation's Line of Departure.

"The objective is to sweep through the villages, approximately two and one-half miles east and then move north to the Cau Do River where Company D and the reconnaissance detachment will move across the river by 3:00 P.M. and establish a base of operations before sunset."

"Sounds fairly simple," one reporter said, smiling.

The colonel, never losing his friendly expression, said, "It could be, but then we don't really know what intensity of resistance they will face. It could get pretty tough, and that means slow going."

The major who stood next to the map paused for the two men and then said, "Yes, sir, Colonel, it could get fairly tedious for Company D. We have reports of a sizable enemy population that has been entrenched in that area for more than a decade, and reportedly since the French were here after World War II. Vietnamese intelligence sources report they have seen concrete-reinforced underground tunnels and various earthworks camouflaged by village structures. Our Marines must move with caution since intelligence reports that there are all sorts of traps, snares, and mines throughout.

"Again, we don't know if the enemy will turn and run or if he will stand and fight. We have reliable reports that in Cam Ne (2) alone, there is a company-sized contingent of Viet Cong operating from there.

"Given the enemy population, we expect that with two companies from 2nd Battalion, 9th Marines, flanking the north and with 1st Battalion, 3rd Marines, flanking the south, when Company D moves in from the west, there could be a pretty solid fight. We are exercising the hammer and anvil prerogative with elements from both 3rd and 9th Marines ready to launch, should Company D encounter excessive enemy resistance.

"One of the great problems we anticipate is that the enemy historically has fought from within the ranks of civilians. In other words, we may encounter a firefight where the enemy may attack us from the cover of a hut or other structure occupied by a civilian family. The French encountered this a decade ago, Viet Minh attacking them while using women and children as shields. It's a very ugly business and we expect that it will not change."

General Walt stood and the major stepped back to the side of the large map. The general then looked at the several officers and reporters, and repeated a directive that he had earlier issued but which he wanted to emphasize.

He said: "It is imperative that all officers and men understand the nature of the Vietnamese conflict, the necessity of winning the support of the people, and the primary importance of protecting and safeguarding civilians whenever possible. The indiscriminate or unnecessary use of weapons is counterproductive. The injury or killing of hapless civilians inevitably contributes to the Communist cause, and each incident will be used against us with telling effect. However, this order must not infringe on the inherent right of an individual to defend himself from hostile attack."

General Walt paused and then said, "If Captain West's Marines receive fire from a position, hedgerow, trench line, bunker, spider trap, hut, or any other location, they are to overcome and destroy. Furthermore, if they encounter an enemy military complex, no matter what its appearance, they will get rid of it."

The colonel stood and cleared his throat and General Walt looked directly at him and waited for the question.

"Sir," the colonel said, "does this mean that if our Marines find that a village is not in fact a complex of dwellings but camouflaged enemy pill-boxes that you are giving your permission to destroy those huts?"

"Yes," the general said. "The men have my permission to burn those thatched houses that hide or camouflage enemy pillboxes."

Helicopters carrying supplies to 1st Battalion, 3rd Marines, continued to take off from the long procession of aircraft that now lined the tarmac at Da Nang Air Base. The sun, spreading orange across the sky and casting its dim first light over the flight line, began to crest above the sea. The slight-built colonel stood near the newsmen and waited while General Walt met a group of officers and listened in his usual manner of cocking his head to one side and placing his fists on his hips.

"Looks like he's got to make a decision," the sergeant major said.

"I think it's about the Provisional Air Base Defense Battalion," the colonel said.

One of the newsmen who also watched the general looked at the colonel. "Any kind of a story?"

"Not in my opinion," the colonel said and watched as the fingers that had reached for notebooks now retreated back to hip pockets and waiting. "It's just an experiment that a few of us hoped would increase our economy of force, but didn't pan out.

"Until the nineteenth of last month, 3rd Battalion, 9th Marines, had the responsibility of security of Da Nang Air Base. As an experiment, General Walt organized a Provisional Air Base Defense Battalion, which had a headquarters and service company and 4 infantry companies, manned by 35 to 40 officers and a little more than 900 enlisted men."

The colonel looked across the flight line and saw that the general was not coming soon, and the nonstory explanation seemed to keep the newsmen occupied. Seeing that he had more time to kill, the colonel continued to talk.

"The provisional battalion, commanded by Lieutenant Colonel William H. Clark, was activated on July 19 and immediately relieved Company A, 1st Battalion, 9th Marines. Its purpose was to enable regular infantry Marines to go to operations, like this one, while support Marines, such as the men who work for me at the Da Nang Press Information Center, manned the defense battalion.

"Colonel Clark and other staff officers recommended against the idea because too many support Marines needed for their primary jobs would be required to man the defense battalion, thus creating a backlog of support. In less than two weeks of operations, when General Walt saw that a great number of vehicles were not available for operation—their drivers and mechanics were busy with their sixty days' duty with the defense battalion—he realized that the idea had greater fault than benefit. I have heard that he has already made the decision to disband the provisional battalion and that 3rd Battalion, 9th Marines, just now coming in country will assume the air base defense duty. Odds are that decision is what has the general occupied."

Once the general turned toward the helicopter, a sergeant hurried to the group of newsmen and led them to the waiting aircraft, a UH-1E "Huey," a helicopter that would become almost symbolic with the Vietnam War.

The flight lasted less than ten minutes, and when the newsmen with General Walt walked up the hill from the landing zone, they encountered several frustrated Marines.

"The amtracks are stuck in the mud," the first Marine blurted out. "We're supposed to be attacking the first objective by ten o'clock, and as it appears now, we'll be lucky to be moving upstream by then."

"Verle," the general said, "what's the problem?"

The battalion commander, Lieutenant Colonel Verle E. Ludwig, hurried to meet the general. He had mud covering his boots and trousers to his knees. Ludwig looked at the general and shook his head. "Sir, three of the amtracks are stuck in the mud. We've got others pulling them out into the deeper water. Two of them may come loose, but I'm afraid that we're going to have to reload the troops off the third tractor and get moving. We're going to be an hour behind as it looks already."

"Let's get it done then," the general said and then glanced at the colonel. His expression made it clear to the colonel that this was not a good example for the press to see. The general looked at the newsmen and said to Ludwig, "We have a few gentlemen of the press who can observe this operation from the high ground, here. Some may also move on south to Operation Blastout and cover that. You know the MAF ISO.[3]

[3]Information Services Officer.

His Marines will escort these gentlemen from the press. Give them what you can, but don't compromise your operation on their account."

The lieutenant colonel smiled and offered his hand to the reporters and looked at the general. "No problem, sir. We've got that CBS crew already aboard, so one or two more won't be a big bother." Then he looked at the newsmen and said, "It's pretty boring stuff. Just a village sweep."

The reporters remained with the colonel and the helicopter and watched as the muddy Marines hurried back to their work. From the high ground and from the helicopter, they could observe both Blastout I and the Cam Ne sweep from the air.

Far across the wide river and flat rice lands, where a hedgerow extended from a cluster of grass huts and grew along the dike that held the water in the paddy, a boy stood at the field's edge. He raised on his toes beneath a tree whose limbs hung low, nearly touching the water, and with a steel rod that once might have been a piece of an axle from a small wagon, he struck a foot-wide iron ring whose original purpose had rusted from living memory and now served its inheritors as an alarm bell, which they had hung in the tree by a twisted hemp rope. Its clang chime rang loudly and carried through the villages to the west and south.

An old woman whose wrinkled brown skin almost hid her cloudy, dark eyes within deep slits and contrasted dramatically with her yellowed gray hair, which she pulled back tight and tied in a knot, stood on her shaky, bowed legs. Her gnarled hands brushed straw and grass debris from the black silk pants and blouse that she wore. A boy who had sat near her took up a wooden staff, its middle part worn smooth by many years of handling, and jabbed its end solid against the ground so that when the woman grasped the shaft, she stood firmly supported by it. Nimbly, she tilted her wrist upward and jabbed the staff's tip into the narrow trail ahead of her and stepped forward. The boy said something and tried to take her arm, but she shook him away and ambled slowly on her own.

Ahead of the woman, the boy could already see the men hurrying, carrying bundles and bags into several huts and sheds and lean-tos. Inside the flimsy grass structures, men lifted straw mats and floorboards, and opened entryways into tunnels and spider holes that led to dens and trenches and other hiding places. There they laid the bundles and bags, and then hurried back for other bags and bundles.

In the fields, men drove black water bulls that pulled sledges and carts piled with the muck and straw and other earthen items from farm work. Many men and women entered the wide patchwork of fields and they all looked to the northeast where the distant whining of amtrack engines warned them that the Americans were coming. They worked piling mud along the dikes at the edges of the field, and carried more straw and mud in the carts drawn behind the buffalo and piled that behind and between huts. Other men sneaked along the hedgerows and behind clumps of brush and trees. There they hooked the trip lines and wires that would set off the many snares and traps that they had built for just such a time.

"Jesus!" John DelGrosso said as he rested his elbows against the damp earth above the river's bank and leaned his eyes against the butt of his binoculars, watching the rice field directly ahead of him. At least a dozen men with hoes and grass hooks walked from the distant village to the fields near the river and began working. "I think they know we're coming, I've got twelve men in this field and I can see more walking to those fields there," he said, pointing for Pat Collins who lay hidden near him and watched too.

"Watch 'em disappear when they hear the amtracks coming down-river," the captain said. "Trouble with this whole fiasco, we sure as hell won't surprise anybody with a gang of amtracks landing in the middle of the day and a whole damned infantry company storming ashore. Watch how those guys don't seem to make any headway. If they were really working in that field, they'd be moving around more and not standing at one spot, chopping the same weed for fifteen minutes."

Throughout the rice fields, men, women, and children seemed to busy themselves with every kind of work as Captain West and his Marines now moved up the Cau Do River toward the Yen. They managed to un-stick two of the three bogged amtracks, but with time running far beyond anything acceptable for a successful operation, West transferred the squad of Marines from the stuck amphibian to two others that flanked it.

He asked for full speed, but even at that, moving upstream in a cum-bersome vehicle that could swim at eight knots top speed, West knew that his men would be lucky to see the Line of Departure before eleven o'clock. As the crawling steel giants that resembled squat boxcars on tank treads growled up the wide river, their shrill engines announcing their presence for the countryside, the captain silently prayed that they would at least be across the beach and on their way to Cam Ne before noon.

As the sound of the amtracks echoed up the river and found the ears of Pat Collins and his Marines who had now lain in place for nearly half a day, the captain looked at his watch and then at John DelGrosso.

"Let's get ready to move," he said. "It's nearly 10:30 and I don't want to hang around once these guys land."

John DelGrosso looked at his watch and wrote the time on a corner of his map, which lay on the ground next to him. He then folded it and shoved it in his shirt and looked once more at the suspiciously large number of farmhands working in the fields.

"They're moving out!" John DelGrosso said, feeling sudden frustration.

"Of course," Pat Collins said calmly. "Did you see anything that looked like weapons?"

"No," the lieutenant said.

"Odds are they have them hidden and they're moving to them now that they know where we're coming in," the captain said. "Jesus Christ, we could ding the shit out of them if we could just slip into these villages. We might as well have sent them a letter announcing the plan. They're going to pick the time and place for any fights. They're in control, like it or not."

"Look at this," John DelGrosso said, scanning the distant horizon with his binoculars, "they're all moving out. In five minutes this place will look like a ghost town."

"And it's going to be the same old dose of salt that two-nine's[4] been fighting for the past two weeks," Pat Collins said. "We're going to clear a village and then get shot in the ass. All day long. Looks like we'd wise up after a while."

By the time that the first amtrack lurched ashore and slammed full stop, rocking on its treads a few feet short of the riverbank's crest, only a frightened boy leading a water buffalo along a rice paddy dike remained in view from where Pat Collins's men squatted. Collins's reconnaissance Marines had moved into new positions spread along a line more than 1,000 yards from one end to the other. There they waited for the 300 men from Captain West's company to reach them and then together they would sweep on this 1,000-yard line across the rice fields and into Cam Ne (2).

Pat Collins knelt near his radio operator and watched Herman West's

[4]2nd Battalion, 9th Marines.

Marines leaping from the amtracks, rolling and springing to their feet, running, teeth gritted and growling, charging up the riverbank. Many of these Marines had not yet fought the Viet Cong. Others who had only knew the enemy from a sporadic fight here or there, a sniping or a hit-and-run. Few of them had actually been through a "donnybrook," as Pat Collins might say.

John DelGrosso smiled as he watched these boy warriors' curled faces and listened to their battle cries. He remembered playing football and how he saw similar faces and heard similar growls and shouts as players at practice charged toward sawdust-filled tackling dummies. It was almost the same. Homecoming game, running onto the field, breaking through the man-high paper banner. But here there were no cheerleaders or raving fans. There were no referees. No timeouts. These boys who had muscled their way across a chalked line only a winter ago put their shoulders together at an imaginary line and now embarked onto a field where they played for keeps. Yet they growled steel voices, spoiling for a brawl just the same, and John DelGrosso smiled. He knew. He had made that passage himself.

"Harry," John DelGrosso said to his first sergeant, who crouched next to him, "I want you to pass the word to let these guys know to move out with a little caution. They look ready to take on Red China. We don't need anyone kick-starting a bouncing betty because he's got a hard-on to go whack Victor Charles."

"They're definitely motivated, sir," Harry Rogers said as he stood and motioned to a lieutenant who had just congregated his platoon on line to the right of where Rogers and John DelGrosso waited. The lieutenant bounded up the bank's slope, and John DelGrosso stood and put out his hand.

"Your boys look ready to run the Miracle Mile," John DelGrosso said.

"Shit," the lieutenant said, panting for breath from running. "I'll pit us against anybody this morning. We're ready to kick ass and take names."

"It's good to see Marines motivated for a fight," John DelGrosso said. "You guys get the lowdown on the situation with these villages?"

"Pretty much," the lieutenant said, still breathing hard. "I gave my platoon a good talk on what to expect, hit-and-run, sniping, and watching for booby traps."

"I think that's what we'll see today, but be ready for anything," John DelGrosso said. "From what we observed this morning, the VC have our numbers matched, if not more. But I would be surprised to see him challenge us head-on."

"I'll let them know," the lieutenant said.

"Our greatest enemy will be ourselves," John DelGrosso said. "A Marine gets in a rush and forgets his discipline and tactics, that's when he steps on a mine or trips a Malayan whip and gets slammed in the chest with a yard of bamboo spikes. I had a little talk with my Marines this morning and reminded them about the nail boxes and punji traps and all the dirty shit that Charlie has hidden around here."

"I'll take the advice," the lieutenant said, smiling.

"Can't hurt," John DelGrosso said. "You know, an ounce of caution."

By eleven o'clock the sun stood nearly straight overhead and blistered hot on the land about the 1,000-yard line of Marines who walked step by step from the river. Ahead of them the rice paddies spread westward toward distant lines of trees, behind which other trees stood and beyond them the sea. Dotted among the rice fields were huts and shacks in groups surrounded by trees and hedges and fences made of sticks. Beyond these, to the front of the advancing line, Cam Ne (2) lay visible on the horizon, some two miles away, and somewhere in that distance the sound of clanging steel warned of the Marines' approach.

Each man who walked—his head cooking under a steel helmet, his sweat-soaked shirt open, and his M-14 held at his hip, ready—knew that Charlie had the advantage today. Charlie held the card that said Surprise. He knew that Charlie could pick the time and place of their first big fight, if he would fight at all.

From where the Viet Cong soldier waited, behind a clump of grass and dead wood where a farmer days earlier had pulled down a dead tree and left its mud-clogged roots turned up sideways, he could see the amtracks grinding their way up the riverbank, churning through the rice paddies, and cutting through the dikes. He watched as the Marines walked cautiously between the armored vehicles, their heads bent forward, their shoulders bowed, their rifles held in front of them at waist level so that they could shoot fast.

The soldier judged by the way that these men moved that one shot would be all that he needed to set them off, to make them waste time and ammunition. If he was lucky, he might hit one of the Marines when he shot. But if that failed, it was not important. His objective was to delay the Marines. To frustrate them.

He sighted his Chinese-made SKS rifle on the chest of a Marine who walked next to an amphibian tractor that drove toward the downed tree and in a few more minutes would grind the guerrilla's hiding place to splinters as it passed. The Marine appeared taller than the others, so for this reason the Viet Cong rifleman selected him as his target.

Pat Collins had moved his men to the left of the line that the infantry company had formed, and began to sweep at a gradual angle toward the north of Cam Ne so that when Captain West's men confronted Cam Ne on the east side, he would be in a position to block any Viet Cong retreat or a counterattack against West's flank. As his Marines cleared the first set of rice fields and stopped in the cover of a hedgerow, he noticed a bushy-haired, American-looking man wearing a bush shirt and holding a microphone standing next to one of his Marines. Both men looked toward a Vietnamese man who held a large motion picture camera pointed at them, and the man with the microphone was talking.

"John, where'd he come from?" Pat Collins said to John DelGrosso as the lieutenant squatted next to the captain.

"That's Morley Safer from CBS News," DelGrosso said.

"But he didn't just pop out of the ground, for Christ sake," Pat Collins said.

"He was with Company D when they landed on the beach. You didn't see them?" John DelGrosso said, unlacing his boot so that he could pull up his sock, which had bunched under his heel. "This really drives me crazy, I gotta get some new socks."

"What's the story on this guy!" Collins said, not taking his eyes off the newsman as he talked toward the camera and now put his hand on the shoulder of the Marine who stood next to him.

"Typical bullshit, I guess," DelGrosso said. "Do you miss your mother, who's screwin' your girlfriend, Suzy, while you're out here whackin' dinks. You know, the typical dumb questions that they always ask."

"You talk to this guy?" Pat Collins said, still watching Safer.

"Just before we headed up the beach," DelGrosso said. "I recognized him right off. The cameraman's name is something Can. They seem right enough. Can even offered to be an interpreter, if we need one."

Pat Collins looked at John DelGrosso as he pulled his sock straight and began lacing his boot. "You get that boot on, you can introduce me to these two jokers. I'd better fill them in on a few secrets about this bunch of lunatics that they've decided to accompany into battle."

When John DelGrosso had his boot retied, Ha Tue Can had taken down his camera and Morley Safer had tucked the microphone into the hip pocket of his bush shirt. The Marine who had been talking smiled and began to flush as though he had done something wrong and had been caught at it as the captain and lieutenant came close.

"I hope you kept at least acquainted with the truth, Satchel Ass," Collins said to the Marine and then offered his hand to Morley Safer. "Pat Collins, I command Company D, 3rd Recon. This is John Del-Grosso, my XO."

Safer shook the captain's hand. "Morley Safer and this is Ha Tue Can."

"John had already told me who you are," Collins said. "I think you took a wrong turn at the fork, you probably want to stick with the main body on this operation. They'll end up on nearly the opposite side of the village, and you'll miss a lot of the action if you stick with us. We'll only block any retreat."

"Thanks, but we'll continue with you if you don't mind," Safer said.

"I don't care," Collins said. "Your shot to call. Where do you call home?"

"Can is local and I'm based in New York, although I am from Canada," Safer said.

"I've trained up there. Worked with both Royal Marine Commandos and Canadians," Collins said.

Safer smiled.

"For the most part the Canadians were a good bunch," Collins said.

"Where's home for you?" Safer said.

"Grosse Isle, Michigan," Collins said and then looked at DelGrosso. "Then there's our boy from Brooklyn who has probably butchered every word in the English language at least two different ways."

John DelGrosso shrugged as both men laughed. Pat Collins looked at DelGrosso and then at Safer. "Since you're here, you might as well hang with this squad. You need anything, just ask Lieutenant DelGrosso or me, otherwise I'm sure one of these star-struck Marines will be glad to do anything to get their mugs spread across the silver screen."

Before Safer could say anything in response, the sudden crack from a rifle shot echoed across the flat countryside. And every man ducked for cover.

"See?" Collins said, looking at Safer who now searched the hedgerows and fields ahead of them, looking for the origin of the shot.

"I'm hit," cried the tall Marine who had walked next to the amtrack. His cry drowned in the sudden volley of gunfire that erupted as the Viet Cong soldier who had shot him dashed from his hiding place behind the dead tree and dove through the tall grass that grew along a nearby embankment that led to a tunnel. In a flash the man disappeared, but the Marines, aching for a fight, kept shooting, chopping the wood of the dead tree and sending clods flying along the embankment.

While the Marines concentrated their fire on the dead tree and the grassy embankment, several Viet Cong soldiers opened fire from the next tree line. In a second the end of the 1,000-yard line of Marines farthest from Pat Collins and Morley Safer turned their concentration of fire on the distant enemy. Then, just as the Marines shifted their fire, another group of enemy guerrillas began shooting from behind the trees nearest to the village.

Captain West hurried to the downed Marine and when a corpsman had plugged the wound with gauze and wrapped the Marine's chest tight, he turned to the captain and said, "It looks like a clean hole. His shoulder may be broken, but otherwise the wound isn't bad."

"Nobody hit that guy? He was right in front of us," West said, feeling the edge of frustration begin to work on him. "I knew it was too good to be true, making it through the rice paddies without getting hit. They've disbursed their forces into small groups scattered all over creation. They aim to give us a death of a thousand cuts. We've got to get on over to that tree line where we have some cover. These open paddies are bad business. We've got one more wounded over by that recon bunch. Somebody got trigger-happy and zapped the guy in the ass. The bullet cut through the fleshy part of his butt, and Pat Collins told me the boy's more embarrassed than anything."

"That guy from CBS see this?" the corpsman asked as he worked on the wounded Marine.

"I imagine so," West said. "The guy is right with them. What's it been, Doc, ten minutes since we started?"

"Almost on the button, Skipper," the corpsman said. "It should go better once we can move with a little cover."

"If we don't start blowing ourselves to bits on mines and booby traps," West said. "I think I'll lead our squads in behind the amtracks. If they have any antipersonnel mines or punji snares set, the tracks ought to set them off."

"Tomato cans and bouncing betties," the corpsman said, "but what about anything bigger?"

"I guess we'll find out, won't we," the captain said. "But it doesn't make any difference for the tracks whether my men are in front or behind, and if the tracks can blow a few booby traps along the way, it will make going for the Marine on foot a lot easier."

Pat Collins watched as Morley Safer and Ha Tue Can followed the reconnaissance squad as they made their way along the hedgerow behind three amtracks, still carefully looking for trip wires while at the same time watching for movement ahead that would signal an ambush. Collins could hear the shrill whine of the amtrack engines as the heavy vehicles gunned themselves forward, up the hedgerow, and he had just turned to watch them when the hollow-sounding *karumph* of an exploding booby sent Marines ducking. In the distance he could see the gray smoke and black debris shower through the air and over the front of the amtrack that triggered the deadly mine. Yet it was meant for a man, not a machine, and the heavy tractor pushed forward.

Another *karumph* echoed from another tractor, then another. In less than ten minutes, the sound of exploding mines seemed common, and the Marines quit ducking unless one detonated uncomfortably close.

"I hope our newsman is paying attention," Collins said to John DelGrosso as the patrol now pushed closer to Cam Ne.

"He's pretty close to those tractors, bet all he hears is the engines," DelGrosso said.

"And if he hears it, bet he thinks it's our ordnance exploding out there," Collins said.

His remark brought a curious smile from John DelGrosso. "Maybe we should tell him."

"We've got plenty to do without worrying about CBS News," Collins said. "When he comes face-to-face with one, he'll figure it out."

"Shit!" the lance corporal growled under his breath as he froze, feeling the tug of the trip line that pressed against his shin.

"What?" the Marine behind him asked and then looked down. "Shit a brick, man! You fuckin' don't even think about moving!"

"What's it tied to?" the lance corporal groaned, trying to stay still as stone.

"We've got about a twelve-foot-long pole pulled back around this tree, and on its end a rack with about a hundred foot-long dung-soaked punji sticks on it," a sergeant said as he traced the pole with his hand and found the release rope tied to the trip wire. He held the rope with his hand and kept the tension on the trip wire. "Okay, jughead, take a step back. I want all you assholes to clear that area there and get on this side of me so you'll be out of the way."

When the lance corporal joined the other Marines who now waited behind their squad leader, the sergeant released the line and the pole sprang across the trail, whooshing the air with the spikes and then falling to the trail once it reached the end of its deadly arc.

"Goddamn Malayan whip!" the sergeant said. "I've seen them long as a fence. Take out a whole squad."

"Fuck me to tears!" the lance corporal said. "I was that close."

"You got it, Jack," the sergeant said. "You came about a cunt hair too close. You just about took the big ride. Stateside in a box." Then the sergeant looked at the other Marines and scowled. "Right now, I want you'se to break off a stick about a yard long and thick as your pinkie."

The Marines immediately rustled in the brush and began breaking sticks while the sergeant watched. "Your pinkie," the sergeant said, holding his little finger in the air to show what he had meant to one Marine who pulled hard on a much-too-thick limb, "not your dick, Einstein! The object is to get it small enough so that you can feel any trip wires with it by your fingertips. Got that?"

By the time that the infantry company halted on the outskirts of Cam Ne, nearly every Marine led himself with a feeler stick as he watched the hedgerows and dikes at his sides and ahead for snipers or small groups of Viet Cong. Sporadic gunfire had accented their march beyond the first tree line. With every advance closer to Cam Ne, a hit-and-run ambush would send a section of Marines diving for cover while another section would send a volley into the ambush. But there was rarely a return. The Viet Cong would shoot and then move, shoot and then move, and then shoot again, but never hold a position more than a minute.

Herman West looked at his watch. Twelve o'clock. Sweat and dirt mixed on his arm and glistened. He wiped it with his hand, leaving a muddy smear. "We're never going to make the objective by fifteen-hundred," he said to the lieutenant who knelt next to him at the trees that skirted the eastern side of Cam Ne. "We have this village to clear and another, and then push to the river. If the other side of this ville is anything like this side, we can forget it."

"Sir, what next?" the lieutenant said.

"I've got to make a report to Colonel Ludwig," West said.

As he listened into the handset for the operator on the other end to put Lieutenant Colonel Ludwig on the microphone, the hot chatter of automatic rifle fire rang from a hut just inside the village. West could see the white puffs of smoke in the shade of the hut's doorway and knew that the rifleman was somewhere behind, in the darkness.

Several Marines fired into the doorway and then there was silence. "Did they get him?" the lieutenant asked West.

"Maybe. We'll see once we get over there," West said, and then the same kind of automatic rifle fire came from a hut far to the right of the first. The Marines fired into the second hut, and then a rifleman in the first hut fired. "Tell those guys with the 60s to launch a few mortar rounds into those huts. We've got to get moving."

A third rifleman began firing from another hut and in the midst of the firing, the Marines could hear several children screaming as the first mortar round landed between two huts. Near it, a wood pile and a large clay pot exploded, sending their debris skyward.

"Sir, they've got civilians in there," the lieutenant said. "They're using them for cover. And we've got secondary explosions, so the place is probably wired."

"Sir," West said as Lieutenant Colonel Ludwig came on the radio, "right now we are closing on Cam Ne (2) and we're receiving sporadic fire from the huts. The enemy appears to be using the civilians as shields. I've got my mortars directing their fire into automatic rifle positions and we are setting off secondary explosions, probably their ordnance storage of other booby traps, but I can't guarantee you anything about civilian casualties. If we're not careful, it could get very nasty."

"Do your best, but suggest that we just take it slow and move with caution, remember that we don't need any civilian casualties if we can possibly avoid them," the colonel said.

"I think the damned VC know that," West said, "that's why Charlie's using them for cover."

Several more 60-mm mortar rounds landed in the village, setting off other explosions. One mortar, however, found its mark on a hut where a Viet Cong guerrilla had been firing an automatic rifle. The hut exploded with several tremendous booms, sending straw and bamboo poles scattering and the thick thatched roof slamming to the ground with a dusty *whoosh*. Several women began screaming from the rubble and a Marine shouted, "Hold your fire!"

Three women and a young man struggled from under the debris, clearly in shock and limping from wounds. Another woman cried out and fell to her knees at the edge of the debris. All shooting stopped and the Marines watched as other men and women hurried to the hut and pulled away the collapsed structure and then lifted the limp body of a ten-year-boy from it.

West asked his commanding officer to stand by and then shouted to the lieutenant, "Let's get a squad up and move into the village."

As the Marines edged their way past the stick fences, the villagers laid the dead boy on the ground next to the flattened hut where the mother sobbed.

"Sir," West said again to the colonel. "I will call you in about ten mikes. We're moving into the village. I will give you a report then."

Squad by squad the Marines began enveloping the village, reaching a hut and stopping, lifting basket tops with their rifle muzzles, peeking behind straw screens, and lifting floor mats. Several of the structures had walls rigged to cords that lifted them straight up opening the side of the hut for a machine-gun crew to operate there. Hut by hut the Marines found hidden explosives, ammunition, and a few weapons, but mostly they uncovered the concrete-lined bunkers and holes, and the trenches and traps. Quickly Captain West began to realize that few of the huts served the sole purpose of shelter; most camouflaged a cunningly constructed Viet Cong fortress.

As he squatted next to his radio operator, waiting to make his report to Lieutenant Colonel Ludwig, he could hear the sporadic crack of rifle fire deeper in the village. As a patrol would pass a cluster of huts, a sniper would attack them from the rear. Three Marines now lay with the other wounded man at the east side of the village, waiting for the helicopter that would evacuate them to Charlie Med in Da Nang.

"Sir," West said, "here's the situation. We took fire moving in and sustained one Marine wounded. Coming in we uncovered 267 punji stick traps and pits, 6 Malayan whips, 3 grenade booby traps, 6 antipersonnel mines, and a daisy-chained hedgerow with about a dozen or more grenades strung out in a series along a wire. I got three more Marines wounded once we got into the ville. We suspect killing a couple of VC, we found drag marks and blood, but no weapons or bodies so we're pretty frustrated at this point.

"Problem with this village is that we get hit by the VC but we can't engage them. They shoot us and then duck down a trench or a hole and then pop up somewhere else. We've been blowing bunkers all morning, but this place is a regular fortress and given the number of fortifications and storage lockers hidden under these huts, we won't get this place cleared before dark."

The radio crackled dead air and then Ludwig said, "What about destroying the fortifications. We don't want to leave a fortress behind."

"We can burn them as we go," West said.

"What about the civilians," Ludwig considered.

"Lots of them," West said. "We've got women and children, but they're living in huts that are otherwise ammo lockers or pillboxes. We've got some flamethrowers and we can torch them as we go."

The sporadic firing had lasted for the past hour and now Pat Collins could see the columns of dark smoke rising from the village and he could hear the secondary explosions as ammunition and ordnance hidden in huts ignited.

"Guess they're gonna burn the place, " John DelGrosso said.

"They should have started that a long time ago, there are at least 500 huts in this little burg, and odds are that nearly all of them are either an ammo stash or bunker," Pat Collins said as he watched a squad of his men investigating a tunnel and underground bunker built beneath a hut.

"Fire in the hole! Fire in the hole!" one of the Marines shouted and then the ground shook as an explosive charge brought down the roof of the tunnel and bunker, leaving a caved-in hole filled with broken beams, bamboo poles, and collapsed remains of the hut.

Morley Safer and his cameraman, Ha Tue Can, had followed the squad into the village and there filmed as a Marine with his flamethrower laid a fountain of fire on the wall and roof of a hut. Near him other Marines with flamethrowers worked while others tried to burn structures with white phosphorus and termite grenades.

Safer stood in front of the camera and said, "It first appeared that the Marines had been sniped at before and that a few houses were made to pay. Shortly after, one officer told me he had orders to go in and level the string of hamlets that surround Cam Ne village. And all around the common paddy fields a ring of fire. One hundred fifty homes were leveled in retaliation for a burst of gunfire. In Vietnam, like everywhere else in Asia, property, a home, is everything. A man lives with his family on ancestral land. His parents are buried nearby. These spirits are part of his holdings. Today's operation shows the frustration of Vietnam in miniature. There is little doubt that American firepower can win a military victory here. But to a Vietnamese peasant whose home means a lifetime of backbreaking labor, it will take more than presidential promises to convince him that we are on his side. If there were Viet Cong in the hamlets, they were long gone."

While Safer stood in front of the CBS News camera on one side of the village, burning huts in the background, Herman West had given the order for his Marines to withdraw. He had discussed the situation with Lieutenant Colonel Ludwig, and they both concluded that the objective could not be achieved and that a withdrawal was in order. West had asked that they withdraw back to the Yen and float the amtracks to the south bank of the Cau Do where they could attack from the north and accomplish a greater share of the mission, but Ludwig overruled that. He told the frustrated captain that given the type of battle he had faced, he and his Marines had done well despite not reaching the objective.

According to Marine Corps figures, a total of fifty-one huts had been destroyed by the Marines along with thirty-eight trenches, tunnels, and prepared positions, despite the fact that they had only gotten one quarter of the way to their objective. Furthermore, despite the way the Viet Cong had attacked by sniping throughout the day and using the local peasants as shields, only one civilian death and three others wounded had resulted from the fighting.

Pat Collins watched as Morley Safer and his cameraman jogged with the squad of Marines as they withdrew from the village and dashed for the tree line. Already Herman West's men had cleared the first hedgerow and hustled across the open rice paddies. The Marines had little more than cleared the last man from Cam Ne when a barrage of gunfire from more than one hundred Viet Cong cut across the fields at the men.

"Beautiful. Just fuckin' beautiful," Collins said as he slid into cover behind the trees and looked back at the village. "No way that hacking and burning did enough good there, that whole goddamned VC company probably sat out the entire day underground, and when they saw us leaving, they wanted to let us know who really had the upper hand here."

Herman West crouched next to his radio operator and called in the situation to his colonel. "We have a substantial force of between eighty and one hundred Viet Cong attacking our rear."

Ludwig returned, "Hold your position, we will call in a fire mission for the 105s and the 81s."

In five minutes, twenty-four 105-mm howitzer shells from Battery D, 2nd Battalion, 12th Marine Regiment, and twenty-one rounds from the 81-mm mortar section of 1st Battalion, 9th Marines, showered onto the Viet Cong positions. The Viet Cong guns again fell silent.

As Herman West withdrew, he counted what he believed were seven dead Viet Cong. However, the Marines were never able to verify the number of enemy dead or even the actual size of the force that attacked them.

As they departed, Morley Safer watched a helicopter flying over the village and tried to count the multitude of smoke columns rising from the hamlets. From where he had watched the sweep, he had not seen the enemy. He had only heard sporatic rifle fire and then the Marines launching their mortars and other explosives. He saw no enemy weapons. He did not recognize the earthworks and fortifications as anything out of the ordinary from any he had seen in nearly every Vietnamese village he had ever visited. He saw concrete foundations and what he believed were shelters, built years ago under the old Strategic Hamlet Program and with American concrete. As he left with the Marines, Cam Ne burning behind them, he felt sick at the sight. To him this seemed an overkill. A cruel punishment for a village that refused to pay taxes to General Thi and his local warlords.

## • 5 •

"WE DON'T TALK TO ANYBODY WHO ISN'T WEARING A GODDAMMED uniform!" Pat Collins said as he slammed down a copy of *Pacific Stars and Stripes* that carried the Associated Press story of Morley Safer's report on Cam Ne and a photograph of a Marine casually setting fire to a hut with his Zippo cigarette lighter. "That asshole in the picture is one of ours!"

John DelGrosso looked at the photograph and then stepped outside the tent where the air seemed more breathable. He held the newspaper, staring at the front page, and then looked at Pat Collins. "There was a concrete bunker under that hut. We were going to blow the damn thing anyway."

"Your friend Morley Safer is on everybody's shit list," Collins said. "I have heard that Safer actually asked that Marine to torch that hut because he needed film of Marines setting fires close up, and then he had his cameraman shoot film of some old woman sitting by the trail crying. He made it look like this guy is casually burning the hut while the old woman pleads and cries for him to spare her hootch."

"Safer did seem a little hinkie from the start. He was out to get us," DelGrosso said.

"Walt wants the son of a bitch out of the country. He told Westmoreland that Safer is banned from I Corps," Collins said.

Morley Safer had cabled New York on the evening when he returned from the field at Cam Ne. He told his superiors at CBS News headquarters that an officer on the scene had said that the Marines had orders to burn the village to the ground if they received even one round of enemy fire. Someone had fired an automatic rifle from an unidentified direction and the Marines responded with rockets, grenades, and machine guns. Despite the pleas of elderly villagers, they used cigarette lighters and flamethrowers to destroy 150 dwellings. He said in his cable, "I witnessed the foregoing and heard that another Marine unit on the opposite side of the village wounded three women and killed one child. Two

Marines were wounded by their own fire. Marine sources deny this. Prior to the burning, townspeople were urged in English to abandon their shelters and remain in their positions. This reporter offered services of South Vietnamese cameraman to give desired instructions in native tongue. Marines had no official interpreters, only three Vietnamese who spoke no English. Defense Department says all our troops constantly reminded of need to protect civilians. Marines have lost men helping civilians in Da Nang area."

Harry Reasoner began the CBS Evening News by reading Safer's cable on August 3, 1965, and on August 5 he showed the film of Cam Ne that included the Marine from Pat Collins's unit casually lighting the hut while the old woman cried. In the same newscast, CBS News also disclosed that the hut that the Marine was burning did cover the concrete entrance to a tunnel, but that the casual nature of the Marine burning the hut did not appear as though he was under fire.

A *New York Times* story written by a reporter who flew over the burning complex in a helicopter generally backed Safer, and reported that there were some 300 huts left burning as the Marines departed.

It didn't take long before Morley Safer faced a growing number of critics who wanted the truth regarding the charge of him asking the Marine to light the hut. One version of the story even suggested that Safer had handed the Marine a lighter when the Marine said that he had none. However, once the Marine Corps investigated the story, they conceded that Safer did not give the Marine a lighter and ask him to burn the hut.

Safer followed the Cam Ne report in successive days with interviews of Marines where he asked them how they felt going up against children, women, and old men. He also asked about the need to burn Cam Ne. The Marines tried to explain how it was tough to fight an enemy that used old men, women, and children as combatants, however, their choice of words left them looking bad. That the civilians were the enemy "until proven innocent."

One week later, after General Walt's demand that Safer be barred from I Corps had been overturned, Assistant Secretary of Defense Arthur Sylvester was demanding that CBS recall Safer.

This demand had less to do with the Cam Ne incident, and involved Safer violating the ground rules. On August 11 he reported that U.S. airborne units were on the move to Pleiku and might relieve a Special Forces Camp at Duc Co that had been badly battered by continual enemy attacks.

Sylvester wrote to CBS News President Fred Friendly and gave him a detailed account of the action at Cam Ne, and said that Morley Safer's premature disclosure of the movement of American paratroopers on Pleiku clearly demonstrated the reporter's ill will toward the military. He also told Friendly that Safer had a reputation in Canada as being against the military.

Friendly called Sylvester's letter clearly a case of character assassination, and that the films taken by Safer and his cameraman had shown that the Marines burning the huts did not appear to be under fire, nor did any of the footage disclose any evidence of trenches or other fortifications. He stood by the CBS version of the Cam Ne story, backed his reporter, and refused to recall Safer.

The ISO stood next to General Lew Walt and watched as South Vietnamese soldiers lowered their yellow-and-red flag as the sun lay low over the Annamite Mountains whose dark green face looked nearly black this evening. "I think it's a good idea for you to sit down and have lunch or dinner with Safer. They're keeping him here, and it is better to work toward a positive footing," the colonel said.

Walt's jaws tightened and he looked at the colonel. "I don't think I can ever forgive the man. I'll eat with him and be cooperative, but I don't have to like him."

"I don't either," the colonel said. "But we must get along with him."

"I gave the bastard a lift to the field in my own goddamned helicopter, Tom," Walt said. "He sat right there and heard me give permission to the commanders in the field to burn those thatched houses that hid or camouflaged pillboxes. He knew what was going on, but he sure as hell misrepresented the facts."

"Barry Zorthian told me about a little tiff where Arthur Sylvester had told Safer and some other correspondents that the press ought to be the handmaiden of government in a time of war," the colonel said.

Walt looked at the colonel.

"Safer got really pissed off and walked out," the ISO said. "Maybe he's just being careful not to be misidentified as anybody's handmaiden."

*Two months later* Marine Corps Gazette *published a full account of the Cam Ne incident and the Safer report. They concluded that balanced reporting, accuracy, and fairness should be the hallmarks of journalism. The magazine summed up the Marine Corps' position by stating: "War is a stupid and brutalizing affair. This type of war (Vietnam conflict) perhaps more than others. But this does not mean that those who are fighting it are either stupid or brutal. It does mean that the whole story should be told. Not just a part of it."*

*Two years later* Newsweek *reporter Francois Sully commented about Cam Ne, saying, "The Marines' orders and efforts to avoid antagonizing and to try to win the cooperation of the local populace were misplaced in regard to the people of Cam Ne, and breaking up the group and leveling of the village structures were the only feasible actions short of a military assault."*

*On August 18, 1965, the Marines returned to Cam Ne. For two days they searched and cleared the entire complex and established 1st Battalion, 9th Marine Regiment's command post on the south shore of the Song Cau Do. During the weeks that they spent there, they rebuilt huts that they had earlier destroyed.*

*On each occasion that the Marines had gone back to the villages in or near Cam Ne, Pat Collins's reconnaissance teams had located sizable enemy forces, yet when the main body of Marines attacked, the enemy hid. Collins held that because of the size of the forces that the Marine Corps launched, it would have taken a blind person to not see the punch coming. The Viet Cong were simply not yet ready to fight in great numbers.*

*For Pat Collins and other Marine Corps leaders, Cam Ne served as an example of how the Marines had blundered their way in early critical encounters with the Vietnamese people, and even more critically with the enemy. It was obvious to Collins and others that they had much to learn in regard to dealing with the local people, the press, and more so with engaging the enemy effectively.*

*Sadly, Cam Ne represented a milestone in the war in South Vietnam that deeply alienated the military from the press and the press from the military. Neither trusted the other.*

*The military attitude, based upon Cam Ne and similar instances, was that the press was on the other side, that the press was out to get them, that the press was an anti-American villain.*

*For many of the press, the military represented an arm of a corrupt and evil regime. Soldiers were pawns, often unwitting, and always wound up on the dirty end of the stick. Nearly always misguided, cruel, and insensitive to the Vietnamese people because they were small, brown-skinned, and slant-eyed.*

*The only certain fact about Cam Ne is that it was a monumental tragedy in the history of the Vietnam War. A tragedy for the resident villagers, a tragedy for the press, and a tragedy for the American forces.*

*The tragedy of the press and the military was their misunderstanding of each other that grew from that day. Unfortunately, the people in America saw the war primarily from the perspective of the press and were most significantly affected from the pictures of the war. The pictures always told of tragedy, sadness, and despair. The pictures showed the heartache and ugliness that every Marine who has ever served in combat knows too well. Too often the pictures and words behind them did not match. While the words told of American forces progressing against a ruthless enemy, the pictures showed the tragedy of war. Pictures always win.*

*In Cam Ne, where some of these first sad pictures were taken and sent to America, that day was a tragedy in the lives of the poor people who were caught between the Viet Cong and the American forces there. Morley Safer saw this and deeply felt its impact. He reported this truth to the world, raising a controversy that lasted the whole life of that war and will continue as long as the Vietnam conflict is discussed.*

*Safer knew that during the Agrovilles and Strategic Hamlet programs, the South Vietnamese government developed Cam Ne, and other village complexes like it, as defendable enclaves for the peasant farmers. They provided these peasants with American concrete with which to construct shelters and other fortified positions so that they could protect themselves from the growing bands of Communist guerrillas. When Diem and his brother, Nhu, herded the peasant farmers together, forced them to move from their native lands to these Strategic Hamlets, and did not allow them to even elect their own village chiefs, the people of these hamlets turned against the established government. They may or may not have all been Viet Cong, but they were certainly not friendly with the government or the Americans.*

*Odds are very good that not a single Marine who swept Cam Ne on August 3, 1965, knew or realized any of this.*

*Morley Safer also had heard that South Vietnamese government offi-
cials in Da Nang had sent word to the people of Cam Ne that if they did
not pay their taxes they would be punished. Historically, Major General
Nguyen Chanh Thi, Da Nang's South Vietnamese Army warlord, had
been against the Americans going south to the areas around Cam Ne.
Had there been a manipulation to use the Marines to punish the people
of Cam Ne for not paying their taxes, it came from outside the ranks of
General Thi. It is also possible that the threat of punishment for nonpayment of taxes came after the fact that the Marines would attack Cam Ne
became known. In this context it certainly would have played much to
the advantage of the Viet Cong in their psychological operations of keeping the peasants angry with the South Vietnamese government and the
Americans.*

*Again, it is a safe bet that not a single Marine who swept Cam Ne
that day knew any of this, either.*

*With the knowledge of the Strategic Hamlet Program's development
of shelters in the villages and the knowledge of the rumor that somehow
Cam Ne was to be punished for nonpayment of taxes, Safer's perspective
becomes clear. He saw trenches and concrete structures beneath the huts,
but to him this was normal and consistent with the Strategic Hamlet Program. He was also new to the Da Nang area, and this was his first outing
with Marines there. Thus he had little or no knowledge of the previous
fighting that had occurred in the area of Cam Ne.*

*Had the Marines who swept Cam Ne been aware of the facts sur-
rounding the origins of the fortifications that they saw beneath and surrounding the huts, perhaps their perception might have been different.
Perhaps they would not have seen these trenches and holes as fighting positions but as shelters, as Safer had seen them. However, considering the
Marines' prior experiences in the village of Duong Son and Cam Ne, their
perceptions, no doubt, would have been that the fortifications beneath
and around the huts at Cam Ne may have originally been constructed as
shelters, but in the past few weeks they had been used as fighting positions against them.*

*Thus, from Cam Ne came the truth of Morley Safer's report, and the
truth of the Marines' experiences. Both were truthful, but each saw the
whole affair from completely different perspectives. This is the other
tragedy of Cam Ne.*

*The only question still remaining regards whether or not Morley Safer asked the Marine to light the hut for the camera to film, or that he provided the Marine his lighter, or that he both gave him the lighter and asked him to set fire to the hut for his camera. All three versions are commonly told among Marines. Morley Safer strongly holds that it is all a pack of lies.*

*God, Morley Safer, and the Marine who torched the hut know the truth. I have talked to Mr. Safer. I cannot find the Marine who torched the roof of the hut in question; perhaps he died in the war. Thus it stands, and one must give Mr. Safer the benefit of his innocence.*

# HUNTING CHARLIE

•1•

HE LOOKED AT HIS WATCH AND IT WAS TEN O'CLOCK. HE WONDERED if he could sleep, even though he had been patrolling since dawn two days ago. The sun bore down on the green canvas tent that sheltered the two rows of cots, and even with the flaps up, the heat had become more than B. C. Collins could stand.

"This shit ain't gonna work," he growled to himself and began pulling at the buttons on his shirt. He dropped the garment on the floor at the side of his cot, and then yanked down his trousers, which caught around the tops of his boots. "Goddamnit!" he snarled again and dropped his bare butt on the cot and bent over to unlace his boots.

"B.C.!" a voice called outside.

"I thought I told you lads to hit the rack, Freddy!" B. C. Collins said angrily to Lance Corporal Freddy Murray.

"We did, B.C.," Freddy Murray said, walking to Collins's cot where the wrathful corporal sat naked with his trousers wrapped around his ankles. "We're all crashing in our racks when that mousy-assed corporal that works for the sergeant major comes in and rousts us out to join his sandbag detail."

"Of course you told him that you lads just got off patrol," Collins said.

"Right," Murray said. "I stood ground with him, ready to toss hands too. But he kept saying he had orders from the sergeant major to take anyone lounging around the compound, and if we made trouble, we'd be talking to him. The team went with the corporal, and I've been looking for you."

"Where is this bastard?" Collins said and pulled up his trousers and snugged his belt tight.

"I'll take you there," Murray said, smiling.

As the two Marines made their way past a row of plywood-enclosed privies, B. C. Collins pulled his arms through the sleeves of his shirt but left it unbuttoned and flapping behind him as he walked at a furious pace. In the distance Collins could see several of his squad, shirtless and hacking at the hard earth with picks and shovels and filling sandbags. Near where they worked, the corporal in question sat on a box, watching.

"I told you lads to hit the rack," B. C. Collins shouted in his coarsest voice to his men who already had dropped their tools when they saw him approaching.

The corporal sitting on the box stood, ready to face the incensed squad leader. B. C. Collins towered over the Marine and his raw breath hit the man directly in the face, making him take a step back.

"Let's get something straight, lad," Collins barked, poking the corporal hard in the chest with his index finger and his gravelly voice rumbling deeper and more forcefully than any of his men had ever before heard. "You want to put anyone in my squad to work, you come see me first. And in the second place, these guys just got off patrol and haven't slept in two days."

"Wait a minute, Collins," the corporal snapped, trying to sound just as tough as his much larger counterpart but managing only to yap like a terrier. "You can't talk to me like that, I've got time-in-grade[1] on you."

B. C. Collins's bloodshot eyes popped wide and then snapped tight to narrow slits. His face flushed a sudden deep red and he boomed, "You goddamned little chicken-necked, pencil-pushin' fuck!" And in that

---

[1] The amount of time a Marine has served at his current rank since the date that he officially attained the rank. Usually this is the first day of the month in which he or she is promoted.

moment of explosive rage, B. C. Collins doubled his left fist and drove it deep in the corporal's stomach and followed with a hard right upper-cut that lifted the Marine off his feet and sent him sliding backward across the ground. The corporal shook and then stiffened and then re-laxed, still.

Freddy Murray, not totally surprised by Collin's sudden attack, grinned. "Shit, B.C., I think you killed the dumb bastard."

"No," Collins said, kneeling at the unconscious Marine's side while his squad crowded around. "But I sure as hell broke his jaw. He's gonna be eatin' through a straw for a couple of weeks. You better get a corpsman. I'm gonna go see Doc Blanchard before this gets blown outta shape."

B. C. Collins buttoned his shirt and realized that he had forgotten to put on his cap. He looked at Murray, a Marine similar to Collins in size and strength, and snatched the green sateen utility cover from his head.

"Well, lads, wish me luck," he said with a defiant smile and pulled the cap on the back of his head. Then he casually walked away toward the battalion headquarters, stopping for a moment to blouse his trousers above his boot tops.

When he reached Doc Blanchard's door he had already given himself as close an inspection as possible, and other than smelling rank from the two-day patrol, he felt fairly presentable for the battalion commander.

"Sergeant Major," Collins said, centering himself in front of the bat-talion top sergeant's desk, "Lieutenant Colonel Blanchard's gonna want a piece of my ass, so I need to turn myself in so he won't take such a big bite."

The sergeant major frowned at the corporal and said, "You're break-ing the chain of command. You need to see First Sergeant Henry and then me."

"I broke your corporal's jaw," Collins said, trying to sound sorry, but managing only to sound a bit triumphant.

The sergeant major raised his eyebrows and looked across at the desk where his man normally worked. "I sent him out to organize a working party. What the hell happened?"

"He snatched up a bunch of my boys after they just got back from pa-trol and had them filling sandbags, and he never asked me a thing about it," Collins said.

"So why'd you break his jaw?" the sergeant major said, walking around his desk.

"The bastard tried to pull rank," Collins said calmly.

"We'll talk to Colonel Blanchard," the sergeant major said, anger rising in his voice, "but if I have any say he'll run you up and disk you at battalion office hours."[2]

"Hell, that won't be anything new, Doc Blanchard loves the taste of my ass," Collins said smartly and watched the sergeant major's jaws clench tight.

Two days later B. C. Collins dropped his seabag on a cot in a new tent occupied by noncommissioned officers who worked at the battalion headquarters. They were mostly clerks and drivers, and B. C. Collins grumbled and refused to talk to anyone as he unpacked in his new home.

Doc Blanchard knew that extra punishment duty had never really bothered Corporal Collins, he took it in stride. However, Blanchard also knew that Collins prided himself on leading Marines in combat, and lived to go on patrol. Blanchard knew that to deprive Collins of his position as squad leader and to deny him going out with his squad would certainly work as punishment. Thus, Doc Blanchard committed B. C. Collins to a duty that many other Marines would take as a reward. No more spending days and nights crawling in the muck. No more dodging bullets or risking the loss of life or limb from a mine or booby trap. No more leading a squad and no more patrolling.

For punishment, Doc Blanchard assigned B. C. Collins to duty as a clerk in the headquarters operations office where he would push pins in a map and answer the telephone.

· 2 ·

I'M LEAVING IN A FEW WEEKS," DOC BLANCHARD TOLD PAT COLLINS. "When I'm gone, you can have Corporal Collins. But I want you to wait awhile. Let him soak."

---

[2]A commander's authority to issue nonjudicial punishment as prescribed under Article 15 of the Uniform Code of Military Justice. Marine Corps slang term for this is office hours.

Pat Collins smiled. "He's one of the gutsiest Marines around. The guy loves to fight and is as mean as a snake. I hope he doesn't level the three-shop before he gets back in a platoon."

"He's like a lamb," Blanchard said, chewing on his cigar and spitting bits of tobacco off the tip of his tongue. "I think he has it figured that when I leave, someone will hit up Roy Van Cleve for him, and he wants to be able to go."

"You tell him?" Collins asked.

"No," Blanchard said. "He's got it figured. Van Cleve won't stand in your way because the sergeant major wants Collins out of there worse than Collins wants to get back with a platoon."

"I'll give him a couple of weeks," Collins said. "That'll make it mid-September."

"You may want him before that, and that's all right," Blanchard said. "You're going to be busy as hell now that Walt's approved our plan of farming out the companies to the regiments and making your Dingin' Deadly Delta the general support company for the division. Walt likes you and told me he wanted you working directly for him. We've agreed on an arrangement, but your battalion commander will still have a say. I know Roy Van Cleve and he will want to be kept in the loop."

"Of course, you're aware of the little night raid that we're pulling on that island just off the coast from the Hai Van Pass," Collins said.

"Sure," Blanchard answered. "They say Charlie uses it as a supply dump. The two-shop spooks believe that because we have pretty well blocked off any avenues into Da Nang from the west that supplies have to be coming in from the north, get dropped there, and then are infiltrated through Da Nang in those little round basket-type boats, the ones they weave from elephant grass and then paint the bottom with tar."

"General Walt's hot about nailing down the logistical lines that Charlie's using to support VC around Da Nang," Collins said. "If you ask me, they're coming right under the canopy in broad daylight.

"We can fly all these aerial recon missions and those guys won't see a thing. I've been in there and up on the Hai Van Pass and along that ridge, there's triple canopy in places. Hell, you can run a herd of elephants through there and never be seen."

"There are theories too that the VC float the shit in by sea," Blanchard said, chewing another soggy strip of tobacco off his cigar.

He clamped the handmade Churchill in his teeth and took out a box of matches, striking one and holding its fire just out from the cigar as he sucked the flame into the tobacco. A fog of fresh smoke surrounded his head and he looked at Collins. "I've heard speculation that Charlie loads up these little round boats by the dozen and floats them down, just off the coastline. They may not stop at that island at all."

"I'd put money on that it's all of the above," Collins said.

"So how do you stop Victor Charles," Blanchard said.

"Special boats and foot patrols. Lots of them," Collins said. "Like I said, you can look all day from the air and you won't see shit. On the ground you'll ding the bastards."

"So how do you convince the old man?" Blanchard asked, the cigar bit between his teeth.

"I'll take the whole damn company," Collins said, "all eighty of them. We'll march in daylight and Walt can launch all the airplanes and helicopters he wants and he won't see a thing. I've even worked out a plan for patrolling up there."

"What's that?" Blanchard said.

Pat Collins smiled. "I call it the Great Train Robbery. If we walk up, we'll take two days just to get started. If we ride in or fly in, the VC will see us just like all these other operations. The only thing that really makes it through without getting hit is that little train that runs north. It has all those switchbacks going up the Hai Van Pass. I figured that I could dress my guys up in local garb, you know, black pajamas and coolie hats, and ride the train up. When it hits that last switchback near the top, we jump off and disappear in the woods. Just like that," he snapped his fingers. "Beautiful."

"If you do it, and I'm not giving you permission, but if you do," Blanchard said, "do it before I leave. Roy Van Cleve would never consider such a crazy-sounding stunt."

"I don't think I'll ever get it off the ground," Collins said, "but it's sure a great idea."

• 3 •

JOHN DELGROSSO RUBBED CAMOUFLAGE PAINT ON HIS FACE FROM A two-toned stick that he heated with his cigarette lighter to soften the wax-based makeup. He alternated dark green and light green stripes on his face, trying to create a pattern that would somehow make him look fierce. Many Marines tried to accomplish this as they applied the cammy, and they had each developed their own style of applying it in a particular pattern uniquely their own—like an American Indian would paint on his war face.

While John and his men rubbed the green grease on their cheeks, eye sockets and foreheads, ears, chins, and necks, Eddie Adams took pictures of them. He had a short lens on his camera and held it close to the faces of the Marines, hoping to capture a portrait that showed the camouflage makeup accented by the cammy-green bush hats that more and more of the reconnaissance Marines now wore. He especially liked Pat Collins's because he pinned the front of the brim back with a Marine Corps emblem in a style that reminded Eddie of the way Gabbie Hayes had worn his hat in Roy Rogers westerns.

"Better cammy up, Ed," John DelGrosso said, seeing Adams busy with the camera, trying to capture as many faces as possible before darkness ended his photography work.

Eddie caught the cammy stick that John DelGrosso pitched to him, and as he rubbed the paint on his face, he heard the Navy LCU[3] rumbling just beyond the crashing surf in the lower bay of Da Nang, north of the air base.

"Let's get our teams together and mount up," John DelGrosso said, directing his men to their small, inflatable boats that lay along the beach.

In twenty minutes the half-dozen rubber boats bobbed behind the landing craft as it pulled them out to sea. In the darkness the black ocean and the black sky melded together, and the only reference the men could truly establish was the tail of the landing craft ahead of them and the twinkling shore of Da Nang behind them.

Each man sat astride the round, black sides of the inflatable boats, and held tight to the ropes that laced along the gunwales. Their packs and other equipment lay in the bottom of the boats, tied snugly so that if they capsized, they would not lose the cargo. One Marine sat at the rear of the boat and held his paddle in the water, using it as a tiller. As coxswain, he guided the little craft, keeping it turned into the wake of the LCU.

[3]LCU is a utility landing craft with a forward-dropping ramp and is capable of carrying troops or small vehicles.

Three Marines each lay in the prow of three of the boats. These men wore tiger-striped camouflage shorts, green T-shirts, frog fins, and clutched a diving mask. They had knives strapped to their utility belts along with waterproof lights. They rested now since as scout swimmers their work would come when they would swim ahead of the boats and guide the crafts safely ashore.

In an hour, the boats bobbed six miles offshore, tugging and jerking on their lines behind the LCU as it turned toward its destination where the Marines would untie their rubber boats from behind their tug and then paddle silently eastward five miles to the island that lay off the coast below the Hai Van Pass.

Eddie Adams strained his eyes to see anything under the moonless sky; then as the night darkened the stars became vivid, glittering like sequins on black velvet. As he paddled at his corner of the boat, keeping in sync with the other Marines, he marveled at the tremendous number of stars, and then he noticed below them that he could see the shadowy shape of land.

Far to his left, the lights of Da Nang reflected off the water while to his right the stars disappeared into uneven blackness. Straight ahead, he could see the towering mountains of the Hai Van and below them the dark hump of an island jutting up from the sparkling black sea, and he felt his heart race.

John DelGrosso motioned for the scout swimmers, and they slipped silently into the ink-dark sea and disappeared into the night without a sound. "No talking," he whispered. "A voice can carry for a mile over open water."

Eddie nodded his understanding and he felt a now familiar lump that he had come to know before battle tighten in his throat. He knew that he could not talk even if he tried.

The surf crashed against the rocks, and as the platoon of dark-faced, dark-clad Marines bobbed and rolled through the waves in the six small boats, the sound of the breaking water rumbling into foam around the jagged boulders that lay at the edge of the island grew loud. Three faint flashes of light blinked from the shore. The swimmers had landed and now marked the approaches for the boats.

John DelGrosso heard himself grunting as he strained against the paddle and pulled hard to guide the boat between the rocks. Even with the now-loud roar of the surf, he could hear Eddie breathing hard, blowing out air with each stroke of his paddle, and the sense of struggle that the photographer endured made John feel close to Adams. He truly was one of them. A friend.

One by one the boats slid against the jagged shore and the Marine who sat astride the right front of the boat climbed up the rocky bank, pulling the boat by the lead rope and holding it tight against the island while one by one the Marines unsaddled themselves and scrambled to the security of dry land.

The men all wore green canvas shoes with black rubber soles that resembled basketball sneakers except for their color. They even had a round patch with U.S. in raised, black rubber letters cemented to the canvas top at the point of the ankle bone. Eddie remembered seeing similar shoes in Korea when he worked as a Marine Corps combat correspondent. Chinese soldiers had worn them because they were cheap and easy to manufacture. Then the Marines had joked about them. Now, a decade later, they too wore them.

Water gushed from the shoes' sides as the Marines sloshed up the steep bank and dragged the black rubber boats into the brush where they covered them with layers of grass and branches. Then as the swimmers pulled on shoes, trousers, and shirts and armed themselves, team by team the men squatted in a circle and waited for John DelGrosso to begin the night's search-and-destroy patrol.

Each team had to move in concert with the other, and together sweep along the coastal points of the island first. After that they would sweep across one side and then the other of the island's interior, hoping to find the VC's supply dump.

The night creatures croaked and squawked and twittered as John DelGrosso walked quietly, a step at a time, feeling for footing and then letting down his weight. He gripped his rifle in his right hand and in his left he gently held a feeling stick, with which he searched by touch for trip wires and booby traps.

An hour passed and then another. Not a sound. Not a sign of any human life on the island. Only the frogs and bugs and birds and other various small creatures that live beneath the umbrella of heavy tropical growth. Completing the circle, John DelGrosso signaled his platoon to begin working across the western side of the island, moving in the same quiet and careful way.

Eddie Adams followed close to John DelGrosso. He held his camera, which hung from his neck by a thick canvas strap, close to the chest with his left hand. He had taped several film cans to the strap and then had gone over everything that he could find that might rattle or click and wrapped it with the same black cloth tape. He didn't quite know what he would do if a fight started in the dark since he could not use flash and the night was too dark to expose his film, even with an open shutter. However, the opportunity might arise. Pyrotechnics might explode overhead, the enemy might send up flares. Who knew. Whatever the case, he was ready.

The spread of reconnaissance teams had little more than crossed one hundred yards of island interior when the night quietness shattered with the terrified screams of several Marines. Birds leapt from branches and launched skyward in the blackness, squawking as they climbed away from the commotion on the ground.

John DelGrosso froze in his tracks, Eddie behind him and Harry Rogers behind him. They waited and again the screams came, but now more screams joined the others and the men could hear a panic ahead of them. Men crashing through the brush, running blindly toward them.

Suddenly the air above them seemed to hum like the sound of an electrical transmission line outside a power plant. The hum grew louder and the screams and crashing came closer.

"Run!" John DelGrosso shouted, swatting something that landed on his face. Then another large insect and another until the swarm of jungle hornets had spread its cloud of thousands to the waiting Marines and photographer. Without another thought, the men turned and ran almost blindly toward the coast where they knew that they could rush into the sea and get away from the sky full of hornets.

Once in the water, several yards from the land, John DelGrosso and his men relaxed. The threatening insects seemed intent to remain in the jungle and left the open air and water to the Marines. This island was theirs and they shared it with no man.

In half an hour John DelGrosso crept to the shore and led his men to the safety of their hidden rubber boats. "There's nothing on this island," he told Eddie, who sat close to him. In a loud voice he spoke, "Light 'em if you got 'em. I'm declaring this island secure, except for those yellow jackets."

Eddie peeled out a pack of Pall Mall cigarettes from a two-piece plastic box and handed several to the other men who smoked. As he relaxed, waiting to hear what the platoon would do next, a corporal with several large welts on his neck and face crawled next to John DelGrosso.

"Sir," the Marine said, "I've got two guys in pretty bad shape with the bee stings. Doc Thomas says I should tell you that they could get serious and ought to get medevacked by chopper at first light."

DelGrosso climbed to his feet, his uniform bagging wet on his tall, lanky body, and he sloshed in his soaked recon sneakers over the rocky shore to where Doc Thomas worked on the two Marines.

"What's the score, Doc?" John DelGrosso asked.

"About half the platoon got the shit stung out of them," the corpsman said. "I've given several guys shots that will help the swelling. These two are pretty bad. They have stings over a lot of their bodies. The damned hornets got down inside their uniforms and really went to work. They're both going to be hospitalized, and we could have some serious problems with them between now and daylight if either of these men are allergic to insect bites. Those damned hornets can kill a friggin' water buffalo. We're lucky as hell it's not worse."

The corporal next to DelGrosso shook his head. "The whole fuckin' island is full of these goddamned nests. We're going along on point and next thing I know I hear something go *thump* on the ground and all these bees start buzzing. Someone screams and I run. Everybody starts running. Then I see all these other nests. Everywhere. Guys are running through the bushes and knockin' the shit out of more hornet nests. By the time I can see the ocean, I've got millions of them all over me. All I can see are hornets. Everywhere. The sound of 'em. It was so loud!" the Marine said, shaking.

John DelGrosso put his arm over the young man and felt several welts swelling on his skin under his wet uniform. "These two men the only ones we've got to worry about?"

"So far," Thomas said, "but I plan to work through the night and keep an eye on everybody. I'll catch some z's tomorrow, once we're back."

DelGrosso put his hand on the corpsman's shoulder and then stood. Even the doc had welts swelling. "I'll get on the horn now and arrange for a chopper at first light," the lieutenant said and sloshed his way back to where Eddie and his radioman lay, enjoying their cigarettes.

• 4 •

WHILE GENERAL WESTMORELAND AND OTHER MILITARY LEADERS met in Hawaii to decide whose units would be included among the Phase I Forces—the additional troops to bring strength in South Vietnam to 125,000—Pat Collins sat looking at his company roster, still frustrated by his shortage of men.

He had already been to the brig looking, and he had drawn a line in the dirt and his entire company formation stepped across it, volunteering their extended service to him. Yet he still needed more men.

While John DelGrosso and his platoon had made their infamous Hornet Island raid, Collins had taken the remaining platoon up the Hai Van Pass, into the mountains that bordered Elephant Valley. They had flown in by helicopter because even General Walt felt disturbed at the idea of Collins's recon Marines taking a clandestine ride on the local railway.

Once on the ground, Collins marched his company in full daylight straight into Da Nang without ducking once while search planes and helicopters tried to spot them. He proved his point that Charlie could move with ease under the canopy, but now he needed men to go and get Charlie.

His PRC-10 radios were unreliable. He had to have extra men to carry batteries. He had to have extra men to cover the flanks of the enlarged patrols.

General Walt sent out word asking for volunteers. With the voluntary extensions among the men he had, and now a trickle of volunteers coming, his company slowly began to grow. Yet most of those who came had rough skills.

Among them were Charlie Scarfano and Gary Smith, gutsy lieutenants, but the men had trouble reading even an Esso road map. Scarfano tended to find a high place, locate a roadbed or railway track, and follow it back, frequently the longest route home. He had been with the unit only days and already he had become known as Railway Track Charlie Scarfano.

On one occasion, Collins had sent Gary Smith out with a squad on a patrol along the north face of Dong Den, overlooking Elephant Valley. The route was simple, out and back. A training exercise more than anything, but as the day wore toward evening, Collins knew that Smith had become lost, as usual.

"Come on, Harry," Collins said to First Sergeant Rogers, who was sitting in the corner of the command post tent reading a boxing equipment catalog. "You can go with me to find the Lost Patrol."

Rogers rolled the magazine-size book in his hand and shoved it into the cargo pocket on the side of his trousers. "We've got money coming from special services," he said as the two men walked toward the flight line where several rows of Huey helicopters sat.

As they passed a Quonset hut that had a border of white-painted rocks laid in a line along the walkway that led to its front door, Pat Collins picked up a smooth stone the size of his fist and shoved it in his pocket as he walked.

"So what's your idea?" Collins asked, not breaking stride.

"I used to do a little boxing," Rogers said.

"I know," Collins said. "One look at your nose and anybody could tell that."

"Some of the troops have asked me to teach them to box," Rogers said. "I can buy some gloves, a few bags, and headgear, and we can have our own little program. Smokers every Saturday night. We can challenge other units."

"Okay," Collins said, "but one thing at a time. Boxing smokers between platoons or companies, but let's keep this thing under control."

Harry Rogers smiled and pulled out the catalog, and thumbed his way through more pages as the two Marines walked inside the light helicopter squadron operations hut.

In thirty minutes Pat Collins and Harry Rogers sat at each side of a Huey looking out its open doors at the valley below. The helicopter turned and tilted high above the treetops as it zigzagged its way around the cloudy-topped mountain called Dong Den.

It didn't take long before Harry Rogers tugged Pat Collins and pointed down. There he saw the squad, standing in line, waving their arms at the helicopter.

"Bring it down," Collins shouted to the pilot through the mouthpiece of the communications headset that he wore. "I want to hover just above those guys."

Pat Collins pulled the white-painted rock from his pocket and put it between his feet. Then he reached inside his shirt pocket and took out a folded piece of notebook paper. He spread it across his thigh and began to scrawl on it with a black grease pencil. *"Go down the hill to the river. Turn right. Go to the ocean. Turn right and you're home."*

He folded the note once more and wrapped it around the rock. He took a roll of string from his pocket and made several turns around the note-covered rock. He tied the bundle tight, snapping off the excess string and stuffing it back in his pocket. Then he leaned out the helicopter door and shouted to the pilot, "Come a little to your right. I want the squad on your left side."

As the helicopter drifted to the right, Pat Collins could see Gary Smith looking up. He let fly with the rock and several of the Marines scattered, thinking that it was a missile with which the captain had meant to crown the lost lieutenant. The lieutenant turned to duck too, and the rock slammed into the back of his pack, nearly knocking him down.

When Pat Collins saw one of the men unwrapping the note, he signaled the pilot to fly home.

Harry Rogers didn't say a word as the two men walked back to the company headquarters. He had his own problems with land navigation. However, his troubles had stemmed from not taking note of instructions.

A week earlier Collins had noticed him not jotting down vital information, such as grid coordinates, rally points, and assembly areas as the captain briefed the company for a patrol. Roger just sat and listened, as though he already knew the script. Pat Collins had always been wary of men who did not take notes. No one, not even himself, could memorize the six-digit and eight-digit coordinates they used to fix on a map the various patrolling, reporting, and assembly locations. He knew that Rogers was familiar with most of their operating areas, but when he didn't write down the data that fixed the various thrust points, he decided to teach the first sergeant a lesson.

Once the company had spread into squad-size teams across the patrol area, Collins crawled to a hill that overlooked the broad, rolling valley where his Marines patrolled. He sat there with his binoculars and radio and called Rogers.

"I want you to meet me at Thrust Point Tango," Collins said as he focused his binoculars on the Marine a quarter of a mile below him.

Rogers agreed and then began walking.

Pat Collins lay in the grass, watching the first sergeant in the distance wander to one knoll after another, circling and doubling back, looking for the captain. After several hours, Collins called Harry Rogers.

The captain growled over the radio, "Next time, take notes!"

Harry Rogers developed his boxing program and became widely respected as both an outstanding coach as well as a fighter. Coming from Boston, Rogers had grown up boxing in Golden Gloves, Police Athletic League, and other junior programs.

When the boxing smokers got well under way, Rogers found himself with few matches. Many of the big guys refused to box him and said, "I don't want to hurt you, First Sergeant." But Rogers and the other Marines knew better. Rogers could whip nearly any man in the company, and most in the battalion.

During those weeks before and after the incident at Cam Ne, Pat Collins had alternated his patrolling patterns to where he sent a squad west to the mountains four or five days and then south five to seventeen days. The extent of their patrols depended to a great degree on how long their radio batteries lasted.

He developed a system by which he would work an area with seven patrols that operated near each other's flanks so that one could cover another in case they ever ran into trouble. As the final bailout, Collins assigned an eighth patrol that remained in the rear as a pickup and recovery team. These men worked at the combat operations center and acted as a liaison between the seven patrols in the field and the fire support and air units. They made sure no one shot the recon teams in the field.

Pat Collins usually worked areas where his units were the only friendly forces around. This way, he knew that anything that moved was not friendly.

In most of those situations, the artillery had a range that could hit both the reconnaissance teams and the enemy, and tended to be very active throughout those free-fire zones. Thus Collins depended heavily on the competence of the men he left in the rear. His standing order was that in every case the rear reconnaissance team ensured that fire support and air kept a clear zone of 1,000 meters around the operating teams. He made sure that his men knew to clearly identify for the artillery and air units where the seven patrols were and kept them abreast of their progress. Collins called it his "Jesus factor."

He trained all the newly assigned reconnaissance Marines in his own brand of patrol operations. When in the jungle, usually in the western hills, they moved in the daylight observing night tactics.

For example, he taught his Marines to pick out a clandestine assembly area where they could spend the night, but move past it. Then after dark, they would move back to it, form a triangle, and set up for the night.

Collins required each of the nine men on the patrol to stand a half-hour watch. That way, all the men rested. He claimed that it was better to have one man wide awake during his half-hour watch than have him groggy for three or four hours and then wasted all the next day too.

His men would sleep in the triangle, one man sitting up, fully alert in the center. They slept with all their clothes and equipment on and passed the watch to the right. Sometimes one or two of the men would pull two watches in the night, but they were always fully alert.

About 40 minutes before dawn, he would awaken everyone and they moved again, approximately 180 meters. This way, if the enemy had watched the team set up for the night, and planned to attack after nightfall, the team would not be where the enemy had last seen them. If during the night the enemy happened to discover their position, by dawn the team would be gone again.

When in the lowlands, Pat Collins's Marines only patrolled at night. They would not move at all in the daytime. The teams would sleep through the day, using the same half-hour watch tactic, and hold up in an abandoned hut or a swampy area, sleeping in the water among the reeds and high grass.

Pat Collins normally trained new patrol leaders in several phases of increasing responsibility: first as an observer, then on two patrols as assistant patrol leader, and then two patrols as leader with either Collins himself, Harry Rogers, or John DelGrosso on patrol to watch. After that the new patrol leader would lead his team on three outings into very controlled areas.

Every patrol stood inspection before going out, and the men knew Collins's Essential Elements of Information backward and forward.

They knew their warning orders, and their rally points. They knew the point in front of them and the one behind them, and knew to signal as they passed. They knew that the tentative rally point was in front and the en route point was behind. They knew all their pickup points should something go wrong. Trouble and they would scatter, but automatically went to their primary, secondary, or tertiary pickup points. Once the situation had settled, the leader could go to those points and regroup his Marines.

In the weeks that led into August, although shorthanded, Pat Collins's company grew from merely qualified to highly skilled patrols. When he began he had lieutenants and staff noncommissioned officers leading patrols, but as time passed, he now had corporals and sergeants leading them. But in every case, he knew that these men were good.

## •5•

JOHN DELGROSSO STOOD OUTSIDE THE COMPANY HEADQUARTERS tent where inside Harry Rogers busily stuffed boxing gloves and headgear into a seabag. They were going down to the Seabee compound for a few days and he knew that there would be plenty of chances for some rousing smokers between his Marines and the Seabees.

"I think old Railway Track Charlie would have been better off running the beach operations," DelGrosso said.

Inside the tent Harry Rogers called out, "Lieutenant, look at the good side. We've got a few good days coming while the Mad Man and Railway take the troops looking for Indians up in the mountains. In a couple of days any of those guys will gladly trade places with us. We'll have the Life of Rielly. Eating Seabee ice cream. Watching their movies."

"Don't forget that we've got the beach patrol and the little problem of Viet Cong infiltration between the Seabee camp and the marine compound," John DelGrosso said. "I think they've had three firefights this week and never saw dink one."

Harry Rogers hauled the bag out to the jeep and tossed it into the short, two-wheel trailer that they had hitched to the back bumper. "Got an idea for EPD," he said, smiling, walking back for another load of boxing equipment.

"What's that?" John DelGrosso asked, watching the stocky first sergeant.

"Those beach patrols," Rogers said, now laughing to himself.

"There's nothing tough about the beach patrols," John DelGrosso said. "We just run the jeep down China Beach and stake a fifty up on Monkey Mountain. If we make contact, we run Charlie up the beach where the guys on the mountain ding 'em with the fifty. I don't see anything shitty about that."

Rogers laughed out loud. "Shitty! You missed it."

John DelGrosso scratched his head and smiled at the first sergeant. "Maybe I'm just not that bright, Harry. What's so goddamned funny?"

"All these dinks," Rogers said. "Where do they dump their honey pots? Where do they hang their asses by the dozens to take a shit? Where is there more shit lying on the ground than anyplace in this shit pile of a country?"

John DelGrosso laughed. "China Beach."

"Give the man a cigar," Harry Rogers said. "When we run those jeep patrols, our guys aren't just going to drive along the coast where the sand is pretty and all the little girls go swimming. They're gonna be driving on the back side, in the boonies, in all those shitty spots."

"Shit's gonna splash all over the jeep, and somebody's got to clean it up," DelGrosso said.

Rogers gleamed, and dropped a wooden box inside the back of the jeep. "I've already got a list of prime candidates, although a lot of them are with the skipper and Lieutenant Scarfano. However, I think that this is EPD right up there with burning shitters."

I N THE DISTANCE HE COULD SEE THE PARALLEL RUNAWAYS AND THE huts and buildings that surrounded Da Nang Air Base. Beyond the runways he could see the bare earth and green tent tops of the various battalion compounds, including his company's.

Pat Collins stopped and looked to his left and traced the winding orange scar of a roadway that cut through the green of Hill 327 and he tried to count tents there too. He lost track after eighteen and felt good. If it confused him, it probably confused the enemy too.

Next to each tent, he could just make out the wooden uprights of the new sea huts, as they called them. These were the more permanent barracks for the Marines who still lived in tents. Sea huts, made of wood-frame uprights set in a waist-high arrangement of red tile bricks and then covered with canvas and plywood sides, big screen wire windows, and tin roofs, were springing up everywhere. Once the Seabees finished a building, Marines immediately stacked a double-thick ring of sandbags around the red tile bricks before they moved inside.

He looked at his watch and then motioned to Charlie Scarfano, who sat whispering in conversation with Corporal John Dobbs and Gunnery Sergeant Bob Holt, that they should get to their feet and push westward. They had to hurry before they reached the point where Pat Collins had planned for them to spend their first night under the canopy of the jungle on the western hills.

During that first night Pat Collins awoke twice. The ground was hard and he looked around the hillside where his squad slept and saw a shed with a thatched roof. When he stood the Marine sitting watch looked up at him and smiled. It was very dark, but the moon shone down between the thin cover above their heads and lit the place well.

"I'm gonna rack out on that shed," he told the Marine and he nodded. "Make sure that everyone knows it's me up there and not some gook."

The Marine nodded again.

Pat Collins had six squads scattered across the hill at one place or another. He was at the center and he planned to move to a point 200 meters southwest before dawn.

When he rolled over and saw the light and the fog rising from the ground and around the jungle like smoke, he started to leap off the shed and yank up whoever fell asleep on post and rattle him good. But he saw no one.

A sudden twist of concern wrenched him and as he started to slide from the roof, several pops from rifles firing cracked through the air and echoed in the forest. Next, a sudden explosion in his back, striking him in the center of his rucksack, knocked him off the shed.

I've been shot! Pat Collins thought as he fell hard against the ground, flat and spread on his stomach, which knocked his breath out for a moment. The pain in his back burned and he tried to move.

His ears rang with the chatter of several rifles firing across the forest, and he knew his Marines had opened up against a VC and he was somewhere between the two. So he lay as flat as he could and waited.

"Goddamn, Skipper!" Pat Collins heard a voice say as he felt hands grab him. "That fuckin' dink shot the shit out of your pack. Fucked up your lunch, I guess. How's your back?"

Six of his men crowded close and Pat Collins looked at the corpsman. "Hurts like a bitch, Doc, but you tell me."

"You'll live, Skipper," the corpsman said, lifting up the captain's shirt and looking at the damage to his back. "It didn't break the skin. Just left a purple welt about the size of a dollar."

Bob Holt squatted and helped Pat Collins repair the damage done to his pack, taking some communications wire and knotting it around the tear that the bullet left. "Good thing they got shitty ammo, probably loaded it themselves with homemade gunpowder."

Pat Collins reached behind himself with his right hand and shoved it up near his shoulder blade and rubbed the sore spot with his index finger. "Just not enough power," he said. "Did you get him?"

"Shit no," Holt said.

Pat Collins slipped on the pack and looked at Holt. "That one matches the bruises still on my ass and legs."

Holt laughed. "Yes, sir. I thought about that. I started to say something but you didn't seem in the spirit so I let it go."

Two weeks earlier Pat Collins had walked into an ambush with Holt and the Viet Cong had opened up with an A4 machine gun directly on Collins. The bullets struck the captain across the legs and butt and sent him head over end, tumbling into a rice paddy.

"I thought that bastard had blown my legs off," Collins said with a laugh, which helped him release the anxious pressure that built in his chest. He could not help but think that he might be dead had the enemy good powder, decent ammunition, and arms.

"You live a charmed life, sir," Holt said, slapping the captain across the shoulder and giving him a hand up.

"We've had our share of scrapes," Collins said, adjusting his shoulders again under the weight of his pack.

"That's why I like to patrol with you," Holt said. "You scare the shit out of everyone, but we come out alive. You're like Superman. Bullets just bounce off you."

"Come on," Pat Collins said and began walking. "That VC knows where we are and he's told his buddies, so stay alert. How come it's daylight and Charlie gets the jump on us?"

"On you," Holt said. "I didn't perch your ass on that shed. We were up and heard the bastard stumbling around in the dark. He was focused on your chain-saw snoring. We waited and opened up as soon as we saw him."

Throughout that morning, the patrols moved cautiously over the lower hills and started up the side of a mountain that seemed alive with sign. At nearly every turn the men found broken bits of blue and red plastic, clearly marking trails.

Pat Collins remembered patrolling with Frank Reasoner and seeing the same kind of plastic markings and began noting the locations on his map.

"I think we're getting into some heavy shit," Bob Holt told Pat Collins, who stood counting the markings on the map.

"Can we raise division?" Collins asked the lance corporal who stood behind him packing the radio.

The man nodded confidently and began making the call.

"Some of these trails looked pretty well traveled," Charlie Scarfano said to Collins on the radio. Scarfano had moved with another patrol and now sat at the other side of a draw that extended up the side of the high ridge that the company now climbed.

Ledge by the ledge the trails showed the wear that Scarfano had noticed on the southern flank and now Pat Collins saw too. The traffic seemed to be by foot because even a bicycle would not handle the sheerness of some of the cliffs.

"I've got tracks up here," Scarfano said on the radio. "Somebody's got rolling stock in the neighborhood."

His patrol had moved to the crest of the ridge and found what looked like a roadway.

"What sort of tracks?" Collins said.

"Vehicle. I can't tell, but somebody's got dual wheels on at least one of whatever it is," he said.

"You sure they weren't left there by our people?" Collins said. "You know the ARVN has been all over this country."

"Could be, sir," Scarfano said, "but they look fairly recent and we got more little bits of blue plastic every few yards that runs parallel to this trail."

Once Pat Collins saw the trail he knew that major supplies had to be passing along this route. He didn't know how far he had to travel yet to find the supply point.

"Let's just follow along the ridge," Collins said. "North or south. Take your pick."

Scarfano said, "I like north. Bet they're headed south."

"We go north," Collins said and walked back to where Bob Holt had waited with the other patrols.

"We'll cover each side of the ridge and parallel this road," Collins told Holt. "Scarfano has the east side of the ridge and we'll take the west."

Slowly and silent the patrols, working in six teams, spread down each side of the ridge that soon became known as Dodge City, which overlooked another hellhole called Happy Valley. They pushed northward through the rest of the day.

Pat Collins saw that the forest had become darker, and felt the chill of an oncoming shower. He knew that it would help in their movement but would limit their ability to see as the day dwindled toward dusk. Other than the one VC who shot him that morning, they had seen no other enemy.

It was the quick flash of movement that first caught his attention. He had learned long ago to see not only through the front of his eyes but through the sides as well, and it was through his peripheral vision that he first noticed the split-second flicker.

On the periphery of his right, he saw Bob Holt freeze too and he knew that it had not been a bird or monkey. Slowly Pat Collins knelt and waited and sniffed the air. In the few months that he had led reconnaissance patrols in Vietnam, he and his men had learned to smell the enemy, and he now caught a whiff of the distinctive odor of human sweat mixed with the foul fish stench of nuc mom, a concoction of fish and vegetables fermented in their own juices and buried in an earthen jar. It was VC C-rations, and when the enemy sweated he smelled of the stuff.

Collins pointed to his nose and then pointed ahead of him at the blind of trees that dropped behind a draw. Holt nodded and Pat Collins heard him sniff the air.

With the quietness of a still hunter, Pat Collins crept forward, easing an inch at a time, careful not to break a twig or rustle the soggy mulch-covered forest floor.

It was almost like hunting deer; that was the similarity that ran through Pat Collins's mind when the Viet Cong guerrilla suddenly saw him and bolted like a frightened buck, leaping straight up and jumping down the draw.

Pat Collins heard Bob Holt's heavy footsteps behind him, already started for the fleeing guerrilla. Collins sprang forward and jumped down the draw too. His feet struck the loose bed of leaves and broken, rotting twigs and slid, and he grabbed branches to keep from sliding over the rocky cliff that suddenly appeared ahead of him.

"The bastard's down there," he grunted with a deep breath to Holt, who stood at the top of the draw.

"Look out, Skipper," Hole said, "he's liable to blow your head off if you stick it over the cliff."

Pat Collins stood, and as he reached his full height, he saw the frightened soldier. The captain had nearly gotten his rifle pointed at the man and was about to shoot when he saw the guerrilla's arm swing hard above his head and release an object that looked like a black can with a brown stick coming out of the end.

"Grenade!" Pat Collins heard Bob Holt shout just as the object struck him squarely between the eyes, snapping his head backward and sending a severe, driving pain straight through the center of his head.

Bob Holt crashed on the ground, breaking low branches and letting out a loud grunt as he landed. Pat Collins heard himself say, "Shit!" as he looked between his feet and saw the Chinese-made grenade still spinning between his feet.

His stomach turned as the small bomb stopped spinning, and in a second Pat Collins leapt into space, landing six feet below at the bottom of the cliff. He waited for the explosion but it never came, and he climbed back up and looked at the grenade.

Bob Holt lay at the top of the draw and peeked down to see Pat

Collins climbing back, his face bloody and a lump the size of a hen's egg rising between his eyes.

"You better have the doc take a look at that," Holt said.

"Shit," Collins said, "I'm punchy, hurt, but I'm still alive."

"Like I said"—Bob Holt smiled—"you're the luckiest man I know. Spent bullets and now a dud grenade. Pure luck."

"Bad fuckin' ammo," Pat Collins said.

"That's good for us," Bob Holt said.

"Right," Collins said, holding a wet bandanna against the wound.

Pat Collins prided himself on the fact that every man in his company sported some sort of battle scar, yet he never considered what might constitute a Marine deserving a Purple Heart medal until he noticed men from other units receiving the medals for what he considered incidental injuries Thus many minor bullet wounds and punji stick injuries among his men went unreported.

Often these wounds were only a welt rather than a hole because of the Viet Congs' frequent use of homemade ammunition with crudely concocted gunpowder, or out-of-date ammunition and ordnance supplied to them by the Soviets or Chinese at high costs.

Despite the conservative criteria that Pat Collins maintained in the awarding of a Purple Heart, before the end of August 1965 every man in Company D, 3rd Reconnaissance Battalion, had received at least one Purple Heart by Collins's standards.

While Pat Collins and his patrols pushed ahead, looking for the lone guerrilla, Charlie Scarfano, hearing the call on the radio that the captain had been slightly wounded by a dud grenade, had pushed to sweep to an angle of Collins's flank in hopes of cutting off the fleeing Viet Cong. When he tried to get back on line and resume the patrol at Collins's flank northward, he discovered he had lost his orientation to the supply route.

"Goddamnit, Charlie," Collins complained on the radio, "I'm not going to walk over there and show you where you are. You'll have to figure it out. Climb a damned tree or something. But there sure as hell aren't any railway tracks around here!"

Scarfano saw a tree on the ridge above him and he felt certain that if he climbed it, he could pick out the faint roadway and by that find the locations of the other teams and Captain Collins.

He left his rifle with his radio operator and sneaked quietly to the tree and began working his way up to the higher branches. The lieutenant had hardly made it halfway into the lower limbs when twenty feet below him he heard the sound of heavy breathing. As he looked down between his toes, he saw the top of the head of a Vietnamese man wearing a khaki shirt, black shorts, and he had a rifle in his hands. His head darted from left to right as he stood beneath the tree, looking where to move next.

A sudden chill filled the lieutenant's entire insides. He squatted on the branch, totally unarmed. All the guerrilla would have to do is look up. My God! he thought, I'm dead!

Thirty feet away, he could see his radio operator, lying quietly and looking up the rise, trying to see the man. He had heard him too, and even though he had his rifle up, ready to shoot, he could not see the enemy soldier.

He didn't even think, he simply jumped.

Charlie Scarfano hit the soldier with both feet directly in the middle of his back and drove him to the ground with an awful crunch. The sound of the Viet Cong's snapping collarbone and shoulder cracked nearly as loudly as a rifle shot and the man cried out in brutal pain. Railway Track Charlie had captured a prisoner.

"That's the same bastard who clubbed me with the grenade," Pat Collins said, watching the corpsman as he bound up the prisoner's arm and shoulder into one tightly wrapped bandage.

"I want to go back up that tree," Scarfano told Pat Collins as the corpsman worked. "There was something that I saw before the VC got under me. It may be nothing, but let me take a look."

Pat Collins walked up to the high tree and gave the lieutenant a foot lift up to the lower branches. As the Marine climbed higher and higher he kept looking more and more until he was nearly at the top of the tree and he stopped.

"What is it," Collins asked in a low voice, and the startled look that came over the lieutenant's face at the sound of his words told the captain that they were dangerously close to trouble.

The lieutenant came down the tree fast and when he slid to the bottom he looked squarely in the eyes of his captain and said, "You're not going to believe this. Nobody is."

"What?" Collins said.

"Let's get a patrol and move forward and you'll see. Not even three hundred yards down that side of the ridge. Charlie. Big time," the lieutenant panted.

Slowly the patrol crept forward and Pat Collins peered through his binoculars and watched dozens of soldiers, rifles on their backs, stacking boxes and staging supplies, ready for movement.

"They've got trucks either hauling it in here or hauling it out of here," Pat Collins said.

"How many you suppose down there," the lieutenant whispered.

"Not enough," Collins said. "They have about eighty or ninety and all told we've got fifty-six, if we mass the six teams. By my three-to-one rule of thumb, we outnumber them twofold."

Bob Holt slid close to Pat Collins and said, "We've got the company laid on an angle at two sides of these guys. One team has made a recon of the area and these guys no doubt think they're alone."

"What's our prisoner say," Collins asked.

"*Chu hoi*," Holt grumbled. "No English, but all he'll say is *chu hoi*, don't shoot."

"I want a rear guard, just in case," Collins said. "I'll take four teams and clear this out while you take two teams and keep security. If they have help, they'll come running when we start dinging these bastards."

The Viet Cong never had a chance and the battle was over almost in minutes. As Collins and his men set fire to the supplies and used grenades to destroy the boxes of munitions, all old and badly decomposed, they heard the sound of rifle fire down the ridge where Bob Holt had circled to catch any fleeing enemy.

· 6 ·

BY AS EARLY AS JULY 21, BASED ON INTELLIGENCE REPORTS AND other sources, General Walt had concluded that Chu Lai was vulnerable to attack by an enemy force of as many as three regiments. Realistically, many of General Walt's staff believed that the Viet Cong would not risk such a large concentration of force against American firepower, but they agreed that Charlie might very well attack Chu Lai with a reinforced regiment in a hit-and-run assault.

When operations in the south began, heavy concentrations of enemy moved against Marines in hit-and-run assaults, yet the later operations such as the sweep through Cam Ne on August 3, and the operations in areas south of there in Blastout I netted few Viet Cong captured or killed or even seen. The only conclusion that General Walt and his staff could reach was that the enemy had moved out in force.

Now, given the indications that heavy supplies still moved to the southeast from the mountains to the northwest and west of Da Nang, the threat on Chu Lai grew darker and darker as each day passed. The critical question remained: Where had the enemy gone? Where were they hiding?

• 7 •

I THINK I HIT HIM, LIEUTENANT," THE VOICE IN THE FADING DARKNESS said, "I can see a blood trail on the ground."

Below them several splotches of red shone at the edge of the roadway that ran between the two camps. The lights that lit the perimeter wire reflected across the road and with his hands cupped around his flashlight, holding it near the ground, John DelGrosso could see the deep red color of the fluid that lay in three wet, quarter-sized puddles.

"See any others?" John DelGrosso asked Harry Rogers, who squatted in the weeds near the roadway.

"A few more on down the road where they trampled in the grass, but it doesn't make sense," Rogers said. "If the kid hit him, I think that there would be blood drops at regular intervals."

John DelGrosso knew that the single shot in the dark had most likely ruined any chance they might have of catching the infiltrators at their work. With hardly an hour before daylight, the odds of the VC returning were slight.

"We going in?" Doc Thomas asked hopefully, realizing the odds.

"I'm thinking," DelGrosso said. He looked at Harry Rogers, who squatted quietly, relaxed and not really caring if they quit or waited longer.

"What do you think?" Rogers said, seeing the lieutenant's pondering.

"We saw one guy with a rifle," DelGrosso said. "One shot fired and no kill. Just something that looks like blood, and some bent grass. Let's try to track them. We won't take more than a couple of hours."

"It's no trail," Rogers said. "It's just a fluke we saw what we did in the dark."

"If we're lucky, maybe we can find some more," John DelGrosso said. "Besides, we're getting enough light now that we should be able to see any significant amounts of blood. Anyway, I'd feel better going through the wire in full light of day. These guys are still too jumpy around here, and I don't like the idea of moving into the wire in subdued light after we cranked off one round."

Slowly the black-faced patrol waded step by step through the marsh grass and brush that lay in the sandy wetlands that stretched south and west of the encampments where on both sides of the roadway nervous Seabees and Marines in the first gray light of a new day watched their perimeters for infiltrating sappers.

More than an hour had passed and now John DelGrosso's patrol had searched along the path of broken twigs and random splotches of red goo in a large circle that brought them back to a point less than fifty yards from where they had begun the trek.

John DelGrosso smiled as he looked to his right where Harry Rogers had already realized what the enemy had done. Slowly the lieutenant crawled next to the first sergeant and whispered, "Form a V right here and let's wait."

In less than ten minutes the nine men had positioned themselves so that their fire would interlock across a small path that led through the marsh grass and back to the roadway near the canal. John DelGrosso knew that the infiltrators were still here and that they would depart this way in order to get back to the canal and their boats without being seen while the Seabees and Marines exchanged fire.

The first rifle shot caused him to jump and he looked hard at the horizon where the lights from the camps still flickered against the gray sky.

Suddenly the thudding sound of running feet made John DelGrosso's finger tighten on his AR-15 carbine's trigger. He looked over the top of the handle that served as sights and saw the two silhouettes, men clearly carrying rifles, running.

In that instant he pulled hard on his trigger and sent an automatic burst of fire that seemed to ignite an entire war. Muzzle flashes crackled around him as other AR-15 rifles and heavier caliber M-14s sent a hail of interlocking lead that immediately killed both Viet Cong before they fell to the ground and then tore at their bodies, ripping them to pieces.

"Cease fire!" Harry Rogers shouted. "They're dead already! For cryin' out loud. There's only two of 'em. Shit! You guys worked 'em over like hamburger."

John DelGrosso reported the results on the radio as his men sat and waited for the gray sky to grow bright enough so that they could safely return home.

Harry Rogers sat next to the bodies and with a stick he opened the mouth of one of the men. Then he pried the other's open. With his two fingers he felt in the pocket of one man and brought out a bag. He dug in one finger and brought out a load of crushed pulp made of seeds and leaves that had the slight scent of lime and shone deep red in the orange morning light that now spread over the flat marshes and sandy clumps of brush.

"Betel nut," Harry Rogers said. "I knew that wasn't blood we was seein', Lieutenant. It was their spit full of betel nut juice. The dumb shits were chewing betel nut and spittin' a trail for us. What a dumb couple of dead gooks!"

# CORNERING CHARLIE

•1•

ENERAL WESTMORELAND HAD ALWAYS BEEN AN AGGRESSIVE SOL-
dier. His years at West Point had made him into an officer who focused on an objective and he was quick to shed anything that restrained
him. Watching the Marines' slow progress in the north through July,
Westmoreland called Walt and questioned him about the pace.

During July the 1st Viet Cong Regiment had attacked the garrison at
Ba Gia, twenty miles south of Chu Lai, overrunning the hamlet, killing or
wounding 130 Vietnamese defenders and making off with more than 200
weapons, including two 105-mm howitzer artillery pieces.

The seemingly freewheeling activities of the 1st VC Regiment left
General Westmoreland frustrated since the Marines had yet to engage
them. Both III MAF and MACV intelligence had received reports that the
1st VC Regiment was now in the mountains west of Chu Lai and moving
in for the kill. Now, with the threat of Chu Lai in question, per the reports that the 1st VC Regiment was moving in strength, it left the general
concerned.

He called General Walt and asked him why his Marines had not expanded their operations more quickly. He told Walt that he expected the

Marine commander to take a greater role in operations with the South Vietnamese forces in the region, moving greater distances and covering greater areas.

General Walt reminded Westmoreland that under the May 6, 1965, Letter of Instruction that he must follow, III MAF was restricted to reserve and reaction missions in support of South Vietnamese forces heavily engaged with an enemy force. As he saw it, they were restricted mostly to defense of their enclaves and bailing out the South Vietnamese forces that had gotten in over their heads.

Westmoreland said, "These restraints are no longer realistic." He told Walt to rewrite his instructions, working into them the authority he needed to adequately move against the enemy and to submit it to him as soon as he could. He told General Walt that this revised Letter of Instruction would be approved.

On August 6, 1965, Walt's revised Letter of Instruction was signed, and he received the permission that he needed in order to move against the enemy that threatened Chu Lai.

That day, General Walt released one battalion from the 4th Marine Regiment to join the 51st ARVN Regiment to search the area south of the Song Tra Bong. The operation, code named Thunderbolt, lasted two days and covered an area seven kilometers south of the river and west of Highway One. They made little contact with the enemy, found few signs of any kind of Viet Cong force, and suffered two Marines wounded while forty-three Marines went down because of heat sickness in the 110-degree temperatures.

Although they found little to no evidence to support the belief that the 1st Viet Cong Regiment was closing in on Chu Lai, it did not lessen the concern. General Walt ordered his staff to keep pushing until they found the enemy regiment. He knew that with the arrival of the 7th Marine Regiment in a matter of days,[1] he could quickly move with telling effect on the 1st VC Regiment. If only he could find them.

---

[1] 7th Marines represented part of the buildup of U.S. strength in South Vietnam to 125,000, called Phase I Forces, which was approved after McNamara's visit in July. The regiment landed at Chu Lai on August 15, 1965.

## • 2 •

THE MAN WAS THE BIGGEST HUMAN THAT PAT COLLINS HAD EVER seen in his life and he was laughing. He grumbled to himself, "Not only is this guy big and ugly, but he's crazy too."

Pat Collins stood and looked at the major who sat in the helicopter operations tent. "Are you serious about this guy? You wouldn't be dumping one off on me."

The major smiled and looked at the huge Marine captain and then at Pat Collins. "He's the only man who had the balls to volunteer. You're not exactly known as Joe Cool. You've got a reputation. They don't call you Mad Man for nothing."

"Don't let looks fool you, Captain," the mammoth captain said to Pat Collins. "I can outfly any of these jocks in my sleep. You want a chopper pilot to take you out to snatch VC? I'm the driver who can do it."

"General Walt wants us to get prisoners to interrogate," Collins said. "I need a pilot who can fly into a village, finger a guy, set down, we grab him, and then get out in a matter of seconds with everybody alive, including the prisoner. You fuck up and we're all dead."

The big man smiled and zipped up the front of his flight suit, catching a crop of chest hair between the brass teeth. Pat Collins watched as the Marine winced slightly. Then when the pilot looked down and saw the hair caught in the zipper, he yanked the front of the flight suit, ripping out the hair by its roots, and then looked at Collins. "Come on. We'll go take a test run."

When Pat Collins walked outside behind the big man, Harry Rogers trotted across the tarmac and walked next to him. Rogers smiled at Collins and said, "Gunny Holt said you're organizing a snatch team."

"That's right," Pat Collins said, walking toward a UH-34 helicopter where two Marines sat in the aircraft's open doorway.

"Bob Holt said that you already picked him and Satchel Ass Dobbs," Rogers said.

"That's right," Collins said, stopping and looking directly at Rogers.

"Well?" Harry Rogers said, smiling.

"Well what, Harry?" Collins said.

"Well, you know?" Rogers said.

"Come go flying with me, and let me think," Collins said, trying hard to hide the delight at teasing the first sergeant, and he knew that it was showing on his face.

"Flying where?" Rogers said.

"Test ride," Collins said. "We're going to see if this crazy captain can pass the snatch test."

Harry Rogers looked at the giant Marine walking around the old helicopter, a black spray of oil on its cowling behind the engine. He saw a number of scrapes along the underside of the aircraft and then he noticed all the holes and the patches that obviously covered other holes. "In that piece of shit?"

The huge pilot had put on a flight helmet with great catlike eyes fashioned in reflective tape on its top. He looked fierce in the helmet and reminded Harry Rogers of a character from a movie about gladiators that he had seen several years ago.

"It ain't a piece of shit," the pilot barked at the first sergeant.

"Hey, no offense, Captain," Rogers said, realizing that the man had superhuman hearing to go along with his size.

"Looks like it's seen a good deal of action, though," Harry offered in an attempt to soften the bristled Marine.

"I got it new," he said. "Drove it almost a year now, and no breakdowns. Just normal maintenance. We've seen plenty of action. Mostly with ARVN and Vietnamese Marines."

The two other Marines who had been sitting in the helicopter's open door now had begun working inside. One man climbed into the cockpit and sat in the right front seat and the other man looked at the two passengers. "You want to strap into a seat or use gunner's belts?" he asked.

Rogers looked at Collins and then at the Marine who obviously was the helicopter's crew chief and said, "Gunner's belts. We need to move around."

"You know how these things work?" the Marine said, handing Rogers a five-inch-wide web belt with a heavy metal clamplike fastener sewn into the nylon webbing and then a heavy leather flap sewn behind that. On the back of the wide belt, a six-foot-long, adjustable nylon strap hung with a heavy metal clip looped on its end.

Rogers wrapped the belt around his waist, snapped the buckle, and then took the inch-wide adjustable strap and flipped it over his shoulder, taking the heavy metal clip in his hand and looking at the crew chief. "This hooks into the cargo rings on the floor, right?"

"You got it, First Sergeant," the Marine said.

Rogers looked at Pat Collins, who had knelt to one knee and now dug his fingers at the wide belt, working loose the loop that it made into the main buckle so that he could let it out to fit his waist. "What'd they do, give you one for a midget?" Rogers asked.

"Goddamned beanpole, I guess," Collins said, finally pulling the loop loose and sliding the belt material so that it lengthened enough to allow him to fit it around his middle.

When Harry Rogers and Pat Collins climbed aboard the helicopter, the huge pilot had already climbed into the cockpit and leaned back down to look at his two passengers. He shoved a long arm down and said, "Shake. Name's Slyde."

Pat Collins took his hand. "I saw it on the leather patch on your flight suit."

"We never introduce ourselves," the pilot said and Pat Collins smiled. "Slydell. But call me Slyde, like Clyde but with an S."

"I'm Pat Collins, this is First Sergeant Harry Rogers," Pat Collins said.

"I've heard them call you Mad Man. You go by that?" the pilot said.

"No," Pat Collins said. "I guess I grew that moniker among the rear-echelon commandos."

"I didn't know," the pilot said. "In the wing, everybody's got some sort of oddball name, like a call sign. I don't know anybody by their Christian name, only hooks like Blackjack, Ace, Grave Digger, Werewolf, you know, crap like that. My first mate up here is Lieutenant White, we call him Rodeo. He's an Aggie from Texas A&M. Rode bucking horses down there, so I guess flying close to the ground is second nature to him. Crew chief there is out of Buffalo, Sergeant Katz. We call him Kitty, but that pisses him off." The huge captain laughed. "He likes to be called Robert, but don't call him Bob. Bob Katz!" He laughed hard again. "That pisses him off too."

"My friends call me Robbie, sir," the sergeant said, checking the hookup on Harry Rogers's and Pat Collins's gunner's belts.

"Thanks, Sergeant," Harry Rogers said.

"Hell, they have their fun, but we really get along," Katz said. "The skipper, though, he's a wild man. Scares shit out of me every flight, so you'd better hang on."

The sergeant jumped outside the helicopter, and in his hand he held several wide loops of a long, black electrical cord connected to his helmet that allowed him to talk to the pilot while he turned up the engines.

In a matter of minutes the sergeant rolled inside the open door and the helicopter lifted up and away at that second.

Pat Collins looked up and saw between the two pilots a familiar-looking wooden box. He poked Harry Rogers and pointed at the box. The first sergeant looked wide-eyed and began laughing. "A box of frags," he shouted.

"He throws grenades at gooks on the ground," Katz shouted in Collins's ear. Then he ambled to a gray-painted metal box bolted to the deck and lifted the lid. He took out two sets of intercom headsets and handed one each to Collins and to Rogers.

When Pat Collins had plugged his headset into the junction box located above his head, the chopper took a sudden hard turn to the right and then one to the left. Katz immediately scrambled to open the port where he had tied down a .30-caliber machine gun. He knew by the tilting and diving that they had come under fire.

Slyde banked hard left, turning the helicopter on nearly a 90-degree bank angle, and Robbie Katz was looking straight down at the jungle where he could see men with rifles now running.

Katz opened up with the machine gun and sent spent brass bouncing throughout the passenger compartment. He never stopped firing as the copter drove to the treetops and then zigzagged back after the enemy.

Through all of this Pat Collins could hear the huge captain at the pilot controls howling with laughter.

Harry Rogers had crawled to the open doorway and sat there with his legs dangling down, his toes seeming to be only inches from the trees. Pat Collins sat next to him and rested his rifle in his lap, ready to shoot between his feet.

"You hear that big son of a bitch laugh?" Pat Collins shouted at Harry Rogers.

The first sergeant looked at Collins and smiled, shouting, "Crazy! Fits right in with the rest of our gang!"

Pat Collins felt down the wire hooked to his headset and when he found the talk button, he spoke into the microphone suspended in front of his mouth by a wire boom that was anchored to the left side of the headset. "How about we take a look through a couple of villages and I'll show you what I want," Pat Collins said to the pilot.

"Roger," the captain said and turned the helicopter. "How low should we pass?"

"I want to be able to see in the huts," Pat Collins said. "Do you think you can get that low?"

"You just tell me when," Slyde said and laughed hoarsely.

Pat Collins noticed the chopper suddenly drop when it crossed over the rice paddies. He could see the spray of water behind the helicopter and knew that this pilot would certainly do, if he didn't crash first.

He leaned slightly forward and saw the village ahead and the pilot kept the helicopter skimming along with its wheels only a foot or two above the earth. As they zoomed past the first cluster of huts, Pat Collins could only see the flash of some faces, wide-eyed and very frightened, just inside the doorways. Behind them, baskets, jars, rakes, bicycles, chickens, walls from huts, all seemed to tumble together in a dusty whirlwind left by the speeding helicopter.

"You're too goddamned fast," Pat Collins shouted.

The pilot howled and hawed, and laughed so loudly that Pat Collins and Harry Rogers could have heard him above the roar of the chopper's engine without the aid of the headsets.

"Good altitude. Hold that," Collins said, "but slow down so I can see inside the huts. We're past them before I can make out anything other than eyes and teeth."

Slyde turned the helicopter with its nose raised and came back, barreling nose down for the village again. Then, just as the copter reached the huts, he raised the nose and roared past the huts much more slowly.

This time Pat Collins could see the frightened faces of children hugging their mothers, fathers hugging the mothers and the children, all of them looking out the doorways in disbelief. He could tell that they were only farmers, at least for now. He knew then that he could not have found a better pilot or more perfect finger man for the job.

•3•

S IR, HERE'S THE LATEST RECON SITREPS," B. C. COLLINS SAID AS HE
entered a room where Colonel Leo J. Dulacki, a brilliant Marine officer who had proven himself as a highly talented intelligence officer, plotted enemy points of contact on a large map. Dulacki would eventually
rise to the rank of lieutenant general. Dulacki stood next to a master sergeant and a major, each holding stacks of papers, clipped together, and
reading information to the colonel from them.

"Over there, Corporal," Dulacki said.

"Like a Chinese crossword puzzle," B. C. Collins said. "Charlie's all
over the place."

The colonel took the reports that gave him reconnaissance sightings
of enemy units, times and places, strengths and activities, and one by one
he plotted the coordinates on the big map. Then he handed the papers to
the major.

"See," the colonel said, stepping back.

"Lots of sightings," Collins said.

"But there are sightings and there are sightings," Dulacki said wisely.

"The enemy covers his tracks so he makes contact on purpose. These
are the aberrations," the colonel said. "Look at the picture once you discount these. You see? Truly the 1st Viet Cong Regiment is on the march
to Chu Lai. They are close. But exactly where?"

"Well, 4th Marines sure didn't see them down there, sir," Collins
said, pointing to the area where the battalion from the 4th Marine Regiment and the 51st ARVN Regiment had patrolled south of the Song Tra
Bong, nine miles below Chu Lai.

"I know this as sure as I'm standing here," the colonel said, looking
at the map and then at the major and the master sergeant, "that regiment
is down there, slowly but surely closing on Chu Lai."

"Send recon down there," B. C. Collins said. "We can find 'em."

"General Walt has been very jumpy," the master sergeant said, looking at the map and marking other positions. "You know, we have a lot of
Marines here who fell victim to the Chinese in Korea, at the Chosen
Reservoir. The colonel here had a battalion in 7th Marines. We pushed
too far and got cut off and surrounded by the bastards, and we sure don't
want to see that happen here. The thought of the enemy lying in wait

somewhere around southern I Corps in near-division strength ready to overrun Chu Lai, has General Walt pushing hard. Right now, that air base and enclave is like a goat tied to a stake, waiting for the stalking tiger to gobble him up."

The colonel walked back to the map and gave the master sergeant and B. C. Collins a sly wink, both of whom now stood at the map, puzzling at the dozens of marks on it. Dulacki stared at the board and looked west of Chu Lai. "The best information we have reports that the 1st VC Regiment is somewhere here"—and he swept a circle over the map with his finger—"west of Chu Lai and on the march. And by the way, Corporal, we have recon looking."

"Shit," B. C. Collins said and then realized his comment had been out of place. "Excuse me, sir. But Colonel Blanchard nailed me to this office work because I punched out another corporal. I just get pissed off every time I think about it. I ought to be out there with those guys, with all due respect, sir."

Dulacki smiled and said, "You've done a good job here, perhaps that will count for something. Maybe you can get a few days off to go hunting. Captain Collins is always on the prowl these days. General Walt has him looking under every rock. Maybe they could fit you in."

"Never," B. C. Collins said. "Doc Blanchard, he'd rather die and go to hell. No, sir. Don't get me wrong, I ain't going sour on the man. He did good by me because anybody else would have locked my young ass up. I got what was coming, but there's no way Colonel Blanchard will slack off."

"Don't say never, Corporal," the master sergeant said. "Talk to Captain Collins or his first sergeant. There's always a way. Take my word for it."

• 4 •

LISTEN, YOU OUTLAW," PAT COLLINS TOLD B. C. COLLINS AS THEY walked to the flight line, "I've got my ass way over the edge getting you on this mission. I don't know what you and Holt have cooked up, but don't screw up here."

"Skipper," B. C. Collins said, "I'd rather shit razor blades. . . ."

"Yeah," Pat Collins said, cutting off the corporal, "I'm counting on

that. You belong to Gunny Holt. He wanted you on his snatch team because you're big and strong and you got more balls than brains. But don't
forget, you still have pencils to push once we're back, so don't start laying claim to any rack space back at Dirty Delta's hootch."

"Yes, sir," B. C. Collins said, feeling his enthusiasm fade. The idea of
landing a slot on the prisoner snatches made him gain hope that he had
pushed his last pin in a map, even though he had learned a great deal
from his daily trips to the III MAF G-2 where he became familiar with the
big-picture perspective of the war. However, he longed to be on patrol
and the captain's reminder that this evening's work was only temporary,
a one-night stand, left him depressed.

He slowed his pace and now walked behind Pat Collins and Harry
Rogers. Then an arm came over his shoulder and he saw that it was Bob
Holt. Beside Holt walked Corporal John Dobbs and Staff Sergeant Dutch
Miller.

"He's ridin' your ass hard because he wants you in the company,"
Holt said softly so that the captain could not hear. "Doc Blanchard made
the skipper take a blood oath about you. You've got to serve your time
with the lace-pants crowd until Blanchard has gone. Old Paddy said he
would wait two weeks after the colonel has caught the freedom bird back
to the World. That puts you about a month off, with good behavior. I told
the skipper I could use a guy like you on my team. I told him that if he'd
take you on this mission I'd watch you. Don't forget, sports fan, I'm one
of the few bums around here who can whip your ass. I'm telling you this
because I don't want you to go lettin' the skipper down by seein' you
draggin' your chin. He might change his mind about you. Figure you're a
pussy or something." Holt shoved B.C. hard. "And keep a tight lip on
this little conversation. Skipper'd bust my ass."

B. C. Collins held his head up and walked alongside Pat Collins. The
captain eyed him cautiously.

"Sir, I needed to get back to the field, so thanks for taking me," B.C.
said casually as the men walked toward the helicopter. "I was starting to
wear skivvies again, and liking it."

Pat Collins laughed. "Okay."

"I know this is one day only, but it means a lot, sir. I won't forget it,"
B.C. said.

## • 5 •

WHEN THEY HAD SWEPT UP THE STREET OF THE FIRST VILLAGE, looking through the front doors, eyeing the frightened inhabitants watching the green Marine helicopter rush past, kicking up baskets, chickens, dirt, and knocking over walls and fences in its wake, B. C. Collins felt his heart nearly stop. Wide-eyed, he looked at Bob Holt, who sat relaxed next to him, gazing at the huts and the shaken people inside them. Holt looked back and B. C. Collins could read his lips and almost hear him when he shouted, "Relax!"

Bob Holt had gotten used to the daily flights and the sound of Captain "Slyde" howling and laughing as he ripped through another village, blowing away all that was not tied down.

"Wait until he starts chucking grenades out the window at VC," Holt shouted close to B. C. Collins's ear.

B. C. Collins listened to the almost crazy-sounding laughter, despite the loudness of the engines, coming from above him where the pilot sat, driving the helicopter only inches above the ground. He looked across the helicopter and saw Pat Collins looking out the gun port, seemingly as relaxed as if the aircraft was flying above the trees. The corporal tried to relax too, but he knew that would be impossible.

Just as the trees nearly kissed the front of the cowling of the helicopter, Slyde would pull hard on the controls and cause the chopper to almost leap straight up, clearing the jungle. He shoved the nose down and the copter raced away, following the contours of the rising hills toward the mountains.

"That's Chu Lai out yonder," Holt shouted to B. C. Collins as the helicopter turned right to climb higher.

Just off the rear right, B. C. Collins could see a cluster of new construction and the air strip and beyond it several ships lying well off the coast. He knew that they were the Navy task force landing the 7th Marine Regiment.

Beneath them, there were only trees. A trail would open into a clearing and the helicopter would circle and the men inside would look close, but they had seen nothing. Pat Collins knew that with the several reports, all of which had come from Vietnamese sources, that the 1st Viet Cong

Regiment had marched northwest from Ba Gia, into the mountains west of Chu Lai, then there should be some sign, some track.

"Ten minutes, we go back for gas and a drink of water," Slyde said on the intercom to Pat Collins.

He pushed the button on the line coming from the headset, keying his microphone, and said, "Then let's move over that next ridge and take a look. After that we'll pack and go back."

The helicopter zigzagged down the valley and followed the contours of the land up the ridge and over the top. The pilot, the crew chief, the copilot, Pat Collins, all the snatch team scanned the horizon and then down along the ridges and draws and humps and dips of the land, and they did not see what B. C. Collins and Bob Holt saw, who sat in the open door, their legs hanging down and looking at the ground passing between their toes.

It was just a flash. A flicker of a glimpse, but it was all Bob Holt needed to pick out the scramble of the several soldiers from a sunlit spot. They crawled and dragged and scuffed through the dirt, hurrying to get to the cover as the American helicopter flew overhead. B. C. Collins blinked as he looked at Holt and both men shouted, pointing to the ground passing beneath them.

Pat Collins pressed the talk button. "Make a slow turn, very wide and slow to the right and come back over that spot again. We saw something and I don't want to spook these guys."

"We'll drop low so you can look ahead and see below the trees," Slyde said. "Maybe we can get a good look."

On the second pass, Pat Collins had his binoculars ready and when he saw what looked to be men low and to the right of them, he put up the glasses and saw clearly several uniformed troops crouched in the shadows, half hidden in the brush.

"Turn back, and head east," Pat Collins said over the intercom. "We'll come back after dark."

The reported sighting of uniformed soldiers, possibly North Vietnamese, caused speculation but didn't answer anything about the location of the 1st Viet Cong Regiment. Pat Collins hoped that when he returned that evening, with a reinforced platoon, and Golf Company, 2nd Battalion, 9th Marine Regiment, he could grab a prisoner or two who could supply those answers.

B. C. Collins never left the helicopter. He volunteered as the gear watch and waited for fear of being left out. His day was already over, but the night had only begun, and he wanted to hold on to the mission. He sat, chewing crackers smeared with peanut butter, washing it down with coffee that Robbie Katz had brought out. Katz wore a tiger-stripe camouflage uniform similar to those worn by the South Vietnamese Marines and U.S. Marine advisers. Several of the Marines who had come to Vietnam in 1964 as crewmen on the helicopters that supported the South Vietnamese forces wore the uniforms, which made them stand apart from the rest of the Marines. Many wore them more as a symbol of their seniority in country, but that meant little to B. C. Collins. For Robbie Katz, it reminded him that he would soon leave, that his year was nearly at an end, until tonight, when he got the news.

Katz slurped coffee to wash down the peanut butter that clung inside his mouth. "Fuck it," he said, shoving the half-eaten can of peanut butter back into the C-ration box and brought out of it a can of peach halves in heavy syrup. As he worked the can opener, which he had strung on his identification tag necklace, he looked at B. C. Collins. "How long before your rotation date?"

"I only got here in May," Collins said, crunching more crackers and slurping coffee. "Hell, I'm still shittin' stateside chow."

"Well, I'm fucked," Katz said, "and so are about half the guys in Vietnam and nearly everyone in the wing."

"I heard rumbles of involuntary extensions all summer," Collins said, sensing the trouble.

"Word went out yesterday. Everybody in the operations hootch is talking," Katz said. "Involuntary extensions are officially in effect for four months. I'll get home by the holidays, if I live that long. Once I leave here I still gotta go to Pendleton and get out of the Crotch, probably a week, then I'll be hitting the Port Authority Bus Terminal off Thirty-fourth Street in midtown Manhattan and home, a few blocks away in Hell's Kitchen. I was counting on being there in time to catch when the Yankees wrap the season with their annual home stand against the Red Sox up in the Bronx."

B. C. Collins said nothing. He chewed more crackers and peanut butter, and slurped more coffee.

"Fucked," Katz said. "Fuckin' Red Sox will probably sweep anyway. Who really gives a shit. Goddamn four months! What a giant green turd."

One by one the helicopters carrying the Marines from Company G, 2nd Battalion, 9th Marines, disappeared over the mountains west of Da Nang as the sun turned red ahead of them. The aircraft followed the leader by one and two or a clutch of three together.

During the past week, more and more flights carrying companies of Marines into the west and southwest, where the mountains drop to the rice lands and the sea, launched from the airfield at Da Nang. Thus this evening's activity fit well with the night and day before, and the night and day before that and before that too.

Pat Collins, John DelGrosso, his platoon, and the snatch team had flown from Da Nang two hours before the rifle company and had found a clear hill where the infantry could land two or three helicopters at a time. Once there, Company G divided into platoons and hiked up and over the next two ridges, following three reconnaissance teams that Collins had left for them as scouts. Once they had crossed the second ridge, at a spot that Pat Collins had picked, they again assembled their unit.

B. C. Collins had painted on his war face at the helicopter that afternoon, between eating crackers and listening to Robbie Katz complain. Then, as a sour joke, he told Katz that he would probably not live until Christmas anyway, considering the flying habits of his captain. The sergeant called B. C. an asshole and left Collins alone at the chopper until the crew and snatch team returned. Then Katz slapped B. C. Collins across the back and said, "You know, you're probably right. That's what pissed me off."

Now, as the corporal added fresh paint to his already dark green face, he thought about what Katz had said. It preoccupied him and Bob Holt noticed the Marine's sullen expression.

"You about ready to snoop and poop?" Holt asked, gouging B. C. Collins in the shoulder with his elbow.

"That crazy chopper crew gonna wait up at the LZ 'til we get back?" B. C. Collins asked.

"Why should you care?" Holt said.

"I wondered," Collins said.

"Matter of fact, the skipper cut 'em loose and I guess they headed for the barn," Holt said. "We'll hitch on with Golf Company."

"I hate ridin' with that bastard," Collins said, feeling a great relief.

"Yeah, he does get a little hairy," Holt said, looking at the sky, now growing dark and more and more stars becoming visible.

"You ever flown with him at night?" Collins said.

"No, thank God," Holt said, "and I hope I don't. Bad enough in the daylight when you can see what you're missin'. It'd drive me bats to wonder about it. You know, not see it comin'."

In the bottom of the valley that lay between the ridges, John Del-Grosso had found a trail where a large group of people had pushed their way through the elephant grass that grew there. He estimated that fifty to one hundred troops had passed along that route recently, perhaps within hours. When he told this to Pat Collins, the captain decided that they would position the rifle company on the side of the ridge where they could see across the valley and provide cover fire if his scout teams needed to make a hasty withdrawal.

Collins then divided his reconnaissance Marines into four teams of four men each. These scout teams would fan across the valley, generally following the direction that the trail of broken and bent elephant grass led them.

It was a waving sea that seemed to engulf B. C. Collins as he pushed his way into the chest-high grass, taking his turn at the point. The clear, warm August night smelled fresh in the valley where the men could smell only the damp earth, the trees, and the deep grass that bled its sweet odor as they broke its thick stems, pushing on. Ahead, B.C. could see the dark cut that the trail made through the grass and saw how it tended more southerly as the team neared the other side of the valley where a thick line of trees and low brush grew as the ground again sloped upward on the next ridge.

Once at the edge of the valley B. C. Collins knelt and saw fresh tracks that crossed into the trail from another direction, and then as he walked another hundred yards, another trail came into this one. He stopped and held his hand in the air to signal Gunnery Sergeant Holt.

"We're getting close, and these jokers have been in and out of this place a number of times, judging from the wear they've been giving these trails," B. C. Collins said in a deep, hushed voice as he leaned next to Bob Holt's ear.

"You see how the traffic seems to head for that little finger that pokes out in this valley?" Bob Holt said.

"Right," B. C. Collins said, his eyes following the paths to the darkness of a raised tree line that jutted into the deep grass.

"But we don't have to go too far past or even up that finger before we see something of them," Holt said. "Why don't you let me walk up ahead by myself. I'll take a look over that rise and give you the high sign to follow."

He had crept less than a hundred yards farther and had quietly crawled through the brush to the top of the lower end of the finger when he heard the voices. Men talking and laughter. In ten minutes he had B. C. Collins, John Dobbs, and Dutch Miller kneeling at that same spot where they too heard the sounds of the North Vietnamese soldiers carrying through the forest from where they had camped for the night.

"Let's get back and call the skipper," Holt said. "We've got to make a plan before we get any closer. They can't be more than a hundred yards down in that little flat part of the draw that runs by this finger. My guess is that they figure they're far enough away from civilization where they don't have to be too careful."

In less than half an hour, Pat Collins squatted in a circle with John DelGrosso, Bob Holt, and Harry Rogers while the reconnaissance platoon crouched nearby in a large triangle, looking out, into the night, watching and listening for the sound of any enemy patrol that might approach.

"Bob," Pat Collins said, "you and I are going to sneak up that little rise and see if we can eyeball these unlucky bastards." Then he looked at John DelGrosso as he pulled a map from inside his shirt and unfolded it. "You've got the tribe until we get back. Once I see what this camp looks like, we'll decide how we're going to deal with them. Our friendly line is back here," he said, pointing to the lower ridge on the map where Golf Company waited. Then he pointed to three other plots on the map between that ridge and their present position. "These are our pickup points. If you hear shooting, Bob and I will go two different directions and come back here on your right and left. If someone comes charging straight at you, shoot because, coach, it won't be us. And if this world starts shittin' Chinamen, take immediate action and scatter to these pickup points. If we have to bug out to Golf Company's position, we'll circle up to their right flank and come in there. That will give those guys a chance to cut off these bastards broadside in that valley if they give us a chase."

John DelGrosso marked his map and shoved it inside his shirt and sat again in the dark, looking toward the dark rise as Pat Collins and Bob Holt disappeared into the forest.

As the voices and laughing grew louder, Pat Collins could hear his heart pounding, pulsing in his ears. He watched as Bob Holt moved cautiously forward and then he moved. Then as they moved down the side of the finger, and saw the slope gentle off into a hidden cove of a draw, he saw the flickering of several fires.

"Jesus Christ!" Pat Collins whispered. "These guys are on a goddamned camp out. Look at those fires."

"They're afraid of ghosts," Bob Holt said. "Duc told me that."

"Too bad he's not here now, I'm sure he'd have a full explanation," Pat Collins said of the South Vietnamese Marine captain who had been assigned to them for a month and who had accompanied them to Binh Thai on their first flight.

"I'd bet a month's pay, sir," Holt said. "This is August, remember in Okinawa when they used to have all the festivals for the dead and they'd pour salt in the doorways to keep spooks out, and how they'd go to the graveyards and take food?"

"Oban," Pat Collins said. "The festival of the dead. All the spirits, good and bad, are supposed to be up and around. Has something to do with the August moon, like in Europe on All Hallows Eve."

"Yes, sir, gooner Halloween," Holt said. "These aren't Okinawans, but ten to one these chisel-heads have something like that, and look at the moon. It's going on toward being full. Bet you that when it gets full, in another week or two, these guys will be scared shitless of anything that moves in the night."

"I'll buy it," Pat Collins said. "Sounds about as reasonable as any other excuse I could imagine."

"We could put her to the test," Holt said.

"Let's get a plan put together first," Pat Collins said. "It's also just as likely that you're wrong, coach."

"Bet I'm not," Holt said. Then the two men crept back up the hill and down to the flank of where John DelGrosso and the platoon waited.

In an hour, the platoon had rechecked their equipment, their rifles, ammunition, and made sure that nothing on them had worked loose and now rattled or clanked. Pat Collins quietly issued his plan of laying in a line along the upper ridge, above the encampment, while Bob Holt and his snatch team located and took a prisoner.

Cupping his hand around his watch and looking into it, B. C. Collins could see that it was almost straight up midnight. He looked to his left and saw Bob Holt lying on his stomach, gazing just ahead of them at the circle of light made by the campfires. John Dobbs lay to his right and beyond him Dutch Miller, who had crawled so low that he could only see the tops of the Marine's boot heels.

The first hoot nearly set B. C. Collins on his ear, and he felt the sudden sheet of cold sweat suddenly bead on his face, dripping through the green camouflage makeup that he wore on his face. When Bob Holt cried out again, sounding like every idea of the way a ghost ought to sound that B. C. Collins could ever imagine, the corporal whipped his head to the left and glared at Holt. He could not talk, he could only wish that he could clamp both his hands around Holt's neck and squeeze. He's trying to kill us! Collins thought, feeling the tightness of panic trying to lock his body.

The voices and laughing stopped with the first hoot and one of the soldiers, in a loud voice with a sour tone, said something in Vietnamese that neither Holt, Dobbs, Miller, nor B. C. Collins could understand. When Holt cried out the second time, none of the men answered. They just sat close to their fires, holding their rifles, and, blinded by the brightness of the firelight, looked out into the frightening blackness of the night.

B. C. Collins watched as one of the men, a thin man wearing a pistol belt, stood and spoke loudly to the men. He seemed to be scolding them, and he walked to one man who crouched next to the fire and kicked him, knocking the soldier off his haunches. Several of the others laughed and stood, and then, with their rifles raised, they walked directly to where Bob Holt lay. B. C. Collins glanced at Holt and prepared to shoot, but Holt simply lay there.

Suddenly another hoot, much like the first one came from the other side of the circle of fire, and the men stopped.

B. C. Collins looked to his right and he could not find John Dobbs nor Dutch Miller at first, but in a moment he saw the dark shape of Dobbs's stocky build creeping back toward him. He watched as Dobbs squatted and cupped his hands around his mouth and in a soft, almost womanly cry, wailed.

He had heard the old Irish legend of the banshee as a child, and remembered how they believed that when one hears her mournful cry in the middle of the night, a loved one would soon die. B.C. thought to himself that John Dobbs made a wonderful banshee, and he hoped to God that in North Vietnam a banshee's wail was observed much the same way as in Ireland.

John Dobbs crept back to the right of where he had cried out, and then he knelt and gripped his rifle, ready to shoot.

The Vietnamese soldiers obviously had no idea of who or what lurked in the blackness. While their logic told them that it had to be an intruder, their strong beliefs in supernatural powers kept them crouching close to the fires, snuggling behind their rifles, fully alert and extremely frightened.

"Did you shit yourself," Bob Holt whispered in an almost silent breath in B. C. Collins's ear and made the corporal jerk hard, knocking his head into Bob Holt's.

"I thought I was wacky," Collins whispered back. "You have completely left the planet! In about a minute these guys are gonna come huntin' us!"

"I'll lay odds they stay put," Holt whispered back. "It's Oban, man. The dead are all up, walking around. These guys won't move. I promise."

Collins showed Holt his middle finger and said in a louder, more raspy, and angry whisper, "You better fuckin' hope, or we're all goin' home in the hold baggage."

Holt put his arm over Collins and gave him a reassuring hug and then patted his head. "Settle in, we're gonna let these guys crap out. By daylight, they'll all be sound asleep. We'll walk in, grab that captain who kicked that guy's ass, and run for it. I'll snatch the guy and you three'll hose the camp down like Dillinger and give us enough rearguard action so we can get out of here."

The fires flickered in the night as the soldiers kept the wood stacked on them, keeping the flames high. The four Marines lying just outside the camp, waiting beneath the brush in the blackness, kept quiet. The quietness seemed to unsettle the soldiers even more, as though the phantoms that had howled at midnight now quietly waited until the men could no longer stay awake, and then would rob them of their souls.

The almost hypnotic flashing and blinking of the fires left B. C. Collins feeling his eyelids becoming thick and heavy. He watched the soldiers nodding and yanking their heads up in reaction, and he felt his own head drop and rebound reflexively. Pulling his wrist close to his face, he squinted at the watch dial and sighed. The four men had lain at the edge of the camp for four hours. When would they fall asleep? he asked himself.

Slowly the blackness of the night began to turn gray, and B. C. Collins caught himself just as his head nearly hit the ground in front of him. A hand took his shoulder and he heard Gunny Holt whisper, "Now."

B. C. Collins looked at the camp. The fires burned low in their beds and gave off white smoke that mixed with the fog that settled on the little hidden valley. The soldiers lay curled by their rifles. All of them had fallen asleep.

Without a sound, the men crawled forward guiding on the dim coals and low flames from the fires, and the dark humps that were the sleeping soldiers. Even though the darkness had begun to brighten, the night still dominated and with the fires burning low, giving off little light, the Marines now found themselves unsure of their positions in relation to the encampment.

As they slowly crawled forward, each man on his own track several yards from the other, B. C. Collins soon began to realize that they had crawled too close to the fires and had now surrounded themselves with sleeping soldiers. Some of them began to stir, and when one man stood and stumbled to the bushes behind B. C. Collins and began urinating near the spot where the Marine had spent so many hours waiting, his heart nearly stopped.

Bob Holt and John Dobbs and Dutch Miller also began to realize that they had placed themselves in the midst of the NVA company encampment, surrounded by sleeping and now waking soldiers. Bob Holt looked to his right and saw B. C. Collins lying motionless, flanked by three soldiers who now also began to stretch in their sleep.

The sound of splashing water and a healthy fart made Bob Holt turn and look to his left. There, not twenty feet away, stood the North Vietnamese captain. He shook off the last drops and dipped his knees as he buttoned his fly. He had a map case across his shoulder, and as he turned toward the Marine, he buckled his pistol belt.

Bob Holt lay motionless, his head resting on his hands in the still dim grayness of the early morning, where everything still seemed colorless in shades of black and white. The captain walked and farted again, shaking a leg and saying something in Vietnamese.

He stopped by the fire, four feet from where Bob Holt lay, and dropped on several sticks of wood. When he coughed from the smoke shifting in his face, as it always seems to do when a person tends a fire, Bob Holt quietly pulled his legs underneath himself and squatted on the balls of his feet, coiled.

The captain took one step and Holt jumped to his feet.

"Boo!" he said in a voice that came deep from within him and bellowed over the quiet campsite.

The captain dropped open his mouth, about to shout, and Bob Holt closed it for the enemy officer with a hard right uppercut that crushed the man to the ground with a sound *thud*.

He was out cold.

Holt pulled the officer up by the front of his green canvas shirt, and like a long sack of rice, the Marine heaved the moaning officer over his shoulder and ran for the trees.

"Wake up, you motherfuckers!" B. C. Collins roared as he opened fire with his M-14 selected to full automatic. He spent that magazine and shoved another in the rifle's well and fired again.

John Dobbs and Dutch Miller joined the action, each running their full automatic rifle fire across the ground where the NVA soldiers tried to scramble to their feet.

They did not stop to look or even think of numbers wounded or killed. The Marine snatch team knew they had killed several and wounded many more, but now, with rifle fire cracking all around them, they could only think to run and shoot.

Pat Collins didn't have to rouse anyone. The sudden chatter of a hundred guns firing awoke those who slept in an instant. Even across the wide valley of elephant grass, the sleeping rifle company came fully alert.

"Don't shoot until you see who they are," Pat Collins called out to his men who now lay ready to open fire on the first thing that came crashing through the trees at them.

Bob Holt crashed up the hill first and shouted, "Collins, Dobbs, and Miller are right behind me!"

The gunny didn't slow his hard pace as he leapt over a Marine who lay ten yards from John DelGrosso. Holt kept running, finding the trail at the edge of the valley, and he shouted so loudly that his voice echoed up the wide valley, "Skipper! I wouldn't wait here! We got at least a hundred coming after us fast! We better scatter!"

When B. C. Collins leapt through the trees at the top of the low ridge that reached into the valley, and Dutch Miller and John Dobbs crashed through the line of Marines at the lower end, the air seemed to come alive with the crack and pop of hundreds of bullets in flight overhead.

Below them, the crash and bang of a hundred bodies running through the brush and small trees that grew thickly on the rise, snapping and breaking them, and the shouts of the North Vietnamese soldiers left no doubt in Pat Collins's mind that Holt had not exaggerated his count of the enemy. There was no match here, and Pat Collins shouted, "You heard the gunny. Let's go!"

The teams of reconnaissance Marines broke from their positions like a flock of quail, and darted down and up, but always away from the angry crowd of North Vietnamese soldiers who had seen the Marine run from their camp with their captain lying over his shoulders.

From the other side of the valley, Golf Company's platoon leaders watched through their binoculars and saw several bush-hatted heads bobbing in the sea of elephant grass, running northward, parallel to the rifle company's line. They could also see Bob Holt leading the hare-and-hound chase with the officer held tightly on his shoulder. The dozen and more other Marines ran and shot, ran and shot, trying to keep the North Vietnamese soldiers at bay, but had little luck.

However, once the captain who commanded Golf Company saw the clear line between Pat Collins's Marines and the enemy, he called for the platoon on his far left flank to open fire.

Bob Holt heard the deep-throated chop of an M-60 machine gun driving its fire behind him and he turned to see the spray of red tracers coming off the ridge to his right. Yet in that moment that he stopped, he also heard the bullets fired by the NVA clipping through the air around him and he knew that he had not yet crossed the goal line for his touchdown.

He had just decided to turn toward the ridge when the bullet struck, almost knocking him off his feet. Bob Holt felt nothing, but knew he had certainly been hit.

"The gook took a round!" John Dobbs shouted behind Holt who now stopped to try to find the wound. "Keep running, Gunny! Collins and Miller are already crossing the valley. Let's go!"

Bob Holt could feel the wetness of the officer's blood running over his back and knew that the man was bleeding badly. The man moaned but did not try to struggle at all, now.

"He's leaking pretty bad, Gunny," Dobbs said.

"We've got to get him to Charlie Med, that's our only chance," Holt shouted, gasping for breath.

In a moment the two Marines cleared the tree line on the edge of the valley and bounded up the ridge to the line of Gold Company Marines who now fired above the two men's heads at the North Vietnamese soldiers in the valley.

Pat Collins took one look at the officer and knew that they had to race against time to keep this man alive so that they could find out what he knew.

Doc Thomas looked at him and shook his head. "This compression bandage will slow the bleeding, but he's gonna die unless a surgeon cuts him open and closes those ruptured arteries. If we could medevac him, I think he would make it."

The recon Marines took turns carrying the wounded officer down the ridge and up the next to the landing zones where the choppers had dropped them the day before. Now as the morning cooked on, Pat Collins shaded his eyes with his hands, searching the sky for the first helicopter, and stood next to the NVA officer who had now turned pale and drifted in and out of consciousness.

Pat Collins had arranged with Golf Company's commander to put the wounded enemy on the first helicopter that landed and he would send them directly to Charlie Med. Collins rationalized that since this wounded enemy officer was the object of their two-day mission, and that even considering that the officer's map case was filled with valuable intelligence information, if the man died the intelligence loss would make the result of their mission hardly worth talking about.

When the Marines heard the engines of the first helicopter echoing from behind the ridge east of them, Pat Collins tossed a red smoke grenade into the center of the landing zone. Even before the chopper had settled on its wheels, three Marines and the corpsman ran toward the aircraft, carrying the wounded enemy.

Pat Collins grabbed the crew chief and shouted, pointing to the NVA officer, "Take him to Charlie Med! Make sure they keep him alive! He's bleeding badly so they've got to get right to him! It's goddamn important that you get him there alive!"

The crew chief said something to the pilot through the microphone that stood out on a wire holder attached to the Marine's helmet. Then he gave Pat Collins a thumbs-up and bailed on board.

"We should have sent one of our guys with him," Bob Holt said.

"Too late to think about it now," Pat Collins said, hanging the enemy officer's map case over his shoulder and patting it securely with his hand.

That afternoon when Pat Collins called Charlie Med, they had no clues regarding the enemy soldier. He never even made it to Da Nang. Two days later Pat Collins learned that some Shore Party Marines at Chu Lai had found the officer dead, lying on a stack of wooden crates where he bled to death.

· 6 ·

THE LOSS OF THE NVA OFFICER HAD SEEMED TO PAT COLLINS THE ultimate exercise in frustration. However the setback was rescued when that same day a Viet Cong officer from the 1st VC Regiment deserted and surrendered to the South Vietnamese forces near Chu Lai. They took him directly to General Thi in Da Nang where the general personally interrogated the man.

Thi called General Walt and told him that he had learned from the deserter that the 1st VC Regiment was only twelve miles down the coast from Chu Lai at the village complex called Van Tuong, positioned there to attack the Chu Lai enclave. The deserter had disclosed that two of the regiment's three battalions, the 60th and the 80th battalions, were at Van Tuong. Also, the VC regiment was reinforced by the 52nd VC Company and the 45th Weapons Battalion. All told, the Viet Cong had a force of more than 1,500 men four to five hours' march from Chu Lai. They could attack at any time.

The South Vietnamese general concluded his story to General Walt by telling him that in all of his years of fighting, he regarded this information as some of the best he had ever obtained. He said that he completely believed what the man had told him and he urged General Walt to make haste. There was no time.

When Colonel Dulacki told General Walt that he had information that upheld what the deserting Viet Cong had told, the general sent him straightaway to Colonel Edwin H. Simmons, the III MAF operations officer, told him to start working on a plan.

That same day, General Walt called a council of war together at Chu Lai, and laid it out to his senior commanders. Among them, Brigadier General Fred Karch had returned to Vietnam on August 5 and had established his headquarters at Chu Lai where he was the coordinator of activities. Additionally, the commanders of the 4th Marine Regiment and the newly arrived 7th Marine Regiment were there.

General Walt looked at the men and said, "General Thi says that this is the best information that's come out of I Corps in the whole Vietnam War. So that leaves us two obvious courses. We can wait in our defensive positions until the enemy attacks, or we can go out and hit the VC before they're ready to move."

He looked at Colonel Oscar F. Peatross, a veteran of Iwo Jima and Makin Island, where on that raid he earned the Navy Cross, and a man who besides commanding the 5th Marines in Korea had served as a battalion commander under Walt. "If we go out and hit the VC first, we'll have to reduce the number of Marines manning the Chu Lai perimeter. But with 7th Marines here, that's now acceptable."

Walt sat silently and waited for any comment. He knew that the men agreed. "At most, all we're going to dig up is two battalions. If we dig up as many as two battalions, we have got to have the amphibious means of making a landing, and our ultimate action depends upon how well we come to grips with this thing."

He looked again at Oscar Peatross. "Pete, you're the only one available."

Peatross nodded.

General Walt returned to Da Nang and for the next two days, after he received General Westmoreland's approval, 7th Marines went to work assembling their forces while the III MAF staff worked nonstop preparing the plans for the first major operation of the Vietnam War, an operation that would call for a two-battalion assault, one over the beach and the other inland by air.

The first movement reassigned two battalions formerly under Peatross back to 7th Marines. These would be the assault battalions and were 2nd Battalion, 4th Marines, commanded by Lieutenant Colonel Joseph R. Fisher, and 3rd Battalion, 3rd Marines, commanded by Lieutenant Colonel Joseph E. Muir, a Marine who would die in action in less than three months, on November 9, 1965.

General Walt also received approval from Admiral Ulysses G. Sharp, Commander in Chief, Pacific, to task the Special Landing Force aboard the amphibious task force at Subic Bay, 720 miles away, as the operation's third battalion. They would stand aboard ship as the operation's floating reserve. Their two-day transit time would place them off the coast of Chu Lai on August 18, 1965. D-day.

The objective area for the amphibious assault, now named Operation Satellite, lay over a ten-mile stretch of land, flat except for a few wooded knolls, and interlaced with canals. The villages were surrounded by both rice paddies and dry crop fields.

While still airborne on an aerial reconnaissance of the operation's objective and the beach areas, Colonel Peatross and the battalion commanders reached a conclusion on which beach they would make the amphibious assault landing and the locations of the helicopter landing zones. After examining two beaches, the men decided to land on the coast just north of a small fishing village called An Cuong (1). They called that place Green Beach. A force there would block any attempted VC escapes to the south. The three helicopter landing zones, LZ Red, LZ White, and LZ Blue, lay five miles east of Highway One and a mile inland from the coast, plotted in a triangle spaced two kilometers apart and two kilometers from Green Beach. The Marines could then move northeast toward the South China Sea from these positions.

It was a simple strategy. Surround the 1st Viet Cong Regiment from the south, southwest, west, and northwest, and force them out on the hump of land that jutted into the South China Sea along the Nho Na Bay and the Phuoc Thuan Peninsula. The assaulting forces, leaving the blocking forces on the surrounding high ground, would come together along a line, which the Marines had named Phase Line Banana, that sealed off that chunk of land where the 1,500 Viet Cong had congregated, and would then push the enemy into the sea.

Led by Joe Muir, the 3rd Battalion, 3rd Marine Regiment, would launch the attack with their landing at 6:30 A.M. on August 18 at Green Beach. Kilo and India companies would land abreast, K Company on the right, while Lima Company stood as their reserve and would follow ashore once the two companies had gained ground. While I, K, and L companies landed on the southern flank and swept westward and then northwestward to Phase Line Banana, 3rd Battalion's remaining company, Mike, had remained ashore at Chu Lai and would move overland to a ridge line that overlooked the northern end of the phase line and there they would block any possible retreat that the VC might attempt to the north.

Once H hour passed, UH-34 helicopters from Marine Medium Helicopter squadrons HMM-261 and HMM-361 would land Joe Fisher and his 2nd Battalion, 4th Marine Regiment, into the three landing zones, LZ Red, LZ White, and LZ Blue.

The two battalions would link up at a hamlet called An Cuong (2) when Hotel Company, 4th Marines, had moved from LZ Blue up a forty-three-meter-high hill and then down to the An Cuong village while India Company pushed northwestward 1,800 meters from Green Beach. From there, it was a matter of the two battalions tightening the noose toward the sea, while artillery batteries at Chu Lai provided them fire support, and two destroyers, the USS *Orleck* (DD 886) and the USS *Prichett* (DD 561), and the cruiser USS *Galveston* (CLG 3) provided naval gunfire. Marine Aircraft Groups MAG-11 and MAG-12 would fly close air support.

One of the plan's greatest advantages lay in the fact that because 7th Marines had just landed at Chu Lai, the Viet Cong were not concerned about the sight of the Navy ships off the coast. And with the arrival and departure of other ships ongoing, it seemed like business as usual when the amphibious task force came on the horizon. When the amphibious assault force back-loaded on the ships, it would seem a normal activity. Thus, despite the presence and movement of the ships, Charlie had no idea of the impending landing. The element of surprise would no doubt hit him a very hard blow.

## • 7 •

"HERE IT IS," THE CORPORAL TOLD THE PRIVATE FIRST CLASS WHO sat at the typewriter, hammering the keys, trying to keep pace with the avalanche of paper that seemed to grow taller on his desk.

"What is it?" the private moaned.

"Final chop," the corporal said. "We can get this thing typed smooth on the mimeograph stencils. Colonel Simmons has to have it first thing, no matter if it's 3:00 A.M."

The private looked at his watch and then glanced at the darkness that had descended on the day. He had worked through it without stopping. He ate a sandwich instead of going to the chow hall; now the corporal told him he had to bang away until 3:00 A.M., if that's what it took.

"It's already nine o'clock!" he said harshly. "I've only been at this for twelve hours."

"A couple more, man," the corporal said. "Take it slow and easy, and no mistakes. I'll start cranking copies off the machine once you get it typed, so hurry up and give me that first page. I've had twelve hours of this shit too, you know."

The private had hardly slipped the first stencil sheet into his type-writer when the lights went out. All around them darkness and silence. They sat still and listened for shooting. When there was nothing, not even the sound of the engines that drove the electrical power plants, the corporal cried out in the darkness, "Beautiful, just fuckin' beautiful!"

"What do we have to do," the private chided, "type this shit by starlight?"

"Hang on, Tony," the corporal said, "I'll go down in one of the bunkers and get some candles. We still gotta get this shit done."

In ten minutes the Marines sat in the office, bent close to their work, typing and printing out the operation plan. They had to hurry. The landing was a day away.

## • 8 •

"ED," GENERAL WALT GROWLED INTO THE TELEPHONE, "COME IN HERE."
Colonel Edwin Simmons stepped inside General Walt's office, and Walt looked up. "Did you read this operation plan?"

"Yes, sir," Colonel Simmons said, "and I saw it already. I was about to come to see you."

"There isn't time to change it," Walt said. "I'd like to know how it happened."

"Generator failed last night," Simmons said. "The boys had to type it by candlelight."

"Everything else is correct," General Walt said. "Landing set at zero-six-thirty on the eighteenth. The name sounds fine, though. Spelled a little unusual. People may have trouble with it. I can see how a kid can get it mixed up with 'Satellite' in the dark. It's okay. We'll just change the name. No time for anything else."

"I'll tell those responsible," Simmons said. "Operation Starlite it is then, sir."

# STARLITE

## •1•

**T**HAT MORNING, JOHN DELGROSSO AND HIS PLATOON HAD WATCHED Mike Company, 3rd Marines, clustered on top of a platoon of amtracks, drive out of Chu Lai, headed south on Highway One. That was August 17, 1965.

There was nothing unusual about the departure; for weeks other companies had ridden out of Chu Lai, headed north on Highway One or south, and sometimes they boondocked over the flatland to the west. But DelGrosso and his men knew that this was the prelude to the big one. A battle that none of them could imagine what its result might be. They knew Charlie was south of Chu Lai, but there had never been a big battle like this one. Not here, yet.

As the day went on, there were few events that Mike Company encountered on the trail. Once they reached the Trung Phan Peninsula, the company marched eastward through the night and set up at their blocking position, reporting they had dug in for the night, and stood ready at 5:00 A.M. on the morning of August 18, only seventy-five minutes before H hour for Operation Starlite.

Meanwhile at Chu Lai, Lieutenant Colonel James P. Kelly moved his

1st Battalion, 7th Marines, ashore on August 17 and relieved Joe Muir and his 3rd Battalion, 3rd Marines, on the Chu Lai perimeter. Two other companies, one borrowed from Da Nang and one from Phu Bai, joined with Kelly's Marines in guarding Chu Lai, picking up the slack left from the departure of Joe Fisher's 2nd Battalion, 4th Marines.

Through the day, while John DelGrosso and his platoon prepared for their night operation up the coast, out of the war, another attempt at snatching Viet Cong for interrogation, they watched as platoon after platoon casually rode out to three ships standing offshore: the amphibious assault ship USS *Bayfield* (APA 33), the landing ship dock USS *Cabildo* (LSD 16), and the tank landing ship USS *Vernon County* (LST 116). Along the beach, three flame tanks from 7th Marines and an M-48 assault tank from 3rd Marines churned through the sand and rolled up the ramp of an LCU as its engines churned the water, keeping its front gate down against the beach. Next to it another LCU plowed into the shore and the four remaining M-48 tanks from the platoon of five chugged aboard it. Other rolling stock, ontos[1] and other lighter assault vehicles, already stood ready on the decks of the landing crafts aboard the ships. The two LCUs moved slowly out to sea and then waited.

By 10 P.M. John DelGrosso and his platoon clung to tow ropes behind an LCM that chugged slowly out to sea. He could see the ships moving slowly away in the night, the small lights twinkling on their decks as they headed eastward to the horizon. Once beyond sight of land, they would turn southwest and rendezvous with the two LCUs holding the tanks, and with the cruiser USS *Galveston* and the destroyer USS *Orleck*, at five o'clock on the morning of August 18.

Most of the Marines under Pat Collins's command had a difficult time handling the surf. They spent more time working on tactics and less time working on methods of entry. Captain Dave Whittingham commanded 1st Force Reconnaissance Company and his Marines handled surf operations, as well as scuba or parachuting, nearly flawlessly. Whenever they came in contact with Collins's men, the force recon Marines boasted about their abilities while the Delta Company Marines grumbled,

---

[1] A tracked assault vehicle, smaller than a tank, with its most distinctive feature being several main guns mounted on it rather than the main single gun as seen on its larger cousin, the tank.

knowing how inadequate they were in that often flamboyant aspect of their work.

However, Pat Collins taught his men that method of entry was a small part of the overall package, and that man for man he believed that his Marines were better warriors and tacticians than anyone, especially the 1st Force Reconnaissance men.

Collins's proof came, though, in a sad lesson when the force recon Marines had conducted a landing survey for 4th Marines and used the same method of entry at the same place three times running. On the fourth landing, the force reconnaissance team walked into an ambush and a Marine corporal died in the fight.

Now, as the summer ended and Operation Starlite ushered the Marines into a full-scale war, General Walt ordered Whittingham and his 1st Force Reconnaissance Company assigned to 3rd Reconnaissance Battalion for training. It was a bitter medicine for the force recon Marines, but they took it and now worked with Pat Collins and the other 3rd Reconnaissance companies, walking patrols, learning tactics.

The event had boosted the egos of John DelGrosso's platoon, as well as others, but it didn't improve their abilities in the surf.

Now as the LCM chugged away, leaving the recon platoon bobbing outside the surf line, John DelGrosso sighed as he saw how roughly the waves were breaking this night.

"You see any lights?" John asked Staff Sergeant Dutch Miller, who sat in the rear of the boat that bobbed next to the lieutenant's, holding his paddle down as a tiller.

"Nothing," Dutch said.

John DelGrosso took the coxswain's position in his boat too, so that he could command rather than getting lost in the business of paddling. A business that demanded maximum muscle and stamina and tended to drain the brain because of the toil.

"Those two swimmers should have given us a signal," John DelGrosso said, trying to listen for any gunfire ashore but only heard the loud pounding of the heavy surf.

"Time to move up the coast, sir?" Dutch Miller said.

"Let's go," John DelGrosso said, "but let's keep our eyes open for lights."

As the boats moved northward, the men tried to battle away from the pull of the tide that would throw them into the ripping and churning waves as they broke and crashed. In a matter of minutes, however, the current had taken them and now the men fought hard just to stay with the small, inflatable boats.

John DelGrosso could feel his stomach tie in a knot as he pulled hard with his paddle, steering the boat and trying to keep the dry side up. But there was no dry side now and the boat went over. The men hung to the ropes and paddles as they tumbled through the surf and in a few seconds they had the boat righted and climbed onto the craft as it drove toward the shore, lurching hard with each new wave.

"God I hate that!" John DelGrosso said and saw Dutch Miller and his men ride their boat smoothly over the breakers and come sliding alongside.

"Kind of like jumping out of the window instead of using the stairs," he said and laughed. "But if you're looking for lights, they're dead ahead."

John DelGrosso looked and he could see two lights blinking, and then to the right of them several firelights.

"Guide on the two lights," he said.

As the platoon paddled now smoothly, on line, Dutch Miller pointed and called to John DelGrosso, "Looks like trouble!"

On the beach, the two swimmers ran hard toward the south, away from where the firelights twinkled. Then as the boats struck sand, John DelGrosso could see the figures of several men and women crowding near the fires, some standing and some squatting. On each figure, John could see the unmistakable silhouette of a rifle, strapped across their backs.

"Go for it!" the lieutenant shouted and began shooting as he ran in the surf. His platoon splashed through the waves too and began shooting at the Viet Cong who had landed their sampans and junks, and had been enjoying a beach picnic stop while hauling supplies south, probably for the 1st Viet Cong Regiment now just south of Chu Lai.

"They're running for their boats!" Miller shouted as he shot, seeing the Viet Cong take flight from the attack.

John DelGrosso turned and nearly knocked over the Marine who packed the radio and tried to keep on step behind his commander.

"Get naval gunfire," the lieutenant shouted, "before they get away!"

"No dice, sir," the radioman cried back, the surf breaking against his knees and waist.

"Call for the reaction force, give them the coordinates and direction that the boats are sailing," DelGrosso said. Then he looked to where Dutch Miller had stopped and was now shooting with careful aim at the several Viet Cong who had run inland. "Dutch! Let's get some teams together and move up the beach and try to pick up some prisoners."

John DelGrosso wanted badly to come out with at least something after such a terrible start. He couldn't imagine the odds of landing in the middle of a VC beach party, and now he wanted at least something to show for it. After he had consolidated his Marines, he sent them out in their normal fashion of working in overlapping patrols where one team could assist another and if the fight got bad, they could band together and fight as a platoon.

Slowly, DelGrosso led his teams to the outskirts of a small fishing village where his men had tracked the fleeing enemy from several blood trails.

"Send in one man and we'll set up out here," he told Dutch Miller over the radio.

A tall, lanky Marine slowly crept to the dark, quiet village. He had hardly closed within twenty feet of the first hut when he saw the VC standing next to the hut. Keeping his cool, he turned around, hoping that no one had heard nor seen him, and tiptoed back. The Marine held his rifle above his head with one hand and took high, exaggerated steps and made John DelGrosso think of Mickey Mouse or some other cartoon character with his animated movement.

When the man had stopped, the VC had already seen him and was about to shoot, but when the Marine had turned to walk away, the enemy soldier decided to follow him, thinking that only one Marine had ventured to the village and now hoped to get back to his men. Apparently the guerrilla wanted to follow the Marine back to his company so that he could return and bring the VC force with which they could attack the Marines.

Ten feet behind the sneaking Marine, the VC soldier stalked, taking identical high steps and holding his rifle in the air too. John DelGrosso had to bite his cheek to keep from laughing.

"There's your man," he said into the radio, meaning that here was a prisoner. All that the nearest team had to do was run out and grab him, but the words had no more than left his lips when the entire flank sparkled with muzzle flashes and a hail of bullets took the man off his feet and dispatched him to the promised land in that same second.

• 2 •

H E AWOKE WITH A SUDDEN JERK AND HE LOOKED AT THE EARLY morning sky but he saw no clouds. Another rumble and another, and John DelGrosso knew that the thunder was the opening salvo of 155-mm rounds exploding on the knolls and low ridges west of Chu Lai where the Marines from Hotel, Golf, and Echo companies, 4th Marine Regiment, would soon land. The heavy guns from 12th Marine Regiment had begun the preparatory fires for Operation Starlite that with the first explosion was now under way.

While 12th Marines pounded LZs Red, White, and Blue, twenty jets, A-4 Skyhawks and F-4 Phantoms, dove in between salvos and dropped eighteen tons of napalm and high-explosive bombs on the landing zones and nearby places where the enemy might hide. Because Green Beach was so close to the fishing village of An Cuong (1) the A-4 Skyhawks from MAG-12 could only strafe the stretch of shoreline with their 20-mm canons.

John DelGrosso looked at his watch, 6:15 A.M., as he walked with his men, patrolling their way back to Chu Lai. He could see the jets taking off in tandem. As he watched them, he noticed that their wheels never went up: they took off, dropped their loads, and landed, almost in a circle. The war was that close to home base.

He felt grubby and rotten as he walked. Besides his skin burning from the sea's salt and the rubbing of beach sand under his clothes, his feelings burned with the frustration he felt at losing his prisoner. What a dumb thing to have happen, he thought. The guys are just too trigger-happy. The skipper will not let me forget this one, he told himself. "God, what I wouldn't give for a hot shower," he said and Dutch Miller just looked at him and smiled.

However, while India and Kilo companies, 3rd Battalion, 3rd Marines, landed at Green Beach and began to move inland on their sweep to the northwest, dodging only a few snipers' rounds, and as Hotel, Echo, and Golf companies now landed at LZs Red, White, and Blue, Pat Collins and Company D sat on a ridge called Bach Ma, just 10,000 meters east of another ridge that they would come to know as Dodge City, which overlooked another bad land that they would come to know as Happy Valley.

He looked at his watch and it was already after 7:00 A.M. and he began to fume. "Where are those goofy bastards!" he asked Harry Rogers, who had now stretched out and looked across the valley to Dodge City.

"That was them that flew by a minute ago," he said.

"Hell," Collins said. "There've been choppers up and down these ridges all morning. How do you know?"

"These guys went west," Rogers said. "All the others were flying north and south."

"What, they screwed up and are looking for us over in west Jesus?" Collins said as he lay back on his elbows and looked to the west hills too.

"Give them twenty minutes and they'll figure out that we're not over there," Rogers said philosophically. "Old Slyde will cruise back to the coast and turn and count ridges again. This time, I'll have some guys standing in the LZ to flag him down."

It took fifteen minutes, but nonetheless the Marines heard the chopping roar of the UH-34's engines coming from the east and when Bob Holt and a corporal named Posey stood in the landing zone and waved, the chopper set down.

"Jesus beaver! I've got something to tell you!" Slyde said, scrambling out of the cockpit of the chopper.

"You got a tail full of lead," Pat Collins said, walking to the helicopter and looking at several fresh holes in the aircraft's skin.

"I saw this big cleared area, a lot of guys standing around, and I thought it was you," Slyde said.

"If you'd read your chart right, you would have seen this ridge and the words 'Bach Ma' to the side," Collins said, feeling a little disgusted. "I don't know what the hell that place is that you went into."

"Goddamned Dodge City is what I call it," Slyde said. "There were more bullets flying when I dropped in than on *Gunsmoke*. I think I even saw Chester and Matt Dillon out there slingin' lead at me. They wanted to blow me down real bad. Man! All I could do was grab a handful of collective, punch this old cow in the ass, and pray."

"What was it, a VC compound?" Collins said more seriously.

"More than that," Slyde said. "I saw trucks. A bunch of them."

"Harry, you and Holt, Posey, and Dobbs get in the helicopter," Collins said. He looked at Charlie Scarfano and a new lieutenant, Tobin Meyers, and pulled the map from his shirt. "Over here, sports fans."

He pointed to a ridge south of their position and said, "Move here, clear this LZ, and wait. I'll contact you once we spot the VC. We're going to take a second look at that compound and then find a flat spot and see if we can grab one of those guys. It shouldn't take more than a couple of hours for you to get to this spot so while we're going after these bozos, stay low and don't attract any attention to your new position. If they saw these clowns go down over there, they more than likely watched them land over here, so you'd better not waste any time moving off this spot."

Pat Collins took a second look at Scarfano and Meyers and then pointed south. "It's right over there. Go east, down this slope, walk south down that valley, and go west, up the hill."

When the chopper lifted away from the hill, Scarfano and Meyers had already gone with the company, hoping that if the VC had come to check out this spot that they would find no one and assume that all had boarded the helicopter and flown out.

Slyde kept the 34 flying low and hugged the draws and runs that snaked around and between the ridges westward. As they swept south and then turned back north after clearing the second line of peaks, the pilot spoke to Pat Collins over the intercom. "Just ahead. You can see that red scar where they've been scraping a flat spot, maybe building something there."

Pat Collins looked out the gun port and saw the spot, and just beyond it, under the trees he saw the trucks. "I count twelve trucks," he said. "Boxes of supplies and something covered with tarps, could be a couple of those big-ass mortars that they've got to pull with trucks."

"Bet those are rocket launchers on those trucks," Slyde said. "Fires about fifty rockets at once."

"Could be," Pat Collins said and then noticed the soldiers on the ground aiming their rifles at them.

The helicopter banked hard right and flew up the ridge and over while another shower of lead banged through the body of the chopper.

"Everyone still holding fluid?" Slydell said.

"Yeah, we're okay," Pat Collins said. "Let's snake around to the north, and go west and try to drop down behind those guys. They'll be watching the east, but I'll bet the west side is open. Meanwhile, let's plot and report that position to III MAF, that ought to show them that there's more than meets the eye out here."

Slyde Slydell flew the helicopter low and slow as he lumbered east and then north. They could see Da Nang lying quietly in the distant haze that disappeared with the pale blue where the sky and sea met. While they flew, Pat Collins spoke in short cryptic sentences that gave III MAF intelligence the grid coordinates of the compound, and as he spoke, Harry Rogers and the other three Marines sat nervous and quiet. They too saw the trucks and equipment, and they knew that with that much hardware, there had to be more than the cluster of riflemen who shot at them as they flew along the ridge.

The helicopter came in low again, but this time from the west. With the day wearing on, Pat Collins hoped that they could drop in, grab a man, and fly away. He didn't like the idea of dropping in, waiting until dark, and moving on the camp. The comfort factor wasn't there with five of them and at least thirty VC that he saw around the trucks.

"Slyde," Collins said.

"Roger," Slyde said.

"Come in fast, drop us, fly out," Pat Collins said. "We'll call you back in. If it looks like we have to wait until dark, make a hard run back to Da Nang, refuel, and then meet up with the company at the LZ. I'll call you in."

"You know we're sitting ducks over there if we stop to wait in that LZ," Slyde said.

"I know," Pat Collins said, "but you've got to be here fast. I don't want to wait once we grab a guy. I don't care what you do, but you better be here, or hope I get killed."

"We'll be here," Slyde said and then laughed loudly and yelled like a cowboy as he drove the chopper over the rise and down the valley, slapping treetops with the bottoms of his wheels.

When he saw the clearing break ahead of them, Slyde pulled the chopper's nose high and was about to set it down when he yanked the controls hard and jumped the aircraft straight up and turned.

"Goddamned punji sticks six feet long," Slyde shouted over the intercom. "You sure you want to set down here? They've got that whole clearing crisscrossed with those damned things like a pincushion. They could have a goddamned NVA division in here and we wouldn't know it!"

Pat Collins knew that the pilot was right and the sight of the field full of sticks meant they could be dropping in and never getting out. He was about to tell the pilot to head home, that the intelligence find of the compound and now this punji-staked landing zone were ample rewards for this mission when he saw the lone NVA soldier run for the ridge and the compound.

"Let's get him!" Collins shouted and the helicopter went nose down toward the ridge.

"How about here," Slyde said, pulling the helicopter to a halt and hovering over a big bush. "Just jump out! It's clean."

Pat Collins yanked off the headset and stepped out with one foot on the wheel strut and was about to let go and drop into the bush when he saw the face of a Vietnamese soldier looking up at him and pointing his carbine straight up.

"Goddamnit!" Pat Collins screamed, but no one could hear him. "Let me back up! A goddamned VC!"

Just then the soldier opened fire and Pat Collins held to the chopper with one hand and pointed down his AR-15 with his other and held back the trigger. He hoped that his shooting would alert the men inside to pull him up, but Harry Rogers now tried to climb out too, seeing the NVA soldier disappear up the ridge, and began pushing the captain out the door.

"Goddamnit! Stop pushing, Harry!" Pat Collins screamed.

"Go on, Skipper! He's getting away!" Harry Rogers screamed back.

When Robbie Katz saw Pat Collins empty his rifle at the ground, he immediately realized that an enemy must be down there, and he yanked out the M-60 waist gun and jammed it out the port over Harry Rogers and opened fire. However, he could not angle the bulky machine gun low enough, and as the ammo belt jumped through the smoking weapon, the rounds, with a tracer at every fourth spot in the links, danced across the field and up the ridge and back down. He wasn't even close.

Just as Harry Rogers too realized that Pat Collins was wanting back inside because he was busy dodging bullets from the Vietnamese soldier hidden below them, a burst of heavy machine-gun fire erupted from the ridge, ripping through the side of the aircraft.

When he saw the stream of tracers pour out over the trees, Slyde yanked his controls and drove the chopper up and tilted in a steep right turn and climbed away while Pat Collins clung to the doorway. His feet dangling free in the air, his rifle hanging looped from his elbow, and Harry Roger's and Bob Holt's arms swiping through space trying to grab hold of his shirt before he fell.

That evening Pat Collins briefed General Walt, who had spent the day closely watching the progress of Operation Starlite. He agreed that the snatches had not proved successful, and that when even Pat Collins began to complain about not being able to take the excitement, perhaps they were too hazardous. He told Pat Collins to suspend the operations and to look into clearing the rivers. Riverine operations might prove more productive.

· 3 ·

NO ONE KNEW, WHEN THE BATTLE BEGAN, WHAT MEASURE OF SUC-cess the Marines might achieve in Operation Starlite, or if they might end in an embarrassing no-show, except this time on a grand scale.

It almost seemed that way when 3rd Marines moved northwest off Green Beach. It also did as Golf Company landed at LZ Red with little to no trouble. However, when Joe Fisher moved off to LZ White with his command group and Echo Company, and the men casually sauntered out of the landing zone and into a hedgerow, they quickly discovered that this would be a show to which the enemy had bought a ticket after all.

It was just past 7:30 A.M. on the morning of August 18 when Joe Fisher's Marines, not taking any fire from the first helicopters, strolled out of the landing zone. But when they moved eastward through the first line of trees, the world came alive with gunfire from a ridge that overlooked the field. A few kilometers south of their position, Hotel Company already received stiff resistance as they moved off of LZ Blue and pushed toward Hill 43. But it was Echo Company that opened the day with the first sizable fight.

For Lieutenant Colonel Fisher and his Marines at LZ White, which was the center landing zone, due west of Phase Line Banana, it was as though the Viet Cong had heard they were coming and were there waiting in force. They attacked the Marines, from dug-in emplacements on the nearby high ground, with mortars, machine guns, and small-arms fire. Trying to maneuver out of the field of fire, the Marines spotted at least one hundred enemy soldiers set in the open, firing.

Fisher called for artillery and reported the grid coordinates of the Viet Cong position. In literally a matter of minutes, helicopters lifted 3rd Battalion's, 12th Marines, 107-mm mortar battery (Howtar[2]) to the ridge held by Mike Company, 3rd Marines. The Howtars fired their first salvo in short order. The artillery barrage struck the one hundred Viet Cong and killed most of them. Joe Fisher observed that at least ninety enemy lay dead in the open.

While Echo Company fought their way out of LZ White, Joe Muir had established his initial command post on Green Beach where Colonel Oscar Peatross joined him after 7:30 that morning. Several Marine generals including Walt, Karch, and Lieutenant General Victor Krulak, visiting Vietnam from his headquarters in Hawaii, also landed at the 3rd Marines CP through the next two days.

Muir and Peatross watched as the tanks and ontos pushed ashore and moved forward to support the advancing Kilo and India companies. Once the sweep had turned northwest, Lima Company landed and set up security for the beach supply area.

As Kilo and India companies pushed northwest to rendezvous with Hotel Company, 4th Marines, the Hotel Company Marines had to fight their way past that forty-three-meter-high mound of tree-covered earth and then down across rice paddies that left them open to an increasing concentration of enemy fire.

As the three units converged on their attempt to link up at An Cuong (2), Kilo Company approached Phase Line Banana and bogged down against an entrenched enemy there. Lieutenant Colonel Muir now established his rear command post, inland, and ordered Lima Company into the fight at that point to help Kilo Company overwhelm that resistance.

However, the pot began to boil as Hotel and India companies moved close and found themselves in an area one kilometer square, bordered by An Thoi (2) at the north, Nam Yen (3) on the south, and An Cuong (2), their initial objective, on the east. They quickly discovered that this was

---

[2]Howtar is the 107-mm mortar that is set on wheels and looks very similar to a howitzer field artillery piece but somewhat smaller.

where the 60th Viet Cong Regiment lived. In fact, LZ Blue had been nearly on top of the 60th VC Regiment's command group.

The 60th had let the first helicopters land, but then opened fire as the others came in. The whole area grew hotter by the minute, to the point that one pilot, Captain Howard B. Henry from HMM-361, said, "You just had to close your eyes and drop down to the deck."

UH-1B Huey gunships from the U.S. Army's 7th Airlift Platoon attacked Hill 43 while First Lieutenant Homer K. Jenkens, commanding Hotel Company, led the Marines out of the landing zone and pushed the Viet Cong back. Jenkens, however, had no idea of the size of force he was facing until he had ordered one platoon to take Hill 43 and the rest of the company to clear Nam Yen. Soon both attacks bogged down and he realized that here was the enemy.

He pulled his forces back, called in air strikes on the village and on the hill, and attacked the hill with his full force. Although the VC fought hard, they could not withstand the pressure from the Marines and the air strikes. As Homer Jenkens pulled forward from the hill, his men saw numerous dead Viet Cong scattered in the brush as they departed.

India Company, 3rd Marines, had also closed toward Nam Yen and had to pull back because of the air attacks. In fact, they were so close at one point that fragments from the Marine air strikes wounded two of India Company's men.

Commanded by Captain Bruce D. Webb, India Company moved away from Nam Yen and turned along a streambed toward An Cuong (2), where they met more heavy fire coming from several of the hamlets. Webb attacked An Cuong (2), a heavily wooded hamlet surrounded by trees that severely limited Webb's fields of fire.

Working forward from the rice paddies, lined by hardwood trees and bamboo, into the strongly fortified village, interlaced with trenches and tunnels and bunkers, Bruce Webb finally managed to enter the hamlet. He and three other Marines had only begun clearing the huts when a grenade exploded, killing Webb and wounding the three Marines. Then three 60-mm mortar rounds struck the unit, wounding three more Marines.

Seeing the situation growing sour by the minute, First Lieutenant Richard M. Purnell, Webb's executive officer, assumed command and called in his reserves. This was the muscle needed to push the enemy back, and give the Marines the village. As India Company departed, they reported fifty dead Viet Cong counted in the village alone.

At eleven o'clock on the morning of August 18, Homer Jenkens, thinking that India Company had cleared Nam Yen, advanced Hotel Company past the village, and when his Marines moved forward of the hamlet, maneuvering with the support of five tanks and three ontos, the Viet Cong opened fire from Nam Yen and put the hapless company in the center of a deadly cross fire.

As mortars began to fall on his lead platoons, he ordered the tanks and ontos into a circle and deployed his infantry after the enemy positions. One squad attacked a machine-gun position and killed nine Viet Cong, but lost that hold when small-arms fire began cutting through his position.

Realizing that he could not hold off the battalion-size force that he now faced, Homer Jenkens swallowed his pride and ordered his company to withdraw back to LZ Blue while A-4s and F-4Bs attacked Nam Yen and a thirty-meter-high hill just beyond An Cuong (2).

By 2:00 P.M., Jenkens tried to move his company back on the landing zone. The lead platoon had to alter its course when medevac helicopters tried to land. When these Marines moved away from the landing zone they encountered a Viet Cong ambush, and during the fight they managed to link up with several of India Company's Marines who had guarded a helicopter that had crashed nearby and the men now tried to get back to their company.

As this small group of Marines fought their way out of the one ambush, they fell into another by a much larger Viet Cong unit. Even though they were only a handful of Marines led by Corporal Robert E. O'Malley, a squad leader from India Company, 3rd Battalion, 3rd Marines, they fought with devastating effect on the enemy as they clawed their way to An Cuong (2).

With Hotel Company fighting a delaying action on their way back to LZ Blue where they were to hold a defensive perimeter until reinforcements arrived, and India Company withdrawing from An Cuong (2), pushing back to 3rd Battalion's rear command post, the Viet Cong began to attack in force.

An unlucky supply column headed for An Cuong (2) got lost in the deadly triangle between An Thoi and Nam Yen. As the Viet Cong pushed, they struck the line of vehicles, a mix of tanks, amtracks, and ontos manned by only twenty-three Marines. The Viet Cong hit the column with mortars and other explosives, disabling several vehicles. All the column could do was turn their guns at the enemy and try to hold them off until help arrived.

Major Andrew G. Comer, 3rd Battalion's, 3rd Marines, executive officer, heard the frantic cries of a panic-stricken Marine calling for help on his disabled amtrack's radio while the Viet Cong closed on the trapped supply column. Comer immediately organized a rescue effort, employing Lieutenant Purnell and India Company who had just arrived at the rear CP from An Cuong (2).

Hearing that the Viet Cong were about to overrun the entrapped supply Marines, he mounted out a fast-moving column of a few amtracks, a few ontos, and the single remaining M-48 tank. This was the last of the chips, but realizing that this push might be a drive through which the Viet Cong might break out of the tightening noose around them, Colonel Peatross approved the rescue effort.

Major Comer's patrol moved westward from the command post, across the streambed, and past An Cuong (2) without any trouble. But as they topped the thirty-meter hill between An Cuong (2) and An Thoi (2), a recoilless rifle opened fire on the single M-48 tank, knocking it out of commission. When the other vehicles jammed together, the Viet Cong opened their ambush and struck the column with mortars and rockets and small arms. Within moments, five Marines lay dead and seventeen others were wounded.

It soon dawned on the Marines that the Viet Cong had been fighting them from underground earthworks, deeply dug, so that when they saw an opportunity for attack, they took it, but when the Marines retaliated with force, the enemy quickly disappeared.

Major Comer sent India Company into An Cuong (2) to search for the missing supply column, leaving a rear guard at Hill 30 to help evacuate the wounded, and he led his command group trying to cover India Company's flank through the outlying rice paddies. However, Comer had little more than gotten into the open paddies when his party fell prey to another ambush that struck from trenches and from a wooded area outside the village. He and his Marines began to fight their way out, taking cover in the rice paddy and moving from dike to dike while under fire. But as they fought, many more men were wounded and it soon became apparent that they might not make it out of the field.

Moving under fire, Corporal Robert O'Malley, leading the mix of Marines from Hotel Company and those from India Company who had guarded the downed helicopter, saw the fighting. O'Malley quickly realized the helpless situation in which Major Comer found himself so he attempted to push across the rice paddies and link up with Comer's men. However, the grazing enemy fire sweeping through the fields held his advance.

Robert O'Malley could see the enemy in a trench at the edge of the rice paddy where his men and Major Comer's hugged the ground, sliding through the deep muck, trying to link up and stay alive. This was a key Viet Cong emplacement and dominated the rice fields. The Viet Cong fire was fierce and eventually, unless someone took the initiative, O'Malley knew that many of his and Comer's men would surely die.

With complete disregard for his own life, Robert O'Malley bolted from the Marines' worsening position and ran through the muddy field, single-handedly attacking the trench while the enemy bore down on him with their fire. With total abandon, he fought his way through the water and muck and outmaneuvered the Viet Cong, finally reaching their emplacement.

Jumping in the Viet Cong–held trench, he opened fire with his rifle and tossed grenades at the enemy, killing all eight men there. Now wounded, he reloaded his rifle and began firing at other enemy positions with deadly accuracy and moved back to his Marines. Still under fire, he led them safely to where Major Comer had now moved and tended to his wounded Marines.

As India Company fought strong Viet Cong resistance while hoping to locate the stranded supply column, Major Comer told Lieutenant Purnell that his priority was getting the supply group out. And in a gallant gesture, Comer told Purnell that he would provide him whatever support that he could.

For Major Comer and Corporal Robert O'Malley, the fight was far from over. Many of Major Comer's men needed immediate medical aid. The wounded Marines had to reach the evacuation area back at Hill 30. Without regard for himself, O'Malley immediately led a detail, carrying the wounded to the evacuation area under continued heavy fire. Once these men were safely aboard helicopters, O'Malley returned to Major Comer to lend further assistance.

Several of O'Malley's men suffered wounds, including O'Malley himself; he had taken three rounds, but he insisted on continuing to fight. Despite O'Malley's insistence on staying with the fight, Major Comer ordered the corporal to take his men straight away to the evacuation area. They had done enough.

Under heavy fire, and with he and his men all now badly wounded, the band of Marines led by O'Malley continued to fight with telling effect against the enemy as they maneuvered back to Hill 30 where helicopters could get him and his men out.

Time after time helicopter crewmen tried to get O'Malley to climb aboard one of the aircraft, but the corporal refused, seeing that he still had men remaining to get aboard and that the whole site was besieged by enemy fire. Despite his wounds, O'Malley remained in the open, firing his rifle, suppressing the Viet Cong's determined attack on the evacuation.

The corporal held his ground, even though he might be killed at any second, until his last man had finally struggled aboard the helicopters. Only then did he allow himself to withdraw from the fight. He collapsed in the arms of the crewmen as they pulled him into the aircraft's doorway and flew him and his Marines to safety and medical care.

For his repeated acts of uncommon valor where he totally disregarded his life for the lives of many Marines that day, Corporal Robert E. O'Malley, a green kid from the Hudson Valley in New York, earned the Medal of Honor.[3]

Seeing India Company encountering strong resistance and seeing Hotel Company in a similarly bad situation, Oscar Peatross realized that the Viet Cong could break the operation by pushing through at that highly straining center point of the attack. Faced with what could be the breaking point of the fight, Colonel Peatross made the decision to commit two companies of his reserve battalion aboard ship.

General Krulak had been standing in the command post with General Karch when the heavy fighting at An Cuong (2) had begun. General Walt

[3] This represented the first Medal of Honor awarded in Vietnam, although Frank Reasoner would later have the medal presented posthumously to him for his action in July.

had been there earlier, but he left before the action started. When Colonel Peatross knew that he would need the reserve battalion, he also realized that neither he nor General Walt had the authority to order them ashore. These Marines belonged to the Navy commander of the task group since they were the Special Landing Force. Approval for them to come ashore had to come down the chain of command.

Lieutenant General Krulak quickly came to the colonel's aid and suggested that they go to the ship and talk to the Navy. It did not take long before India and Lima companies from 3rd Battalion, 7th Marines, were aboard HMM 163 choppers heading for the thick of the fight where Major Comer, Lieutenant Purnell, and Lieutenant Jenkens held their ground against a major thrust by the 1st VC Regiment.

With the increased strength that the two additional companies added, the 60th Battalion broke off the fight and went back underground.

That evening while Colonel Peatross reported to General Walt that the situation had improved, but that it appeared that the Viet Cong were not going to consolidate their forces but would fight from selected locations, the USS *Galveston* and the USS *Orleck* fired illumination rounds over the troubled center just west of Phase Line Banana.

Throughout the night, while the illumination rounds kept the wooded trails and wide rice paddies around Nam Yen, An Thoi, and An Cuong bright, the Marines held. No one knew of the supply column's exact location, but those stranded Marines had finally managed to get word to Joe Muir that they were no longer under fire. Muir told them to hold until daylight when someone could get to them.

On the following day, when the Marines pushed again, there were no Viet Cong. The enemy had again disappeared.

The Marines realized that even though they did not see the Viet Cong, they were still within their tightening circle. They knew that Charlie had gone underground, but he had not escaped. And as a Marine patrol would push across a rice paddy, usually surrounded by hardwood and bamboo hedgerows, Viet Cong would attack them from the rear, popping out of hidden positions within the dikes and from tunnels and bunkers in the hedgerows.

At nine o'clock that morning, India and Mike companies from Lieutenant Colonel Charles H. Bodley's 3rd Battalion, 7th Marines, moved out from An Cuong (2) and shortly found the missing supply column. Of the twenty-three Marines in the convoy, five were killed and nine were wounded. Nine men remained in action through the fight. When Charles Bodley cleared the area, he counted sixty dead Viet Cong killed in the fighting by the handful of supply Marines.

The nineteenth of August passed with no major battles. As they would attack from their holes, Marines would converge on them and pry them out of the ground. The Viet Cong edged farther and farther toward the sea, and little by little more of them died.

Although Operation Starlite would extend more than a week, the main battles ended after the second day. In those two days the Marines had killed an estimated 800 enemy with an actual body count of 614 Viet Cong dead, most of whom were members of the 60th and 80th VC regiments. They had taken only 9 Viet Cong prisoner. On the other side of the ledgers, 45 Marines had died in action and another 203 had been wounded.

One major factor in the success of the operation was the impressive firepower that the Marines were able to direct on the enemy. The Chu Lai artillery group, under the command of Lieutenant Colonel Leslie L. Page, and composed of various batteries from 11th and 12th Marines, using artillery ranging from eight-inch howitzers down to the 107-mm Howtar batteries, placed more than 3,000 rounds into enemy positions during the two days. Other batteries in support of 7th Marines pumped in an additional 2,400 rounds, and the destroyers *Orleck* and *Prichett* and the cruiser *Galveston* added nearly 1,600 additional rounds of heavy gunfire.

On one single fire mission, the *Orleck*'s gun crews, spotting more than one hundred Viet Cong running up the beach, attempting to escape, fired rapid salvos with the ship's five-inch guns, stopping the enemy in their tracks. The ship also sank seven sampans in which other Viet Cong attempted to flee.

Air support also weighed heavily in the success of Starlite. More than 75 Marine A-4s and F-4Bs flew more than 290 sorties during the operation, dropping their payloads with extreme accuracy, sometimes within 50 meters of friendly positions. The aircraft dropped 65 tons of bombs, 4 tons of napalm, 523 rockets, and shot more than 6,000 rounds of 20-mm canon ammunition. In the first two days of the operation, this represented the most sorties in history ever flown in support of any attack group. The planes quite literally attacked the enemy off the end of the runway.

The press praised the operation's success, but the South Vietnamese military leaders remained ominously quiet. The Marines, at first not understanding this, later learned that the ARVN had seen these same Viet Cong battalions wiped out before, only to return. They knew, as the Marines would later discover, that the 60th and 80th VC battalions with the 1st Viet Cong Regiment would be back.

For the Marines, Operation Starlite renewed their faith in their ability to fight. They had taken a beating from people like General Westmoreland who complained that all the Marines wanted to do was stay inside the safe confines of the bases, and that he had to prod them out to pursue the enemy. This action ended that commentary from him.

# CHARLIE REGROUPS

## • 1 •

COME WITH ME, COLLINS," PAT COLLINS SAID TO B. C. COLLINS AS he stood up from behind the desk where he had worked in the battalion operations section since breaking the corporal's jaw.

"What's up, Skipper?" B.C. said, walking behind Pat Collins as he marched from the hut and did not look back to see if the corporal was following him.

"Nothing's up," Pat Collins said, not losing step. "Just come with me."

B. C. Collins tried to think. What could the captain want? he asked in his mind as he kept pace with Collins. Has he gotten wise to the laundry caper? Has he figured it out that I've been getting his laundry on purpose?

For several months, B. C. Collins had intentionally switched his laundry with Pat Collins, paying for the captain's since he usually had fewer items, and then later switching, taking advantage of the difference. It was always a straight trade, even though B.C. always had the much larger laundry package.

"Sir," B. C. Collins said. "Is this about us getting our laundry mixed up every week? I mean, I'll pay you the difference if that's it. It just happened by accident the first time, and with you putting your stuff in regular, and me letting mine mount up. You seemed so happy just to switch straight across."

Pat Collins stopped and bowed his neck and glared at the corporal. "No, this isn't about the laundry," Pat Collins said, "but don't think you were fooling anyone. I wised up to you a long time ago, you know. I figured you were making a little beer money, letting me subsidize your laundry bill by the straight trade. I've got news for you, though, lad. I let you get by because I figured you needed it, locked away in the rear. Made you feel like you were getting over, kept you going. But that's all done. You're comin' with me."

B. C. Collins began to smile and followed the captain, who walked to a newly built hut and pointed inside.

"This is Dingin' Deadly Delta's NCO quarters," Collins said, trying to sound gruff but now clearly losing his camouflage. "Go get your trash and move in. You know Satchel Ass?"

"Yes, sir," B.C. said. "Corporal Dobbs?"

"Right," Pat Collins said, "he'll get you settled."

"What about Colonel Van Cleve?" B. C. Collins said.

"What about him?" Pat Collins said. "As far as he's concerned, you've been assigned to Delta Company since he took command two weeks ago."

"And I've been up there pushin' pins and makin' coffee! For two weeks?" B.C. said.

"You served your time," Pat Collins said. "I need a good squad leader. Just save your right hook for Charlie."

B. C. Collins bolted in a dead run for his old quarters when Pat Collins shouted to him. "Two things," the captain said. "First. You're the only man in the company who doesn't have a Purple Heart. We'll change that in short order. Second. I want my herringbone utility jacket back. I know you've got it. You kept it out of my laundry two weeks ago."

"I intend to preserve that record, sir," B. C. Collins said, "and I'll give a look for your shirt when I pack out of the hootch."

## • 2 •

WHAT THE HELL AM I DOING HERE, EDDIE ADAMS ASKED HIMSELF AS he walked along the dusty roadway toward a village that lay on the low plains of South Vietnam's Central Highlands. He had joined in several Army patrols, and though the soldiers seemed a good lot of fellows, hardly different persons than the Marines he had come to know so well in this war, he had never found that sense of comfort that he felt with Pat Collins or Marines like him. Eddie sensed that perhaps the officers did not identify so well with their troops. That unlike Marines, the officers held themselves apart from their men.

Eddie missed the comradeship. He missed the closeness. He missed the sense of family. That's it! he told himself. Family!

He walked farther and as the patrol approached the cluster of huts, he thought what a crummy idea this had been. To come down here.

When Secretary of Defense Robert McNamara had persuaded President Johnson to bolster the American forces in South Vietnam by allowing them to bring strength up to 125,000 men in August, besides the 7th Marine Regiment coming ashore at Chu Lai, several U.S. Army units also landed in the coastal regions of the Central Highlands called II Corps.

Eddie Adams covered Operation Starlite, but when the next operation, another regimental sweep to clear a reported enemy buildup farther south of Chu Lai, called Operation Piranha, had netted 163 Viet Cong dead in three days, it quickly became apparent even to the photographer that the Viet Cong were not going to engage the Marines in any kind of mass. Eddie knew that with the Army now patrolling to the south that he might find fresh material there.

"Sergeant," the lieutenant said in a voice that he tried to make deeper than its naturally high pitch. He didn't want to sound like a twenty-one-year-old kid. He wanted to exert his voice of authority. Forcefulness, he had learned at his Army ROTC class, commanded immediate respect. His instructor also told him that the troops bear watching, or they'll gain the upper hand.

"Sergeant!" he said now more forcefully and in a voice that actually sounded silly, even coming from a fully mature man.

"Yes, sir!" the sergeant said and snapped his heels together.

Eddie could see clearly that a deep division existed between these men. He had seen enough to know that the troops only tolerated the lieu-tenant, possibly because the officer regarded his soldiers as chattels rather than men, or better yet brothers.

"Take four men from your squad and climb over that fence," the lieu-tenant said, pointing to a typical Vietnamese bamboo stick fence. "I want you to go inside that hut and investigate. See if there are any VC or arms. Look for trapdoors, spider holes, you know."

"Sir," the sergeant said, but then changed his mind.

"Lieutenant," Eddie said, suddenly feeling his frustration drive hard at his emotions, "I think what the sergeant wants to tell you is that it's a bad idea to tell those guys to climb that fence."

The lieutenant glared at the sergeant and then looked at Adams. "Sir, this is not your business. It's mine."

"Listen, Lieutenant," Eddie said, now pleading, "don't do this. You'll get one of these guys killed. Why don't you take an M-79 and launch a grenade into the fence. Blow it down and then investigate. That fence is mined. I've seen 'em. I know what I'm talking about."

"I want you to mind your own business," the lieutenant said to Eddie. "You coming along on this patrol presents a greater hazard. If you cared about these men, you wouldn't be here. Now, mind your own business."

"Fine!" Eddie said angrily. "Go ahead. You Army officers are all the same. Two days ago, I tried to tell a captain not to send his men up a road. We'd been walking through dense brush, not far from here, and the captain got tired. We were going too slow. He ordered his men up on the road and told them to move out. I tried to tell him about ambushes and booby traps, but just like you, he told me to mind my business. I fought in Korea. I was in the Marine Corps. I've also seen more combat than most of the majors and some of the colonels in this war. That captain didn't listen to me, so I stayed in the rear and watched him march down that road. The VC had set up claymore mines in the trees, and when that fool marched his company through there, a bunch of his men died."

"Mr. Adams," the lieutenant said calmly. "We can't just go blowing down fences and huts. You press people would have a field day. We have rules against that. My men will climb that fence and you will mind your business."

"Fine," Eddie said. "I'll stay back here and take pictures of your men getting blown to hell. Their families will love seeing them!"

Eddie pulled up his camera and began clicking photographs. He crouched on one knee as the sergeant and four men walked to the fence, and he tripped the shutter again and again as the sergeant grabbed hold of the fence and began to shake it. Eddie fell back, shooting the last frame, just as the fence exploded.

That night Eddie flew to Saigon and spent a few days resting and filing his photos. He told Malcolm Browne that he did not intend to go back out with any other Army units. Furthermore, come hell or high water, in December, he was going back to the States. He had promised his wife and three children, who were in New Jersey, just across the Hudson River from Manhattan, that he would be home with them before Christmas.

### •3•

THROUGH THE FALL OF 1965, PAT COLLINS AND HIS MARINES searched deeper and deeper for Charlie. As the big operations began to net fewer and fewer results, Collins and his men looked for new ways of getting the Viet Cong. He knew that even though the VC would not mass a force against the Americans, they continued to build their strength. They had clearly chosen the warfare of a slow, complex fight of wearing down the opponent with hit-and-run, the death of a thousand cuts.

Fleet Marine Force, Pacific commanding general, Lieutenant General Victor H. Krulak, had devised the Enclave Plan, which basically contradicted the war-fighting strategy that General Westmoreland proposed.

Westmoreland, a U.S. Civil War student for many years, saw the tactics employed then as ideal for counterguerrilla action. A war of movement. Historically, the Civil War had been the only time such a bloody and difficult style of battle had ever been used by American forces. Vietnam, the situation of no lines and an insurgent enemy, offered the ideal setting for Americans to again fight this kind of war. A war to the death where one army kills the other. Terrain is immaterial. Only pursuit and elimination of the enemy can be the objective.

General Krulak, for generations a student of the Far East and a scholar regarding Oriental customs, traditions, and histories, a man who spoke and read and wrote in fluent Mandarin Chinese, called for a different plan. A spreading ink blot, as many called it. Enclaves that not only served as supply bases, sources of refuge and stability, but a growing positive influence on the people who were aided by their presence. Winning the hearts and minds of the people.

Westmoreland envisioned numerous, fast-moving assault forces, maneuvering over the vast countryside, not tied to any land spot, but ready to go and destroy the enemy at a moment's notice. He apparently did not consider the structure of the terrain and environment in which these fast-moving assault forces, who would ferret out and eliminate the enemy, had to operate. As time would tell, weather, steepness of terrain, and lack of proper equipment would take their toll on them. These assault troops would take days to move only a few miles, and Charlie easily skirted them time and again. For this plan to work, General Westmoreland needed a greater degree of commitment by America's politicians and many more men.

General Walt understood and agreed that the most effective way to fight the Viet Cong was with a multitude of patrolling small units, scattered across the backcountry, interdicting the Viet Cong. However, he also understood General Krulak's more long-range objective of converting the people as they sought out the enemy, using small-unit tactics, but enjoying the advantages of solid lines of support.

This is where the French failed, losing their supply lines. This is where so many plans failed, and Krulak, one of the Marine Corps' greatest military thinkers, knew this too.

Thus as the fall of 1965 approached November, a full-scale war of movement was under way. However, a Pacification Program in conjunction with spreading enclaves, reaching northward, to eventually sweep the DMZ, had also begun.

Many Marines now worked in the Civic Action Program, and lived with the Vietnamese peasants in their villages. They armed, taught, and trained Combined Action Companies. The first were established in the Hue and Phu Bai areas and had become resounding successes. The villagers received medicine and food from the Americans who befriended them. The Americans protected their crops and allowed them to harvest their rice without the enemy taking it.

U.S. decision makers saw that Civic Action was the route to take. Charlie could rebuild with great effectiveness his battalions and regiments again and again, but if he lost the support of the people, if he had no place to hide, no place to go, he would be beaten back. It would literally put the Communist Insurgent Doctrine in reverse.

Yet the politics and interservice rivalries, the feelings of so many in authority who had to be placated, caused every plan to lose effective force. They received only partial effort and no full or lasting commitment. In that situation, no plan had a chance of working.

Thus Pat Collins, like so many other brilliant military officers who fought the war from the ground, who knew the conflict, the problems, and the means of success firsthand, became frustrated and disgruntled. It bothered him to see air strikes on wastelands. He didn't understand how bombing the back woods did any good. "Why not Hanoi?" he often asked himself. "All the B-52 strikes are ever going to do is piss off the monkeys," he would say again and again. But he would conclude, like all the other captains and majors and sergeants and lance corporals, "What the hell. It doesn't mean a thing." And he would walk on.

As a matter of sanity, he simply tried to keep focus on his small world, his part of the war. He decided not to worry about the way things would end. It was all headed down a slippery slide, unless something drastic changed, and there was little he or anyone he knew could do to stop it.


• 4 •


B OOBY TRAPS BECAME A WAY OF LIFE FOR PAT COLLINS AND HIS Marines. However, he noticed that the farther west he patrolled, the fewer he saw. But near Da Nang, every ditch and fence and road, every stalk of sugar cane or rock in the road had a bomb tied somewhere to it. Charlie had chosen his brand of warfare: passive assault, snipe, and depart. Cut and cut and cut. Bleed them slowly but surely.

Operation Black Ferret, a three-day regimental sweep of the same area where Operation Starlite had struck the Viet Cong hard, began on November 3, 1965. At the end of the operation, the regiment accounted for only two dead Viet Cong. Yet the Marines had eight men and a Navy corpsman wounded, and renowned correspondent Dickie Chapelle—a journalist who had covered Marines in combat beginning with World War II—was killed. She died on the second day, November 4, 1965, when she or one of the Marines near her tripped a VC booby trap, detonating a hand grenade and an 81-mm mortar round.

"Eddie actually cried," John DelGrosso told Pat Collins as the two men sat, taking a break, far west of the artillery fan that Da Nang provided. It was a favorite haunt of Collins's.

"He should have come along," Pat Collins said. "I think things work out better way out here. You lose a buddy, get out in the boonies, work it out. I love it out here."

Pat Collins paused and looked out into the jungle that surrounded them. "This is where the enemy lives. He stages right out here, outside the artillery fan, and he traverses our boundaries, and moves through the H-and-I fire zones, no sweat. He's anyplace out here where you don't have people, and the artillery isn't hitting shit."

He looked at John DelGrosso and narrowed his eyes. "Westmoreland's right in one respect. We'd better be working in the woods or Charlie is going to just sit back and laugh at us.

"He sees us coming every time. Look at that operation where that reporter was killed, they didn't get shit. We had recon units down there a week before the operation and the VC were everywhere. Then we start moving in the heavy trucks and setting up tents, and then the VC catch on and disappear. Where a week before there was Charlie under every bush, two days before the operation, there wasn't shit there."

John DelGrosso relaxed and looked at his captain, who had worked up his anger and now breathed heavily, trying to shake it off. "What the hell," he said.

"Look at this map," Pat Collins said, pulling the sectional chart from inside his shirt. "Once we cross this next ridge, we will drop down in this valley where there is supposed to be little farming villages. Not much there, but we might get a shot or two. I'm going over to T. C. Meyers's platoon for this."

"I hear that Colonel Van Cleve is talking about a battalion-size operation out here," John DelGrosso said.

"That's the story," Pat Collins said as he stood and dusted the dead leaves from his uniform. "Don't bet on any raids, though. The man's a purist. Roy R. Van Cleve and Doc Blanchard are like black and white. Blanchard went along with the old 'You find 'em, we'll bail you out' routine. But Van Cleve says that reconnaissance is seeing and avoiding contact. No more raids. Our only hope is with these SOG operations."[1]

"Your son," DelGrosso said with a smile, "B. C. Collins, may eliminate that opportunity with his last escapade."

Pat Collins laughed and took two steps away and said as he walked, "He and his team got back alive. Shook the shit out of the NVA too."

Two weeks earlier B. C. Collins had taken a SOG mission into Laos. His spirit for adventure tended to overpower him at times. The idea of going into enemy compounds, throttling them with piano wire, or shooting them with silenced pistols excited him. As he and his team of four crossed the border into Laos, he knew that they had no way out except by their courage and tenacity.

In two days he had led the patrol directly to the edge of an NVA compound. He marked his maps and snapped photographs, and then, just as they began to climb back up the ridge that would lead them to the trail back to South Vietnam, a bullet clipped past his head.

"Shit!" B. C. Collins growled, and then he wheeled on his toes and opened fire on a guard patrol that had happened upon them.

For the next three days B. C. Collins and his patrol fought as they edged their way slowly back to the border. His team moved around the clock, in an almost constant gun battle until they crossed back into Vietnam. It took another day to reach the landing zone, and when the helicopter landed, everyone on the pickup team knew all about the sortie.

"There've been complaints," Bob Holt told him. "Laos claims that we've invaded her sovereignty. Of course we deny it. But I think this might not be a good time to ask for a second mission over there."

As the sun dropped behind the mountains to the east of where Tobin C. Meyers and Pat Collins waited with his patrol, the lieutenant rubbed fresh camouflage on his face. He still had much to learn about night patrols, and the man who one Associated Press dispatch called the "Battlefield Messiah" was about to give him another lesson in that art.

A light rain began to wet the treetops above them and the thumping of the water, dripping and falling, striking the leaves as it fell through the canopy and splashed to the mulch-covered ground, covered the patrol's

[1] Special Operations Group, usually U.S. Army Special Forces assisted by Nungs and other mercenaries. They were long-range, often clandestine missions.

footsteps as they slipped down the ridge to the valley. He could see the two huts set under the trees at the edge of the valley, and they looked peaceful, almost like a postcard. To the young lieutenant, it looked beautiful.

A sergeant named Malone walked ahead of the lieutenant, and behind him John Dobbs, old Satchel Ass, as Pat Collins affectionately called him.

Apparently, John DelGrosso's patrol had flushed two Viet Cong who did not want to fight, and they had slipped from the other platoon's sight without being seen. Once the two guerrillas thought they had cleared the patrol's view, they ran freely, holding their rifles high and breaking wood, which called Tobin Meyers's attention.

"Stop!" he called and then shot at the men.

The Viet Cong took one look and ran to the distant huts.

"Why'd you do that?" Pat Collins said.

"I don't know," Meyers said, shaken slightly.

"Okay, coach," Collins said, "they're over in that hut. Why don't you move up and investigate while we cover you. Remember, we'll be right behind you."

The rain now fell with greater force and soaked the Marines. Water ran from Tobin Meyers's bush hat as he approached the hut. He pushed the brim up so that he could see without a cascade running on his face.

The lieutenant could hear coughing and then he saw a man with a rifle duck back in the hut. As he took a step closer, a single shot cracked out from the hut and struck the tree that stood a few inches from him.

Rather than shoot blindly, he decided to get close and perhaps he could get a clear shot. He stepped cautiously across the bare earth in front of the hut, and was about to look inside when he heard the unmistakable sound of a rifle bumping something, perhaps the doorway or an upright.

The sound sent his heart twisting in his chest, beating wildly, almost driving him blind, and he fired. He could not see a thing but he shot and shot and shot until he was sure that whoever had stood, about to shoot him, was dead.

He hadn't even caught his breath when he heard the muffled cry of a child and the jabber of her mother, trying to hush the baby. Tobin Meyers's heart beat hard as he reached for his light and leaned in the hut, shining it down.

There, in the doorway, lay the two Viet Cong, both shot several times by his rifle. But the light also caught the terrified faces of the baby girl and two other children shivering and clinging to their mother, looking at him as if he were about to shoot them too.

"Oh, God, what have I done?" the lieutenant cried as he stumbled backward where Pat Collins caught him in his arms.

John Dobbs sat on the side of a fallen tree and wiped sweat from his face. He felt it running over him as though he had just stood in a shower. They had marched uphill all morning and he hoped that they would soon get to a high enough altitude where the temperature would cool.

At first Dobbs thought that the lieutenant was just tired, hanging his head, but when he saw the man's shoulders shaking he knew that he was crying. The corporal stood and walked up the trail where Pat Collins sat.

"Skipper," Dobbs said, "maybe you better talk to Lieutenant Meyers. He's been shook all morning about last night. Those scared kids really got him going."

The captain stood and clapped Dobbs on the shoulder. "Thanks, Satchel Ass."

"What's this shit, Lieutenant?" Pat Collins said, tapping Meyers on the foot with his toe.

"I just can't get it together," Meyers said. "I keep seeing their faces. Those beautiful children, terrified that I would kill them. My God, Captain! I could have killed them too."

"You sure as hell could have," Pat Collins said in a strong tone. "Some knucklehead next week might whack them too. Some VC might. Hell, a goddamned bomb might land right on that hut and blow those beautiful children straight to kingdom come. They do it every day, T.C.! That's war! Now you've seen it up close. Now you know what it's like. But you better get hold of yourself; sitting here crying on a log won't keep your men alive. They depend on your stability."

The lieutenant looked up and shook his head. "I know, but I can't help how I feel. I'm not a barbarian."

"Goddamn right," Pat Collins said. "There's not a barbarian in my company. Not even that crazy outlaw Bryant C. Collins or Harry Rogers or Bob Holt. Every one of them feels like you do. But you can't let this affect your judgment or your will to fight. These guys have to see leadership. They expect you to be as strong as they are, because to tell you the truth, pal, every one of us has felt like sitting down and crying too. You want to know how to get past this shit?"

"Yes, sir," Meyers said. "This is killing me."

"Next time lead flies," Pat Collins said, sweeping his right hand up, "you've got to sail right in. Let it go. Guns blazing. Just turn that devil loose."

The lieutenant laughed and Pat Collins slapped him across the shoulders. "It happens to a lot of guys, coach. Just shake it off. It'll go."

In three hours Tobin Meyers walked at the point. Pat Collins had gotten the patrol lost and now he walked at the center of the patrol, looking at the map and trying to identify a terrain feature beneath the canopy that matched.

"I've gotta climb a tree," he said and Tobin Meyers turned and smiled. "Too bad old Railway Track Charlie got wounded and sent out, he would have loved this moment in history. Pat Collins, Battlefield Messiah. Lost!"

"Don't let this go to your head, pal," Pat Collins said as he pulled himself up the branches of a tall hardwood tree. "You're lost too, you know."

Pat Collins had leaned his rifle against the bottom of the tree, and as he climbed he could see ahead in the trail. What he saw made him feel that God truly walked next to him.

"Ambush!" Collins shouted after seeing the Viet Cong patrol lying on the slope, their rifles poised at the trail just ahead of his Marines. In that same instant he simply let go of the tree and jumped, just as the shooting started.

John Dobbs ran after the lieutenant when he saw him suddenly charge forward, hearing Pat Collins's warning. Tobin Meyers shouted a war cry, waving his pistol in the air, and charged into the ambush, firing the .45 at almost point-blank range.

The corporal, shooting his rifle only a few seconds, absorbed several rounds in his chest and stomach and went down hard.

"Dobbs!" Meyers shouted and turned to his fallen Marine. Just as he turned, a bullet shattered through his hand and sent his pistol flying in several directions. He could feel other bullets strike his legs and his back.

The burning pain ached in his right hand and arm, but Tobin Meyers refused to look at it as he grabbed for John Dobbs and dragged him back to cover with his one good hand.

Sergeant Malone crawled near the two Marines and guarded them. He too had suffered a bad wound in his arm.

John DelGrosso heard the shooting and immediately turned his patrol toward the flank of Tobin Meyers's position, and attacked the Viet Cong from their rear. At that point the VC split in several directions, dragging their dead and wounded with them.

"Holy shit, Skipper," Harry Rogers said as he moved close to the tree where Pat Collins now knelt. He held Tobin Meyers's mangled hand and with his folding knife cut away what was left of the lieutenant's fingers and began binding a gauze wrap tightly over the remaining hand.

"Shit, man, I know I said come out shooting," Pat Collins said as he worked, "but next time don't take me so goddamned literal."

Doc Thomas knelt next to John Dobbs, who lay clay white and clearly near death.

"We're gonna lose him, sir," Doc Thomas said, wetting a bandage on John Dobbs's middle.

Pat Collins looked at the Marine corporal and he felt those same horses pulling his heart that had trampled over Tobin Meyers's the night before. "You're looking pretty bad, Satchel Ass," he said and saw that the Marine had not even heard him.

"We've got a chopper coming, but it's already full. They can only get one man," Pat Collins said after finally getting a radio signal to reach Dong Den where John Henry and a detachment from A Company sat operating the radio relay site.

Tobin Meyers looked at his hand and legs and then looked at Sergeant Malone. "What's it to be, Captain?"

"I'll tell you what," Collins said, "if we don't get old Satchel Ass out of here right now, well, pals, he ain't gonna make it. He may not make it anyway. If I don't get you out, T.C., you'll lose all of that hand and part of your arm. I guarantee it. Sergeant Malone, the same with you. You can save your arm if you take this bird out. Dobbs may be a goner anyway, so I'm putting the ball in your court. Both of you. You tell me."

Neither Marine blinked. "Dobbs," they both said.

Their gamble for Corporal John Dobbs paid off. He lived, although he suffered permanent disabilities that left him in a wheelchair. Malone lost his arm. So did Tobin Meyers.

Tobin Meyers, medically retired from the Marine Corps, became a missionary and then went back to Southeast Asia. Perhaps, he could never stop seeing the children's terrified faces from that night.

• 5 •

BY EARLY NOVEMBER, JOHN DELGROSSO COULD FEEL THE SLIGHT change in the air. It was really getting cooler, especially after dark. In fact, he began to shiver on the night ambush that they conducted the day Tobin Meyers, Sergeant Malone, and Satchel Ass had departed.

Dobbs had hardly known them when they tried to see him as he clung to life at Charlie Med, but both Meyers and Malone looked well. They promised to stay in touch, and John DelGrosso wondered if they would.

That night, he had his sleeves down, and he wished that he had a field jacket. It felt cool to him as the slight breeze had begun to blow off the sea, sweeping across the rice paddies and across the dry crop field where he, his platoon, and Pat Collins lay waiting in yet another ambush.

They had found a grassy dike that divided the field and formed what the lieutenant called a "Bar Ambush." He swore that he learned about it in his Basic School class at Quantico, now more than a year ago. Pat Collins looked at the setup and frowned.

"You sure that you didn't dream this shit, and just think you had a class on it at TBS?" he asked.

"Absolutely!" John protested.

Now as the men lay on the grassy dike, pointing out both ways, alternating every other man in the opposite direction, he hoped that he remembered the whole class. As he looked out and the moon began to rise over the hedgerow beyond him, he hoped that this idea would work out. After all, even though he would go home in a month, he still planned to stay in the Marine Corps as a career officer.

Pat Collins lay six men down from John DelGrosso and looked the opposite direction. He could see the hint of shadows and realized that the moon must be rising. He took hold of the communications wire that the men had strung between them from first man to last, and he slowly drew the slack from it, feeling someone down the line draw it back.

At least someone besides me is staying alert, he told himself. He really did not like the idea of lying across a dike like this. He had a more conservative nature when it came to ambushing. He believed that getting too complicated gave the Marines manning the legs too much to think about, too much to have to remember. A simple L or a V were time-tested. Variations like horseshoes kept the killing zone in a cross fire and the enemy on the inside of the circle having to break out, not the other way around.

The more he thought, the later it became, and the later it became the happier Pat Collins grew. Perhaps we won't have to put this to the test, he told himself. That was when the stick snapped.

He felt a sudden tug and looked to his left. When he saw nothing, he turned his head over his shoulder and tried to see behind him. Still nothing.

Again the communications wire yanked on his fingers, and he looked, this time searching even next to the dike. Still nothing, but he could hear something, a scraping sound and a blowing sound. Like someone with a cold.

He put his head down and held his rifle, ready to snap it up and release a stream of lead at the unlucky VC who thought he was sneaking along the grassy edge of the dike. He felt certain that the man had seen them go into the field, and expected them to set up in an L or V in the hedgerow. Once in a while DelGrosso comes up with a good idea, he told himself. This joker will really be surprised.

When he clearly heard the rubbing of a body against the dirt side of the dike, Pat Collins raised to his elbows, began to tilt his rifle stock up, into his shoulder, and he lifted his head so that he could see over the grass and clearly view the intruder.

It may have been the clawing of the earth in front of him that startled him at first, but he felt certain that he had never been so scared before and not screamed. The pig, a black one with a long and very muddy nose, decided to climb the dike right at the point where Pat Collins lay. Just as the pig started up, so did Pat Collins and the two met, nose to nose, eye to eye. He could smell the filthy beast's breath!

The captain almost shot the animal, he was so angry, but he felt good that all the men had kept their cool and did not shoot even when the large black boar charged off the field, like a dog with its tail pelted by a blast of rock salt. Pat Collins had never realized that a pig could run so fast.

At four o'clock in the morning, Pat Collins began to wonder if Charlie would show, and he decided that it was almost time to pull the men up and move out of the open before the sun caught them. He had seen a hut near the river where they could hold up for the day, and if they had to get away, they had several avenues down the river, across it, or in it.

Pat Collins was thinking about the hut, how he would set up his watch, when he almost missed seeing the first Viet Cong walking on his tiptoes. The captain pulled the communications wire, but no one pulled back. He pulled again and saw six more men, tiptoeing across the field. Then he heard what the Viet Cong heard when they stumbled on the ambush. Snoring!

Every man in the platoon, including John DelGrosso had fallen asleep, and now that he noticed, Pat Collins could hear them all sawing away.

"Damnit!" the captain shouted and began to shoot, but all too late.

# MAD DOGS AND RIVERINES

• 1 •

RAIN PELTED THE COMPOUNDS ALMOST DAILY WHEN OCTOBER ended. For Pat Collins and his men, the 190th birthday of the Marine Corps, November 10, 1965, meant shivering in a downpour, high on a windswept mountain west of Elephant Valley, eating soggy chocolate nut cake from C-ration tins. They had dropped in at a clearing several miles below, and under the cover of the rain had climbed this mountain where they stopped for chow.

Even though they were wet, and the rain seemed never to end, the men sat laughing. It was a party. Charlie was far below, huddled in hootches, watching for shadows lurking in the downpour, while Delta Company sat out in the rain, soaked to the skin, having their traditional Marine Corps Ball.

They were laughing because they had started telling stories, sea stories the Marines call them. "You know the difference between a sea story and a lie?" Collins had said. "A sea story begins with 'This is no shit!'"

"Well, this is no shit!" John DelGrosso said. "The guy who decided that taking dogs on recon patrols ought to have one, the biggest stinking German shepherd of them all, and we ought to shove it up his ass."

"Tell about the last time out, Lieutenant," B. C. Collins said and laughed hard and slurped soggy chocolate nut cake from his hand. "You know, fuckin' Rin Tin Tin! Even that handler looked like that dumb fat kid, Little Rusty."

All the men laughed. It felt good to laugh, and they laughed at every stupid quip, even if on any other day it would have drawn only a groan.

John DelGrosso pulled his poncho down so that his hands and feet tucked nicely inside and the hood shed the water off his face. He looked at the guys and smiled. "You know the honeycomb of tunnels all around Cam Ne?"

The men nodded. They remembered them well. Several even thought of next week when they would be back there, working along the river again, searching tunnels and trying to demolish them. That seemed to be a favorite pastime for planners at III MAF, send division recon down the river when there's no other work.

"Sure," B. C. Collins said, "too well, Lieutenant, too well."

"We pulled a patrol west of there, up in those low hills, so we have to do a little walking," DelGrosso continued. "We cover eight or ten miles a day on some of those little marches. We get the word that we've got dogs going too. Fido is going along to sniff out Charlie, so's we can whack him. And this is at least a five-day patrol."

"Fuck yeah," Bob Holt said. "For every day you're gonna be out, you gotta carry two of those number-10 cans of dog meat for these mutts. Now three dogs, and none of 'em like each other either, they eat six cans a day. You go for five days, that's thirty cans of food. Big fuckin' cans!" The gunny looked at the lieutenant. "Sorry, Lieutenant. But I hate those fuckin' dogs. The gooners keep 'em around their hootches and then eat 'em like we eat pigs. They're always barkin' when we try to do beach ops, and we have to paddle out—in and out, in and out—because these god-damned mutts start barking. Now, we gotta take 'em with us on recon! We gotta drag along their screwy, outta-shape handlers, and then on top of our load we gotta hump about six-fuckin'-thousand pounds of dog food."

John DelGrosso waited and then said, "Just like gunny said, we end up lugging six thousand pounds of dog food, and on patrol I don't have to tell you how much extra weight that is per man. Adding this with the extra batteries and radios, hell, we're all needing wheelbarrows.

"Anyways, we push off to the west and move up the first set of hills, going at a good clip, and we gotta stop. The dog handler says Fido has to rest.

"We stop and these dogs lap up a little water. Then we move on and in half an hour, we're stopping again. I asked this handler what's the problem and he said it's too hot. He tells me, these are German shepherds. They do great in average to cool climates, but in the tropics forget it.

"After one day, we actually started having to carry these friggin' dogs. Really!

"I called in and kanked the patrol, so we turned around and headed home. And we're still having to carry the dogs. I finally got so pissed off, I told the senior handler, 'Either those dogs walk or we eat 'em!'"

All the men laughed.

"Skipper," DelGrosso said with a sigh, "I hope we don't see another dog, at least not with us."

"Fuck the dogs," Pat Collins said, "I've still got elephants on my mind."

"Oh, God! Colonel Wheeler," Harry Rogers groaned. "I've heard a rumor about him and elephants."

"It's the damned truth," Pat Collins said. "I thought it was a joke and got my ass reamed."

"How's that, sir," B. C. Collins said.

"I walked into the 4th Marines CP the other day and Colonel Wheeler is stomping around out back looking at this big, goddamned pit he had dug with a fence around it," Pat Collins said. "It was a goddamned pen for Dumbo!

"I open my big mouth and ask what the hell this thing is, and Wheeler looks at me with a straight face and says, 'It's my elephant pen.'

"I started to laugh right there, but since he wasn't smiling, I didn't. You never know when this guy's on the level or when he's taking an at-bat with your brains. Old Ed Wheeler says to me, 'Paddy, do you think you can find an elephant?'

"I tell him, 'Sure.'

"He tells me, 'Make me a plan and come back and tell me what you're going to do.' So in an hour I walk back there and I say, 'Colonel, I've got that elephant plan all worked out.'

"He says, 'Shoot.'

"I tell him, 'First, I'll go draw a 3.5 rocket launcher. Then I'll ambush this elephant, point this bazooka at him, and tell him to stick up his trunk. If he doesn't come along peaceful, I blow his ass off.'"

All the men laughed hard, and Pat Collins laughed too.

He strained to keep his words together as he laughed and then said, "Goddamned Colonel Wheeler was serious! He wanted to kick my ass. Called me insubordinate! Shit, I thought he was joking. Who wouldn't!"

"I hear that he's got everybody looking for elephants," Harry Rogers said.

"If you see one, don't tell anybody," Pat Collins said. "We have a hard enough time taking VC prisoners. I'd have no idea how to deal with an elephant."

"I don't know which is worse, elephants or dogs," John DelGrosso said, still laughing.

"You ever seen an elephant turd?" Pat Collins said and laughed. "That oughta give you a clue, sports fans."

"I'll tell you something worse," B. C. Collins said in a low and serious voice. "All these strap hangers. Observers, they call them. They go on patrol, and we're talking about some serious shit. These guys don't know if it's today or tomorrow. They come expecting the Easter Parade. Skipper, you know what I tell 'em?"

Pat Collins, still smiling, shook his head.

B.C. said, "I tell 'em you join my patrol, you better be ready to stay with me, fight like hell, or get left in the bush."

Pat Collins nodded, then he said, "More and more we're getting all sorts of people who want to go out with Recon. Some sort of goddamn ego trip. I'll give you lads a bit of advice. Tell them what I do. Before we go, I let them know that they have to carry what we carry. Either you do as we do, hump the same kinds of weapons, or you're on your own, coach. That gets their attention."

"Jesus H.," John DelGrosso said, "we had a gaggle of officers wanting to go out, and all they had were pistols and canteens. They didn't want to be loaded down!"

"I remember that goofy bunch," Pat Collins said, "I told them, 'Listen, you have to understand something, coach. This isn't a class on The

Company in a Daylight Attack back at The Basic School. There isn't room for observers and directors on small patrols. All of you are participants and you had better be prepared to act!'"

John DelGrosso laughed and said, "Those guys just walked off. Didn't they, Skipper!"

Pat Collins nodded and smiled. "They weren't too thrilled about it. But Walt backed us up. They didn't give us any shit."

His company had wasted a good portion of the afternoon, celebrating the Marine Corps' birthday in their own way, but Pat Collins knew that he had to push them back into action. They would patrol south and eastward this night and then link up with Golf Company, 2nd Battalion, 9th Marine Regiment, and patrol in force through the farming country in the lower hills: increasingly dangerous country because of the booby traps.

Soggy and shivering, the men got to their feet, their joints and muscles aching from the cool air and rain, and they sloshed their way off the top of the mountain. They headed back under the canopy where although it was warmer, it was just as wet and Charlie might lay at any turn.

· 2 ·

WHILE HIS MEN HAD RESTED AND EATEN IN DISCOMFORT BUT safety, Pat Collins had planned the work for the night. He decided that since they would be patrolling through Elephant Valley, a wide stretch of fertile river bottom country that broadened out flat and led to Da Nang, that the many farm fields there might provide the perfect cover for ambushes and, perhaps, an opportunity to take a prisoner for interrogation.

He divided the company into teams and spread them out so that they could operate as small units, but that no one was too far away so that if they needed help, they could get it.

Pat Collins chose his team and took two new men, a corpsman and a sergeant named Ratliff. That night, he led them to a field that reminded him of their Bar Ambush fiasco a few days ago. Only this time, he would make sure that none of the team fell asleep.

Sergeant Ratliff lay adjacent along the trail to Pat Collins. Instead of them lying in the center and pointing out, butt to butt, they lay alternately spaced shoulder toward shoulder at intervals wide enough so that they had clear fields of fire, but close enough so that they did not have any dead space. Pat Collins hoped that by doing this they might grab someone. Just reach out and yank his feet out from under him. If a small band of VC came along, one Marine would grab the ankles of one man and the rest of the team would shoot the others.

One problem did surface, however. Pat Collins discovered finally at 5:00 A.M., when they had seen not one other human being, that he had picked a beautiful spot for an ambush and snatch, but it was apparently too far off the beaten path. He had picked a place for an ambush where few people ever passed.

"I've gotta take a dump," Pat Collins whispered across the way to Sergeant Ratliff. The horizon had already turned pink and the captain had an hour ago concluded that they were destined to come up with empty hooks at this fishing hole.

The trail upon which they had lain had earthen dikes running down either side, covered with foot-high grass, and Pat Collins slid back and over the berm that lay behind him. He left his rifle on the trail. It was only two or three feet away, and he had seen no one all night.

The relief felt good, since the nut cake had lain like a brick in his stomach. But he had no more than turned loose of the first load, when suddenly he could hear shooting from the trail. Since he was squatted with his trousers around his ankles, he lay forward on his belly and looked up the dirt incline toward the trail until the shooting stopped. Only a few seconds.

A light drizzle had begun to fall, limiting his vision so that when he saw several figures standing on the other side of the trail, he assumed that it was Sergeant Ratliff and the rest of his team.

"Shit, they let the only VC we see all night get away, and I'm down here in the rice paddy with my pants around my ankles taking a crap," he grumbled to himself as he wrestled his trousers up and buttoned them. "And now they're just gonna stand around up there so that the whole goddamned VC Army can get a fix on them."

He was about to stand and tell the men to get down when one of them quickly turned, noticing something apparently coming nearby. The men quickly and quietly jumped down the side of the berm on each side of Pat Collins and hid.

Even though the dawn sky lay pink across the horizon, the early morning rain and remaining darkness limited Pat Collins's visibility so that he could barely make out the shapes of the men at either side of him. He waited quietly and when the man on his right got to his knees and began to crawl, so did Pat, right behind him, and the man behind the captain did the same.

They moved well down the trail that crossed the large rice fields, one of which now brimmed with water from the rains. When they approached the hedgerow that bordered the fields, the men stood and began to run.

The rain had slacked and the dawn had brightened now, and as Pat Collins jogged behind one of the men, he noticed that he wore black and no bush hat. He noticed that the man carried a Chinese SKS rifle. He noticed that he wore sandals.

Shit, coach, I'm off sides! he said to himself, I'm in the middle of a VC column bugging out. And he immediately dove on the trail and rolled on the other side, splashing into the muddy water.

The Marine captain held himself beneath the water's surface and counted to thirty, and then slowly, like a turtle, he let his head slide above the surface. He looked first left and then to the right where he had last seen the Viet Cong jog toward the trees. They had not left, but now squatted and surveyed the field. He held himself below the water and allowed only the top of his head, his eyes, and his nostrils to remain above the rice paddy's cover.

Slowly the Viet Cong soldiers slipped into the trees, and when Pat Collins could no longer see them he carefully slid down the side of the dike, keeping his body below the water.

When he reached the spot where he thought he had left Sergeant Ratliff, he slid up the embankment, through the grass and weeds.

"Ratliff!" he whispered.

"Here!" Ratliff whispered back.

"Where!" Collins whispered.

"On the other side!" Ratliff whispered.

Pat Collins then saw the sergeant looking right at him, not ten feet away.

"Who shot?" Collins said.

"I think those VC got hit by our flank team, over behind that hedgerow," Ratliff said. "At first I thought it was one of our guys shooting. It sounded pretty close. We were waiting for you to open fire, but you didn't. By the time I decided to shoot, something spooked those VC and they disappeared."

"Whatever spooked them sent 'em jumping right down where I was taking a shit," Pat Collins said. "I thought it was you, so I fell in. Shit, they're just over in that hedgerow."

"So what do we do?" Ratliff asked.

"We can follow them, or we can lay here and gamble that they'll come back wanting to hit our other team," Pat Collins said. "My guess is that they'll go after our boys. I vote we stay here."

"Roger that, sir," Ratliff said. "You can pull back to your spot and I'll get back to mine."

"Just pass the word in a whisper to sit tight and wait for my signal," Pat Collins said.

The men waited nearly twenty minutes and the brightness of the new day had begun to show color, although the drizzle and fog held the darkness and kept the visibility low, limiting what any of the men could see.

Since the sergeant and the corpsman were new to the team, Pat Collins had kept them closest to him. He noticed that the corpsman, a tall, lanky midwesterner who wore black horn-rimmed glasses, seemed high-strung. Perhaps too nervous for good reconnaissance work. Since he had his doubts about the man, he looked to where he lay. The new doc hugged the ground and held his M-14 tightly. It looked as though he had not moved a muscle all night.

He'll be alright, the captain reassured himself, remembering that the corpsman had expressed no qualms about carrying a rifle and joining any fight. He had given the doc his short speech about how every man on the recon team was a participant, a lead slinger, even the corpsman, and the new man had agreed. It seemed logical that he should, the man had told him. Yeah, just a little nervous, but his mind is right, the captain said to himself.

Then he looked to Ratliff, who lay calmly and quietly and slowly shifted his head from left to right, searching for the Viet Cong to return. He'll be fine too, Collins said to himself.

As the rain let up, Pat Collins could see that one of the Viet Cong had ventured again out on the trail, and he walked crouched over with his rifle at the ready.

"I'll grab him by the ankles when he comes by us," Pat Collins told the men at his sides.

Suddenly he heard a splash. Not a big one, but a muffled gurgle and glub that water makes when a body slips into it. He looked and the corpsman was not in his place. Then, as Pat Collins searched with his eyes, the sound of the water made sense.

The captain raised to his elbows and peeked over the other side of the trail and saw a butt slowly emerge above the water. It rose higher and higher until it stood well above the water, making the corpsman look like a duck gone bobbing for a fish.

Pat Collins immediately glanced up and saw that the VC soldier stood fully erect, and for a moment he just looked in amazement at the corpsman in the rice paddy with his head and shoulders underwater and the greater part of his back and butt in the air.

"Get him," Pat Collins said as he rolled on his side and began to shoot. But the Viet Cong had already begun to run and then in one motion, the man, like a Chinese acrobat, sprang in a straight-legged flip, his arms out and his body rigid, and he dropped over the side of the berm and disappeared.

• 3 •

PAT COLLINS AND JOHN DELGROSSO SAT TOGETHER, LOOKING AT their maps, now trying to decide how best to move the company to the lower hills where Golf Company was to meet them. After the VC had fled, Pat Collins regrouped the company and tried to sweep the hedgerows where he had seen the Viet Cong disappear. However, they had little luck.

"They'll just have to get along without us," John DelGrosso said, trying to work a smile across Pat Collins's face.

"They might," Collins said and didn't smile. "But we could get another shot, if we work in force."

He looked at his map and pointed at a low bend that led around Dong Den and placed them at the head of a valley that ran north and south. "We can go here and sweep straight down to here, where Golf two-nine is waiting. Maybe we will flush something into their patrol lines. We'll move through the canopy until we lose cover and set up in an ambush tonight, with our full company."

By an hour after dark, the company had moved from under the canopy of the high mountains and now maneuvered their way over the low, bushy hills that gently surrounded small farming areas that clustered along the several small streams that flowed into the Bay of Da Nang.

A narrow roadway wound its way through the high grass, brush, and low trees, and Pat Collins studied the area for a long time before he chose a spot on that road where he would lay his full company in ambush. He was angry now.

The rain continued to fall, and with no moon or stars shining, the blackness of the night seemed darker than ever.

"Get out the comm wire," Pat Collins told Harry Rogers, who sat in the circle of platoon leaders and sergeants as the captain held his council of war. Tonight there would be no mistakes.

"It's gonna be a bitch seeing anybody in the killing zone," Collins said, "so everybody's gonna have hold of the comm wire. If a VC patrol enters from the left, the man on the left tugs once. If on the right, the guy there does the same. Once the VC patrol is completely in the killing zone, I want to feel two good pulls, either from the guy on the left or the one on the right, according to which direction these bastards are coming from. We've gotta make sure that we nail the enemy in the killing zone. If we hit the front of his column or the tail end of it, and he's got people outside, they can turn on our flanks and blow our shit away."

In the darkness, the men nearly had to feel their way to the various positions along the trail. For the men on the left, it became confusing. Several of them found their line jagged and it seemed odd, yet they all lay overlooking the trail. They shrugged it off as just another odd twist that did not have to make sense to them; after all, this was South Vietnam.

The rain fell hard and for several men on the left, the suddenly moving shadows had seemed unreal, as though they were part of the storm. But when Sergeant Ratliff looked up and saw two legs standing over him, all he could do was scream and shoot.

Pat Collins felt one tug on the wire from the left and then two more, very quickly, just as Ratliff fired. However, Collins could not see a single soldier, nothing at all.

"They're behind us," he called out in the night, and quickly rolled over and sat up and opened fire with his rifle.

Every Marine around him did the same, and he heard a grunt and a hard *thud* in the blackness.

"We've got some of them," he called out, knowing by the sound of the fall that several VC had obviously bunched together in the rain and his sudden hail of fire had brought them down together.

He could hear other shooting at each end of the column and by the sound of it, Charlie had gotten caught dead center.

Once the shooting stopped, he called for a head count and status of any casualties. Harry Rogers let him know that they had not lost a single man. However, Sergeant Ratliff was fairly well shaken because the Viet Cong had walked right over the top of him.

"How's that possible if he's off the side of the trail?" Pat Collins asked the first sergeant.

"Sir, I guess he got mixed up," Rogers said. "There's a weird bend in the trail right on our left flank, and apparently Ratliff thought he was at the side but got dead center. It'll be light soon and we can take a look at it."

As the sky began to brighten, the rain also died to a foggy mist. Pat Collins and Harry Rogers walked out to investigate how many Viet Cong they had killed, and there, instead of any lifeless VC, they found one very dead water buffalo with more than 400 bullet holes in it. There had been Viet Cong, but by the time the Marines realized that the enemy had moved behind them, the VC had scattered, leaving the animal.

Pat Collins and several of his men walked back to where Sergeant Ratliff had lain and had the Viet Cong walk over the top of him. Sure enough, he had lain at the side of the main trail, but right in the middle of the second trail that branched and ran behind the ambush.

· 4 ·

WHEN COMPANY D CROSSED THE LAST LOW HILL, PAT COLLINS could see the several dug-in fighting positions that Golf Company had established for their night defense. The sun lay low in the sky and his men had not slept in nearly two days. He radioed the company commander and then moved into their perimeter for the night. Golf Company had seen no one that day except the reconnaissance Marines.

By daylight the next morning, Company D and Company G had already broken into patrols and moved southeasterly toward the bend in the Cau Do River where the Yen River meets it. Pat Collins felt sick in his stomach as they came closer to this low hill country where the Viet Cong sniped and ran, or rigged a booby trap at every opportunity.

For the Marines on patrol, the booby traps represented a vicarious attack that could as likely kill a child or a cow as it was likely to kill a Marine, and the thought of tripping one kept many of the veterans unsettled. They knew as they drew closer to the coastal areas that Charlie had become shy. Now Charlie mostly fought the Marines with his traps; many amazed even the most hardened veteran of two previous wars who would swear he had seen it all.

Yet there was always something new, something very frightening but very creative that Charlie would show him. Nail boxes and bear traps. Grenades that swung on a line and exploded in a man's face or bounced up at his waist. Dud ammo converted into a mine, set off with a spring, a nail, and a length of line along with a single cartridge or grenade. That's how the reporter Chapelle had lost her life. It was also how an increasing number of Marines were losing theirs.

Pat Collins had broken his company into teams and the teams had attached themselves to Golf Company patrols. Together they moved back toward the badlands south and southwest of Da Nang.

Once in the Cam Ne complex area, where 2nd Battalion, 9th Marines had a command post established, Collins and his men would spend the next several days working the rivers from small boats, probing the banks, looking for holes and tunnels where Charlie might hide.

As they drew closer, the patrols came across more and more clusters of huts built at the edges of more and more rice fields and dry crop fields. They all had hedgerows and fences, a favorite place for Charlie to plant his creative little bombs.

Several new Marines patrolled with the platoon that Pat Collins had chosen to follow. He watched them making mistakes and their platoon sergeant, a staff sergeant named Rhodes, trying to correct them before one of their errors reaped a deadly payoff. However, Pat Collins knew that this man could not see everything at once, so when he saw a new Marine approach a trail that led to a fence, the captain stopped the boy.

"What's your plan, son," Collins said, taking the Marine by the shoulder.

The young private, a tall, muscular boy who had a tight build and was clearly an athlete, looked at the captain and stammered, "I was heading for those hootches, sir."

"I can see that, but do you have a plan, lad?" Pat Collins asked again.

"No, sir, I guess I don't," the private said.

"Best way to stay alive is have a plan," Collins said. "I see you head-ing up this nice hard-packed and well-worn footpath. No mines here, right? Good hard clay. Can't hide a mine there. But how about that fence?"

"Booby-trapped?" the Marine asked.

"Maybe and maybe not," Pat Collins said. "But I sure wouldn't go up and open that gate. Trees right there, and bushes."

"Yes, sir," the boy said, still slightly stammering.

Pat Collins turned to wait for the staff sergeant to reach him when he saw the Marine's jaw drop and his eyes widen.

"Stop!" the staff sergeant called, and Pat Collins wheeled back, turn-ing on his toes, just in time to see the private, the same Marine he had just warned not to open the gate, reaching for its wooden picket top.

In an instant, Pat Collins dove to the ground along with several other Marines who either recognized the potential danger or saw the captain drop and reacted with him.

Just as the boy pulled the gate open, he heard a spring sing out and suddenly something snapped around his ankles and swept his feet from under him and yanked them straight up.

The world moved in slow motion for the young private whose eyes now took in every detail that surrounded him. He saw the dust billowing around the other Marines as they bellied into the path and scrambled for cover. He saw his staff sergeant's mouth open, his face bright red, the cords in his neck standing out as he shouted at him. He saw the line that suddenly dropped in loops in front of him as his feet swung up, and as he looked up toward his feet, he saw the 60-mm mortar shell falling.

All Pat Collins could see was suddenly the boy was yanked off his feet, immediately pulled into the air, and with his head swinging down, his hand reached out and grabbed the 60-mm mortar shell by its fins.

The private said nothing. He simply swung from his feet, his head a foot from the ground and his right arm rigid in front of him, holding the mortar round two feet above the earth.

## • 5 •

T HINK YOU'LL SINK, HARRY?" JOHN DELGROSSO SAID TO HARRY
Rogers as the two men climbed atop the LVT. The first sergeant
wore a large, very bright orange life jacket.

"I can't swim, and I don't want to drown, Lieutenant," Rogers said
and put a long cigar in his mouth.

"Makes a beautiful target," Pat Collins said as he climbed up the amtrack and sat on the round, inflated side of the rubber boat that they had
strapped to the vehicle's top.

They had tied three of the inflatable rubber boats to the amtrack and
planned to ride it down the river where they would untie and paddle
along the banks, looking for tunnels to demolish. The LVT served them
as a supply base, so that they would move back and forth to the amtrack
as needed.

Pat Collins and his men had learned that behind nearly every village
along the river, they could find a network of tunnels if they looked hard
enough. When they eliminated the tunnels it was remarkable how the villagers suddenly became much more cooperative. Thus the captain and his
Marines regularly began working along the river, watching for smoke
coming from the ground, probing with sticks, flushing out the Viet Cong,
and then blowing up the tunnels.

As the vehicle drove into the water and began to swim upstream, the
Marines watched as it pushed against the current. They knew how hard
it would have been to paddle to their starting point, several miles against
the flow.

Harry Rogers had already lit his cigar and he sat on his boat, wearing
his large orange jacket, and looked like the king of the Mardi Gras with
the stogie bit between his teeth.

The three teams of Marines wore their bush hats, tiger-striped camouflage shorts, and black-and-green recon tennis shoes. Each man had a
rifle and a knife.

For November, the day seemed warm. It had stopped raining the day
before, and now, for a rare occasion between October and February in
this region of I Corps, the sun shone in an almost summertime brightness
and warmth.

It was almost too nice and they were enjoying it too much when the rushes and tamarack came alive with small-arms fire.

"Cover!" Pat Collins shouted, but there was nothing. The Marie sitting on the open hatch of the amtrack had dropped down and slammed the lid shut in half a heartbeat.

Harry Rogers immediately began firing his M-14 at the brush on the river's edge, and then instinctively so did the other Marines. And even though the men sat atop the amtrack with no cover as it churned its way through the water, slowly past the ambush, not a man suffered even a scratch and none of the inflatable boats sustained a puncture.

"You goddamned cowards!" B. C. Collins roared and beat his fist on the tight hatch. "Come on out of there and face your maker."

When the Marine finally did emerge from the hatch, Pat Collins took one look at him and grumbled, "You better hope that you never go on patrol with me or any of them." And he pointed to the others.

The Marine in the amtrack said nothing, he just kept on his helmet and talked to the driver below him until the LVT reached the turn in the river where it joined with the Yen.

Pat Collins looked at the crewman and said, "Now it's our turn. You can float around out here like a sitting duck, waiting for the mortars, while we go to work close to the banks where we can take cover."

The crewman said nothing as the three boats slipped off the amtrack and the recon Marines moved along the riverbank and began probing for tunnels.

"Push it in closer," Pat Collins said to Harry Rogers, who sat at the back of the rubber boat pushing with his paddle while clenching the cigar in his teeth and cradling his M-14 in his lap. He had buckled the front of the orange life jacket, and because of its bulkiness around his waist, he had a tough time pulling on the paddle.

"Can you lean over the front and feel down three with your arm?" Rogers asked.

Pat Collins lay over the front of the rubber boat and felt just below the water where the bank seemed strangely dark.

"It's a tunnel," Pat Collins said after he reached under the water and stretched his arm up and found where the tunnel led above the waterline beneath the bank. "Probably runs all the way to the village. This is how

they escape. Slide right down the tunnel and into the river, below the water. We'd never see them."

He was about to pull his arm out of the hole when suddenly someone
grabbed it and pulled hard, yanking him off the boat and into the river.
Then a grenade broke the surface of the water and splashed back down,
behind him. Pat Collins thought the grenade would blow his legs, or at
the very least his testicles, off as he managed to pull free from the VC in
the hole.

When the grenade exploded, the captain shut his eyes and put both of
his hands between his legs. He felt some sharp stinging along the backs of
his legs, but he seemed fine in general.

He looked behind himself and the boat was gone. Blown to bits. But
where the boat had been, Harry Rogers now bobbed, life jacket intact,
snug around his chest and neck. The first sergeant, still clenching the cigar between his teeth, leveled his M-14 at the riverbank and began shooting through the mud.

After the fourth shot, next to the tunnel entrance, a body floated up.
In twenty minutes, after they had stuffed a healthy charge of explosive
into the hole, Pat Collins and his men watched as the ground belched and
then collapsed in a huge crater on the riverbank.

"It should be a day or two before they can use that one again," he
said.

# ROUND-EYED CHARLIE

## •1•

"Y OU'RE GONNA GET CAUGHT, AND FIND YOURSELF IN A WORLD OF shit, B.C.," the corporal lying on the cot next to the door said.

"I've been doing this for two months, and it works like a charm," B. C. Collins said, buttoning up the front of Captain Pat Collins's herringbone utility jacket. Then the corporal took out the set of captain's bars, also borrowed from the skipper, that he kept in his foot locker, and dropped them in his pocket. "With Paddy Collins out in the bush with DelGrosso, who's gonna know? You gonna tell 'em, Posey?"

"No," Posey said, "I'm no rat. But impersonating a commissioned officer is serious shit. They bury you under the brig for that."

"The ducks and the zoomies at the White Elephant, they don't know one jarhead from another. The skipper don't go there enough to get a reputation, so this works," B. C. Collins said, picking up his bush hat and tightening the Marine Corps emblem that he had screwed to the front of the brim, just the way the captain wore it.

"What will you do if you see someone who knows you?" Posey said.

"Duck out the back," B.C. said and swaggered out the door.

He caught a ride on a supply truck, and in a few minutes he stood at a corner in Da Nang where he could see the infamous Da Nang Open Officers' Mess, commonly called the White Elephant, a place where loud music rocked, beer and liquor flowed around the clock, and the best local girls worked the clientele. Officers made more money, and who knew, the working girl might hook that big fish, a young lieutenant or captain, who would take her to the so-called "Big PX," stateside.

At the doorway, a chubby-faced man wearing a white bush shirt sat on a stool behind a wooden lectern. On the makeshift desk lay a book and a list of all officers allowed in the club.

Corporal Bryant C. Collins looked at himself in the window of the corner restaurant where he stood. He took the captain's bars from his pocket, and watching his reflection, he carefully centered each of the silver double-bars on the herringbone utility shirt's collar. He checked his fresh haircut and checked the fresh polish on his boots.

With the bush hat tilted forward he strolled to the man behind the lectern and said, "How's it going, pal. Anything happening inside?"

"No, Marine," the man said, giving the corporal the eye and then glancing down at the sheet listing all the officers and their units, "really slow this afternoon. Just a few pilots talking with their hands. What's the name?"

"Collins," B.C. said, pointing to the name and unit stenciled on the herringbone jacket. "Third Recon Battalion."

The man ran his finger down the page and his finger stopped. "Right, sir. Captain Collins, P. G. Step right inside, sir."

For B. C. Collins, it had not been a lie. He was Collins of 3rd Recon. He felt that the only place where he had really gone afoul was wearing the officer's rank. He knew that was serious if seen by the wrong eyes. But he also felt confident that Pat Collins would treat him with understanding. He knew that the skipper saw his toughness and courage and his loyalty to the unit as far more important than busting him for sneaking into the officers' club for a beer. He knew that he had become one of Collins's special people when the captain had started calling him by the pet name Smedley.[1]

Everyone in the platoon thought that Pat Collins had gone on patrol for the day with John DelGrosso. The captain had gotten excited when he

[1] Based on Marine Corps General Smedley D. Butler, recipient of two Medals of Honor.

heard the reports that patrols had now spotted what looked to be Americans operating with the Viet Cong.

A week earlier he had been on patrol and a man in a camouflage uniform crawled out of the grass near him. Collins thought he recognized him as one of his men and stopped him.

"Hey, pal," Collins said, "what are you doing out of position?"

The man looked at him as though he did not understand, and that was when the captain noticed the soldier was wearing tennis shoes. He tried to grab the man, but he jumped back in the grass and fled from sight. Pat Collins had not heard the man speak so he did not know if he had been a French deserter, a Russian, or an American college student who sympathized with the Communists and had come to Vietnam to fight on that side.

For many weeks, Pat Collins, as other Marines, had heard rumors. None of them saw or heard anything that stood as fact, however. But today, several facts stared them in the face regarding round-eyed people fighting on the side of the Communists. It appeared that two French deserters, one white and one black, had killed two U.S. Army sergeants at a club in Saigon. They had taken the two dead Americans' identification cards and then fled.

No one had seen the two men until a few days ago when using the identification cards they infiltrated a U.S. Army compound outside Pleiku and had set a fire. A day ago there had been a suspicious fire at Da Nang Air Base. That same day two "American-looking" individuals, one white and one black, the black man wearing a blue rain cape, were spotted near Hill 327, watching traffic there.

John DelGrosso had taken his patrol out, scouting the western side of the hill, and Pat Collins had joined the patrol. After tramping along the fringes of the hill, Pat Collins decided that he'd had enough, and that he would head back to the compound. He had some paperwork to finish, and would be near the radio, in case something happened.

B. C. Collins had little more than left the 3rd Reconnaissance Battalion compound and had caught his ride to Da Nang when Captain Pat Collins came to the NCO hut looking for his men. He wanted them on alert, just in case DelGrosso got a lead on the two westerners.

"Posey, where's Smedley?" the captain asked.

"Liberty, sir," Posey said, not knowing how else to answer.

"I hadn't authorized any liberty," Collins said. "First Sergeant Rogers let him go?"

"I guess so, sir," Posey said, hoping that this would satisfy the captain's curiosity.

What the hell, Pat Collins said to himself as he looked at his watch and saw that the day was nearly gone anyway. The idea of a cold beer in the ville sounded good to him, and he had an excuse, he rationalized. He was looking for his lost corporal.

As Pat Collins approached the White Elephant, he took off his bush hat and slapped it across his trousers, knocking the dust from them. Crap, I hope they let me in. I'm a little filthy for company, he said to himself as he approached the man seated behind the lectern at the door.

"Is this okay? I know I'm a little dirty," the captain said, trying to be as diplomatic as possible.

"Normally," the man said, "I'd send you back to get a shower and clean fatigues, but there's not much business today. I guess it's okay for now."

The captain started to step past the chubby-faced man in the white bush shirt, but the man's fat arm jutted out.

"Hold it a second, sir," the man said. "Let me check you off the list."

"Name's Collins, P. G.," the captain said and started to walk again.

"I'm sorry, but I don't have you on the list," the man said.

"What do you mean?" Collins said. "I've been here a dozen times! Look on your list. P. G. Collins, captain, 3rd Recon Battalion."

"I'm sorry," the man said, "but apparently you have a double. You're already inside. Shall we call the manager and get this straightened out?"

Pat Collins started to say yes, but then he realized that his outlaw corporal had gone on liberty. "No, that won't be necessary."

The man then looked at him with a scowling expression and said, "I suggest that you move on then, sir. I probably ought to call the military police."

"No trouble, pal," Pat Collins said, feeling his fury rise up through his neck and fill his face. He walked to the restaurant at the corner, sat on a stool next to the open door, and ordered a San Miguel beer. The waiter brought him a warm one, which did not improve his very sour disposition.

The captain struggled to finish the one beer. Its warmth and his anger

unsettled his stomach. The acid burn increased his foul mood, and he sat
and pondered how he would take care of his double.

Pat Collins watched as more and more officers walked inside the
White Elephant, several coming from the Da Nang Press Center nearby,
and civilian journalists accompanied them to the club.

Place is heating up again, the captain told himself. He's smart enough
to know that he'd better get out of there before a large crowd gathers. He
ought to come out at any second.

He left the empty San Miguel bottle standing on the bar with no tip,
and he began to walk close to the front of the White Elephant. Several pilots came out and in the middle of them, he saw B. C. Collins. The pilots
slapped him on the back, and the corporal wearing the herringbone utility shirt and the bush hat with the emblem pinning the front brim back,
and Pat Collins's captain's bars on each collar, turned, still smiling.

When he saw Captain Pat Collins, the smile quickly shrank and the
corporal froze in his steps. The chubby-faced man wearing the white shirt
swiveled on the stool and leaned one elbow on the lectern and watched
the encounter unfold.

"Who gave you the liberty card, Smedley?" Pat Collins said.

"I, ah, kind of slipped it out of the logbook in the first sergeant's
hootch, sir," B.C. said honestly.

"What'd you tell that man in order to get inside?" the captain then
asked.

"The guy asked me my name and I told him Collins. Then the guy
asked my unit and I said 3rd Recon," B.C. said.

"You didn't lie to him?" Pat Collins asked.

"I didn't *tell* him anything that wasn't true, if that's what you mean,
sir," B. C. Collins said.

"When did you get commissioned and promoted to captain?" Pat
Collins said.

"I promoted myself about two hours ago, sir," B. C. Collins said.

"Well, Smedley, I'm busting you back to corporal," Pat Collins said
loud enough for the doorman to hear. The chubby-faced man smiled and
took off his horn-rimmed glasses and wiped them with the handkerchief
that he took from his hip pocket. Then he wiped the sheen of sweat from
his face and put the glasses back on.

"You got more balls than a goddamned bowling alley," Pat Collins told the corporal. "Let's go home."

"What about this, sir?" B.C. said in a low voice and handed Pat Collins the captain's bars.

"It's done. You leveled with me," Pat Collins said. Then he turned and stood nose to nose with the corporal. "Next time you decide to pull something like this, Smedley, you just make sure I know where I'm at!"

· 2 ·

PAT COLLINS TOOK THE HERRINGBONE UTILITY SHIRT AND STUFFED it in his laundry bag, and then walked to the front of the hootch where Harry Rogers sat, chewing his cigar, feeling foul.

"Sir," Rogers said, "just letting him go like that, and then laughing about it. That's bad for the boy. He'll think he can get away with anything now. I won't be able to control him."

"You just want a piece of his ass and that's all, Harry," Pat Collins said. "You have to understand that Marine. He's like a lot of these outlaws, a double load of guts. Back in garrison, they're not intimidated by getting into trouble. Out in the bush, they're not intimidated by Charlie. You're a goddamned good example, Harry. I'm sure you never pulled a stunt."

The first sergeant just chomped his cigar and stared out at the western hills and then looked back at the captain. "It's not punishment, but it could serve as a lesson and keep him out of trouble," he said.

"What the hell are you talking about, Harry?" Pat Collins said, sitting at the table where two radio operators sat reading L'Amour westerns and listening to the static over the communications network. Every few minutes a voice from a patrol would crackle and issue a situation report. One of the men would jot the information on a yellow pad and let the patrol leader know that the message was received.

"B. C. Collins, sir," Rogers said.

"What do you have in mind, Harry?" Collins said.

"Send him and his team down to two-nine, let them work on those spider holes and tunnels along that river. That'll keep him out of trouble," Harry Rogers said.

"Good idea," Collins said. "Any word from DelGrosso?"

The radio operator said, "Only one sitrep. They picked up a place where it looked like a couple of people camped and there was a crushed Winston cigarette wrapper thrown down there."

"Could be our boys," Collins said.

The trail had gone cold after his team had found the campsite. John DelGrosso guessed that two westerners slept there since the cigarette wrapper had obviously come from the military exchange, although more and more they were growing common on the black market. But the Viet Cong didn't leave trash like that behind. He guessed that because there were no butts, just matted grass where the two men had lain, large areas consistent with large Western bodies, that whoever dropped the wrapper had not known it. DelGrosso guessed that it had been a fortunate accident.

They followed the tracks, and then lost them in a stream that cut through the hills and led down to the area south of Da Nang.

"My guess is that they're working with that VC organization at Cam Ne," John DelGrosso told Bob Holt as they followed the stream.

"We might as well cut back north and get home," Holt said.

As they walked quietly between the low bushes and through the knee-high grass that grew on the low rolling hills, John DelGrosso kept seeing something flash through the brush just ahead of them, as though someone was watching them and keeping on the move at the same time.

The lieutenant dropped to one knee and pretended to retie his boot. He slowly tilted his head slightly up so that he could just see the clump of trees ahead of him and he saw the black man's face.

DelGrosso slowly stood and walked to his left, keeping the hiding man in the corner of his eye. He came close to Bob Holt and whispered, "They're in that bunch of bushes watching us. Let me have your canteen."

John DelGrosso took a drink and then handed the bottle back to the gunny. "Why don't you walk to that side and send those guys in from the flank. I'll walk back to my position and wait until our guys get around back and then we'll just run at them."

The two men who hid in the bush watched John DelGrosso walk back and slip off his pack. He dug inside and then tied up the sack, slung it on his back, and picked up his rifle. Then he shouted and ran straight at them.

Their first inclination was to run out the back of the bushes, but they didn't. They charged straight at the shouting lieutenant, only they did not see Bob Holt come at them from the side. He took out both men with a rolling block, sweeping them off their feet and sending them tumbling in the dirt at John DelGrosso's feet.

"Get up!" DelGrosso growled at the two men. They both wore khaki shirts and jeans. The black man had a blue rain cape rolled and tied on his belt.

"Show me some ID," Holt said, jamming his rifle into the black man's ribs.

The men said nothing. They both squatted on their haunches and waited.

"Sir," John DelGrosso said on the radio, still breathing hard. "We caught them!"

Pat Collins nearly knocked the radio off the table, leaning across to grab the handset from the operator.

"Who the hell are they?" Pat Collins said excitedly.

"Don't know that," DelGrosso said. "They won't talk. You want to send a chopper to pick us up. I don't want to risk losing these two by walking."

"Roger," Collins said, "we've got air coming. Tell me, do they understand English?"

"I think so," DelGrosso said. "When Gunny Holt spoke, they responded pretty fast."

Pat Collins thought for a minute and then said, "I haven't called for air yet. Why don't you do this. If they won't talk, just kill 'em!"

"Sir!" DelGrosso said. "You said, 'Kill them'?"

"Roger that," Collins said, smiling smugly.

John DelGrosso took the muzzle of his AR-15 and pressed it onto the forehead of the white man and pushed his head up until they made eye contact.

"Boss says you don't talk, I'm supposed to kill you," John DelGrosso said in his best Brooklyn-tough-guy voice. "What'll it be, pal?"

"Time out!" the white man said, clearly shaken by the serious-acting Marine lieutenant.

"Shut the fuck up!" the black man said. "They won't shoot anybody."

"Goddamned Americans!" Bob Holt said, shoving his boot square on the black man's chest and holding his M-14 rifle's muzzle flat against the man's nose. "Fuckin' traitor! Here's a one-way ticket to hell, you son of a bitch!"

"Stop, man!" the white man said, seeing that the Marine gunny was really about to shoot his partner. "We're Green Berets. We've got ID, man! Fly us in and we'll check out. We're just trying to infiltrate the VC, man."

The two men were in fact U.S. Army Special Forces soldiers who had dressed to impersonate the two French deserters. DelGrosso and Collins never saw the two men again.

Regarding Americans serving with the Viet Cong, many Marines continued to report sighting them. In 1968, when Pat Collins returned to South Vietnam, his rifle company would come across a platoon of Viet Cong and kill several. Among the dead were two Americans. One, a girl who had been a student at Oberlin College in Ohio.

· 3 ·

B RYANT C. COLLINS TOOK A SIX-MAN TEAM TO 2ND BATTALION, 9th Marines, and began work on the Cau Do river, and in a week he had moved all the way to the Yen.

Now as Collins and five other Marines paddled a rubber boat behind an amtrack, B. C. Collins began to notice that they had gone too far.

"Hey, lads," B.C. said as he pulled on the paddle, trying to keep his boat abeam the amtrack that worked as their point vehicle and source of supplies and explosives. They had blown a half-dozen holes that morning and found several others at a point where a berm that bordered a rice field butted the raised side of the riverbank.

"Yeah," the lance corporal who was Collins's assistant team leader said, "gettin' tired?"

"Shit no," B.C. said, "but weren't we supposed to turn around at that last bend?"

"I hadn't paid that much attention," the lance corporal said. "If we'd gone too far, the amtrack would have stopped. We're all right, anyway. Let's get these blown and go home."

"You got a deal there, lad," B.C. said cheerfully, deciding that they would call it a day.

None of them had realized, however, that they had worked themselves into a place along the Yen River where 2nd Battalion, 9th Marines, had swept against the Viet Cong who had fled across the river, ducked into the tunnels, and slipped into the village that lay 300 meters to the east while the recon team had worked on the holes upriver and out of sight.

Now as they floated around the bend and found the tunnels that the escaping VC had used, the first rounds began clipping through the air overhead.

"Shit, B.C.," the lance corporal said, ducking down, "we've got somebody shooting across the water at that village."

"Let's get downstream," Collins said, pulling hard on his paddle. He knew that they could go much more rapidly with the current and get out of the cross fire of the Marines and the VC.

The boat began moving ahead of the amtrack, whose crewman atop the vehicle now heard the firing too, and seeing the Marines paddling hard began to pull up his M-79 grenade launcher.

Suddenly rifle fire opened from the east side of the river, and began pinging off the amtrack.

"Ambush!" one of the Marines behind B. C. Collins shouted. Then the six men heard the unmistakable *thunk* of the blooper launching a grenade. All the men turned to look behind them where the amtrack churned away and saw the grenade sailing through the air directly at them.

"Jump!" Collins screamed as he fell off the rubber boat and swam toward the bank.

The explosion sent shrapnel stinging into his back as the grenade detonated in the center of the boat, leaving only black shreds of nylon-reinforced rubber sinking behind them.

The six Marines started to swim to the amtrack, but it was now taking heavy fire from the village, and from their low position on the riverbank, they decided against that plan.

Quickly, the six Marines crawled up the bank, careful to stay beneath the brush. Once they had gotten together on the bank, B.C. looked around.

"Any of you lads know where we are?" he said.

The five men shook their heads.

"Let's take a look at our situation," Collins said, now realizing the pickle in which they had landed. "We have one M-14 with one magazine in it. Everything else went in the drink. How many rounds you got in that?"

"Four," the Marine with the rifle said.

"Over on the west side, coming down like gangbusters, we have the Marines, shooting everything that moves," Collins said. "Right here on this side we have the VC holding up in the village. I vote that we hustle into that village, hide in a hootch, wait there for the Marines to invade, and show the white flag."

"How do we get in there without getting blown away?" the assistant team leader said. "We got only one rifle with four rounds."

"If we ding any VC we just grab their gear," B.C. said.

One by one each man ran along the dike, barefooted and wearing only swimming trunks. The Marine with the rifle ducked inside the first hut and waved the others to come ahead. As the remaining men ran to the hut, Marine mortars began to walk into the edge of the village.

Pat Collins sat on the hill, across the river at the flank of 2nd Battalion, 9th Marines. He had watched the operation for much of the morning, and at the same time he had also watched his six recon Marines work above the operation on the riverbank. When he saw them float past the bend that marked the end of their patrolling area, he told his radioman to get 2nd Battalion's operations section on the radio so that he could advise them that he had six Marines on the river, right in the path of their attack.

As he waited to speak to someone in the battalion's S-3, he saw the boat explode and the men swim to the bank. He also watched as they ran to the village.

"We gotta get to the other side of this ville," the lance corporal said. "In about two shakes, those mortars will have us dead on."

B. C. Collins took the M-14 rifle and dashed from the hut to another grass-and-thatch house several yards farther inside the little hamlet. Just as he ducked through the doorway, he met two Viet Cong guerrillas dressed in black pajamas and wearing straw hats. He didn't hesitate for an instant as he shot each man, center mass, and used two of his four rounds.

"He's waving at us," the lance corporal told the others and they ran to the hut where B. C. Collins had already undressed one dead VC and began putting on his clothes.

"Get dressed, lad," B.C. said to his assistant as he pulled the small black shirt together tight across his chest and began buttoning it. "Grab their AKs, and let's go get some more."

In five minutes, they had already invaded another hut and killed two more, and then they killed three. The men dressed in the black clothes of the Viet Cong and tied the straw coolie hats on their heads.

"The rest of these dinks are gonna know we're Americans," the lance corporal said, taking a look at how the pants on all the men struck them at nearly mid-shin.

"We'll kill 'em if they do," B.C. said. "It beats not doing anything. Let's go!" And he ran out of the hut and charged across the village to the other side, the M-14 on his back and an AK-47 in his hands.

The five other Marines, each carrying an AK-47 or Chinese SKS rifle, followed the corporal and ducked into another hut, killing two NVA soldiers who had gone ahead of the Viet Cong and possibly had been advisers to this particular unit flushed by the 2nd Battalion, 9th Marines, sweep.

The Marines stood in the doorways of the two hootches and waved to each other.

"Good," B.C. said to his assistant, "our team is still intact and nobody's dead or wounded. Now we just wait."

He had little more than said that when he saw the Huey gunship turning on its side and coming down fast in a strafing run through the village. The Marines hugged the ground as the machine guns chopped through the village, blowing dirt and straw through the air as it passed.

"I've got a group of six or eight VC spotted on the far side of the village," the helicopter pilot said over the radio.

"Give me that radio," Pat Collins said to his operator, and he keyed the microphone and talked to the helicopter pilot. "Those are my men!"

"Whose men?" the pilot responded.

"They're recon. My men," Pat Collins said.

"Negative," the pilot said. "These are six to eight VC, dressed in local garb. Black pajamas, not Marines."

"Like I said," Collins said. "Six recon Marines dressed like VC. They're my men."

The helicopter turned back when the pilot then saw B. C. Collins running through the village toward the advancing Marines, his shirt and hat off now, waving his arms above his head.

In ten minutes a helicopter pulled the six reconnaissance Marines from the village and flew them to Hill 327 for a thorough debrief. That evening, Pat Collins strolled past B. C. Collins's hootch. He kicked open the door and tossed in two six-packs of beer for the corporal and his team.

"Jesus Christ, Smedley," Pat Collins grumbled and stepped away from the door, letting it slam. He took a few steps and looked back at his Marines, already popping open the cans. "You and this gang of maniacs are gonna drive me completely over the edge."

# BIRDWATCHER

•1•

A S DECEMBER CAME, MANY THINGS IN SOUTH VIETNAM CHANGED.
Among them, a number of Marines went home.

John DelGrosso packed his seabag and looked out at the rain that
fell. It was snowing in New York and he could almost smell the smoke
coming from the street vendors' carts, selling hot chestnuts and giant
pretzels near Rockefeller Center. He thought of Radio City Music Hall
and its annual Christmas spectacular, the skating rink in front of the RCA
Building where Johnny Carson hosted *The Tonight Show*. Maybe he
could get tickets. Then there was the giant Christmas tree right there; it
would be lit by now, he thought. And the giant snowflake hung in the
center of the intersection of Fifty-seventh Street and Fifth Avenue. New
York at Christmas. But more than that, there were his friends and family.

"Say, Ed," John DelGrosso said as he looked out at a figure standing
in the doorway of the sea hut. "You get to New York, give me a yank."

"I'm right behind you," Eddie Adams said, and he waved an airline
ticket. "I just came to tell you good-bye."

"We're all getting out of here," DelGrosso said. "Captain Collins has
orders home too. He'll leave in a few days. Right after I do. He's busy

getting those guys from 1st Force Recon launched. General Walt's letting them take another stab at independent operations. But so far it hasn't gone too well."

Eddie sat on a box and watched as the lieutenant stuffed clothes down in his seabag. "What's their problem?"

"Nothing that everybody else isn't suffering from," John DelGrosso said. "They get guys trained and competent, and with this Christmas rush, getting everybody home, they got left a little short. They've got a tough mission too. Lots of SOG operations and weird shit. Takes a lot of training for that."

"What's Pat doing?" Eddie asked.

"He's helping them get organized on a mission with some Greeny Beanies out to the Laotian border. Some kind of cloak-and-dagger stuff," John DelGrosso said.

"Can we find him before I go?" Eddie said.

"Sure," John DelGrosso said. "Let me put a lid on this and we'll go."

· 2 ·

WITH MUCH RETRAINING UNDER THEIR BELTS, 1ST FORCE RECON-naissance Company had again gotten approval from General Walt to send out patrols. However, this had been only a marginal approval, and their future independence as a unit depended heavily on the quality of their tactics and successes.

They joined Australian and U.S. Army Special Forces, who served as patrol leaders for Vietnamese Civilian Irregular Defense Group (CIDG) soldiers, on deep operations. Special Operations Groups missions went deep into the far reaches of South Vietnam.

Also accompanying them were Nungs—Chinese-descended people originally from northern Vietnam. Nungs had gained a frightening repu-tation for their martial skills.[1] Marines who had gone on missions with

---

[1] The Nungs had allied with the French in the 1940s and '50s, and when the French fell in 1954, the Nungs moved south. At one point the South Vietnamese had established a Nung regiment, but as the regiment grew stronger, the government feared that it might become too great a threat and had it disbanded. After that, the Nungs hired on as mer-cenaries, coming under the various controls of organizations involved in unconven-tional warfare. They were especially effective on clandestine and special operations missions with specially trained U.S. military units.

Nungs always returned telling amazing stories about these soldiers' hardness and absolute fanatical bend on their work. Nungs had an ability of frightening even the toughest men.

On November 27, second platoon left 3rd Reconnaissance Battalion control and went to Special Forces Camp A-106 at Ba To, forty-two kilometers southwest of Quang Ngai. A week later, third platoon departed for Special Forces Camp A-107 at Tra Bong, twenty-seven kilometers southwest of Chu Lai, on the upper reaches of the Tra Bong River. Their mission—code-named "Birdwatcher"—was to test the feasibility of truly deep patrols.

In another week, December 15, three reconnaissance teams moved out to find VC units. Their force consisted of thirteen Marines and seven CIDG troops, and a sixty-one-man base defense reaction force made up of U.S. Special Forces soldiers, Nungs, and CIDG troops, and was led by a Vietnamese lieutenant. During the next two days they spotted seventy Viet Cong.

Although their reconnaissance seemed to go well, their tactical decisions and thinking lacked and cost them the ultimate price.

For the two days and nights that they patrolled, the lieutenant had not thought to move the base, and on the third day, a heavy fog shrouded the area. They had to scrub plans of moving back to Ba To and the eighty-one-man force was stuck at the same spot for another night. The only saving grace in this whole picture was that they had established the encampment on a hill, the best defensive terrain in the area.

At dusk that day, Gunnery Sergeant Maurice J. Jacques, a Marine who had taken the last three months of retraining under 3rd Recon as a serious insult to his unit, watched nervously as the rain continued to fall. He knew that the Vietnamese lieutenant had made a grave error.

When the first Viet Cong mortar struck below him, and then began to walk mortars across the patrol base, he saw that the problem had now become greater than just winning a battle. It meant survival.

The Vietnamese lieutenant in charge of the patrol died when one of the mortar rounds struck by him. Also, one of the Green Beret sergeants lay wounded. As the mortar shells continued to hit their camp, enemy machine-gun fire swept in.

Maurice Jacques could not believe what he saw next. It seemed as though the gates of hell had opened and had released its wrath on the camp. As the machine-gun fire found its mark, nearly 200 Viet Cong attacked.

For Jacques, tactical choices suddenly became very limited. In seconds, as the Viet Cong charged their position, the South Vietnamese troops fled, leaving the few Marines and Green Berets and Nungs to stand alone.

All the gunny could think to do was find every Marine that he could and organize them into a small unit. He knew that if he could get them together, they could withdraw into a tight perimeter.

He counted all but five of his thirteen Marines, but while trying to get organized, one of his Marines was killed and his corpsman and another Marine were hit, so he again moved the men, this time to a clump of banana trees where they hid until morning.

During the night, the men lay awake, facing out from their little circle. The men could hear the brush rustling near the banana trees, but in the darkness they could see nothing. The small band of Marines held their fire, for fear that they would attract the Viet Cong. They prayed as the steps came closer. Then Jacques lunged from the trees and grabbed the man from behind. To his relief, the intruder was one of the five lost Marines, however that still left four others still lost and one man known dead.

When dawn came, the fog remained. Gunny Jacques realized there would be no chance of any aircraft seeing his small band, thus Jacques began leading his Marines through the bush in search of the trail back to Ba To.

The men literally crawled through the foliage as they climbed toward the trail. Then from its vantage they could see dozens of Viet Cong sweeping through the area where they had just departed, looking for stragglers.

Seeing the Viet Cong in such great numbers, the gunny knew that he could not follow the trail, that the men had to move through the cover of the bush. The men crawled slowly and silently for more than four kilometers before they found thicker cover that would enable them to walk to the top of a ridge line that they knew would take them back to Ba To.

During the night, a Vietnamese CIDG had also joined them and accompanied the men on their trek home. While stealing their way along the ridge line, they heard someone coming through the brush and were ready to fire, but the Vietnamese told the men to hold their fire.

The growing band of survivors lay ready to fight, if necessary, but hoping that if these were enemy soldiers that they would walk past them. The sound came closer. Then two men stepped out of the bush—both were CIDG troops. They also joined Jacques's group of stragglers and headed for home.

The men again found the trail, but considering the night they had experienced, they chose to stay in the cover of the bush. The wind picked up the next day and covered the sound of their steps, allowing them to move more quickly through the bush until they reached Ba To.

Hardly an hour had passed since Gunny Jacques had made it back to Ba To when the last Marine survivor entered the camp.

Not a man in the camp at Ba To had ever seen such a sight. It would have been comedic had Lance Corporal Donald M. Woo, one of the four missing Marines, not suffered so greatly from his crippling wounds.

All through the night, he fought to survive. He had hidden in bushes, but the Viet Cong had found him when they made their sweep looking for stragglers. The men who took him prisoner had discounted his ability to fight, and he pulled his knife, hacking the men and escaping. The lance corporal had seen the trail left by his comrades and tried to follow. But again that night, he fell captive when an NVA patrol found him. Again he hid his knife and let them underestimate his ability to fight, even though he suffered severe wounds.

He knew that he could not make it on his own, in his condition, so he set out to remedy that. This time, when he made his escape, he lay in ambush with his knife ready. Then when two NVA soldiers crept past where he hid, he lunged out and captured them. Threatening them at knife point, the Marine lance corporal forced the two men to carry him back to Ba To.

Four days later, a patrol found fourteen bodies of the missing members of the ill-fated reconnaissance force. They included the three missing Marines, the Special Forces sergeant, the Vietnamese lieutenant, and nine CIDG troops.

Previous to the Ba To incident, force reconnaissance patrols were instructed to split up if they were discovered and each man to evade capture on his own. However, after Ba To, the policy changed. Reconnaissance patrols from here on would go in together, stay together, and come out together.

A week after Ba To, the 2nd and 3rd Force Reconnaissance platoons returned to 3rd Reconnaissance Battalion. The force recon Marines continued their deep work, but, to their continued frustration, as part of 3rd Recon Battalion.

## • 3 •

JESUS CHRIST WE'VE GOT A CRISIS!" PAT COLLINS SAID, SLOSHING through the mud in front of the hut where John DelGrosso and Eddie Adams sat.

"We were just looking for you," Eddie said.

"I've been over at the head shed," Pat Collins said. "Reasoner's getting the Medal of Honor. They're naming 3rd Recon's compound Camp Reasoner. If they're givin' Reasoner the Medal of Honor, they sure as hell ought to give that outlaw Smedley one too."

"Why wouldn't they?" DelGrosso asked.

"You damned sure ought to know why," Collins said. "That incident where he poked that corporal and broke his jaw. I think that pissed off enough people that they didn't want an outlaw getting the spotlight. Hell, they put him in for a goddamned Bronze Star, for Christ sake."

"Bill Henderson won't let that fly," DelGrosso said. "He's Krulak's godson. Hell, his dad's the general they named Henderson Field on Guadalcanal after. They won't push him around. Smedley will get better than a Bronze."

"If Henderson's summary of action flies, he will," Collins said. "But for Christ sake, it won't be a Medal of Honor. Nobody deserves it more."

Eddie looked at Pat Collins and said, "That the crisis?"

"Oh, shit, no, it's that hard case Harry Rogers," Pat Collins said. "Our patrol last night, when that water buffalo charged Harry?"

"And he blew the shit out of it with his M-14?" John DelGrosso finished.

"There's a whole goddamned South Vietnamese delegation over at General Walt's office right now demanding Harry's head. They branded him Water Buffalo Killer."

"We can talk while we walk over to the club for a farewell beer," John DelGrosso said. "All of us going home, we need a little farewell party."

The men slogged down the hill to a jeep and rode to the White Elephant together for one last good-bye. The same fat-faced man sat inside the doorway as the three men entered together for the last time.

Inside, Pat Collins began to talk with his Irish brogue. He swore about how the war was getting out of hand, and nobody knew what the hell they were doing. Eddie and John gave him their A-men.

He complained that the reconnaissance patrols were turning into a joke. "Hell, they're looking like Foreign Legion patrols with all the gear they're lugging around."

"I hear that 1st Marine Division is coming in country down at Chu Lai in a couple or three months," John DelGrosso said.

"Shhh," Pat Collins said as he sipped his beer, "no one's supposed to know that. Like everything else. It's a damned secret. Except everybody knows about it."

## • 4 •

THE RAIN HAD CLEARED AND EDDIE ADAMS AND JOHN DELGROSSO had been gone from South Vietnam for more than a week. Pat Collins found himself wandering around the compounds, as though he were a stranger. He was ready to go home.

He walked to the NCO hut where Corporal Posey lay on a cot near the front. Inside, Corporal B. C. Collins sat rubbing oil into his boots, trying to waterproof them.

"Smedley," Pat Collins called as he stepped inside.

"Sir," B. C. Collins said.

"I'm gonna do you boys a favor."

"What's that, sir?"

The other Marines in B. C. Collins's team turned to listen too. He had said you boys, and they knew that it meant them all.

"I'm leaving for the States, and I don't want a lot of these gas bags dumping on you lads, so I'm sending you up to Phu Bai," Collins said and chuckled.

"Shit, sir," B. C. Collins said. "Don't you remember back when General

Walt held that Marine Corps birthday ceremony? It was just before we went up in those hills on the actual Marine Corps birthday."

Pat Collins nodded. "Sure. That's when General Walt threw the Ka-Bar[2] into the cake."

"He walked outside and looked up at Hai Van Pass and those mountains way up there," B. C. Collins said. "Remember? And he said, 'I wonder what's up there?'"

"Right," the captain said.

"Me and old Ratliff," B. C. Collins said, "Van Cleve sends us up there. We climb for what, a week? We froze our asses off and the only thing we found were three chicom grenades. We buried 'em too, because we knew if we told about them, Walt would have us up there patrolling every day."

"Believe me," Pat Collins said, "I'm doing you boys a favor."

The next day B. C. Collins and several others who felt blood close to Captain Pat Collins walked with him to the airplane and shook his hand good-bye.

In a week B. C. Collins and his team transferred up to the high country of Phu Bai. But a week after that, they went to Hawaii for two months of submarine training.

Pat Collins knew all along.

---

[2] Marine utility knife made with a single steel shank and blade about ten inches long and features a stacked leather handle. Highly regarded as a field tool as well as a weapon.

# B.C.'S BEER BUST

•1•

CHRISTMAS HAD NOT GONE THAT WELL FOR EDDIE ADAMS. HE FELT guilty. He told himself that coming home is never like a man imagines it. The hugs and kisses and bliss. Then the world comes back and crams it in the old back door.

Every day that Eddie toasted the holidays with friends, every time people sat and talked about things in general, nobody mentioned the quarter of a million American boys who Eddie knew were hanging their lives on the line in South Vietnam.

A cold wind blew up Sixth Avenue in Manhattan as Eddie Adams turned the corner, eastward, and walked along Fifty-second Street to the corner where the Associated Press Building overlooked Rockefeller Center, a block south. Typical of any New York day, hot or cold, the yellow taxicabs skidded around the corners and roared past as fast as they could travel between blocks.

When he turned the corner and walked to the front of the AP Building, he could see a familiar green uniform on a young man, standing across the street, who also looked very familiar.

The boy had two stripes on his green serge uniform, green stripes on a red felt background. Three rows of ribbons graced his left breast, below which hung a silver Marine Corps Expert shooting badge. From the decorations, especially the purple ribbon on the top row, Eddie knew that this Marine corporal had seen combat. As many Marines knew, Eddie realized that a Purple Heart let a person know that this man had at least been close enough to the enemy to feel his wrath.

Eddie waved at the corporal and the Marine smiled. He stepped into the street, leaning on his crutches, and then a yellow-colored taxicab screamed around the corner. The driver made no attempt to serve to miss the disabled veteran. He drove straight at the kid. Eddie saw the Marine fall backward, and he prayed that the taxi had only come uncomfortably close.

When he rushed to the Marine's aid, and not one other person seemed to even notice the man, even though there had been a hundred other people just as close, looking at the Christmas decorations around Rockefeller Center, Eddie felt something inside his heart give way.

He helped the Marine to his feet, and watched him hobble away on the crutches. He watched as people rushed by the Marine and hardly gave him notice. Eddie knew then that the price paid by Vietnam veterans would never count for much in the minds of most Americans.

When Eddie walked through the busy Associated Press offices and saw that the people had many other, more important things going on in the world of public priorities and news, he became angry. These people did not care. The war meant nothing to them.

Eddie Adams became so angry and so hurt that even though he had been away from his wife and children for a year, and he had only been home a month, he knew he had to go back to South Vietnam. He had to go back because no one here cared about the soldiers and Marines and airmen and sailors over there.

That pissed him off. Because Eddie cared.

· 2 ·

H OW MUCH FOR THE CASE OF BEER?" THE SERGEANT ASKED B. C. Collins, who sat at a table under a canvas tent fly at Camp Reasoner. Behind him he had charge of a container box filled with beer.

It was midsummer 1966, a week away from his flight home from

South Vietnam, and with his year-long tour about finished he had the dubious duty of selling the special services beer supply to the Marines of 3rd Reconnaissance Battalion.

He had worked in the rear area, first doing supply and then operations assistance, and now special service since Memorial Day. That was when General Walt pinned the Navy Cross to his pocket and shook his hand.

The Bronze Star recommendation that the battalion had originally submitted for his heroism in the battle in which Frank Reasoner had lost his life and had won the Medal of Honor was upgraded to the Navy Cross.

Some thought that was too good for such a salty Marine corporal who had such a reputation and propensity to brawling and other disreputable incidents that would give any commanding officer nightmares. Although everyone agreed, including B. C. Collins, that he had a great way to go before anyone could declare him housebroken, many disagreed that his surly nature should discount any act of heroism that he might perform. Pat Collins would always feel that way about this Marine he nicknamed Smedley.

Thus, for the last days of his tour in South Vietnam, B. C. Collins sat out of the way, and out of trouble, doling out the beer supply, which as a matter by itself he did not find all that distasteful. He was a Marine who did enjoy his ration of brew.

"Okay, lad, what'll it be?" B.C. growled in his naturally gravel-coarse voice to the sergeant who stood in front of him.

"I need a case for my squad," the sergeant said. "Can I get as much as a case?"

"Sure, Sarge," B.C. said. "You want ten cases, I'll sell you ten."

The sergeant smiled.

"How about three cases?" he asked.

"You got it, pal," B.C. said.

"How much?" the sergeant asked, pulling his wallet from his hip pocket.

"How's a buck a case sound?" B.C. said.

"Something wrong with it?" the sergeant asked.

"Hell no, this is good beer. Budweiser. Pabst. Even got old Oly. It's all good beer," B.C. said.

"At that price give me six cases," the sergeant said.

"You got it, lad," B.C. said, and pulled six cases of Budweiser from the container.

In a matter of a few hours, a line had formed in front of B. C. Collins's table and Marines walked away with cases of beer at a time.

"They'll court-martial you, B.C.," Posey said when he went to lend his buddy a hand in manning the beer supply. "You can't just pick a price out of the blue and sell beer for it! What in hell are you going to do when you run out and Colonel Van Cleve comes asking what happened."

"Well, lad," B.C. said, "I got a plan. I've got my eye on a six-by truck. See it over there?"

Posey looked and saw the truck. "Yeah, and you'll go down to the Force Supply Group in Da Nang and just load up with a fresh supply. What the hell you gonna use for cash?"

"You're gonna let me in the armory, and I'm gonna get three of those AK rifles that we captured," B.C. said.

"You're crazy!" Posey said. "That's so dumb, I think you're just going on. I call ya. Go ahead. I want to see how far you'll go."

B. C. Collins looked at his buddy and then walked across the compound. He looked back and said, "You wait there and keep the beer moving. I'll be back with a fresh supply."

In five minutes he had the truck started, had gone inside the armory, and had taken three AK-47 rifles with three magazines full of ball ammunition.

He wheeled the truck down the hill and drove straight to Da Nang, where the supply warehouses stood in long rows. At the end, surrounded by concertina wire, he could see the special services supply. A large red and gold sign on the chain-link fence that surrounded it announced, DA NANG CONSOLIDATED CLUB SYSTEMS, SPECIAL SERVICES, III MARINE AMPHIBIOUS FORCE, REPUBLIC OF SOUTH VIETNAM.

A small Vietnamese worker pulled open the high gate when B. C. Collins honked the truck's horn and began backing the huge vehicle toward the warehouse. Once inside the fenced area, B. C. Collins climbed out of the truck and looked at the Vietnamese worker, a forklift operator. He then glanced over to the gate where a first sergeant stood, dusty and tired-looking.

He waved at the Marine, who waved back, and then the corporal walked over to where the Vietnamese man had already climbed back onto the seat of his forklift.

"Fill her up, pal," B.C. said, looking at the man.

"Need paper," the Vietnamese said.

"I got my paper. You just hold on and I'll show it to you," Collins said. He walked back to the front seat of the truck and pulled out one of the Communist-made rifles. The Vietnamese forklift operator watched the corporal walk back to him, shove the magazine into the rifle, and then jack a round into the chamber.

Pointing the muzzle of the rifle at the forklift operator's head he said, "Here's my authorization, pal. Fill her up."

The tires squealed as the Vietnamese man raced the forklift around the concrete floor of the supply warehouse, hooking up a pallet of Budweiser. Then one of Schlitz.. Then Olympia.

"Hell," B.C. said, "the guy thinks he's a civil service worker pushing for a pension. Look at him go."

The first sergeant watched and said, "I came to try and get them to sell me a case of soda for my grunts. They wouldn't do it. Some sort of quota. You think you could throw on some sodas?"

"You got it, First Sergeant," B.C. said. Then he called out to the driver. "Hey, little man!" The driver looked at him. "Throw on a pallet of soda for the first shirt over here."

The first sergeant helped B.C. pull the tarpaulin down over the load and tie up the back. He was about to climb in the truck when a master sergeant walked out the warehouse door.

"Where in God's green earth do you think you're going with that load of beer," the master sergeant shouted. "We've got quotas. Everything's got quotas. I didn't see any paperwork for all this beer."

"How about this," B. C. Collins said and tossed an AK-47 with a full magazine to the master sergeant. "That a fair trade?"

"Shit, fella," the master sergeant said. "But what am I gonna tell the officer in charge here. He's gonna have to come up with some sort of cover."

"Give him this," B.C. said and tossed another rifle and magazine to the Marine. "I'm sure he'll think of something."

In two hours exactly B. C. Collins had driven back past the first sergeant's compound, off-loaded the pallet of soda, and then drove back to Camp Reasoner where an enthusiastic crowd of Marines unloaded the truck, filling the container box plus a supply tent with all the beer.

•3•

"COME OVER HERE, COLLINS," LIEUTENANT COLONEL ROY R. VAN Cleve shouted to Corporal Bryant C. Collins.

"Yes, sir," the corporal said, snapping to attention in front of the colonel.

"I think you've just bumped the XO off his flight home tomorrow," Van Cleve said. "I got word of rumblings about that beer run yesterday. The XO is due out tomorrow, but I think you had better be on that plane."

•EPILOGUE•

BRYANT C. COLLINS GOT OUT OF THE MARINE CORPS AFTER FINISH-ing his first tour of active service. He went from Vietnam to Quantico, Virginia, where he worked as an enlisted instructor at The Basic School. He reenlisted in the Marine Corps a year later and went back to Vietnam in 1969. He retired from the Marine Corps in 1985 as a gunnery sergeant after completing a tour of duty in Beirut, Lebanon, in 1983 where he again crossed paths with Colonel Patrick G. Collins. He never attained the rank of master sergeant because he called his commanding general at 2nd Marine Division "a midget." In twenty years he hardly changed.

B. C. Collins always said of Pat Collins that he would follow him into hell. Pat Collins returns the regard to his friend by calling him one of the bravest Marines he has ever known.

Colonel Pat Collins retired from the Marine Corps in June of 1989, as did Colonel Carmine J. DelGrosso, who quit calling himself John after returning from Vietnam and readopted the name his Irish mother called him, Sean.

Sean DelGrosso finished his career at Quantico, Virginia, first as the commanding officer of the Marine Security Guard Battalion, the Marines who guard American embassies throughout the world.

When he finished that command, he joined Pat Collins at Quantico in the War Fighting Center. In the closing months of their careers, the two of them put on paper many of the lessons that they learned firsthand in combat.

This input helped to build the book that the Marine Corps uses today in training recruits and first-tour Marines to be warriors. Thus a bit of their experience will continue in the Marine Corps' legacy and traditions to come. Truly no greater honor could any Marine ever earn for himself.

Jim Shockley recovered from his wounds, although today his leg still remains painful and requires a special kind of courage from him.

He too had gone to Quantico, Virginia, to be an enlisted instructor after Vietnam and after his wounds had healed. Even though his wounds presented physical problems, he continued to keep in shape so that he could pass the Marine Corps' physical fitness requirements. He completed his tour of active duty and went to college.

He returned to active duty as an officer, thanks to the help of Sergeant Major John O. Henry and the secretary of the Navy. Jim Shockley served first as an infantry platoon commander, and then entered the Marine Corps' Staff Judge Advocate program and earned his Doctorate of Jurisprudence.

He retired as a major in 1988 and entered politics in his home state of Montana. He has always kept in touch with John Henry, even through all the years he served in his various capacities as a Marine officer.

Sergeant Major John O. Henry also retired from the Marine Corps and resides at Quantico, Virginia, where he is a respected businessman today.

# ACKNOWLEDGMENTS

My thanks to Mr. Eddie Adams, my friend who shared with me many of his private moments and helped to make this book possible.

I owe a special debt of thanks to Colonel Patrick G. Collins, USMC (Ret.), and to Colonel Carmine J. DelGrosso, USMC (Ret.). The hours that I spent talking to them and the insights I gained from them regarding not just their experiences in Vietnam but their overall view of the war's history have added a great deal to my perspective, and have contributed immeasurably to this book. I also want to thank both gentlemen, and especially Colonel Collins, for their enthusiastic and faithful efforts on my behalf.

I thank Major James Shockley, USMC (Ret.), for his patience and time, recalling some painful memories and sharing them with me. Also I thank him for his continual support and persistence with the facts.

Thanks also to Gunnery Sergeant Bryant C. Collins for his support and time, and to Sergeant Major John O. Henry, USMC (Ret.), who shared with me some of his most sensitive recollections but still remained enthusiastic toward my efforts. I also thank the many other Marines of the 3rd Recon Association who served with these gentlemen, such as Sergeant Major Freddy Murray, USMC (Ret.), who took the time to share their memories with me and review my work.

I thank my wife, Lillian, who has endured these many years as this Marine's best friend and partner, and remains the greatest fan of my writing, as well as my toughest critic.

# BIBLIOGRAPHY

## • BOOKS •

Hammond, William M. *Public Affairs: The Military and the Media, 1962–1968*. Washington, D.C.: Center of Military History, United States Army, 1988.

Johnson, Charles M. Major, USMC, and Jack Shulimson. *U.S. Marines in Vietnam: The Landing and The Buildup, 1965*. Washington, D.C.: History and Museums Division, Headquarters, U.S. Marine Corps, U.S. Government Printing Office, 1978.

Simmons, Edwin H., Brigadier General, USMC (Ret.), (Editor-in-Chief). *The Marines in Vietnam, 1954–1973: An Anthology and Annotated Bibliography*. Washington, D.C.: History and Museums Division, Headquarters, U.S. Marine Corps, U.S. Government Printing Office, 1974.

Stolfi, Russell H., Captain, USMCR. *U.S. Marine Corps Civic Action Efforts in Vietnam March 1965–March 1966*. Washington, D.C.: Historical Branch, G-3 Division, Headquarters, U.S. Marine Corps, 1968.

U.S. Marine Corps. *Amphibious Reconnaissance [FMFM 2-2]* (PCN 139 000125 00). Washington, D.C.: U.S. Government Printing Office, 1976, 1979.

U.S. Marine Corps. *Counterinsurgency Operations [FMFM 8-2]* (PCN 139 000700 00). Washington, D.C.: U.S. Government Printing Office, 1973 (with change incorporated 1975), 1976.

Whitlow, Robert H., Captain, USMCR. *U.S. Marines in Vietnam: The Advisory and Combat Assistance Era, 1954–1964*. Washington, D.C.: History and Museums Division, Headquarters, U.S. Marine Corps, U.S. Government Printing Office, 1977.

## •INTERVIEWS•

(Totaling more than 20.5 hours recorded on audio cassettes)

Adams, Eddie. Personal interview, March 1988, New York, NY

Adams, Eddie. Personal interview, May 1988, New York, NY

Adams, Eddie. Personal interview, July 1988, New York, NY

Adams, Eddie. Personal interview, October 1988, New York, NY

Collins, Bryant C. Telephone interview, July 1988, Jacksonville, NC

Collins, Bryant C. Telephone interview, September 1988, Jacksonville, NC

Collins, Bryant C. Telephone interview, November 1988, Jacksonville, NC

Collins, Patrick G. Telephone interview, March 1988, Fairfax, VA

Collins, Patrick G. Telephone interview, May 1988, Fairfax, VA

Collins, Patrick G. Telephone interview, July 1988, Fairfax, VA

Collins, Patrick G. Telephone interview, November 1988, Fairfax, VA

Collins, Patrick G. Personal interview, December 1988, Fairfax, VA

Collins, Patrick G. Telephone interview, September 1989, Fairfax, VA

DelGrosso, Carmine J. Telephone interview, March 1988, Quantico, VA

DelGrosso, Carmine J. Telephone interview, July 1988, Quantico, VA

DelGrosso, Carmine J. Telephone interview, November 1988, Quantico, VA

DelGrosso, Carmine J. Telephone interview, July 1989, Fairfax, VA

Henry, John O., Jr. Telephone interview, September 1988, Triangle, VA

Henry, John O., Jr. Telephone interview, April 1989, Triangle, VA

Murray, Freddie L. Telephone interview, March 1990, Havelock, NC

O'Malley, Robert E. Various personal conversations, October 1988 and
    November 1989, Camp Smith, Peekskill, NY
Safer, Morley. Telephone interview, July 1989, New York, NY
Shockley, James G. Telephone interview, November 1988, Jacksonville,
    NC
Shockley, James G. Telephone interview, April 1989, Victor, MT
Westmoreland, William C. Telephone interview, February 1989,
    Charleston, SC
Zorthian, Barry. Personal conversation, October 1987, New York, NY


                    •RECORDS AND DOCUMENTS•

Collins, Bryant C., Corporal USMC—Navy Cross Citation and Sum-
    mary of Action, for Extraordinary Heroism as a Scout Team Leader
    in Company A, 3rd Reconnaissance Battalion, 3rd Marine Division
    (Forward), Fleet Marine Force, on July 12, 1965.
O'Malley, Robert E. Corporal USMC—Medal of Honor Citation and
    Summary of Action, for Conspicuous Gallantry and Intrepidity in
    Action Against the Communist (Viet Cong) Forces at the Risk of
    His Own Life Above and Beyond the Call of Duty while serving as
    Squad Leader in Company I, 3rd Battalion, 3rd Marine Regiment,
    3rd Marine Division (Reinforced), Fleet Marine Force, on August
    18, 1965.
Reasoner, Frank S., First Lieutenant, USMC—Medal of Honor (Posthu-
    mous) Citation and Summary of Action, for Conspicuous Gallantry
    and Intrepidity at the Risk of His Life Above and Beyond the Call
    of Duty while serving as Commanding Officer of Company A, 3rd
    Reconnaissance Battalion, 3rd Marine Division (Forward), Fleet
    Marine Force, on July 12, 1965.
April 16, 1965—*Report of Patrol Incident of 162100H April*. The re-
    port of first action in which U.S. Marines are wounded in action
    against the enemy after the landing of the U.S. Forces in South Viet-
    nam. Attached to the report are Situation Reports 24, 25, and 26
    that detail the action in which the Marines were wounded.
April 17, 1965—*Operations Summary No. 1*. Message detailing opera-
    tions by the 3rd Marine Regiment with detachments, such as

elements from 3rd Reconnaissance Battalion, led by Captain Patrick G. Collins, during the period from April 11 through April 17, 1965.

April 22, 1965—*Debriefing Statement for Flaming Dart Mission, and Daily Summary for Marine Fighter/Attack Squadron-531*. Highlights first offensive ground action against the enemy in Vietnam, encountered by company-size reconnaissance patrol led by Captain Patrick G. Collins.

April 23, 1965—*Patrol Report, Intelligence Observations and Comments*. Report documents first offensive ground action against the enemy in Vietnam, encountered by company-size reconnaissance patrol led by Captain Patrick G. Collins.

April 24, 1965—*Operations Summary No. 2*. Message detailing operations by 3rd Marine Regiment with detachments, such as elements from 3rd Reconnaissance Battalion, led by Captain Patrick G. Collins, during the period from April 18 through April 24, 1965.

May 3, 1965—*Command Diary: 3rd Marine Regiment for 1–30 April 1965*. Submitted to the Commanding General, 9th Marine Expeditionary Brigade, Da Nang, South Vietnam.

May 9, 1965—*Command Diary: 9th Marine Expeditionary Brigade*. Submitted by the Commanding General, Brigadier General Frederick Joseph Karch, to Commandant of the Marine Corps (Code A03E).

July 10, 1965—*Operation Order 124-65* (Ref: (a) Map: Trung Phun, 1:50000, Sheets 6658 IV). Operation order for Company A, 3rd Reconnaissance Battalion, prepared by First Lieutenant Frank S. Reasoner, USMC, setting out patrols into area south of Dai Loc, in which Reasoner is killed in action.

July 12, 1965—*After Action Report of Patrol "SCAT A," Company A, 3rd Reconnaissance Battalion, Da Nang, VN* (121530 H July 1965). Report submitted by Second Lieutenant W. T. Henderson, USMC.

July 12, 1965—*Sketch of Zone of Action*. Enclosed with After Action Report (121530 H July 1965) submitted by Second Lieutenant W. T. Henderson, USMC.

July 12, 1965—*Chronological Summary of All Radio Messages from Company A, 3rd Reconnaissance Battalion, Da Nang, VN*. Enclosed with After Action Report (121530 H July 1965) submitted by Second Lieutenant W. T. Henderson, USMC.

July 13, 1965—*Statement of Action.* Personal account of action with the enemy in An My Hamlet on July 12, 1965, encountered by SCAT A Patrol, Company A, 3rd Reconnaissance Battalion. Statement composed from personal account of Lance Corporal Freddie L. Murray, Private First Class Thorace L. Panwell, Private First Class Kenneth R. Hahn, Corporal Bryant C. Collins, and Private First Class Thomas Gatlin. Enclosed with After Action Report (121530 H July 1965) submitted by Second Lieutenant W. T. Henderson, USMC.

July 13, 1965—*Signed Statement from Corporal Bryant C. Collins, USMC.* Personal statement of action with the enemy in An My Hamlet on July 12, 1965, encountered by SCAT A Patrol, Company A, 3rd Reconnaissance Battalion.

July 13, 1965—*Signed Statement from Private First Class Kenneth R. Hahn, USMC.* Personal statement of action with the enemy in An My Hamlet on July 12, 1965, encountered by SCAT A Patrol, Company A, 3rd Reconnaissance Battalion.

July 17, 1965—*Silver Star Medal, recommendation for.* A letter (1:WAF:hhl over 1650 dated 17 Jul 1965) from Lieutenant Colonel D. H. Blanchard, Commanding Officer, 3rd Reconnaissance Battalion, to Commanding General, Fleet Marine Force, Pacific, recommending Lance Corporal Freddie L. Murray for the Silver Star Medal for his action on July 12, 1965, in An My Hamlet.

# WOMEN

## AND

# PAIN

# WOMEN
## AND
## PAIN

## Why It Hurts and What You Can Do

*Including Complementary and Holistic Remedies,*

*as Well as Traditional Medicine*

MARK ALLEN YOUNG, M.D., F.A.C.P.

with KAREN BAAR, M.P.H.

HYPERION

New York

Library of Congress Cataloging-in-Publication Data

Young, Mark A.
women and pain : why it hurts and what you can do including
complementary and holistic remedies, as well as traditional
medicine / Mark Young with Karen Baar.
p.  cm.
Includes bibliographical references and index.
ISBN 0-7868-6794-9
1. Pain—Popular works.   2. Women—Diseases—Popular works.
I. Baar, Karen.   II. Title.

RB127.Y68  2002
616'.0472'082—dc21
2001039248

FIRST EDITION

10  9  8  7  6  5  4  3  2  1

Book design by JoAnne Metsch

## ACKNOWLEDGMENTS

I wish to lovingly acknowledge the help and ever-present support of my wife, Marlene Malka Young, whose supreme culinary skills contributed greatly to this work. Her devotion and stalwart dedication to her physician-author husband and to our children, Michelle, Michael, and Jennifer, have helped to make this book a success.

Kindest gratitude is due my agent, Janis Vallely, who brought the idea for this book to life and helped me navigate the uncharted waters of book publishing; to Karen Baar whose literary skill and editorial expertise were invaluable to the process; and to my editor, Leslie Wells, who truly helped to make this book a reality.

Acknowledgments also are due to my many colleagues in academic medicine and to the many scientists and researchers around the world who have helped us fathom the mystery of pain, its effects on women, and its treatment using the best of traditional and complementary medicine.

Special thanks to Debra Walters, Nicole Royer, Jennifer Ryan, Stanley Kornhauser, Joseph Powers, Howard Hoffberg, Michael Lesser, and Evan Young for technical assistance.

—*Mark Young, M.D.*

Thanks to Mark Young, for his innovative approach to pain, to our editor, Leslie Wells, whose enthusiasm for this project was so exciting, and to Janis Vallely, who got this book off the ground and helped keep it afloat. I also appreciate Carrie Covert's flexibility in the face of an impossibly tight schedule.

Love and gratitude to the people who have sustained me during a very difficult time—Sally Connolly, Katherine Grady, Pamela Hort, Jean Larson,

David Paskin, Semeon Tsalbins, and Carol Ripple—I couldn't have done this without your love, encouragement, and support. And to my agent, Angela Miller, who is always a staunch ally and trusted friend and adviser.

Finally, to my treasures, Kate and Emma: I cherish you more each day.

*—Karen Baar*

# CONTENTS

# Tell Me Where It Hurts

Do you suffer from constant, agonizing pain? Have you been to doctor after doctor, only to receive nothing that helps or be told "it's all in your head," "it's stress," or "you're just getting old"? If so, you're not alone.

Women have said it—and men have denied it—for years. Now we know that it's true: Women feel more pain, seek help more aggressively, and make more active attempts to cope with pain than men.

Unfortunately, we also know that too frequently women aren't taken seriously. Although we think of medicine as a professional discipline, rooted in science and free of bias, this isn't always the case. Frankly, our health care system often disregards women in pain. At best, it's ignorance of gender differences. But some physicians stereotype women as complainers who are less self-controlled and more likely to overreport symptoms than men. They dismiss female patients with antidepressants, antianxiety drugs, and platitudes. This adds insult to injury. When you're in pain, it's the last thing you need.

Given how much we know about pain, it's scandalous that women suffer needlessly. As a physiatrist, a physician board certified in physical medicine and rehabilitation, I specialize in treating disabling painful conditions with gentle, simple conservative modalities. Using my skills in acupuncture and complementary medicine, I have helped thousands of people find relief from pain. My background as a member of the teaching faculty of Johns Hopkins University has instilled in me a strong commitment to patient education and empowerment. Since my specialty places so much emphasis on properly balancing the emotional and physical needs of patients, often people with painful chronic disabilities, I am keenly aware of the frustration, anger, and depression that many women patients face when they are in pain and don't know where to turn for help.

## IRENE'S STORY

Irene is a sixty-four-year-old woman who works as a stadium vendor, selling pretzels at the local ballpark. She spends most of her workday on her feet.

She came in to see me complaining of a dull ache in her right heel, along with pain, swelling, and decreased movement in her knee. She'd had discomfort for a while, but the pain was becoming considerably more disabling. Although she had developed a mild limp, that wasn't the worst of it: "Doc, at the end of the day, my foot feels like it's about to fall off and my knee hurts like the dickens."

Irene was feeling desperate. She had been to a couple of other doctors and had gotten little relief. But something else was also eating away at her: "They keep telling me that it's just because I'm getting old, and they say I have to quit my job. But I love my work; it's so much fun to be out there, especially when the Orioles win! Besides, I need the money," she confided.

When I examined Irene, I discovered that she had a large heel spur and an osteoarthritic knee. I knew right away that we could come up with a plan that would relieve her pain and let her keep working.

Irene usually wore the same shoes day in and day out, a pair of worn-out espadrilles she picked up at Payless. I told her she needed to invest in comfortable, cushioned sneakers to wear at work. I also recommended that she buy a viscoelastic horseshoe-shaped heel cushion (which allows the spur to "float" without direct contact) and to think about getting fitted for custom-made orthotics. It was essential that she provide some padding for that heel. Also, what goes on in your foot affects the rest of your leg, so good footwear would also have a positive impact on her arthritic knee.

In addition, I suggested that she soak her feet in an herbal bath after work each day. She laughed when I suggested that her husband learn the arts of foot massage and acupressure, but she took the handouts and put them in her purse.

For her knee, I suggested glucosamine and chondroitin supplements, two nutritional remedies that effectively relieve osteoarthritis. I also showed her how to do quadriceps strengthening exercises to bolster the stability of her knee joint, and urged her to add some light aerobic exercise to her daily routine.

I ran into Irene the next time I went to a game. She was in the next section of the stadium, but when she spotted me, she flashed a big smile and gave me a thumbs-up. After the game, she caught up with me. "The pain is so much better, Doc, and my limp is gone." Then, she winked and said: "And those foot massages are great!"

## GENDER MATTERS

Happily, times are changing. Gender has become a "hot button" issue on the national research agenda, so important that a conference on gender and pain was held at the National Institutes of Health (NIH) in 1998. Eye-opening biomedical research presented there concluded that:

- Women experience more pain than men.
- Women discuss pain more than men.
- Women cope better with pain than men.
- Society's attitudes toward men and women in pain may influence physicians' treatment.
- The open expression of pain sometimes helps people obtain better pain control, but being seen as "too emotional" may work against a woman and lead to inadequate care.
- Pain treatment that works for one sex may not work as well, or at all, for the other.

Some of the most galvanizing research concerns the medications we use to treat pain. This work calls into question the age-old pain management practice of "one size (or one drug) fits all." For example, a series of landmark studies has shown that morphine-like drugs, called kappa-opioids, produce significantly greater pain relief in women than in men. (These drugs work through receptors in the central nervous system. There are multiple types of opioid receptors—kappa, mu, delta, and sigma. The mu and kappa categories are the two major classes thought to be responsible for analgesia.) Kappa-opioids are not as commonly used as other narcotic pain medications. Drugs that work on the mu-receptors are the standard of care and are much more frequently prescribed. Yet they cause more nausea, itching, cardiac effects, constipation, and depression of the respiratory system. Treating women with kappa-opioids, then, may provide better pain relief with fewer side effects.

Other studies show that common pain relievers do less for women than for men. For example, in a recent study of experimentally induced pain, ibuprofen—the key ingredient in Advil, Motrin, and other over-the-counter

analgesics known as NSAIDS (for nonsteroidal anti-inflammatory drugs) —
was less effective at providing pain relief for women than men. Perhaps
dosages for NSAIDS need to take gender into account.

In addition, many painful diseases and injuries disproportionately affect
women. Even when men and women suffer from the same illness, the
symptoms may be different:

- Osteoarthritis (OA), or degenerative joint disease, is far more common
  among women over the age of fifty-five, and women may suffer from a
  more severe form of this disease. In one recent study, women experienced 40 percent more pain, as well as worse pain. In addition, women
  are more likely to develop inflammatory types of OA that lead to knobby
  deformities of the DIP and PIP joints (the two sets of joints below the
  knuckles).
- Rheumatoid arthritis (RA) occurs two and a half times more often
  among women, and it may also affect them more severely. Women
  have reported more painful joints, more swollen joints, and worse function. And the majority of studies show that RA is slightly more disabling
  for women than it is for men.
- Migraine headaches are more severe, longer lasting, and more frequent
  in women than in men. In addition, women have more nausea, vomiting, numbness, and tingling with their headaches, while men are more
  likely to have a visual aura.
- Tension headaches occur two to three times more frequently among
  women, who also experience much higher levels of tenderness in all
  the muscles surrounding the skull.
- Women athletes experience knee injuries two to eight times more frequently than their male counterparts. This is particularly true for tears
  of the anterior cruciate ligament (ACL).
- Osteoporosis affects both sexes, but women develop it at a much
  younger age and in far greater numbers because of hormonal differences.

Gender differences play out on the operating table, too. In a study recently published in the *British Medical Journal*, women emerged from general anesthesia faster than men. However, they returned to their presurgery
health status significantly more slowly and they experienced more postoperative complications.

## WOMEN AREN'T JUST SMALL MEN

We don't know why these differences exist, but a wide range of scientific studies shows that the sexes differ on nearly every level. From the molecular to the psychological, from the basic genetic codes to the hormones, biology, physiology, and the overall functioning of the immune response systems— men and women are different.

We aren't doing enough to understand and close this gender gap. The prestigious Institute of Medicine (IOM) of the National Academy of Sciences recently issued a call for biomedical researchers to "study sex differences from womb to tomb." The IOM's report recommended that researchers take sex differences into account in clinical trials, including studies of new drugs.

Even when women participate in clinical trials—and more women do now than five years ago—there is little gender-specific information coming out of the studies. Scientists at drug companies and research institutions have largely ignored sex-based differences in their data analysis.

We also know precious little about how drugs behave during pregnancy or breast-feeding. Most women who participate in research are postmenopausal. Admittedly, there are serious ethical concerns about allowing women of childbearing age to enter studies. But there may be other, less worthy issues at stake: Perhaps pharmaceutical companies are worried about the marketing consequences of defining a drug as more effective in one sex than another.

Sticking our heads in the sand is not the answer. We must develop guide lines that allow all women to fully participate in research. Failure to do this has serious ramifications; it could, in fact, be a matter of life and death. For example, of the ten prescription drugs withdrawn by the FDA from the market since 1997 because of adverse reactions, eight posed greater risks for women than for men. (In some cases, the drugs were more widely prescribed to women; however, even with medications prescribed equally to males and females, they were more dangerous for women.) And when you are pregnant, physiological changes may affect your response to a drug; you may be more vulnerable to its toxicity or its effectiveness. When you take a drug, you need to know that it is safe and effective for you.

## TAKE CHARGE OF YOUR PAIN NOW

It's going to take a while until these changes come about. Meanwhile, you're in pain, and pain can leave you feeling powerless. My message is that you can regain control of your life with gentle yet potent pain relief strategies geared to your needs as a woman.

## JENNY'S STORY

Jenny is a twenty-two-year-old college student. While driving on campus during a late-spring rainstorm, she had to stop short suddenly and was rear-ended by the car in back of her. "My neck snapped back and forth, but it didn't hurt," she said. "Later on, though, this dull, aching pain started up, and it just kept getting worse. I guess it's what you call whiplash."

By that evening, Jenny's pain was so terrible she couldn't sleep. She couldn't move her neck freely because every move provoked a new onslaught of excruciating spasms. The next day, a nurse-practitioner in the Department of Student Health referred her to me for an evaluation.

Jenny had a considerable amount of pain, spasm, and range of motion restriction in her neck. I ordered X rays, which were negative, although they did show a flattening in the cervical neck, a common finding in whiplash victims. Her neurological exam was normal and she had no motor deficits or weakness, no sensory loss, and no reflex changes.

Jenny is a rarity—one of the few patients I've had who refuses to take any conventional medications—so I had to be creative. For starters, I recommended white willow bark, an herb that has the same analgesic and anti-inflammatory effects as conventional painkillers. For her spasms, I suggested valerian root tea and long, relaxing aromatherapy baths with lavender. I also told her to take advantage of this opportunity and get her boyfriend to give her a gentle neck massage. In addition, I showed her how to apply a moist heat pack, and I referred her for a couple of sessions of physical therapy.

What really did the trick, though, were my acupuncture treatments. She looked more and more relaxed after every session. To prolong those effects, I sent her home with acupressure exercises to do on her own.

It took about two full weeks, but Jenny made a full recovery.

I have always been deeply motivated by modern medicine's quest to alleviate pain, especially for individuals suffering the indignities of disabling disease. During my early days as a medical student at the Finch University

Health Sciences/Chicago Medical School, I was inspired by the examples of my professors, who conducted research in the pharmacology and physiology of pain. As an intern at the University of Chicago/Louis A. Weiss Memorial Hospital, working at the bedsides of people in pain strengthened my commitment to the art and science of pain management and impelled me to pursue a physiatry residency training at the Albert Einstein College of Medicine/Montefiore Medical Center in New York. And because I enjoy research and teaching in addition to caring for patients, I joined the faculty of the Johns Hopkins University School of Medicine in 1991.

Throughout my career, I've observed the strengths that conventional pharmaceuticals and therapeutic procedures bring to the battle against pain. But I also know their limitations. I am a practitioner of integrative medicine, which combines the best of conventional and so-called alternative—I prefer the term *complementary*—care. Of course, I prescribe drugs and use other conventional pain relief techniques when necessary. But the emphasis in my practice, and what you'll find in this book, is a multifaceted program of complementary alternatives, including dietary, herbal and homeopathic remedies, exercise, recipes, and mind-body techniques.

The therapies in this book are all safe and supported by scientific research, as well as my own experience. They are the treatments most frequently chosen by, and most effective for, women. These remedies, easily incorporated into your lifestyle, will let you finally take charge of your pain and, in many instances, free yourself from it entirely.

At its most fundamental level, medicine is about the relief of pain and suffering. As a rehabilitation doctor, I pay special attention to pain, recognizing that not every patient reports pain or responds to it in the same way. I know how important it is to tailor treatments to each individual's need. Gender affects how we perceive, report, and cope with pain. As scientists continue to untangle the threads—hormonal cycles, genetics, brain structure, anatomical, physiological and biological differences—that weave the intricate web of gender-based pain perception, it's imperative that you receive selective, customized care. I hope *Women and Pain* enables you to take the first step forward into the pain-free future you deserve.

## NOTES ON DOSING

*Herbal remedies*: Doses have been standardized according to the German Commission E Monograph (CEM) and/or the *Physicians' Desk Reference for Herbals* (PDR-H). The German Commission E is the rough equivalent of our FDA. Their monographs about specific herbs, which document the herbs' health risks, benefits, and side effects, are based on decades of clinical trials. Dosages from the *PDR-H* and Commission E are confirmed by the American Botanical Council. Please consult your physician before taking any herbal medicines.

*Dietary supplements*: Quantities are in accordance with the U.S. Dietary Reference Intake (DRI). The DRI are quantitative estimates of nutrient intakes that are useful for assessing and planning diets in healthy people. The DRI standards were established by a consensus of the Food and Nutrition Board of the Institute of Medicine and the National Academy of Science. For vitamins, minerals, or supplements listed, a dose range composed of two values has been included: a lower limit and an upper limit. The lower limit is the recommended dietary allowance (RDA). The upper limit is the tolerable upper intake level (UL). Please note that the UL is not the recommended dose, but is the maximum amount that has been determined scientifically to be tolerated without adverse effects. Both the RDA and UL may vary according to age, pregnancy, nutrition, and lactation status. Please consult a physician.

# WOMEN

# AND

# PAIN

I

—

# The Gender Gap

## BETH'S STORY

Beth is a forty-one-year-old woman who works as an inventory clerk at a local bookstore. She'd been my patient for years, ever since her orthopedist referred her to me for "conservative management." I saw her periodically for mild scoliosis (a sidewise spine curvature), which causes fleeting aches and pains. Otherwise, she had been essentially healthy and strong.

Beth was usually pretty cheerful. But on this day, I knew something was wrong as soon as she walked in the door. She was worried because she had recently noticed the gradual onset of a dull, aching pain in her neck and upper shoulders, as well as increasing fatigue. "These days, it often hurts in the small of my back, too, and I tire easily," she told me. But it wasn't just her physical pain that had her keyed up; there was more going on. She'd been to an Urgent Care Center (she could not get in to see her primary care doctor, since he was too busy), where she was told that there was nothing wrong with her, that it was "just stress," and sent off with a prescription for Xanax, an antianxiety drug.

"I just don't believe it," Beth said. "There's nothing particularly worrisome going on in my life right now. They just didn't take me seriously; besides, they seemed awfully rushed."

Still, she was puzzled and disturbed; what was causing her pain? "It's too soon to be falling apart, isn't it?" she joked. "Seriously, though, I know I'm getting older, but I still feel like I'm in good shape. And I'm not doing anything different at work. So what's up?"

After a thorough review of her most recent spine films, laboratory workup, bone mineral density, and pulmonary function test results (breathing can go bad when the spine is deformed), which were all normal, I performed a thorough physical, including a spine examination. Although her posture appeared to be the same as in prior office visits, she did indeed have more tenderness and spasm in her neck and back. Fortunately, her scoliosis and degree of spine angle were unchanged. Her height, leg lengths, and angle of back inclination, reflecting the degree of spine rotation, had not worsened. Because she hadn't exercised in some time, she did exhibit some weakness in her back extensor and abdominal muscle strength, and her overall hip and back flexibility were not quite up to snuff.

As I explained to Beth, these changes had a major biomechanical impact on her spine, and were probably contributing to her neck, shoulder, and back pain. Making matters worse, Beth spends a lot of time at her job sitting at a desk, punching numbers into a computer to keep track of merchandise. And her neglect of exercise wasn't helping either. She used to work out regularly, but she'd grown increasingly sedentary, especially during the winter months.

Unfortunately, Beth has an ailment for which there is no "cure"; her condition is chronic. Based on her X rays, the degree of curvature in her spine was less than 20 degrees—too small to recommend any specific surgery or bracing measure. And there is no way to reverse or improve her long-standing scoliosis.

My job, then, was to help her cope with her current level of pain and make sure it didn't get worse. I was optimistic, since I knew there was a lot of room for improvement. Beth used to be an avid runner. I suggested that at this time she take up swimming instead, which exerts less wear and tear on the body. Not only would swimming help quell the pain, but it would improve her general level of flexibility, muscle strength, and conditioning. I explained, however, that it would not reverse the scoliosis.

To further increase her flexibility, I recommended that she take up yoga or tai chi. And if she had the time, I suggested she take a light aerobic exercise class to enhance her endurance and lessen her fatigue. High-quality, supportive shoes would provide more stability and dampen the impact of her spine pain. And warm herbal baths at the end of her workday would also give her significant relief.

Finally, I advised Beth to tackle some ergonomic improvements at work. She needed a better chair, and it was important that she not sit scrunched up at her desk for long periods of time. Frequent rest breaks were also critical. Whether she stretched—and I suggested a few simple exercises she could do—or just walked around, she absolutely had to get away from her desk for a few minutes every hour. "My boss is a young guy who's a fitness fanatic. I hope he'll understand," she said.

A couple of months later, Beth returned for a follow-up visit. She had started swimming again and had noticed improvements already. But she waited until the end of her visit to tell me the big news: "I finally got up the courage to ask my boss for a new chair. When he told me he wasn't sure it was necessary, I got nervous. But then he told me why—in my new job, I'd be up and around a lot more. No more crunching numbers. He promoted me to office manager!"

This is an exciting time in medical science. We're unlocking so many mysteries, and learning an enormous amount about what makes us all tick. As they unravel nature's code, the scientists working on the Human Genome Project may ultimately reveal that our individual susceptibilities to disease depend on microscopic genetic differences. Why, then, should it be surprising that gender, a major genetic variation, profoundly affects the way we experience pain?

Yet women's pain has been largely ignored by the medical and scientific community, and women have been systematically excluded from biomedical research. As recently as 1984, the National Institute on Aging published a report called "Normal Human Aging" using data only from men! Except for studies centered on breasts and reproductive organs (sometimes derided as "bikini medicine"), most research on medications, pain, and other disorders was for men only, the misguided rationale being that women's pesky hormonal cycles would just confuse the results. Besides, researchers mistakenly assumed that many conditions don't affect women as frequently, or that when they do, the symptoms are the same. Even when studies included women, the results were not separately analyzed by gender.

Change has come, although it's too little and too slow. In 1990 the National Institutes of Health established the Office of Research on Women's Health. And in 1993, Congress passed a law mandating that sufficient numbers of women and minorities be included in research to allow a valid analysis of any differences. Also that year, the Food and Drug Administration (FDA) rescinded its restriction on permitting women in their childbearing years to participate in medical research. In 1998, the agency began requiring manufacturers of pharmaceuticals and medical devices to report the age, race, and gender of individuals participating in their research trials. Today, some legislators are hoping to pass a law that would mandate an office of women's health in every agency in the Department of Health and Human Services.

Even so, some scientists *still* fail to take women into account. An April 2000 article, "Studies Find Research on Women Lacking," in the *New York Times* reported that three new studies, including an investigation by the Government Accounting Office, found that medical researchers who receive federal money often ignore the requirement to analyze their data to see if women and men respond differently to a given treatment. I think this kind of behavior is reprehensible; and it certainly doesn't serve your needs as a health care consumer (and a taxpayer).

Despite these obstacles, the field of gender-based biology is producing some astounding results, although they are not yet widely accepted or even generally known. Some of the most important research shows that women experience more severe, longer lasting, and more frequent pain.

## MEN AND WOMEN HAVE DIFFERENT "PAIN THERMOSTATS"

Here's the bottom line: Women feel more pain than men. In both experimental and clinical research, women consistently have both lower pain thresholds—the minimum amount of stimulation that reliably evokes pain in an individual—and less pain tolerance—the maximum time or intensity of a painful stimulus that a person can endure. Studies also suggest that women report greater pain than men even when they have the same degree of tissue injury.

The reason for this disparity is not just that women are more emotional or more willing to talk about their pain than men, although some doctors still fall back on that tired old excuse. No, the truth is, men and women are physiologically different. For example, in an experiment published in 1991, not only did the women rate pain from heat stimuli as more intense than the men, they were also better able to discriminate among various intensities of pain. We now know that there are profound, gender-based differences in how women and men perceive pain.

## PAIN MEDICATIONS: ONCE SIZE DOES NOT FIT ALL

Besides differing in their perceptions of pain, men and women also respond differently to analgesics, or pain relievers. For instance, certain commonly used pain medications provide effective relief for men who suffer chronic pain in their reproductive organs, but rarely for women with chronic pelvic pain. Researchers at Johns Hopkins compared thirty-nine women with chronic pelvic pain and twenty-five men with chronic testicular pain. (None of the cases involved cancer.) Each person received one of several types of medications—antidepressants, anticonvulsants, and opioids—known to relieve other pain syndromes. A larger percentage of men than women improved in each case. For example, with antidepressants, the most frequently used medication, nine of eleven men (82 percent) improved, while only four of twenty-eight women (14 percent) did so.

We are also discovering that there are gender differences in how people respond to some of the most widely used pain relievers. In a recent study of experimentally induced pain, ibuprofen—the key ingredient in Advil, Motrin, and other over-the-counter analgesics—was less effective at providing pain relief for women than men. And a Dutch study of the effects of intravenous morphine, which is used for severe pain, revealed clear sex-related differences, even when men and women had similar levels of the drug in their blood. The morphine eased men's pain during the first hour, while women had no pain relief during that time. On the other hand, the effects dissipated fairly quickly among the men but lasted longer for the women. Wouldn't you want your doctors to know about research like this if you were suffering from terrible pain?

Recently, research in the United States on another class of painkillers, known as kappa-opioids, has also produced striking results. The drugs were given to twenty-eight young men and twenty young women who had their wisdom teeth removed. If you've ever been through this procedure, you know that it can produce moderate or severe pain. Women experienced long-lasting, high-quality pain relief from kappa-opioids, with few side effects. But the men received little benefit.

We haven't yet figured out the mechanisms behind these puzzling differences. It could have to do with hormones, the number of receptors on nerve cells, or the ways the brain regulates pain relief. Regardless of the reason, though, these findings matter when it comes to treating your pain. Kappa-opioids have been ignored, for the most part, even though they have fewer side effects than more commonly used painkillers such as codeine, Percodan, and morphine. Why? It's likely that when these drugs were tested by the pharmaceutical companies, their effects on women—if women even participated in the studies—were not analyzed separately. This kind of gender-blindness is outmoded and disgraceful. How much are we missing by ignoring potentially crucial gender differences in biomedical research?

## LAUREN'S STORY

Lauren is a twenty-seven-year-old French-Canadian woman, who came to town to do an apprenticeship in architecture in a local firm. A talented pianist and rock climber, Lauren placed a lot of strain on her wrists. She came to my office complaining of pain in her right wrist, accompanied by numbness in her thumb and second finger. "I wake up in the dead of night with horrible pain and tingling. It's so weird; I have to shake out my hand to get it to ease up." She was also having a tough time opening jars. "I almost lost it the other night. I was preparing a Passover seder for fifteen people and I couldn't open the jar of horseradish!"

Lauren told me that her doctor back home attributed her pain to a "tight nerve" and offered few suggestions. "He minimized the importance of my symptoms and told me to 'just keep on trucking,' " she said. In a telephone conversation, her dad, a retired general practitioner, had urged her to see a specialist, and so she'd found her way to my office.

A careful history and physical revealed that Lauren's symptoms were probably caused by carpal tunnel syndrome, a condition that is particularly frequent among women. She had many of the classical features, including a positive Tinel's sign (tapping above her wrist crease caused numbness and tingling), and some weakness in her grip, as well as a tendency to drop things. Following my suggestion, she underwent a nerve conduction study, which confirmed my diagnosis.

Lauren was concerned about the impact this ailment might have on her life. "I play the piano all the time; besides, I use a keyboard all day at work," she said. At the same time, as a big fan of natural, noninvasive complementary treatments, she didn't want to do anything drastic; no steroid injections for her! I was happy to oblige, and assured her that she'd be back at her piano very soon.

First, we addressed her pain. Although she was only willing to use nonsteroidal anti-inflammatory drugs (NSAIDS) if it got really bad, she was thrilled when I gave her a sample of a natural topical treatment she could apply directly to her wrist. Because it works wonders for carpal tunnel syndrome, we got started with acupuncture right away. I also suggested that she try a TENS (transcutaneous electrical nerve stimulator) unit, which uses electrical impulses to stop the transmission of pain signals.

I taught Lauren some hand and wrist exercises and gave her a "cock-up splint," also known as a dorsiflexion or extension splint, which mechanically repositioned her wrist and took pressure off the carpal tunnel. In addition, to prevent her condition from worsening (or from recurring once she was better) I recommended some ergonomic strategies, including a wrist support to use while working on the keyboard, and taking frequent breaks. Finally, to speed healing, I suggested vitamin B6 and a number of other supplements.

Several months later, Lauren was symptom-free.

## THE UNEQUAL BURDEN OF PAIN

A staggering array of painful illnesses and disorders disproportionately affect women. Of course, you are vulnerable to pain during many stages of your reproductive life cycle, including menstruation, pregnancy, childbirth, and menopause. But you are also far more likely to develop painful ailments that have nothing to do with reproductive health, simply because you're female. To name just a few, these include migraine and tension headaches, backaches, fibromyalgia, rheumatoid arthritis, facial pain, and carpal tunnel syndrome. In addition, women are at greater risk than men for developing chronic pain syndrome after they've suffered the same type of physical trauma.

What really muddies the waters, leading to missed diagnoses and ineffective treatments, is that men and women sometimes report different symptoms for the same disease. You've probably heard about the classic example, which is heart disease. Women less frequently suffer chest pain and more often report pain in the back, neck, and jaw. They experience more nausea, vomiting, abdominal complaints, fatigue, and shortness of breath. What's not as well known is that gender differences also play out in the symptoms of other diseases, such as irritable bowel syndrome, appendicitis, and migraine headaches.

I see this all the time in my own practice. Far more women than men come to see me because of chronic headache disorders. When it comes to migraines, it's probably three to one. My female patients have more nausea, vomiting, and aversion to light. Their headaches last longer, and more often disrupt their sleep. In addition, they have to miss work more often. Yet I know this isn't just psychosomatic, because many of the differences vanish after my patients go through menopause.

## EXPLAINING THE GENDER GAP

We don't yet know why the gender disparities in pain perception, responses to medications, and prevalence of symptoms and diseases exist, but we're pursuing some hot leads. Some researchers believe it has to do with the varying expectations and roles society has for men and women. (Certainly, boys raised on a steady diet of Rambo and watching professional athletes "play through their pain" may grow up to feel that real men "grin and bear it.") Others put it down to psychological differences, such as anxiety or an individual's beliefs about his or her ability to tolerate pain. And biology, such as body size or differences in resting blood pressure, probably also comes into play. I think we're going to find that hormonal, genetic, anatomical, and psychological differences all play a role in explaining the gender gap. And men and women may also have different brain circuitry that partly accounts for this phenomenon.

This is a complex subject to unravel because pain is a complicated biochemical "fact." And it is very subjective. The way you perceive, interpret, and express pain is influenced by your philosophical or religious beliefs. Also, the threshold at which your pain becomes unbearable can vary, depending upon the culture you come from, or the situation you are in. There's a classic example in a book called *People in Pain*, published in 1969. The author, Mark Zborowski, a social anthropologist, studied Irish, Jewish, Italian, and "Old American" (i.e., WASP) World War II veterans and found that the way they reacted to pain—how uninhibited and expressive they were—was strongly associated with their ethnic group and social class.

What's more, your doctor brings his or her own biases into play when assessing your pain. For example, in an Israeli study, Jewish doctors and midwives evaluated the pain of 225 Jewish and 192 Bedouin women during labor; the women also assessed their own pain. Although the women evaluated their pain equivalently, the doctors and midwives reported less pain among the Bedouin women. So a caregiver's ethnic background or beliefs may influence how he evaluates someone's suffering.

What I find especially compelling is cutting-edge research showing that sex-linked genetic characteristics may be involved. In experiments with mice, whose genetic structure is similar to humans, scientists applied a technique called gene mapping to identify specific genes associated with pain and pain relief. They found that gender-linked genetic differences accounted for as much as 50 percent of the variability in pain responses. On female mice only, they found a gene on one chromosome linked to analgesic, or pain-relieving, activity; it appeared to be irrelevant to males. And conversely, a gene on another chromosome affected pain sensitivity, but only on male mice. The conclusion? Males and females have an entirely different genetic basis for pain. In other words, your tolerance for pain, your response to pain relievers, and even possibly your susceptibility to certain painful ailments may have nothing to do with your emotional makeup or with your being "a wimp." Instead, it may be hardwired into your genes. This is exciting news because once we learn more about the genes involved in sensitivity to pain, we may be able to develop innovative, individualized pain therapies.

Given the enormous influence they have in many aspects of your life, you might think that sex-related hormones also affect sensitivity and response to pain. You're right; the hormonal connection to pain is one of the most exciting areas of scientific research, with an impressive array of animal studies as well as experimental and clinical research on humans.

Men and women have different levels of the sex hormones, sometimes called steroid hormones: estrogen, progesterone, and testosterone. Hormones affect nerve conduction, so they may influence how your nerves send their pain messages. Sex steroids can also alter levels of neurotransmitters and other chemical messengers involved in transmitting pain through your central nervous system, as well as your body's own responses to pain. In addition, estrogen and other hormones affect how nerves respond to local anesthetics, and they may affect your body's response to other pain medications.

Besides the obvious hormonal differences between men and women, we also have to take into account the female hormonal cycle. Your estrogen, progesterone, and testosterone levels fluctuate over the course of a month, leading you to respond differently to pain during different phases of your menstrual cycle. You're probably more sensitive to pain during the days between ovulation and the start of menstruation. Known medically as the "luteal phase," it's more commonly called—you guessed it—the premenstrual period. Greater sensitivity to pain during this time may be due to the direct effects of hormones on pain processing. Or it may be indirect. For example, if you're one of the many women who suffer from sleep disturbances when you are premenstrual, it may affect how you react to pain.

What's more, in some conditions, painful symptoms worsen during the premenstrual phase. You may already know this if you have irritable bowel syndrome, headaches, rheumatoid arthritis, or fibromyalgia. And hormonal fluctuations also seem to play a role in the pain of temporomandibular disease. My belief is that as we continue to unravel the mystery of pain, innate hormonal differences, accentuated by the menstrual cycle, pregnancy, and oral contraceptives and other hormonal medications, will play a starring role.

Finally, new, controversial research has emerged on how anatomical features may at least partially explain men's and women's distinct responses to pain. It may be that the existence of the vaginal canal and of sensitive neural mechanisms known as "C-fibers" within the vagina play a key role in women's heightened sensitivity to pain. Here's one possible scenario: Because the vagina and cervix provide ready access to the body, they serve as an entrance for viral and other infectious agents, which may trigger a sequence of reactions through the C-fibers in the vagina, up through the spinal cord and brain. This could cause pain in parts of the body that are far from the original site, accounting for the fact that women more often have multiple areas of what is known as "referred pain," or pain that you feel at some distance from its source.

## ARE WOMEN "BETTER SPORTS" ABOUT PAIN?

Before you go off in despair, let me assure you that the news isn't all bad. Although you may suffer more pain, you are also more adept at coping. The patients I see certainly belie the old notion that women are the "weaker sex." And research confirms my day-to-day observations.

For example, women appear to tolerate pain better than men. A recent study followed twenty-seven women and twenty-one men after they'd had surgery to implant a replacement tooth. In the ten days after the operation, the women handled low levels of pain better than the men, who were more disturbed by the persisting discomfort.

Nature tends to be an equalizer, and most body systems are inclined toward balance. So it's likely that because women experience more pain, they also have more physiological mechanisms for reducing it. Much research needs to be done, but we already know of one example. With the phenomenon known as pregnancy-induced analgesia, a woman's body produces higher levels of endorphins during the late stages of pregnancy to enhance her tolerance of pain. Maybe this is the biological underpinning for the old joke that if it were up to men to have babies, the human race would have been extinct long ago! Seriously, though, it wouldn't surprise me if we eventually discover that women tolerate pain better than men because of the sensitizing experience of childbirth.

Women also have an edge when we go beyond the physiological. You know that women are more likely than men to ask for directions when they are lost. Similarly, women tend to take more advantage of existing resources to deal with their pain. They use the health care system earlier, more aggressively, and more effectively than men. And they have a more open attitude toward innovative approaches to pain care, especially acupuncture, massage, meditation, yoga, and other complementary therapies.

Besides, women are better at taking care of themselves. You probably know how to lighten the emotional burden of pain by allowing yourself to vent your feelings, reaching out to friends and relatives, and listening to your body's warnings to slow down when you are in pain.

In one study, researchers compared men and women with arthritis. On "high pain" days, women were far more likely to use a variety of coping strategies, including relaxation, distraction, and seeking support from others. The day after a high pain day, men reported that their mood was poor, but women did not; suggesting that by taking charge of their pain, they were better able to limit its emotional consequences.

My patient Ramona is a perfect example of how well women cope with pain.

## RAMONA'S STORY

Ramona is a twenty-eight-year-old mother of two, and a proud home-maker. At the tender age of seventeen, she was in a near-fatal car accident that resulted in a spine fracture and several bone fractures. She's experienced pain ever since.

Nevertheless, Ramona is a real trouper when it comes to contending with pain, and she comes to see me regularly. Although her pain can be troubling, she remains optimistic that she will ultimately conquer it. She has an open mind about complementary care, and over the years we have done acupuncture, relaxation and visualization, and biofeedback.

Ramona copes emotionally by relying on her own strength, as well as a solid support network of friends and family, with whom she talks regularly and extensively. Her husband, Rick, a manual laborer, has always been supportive. But he remains baffled by Ramona's ability to endure the pain as well as she does. "I'm a tough cookie, but if it were me, I would have thrown in the towel a long time ago," he told me.

•   •   •

Unfortunately, women like Ramona can't do it alone. Ignorance of gender differences has important practical ramifications. In the next chapter, I'll explain how misguided thinking about gender has affected women's medical care in the past, and may still have an impact on the care you receive today.

# 2

—

# Why Gender Matters

When Professor Henry Higgins asked "Why can't a woman be more like a man?" in *My Fair Lady*, he might have been expressing the opinion of many pain doctors, who simply can't, don't, or won't take gender differences into account when they tailor pain-relief strategies.

But as bad as it is to deny the difference, it's inexcusable to dismiss women's pain as psychosomatic. Yet this has been part of the medical tradition since the time of ancient Greece. The word *hysteria* comes from the Greek word *hystera*, meaning womb. Plato and the other ancients compared the womb to an animal that roamed around a woman's body. The womb's wanderings were thought to be the source of many female maladies. Treatments often consisted of trying to lure that misbehaving womb back to its rightful place in the body.

Fast-forward to the nineteenth century. Any woman unfortunate enough to have pains incompatible with contemporary medical knowledge or symptoms that didn't respond to conventional treatment ran the risk of having her illness dismissed as imaginary. Maybe its source was now in her head, rather than her womb, but it was still hysteria. Hysteria was a shape-shifter, a unique ailment capable of imitating almost any known disease. And pain was one of its most common symptoms.

Unfortunately, this is not just ancient history. With distressing frequency, doctors *still* treat women as overly emotional or don't take their pain seriously. Even today, in the twenty-first century, outdated stereotypes often result in less-than-adequate care for women in pain.

## NICOLE'S STORY

Nicole is a single, thirty-seven-year-old stockbroker who had intense pain in her right buttock. It had started as a dull ache nine months ago, appearing mostly when she sat for long periods of time, climbed stairs, or did squats in the gym. But it had escalated from a smoldering fire to a full-fledged conflagration after she participated in a charity bikeathon for breast cancer research.

A "fitness fiend" who took pride in being in excellent shape, Nicole simply couldn't fathom this angry pain that erupted after her marathon bike ride. "Doc, this burning pain is buried deep in my butt. It feels as though someone has taken a blowtorch to my derriere. Everything hurts; I can't even take pleasure in sitting on the floor with my nephew in my lap."

As we sat in my office and she described her condition, she appeared to be defensive and a bit wary. When I gently prodded, the rest of her all-too-familiar story emerged. Nicole had gone to her primary care doctor, who hadn't been sure what was happening. He ordered X rays of her hip, pelvis, and spine. When they were negative, he "went for the big guns" and ordered an MRI of her spine, which was also normal. Drawing a blank, he referred her to a chiropractor and, later, to a massage therapist.

Although she dutifully made the rounds to all the specialists, Nicole got nowhere. Still in agonizing pain, she'd returned in frustration to her internist. He now dismissed her condition as "psychological," implying that she was simply under too much stress because of the floundering stock market. She had left in tears. Finally, a friend at work, whom I had helped a number of years ago with acupuncture and exercise for a back problem, referred her to me.

After our interview and a thorough physical history, I reviewed her prior X rays and MRI. Indeed, they were negative. Still, I knew this was not a psychological problem; it was regrettable that she'd been treated so dismissively. I had a hunch she had an elusive malady called piriformis muscle syndrome. Because it's not an easy condition to pin down on diagnostic tests—in fact, a negative workup is a hallmark of this ailment—some doctors are skeptical about its existence.

Convinced that the "mystery" would most likely be solved by careful physical examination and muscle assessment, I tried several physical diagnostic maneuvers. We hit pay dirt when I asked Nicole to place all her weight on her left foot. At the same time, I asked her to move her right leg away from her body in a sideways fashion, while rotating it, so that her toes pointed up in the air. When she yelped, I had my diagnosis.

The piriformis muscle lies buried deep beneath the gluteal muscles in the buttocks. The piriformis has its origin at the sacral bone and attaches to the greater trochanter of the leg bone (femur), which is the "bump" on the outside top of the thigh. When this muscle contracts, it causes the leg to move out or away from the midline, and to rotate externally. The sciatic nerve is buried deep below the major muscles, including the piriformis, and in 15 percent of the population it runs right through the muscle. Any type of irritation or swelling of the piriformis sets the sciatic nerve, the largest nerve in the body, on fire.

Nicole was enormously relieved to know what the problem was. She was also highly motivated to get rid of it: "Just tell me what to do. I can't wait to feel better," she said. Because she was in such intense pain, I gave her a local injection of lidocaine and corticosteroid into her piriformis muscle to provide immediate relief. In addition, we started an acupuncture regimen. Once the pain had calmed down a bit, I explained that we had to "reeducate her muscles" with a program of stretching exercises. I also referred her to a physical therapist for ultrasound; by heating muscles, this modality promotes better stretch. Finally, because certain types of foot disorders such as overpronation can contribute to piriformis syndrome, I recommended that Nicole see a podiatrist for a foot orthotic.

Nicole left my office still in pain, but well on her way to relief. More gratifying, though, was that I had confirmed what she had known all along: This pain was not "all in her head."

## BLAMING THE VICTIM

There is no way to measure pain objectively. Because it's an individual perception that we communicate through language and by crying or other nonverbal means, the interplay between doctor and patient is critical. When you see your doctor because you're in pain, how carefully he or she listens to you, and the preconceived notions he or she brings to the encounter, greatly influence the care you receive.

Women are more likely than men to seek medical attention for pain. They are better able—or more willing—to fully describe their pain sensations and to talk about their feelings. Besides, it's also more socially acceptable for women to express emotional distress. You would think that this ability to communicate the discomfort of pain would be an advantage. But I believe that women are, in effect, being punished for their strengths. Too often their reports are viewed with suspicion or their complaints are dismissed as "hysterical."

If you suffer from chronic pain, you're much more likely to be diagnosed with depression or histrionic and somatization disorders—ailments for which no physical cause can be found. In plain English, this means that many doctors will assume it's all in your head, or that you're just depressed.

Even worse, women are more often treated with psychotropic drugs than men. (These are medications that affect your mind; they are used for depression, anxiety, and other psychiatric ailments.) In 1989, researchers analyzed data from the National Ambulatory Medical Care Survey and found that even with the same complaint, diagnosis, and visit history, women were still 37 percent more likely than men to receive an antianxiety medication and a whopping 82 percent more likely to get an antidepressant! These results were confirmed in a later study published in 1998. Statistics like these are disgraceful. Despite enormous strides in improving our health care system's treatment of women, this kind of subtle sexism shows that we still have a long way to go.

Health care providers who doubt your experience of pain, blame you for the pain, or minimize your needs for pain relief add insult to injury. "Blaming the victim" can adversely affect your self-esteem, which escalates your distress and sense of isolation. It may also diminish the likelihood that any care you do receive will be effective. If you're suffering from chronic pain, the most important element in your doctor-patient relationship is whether you feel your doctor believes you. If your experience of pain is validated, you are more likely to be compliant and successful with pain relief strategies.

## STEREOTYPES AFFECT YOUR CARE

Even when doctors or other caregivers know your pain isn't psychosomatic, their beliefs about pain and gender influence their attitudes, and they may treat you less aggressively. Several experiments have revealed that nurses make decisions based on gender stereotypes. For example, when nurses were asked to read and react to identical vignettes of men and women in pain, their care plans included more narcotic pain medication and emotional support for the men. In an actual clinical setting, these nursing care decisions would lead to inadequate treatment for female patients.

Sadly, we also have evidence that women do, in fact, get less pain medication. For instance, among 180 adults who'd had appendectomies, men received significantly more narcotic pain relievers than women for the initial postoperative dose, although the total dose during the recovery period was about the same. Gender bias must have come into play because the difference occurred while patients were still too groggy from surgery to express their needs!

When women do say what they need, however, nurses or doctors may take them less seriously or dismiss them as "whiny." In a study of people who'd undergone coronary artery bypass graft surgery, men received morphine significantly more often than women. Interestingly, women received more sedative drugs for anxiety or agitation. Perhaps this reflected the nurses' belief that women are more emotional and more likely to exaggerate complaints of pain than men. Regrettably, other research has shown that even among patients with metastatic cancer, being female is a significant predictor of inadequate pain management.

Even more chilling is this: Women may undergo surgery more frequently than men for similar pain syndromes. In a series of studies, a researcher compared men with chronic, nonmalignant testicular pain and women with chronic pelvic pain. Both of these ailments last at least three to six months and often have no obvious cause. One of fifteen men (7 percent) had undergone epididymectomy (the epididymis is a long, coiled tube that carries sperm from the testicles to the tip of the penis), while seventeen of thirty-nine women (44 percent) had had hysterectomies, without any resolution of their problems! The researcher concluded that male urologists may have greater reluctance to remove reproductive organs in male patients than male gynecologists have in female patients, a conclusion I find deeply disturbing.

## PUTTING GENDER INTO THE EQUATION

We're at the beginning of a revolution. The science of gender-specific differences in health is relatively new, and some of the findings are speculative. Much more research needs to be done. Still, there are things that all of us — practitioners and patients — can do to increase awareness of gender issues and improve treatment for people in pain.

- Men and women may not experience the same symptoms or may express themselves differently when describing the pain associated with a specific problem. So "typical" descriptions of common pain problems and treatment protocols need to be changed, especially as we uncover more and more sex-related differences. For example, despite abundant information illustrating the importance of sex differences when it comes to heart disease, current recommendations for the evaluation of chest pain in women who have suspected coronary heart disease are *still* based on a male model of the disease.

- New models take a while to develop. In the meantime, I'd advise you to ask your doctor to search the scientific literature and be alert to any findings about potentially different diagnostic signs and symptoms in males and females. This will be especially important as more evidence emerges about the varying ways medications affect men and women. And bring this book with you to your doctor's office!
- Because your menstrual cycle may affect your pain, keep a pain diary to note any possible hormonal fluctuations in your symptoms. Whenever you notice regular variations, let your doctor know. If you have rheumatoid arthritis, for example, and you know it gets worse the week before your period, you might be able to adjust your medication or plan your schedule to avoid strenuous activities during that time.
- Other hormones, such as oral contraceptives or hormone replacement therapy, may also affect your painful symptoms. For instance, hormones can significantly increase the pain of temporomandibular disorder. If you notice a change after starting a prescription for hormones, let your doctor know right away.

Meanwhile, if you're reading this book, chances are you are in pain. In the next chapter, I'll explain how pain works, and how it may work differently for men and women.

# 3

## The Mystery of Pain

### SHAKITA'S STORY

Shakita is a forty-three-year-old woman who works as a nurse's aide for a home health and hospice agency. She has a heart of gold and her clients adore her. In fact, it was one of her geriatric patients who recommended that she see me.

Shakita is diabetic and overweight. When she came in, she told me she had ongoing, intermittent pain and numbness in the side of her left thigh. She had been to a string of doctors, including her family physician, a chiropractor, and several specialists. Although she'd been through an extensive and thorough workup, no one had found an identifiable cause for her pain. "They don't have a clue. I got so desperate, I even went to my neighborhood faith healer," she told me, a bit sheepishly.

Lately, her symptoms had gotten worse; the pain was so bad that she now reported a burning ache over the front and side of her thigh, along with some tingling. "It feels like water rippling down my side," she explained.

When I examined her, it soon became obvious that she fit the description of someone with meralgia paraesthetica, a nerve entrapment syndrome of the lateral femoral cutaneous nerve, which is located in the front, outer part of the thigh. This diagnosis would easily explain her pattern of alternating numbness and pain. Because this nerve is a purely sensory nerve, the ailment doesn't cause any motor loss or other deficits. (There are three types of nerves: sensory, motor, and mixed. Sensory nerves carry signals for sensation, such as numbness, tingling, light touch, or pain. Motor nerves provide power to your muscles and give them strength. Mixed nerves do both.)

Diabetes can be a risk factor for meralgia paraesthetica and can exacerbate its symptoms. So can a tight lumbar corset, or brace, which Shakita often wore because she needed to lift heavy patients. And she was obese, which further complicated her situation. When I advised her to lose some weight, she sighed and said: "Well, Doctor, I've been talking about going on a diet for years. If losing weight will ease this pain, maybe I'll finally have the motivation to do it."

In the meantime, I prescribed a capsaicin cream, made from hot peppers, or a lidoderm patch, a topical anesthetic, to dull her pain. I also started her on Neurontin, a medication used for seizures that also has powerful nerve stabilizing properties. She was intrigued by a chart of acupuncture points I had in my office, so I gave her a few acupressure exercises to try. I warned her to avoid corsets and other tight garments and urged her to start some kind of exercise. "There's a park across the street from my house. I'm up early anyway; maybe I'll take a walk before work," she said.

There's no motivator like pain. Over the next six months, Shakita exercised diligently and watched what she ate. Her symptoms gradually improved so much that she was able to stop the Neurontin and rely just on the topical analgesics.

## WHAT IS PAIN?

When I care for patients, I find that illuminating how pain works demystifies it and makes it less frightening. Understanding the mechanics of pain can help you gain mastery over what may otherwise seem like a dark and powerful force that has taken over your life.

Human beings have tried to make sense of pain for millennia. Pain scares us, not only because it hurts, but because it is intimately connected to illness and hints at our mortality. Emily Dickinson understood this when she wrote: "Pain has but one Acquaintance / and that is Death."

Since the beginnings of time, our ancestors have tried to understand pain. In ancient days they thought it was a supernatural phenomenon—a form of spiritual possession or a punishment, gift, test, or means of redemption from the gods.

As we learned more about the natural world of biological processes, our conception of pain changed. In recent times, pain was reduced to a purely mechanistic model—electrical impulses speeding along nerves.

Today we know that pain is much more complicated. It involves a complex interaction between the mind *and* the body. To paraphrase Gertrude Stein, it is simply not true that a pain is a pain is a pain. Your experience of pain depends not only on cellular, molecular, genetic, and physiological factors, but it is also inextricably tied to your mental and emotional health, personal history, culture, and a host of other individual influences.

Still, gender may be the most crucial factor of all. It profoundly affects how we experience, communicate, and get care for pain. And there's experimental evidence that men and women may have different neuroanatomical and neurochemical pathways for processing, transmitting, and responding to pain.

## HOW PAIN WORKS

What, then, is pain? The standard definition, developed by the International Association for the Study of Pain, is "an unpleasant sensory and emotional experience associated with actual or potential tissue damage or described in terms of such damage." But pain is much more than that. I consider pain the "fifth vital sign," along with blood pressure, temperature, respiratory rate, and pulse. It's a window into the body that shows whether something is awry, a sentinel that you should not ignore. Pain signals the possibility of lurking illness or pathology.

Acute and chronic pain are different. Simply put, acute pain flares up in response to a known cause and then it goes away, either in response to the body's own healing powers or with treatment. Not only is acute pain time-limited, but it also serves a purpose. Acute pain is how your body talks to you. Sometimes it's warning you that you're pushing yourself too hard—remember those sore legs the day after you first tried jogging? Or it may prod you to change your behavior. For example, mild back pain while sitting at your computer reminds you to shift your position or get up and take a break. And what compels you to snap your hand back from a hot stove? Searing pain. So important a messenger is acute pain that people born with a rare condition known as congenital insensitivity to pain suffer frequent injuries and tend to die early.

Chronic pain is another story. It's persistent, dragging on for weeks, months, or even years. And it's often a mystery. Chronic pain may be associated with a long-term incurable or intractable medical condition or disease, like cancer. Or a serious infection may be its initial trigger. Sometimes there's no identifiable cause at all. But for some reason the pain keeps going long after you've recovered from the original problem. And unlike acute pain, which is a biologically useful process, pain often loses its function when it becomes chronic. Worst of all, we can't treat the pain by removing or curing its cause.

## RACHEL'S STORY

Rachel is a thirty-four-year-old homemaker with three kids under the age of six. She suffers from brutal migraines as well as severe dysmenorrhea, or menstrual cramps.

Because of the difficulties of raising three young children, as well as all of her other chores, Rachel's symptoms really get the best of her. Her husband is a surgeon and he keeps crazy hours, so she is unable to unload any of her responsibilities on him.

Never one to complain, Rachel came to me one day looking tired and weary. She had just made it through another week of migraines and menstrual cramps. "Doctor, I've tried to stay cheerful, but I have to confess that I'm beginning to get depressed. My headaches have gotten so much worse lately; I think it's the stress. And my cramps are just awful."

I conferred with her neurologist, who had seen her a few months earlier, when her headaches were much less severe. In addition, I repeated her neurological exam and she showed no abnormalities.

During the course of our conversation, I realized that Rachel's headaches seemed to coincide with her monthly cycle. When I mentioned this, she said, "You know, you're right. My worst headaches come a day or two before my period. I've often wondered why everything happens at once." This wasn't unusual, I explained to her. Many ailments seem to ebb and flow with the menstrual cycle, and migraines are high on that list. Although I understood how stressful her life was, fluctuations of estrogen and progesterone were probably playing the key role in her headaches.

I performed an acupuncture treatment utilizing the traditional cranial points, and showed her some acupressure points she could massage the next time she felt a migraine coming on. I also explained how she could fashion a warm compress steeped in the herb feverfew.

I suggested that Rachel start eating fish on a regular basis. Fish oil, rich in omega-3 fatty acids, is now being used to relieve menstrual cramps. It may also prevent the widening and narrowing of blood vessels that causes migraines.

To bolster her diet, I recommended Tums (calcium carbonate)

and magnesium supplements. These minerals work together to improve muscle tone, which can reduce cramping. And they seem to play an important, though as yet unexplained, role in reducing the frequency and duration of migraines. In addition, I told her, they would also help prevent osteoporosis. "Doctor, I'm too young and too busy to think about that, but I'll take your word for it," she laughed. Finally, I suggested that Rachel try SAMe (see page 94). I have had excellent success using this supplement. Not only does it help treat depression, there's also preliminary evidence that it relieves migraines.

If all else failed, I gave her a prescription for rofecoxib (Vioxx), which is approved by the FDA for dysmenorrhea. Rofecoxib is one of a new generation of pain relievers, called Cox-2 inhibitors, that cause fewer gastrointestinal side effects. It's also an all-purpose pain reliever, so it would help her migraines, too.

Several months later Rachel checked in with me by phone. "Things are so much better I don't need to come back," she said.

## NOCICEPTORS, NERVES, AND PAIN

Although we don't completely understand pain, we've learned an enormous amount over the last few decades. And new techniques continue to stretch the frontiers of scientific exploration. We can now look at images of brain activity in awake human subjects as they perceive pain. Some researchers are revealing special pathways and chemicals involved in pain, and performing cellular analyses of the molecular signals that transmit and receive the pain message. And on every level, men and women appear to be different.

Pain occurs in response to a possibly harmful stimulus, such as a burn or a pinch. It's a complicated drama with many actors directed by the central nervous system—the brain and spinal cord. Nociceptors (from the Latin *noceo*, "hurt," and *capio*, "receive") are unique receptors in the skin and most other tissues. They are the first link in the chain of neurophysiological events that ultimately ends when you perceive pain. Some nociceptors react to several kinds of painful stimulation; others are pickier and respond to heat, perhaps, but not to a pinprick. When these small nerve endings are activated by something painful, they transmit signals through the nerves in the spinal cord to the brain, leading to pain.

Certain sharp pain signals are routed immediately. When you stub your toe, for example, your body instantaneously flashes an emergency bulletin.

Less urgent news—duller, more persistent pain—travels on an alternative, slower pathway.

Activated nociceptors also trigger the release of chemicals, such as prostaglandins, serotonin, and histamine, that are associated with pain and inflammation. And they alert the autonomic nervous system, which regulates involuntary processes such as breathing, blood flow, pulse rate, and the release of hormones like epinephrine (adrenaline).

But let's get back to the nervous system, the neurological hardwiring that allows you to perceive pain. Nerve cells, or neurons, form a highly organized, complex web of nerves throughout the body, extending to the toes and fingers as well as to the heart, liver, lung, and other inner organs. Nerves are constantly gathering information and transmitting it to control central—the spinal cord and brain.

Nerve cells are different from other body cells; they have projections on both ends. At one end is the long, thin axon, and at the other is a shorter, more branching projection called a dendrite. These are the live wires of the nervous system. Each nerve cell is a link in a chain, with its axon in close contact, but not actually touching, the dendrite of the next nerve cell in the chain.

Nerve cells transmit information through electrochemical impulses that travel in one direction only, from axon to dendrite. When an impulse reaches the gap, or synapse, between the axon of one nerve cell and the dendrite of the next, the axon secretes a chemical substance known as a neurotransmitter to bridge the gap.

The speed and complexity of the nervous system is mind-boggling. It takes only about one thousandth of a second for an impulse to jump the gap. And a single nerve cell in the brain may have 50,000 dendrites and communicate with 250,000 other neurons.

When a painful event stimulates the nociceptors, they trigger a cascade of events by sending messages through the nervous system and up the spinal cord to several places in the brain. Some of the brain regions that receive pain signals are also involved in perception, emotion, and movement. The brain responds, sending signals through a different nerve pathway back down to the spinal cord. Recall our example of a hot stove; when you touch it, your brain directs you to move your hand. Your brain's nerve cells may also trigger the release of endorphins, the body's natural painkillers. These actually reduce pain and create a temporary sense of well-being. I'll get back to endorphins shortly.

Our knowledge of gender-related differences in nociceptive, or pain, processing is still in its infancy. But thrilling new research in animals and humans indicates that men and women differ greatly. There are probably distinctions caused not only by hormonal differences but also in the actual biochemical pathways men and women use to process pain. Here are some key findings:

- Estrogen alters the receptive properties of important nerves, and there is also clear evidence that pregnancy and progesterone affect nerve conduction.
- Sex hormones influence many central nervous system pathways involved in pain transmission.
- Electrophysiological and brain imaging studies indicate that sex differences occur at many stages of pain processing.
- Hormones also affect levels of serotonin and other transmitters, as well as other biochemicals involved in processing pain.
- Hormones may affect nociceptor receptivity; for example, nociceptors may be sensitized by ovarian hormones. In addition, the central nervous system pain circuitry may vary, depending on where you are in your menstrual cycle.

## OPENING AND CLOSING THE GATE

In 1965, researchers Patrick Wall and Ronald Melzack proposed a novel explanation of how pain works. Their gate-control theory suggested that whether you experience pain depends on the balance between nonpainful information traveling into the spinal cord through large nerve fibers, and the pain signals traveling on small nerve fibers. When the activity in these small nerve fibers reaches a certain level, a "gate" opens, allowing pain signals to continue on to the brain.

Wall and Melzack also speculated that the body has its own ways to suppress pain. For example, large nerves that are stimulated by nonpainful touching or pressing of the skin send signals to the brain more quickly; once they get there, they slam the gate closed, keeping out pain signals. This explains why rubbing your twisted ankle lessens your pain: rubbing excites nerve cells sensitive to touch and pressure that can suppress pain signals from other cells.

What fascinated researchers and led to a spate of important discoveries was the idea that the gate could also be closed from above. In other words, the brain might have its own ways to block pain messages.

Neuroscientists already knew that chemicals were involved in conducting nerve signals. (Recall that neurotransmitters help messages cross the gap between two nerve cells.) Now researchers began to wonder how opioids —

morphine and other highly effective painkilling drugs derived from opium — worked. When they injected morphine into experimental animals, they found that the morphine molecules fit into receptors on certain brain and spinal cord neurons just as a key fits into a lock, opening the door to pain relief.

The researchers may have figured out how morphine did its job, but their work raised an even more puzzling question: Why would the human brain have receptors for a man-made drug? Solving this mystery revealed the existence of a whole family of naturally occurring brain chemicals that behave exactly like morphine and inhibit pain. There are a number of such neurotransmitters, but we use the term *endorphins*, meaning "the morphine within," to describe them all.

Laboratory experiments have shown that painful stimulation causes the brain to release endorphins, which then circulate in the spinal cord. Receptor sites for endorphins have been found throughout the body. Endorphins do more than suppress pain. You're probably familiar with the term *runner's high*. Endorphins also affect mood and perception. And exercise is a surefire way to get your brain to release endorphins. So the brain does indeed have a built-in mechanism for closing the pain gate. In fact, it probably has more than one. Besides the opioid system I just described, we probably have another, nonopioid circuit that blocks pain information from reaching the brain. Today, we're learning that these pain-inhibiting pathways are distinct in men and women. On an intuitive level, this makes sense, since in various areas of the brain, the neurons involved in modulating pain overlap with brain receptors for sex hormones. In addition, in some studies of mice, both males and females turn on pain-inhibiting systems when they are stressed. However, it appears that females have an additional pathway for blocking pain perception. Perhaps this evolved as a way to ease the pain associated with childbirth.

Whatever the explanations of these differences turn out to be, they have important ramifications when it comes to pain medication. Already, we know that men and women respond differently to certain types of painkillers. For this reason, it's critical that we include gender in clinical research!

## PAIN IN THE BRAIN

Short circuits can occur in any electrical system, and this may be what is going on if you have chronic pain. Scientists believe that nociceptors can get stuck in an "on" mode. In extreme cases, they may become so hypersensitive that even a breeze or a gentle touch to the affected area can cause pain.

We're also beginning to untangle other mechanisms of chronic pain. We know now, for example, that nerve injury may alter how nociceptors respond to noradrenaline, a neurotransmitter used by nerve cells to communicate. And we're also discovering that the body develops long-term memories of pain that can interfere with a healthy response to pain and to pain relief therapies. In some people with chronic pain, it appears that a particular part of the brain's cortex that is involved with pain gets reorganized. As one investigator puts it, in addition to pain at the original site of injury, there is "pain in the brain." Whatever the cause, chronic pain is so real and so enervating that it should probably be viewed not as a symptom but as a disease.

Understanding the basic mechanisms of pain is just the beginning. In the following chapters, I'll show you how you can take charge of your pain with remedies specifically tailored to your needs as a woman.

# THE MANY
# FACES
# OF PAIN

# 4

—

# The Hormonal Connection

Some painful conditions are an inescapable part of the reproductive life cycle, and they can cause ongoing, recurring pain along with the great joys of childbearing and motherhood. In this chapter, you'll find information about problems related to menstruation, such as premenstrual syndrome and cramps. I'll also go into breast and pelvic pain, pregnancy, labor and childbirth, and menopause. As a physiatrist, my interest in these issues first grew out of my work with women with spinal cord injury and other chronic disabilities as they faced these challenges.

Because there is no "cure" per se for most of these conditions, my focus will be on prevention and relief of painful symptoms.

(*Note to the Reader:* If there is any chance that you may be pregnant, please consult with your doctor before trying any of these remedies. Good communication between you and your primary medical doctor or obstetrician/gynecologist regarding all medical concerns is imperative.)

## PREMENSTRUAL SYNDROME (PMS)

### ANNIE'S STORY

Annie, a successful thirty-four-year-old computer consultant, suffered from intense back and neck pain compounded by her full-blown premenstrual syndrome. She was referred to me by her gynecologist. At her first visit, she told me she was at her "wit's end." Although she managed to hold herself together at work, her symptoms were getting the better of her at home. During the week before her period, her back pain flared up, causing her to be irritable with her husband. And, to her intense dismay, she found herself blowing up at her two young children over trifling incidents. In addition to moodiness, she struggled with appetite changes, cravings for sweet and salty foods, and cramping. Her chronic neck and back pain worsened and she also had trouble sleeping. "Sometimes, during those last few days before my period, I feel like I'm going to jump out of my skin," she said.

Annie had tried conventional therapies but had only gotten limited relief. She was hesitant about trying the hormonal treatment her gynecologist had recommended. She was worried about possible side effects and the long-term consequences. Besides, like many women, she'd much rather use a natural remedy than a pharmaceutical one.

Because it is a recurring ailment and there is no "cure," I told Annie that we needed to attack her PMS in a holistic fashion, using diet, exercise, and other simple lifestyle changes that she could maintain over the long term. After discussing my game plan with her gynecologist, I advised her to maintain an adequate fluid intake by keeping a pitcher of water on her desk at work and making sure she drank at least eight eight-ounce glasses, every day. To ensure that she had an adequate intake of calcium, magnesium, and vitamin E, which help fight PMS symptoms, we discussed how she could include more whole grains, fruits, and vegetables as well as other nutrient-rich foods in her diet. Because there is evidence that the essential fatty acids found in fish oil may be helpful, I also encouraged her to eat salmon, tuna, or other "oily" fish several times a week. And I explained the growing evidence that the phytoestrogens in soy foods help address PMS and other hormonal ailments. I also suggested that she cut back on starchy carbohydrate-laden foods.

Irritability, insomnia, and moodiness were big concerns for Annie. We tried simple measures first—cutting back on caffeine and taking warm aromatherapy baths with a few drops of lavender oil. I also gave her a couple of relaxation tapes to try, and recommended a gentle exercise program she could do at home, using a stationary bicycle at low resistive settings.

Annie tried everything I suggested, but at her next visit she told me: "I like the relaxation tapes, but I just don't have the time to do both them and the bicycle regularly. Is there anything else I can try for the irritability and depression?" I recommended St. John's wort, a mild herbal medication that eases anxiety and depression. (Annie was not taking antidepressants, nor did she need to.)

There's a strong connection between emotions and pain, so I knew that tackling Annie's depression and moodiness would also reduce the intensity of her cramps. And for the times when she was actually in pain, I suggested some alternative pain relief strategies. Annie was a big classical music fan, so I advised her to lie down with a warm, moist towel on her belly, listen to her favorite symphonies, and do deep yoga breathing. I also showed her how to use a reflexology point (by pressing on a specific point on the hands, ears, or feet, you can affect related organs in other parts of the body) to ease cramping. At work, when some of these techniques were impractical, she could still rely on Motrin or other pain relievers.

Over time, Annie continued to have PMS, but the intensity of her symptoms decreased significantly. "The cramps are better, the neck and back pain has subsided, and I'm not nearly as ferocious," she said. "Best of all, my husband and kids have noticed the difference. They no longer avoid me one week a month."

## PMS Description

This bothersome monthly malady has been recognized since antiquity. It's linked to fluctuations in hormone levels, including estrogen and progesterone. PMS is an annoying cluster of painful physical and emotional symptoms that occurs during the luteal phase of a woman's menstrual cycle — the latter half of the cycle, or the time between ovulation and the start of bleeding. Your symptoms may begin from two to fourteen days before menstruation starts and should improve shortly after you have begun to bleed. PMS symptoms are absent during the early part of the menstrual cycle.

Researchers have cataloged more than 150 different PMS symptoms. Just as the length and severity of every woman's menstrual cycle varies, PMS has a mind of its own and behaves differently in every woman. Still, it's a nearly universal problem: A recent study reported that 30 to 80 percent of women are affected to some degree by PMS.

Despite the broad array of symptoms, pain is at the heart of PMS because symptoms like breast tenderness and abdominal and pelvic cramping are often the most vexing. Moreover, PMS may also exacerbate existing musculoskeletal pain and aggravate other ailments. If you have carpal tunnel syndrome, for example, the swelling and bloating of PMS can put pressure on your nerves and make it worse. Most of the prescription medications women take for PMS are for pain.

The National Institutes of Health (NIH) and the University of California have formulated well-accepted criteria for the diagnosis of PMS. In addition, PMDS, premenstrual dysphoric disorder, is recognized as a psychiatric disorder and included in the *DSM-IV*, the bible of psychiatric diagnosis. Yet PMS is not always taken seriously. Many women are still told "it's all in your head," and it's the focus of a lot of jokes. What's more, PMS sufferers are all too often urged to "wait it out" or to "grin and bear it." As a result, many women—as many as 81 percent in one study—look to self-help remedies and complementary providers to ease their symptoms.

## Causes

Hormones are chemical messengers produced by glands and organs that are transported through the bloodstream to target organs. They are the major drivers of physiological changes in the body. Menstrual hormones like estrogen, progesterone, luteinizing hormone, and follicle stimulating hormone play an important role in orchestrating the menstrual cycle. Although it was once considered a psychiatric condition, we now believe that PMS is caused by fluctuations in the hormone levels that occur during the menstrual cycle, specifically from a change in the ratio of progesterone to estrogen. Research has also shown that serotonin, the well-known mood modulating brain chemical, may be reduced in women during the premenstrual phase of the menstrual cycle. If you are depressed and moody before your period, this might explain why.

## Signs and Symptoms

The most common PMS symptoms are:

- Abdominal cramps
- Pelvic discomfort
- Headaches
- Backaches
- Other musculoskeletal pain (joint, neck, muscle aches)
- Breast tenderness and swelling
- Weight gain and bloating
- Mood swings (irritability, anger, depression, anxiety)
- Fatigue
- Difficulty concentrating
- Sleep disorder
- Lethargy
- Appetite changes (food cravings for carbohydrates or sweets, especially chocolate)
- Acne

## Keep a Pain Diary

Use a calendar to track when your symptoms begin and end, as well as their severity. If you have PMS, your symptoms will occur during the two weeks before your period *and* they will disappear after your period starts. A diary will also help you learn your body's biological timing. If you can predict when you will have the worst symptoms, you can make adjustments to your schedule, saving big projects or major social events for a better time.

## Conventional Treatments

PMS is short-lived and self-correcting, but it comes back every month. Over-the-counter (OTC) drugs can improve some symptoms. You may have success using Tylenol, Advil, and other analgesics for muscle, neck, back, and joint pain. However, Tylenol can cause liver damage and Advil and other so-called NSAIDS have been linked to stomach and gastrointestinal ulcers, kidney damage, and bleeding disorders.

Despite the severity and diversity of symptoms, there are few tried-and-true "shotgun" approaches for PMS. Nor is there widespread consensus about its appropriate management, even among health professionals. Once you get beyond the OTC medications, your options are likely to include a broad array of prescription medications, each dealing with one aspect of PMS. (Bear in mind, however, that most of these drugs have side effects. For example, diuretics rob the body of potassium; antianxiety drugs may be habit forming and cause sleepiness or seizures, and antidepressants can cause weight changes. Be sure to ask your doctor about possible side effects or interactions with other drugs you may be taking.)

Your doctor may prescribe prostaglandin inhibitor medications, like Motrin, if you suffer from disabling menstrual spasms and cramps (dysmenorrhea). Recently there has been a growing body of literature on the benefits of Cox-2 inhibitor drugs, a new class of NSAIDS. Currently, rofecoxib (Vioxx) is the only Cox-2 drug that has been approved by the FDA for dysmenorrhea. Many women also report that Celebrex (celecoxib), the other drug in this class, is helpful. Other "boutique" anti-inflammatory drugs are in the pipeline.

If you get migraines (see Chapter 9), the risk of getting a headache increases in the four days before your period starts. For severe headaches, your physician may prescribe medications known as beta-blockers or calcium channel blockers.

Some doctors prescribe diuretics (water pills) to minimize water retention and bloating. If you have severe symptoms, including anxiety, your doctor may suggest an antianxiety drug such as Xanax (alprazolam). When depression or moodiness is the problem, he or she may suggest one of the SSRI (see page 316) antidepressant medications, which have been touted to address the emotional issues that so often accompany PMS. One drug in particular, Sarafem, has earned FDA approval. However, Sarafem is the same as Prozac (fluoxetine hydrochloride).

Some doctors prescribe oral contraceptives to regulate hormonal shifts. And in very severe cases of PMS, gonadotropin-releasing hormone agonists—drugs that eliminate the menstrual cycle entirely—are a radical but sometimes used strategy.

## Dietary Strategies (See Chapter 14 for food sources of specified nutrients)

- Overall, a well-balanced diet that emphasizes vegetables, fruits, and whole grains is beneficial.
- Eat a diet that maintains an optimal ratio of estrogen and progesterone. Two simple measures include reducing your consumption of simple carbohydrates (sugars) and cutting back on meat and saturated fat. Simple carbohydrates may lead to fluctuations in blood sugar levels resulting in hypoglycemia (low blood sugar). Hypoglycemia can trigger adrenaline release, which can interfere with the function of progesterone. Studies have proven that there is a strong association between PMS and eating a lot of sugary food. And excessive ingestion of meat and saturated fat may raise blood estrogen levels.
- Diets high in fiber can help promote bowel regularity, thereby reducing the risk of abdominal cramping and constipation, which can worsen your menstrual cramps.
- Reduce salt, which can increase bloating, water retention, and weight gain.
- Alcohol, tea, coffee, and other caffeinated beverages increase your risk of PMS.
- Use a lot of parsley to battle bloating and fluid buildup.
- Calcium, magnesium, and vitamins E, B6, and A have all been shown to reduce PMS symptoms.

## Supplements

Although we don't yet know precisely how they work, these vitamin and mineral supplements have been shown to help PMS symptoms.

## Vitamin A

Vitamin A is thought to increase progesterone levels. High doses of vitamin A can be toxic; the acceptable dose range is 900 to 3,000 mcg.

## Vitamin B6

By promoting the production of their building blocks (tryptophan, tyrosine, and glutamate), B6 may enhance the release of important neurotransmitters, including serotonin, dopamine, and norepinephrine. Deficiencies of these brain chemicals may influence other important chemical messengers, such as prolactin and aldosterone, causing fluid retention and breast pain. B6 may also reduce some of the effects of estrogen. The recommended range is 2 to 100 mg a day. Excessive B6 can cause neurological problems in some people.

## Magnesium

A study published in *Obstetrics and Gynecology* in 1991 indicated that magnesium could help the pain associated with PMS, and several other small double-blind randomized studies also support its value in beating this ailment. We also know that women with PMS have low levels of magnesium in their red blood cells. Magnesium supplementation may have an impact on PMS through a variety of mechanisms: It is important in regulating blood vessel tone, in serotonin and neurotransmitter activity, and in cell membrane stability. The accepted range is 320 to 350 mg a day.

## Vitamin E

This vitamin helps prevent breast tenderness and minimizes PMS. The accepted range is 15 to 1,000 mg a day.

## Chromium

An essential trace mineral, chromium helps regulate sugar levels in the body and may reduce sugar cravings. The recommended daily intake is 25 mcg. No safe upper limit has been established.

## Calcium

Calcium plays a role in skeletal and smooth muscle function, neurotransmitter release, and many other bodily processes. It can keep menstrual cramps in check by helping to regulate muscle tone. I strongly endorse the use of calcium supplements for menstrual cramps. Calcium carbonate (Tums) is the most economical commercial calcium supplement and it has the added bonus of being an antacid. A 1998 study by Dr. Susan Thy-

Jacobs in the *American Journal of Obstetrics and Gynecology* showed that women who took calcium carbonate for three menstrual cycles experienced a 54 percent reduction in PMS symptoms including abdominal cramping, generalized aches, and low back pain; women in the control group had only a 15 percent reduction in their symptoms.

Calcium supplementation is generally thought to be safe in women who may become pregnant. Since many scientific studies have shown that calcium deficiency is linked to PMS, there has been much speculation about the relationship between PMS and other calcium-related disorders, such as osteoporosis. To date, at least two studies have shown an association between PMS and reduced bone mass and osteoporosis in women, raising the possibility that low calcium may be an early warning sign of potential future difficulties. (See Chapter 6 for more information on osteoporosis.)

The acceptable daily dose range for calcium is 1,300 to 2,500 mg.

### Long-chain fatty acids (Essential Fatty Acids, or EFAs)
Evening primrose oil, borage oil, black currant oil, grapeseed oil, and flaxseed oil are all high in gamma-linolenic acid, which contributes to the body's production of prostaglandin PGE1, a potent anti-inflammatory. Besides their value in PMS, EFAs may reduce the pain of fibrocystic breast disease, as well as lower a woman's risk of heart disease. Recommended dose is 3,000 to 4,000 mg a day.

### B Complex
One to two tablets a day may reduce cramping and other PMS symptoms.

### Manganese
This trace element (metal) is found in small amounts in human tissue. It helps create connective tissue, blood clotting factors, fats, and cholesterol. In a 1993 study, women on a diet low in manganese had increased premenstrual pain symptoms and mood changes compared to women placed on a high-manganese diet. The acceptable range is 1.8 to 11.0 mg a day. *Warning*: Manganese can be toxic in large amounts.

## Herbs

### Chaste tree (Vitex agnus-castus)
A study published in the April 2000 issue of the *Journal of Women's Health and Gender-Based Medicine* reported that after three months of using *Vitex* daily, 93 percent of the women studied had improvements in PMS symp-

toms of depression, anxiety, cravings, and breast pain. More recently, in results of a double-blind trial, published in the *British Medical Journal*, a majority of women taking *Vitex* for three menstrual cycles reported a 50 percent or more improvement in PMS symptoms. This herb is approved in Germany to reduce symptoms of PMS. The recommended daily dose is 30 to 40 mg in an aqueous-alcohol extract. Do not use chaste tree if you may be pregnant or if you are nursing.

### Black cohosh (Cimicifuga racemosa)

This popular herbal remedy is thought to work by binding to estrogen receptors, thereby balancing your hormones. A native American herb, it is used extensively by women in Europe, especially Germany, to treat a variety of PMS symptoms. Although the doses of this herb are not standardized, the German Commission E recommends taking an alcohol extract of 40 percent. This corresponds to 40 mg a day.

### Kava kava (Piper methysticum)

This is an herbal alternative for treating tension and anxiety, common features of PMS. The accepted dose range is 60 to 120 mg a day, when needed. CAUTION: This herb may interact with Xanax (alprazolam).

### Valerian (Valeriana officinalis)

This is another useful herb that relieves insomnia and anxiety. The accepted dose is an infusion, made by adding 2 or 3 grams of herb to 150 ml of hot water, steeping for 10 to 15 minutes, and straining before use. To simplify things, I recommend commercial teas, such as Dr. Stuart's, Traditional Medicinals, or Yogi Tea. Drink one cup before bedtime.

### St. Johns wort (Hypericum perforatum)

One of the best studied herbal remedies, St. John's wort is effective in the treatment of mild to moderate depression, although its value in treating severe depression has recently been questioned. Herbalists recommend drinking one cup of infusion three times a day. To make the infusion, use 2 teaspoons of herb in 150 ml of boiling water and steep for 10 minutes. Do not take this herb with other antidepressants.

### Yarrow (Achillea millefolium)

This herb has been traditionally used throughout Europe to relieve menstrual ailments with its anti-inflammatory effects. We believe it's named in honor of Achilles of Greece, who used it to help his bleeding soldiers. You can drink yarrow as a tea or use it in your bath to treat menstrual spasms. To make the tea, steep 1 to 2 teaspoons in a cup of boiling water. Try several cups a day just before and during the first day or two of your period.

## Do-It-Yourself

### Yarrow sitz bath

A warm sitz bath is particularly helpful for painful ovaries or uterine cramps. Fill the bathtub so the water covers your hips and reaches the middle of your belly. Soak in the warm water two to three times a day for ten to fifteen minutes. To further decrease pain and cramps, add a yarrow infusion as you run the water for the bath. You can make the infusion by adding 15 grams of herb to one gallon of water. You may want to cover your upper body with a towel to stay warm.

### Reflexology

In a solid, credible study, women treated with true reflexology (see page 353 for reflexology technique) had a more dramatic reduction in PMS symptoms than women who were given "sham" reflexology treatments. The difference in symptomatic relief persisted for two months after treatment.

For PMS or menstrual cramps, try these points:

- SP-1 (also known as Spleen-1 in acupuncture parlance) is located at the great toe, along the midline portion of the nail bed. This point helps relieve spasms in the uterus.
- SP-6 is located behind the tibia (shin bone) approximately four finger widths above the inner portion of the ankle. It may help to normalize menstrual flow and promote relaxation. Avoid this point if you may be pregnant.
- LI-4 (Large Intestine 4) is in the space between the thumb and second finger. It relieves uterine spasms. Avoid this point if you may be pregnant.

### Contrast baths

Contrast baths relax cramps and spasms by quieting down uterine contractions. Alternate a five-minute warm-water bath (choose your own temperature comfort level) with a one-minute cold bath. To the warm water, add five drops of a fragrant essential oil such as mandarin tangerine (*Citrus reticulata*), which has a refreshing scent. Or try camomile, which is gentle, antiseptic, and relaxing. You can repeat this process four times.

*Warm heat towel*

Applying moist, warm heat to your belly and pelvis is a particularly soothing way to tame the spasms and contractions caused by your period. Take a thick towel and drench it in hot water. Wait for it to cool down, and then wring it dry and apply it. If you prefer the convenience of a pre-packaged, portable hot towel, you can buy a therapeutic heat wrap product called Thermacare, which uses air-activated heat discs that give off a low-level, penetrating heat lasting eight hours.

## Mind/Body

*Guided imagery and relaxation therapy*

In a study published in the *Journal of Holistic Nursing*, researchers found that, when used for six months, progressive muscle relaxation followed by guided imagery lengthened and regulated women's menstrual cycles and diminished premenstrual distress. Other studies have also demonstrated the value of deep breathing and progressive relaxation (see page 340 for instructions).

## Exercise

A considerable amount of evidence shows that regular exercise—specifically, aerobic exercise such as running, brisk walking, biking, or swimming—decreases depression. Studies dealing specifically with PMS confirm this and also show that aerobic exercise reduces fluid retention and breast tenderness. In addition, it may minimize cramping by relaxing muscles and by bringing better blood circulation and more oxygen to your pelvis. Your baseline should be at least thirty to forty-five minutes of aerobic exercise three times a week; aim to exercise daily during your period.

## Seeking Help from Complementary Practitioners

*Massage*

One recently published study of twenty-four women with diagnosed PMS compared the effects of massage and relaxation therapy. Women in the massage group had less anxiety, depression, and pain. And in the long term, massage reduced water retention, pain, and overall PMS distress.

### Red Flags

Check in with your doctor if you experience:

- Excessive bleeding
- Abdominal cramping associated with excessive discomfort
- Fever or chills
- Vaginal discharge
- Urinary frequency
- Bowel changes
- Pain during or after intercourse

## DYSMENORRHEA (CRAMPS)

### Description

If you get cramps with your period, you're not alone. At least half of menstruating women have dysmenorrhea, the medical term for menstrual cramps. There are two types. Primary dysmenorrhea, with its crampy abdominal pains, typically appears in adolescence and can be severe enough to affect your quality of life; it's a major cause of work and school absenteeism. In contrast, secondary dysmenorrhea occurs as a result of endometriosis or some other cause, and starts later in life.

### Causes

During your period, your uterus normally has painless, rhythmic contractions. If you have dysmenorrhea, however, an excess of a certain type of prostaglandin (hormonelike substances found throughout the body) causes these contractions to become longer and tighter. This results in ischemia, or decreased oxygen going to the uterine muscles, and that causes pain.

### Conventional Treatments

Since uterine prostaglandins are thought to play a role in its contractions, prostaglandin inhibitors are a logical means for decreasing cramps. The NSAIDS fill this role. Although they are expensive, the Cox-2 inhibitor-type nonsteroidals are an especially safe choice because they have fewer effects on the stomach lining, so they reduce the risk of bleeding complications.

## Dietary Strategies (See Chapter 14 for food sources of specified nutrients)

- Some studies have found niacin (a B vitamin) to be helpful in relieving menstrual cramps.
- Fish oil and vitamin B12 reduce menstrual cramps. In a study published in 2000, Danish researchers gave four groups of women five capsules a day of fish oil, fish oil with vitamin B12, seal oil, or a placebo. The women were followed for three menstrual cycles. The results? Compared with the placebo group, the group receiving fish oil had less menstrual pain. And the women who took fish oil with B12 had the best results—substantial relief from pain and discomfort.
- Vitamin C is a powerful antioxidant. It decreases lethargy and fatigue and improves the supply of blood to your uterine muscles.
- Be especially careful to avoid foods to which you're allergic; food allergies can contribute to water retention, gas, and bloating, which may intensify your cramps.
- Eat enough fruits, vegetables, and other fiber to maintain regular bowel habits, which can also ease dysmenorrhea.
- Eat raspberries to crimp cramps.

## Supplements

### Fish oils
So significant were the results in the Danish study described above that the researchers concluded that supplements of fish oil and B12 may serve as an alternative to NSAIDS in treating dysmenorrhea. Although I believe your best bet is eating fish three times a week, you can take fish oil supplements along with vitamin B12 daily.

### Calcium
Calcium helps muscle tone, which can reduce cramping. In addition, low calcium intake may contribute to water retention and increased menstrual pain. The acceptable dose range is 1,300 to 2,500 mg a day.

### Vitamin E
Vitamin E can help treat menstrual cramps. It can also cut back on breast symptoms. The acceptable dose range is 15 to 1,000 mg a day.

*Vitamin C*
An antioxidant, vitamin C improves blood flow, nourishes the uterine muscles, and relieves fatigue. The acceptable dose range is 90 to 2,000 mg a day.

*Iron*
Iron helps enhance the oxygen-carrying ability of your blood. The recommended dose range for premenopausal women is 18 to 45 mg a day.

*Vitamin B complex*
This is a group of many different vitamins. They play a role in glucose and amino acid metabolism, cell division, and many other biochemical processes. Both B6 (pyridoxine) and B3 (niacin) may be helpful for cramps. Human needs for members of the B complex vary considerably. The best way to make sure you're getting the right amounts is to take a multiple vitamin/mineral product containing the B complex. If you have liver disease, check with your physician before taking a supplement containing niacin.

*Magnesium*
This mineral works synergistically with calcium, helping to regulate neuromuscular tone. The accepted dose range is 320 to 350 mg a day.

**Herbs**

*Red raspberry* (Rubus idaeus)
Red raspberry leaf can relieve menstrual cramps. Herbalists suggest trying this as a tea, brewed using half a teaspoon of herb for each cup of water, once or twice a day.

*Black cohosh* (Cimicifuga racemosa)
Although this herb can be taken daily to prevent PMS, it is also useful for relieving cramps. The doses of this herb are not standardized, but the German Commission E recommends taking an alcohol extract of 40 percent. This corresponds to 40 mg a day.

*Valerian* (Valeriana officinalis)
Used mostly as a sedative, this herb also reduces muscular contractions. To make an infusion add 2 or 3 grams of herb to 150 ml of hot water and

steep for 10 to 15 minutes. Strain before use. The recommended dose is one cup before bedtime.

## Do-It-Yourself

*Contrast baths (See page 50)*

*Massage*
You'll need a friend or partner to help you with this simple abdominal pain reliever. Lie on your back, flat on the floor. Your partner should kneel by your head, sliding his hands under your back so they meet at your spine; then, pull them out toward your hips. Next, he should firmly pull his hands over your waist and gently draw them back to their starting position. Repeat. Your partner now puts his hands on your belly and circles them in a clockwise direction. Repeat this action, using the fingers to go deeper as long as this isn't painful. Finally, the partner puts his hands over your navel; he should relax and send calming thoughts through his arms and hands into your body.

*Aromatherapy*
Use essential oils made from lavender, jasmine, or rose in your massage oil, your bath, or in a diffuser.

*TENS (transcutaneous electrical nerve stimulator)*
TENS—applying brief pulses of electricity to nerve endings under the skin—is a relatively new pain treatment. Although this is a conventional treatment, often performed in a physician's or physical therapist's office, you can buy home units. A Swedish study published in the *American Journal of Obstetrics and Gynecology* showed that treatment with TENS reduced pain and did not increase cramps.

*Reflexology (See page 50)*

*Posture*
Good posture may reduce your tendency to have menstrual cramps.

*IUDs*
Menstrual cramps can be worse if you use an IUD for contraception. You may want to consider an alternate method of birth control.

## Mind/Body

*Biofeedback (See page 341 for technique)*
You can effectively use mind-body techniques such as biofeedback to influence subconscious (autonomic) processes. There are even computer programs and electronic devices you can buy to perform biofeedback in your own home.

*Yoga (See pages 344–351 for postures)*
The Locust Pose helps relieve pain.

## Exercise

*Aerobic exercise*
Women who get regular aerobic exercise, including brisk walking, biking, running, or swimming, have reduced menstrual pain. Exercise improves blood flow to the uterus and strengthens pelvic muscles. It promotes the release of endorphins, which are natural painkillers, and also provides immeasurable psychological benefits (the "runner's high"). Aim for thirty to forty-five minutes of aerobic exercise three to five times a week.

*Other exercises*
Some exercises can be done around the house without special equipment. My patients find that these are energizing and bring about relaxation.

EXERCISE 1
Stand with your legs 2 feet apart and your feet directed out. Gradually bend your knees and lower your bottom until your buttocks are as low as your knees. Cycle up and down about 15 times. You may also swing your pelvis forward and backward in a regular fashion. (*Note*: Avoid this if you have knee problems.)

EXERCISE 2
Stand in an upright position. Lift one knee up and, at the same time, bend both arms up and outward. Lower your foot to the floor and bring the other knee up while bending your arms up and out again. Repeat this sequence 10 to 12 times.

EXERCISE 3

Increase the blood flow to your pelvis with this simple exercise, which involves circling your hips: Stand with your feet about hip width apart. With hands on your hips, circle your hips 5 times in one direction; then reverse. Repeat.

## Seeking Help from Complementary Practitioners

*Acupuncture*

A study published in 1987 by the world-famous acupuncturist-physician Joseph Helms compared four groups of women who received, respectively, acupuncture, sham acupuncture, extra office visits, or no intervention. Ninety-one percent of the women who got acupuncture cut their monthly pain by half, while only 36 percent of the women in the control groups improved. In addition, the women in the acupuncture group used 41 percent less painkilling medication in the nine months following treatment.

Also, the consensus panel of the NIH has found acupuncture to be effective in the treatment of menstrual cramps and PMS.

## Red Flags

- Excessive bleeding
- Abdominal cramping associated with excessive discomfort
- Fever or chills
- Vaginal discharge
- Urinary frequency
- Bowel changes
- Pain during or after intercourse

# BREAST PAIN (MASTODYNIA OR MASTALGIA)

## Description

In 1829, Sir Ashley Cooper attributed mastodynia to psychological factors, claiming that breast pain occurred in nervous and irritable women. Today we know differently. I have many active, healthy women patients who come to see me for sports injuries. After examining their ankles, knees, or whatever has brought them in, I usually ask, "Does it hurt anywhere else when you exercise?" And many of them mention that they have sore, tender breasts, particularly around the time of their periods.

## Causes

There are three types of breast pain: cyclic, noncyclic, and nonbreast in origin. Cyclic breast pain, which is what we deal with in this chapter, is the most common, affecting as many as 67 percent of women. Sir Cooper notwithstanding, it is hormonal changes that cause cyclic breast pain. The pain fluctuates with the menstrual cycle and it affects both breasts. Typically, your breasts worsen during the luteal phase of your cycle, and the pain and soreness reach their peak as your period begins.

Noncyclic mastodynia affects only one in ten women. It bears no relationship to the menstrual cycle; the drawing, burning, achy, or throbbing pain may be constant throughout the month or intermittent with periodic exacerbations.

Mastodynia that is nonbreast in origin has several causes. Costochondritis is diffuse, localized, noncyclic pain in the mid-chest that may radiate to the underarm or back. Deep pressure on the area usually makes the pain worse. We usually treat it with lidocaine injections. Other reasons for noncyclic breast pain include cervical radiculopathy, or compression of a nerve root, angina, rib fracture, gallbladder or peptic ulcer disease.

## Signs and Symptoms

- Nodularity (lumpiness) of both breasts
- Diffuse tenderness or heaviness
- Soreness
- Fluctuating severity
- Pain may radiate to underarm, arm, or elbow

## Conventional Treatments

A wide range of OTC and prescription drugs are used to treat cyclic breast pain. Besides diuretics, there are a variety of hormone treatments, including oral contraceptives, hormone replacement therapy, progesterone and thyroid hormones, tamoxifen, and gonadotrophin-releasing hormone agonists. Your doctor might also prescribe bromocriptine, which treats excessive levels of prolactin, a pituitary hormone that can cause breast pain. Because of its severe side effects, danazol, a synthetic male hormone available only by prescription, is used only in severe cases.

## Dietary Strategies (See Chapter 14 for food sources of specified nutrients)

- Eliminate caffeine, which can make your symptoms worse.
- Vitamins E, A, and B6 may help reduce the pain.
- There is some evidence that reducing dietary fat decreases breast swelling, pain, and lumpiness.

R E C I P E

### DUTCH COLLARD GREENS WITH CREAMY MASHED POTATOES

Collard greens, like other members of the cruciferous family of vegetables, are rich in the protective phytochemicals indoles and glucosinolates. In addition to their anticancer benefits, these compounds suppress free radical formation, so they are useful for joint pain and inflammation. Collards are also rich in beta-carotene, vitamin E, zinc, calcium, manganese, and iron.

*2 pounds new potatoes*
*2 tablespoons Spectrum Spread*
*1 cup fortified soy milk*
*1 tablespoon olive oil*
*1 sweet onion, chopped*
*4 cloves garlic, chopped*
*1 pound collard greens, coarsely chopped*
*3 green onions, chopped*
*½ teaspoon pepper*

1. Wash the new potatoes and trim off imperfections, leaving the skins on. Cut the potatoes in half and boil them in a pot of salted boiling water until they are cooked through. Drain out the water.
2. Mash the potatoes and add the Spectrum Spread and soy milk as you are mashing. Cover the mashed potatoes and set them aside.
3. Heat the olive oil in a skillet over medium-high heat, and sauté the sweet onion and garlic for one minute.
4. Add the collard greens, green onions, and sprinkle in the pepper. Sauté for 2 to 3 more minutes.
5. Stir the collards mixture into the potatoes and serve immediately.

SERVES 4

## Supplements

### Vitamin A

We think this vitamin alters progesterone levels. High doses of vitamin A can be toxic. The acceptable dose range is 900 to 3,000 mcg a day.

### Vitamin B6

B6 may enhance the release of important neurotransmitters, including serotonin, dopamine, and norepinephrine, which in turn may affect other chemical messengers that cause fluid retention and breast pain. It may also reduce the effects of estrogen. Recommended dose range is 2 to 100 mg a day. Excessive B6 can cause neurological problems in some people.

### Vitamin E

Helps prevent breast tenderness. Recommended dose range is 15 to 1,000 mg a day.

## Herbs

### Evening primrose oil (EPO) (Oenothera biennis)

This treatment is good because it has few side effects yet is very effective. EPO contains a large amount of polyunsaturated essential fatty acids and is considered an effective anti-inflammatory. In a 1985 study, women taking EPO supplements for three to six months experienced a significant decrease in cyclical breast pain. The recommended dose is 3 grams daily.

## Do-It-Yourself

### Bras

There's good evidence that one of the best things you can do for yourself is to buy a well-fitting support bra. In one study, a hundred women with breast pain were professionally fitted for bras; 75 percent of them had complete relief from pain.

## Red Flags

Breast pain is not usually a sign of breast cancer, but don't make assumptions. Any pain, bumps, or lumps in your breast should be evaluated by your health care provider. In addition, be sure to practice monthly breast self-examination, have an annual examination by a physician, and a regularly scheduled mammogram.

# FIBROCYSTIC BREAST DISEASE (FBD)

## Description

This condition is a catch-all description of several different benign conditions of the breast that are common in younger women. Fibrocystic changes are the most frequent cause of breast lumps in women between the ages of thirty and fifty; approximately 60 percent of childbearing-age women have lumpy breasts as a result of fibrocystic breast disease. However, if you are menopausal, FBD is unlikely to occur if you are not taking hormone replacement therapy.

Although FBD is not usually serious, it can be painful, and it is a frequent cause of cyclic breast pain. The pain can be so bothersome that it prevents exercising or other activities.

If you have FBD, you've probably noticed that your breasts become painful, tender, and lumpy before your period. The condition clears up once your period begins, only to return the following month.

You must take great caution to differentiate FBD from other causes of breast lumps. If you have a breast lump, be sure to have it evaluated very carefully by a qualified health care practitioner and ultrasound, mammogram, or other appropriate diagnostic testing to be sure it is not malignant.

## Causes

Your breasts respond to monthly changes in estrogen and progesterone levels by alternately swelling and shrinking. Hormonal stimulation causes the milk glands and related ducts to engorge and other breast tissue to retain water. Your breasts become swollen, lumpy, and painful. After your period, the swelling decreases. As this process repeats every month, your breasts may become firm and pockets of fluid may accumulate in enlarged, obstructed milk ducts and neighboring tissue. After a while, your breasts may contain many irregularly shaped areas of tissue that feel beady in consistency.

## Signs and Symptoms

- Breast pain
- Tenderness
- One or more breast lumps
- Breast swelling

## Conventional Treatments

Your doctor may suggest that you try cold compresses on your breasts. You may also be offered aspirin or other OTC pain relievers, prostaglandin inhibitors, or diuretics to reduce fluid retention. If you have severe FBD, your doctor may suggest a trial of danazol, a synthetic male hormone available only by prescription. Most of these drugs have side effects. For example, diuretics rob the body of potassium and the painkillers called nonsteroidal anti-inflammatory drugs (NSAIDS) can cause stomach and gastrointestinal problems.

## Dietary Strategies

- Although there is some controversy in the literature about the effects of caffeine, it's wise to avoid excessive, long-term use of caffeinated beverages. Caffeine, known chemically as a methylxanthine, has been linked in some studies to a woman's risk of developing FBD.
- Avoid meat and full-fat dairy products. We think the saturated fat in these foods has an adverse effect on the body's estrogen levels, worsening breast symptoms. Instead, try to eat tofu, nonfat dairy products, and fish.
- Eat foods from the sea, such as seafood, kelp, and sea vegetables, to be sure you're getting enough iodine. Some research has shown that this trace element helps alleviate fibrocystic breast disease.

## Supplements

### Vitamin A
Vitamin A may alter progesterone levels. In addition, it helps cells reproduce, maintains healthy cell membranes, and enhances the body's use of iron. High doses of this vitamin, however, can be toxic; the acceptable dose range is 900 to 3,000 mcg a day.

### Vitamin B6
B6 is thought to be the "maestro" vitamin for the metabolism of amino acids, important building blocks for neurotransmitters, including serotonin, dopamine, and norepinephrine, which in turn may affect other chemical messengers that cause fluid retention and breast pain. It may also reduce the effects of estrogen. The recommended dose is 2 to 100 mg a day, either separately or as part of a B-complex vitamin. Excessive B6 can cause neurological problems in some people.

*Vitamin E*
Vitamin E is a potent antioxidant that plays a role in building immunity and preventing infection. It may also have a protective effect on the breast and nipples, and helps prevent breast tenderness. It works together with selenium. The acceptable dose range is 15 to 1,000 mg a day.

*Iodine*
This trace element is necessary for maintaining normal breast tissue and may help relieve FBD. In one study, the authors speculate that iodine has an effect on breast cells, making them less susceptible to circulating estrogens. Although you can take it as a supplement, I suggest you take it as part of a multivitamin. Even better, you can get it through dietary sources, such as fish, kelp, dairy, and sea vegetables (dulse and nori). Excessive consumption of iodine can adversely affect your thyroid function, so use caution. The acceptable dose range is 150 to 1,100 mcg a day. Remember, iodine deficiency is rare since the introduction of iodized salt.

*Selenium*
This mineral, found in Brazil nuts, helps activate an antioxidant enzyme called glutathione peroxidase, which protects against cancer and is important for immune function. As an antioxidant, selenium enhances vitamin E and can help nourish breast tissue. Dose range is 60 to 400 mcg a day.

**Herbs**

*Evening primrose oil (EPO)* (Oenothera biennis)
Double-blind research has shown that daily use of evening primrose oil reduces breast pain and inflammation. Recommended dose is 3 grams daily.

*Chaste tree* (Vitex agnus-castus)
In a study published in April 2000, *Vitex* was found to reduce breast pain after three months. Suggested daily dose is 30 to 40 mg in an aqueous-alcohol extract. Do not use chaste tree if you may be pregnant or if you are nursing.

*Black cohosh* (Cimicifuga racemosa)
This herb is thought to work by binding to estrogen receptors, which balances hormones. Although the doses of this herb are not standardized, the German Commission E recommends taking an alcohol extract of 40 percent. This corresponds to 40 mg a day.

## Exercise

You can reduce breast pain by exercising regularly throughout the month. In a study published in 1987, women who ran forty-five miles per menstrual cycle (or a little more than ten miles per week) had less breast tenderness and relief of other symptoms. Because exercise releases endorphins, it also provides natural pain relief when you have symptoms. My recommendation is thirty to forty-five minutes of aerobic exercise, three to five times a week.

## Do-It-Yourself

### Chest wall and breast massage

The pain and soreness of fibrocystic breast disease often cause a great deal of neighboring "referred" pain in the chest wall area. To decrease pain, improve soreness, and alleviate tension, try this massage: Firmly plant your thumb and fingers on the pectoral muscle (the main chest wall muscle above and to the side of your breast). Using a kneading motion, caress the muscle in an upward and outward direction, toward the shoulder. You can use the same technique on the muscles between the ribs.

### Bras

Be sure to wear comfortable, well-fitted bras. One controversial school of thought holds that women who discontinue use of constrictive bras and go "bra free" have a reduced incidence of fibrocystic breast disease and other breast ailments. The theory is that the bra's constrictive effect on the breast restricts blood and lymphatic flow, causing stagnation. I haven't found good research to support this theory. On the other hand, there is some evidence that a well-fitted supportive bra can reduce breast pain.

## Mammogram Pain

When it comes to medical procedures, mammograms are the quintessential "necessary evil." Although they know it's a potentially life-saving procedure, most of my women patients dread their appointments and anticipate them with trepidation, if not downright anxiety. It's not unusual to experience discomfort during a mammogram, but some women find it to be quite painful. If you are particularly sensitive, try these tips before your next mammogram:

- Schedule your exam at the time in your menstrual cycle when your breasts are the least tender. This is usually during the first two weeks of your cycle, but you know best. (According to some research, if you are premenopausal, a mammogram during this time may also be more accurate.)

- Reduce and, if possible, eliminate caffeine for a week before the exam.
- Taking vitamin E for a few weeks before your appointment may also help. The acceptable daily dose range is 15 to 1,000 mg.
- To reduce fluid retention, avoid salty foods for a few days before the procedure.
- Take an over-the-counter pain reliever about an hour before you go. Take more after the procedure, if necessary.
- Be sure to tell the technician if you're in pain. She may be able to make some adjustments to increase your comfort.

## CHRONIC PELVIC PAIN

### Description

Chronic pelvic pain is continuous or intermittent pain that has lasted for at least six months. It is usually severe enough to affect your daily functioning, social relationships, work, and family. The pain may fluctuate with your monthly menstrual cycle.

Pelvic pain affects one in seven women. It accounts for 10 to 20 percent of office visits to gynecologists, and 20 percent of all laparoscopies. (A laparoscopy is a surgical procedure, requiring anesthesia, that can cause uncomfortable pressure or pain for a few days afterward.) There are many possible causes, including endometriosis, pelvic inflammatory disease and other infections, ovarian cysts, fibroid tumors, ulcerative colitis, irritable bowel syndrome, spasms of the pelvic floor muscles, urethritis or other urinary tract infections, constipation, strains, and trauma. Dyspareunia (painful sex) is also sometimes associated with pelvic pain. Unfortunately, in many women with chronic pelvic pain, no identifiable organic cause can be found, even after laparoscopy.

Close communication with your gynecologist is essential if you have pelvic pain. To get a proper diagnosis, you need a thorough physical exam and history. In addition, you may have lab cultures, ultrasound, abdominal X rays, computerized tomography (CT) scans, magnetic resonance imaging (MRI) or other imaging studies, and laparoscopy. (However, bear in mind that some research shows that laparoscopy is of little value in treating endometriosis, and that attention to organic, psychological, dietary, environmental, and other factors is of more value.) Once your gynecologist has determined your diagnosis, she may send you to a physiatrist for focused pain management help.

In the following section I focus on endometriosis, a frequent cause of pelvic pain. You can effectively deal with its painful symptoms using a balanced therapeutic approach. However, do not use complementary treatments as a substitute for gynecological care.

## ENDOMETRIOSIS

### Description

This disease affects between 10 and 15 percent of menstruating women between the ages of twenty-four and forty. What happens is that tissues usually found in the lining of the uterus (the endometrium) grow in other parts of the body. Although these growths are most commonly found in the ovaries or elsewhere in the pelvic area, they may also occur on the bladder, in the intestines, the lungs, or in more distant places in the body. Like your uterine lining, the growths may respond to hormonal fluctuations of your menstrual cycle, building up tissue and breaking down every month. They can cause internal bleeding, cysts, the formation of scar tissue, and severe pain.

### Causes

We don't yet know the cause of endometriosis. The most popular theory, yet to be proven, involves "renegade" cells from the uterine lining. It's thought that these cells spill into the abdominal cavity when menstrual blood backs up in the fallopian tubes, which connect the ovaries and the uterus. Although this may occur in all women, those with an immune or hormonal problem may develop endometriosis.

### Signs and Symptoms

Common symptoms of endometriosis include:

- Severe pelvic pain, especially before and during periods or during sex
- Painful urination or bowel movements during periods
- Fatigue
- Diarrhea, constipation, nausea, or other gastrointestinal problems during periods

Endometriosis can also cause long-term problems, such as infertility or bowel problems.

## Conventional Treatments

Over-the-counter pain relievers, such as aspirin, Tylenol, or the NSAIDS may help, or, if you are in severe pain, your doctor may prescribe pain medications. There are also a variety of hormonal treatments used to suppress ovulation, including oral contraceptives or Depo-Provera injections; danazol, a testosterone derivative; or medications called GhRH agonists (gonadotropin-releasing hormone drugs).

With or without hormonal therapy, your doctor may suggest surgery to remove or destroy the growths, relieve pain, and/or try to restore fertility. The options range from the conservative — laser ablation of growths — to the radical — hysterectomy, including removal of your ovaries.

## Dietary Strategies (See Chapter 14 for food sources of specified nutrients)

- The liver detoxifies hormones, so it's important to keep this organ happy. Liver-friendly foods include carrots and vegetables in the cabbage family (kale, brussels sprouts, cauliflower, broccoli), beets, artichokes, lemons, and dandelion greens.
- Cut back on caffeine; it's associated with an increased risk for endometriosis.
- Limit your alcohol consumption; it stresses the liver.
- Spice up your meals with ginger and turmeric. The former helps fight inflammation and aids liver detoxification; the latter decreases inflammation and increases bile secretion.
- Make sure you get plenty of dietary fiber, which speeds food through the intestines and contributes to regular bowel movements.
- Reduce your intake of animal protein, especially red meat, which promotes inflammatory prostaglandins (i.e., inflammation and pain). On the other hand, a diet rich in vegetables, soy, nuts, and salmon increases the production of anti-inflammatory prostaglandins.
- Beta-carotene helps enhance immunity and may be protective against early stages of tumor growth.

### RECIPES

## SWEET POTATO SUPREME

Try this delicious side dish, rich in beta-carotene.

> 4 sweet potatoes, baked and peeled
> 2 tablespoons olive oil
> 2 cloves garlic, minced
> 1 red onion, chopped or sliced thinly
> ¼ cup sesame seeds
> ¼ cup pumpkin seeds

1. Cut sweet potatoes into one-inch slices.
2. In a saucepan, add oil and sauté remaining ingredients for 5 minutes, until golden brown.
3. Combine the sweet potatoes and the mixture from the saucepan in a bowl. Serve warm.

SERVES 4

## VEGETABLE RICE MEDLEY

This healthy dish features ginger and turmeric.

> 2 tablespoons olive oil
> 1 onion, diced
> 4 cloves garlic, minced
> 2 tablespoons fresh parsley, finely chopped
> 1 cup raw cashew nuts
> 2 carrots, sliced
> 1 tablespoon low-sodium soy sauce
> 2 zucchinis, cut into thick slices
> 1 cup cauliflower florets
> 1 green pepper, sliced
> 2 teaspoons freshly grated ginger
> 2 teaspoons turmeric
> 1 teaspoon coriander
> 2½ cups plus 2 tablespoons water
> 1¼ cups short-grain brown rice

1. Heat the olive oil in a large saucepan. Add the onion, garlic, parsley, nuts, and carrots. Stir over medium-high heat for 1 minute.
2. Stir in the soy sauce and rest of the vegetables and spices. Pour in the water and bring almost to boiling.
3. Stir in the rice, mix well, cover the pot and reduce heat. Simmer over a low flame for 40 to 45 minutes.

SERVES 6

## Supplements

### Vitamin C
This vitamin enhances your immune system and reduces fatigue. The accepted range is 90 to 2,000 mg a day. Cut back if you get diarrhea.

### Vitamin E
To help correct your estrogen/progesterone ratio, try taking between 15 and 1,000 mg a day.

### Essential fatty acids (EFA)
Both alpha-linolenic acid (found in flaxseed, canola, pumpkin seed, and walnut oil) and gamma-linoleic acid (in borage, black currant, and evening primrose oils) fight inflammation. Take 300 mg a day.

### B vitamins
To help your liver process estrogen, take 1 B-complex vitamin tablet daily.

### Selenium
This mineral is involved in the liver's detoxification processes. It also enhances immunity. Accepted dose range is between 60 and 400 mcg a day. Remember, too much causes toxicity.

## Herbs

### Chaste tree (Vitex agnus-castus)
This herb is showing great promise as a treatment for all sorts of ailments resulting from hormonal imbalances, although the scientific support specifically for endometriosis is lacking. The recommended dose is 30 to 40 mg daily in an aqueous-alcohol extract. Do not use chaste tree if you may be pregnant or if you are nursing.

## Do-It-Yourself

*Sitz baths*
To ease pain by increasing blood circulation and reducing pelvic congestion, add 2 ml of an essential oil—such as clary sage, rose, nutmeg, or geranium—to your bath. Use warm water.

## Mind/Body

*Relaxation and imagery*
Get into a relaxed state (see pages 340, 341). Visualize the inside of your uterus and other endometrial tissue shrinking. Continue to focus on this until you can imagine the painful tissues disappearing altogether. Do the exercise for fifteen to thirty minutes at least five days a week.

*Yoga (See pages 344–351 for postures)*
Try the modified Bridge Pose.

*Biofeedback*
Although biofeedback is often performed with sophisticated electronic equipment in the doctor's or therapist's office, there are many forms of biofeedback that you can do on your own. (See page 341.)

## Exercise

*Kegel exercises*
These exercises strengthen the muscles in the pelvis and pubic floor. They involve contracting and releasing the muscles that start and stop the flow of urine. Start by contracting the muscles for a second and then releasing completely; repeat ten times. Do this exercise five times a day. It is completely inconspicuous, so you can do it during meetings, as you ride the subway, talk on the telephone, or watch TV.

## Red Flags

If you develop fever, chills, bleeding, discharge, or persistent abdominal discomfort, call your doctor.

## MENOPAUSE

### Description

Menopause refers specifically to the cessation of the monthly menstrual cycle. According to the Massachusetts Women's Health Study, the median age for menopause is about fifty-one. However, hormonal and other changes leading to menopause take place gradually, over a period of years. During this transition, sometimes referred to as perimenopause, it's possible to start having troublesome menopausal symptoms as early as age thirty-five or forty, even while you're still getting regular periods.

### Causes

As you approach menopause, your menstrual cycle may become irregular. You may skip periods or find that they are more widely spaced. On the other hand, your cycle may shorten, so you have more frequent periods. You may bleed for a shorter or for a longer time, and your flow may become lighter or heavier. All of these changes result from a natural ending of ovarian activity. Your ovaries are producing less estrogen, and there is also a significant reduction in progesterone production. Your estrogen levels eventually drop so much that ovulation, uterine tissue buildup, and menstruation all stop. These hormonal changes don't just affect your period, they influence every part of your body and your mind. As the changes occur, you may experience a variety of painful, annoying symptoms.

### Signs and Symptoms

Few women experience all of these symptoms. You may, however, have at least a few:

- Hot flashes (flushing of face, neck, and/or trunk)
- Headaches
- Palpitations
- Dizziness
- Night sweats
- Cold hands and feet
- Painful sex associated with vaginal thinning and drying caused by loss of estrogen
- Vaginal pain and bleeding after intercourse

- Vaginal discomfort
- Dryness, pain, and itching of the vulva
- Urinary pain and burning due to urinary tract atrophy
- Insomnia
- Depression or anxiety
- Decreased memory
- Reduced cognition
- Reduced sex drive
- Facial hair
- Hair loss
- Acne
- Irregular bleeding
- Osteoporosis
- Heart disease

In addition, the dramatic drop in estrogen levels leads to a higher risk of osteoporosis and heart disease.

## Conventional Treatments

Your doctor may prescribe estrogen replacement therapy (ERT) or hormonal replacement therapy (HRT). There are a variety of approaches. Estrogen helps relieve hot flashes, decreases vaginal atrophy, and slows the bone loss and fractures of osteoporosis. It may also prevent heart disease, although recent research casts some doubt on that finding. And although it's too soon to say this conclusively, it may also prevent Alzheimer's disease. Estrogen is frequently taken in pill form as conjugated equine estrogens (Premarin). Estradiol, in patch or a gel, facilitates the passage of estrogen directly into the bloodstream. And vaginal creams, although they may take four to six weeks to have an impact, help relieve urinary and vaginal symptoms. But taking estrogen may raise your risk of uterine cancer, as well as blood clots. And some women experience new or increased migraines when they take estrogen.

To reduce estrogen's cancer risks, progesterone (or progestin) is usually included in the treatment; it's then called hormone replacement therapy. But HRT also has side effects, including headaches, nausea, vaginal discharge, fluid retention, swollen breasts, weight gain, and abnormal vaginal bleeding. And the jury is still out on the relationship of HRT and breast cancer risk.

To decrease spinal osteoporosis and increase libido, your doctor may prescribe methyltestosterone (the "male" hormone, testosterone). We don't yet know the long-term effects taking testosterone will have on women. If you're only concerned about osteoporosis, several new drugs, such as Alendronate, have a narrower focus.

## Dietary Strategies (See Chapter 14 for food sources of specified nutrients)

- Compounds called isoflavones found in soy foods may reduce menopausal symptoms. Because they are phytoestrogens, which have a chemical structure similar to estrogen, they provide weak estrogenic action. Soy isoflavones may relieve hot flashes and vaginal atrophy. In one recent study, researchers found that women eating 60 grams of soy protein had a 33 percent reduction in hot flashes after four weeks; this increased to a 45 percent reduction after twelve weeks. Aim for 25 to 50 mg of soy protein a day.
- Smoking, alcohol, caffeine, and spicy foods may increase hot flashes.
- Feed your bones with calcium-rich foods.
- Use alfalfa sprouts in your salad; this member of the pea family contains isoflavones with weak estrogenic effects.
- Eat foods rich in bioflavonoids, plant pigments that enhance absorption of vitamin C and reduce menopausal complaints.

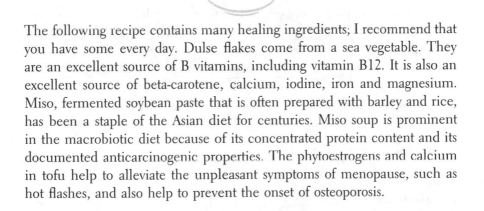

R E C I P E

The following recipe contains many healing ingredients; I recommend that you have some every day. Dulse flakes come from a sea vegetable. They are an excellent source of B vitamins, including vitamin B12. It is also an excellent source of beta-carotene, calcium, iodine, iron and magnesium. Miso, fermented soybean paste that is often prepared with barley and rice, has been a staple of the Asian diet for centuries. Miso soup is prominent in the macrobiotic diet because of its concentrated protein content and its documented anticarcinogenic properties. The phytoestrogens and calcium in tofu help to alleviate the unpleasant symptoms of menopause, such as hot flashes, and also help to prevent the onset of osteoporosis.

### HEALING MISO VEGETABLE SOUP

*1 tablespoon sesame oil*
*1 tablespoon low-sodium soy sauce*

1 onion
5 cloves garlic, minced
1 green pepper, chopped
2 cups fresh spinach, chopped
3 stalks bok choy, including leaves
10 cups water
1 leek
1 parsnip, chopped
½ cup scallions, chopped
½ cup chopped carrots
8 ounces firm silken tofu, cubed
1 tablespoon dulse flakes
½ cup barley
½ cup red or green lentils
1 teaspoon coriander
¼ teaspoon sea salt, or to taste
2 tablespoons sweet miso

1. In a large, heavy stockpot heat the oil and soy sauce over a medium-high flame and sauté the onion, garlic, green pepper, spinach, and bok choy for 2 minutes, stirring constantly. Add the water and heat to almost boiling.
2. Trim off and discard the bottom and green parts of the leek. Chop the leek and add to the pot. Stir in the rest of the ingredients, except the miso.
3. Cover the pot and simmer over a low flame for 1 hour.
4. Take the pot off the flame; remove lid, stir soup, and let cool for 10 minutes.
5. In a small bowl mash the miso with 2 tablespoons hot water and then stir well into the soup.
6. Serve immediately or freeze individual portions to heat daily (do not boil as this weakens the potency of the miso) and enjoy over the week.

SERVES 6 TO 8

## Supplements

### Vitamin E

Vitamin E helps prevent hot flashes and protects your heart. Recommended dose is between 15 and 1,000 mg a day. Check with your physician if you have high blood pressure.

*Vitamin C*
This powerful antioxidant may help prevent hot flashes. The accepted dose range is 90 to 2,000 mg a day.

*Calcium and magnesium*
The loss of these two minerals during and after menopause contributes to the development of osteoporosis. The accepted dose range for calcium is 1,300 to 2,500 mg a day; for magnesium it's 320 to 350 mg a day. If you're not taking estrogen, aim for the higher end of the range, for both calcium and magnesium.

*Flaxseed oil*
Rich in omega-3 fatty acids, this oil helps prevent inflammation and contributes to healthy vaginal tissue. Take one tablespoon a day.

*Rice bran oil containing gamma orzanol*
This dietary supplement may relieve hot flashes. Take 300 mg a day.

*Bioflavonoids*
These are plant pigments thought to have a weak estrogenic effect. Bioflavonoids can decrease hot flashes, reduce muscle cramping and bleeding, ease sore joints, improve vaginal lubrication. Take 500 mg a day; it's best when combined with vitamin C.

*Vitamin B6*
This vitamin enhances the release of important neurotransmitters, including serotonin, dopamine, and norepinephrine. The recommended range for this nutrient is 2 to 100 mg a day as part of a B-complex supplement.

## Herbs

*Chaste tree* (Vitex agnus-castus)
This herb is touted as helping to normalize your pituitary gland's production of hormones. It may take six months before you notice its effects. The daily dose is 30 to 40 mg in an aqueous-alcohol extract. Do not use chaste tree if you may be pregnant.

*Black cohosh* (Cimicifuga racemosa)
This herb, which decreases hot flashes, is available in a standardized tablet form under the name Remifemin. Several double-blind trials have shown it to be safe and effective. In addition, in a policy statement about herbal

remedies in May 2001, the American College of Obstetrics and Gynecology upheld the short-term value of black cohosh in menopausal women with vasomotor symptoms (sweating and hot flashes). The dose is 20 to 40 mg a day.

### Licorice (Glycyrrhiza glabra)

This herb balances estrogen. The recommended dose is 250 mg, or one cup of tea three times a day. Use caution if you have high blood pressure.

### Ginkgo (Ginkgo biloba)

To enhance memory and improve circulation to cold hands and feet, the recommended dose is 120 mg two to three times a day.

### Sage (Salvia officinalis)

If hot flashes are getting you down, and particularly if you sweat a great deal, try a tea made by steeping 2 to 3 teaspoons of this herb in water for fifteen minutes. Drink 2 cups a day.

### Evening primrose oil (EPO) (Oenothera biennis)

EPO reduces inflammation, helps alleviate hot flashes, and curbs breast pain. The recommended dose is 1,500 to 3,000 mg a day.

## Homeopathy

A German homeopathic "cocktail" called Mulimen effectively reduces hot flashes. It contains chaste tree, St. John's wort, and black cohosh. It should be available in your local pharmacy or health food store. Otherwise, you can buy it on-line. Follow package directions.

## Do-It-Yourself

### Reflexology

- SP-6 is located behind the tibia (shin bone), approximately four finger widths above the inner part of the ankle. It helps normalize menstrual flow and promotes relaxation.
- SP-9 is situated in the hollow right below the top (head) of the tibia. It also helps normalize menstrual flow.

## Exercise

*Kegel exercises (See page 70)*
Done regularly, these exercises strengthen muscle tone and prevent uterine and bladder prolapse and incontinence.

*Regular exercise*
Swimming, running, or brisk walking (preferably outdoors in the fresh air) triggers the release of endorphins, natural chemicals that help to diminish pain and improve your perception of well-being. In addition, regular aerobic exercise helps keep your weight under control and lowers your risk of heart disease, osteoporosis, and bone fractures. It also provides specific benefits for menopausal women. Besides alleviating pain, depression, and anxiety, a study of nine hundred Swedish women suffering from menopausal symptoms found that thirty minutes of daily aerobic exercise cut back their hot flashes significantly.

Exercise at least thirty to forty-five minutes at least three times a week. Work hard enough to achieve a 70 percent target heart rate.

*Lift weights*
Strength training (weight lifting) stresses and strengthens the muscles, which begin to atrophy as you age. It also stimulates bone growth. What's more, strength or resistance training helps you keep your weight from creeping up. The reason? Muscle takes more calories to sustain than fat tissue, so as you build muscle mass you burn more calories all day long, even when you're resting.

## Mind/Body

*Yoga*
Menopause may sometimes leave you feeling drained, zapped of energy, and depressed. Yoga is the perfect exercise for you since it improves your endurance and enhances your mood. While the postures increase joint mobility and ease symptoms like hot flashes, yoga breathing and meditation quiet your nerves and ease irritability. I suggest that you try Bow Pose, the Locust, Alternating Leg Lifts, Head to Knee Pose, and Standing Forward Bend (see pages 344–351). Perform these stretching exercises slowly so you can maintain control over your body movements. And don't hold your breath!

### Seeking Help from Complementary Practitioners

*Massage*
Getting a massage helps you relax, relieving irritability, tension, and depression. It also improves circulation, which can be especially helpful if you suffer from cold hands and feet. Use a vitamin E oil to relieve dry skin and vaginal atrophy.

*Acupuncture*
Besides increasing the body's production of endorphins, acupuncture may help balance hormones and relieve flushing and temperature changes.

### Red Flags

Call your doctor if you have persistent hot flashes or a lot of pain. And remember, once the menstrual cycle stops, it stops. If you experience any bleeding six months or more following menopause, contact your doctor.

## PREGNANCY

Pregnancy, in and of itself, is not typically painful. But a number of uncomfortable and sometimes painful ailments can occur.

### Back Pain During Pregnancy

When you are pregnant, your body releases many different hormones, including relaxin. This causes slackness of some of the spinal ligaments, the pubic symphysis (the slightly movable joint at the front of the pelvis), and the sacroiliac joint. Besides, as the pregnancy progresses, your center of gravity shifts and the growing fetus puts a heavy burden on your back. For these reasons, low back pain is a common complaint during this time. For information on treating low back pain during pregnancy, see Chapter 6.

## LABOR AND CHILDBIRTH

### Description

One of my favorite jokes, attributed to Maurice Chevalier, is this:

WOMAN TO MAN: What is the difference between a man and a woman?
MAN TO WOMAN: Madam, I can't conceive!

Unfortunately, the pain of childbirth is no joke. Of all the pains of womanhood, those associated with labor and giving birth are the most vicious. Since biblical times, childbirth has been recognized as a major cause of pain and modern studies confirm this view. Yet contemporary medicine, despite all of its accomplishments, has not identified the optimal treatment for this pain. Controversies rage about the use of pain medications, anesthetics, and other modern treatments and technologies. I feel that the best treatment is a combination of traditional medical interventions, balanced with complementary medicine. For example, the sound of gentle music in the background or the tender caress of a spouse massaging your back can go a long way.

## Causes

During labor, the muscles of the uterus, stimulated by the hormone oxytocin, stretch the cervix, or uterine opening. The cervix gradually widens enough for the baby to emerge. At the same time, uterine contractions push the baby out of the uterus and into the vagina, allowing it to be born.

Physiology and anatomy, the size and position of the fetus, and the nature and frequency of the contractions determine how painful this process will be. But cultural beliefs and customs as well as anxiety and other psychological factors have an enormous impact on pain.

## Signs and Symptoms

*Bloody show*
The small plug that seals the cervix during pregnancy may come out as the cervix begins to open. It looks like pink or blood-tinged mucus.

*Ruptured membranes/waters breaking*
This is a sign that the baby's head is pressing against the amniotic sac. The "water," or amniotic fluid, may come out in a rush or a trickle.

*Contractions*
These pains may feel like menstrual cramps, a backache, or gas. As labor progresses, they become longer and more rhythmic; they also occur more frequently.

## Conventional Treatments

Tranquilizers, barbiturates, or narcotic medications in oral, intramuscular, or intravenous form are often utilized during the birthing process. Like most medication, their use may be associated with nasty side effects. These include nausea, lethargy, drops in blood pressure, slowed contractions or respiration, moodiness and hangover for you, and slowed respiration for your baby. Besides, the effects are often short-lived. For example, many women have said that Demerol, a commonly used narcotic, didn't ease their pain much during labor and made them feel disoriented.

You can also get relief in the latter stages of labor from an epidural block, but this form of anesthesia has limitations. It is highly dependent on the skill of the person performing the procedure. In addition, it is costly and fraught with complications, technical limitations, and risks.

You can use complementary remedies instead of conventional strategies or in addition to them. By doing so, you may decrease or eliminate your need for medications. In addition, you may be able to avoid an epidural or forestall it until it matters most, when your labor is very active.

## Do-It-Yourself

Besides being soothing, these techniques are distracting because stimuli such as heat and cold compete with and diminish your awareness of pain.

### Superficial heat

Heat is calming and comforting. In addition, it lessens your body's fight-or-flight response to stress. During active labor, you can speed up contractions by applying heat to your abdomen over the upper uterine area. Local application of hot compresses to your perineum may be especially helpful during the second stage of labor.

As long as you are careful to avoid burning, using heat is perfectly safe. You can use hot-water bottles, heated silica packs, a warm blanket, heating pads, electric packs, warm baths or showers, or hot, moist towels or washcloths. Your pain threshold may be altered during labor so allow someone else to check the temperature before applying anything to your skin. And when using moist heat, be sure to use extra towels to protect against sudden temperature changes.

*Superficial cold*
The numbing effect of cold decreases pain sensation. It is particularly useful for musculoskeletal pain, so if you have back pain during labor, cold is in order.

Good methods for applying cold include ice bags, gel packs, or rubber gloves filled with ice. Always use some protection between your skin and the source of cold; what you want is a gradual increase from cool to cold. If you are chilled or shivering, do not make matters worse by using cold.

As soon as possible after giving birth, apply ice packs to your perineum to reduce swelling and relieve pain.

*Bath or Shower*
Hydrotherapy, or immersion therapy, is a comforting, age-old treatment. It lowers blood pressure, improves contraction efficiency, relieves pain, and helps you relax. So beneficial is this simple strategy that the British House of Commons Health Committee recommended that birthing pools be made available to women during childbirth.

During early labor, taking a bath may slow contractions, so it's best to wait until you start active labor. Consult your midwife or physician about when to take a bath, how long to stay in it, and the temperature of the water.

The effects of showers haven't been studied as thoroughly as baths, but a warm shower will help you relax and reduce your pain. Try directing the warm water over your abdomen or lower back. Go easy on yourself by sitting on a chair while you're in the shower.

*Keep moving*
If possible, take advantage of gravity by walking. If you are confined to a bed, changing your position frequently will help you stay comfortable and speed the progress of your labor.

*Massage*
If you clench your hands into fists during contractions, ask your partner to provide a soothing massage by kneading, stroking, and applying pressure and friction to your hands. Do the same with any other parts of your body that you tense during contractions. If you like, have your partner use a massage oil with a few drops of essential oil, such as lavender, clary sage, mandarin, or jasmine to enhance the effect and promote relaxation.

On the other hand, you may not want to be touched during labor. Obviously, there's no way to know this in advance, so you'll have to play it by ear.

*Counterpressure*

It's estimated that one-third of women suffer from terrible low back pain during labor. Narcotics and epidurals are not the only answer. Your simplest option is to have someone massage your lower back and buttocks. Bring a rolling pin with you to the hospital or buy a cold can of juice or soda while you're there. Your partner can roll it back and forth over your lower back during or between contractions.

Here are three other techniques your partner or a nurse can use during contractions. These were suggested by physical therapist Penny Simkin:

1. For the partner: Use your fist or the heel of your hand to apply steady pressure to painful spots on her back. At the same time, put your other hand in front, over her hip bone, to offset pressure on the back. Rest between contractions.

2. Sit in an upright chair with good low-back support. Your feet should be flat on the floor and your knees a few inches apart. Have your partner cup each of your knees with the heel of a hand and steadily lean toward you, pressing your knees back toward your hip joints.

3. If you can, get onto your hands and knees; if you can't, stand and lean forward. Have your partner place his hands over the meatiest part of your buttocks. He should then apply steady pressure with his palms, directing the force diagonally toward the center of your pelvis.

*Reflexology*

Stimulation of a variety of reflexology points can help control the pain of labor. Don't use these points before Week 38 of pregnancy, since they can induce premature labor.

- LI-4, located in the web between the thumb and first finger, helps to relieve spasm of the uterus.
- BL-60 (Bladder 60), located on the ankle's outside surface, helps quell back pain and can facilitate the baby's delivery.
- GB-21 (Gallbladder 21), found in the depression on top of the shoulders that is directly in line with the ears, helps speed the very last stages of labor and delivery of the afterbirth.

## Mind/Body

Fear and anxiety about pain, loss of control, or injury to yourself or your baby during labor are common. Being in the unfamiliar environment of a hospital doesn't help matters. Unfortunately, anxiety can magnify your perception of pain, so anything you do to promote relaxation will improve your labor. Try using these techniques between contractions.

## Relax

The pain and anxiety of labor can activate the fight-or-flight response, which increases muscle contractions and may intensify pain. Getting into a relaxed state lowers the heart and respiratory rates, decreases blood pressure, and reduces muscle tension. There are many ways to do it. Whatever you choose—belly breathing, progressive relaxation, or meditation—your goal is to get in to a neutral mental and physical state (see Chapter 18 for details).

## Imagery

Once you are relaxed, you can further distract yourself by concentrating on positive thoughts. Think about your other children, members of your family, or the new baby. Or focus on a calming, beautiful image—a favorite vacation spot or a pleasant memory.

## Autogenic training (See page 341)

## Music

Music has powerful effects on emotion and mood, stress, tension, and anxiety. In relation to childbearing, researchers have found that music reduces agitation, enhances relaxation and concentration on breathing patterns, and decreases pain during labor. During your pregnancy, think about the kind of music you most like and be sure to bring CDs, tapes, and a player to the hospital. You can listen to it simply as a distraction or use it, alone or with imagery, to enhance your relaxation.

## Trance

Hypnosis can reduce pain, shorten labor, and reduce the need for medication. To use this method, however, you and your labor partner must be trained before the big day comes. Ask your midwife or doctor for a referral.

## Seeking Help from Complementary Practitioners

A doula is a trained professional whose only role is to provide you with emotional and physical comfort through hand-holding, massage, suggesting position changes, and continuous emotional reassurance. The doula works alone or with your partner, nurse, midwife, or doctor. Women who use doulas rely less on pain medications, have shorter first-time labor, reduced rates of cesarean section, and a generally enhanced childbirth experience.

## Breast-feeding-Related Ailments

*Sore nipples or engorged breasts*
Here are some tips that may help:

- Reposition the baby. Turning the suckling infant so he or she is belly to belly with you is optimal.
- Nurse first on the breast that hurts less. If there's no difference between your breasts, alternate.
- Each time you start a nursing session, stimulate the suckling reflex by touching your baby's bottom lip to your breast or by expressing a small amount of milk.
- If your baby is able to put a larger amount of breast into his or her mouth, it will result in less nipple soreness and pain.
- Nurse frequently and until your baby is satisfied. The baby will suck less vigorously and this will also help prevent engorgement.
- If your breasts become engorged—full and painful—continue to nurse frequently to encourage your body to adjust your milk supply to your baby's demands. In addition, hot showers or warm water compresses, applied right before nursing, will help.
- Rub some milk on your breasts after nursing to soothe and heal.
- If your nipples are sore, exposing them to sunlight and air will help.
- Clean your breasts with warm water and avoid soap.
- For cracked or painful nipples, one of my Ob/Gyn colleagues recommends gently applying moist tea bags, geranium leaf, or ointments made from comfrey, yarrow, or marigold. Other alternatives are vitamin E oil or calendula cream.
- Change your breast pads or liners frequently.
- Avoid underwire bras or other constrictive clothing.

## Mastitis

An inflammation of the breast, mastitis is usually a swollen, warm, red, and/or painful spot. The area may feel hard. Often, hot compresses, massaging the area, and frequent nursing can ease the problem. However, if you develop a fever, feel tired, achy, or fluey, or if the symptoms don't clear in twenty-four hours, call your health care provider. You may have a breast infection.

### Sunflower oil

Because it is rich in vitamin E, sunflower oil may help ease sore, inflamed breasts. A recent study published in *Immunology* assessed whether dietary interventions, specifically the use of sunflower or red palm oil, had an impact on breast inflammation during late pregnancy and breast-feeding. The researchers found a beneficial role for sunflower oil. If you want to give it a shot, try incorporating it into your diet on a regular basis. It's best not to cook with sunflower oil since it loses its therapeutic potency when heated. Instead, use it in a salad dressing two or three times a week.

### Reflexology

Two points on your ear may help relieve inflammation and provide some relief. One is the apex of your ear, which you can find by folding your ear flaps together and finding the topmost point. The other is the endocrine point on the lower cartilage projection in the front crease of the central hollow of the ear.

Another point to try is GB-42 (Gallbladder 42), located on the top of the foot in the space between the fourth and fifth toes.

## Helpful Hints for Miscellaneous Ailments of Pregnancy and Childbirth

### Morning Sickness

### Ginger (Zingiber officinale)

Thanks to its antispasmodic properties, ginger effectively prevents nausea. However, its safety in pregnancy has not been conclusively proven. Check with your practitioner before trying it. Usual dose is 250 to 500 mg four times a day.

### Vitamin B6

In some studies, this vitamin has been shown to prevent nausea. The safe upper limit for this nutrient is 100 mg a day.

### Acupressure wrist bands

Using these bands to apply continuous pressure to your wrists effectively reduces nausea and vomiting. The bands come with instructions; however, the acupressure point you want to use is between the two central tendons of the forearm, three finger widths from the wrist crease.

*Reflexology*
- LU-8 (Lung Meridian 8), just above the wrist crease, on the thumb side.
- PE-6 (Pericardium 6), two thumb widths above the wrist crease, in the middle of your inner arm.

## Hemorrhoid Pain

To reduce pain, take warm baths with a few drops of cypress, juniper, or lavender essential oil. Applying cool, soothing witch hazel or witch hazel ointment or slippery elm cream promotes healing.

## Postpartum Perineal Pain

After birth, many women experience perineal pain, especially if they've had an episiotomy. In a randomized clinical trial published in 1994, researchers found that adding six drops of lavender oil to a daily bath for ten days after birth reduced discomfort within three to five days.

# 5

——

# Tender to the Bone:
# A Joint Problem

## GLADYS'S TURNAROUND

Gladys is a sixty-three-year-old woman referred to me by her coworker, one of my longtime patients. At her first visit, Gladys's chief complaint was dull, aching, boring pain in her knees and hips that had steadily been getting worse. Gladys didn't usually go to the doctor unless she was really suffering. But somehow we hit it off. She reminded me of my late mom, both in appearance and in personality, and I listened intently as she opened up to me on that wintry day.

A couple of months earlier she had seen her primary care physician. All he had done was suggest Motrin, a pain reliever. He also referred her to a specialist. That's what had precipitated her visit to me. She was scared and depressed. "The specialist told me my only option was surgery. I'm just praying that you can figure out something else," she said.

Gladys's husband had died unexpectedly of a heart attack several years back. It quickly became apparent to me that Gladys loved to take care of people, sometimes at the cost of her own health. She had a stressful job working as an executive secretary at a local college. Although she was approaching retirement, she doggedly spent many hours a day on her feet visiting various administrative departments. "I want to make sure everything is just right for my boss," she explained. On weekends, she baby-sat for her grandchildren, taking them on outings to the zoo and children's museums. Meanwhile, she had let herself go, ignoring the worsening pain in her knees.

Now she could ignore it no longer. Sheepishly, she pointed to her legs: "My knees are turning in; they're so crooked you can drive a trailer truck under me," she half-joked. But her situation was serious; she was having trouble walking.

Gladys was a picture of advanced osteoarthritis in full bloom. Her right hip and knee were markedly worse than the other side. They really acted up when she climbed stairs. Occasionally, her knee buckled when she stepped off a curb. On physical examination, she showed osteoarthritic changes (bony enlargement, motion restriction, pain, and stiffness) not only in her knees and hips, but also in her fingers. Her X rays further corroborated her advanced degenerative joint disease.

While I recognized that joint replacement surgery might eventually be inevitable, my task now was to buy her time. To complement her conventional treatments, which included Tylenol and a nonsteroidal anti-inflammatory drug, I suggested a four-part plan. First, I recommended glucosamine and chondroitin, two nutritional supplements, to fortify her weight-bearing joints. To further strengthen her joints and offer her some aerobic exercise, I encouraged her to enroll in an aqua therapy program at the local community center and taught her several quadriceps exercises.

There was no way Gladys would cut back on her walking. "My grandchildren won't hear of it. They love our weekend outings and so do I!" she exclaimed. Instead, I suggested that she buy a pair of well-cushioned, impact-absorbing walking shoes to avoid stress to her joints. And since her extra weight—she needed to lose about 15 pounds—put more pressure on her joints, I gave her some general nutritional guidelines to follow, and suggested hypnosis to reduce food cravings.

To tide her over until these measures kicked in, I proposed that we start an acupuncture regimen for immediate relief and gave her detailed acupressure exercises to do at home.

Over the course of several weeks Gladys began to notice a change. She still had pain, but it had diminished considerably. Her walking was more confident, less painful, and, best of all, she was feeling good again.

The musculoskeletal system—the elaborate bulwark of bones, muscles, tendons, ligaments, and soft tissue that provides structural support and protection to the body—is a frequent source of pain for women. Among older women, musculoskeletal complaints are also a common cause of disability. Women more frequently suffer from osteoarthritis and rheumatoid arthritis as well as systemic lupus erythematosus, systemic sclerosis, and fibromyalgia. In addition, women and men sometimes describe different symptoms for the same problems.

There are a number of possible reasons for these striking disparities, including hormonal makeup, physical and anatomical differences, and genetic constitution. Social or cultural influences, such as how physically active you are or whether your job is sedentary, probably play a role. Research has also shown that women spend less time than men in organized sports and high-intensity exercises and more time in housework and caregiving activities.

In this chapter, my primary focus is pain from rheumatoid arthritis and osteoarthritis, the two predominant forms of arthritis in women. (Other ailments related to the musculoskeletal system are covered in Chapters 6 and 7.)

Over 43 million Americans suffer from the pain, stiffness, and associated anxiety, stress, and depression of arthritis. Of those, 7 million are limited in their daily activities. In fact, according to the Centers for Disease Control, arthritis disables more Americans than heart disease and stroke. By the year 2020, as the baby-boom generation ages, an estimated 60 million people will have arthritis.

Arthritis affects the joints and their surrounding structures, especially the shoulder, elbow, wrist, hip, knee, and ankle. Arthritis has many faces and forms, and each one affects different parts of the joint. Whatever shape it takes, arthritis all too often wreaks havoc. Along with pain and stiffness, it causes dramatic deformity and misalignment of joints.

## OSTEOARTHRITIS

### Description

Osteoarthritis (OA), a degenerative joint disease, is the most common form of arthritis, affecting nearly 21 million Americans. OA is far more common among women, who may also suffer a more severe form of the disease than men.

OA is caused by degeneration of cartilage, a jellylike material that protects the ends of many connecting bones. When it's healthy, cartilage allows bones to glide smoothly over each other without rubbing together. It acts like a shock absorber to cushion the joints and protect them from the weight and jarring of your movements. When cartilage breaks down, the bones rub together and this causes pain.

OA affects the integrity of joints, which, along with surrounding bone, become thickened and distorted. Bone spurs (osteophytes) may develop, causing more deformity, damage, and pain.

In addition, each joint is enveloped in a capsule with a lining called the synovium, which produces fluid that lubricates the joint, allowing smooth and free movement. This may also be affected by osteoarthritis.

OA worsens over time. It is linked to age-associated joint changes, and there's a dramatic increase in OA in women over the age of sixty-five. As you get older, along with the pain you may experience dysfunction and even loss in the range of motion of your joints.

## Causes

Being a woman increases your chances of developing OA. So does aging, because the years of wear and tear on your joints can trigger the breakdown or wearing away of the smooth cartilage coating that protects joints and adjoining bone structures. Prior trauma to a joint from an accident, sports or work-related activity, as well as poor diet and obesity, also raise your risk.

Other contributing factors are your body mechanics, the health of your nerve and muscle structures, and stress on your ligaments—the structures that connect bone to bone. Particularly relevant in this regard are high-heeled shoes. Over time, by putting added pressure on your knees, high heels can lead to osteoarthritis. Don't fool yourself into thinking that as long as you avoid stilettos, you're safe. It turns out that shoes with chunky high heels are deceptive—they feel more comfortable, so you wear them longer. Even if they're better for your feet, they're just as bad for your knees as thinner heels, according to researchers at the Harvard Medical School.

Finally, genetics may play a role, particularly in OA of the hands. Some of these risk factors are easier to modify than others.

## Signs and Symptoms

- Pain, stiffness, or decreased range of motion in your joints
- Deformity of your joints—they become bony or knobby
- Enlargement of the joints but with little inflammation
- Although OA can affect many joints, it may only strike one or two. The knees, hips, fingers, neck, and back are the most likely to be affected.

## Conventional Treatments

If you're overweight, your doctor will suggest that you drop some pounds to reduce pressure on your joints. She may also recommend a hot pack. To use this, immerse it in hot water, cool it a little, and wrap it in a towel. It imparts moist heat to your aching joints. Even easier to use are electrical moist heat packs. A thermal pack is a new product that involves no electricity; you activate it by crushing and its heat lasts for twelve hours. Hot baths or showers and even heat lamps are also helpful.

There are a variety of drugs, such as Tylenol and NSAIDS, used to reduce pain and improve function.

If you have a local inflammation with swelling, warmth, and redness, your doctor may recommend injecting your joint with steroids. This will provide immediate, albeit short-term relief. And if oral medications aren't helping, another treatment option is a series of injections with synthetic cartilage (hyaluronase) to restore your body's natural shock absorber. These injections are approved for use only in arthritis of the knee; their effects on other joints have not yet been extensively studied.

Splinting or bracing a joint to stabilize and align it and redistribute weight can reduce pain and inflammation and help avoid more damage. Your physician (a physiatrist, orthopedist, or rheumatologist) can evaluate you for these devices. You can buy other aids, such as neoprene sleeves for your knees, at the pharmacy. Finally, shoe orthotics, crafted by a podiatrist or pedorthotist, can correct the way you walk and prevent damage to your joints caused by faulty biomechanics.

Topical gels, creams, and ointments are a great way to avoid the nasty side effects of oral medication. Unfortunately, they are not as readily available in the United States as they are abroad. In many other countries you can buy topical nonsteroidal products for localized relief of arthritic joints over the counter. In this country, you'll have to have your doctor ask the pharmacist to custom prepare topical analgesic formulations.

## Dietary Strategies (See Chapter 14 for food sources of specified nutrients)

*Lose weight*
Both women and minorities are disproportionately affected by obesity and are less likely to exercise. Remember, obesity dramatically raises your risk of developing OA. It doesn't take much to improve your chances: In one study, loss of a little more than 10 pounds over a ten-year period cut the risk of OA in half.

*Avocados and soybeans*
Recently, French researchers have focused on the potential value of an avocado/soybean oil combination. People in their study had less pain and used fewer pain relievers. There was even a suggestion that this combination might promote cartilage growth. You can eat raw soybeans or try commercial brands of soybeans that are lightly dried and toasted to enhance the taste. You can even sample soy chocolate bars. Some of these tasty items provide a whopping 12 grams of soy protein.

*Fish*
Most studies of EPA and DHA, the essential fatty acids found in fish oil, have involved people suffering from rheumatoid arthritis. Still, because they interfere with chemical messengers that influence the body's inflammatory cycle, it's reasonable to use them to fight the pain and inflammation of OA. I am not a fan of fish oil supplements, because they tend to get rancid and become dangerous quite easily. What's more, you can get enough fish oil by eating fish at least two or three times a week. Besides fish, diets that include whole grains, leafy vegetables, and seeds (flax and sunflower) supply the proper ratio of omega-6 to omega-3 fatty acids likely to benefit arthritis.

*Vitamin B3, or niacinamide, helps improve joint mobility.*

*Vitamin E and selenium may relieve pain.*

*Antioxidants*
Antioxidants are natural chemicals that destroy free radicals, those nasty cellular renegades that have been implicated in the development of arthritis and many other diseases. Consuming antioxidants has been associated with reduced risk for OA. The best food sources for antioxidants are fruits and vegetables.

R E C I P E

RED PEPPERS WITH MUSHROOMS AND GINGER

   *2 tablespoons olive oil*
   *2 tablespoons low-sodium tamari sauce*
   *1 teaspoon honey*

*1 tablespoon grated, fresh ginger*
*3 cloves garlic, minced*
*1 sweet onion, sliced very thinly*
*½ cup sweet snow peas*
*1 cup mushrooms, halved*
*3 red peppers, cut into strips*

1. Heat olive oil in a heavy skillet over medium-high heat. Add the tamari sauce, honey, and ginger.
2. Stir in the garlic and sweet onion, and cook for 1 minute, stirring constantly.
3. Add the rest of the vegetables and stir-fry for 4 minutes, or until vegetables are just tender.
4. Serve immediately as a side dish or over brown rice or whole-wheat pasta.

SERVES 4

## Supplements

### Glucosamine sulfate

Some of the most promising developments in treating arthritis come from the world of "nutraceuticals," or dietary supplements. A large-scale meta-analysis published in the *Journal of the American Medical Association* in March 2000 evaluated the use of glucosamine and chondroitin preparations for OA of the knee and hip. Overall, researchers found these supplements to be effective. Here are more specifics.

Glucosamine sulfate is a nutritional supplement that comes from seashells or seafood. It is an important building block for the manufacture and repair of cartilage. More and more scientific literature is emerging to support glucosamine's value in reducing OA pain. A 1998 double-blind study showed that glucosamine, taken for four weeks, was just as effective as ibuprofen in curbing OA symptoms, and it caused fewer side effects. So exciting is the preliminary research on this supplement that the National Institutes of Health (NIH) has embarked on a study to explore its role in cartilage restoration.

You'll see glucosamine in a variety of forms. It's often bundled with chondroitin sulfate and other nutritional supplements thought to be helpful for healthy bones. But there is no evidence that the combination product acts synergistically or is more effective. I recommend glucosamine sulfate or hydrochloride, which have been most extensively studied. Take 500 mg three times a day.

## Chondroitin sulfate

A natural constituent of cartilage, chondroitin helps to provide elasticity and structure. Since cartilage lacks a blood supply, chondroitin plays an important role by allowing water and nutrients to pass to and be retained by the joints. Chondroitin also shields cartilage from destructive chemicals and enzymes, thereby slowing deterioration.

Clinical studies have shown that chondroitin supplementation helps joint function, manages joint narrowing, and reduces pain. Unfortunately, it doesn't repair already damaged cartilage.

Most chondroitin supplements are derived from the tracheal cartilage of cattle and are slow-acting, often taking two months to work. Although the side effects—indigestion and nausea—are minimal, there may be interactions with blood thinners or some herbs. The dose is 400 mg three times a day or 600 mg twice a day.

## SAMe (S-adenosyl methionine)

SAMe is a natural substance produced from methionine, an amino acid, and adenosine triphosphate (ATP), a metabolic chemical associated with energy production. It can significantly improve joint function by enhancing cartilage production, increasing joint mobility, and bolstering ATP levels. It is also an antidepressant. Taken in large doses, it can upset your stomach. The dose is 200 to 400 mg two or three times a day. Do not take SAMe if you take levodopa for Parkinson's disease. This nutrient may trigger manic episodes in people with bipolar disease.

## Vitamin B3

Use of vitamin B3 can lead to improved joint mobility. Although it has not been conclusively shown to reduce pain, people in one study reduced their use of NSAIDS by 13 percent when they took B3. The accepted range is 18 to 35 mg a day. It may cause flushing.

## Vitamin E and selenium

A potent antioxidant, vitamin E has been shown to relieve pain better than a placebo and NSAIDS. It works well with selenium. Accepted dose range is 15 to 1,000 mg a day of vitamin E and 60 to 400 mcg of selenium.

## Zinc

This mineral has been shown to be of value. The accepted range is 8 to 40 mg a day.

*D-phenylalanine*

The jury is still out on this synthetic form of the amino acid phenylalanine. Because it inhibits the breakdown of an enzyme that, in turn, breaks
down enkephalins, the body's natural painkillers, it may help decrease
pain. It is sometimes commercially available in a product called DLPA
(D-phenylalanine with L-phenylalanine). CAUTION: Do not take this supplement if you have phenylketonuria (PKU), diabetes, hypertension, or
panic attacks or if you are pregnant or on antidepressants.

## Herbs

*White willow bark* (Salix alba)

The bark of the white willow tree, native to central and southern Europe
and North America, contains salicin, a substance chemically related to aspirin. This herb is a potent anti-inflammatory and pain reliever. Several
studies focusing on osteoarthritis have found that willow improves function
by relieving pain, especially in the knee and hip. Although its analgesic
action is slow, it is quicker than aspirin. Herbalists suggest these daily doses:
60 to 100 mg in tablets; one or two cups of tea, made by steeping 1 or 2
grams of herb in 200 ml of boiled water for 10 minutes; or 1 or 2 ml of
tincture, three times. Possible side effects include gastritis and ulcers. Do
not use willow if you are allergic to aspirin.

*Boswellia* (Boswellia serrata)

Also known as frankincense and salai guggal, *Boswellia serrata* is a tree
found throughout Asia. It was used in sacraments by the ancient Hebrews
in the Holy Temple. Its key component, boswellic acid, has potent anti-
inflammatory properties. The recommended dose is 400 mg three times a
day.

*Ginger* (Zingiber officinale)

This herb may have anti-inflammatory as well as painkilling properties. You
can make a delicious, healing ginger tea by steeping a teaspoon of grated
fresh ginger in a cup of boiling water. Add sugar if you like. Drink 3 cups
a day when you're in pain.

*Turmeric* (Curcuma longa)

This is the pungent yellow spice frequently used in curry. Its active ingredient is curcumin, which is an anti-inflammatory that also has antioxidant
effects. While eating it in a meal is more fun, research published in Indian

medical journals suggests that taking 400 mg three times a day is effective in some forms of arthritis.

### Devil's claw (Harpagophytum procumbens)

This South African herb is named for its distinctive fruit, which resembles a claw because of its tiny, fruit-bearing hooks. Although it's used extensively in Europe for arthritis pain, there has been little solid research—until recently. A randomized, double-blind, multicenter trial conducted in France and published in 2000 found devil's claw to be as effective as a commonly used conventional drug for osteoarthritis. Recommended use of devil's claw is as an infusion, up to 3 times a day: Combine 1 teaspoon of herb with 300 ml of boiling water and steep for 8 hours; then strain. CAUTION: Do not take if you are on medication for heart arrhythmias, are pregnant or breast-feeding, or at risk for ulcers.

## Herbal Creams and Ointments

### Nature's Chemist

This product contains menthol and a copaiba extract harvested from the Amazon. It's generally thought to be a counterirritant, or a chemical that promotes the release of the body's natural pain relievers. Use it on affected areas three times a day.

### Capsaicin cream (0.025–0.075 percent)

This spicy, therapeutic botanical remedy is harvested from red peppers or cayenne. It can be a potent analgesic. Capsaicin blocks pain by interfering with a neurotransmitter known as substance P. It can also trigger release of endorphins.

Capsaicin is sold under many names, including Zostrix. Use it sparingly, since it may burn. (Cap Max is a form of extra-strength capsaicin that is thought to cause less burning.) Apply it directly to the skin around affected areas three times a day. Avoid contact with your eyes, any mucous membrane, or with open or irritated skin. Do not use capsaicin with heat. Be sure to wash your hands after use.

### Joint-Ritis

This is a new product that combines glucosamine and chondroitin along with menthol, copaiba, and eucalyptus. It's unique because of its composition, as well as its roll-on applicator. You can apply it five times a day.

*Triflora Arthritis Gel*
This is a combination homeopathic gel that you can use to relieve the aches, pains, and stiffness of arthritis. Its ingredients include comfrey (*Symphytum officinale*), poison ivy (*Rhus toxicodendron*), and marsh tea (*Ledum palustre*). A randomized controlled trial recently found that it was at least as effective as Piroxicam gel, a nonsteroidal anti-inflammatory drug (NSAID), in treating osteoarthritis of the knee.

*Arnica (Arnica montana, leopard's bane, mountain tobacco, sneezewort)*
This herb is especially helpful for the aches and pains of arthritis. Use an arnica cream or add several drops of a tincture to a cold compress and apply when your joints are swollen. Do not use on open wounds.

*Aloe (Aloe vera)*
The simplest, least expensive way to use aloe is to buy a plant for your house. Simply break off a leaf and apply to your sore joints the jellylike substance that oozes out.

*Dimethyl sulfoxide (DMSO)*
DMSO is an industrial solvent that has been a subject of great controversy. In its gel form, it may have value. In a recent double-blind placebo-controlled study, its use resulted in a 25 percent reduction in pain. The gel is a standardized dose, so rubbing it on twice daily is enough.

**Do-It-Yourself**

*Acupressure (See Chapter 19 for technique)*
Here are some important pressure points:
1. "HO KU" is located in the web space right by the base of the thumb. Using your other hand, press on this spot for several seconds at a time to relieve arthritic pain in the upper arms and shoulders.
2. For pain in the legs, apply pressure to the outside part of the calf, about four finger widths below the knee joint.
3. Pressing hard on the bottom of both feet should improve pain in the lower legs.

*Heat*
To reduce stiffness and pain, try applying moist heat. Heated pools, whirlpools, warm baths, and showers are helpful. But localized heat applied directly for twenty minutes to sore spots is more effective. You can use moist compresses or microwaveable heat packs wrapped in a damp towel. How-

ever, don't do this when an area is inflamed—signs include redness, swelling, or skin that is hot to the touch. Heat draws blood to the area and increases inflammation.

## Mind/Body

*Relaxation and meditation (See page 340)*
Since there is no cure for arthritis, these techniques will help you cope and relieve stress and depression.

## Exercise

Once upon a time it was felt that arthritics shouldn't exercise because of potential damage to their joints. This myth has now been replaced by widespread acceptance of the value of exercise and fitness. In fact, I was recently part of a national expert consensus panel to formulate specific guidelines for exercise in geriatric patients with degenerative arthritis.

Joints need movement to stay healthy. Exercise can help you limit impairment by increasing your joints' range of motion and your flexibility. Building muscle strength and endurance also reduces pain and helps you better manage your daily activities. Besides, exercise improves your overall fitness and health, boosts your spirits, and helps you sleep. Of course, exercise also helps you maintain or lose weight, and obesity is a major risk factor for osteoarthritis.

Before you begin, you should consult your doctor or find a physical therapist who works with people who have arthritis. Your exercise program should be individualized to work the right muscles and avoid overstressing the affected joints. A physical therapist can design an appropriate home exercise program that you can then continue on your own.

Along with the Arthritis Foundation, I recommend several forms of exercise: strength training, range-of-motion or flexibility, and endurance.

*Strength training*
Strengthening exercises build muscles. This helps stabilize and support the joints and reduces pain by taking pressure off weak, hurting joints. These should be done at least every other day unless your joints are swollen or very painful. There are two types. Isometric exercises work by tightening and building strength in the muscles rather than by moving joints. Isotonic exercises move the joints to strengthen them. Try Quadriceps Sets and Leg Lifts. (See page 334 for exercise.)

RANGE-OF-MOTION EXERCISES

Also called flexibility exercises, these keep your joints moving, preventing stiffness and soreness. Your aim is to systematically, one by one, move each joint. It may help to do these exercises at the time of day when you are most comfortable. Or you may try them first thing in the morning, when your joints are at their stiffest, so you can better meet the challenges of your day. But do them every day. If your joints are swollen or painful, move them gently.

These exercises, recommended by the Arthritis Foundation, focus on the three joints most commonly afflicted in OA—knees, hips, and fingers.

*Hip (CAUTION: If you've had joint replacements, do not do this exercise.)*
1. Lie on your back on a comfortable friction-free surface.
2. Keep your legs straight with about a 5-inch distance between them.
3. With the toes pointing to the ceiling, glide your right leg out to the side (abduction) and then back to midline. Your leg should maintain contact with the ground at all times.
4. Repeat with the left leg.
5. Do this 10 to 15 times with each leg. You can also do this while standing.

*Knee and Hip*
1. Lie on your back.
2. Keep one leg bent, with foot on the floor, and the other perfectly straight.
3. Bend the knee of the straight leg.
4. Grasp the back of your thigh, just above the knee, with your hands and pull it into your chest.
5. Straighten the leg up into the air (extension).
6. Lower it to the floor.
7. Repeat with the other leg.
8. Do this 5 to 10 times with each leg.

*Fingers*
1. Open your hand, keeping your fingers straight and spread apart.
2. Move all of your fingers toward your palm without bending the knuckles.
3. Try to touch the top of your palm with your fingertips.
4. Extend the thumb across the palm so that it touches the creased second joint of your little finger.
5. Repeat 5 to 10 times.

AEROBIC OR ENDURANCE EXERCISES

This type of exercise will help you to control your weight, which relieves pressure on sore joints. Walking, riding stationary bikes, and swimming are good options. I especially like swimming, since the buoyancy of water supports your weight. The water also provides two-way resistance: Although movement seems easier in water, your muscles are actually working harder than they would on land. Unless you have severe joint pain or swelling, aim for twenty to thirty minutes, three times a week.

## Seeking Help from Complementary Practitioners

*Acupuncture*
Both the World Health Organization (WHO) and the National Institutes of Health (NIH) support the use of this age-old healing art for osteoarthritis. And a powerful study of acupuncture published in 1992 found that as many as 25 percent of patients with severe arthritis canceled planned knee replacement surgery because the acupuncture gave them adequate pain relief.

*Massage (See page 326)*
Avoid direct massage for areas that are acutely inflamed, infected, or fractured.

## Red Flags

Call your doctor if you develop fever, weakness in your muscles, or extreme fatigue.

## RHEUMATOID ARTHRITIS (RA)

### THE STORY OF FRANCES

People with rheumatoid arthritis are often consumed with pain and fatigue. Frances, a fifty-four-year-old African-American woman, was no exception. When I first saw her she complained of stiffness, swelling, soreness, and pain in her fingers, wrists, and ankles. She was referred to me by her rheumatologist, who had helped her come a long way, but was referring her to me for holistic pain management.

Frances's pattern of pain was not unlike that suffered by many people with rheumatoid arthritis. She had morning stiffness, occasional warmth and tenderness of her joints, loss of appetite, and fatigue. She jokingly showed me "her battle scars," small bumps on the skin known as rheumatoid modules.

The bigger problem, though, was that she experienced so much pain from her RA that everyday activities of daily living were a chore. The pain and deformity in her hands made it hard to open jars or do housework or clerical tasks. Still, I sensed that she wasn't telling me the whole story; there was another cause for her distress. When I pushed a little, she confided: "I'm embarrassed to tell you this, Doctor, but just taking care of my home, husband, and children is almost too much for me. And I feel so guilty." Needless to say, work was out of the question.

Frances had tried many pain relievers, including NSAIDS (non-steroidal anti-inflammatory drugs), corticosteroids, disease-modifying arthritis agents (DMARDS), narcotics, injections, and other traditional therapies, but nothing had helped her. She was despondent.

I started giving Frances regular acupuncture treatments and I also prescribed a host of nutritional and herbal remedies. At home, she learned to use visual imagery to relax. Frances began feeling better, but I had a hunch that the key to our success would be exercise. Pain doesn't exist in a vacuum; it is highly subjective. When I treat pain, I'm treating the body and the mind, and exercise benefits both. Still, she wasn't thrilled about the idea: "Doctor, I'm fifty-four years old, my body aches, and I've never been able to stick to an exercise routine. Do I have to?" I promised that we'd begin slowly and got her started with stretching exercises, yoga for relaxation, and tai chi. In addition, I gave her some simple acupressure techniques she could do at home while she watched TV.

As she gained confidence, I pushed her to begin a regular swimming routine. As I expected, exercise rallied her endorphins and set a restorative process into motion. Her sleeping and eating improved, as did her interactions with her husband and children. Sticking with the exercise regimen gave her more confidence in her body and empowered her to take control over her pain. I knew she had turned the corner when she told me the next time I saw her: "I feel like I deal with the pain so much more effectively now; it's probably about 75 percent less intense."

Over time, Frances developed a more optimistic outlook; at each visit, she seemed less depressed and withdrawn. She told me she was thinking about expanding her horizons and doing something in the world outside her home, a prospect that had seemed far too daunting before. The real turning point came when she walked into my office with a new suit and a stylish hairdo and said proudly: "I'm taking a job as a volunteer at the local hospital. I feel so much better about myself, it's time to help others."

## Description

Rheumatoid arthritis is a chronic, debilitating, inflammatory condition that causes pain, stiffness, swelling, and loss of function in the joints. The joint linings, bones, and cartilage can all become painfully inflamed.

Joints are surrounded by a joint capsule, which is lined with thin tissue called the synovium. For some reason, the body's immune system begins to attack the synovium, causing it to become inflamed. As its cells grow and divide abnormally, the synovium thickens and the joint becomes swollen. As the disease progresses, the abnormal synovial cells invade and destroy the joint's cartilage and bone. Muscles, ligaments, and tendons surrounding the joint are weakened. The result of the process is pain and deformity.

RA usually occurs between the ages of thirty and sixty. More than 2 million people in the United States suffer from RA and it affects two to three times more women than men. Making matters even worse, RA significantly increases your chances of developing osteoporosis. Risk may be twice as high for women with RA, according to recent research.

RA may also affect women more severely. In one recent study, for example, women reported more painful joints, more swollen joints, and poorer function. And the majority of studies show that RA is slightly more disabling for women than it is for men.

Still, RA varies a lot from person to person. You may have mild RA, with flares (periods of worsening symptoms) and periods of remission. Or you may have a more severe form, where the disease is active for most of the time and results in severe joint damage and disability.

## Causes

We don't yet completely understand what causes RA or why it disproportionately affects women. We do know that it is an autoimmune disease in which, for some reason, the body's immune system mistakenly attacks the synovium, or the lining inside the joint.

Although the causes of RA are elusive, there are several factors that increase your risk of developing the disease:

- Genetic predisposition—Researchers think an inherited trait, combined with a bacterial, viral, hormonal, or other environmental factor, triggers RA.
- Being female—The disease affects far more women than men.
- Hormonal factors—These may influence RA frequency and severity.

For example, in up to 75 percent of women, the disease diminishes during pregnancy; it flares up in 80 percent of women once pregnancy is over. Pregnancy may also confer a long-lasting protective effect because women who have never been pregnant are at higher risk for RA.
· Psychological stress.

## Signs and Symptoms

- · Pain, swelling, soreness, and stiffness of the joints
- · Morning stiffness
- · Joints on both sides of the body are usually affected
- · During a "flare," the joints may feel warm to the touch
- · Joints most commonly involved are the fingers, hands, wrists, knees, ankles, feet, and elbows
- · Loss of appetite
- · Low-grade fever
- · Rheumatoid nodules (small bumps on the skin), especially near affected joints

## Conventional Treatments

The goals of RA treatment are to relieve symptoms, prevent joint degradation, and preserve joint function. Typically, doctors rely on NSAIDS, which can cause gastrointestinal bleeding or ulcers, or the new Cox-2 anti-inflammatory drugs, which don't irritate the stomach as much. If you don't respond to these medications, your physician may prescribe disease-modifying, antirheumatic drugs (DMARDs) such as penicillamine, sulfasalazine, antimalarials, and gold salts. However, these drugs have terrible side effects. Another option is corticosteroid drugs, which are anti-inflammatory and suppress the immune system. But these also have serious side effects, especially when used over a long period.

Rest, cold, and heat applications (except during a flare) are all standard treatments. And techniques to preserve joints, such as splints and other assistive devices, may allow your inflamed joints to rest.

## Dietary Strategies (See Chapter 14 for food sources of specified nutrients)

*Weight*
Controlling or losing weight reduces the stress on the joints.

*Food allergies*

Diet and food may have an impact on rheumatic disease by changing the immune or inflammatory response. In addition, allergenic foods contain antigens, or substances that provoke the immune system, triggering a hypersensitivity that can make the symptoms worse.

*Calcium and vitamin D*

You'll have an increased risk for osteoporosis, so make sure you get plenty of calcium-rich foods.

*Vegetarian diet*

In some studies, a vegetarian diet has been beneficial. Be sure to include plenty of legumes, nuts, eggs, dairy products, and vitamin B12 if you go this route. You can take this further and try a vegan diet, which excludes all animal products. A Scandinavian study found that four months on a vegan diet, along with cutting back on coffee, tea, sugar, and spice, reduced joint pain and stiffness.

*Foods in the nightshade plant family (Solanaceae)*

Eliminating these may provide some relief. These plants contain substances that may increase pain and discomfort by causing inflammation and halting the repair of damaged joints. The family includes potatoes, peppers, eggplant, and tomatoes.

*Flaxseed oil*

This oil contains alpha-linolenic acid (ALA), a precursor of the EPA and DHA in fish oil. Use 1 tablespoon a day. It should not be heated, so it's best used in salads. Smaller quantities of ALA are found in soy, canola, black currant, and walnut oil.

*Green tea (Camellia sinensis)*

Unlike its black and oolong counterparts, green tea is not fermented. This leaves its active ingredients—vitamins, minerals, volatile oils (polyphenols), and caffeine—intact and boosts its health-giving properties. Drink three cups a day.

*Pineapple*

This fruit contains bromelain, an enzyme with anti-inflammatory properties. (See page 324.)

*Fish*
DHA and EPA, two oils found in fish, appear to reduce RA symptoms.

RECIPE

### BAKED SESAME AND OAT-CRUSTED FLOUNDER

½ *cup oat flour*
¼ *cup sesame seeds*
*1 tablespoon coriander*
*1 tablespoon garlic powder*
*1 tablespoon onion powder*
*1 teaspoon cilantro*
*1 tablespoon paprika*
*4 egg whites*
¼ *cup sesame oil*
*4 to 5 flounder fillets, rinsed and dried*
*Olive oil cooking spray*

1. Preheat oven to 375 degrees.
2. Combine the oat flour, sesame seeds, and spices on a shallow platter.
3. Mix the egg whites and sesame oil in a bowl.
4. Dredge the flounder fillets first in the egg mixture and then in the oat-flour mixture, until coated.
5. Spray the bottom of an ovenproof baking dish with olive oil cooking spray. Place coated fillets side by side in the baking dish and bake for 40 to 45 minutes.

## Supplements

*Calcium and vitamin D*
These will help reduce your risk of osteoporosis. The accepted daily dose range for vitamin D is 15 to 50 mcg. The range for calcium is 1,300 to 2,500 mg. Pay special attention to calcium if you are pregnant, breast-feeding, or postmenopausal.

*Fish oil*
A study published in the January 2000 issue of the *American Journal of Nutrition* again corroborated the growing evidence that omega-3 fatty acids

are a wise strategy. Patients who took two fatty acids—eicosapentaenoic (EPA) and docosahexaenoic acids (DHA)—for twelve weeks had less morning stiffness and fewer tender joints. These fatty acids, found in fish oil, interfere with chemical messengers that contribute to the inflammatory cycle of RA. Consuming fish oil regularly may also help you reduce your dependence on NSAIDS. Fish oil may be particularly useful if you are pregnant or breast-feeding as it may help you avoid toxic medications.

While my personal preference is that my patients get their dose of EPA and DHA from eating fish two to three times a week, those who are unable to consume fish may take supplements of fish oil; the dose is 3 grams. Be sure to keep them refrigerated because they go rancid, becoming potentially dangerous, quickly. Consuming flaxseed oil may also be helpful.

### Evening primrose (EPO), borage, and flaxseed oil
These oils help elevate concentrations of a fatty acid called gamma-linoleic acid (GLA), which has potent anti-inflammatory properties. The recommended dose is either 45 mg of EPO or 1,800 mg of borage oil daily. Make sure these supplements are refrigerated.

### Antioxidants
People with low antioxidant levels have a higher risk of developing rheumatoid arthritis. Take 900 to 3,000 mcg of vitamin A (retinol and beta-carotene), and 15 to 1,000 mg of vitamin E (alpha tocopherol) each day. You should also take vitamin C (ascorbic acid). The accepted range for C is 90 to 2,000 mg a day.

## Herbs

### Boswellia (Boswellia serrata)
Boswellic acid, a key component in this tree's bark, has pain relieving and antirheumatic properties. The jury is still out as to its absolute effectiveness but research by Dr. Deepak Chopra has demonstrated that boswellia reduces arthritis pain, especially when used with other Ayurvedic herbs, such as ginger and turmeric. The recommended dose is 400 mg three times a day.

### Turmeric (Curcuma longa)
This is the pungent yellow spice frequently used in curry. Its active ingredient is curcumin, which is an anti-inflammatory that also has antioxidant effects. While eating it in a meal is more fun, research published in Indian

medical journals suggests that taking 400 mg three times a day is effective in some forms of arthritis.

### Ginger (Zingiber officinale)
This herb is used in both traditional Indian healing and Ayurvedic medicine. It works by inhibiting the body's production of inflammatory substances called prostaglandins. You can make a delicious tea by steeping a teaspoon of grated fresh ginger in a cup of boiling water. Add sugar if you like. Drink three cups a day when you're in pain.

### Ashwaganda
Known as "Indian Ginseng," this herb in the pepper family is part of the Ayurvedic medicine chest and is also used in Africa to treat inflammatory conditions. One teaspoon of powder twice a day is the recommended dose. Use caution if you are on sedative drugs.

### Valerian (Valeriana officinalis)
If pain is disturbing your sleep, you can make an infusion by adding 2 or 3 grams of herb to 150 ml of hot water and steeping for 10 to 15 minutes. Strain before use, and drink a cup 30 to 45 minutes before bedtime. I recommend that you obtain a commercially prepared infusion tea, called Dr. Stuart's "Vesper Tea," which blends valerian with limeflower, hops, passionflower, and fennel.

### Ginseng
This popular herbal remedy will lessen your fatigue and improve your stamina. The suggested dose is 500 to 1,000 mg of powdered root once a day or 100 mg in standardized extract twice a day.

## Herbal Creams and Ointments

### Aloe (Aloe Vera) (See page 97)

### Joint-Ritis (See page 96)

## Do-It-Yourself

### Smoking
A recent study of more than thirty thousand women found that smokers have nearly twice the risk of developing early-onset rheumatoid arthritis as do nonsmokers. So *stop smoking*!

*Heat (See page 97)*
Do not use heat during an acute flare.

*Cold*
Cold packs may be helpful after exercising especially if you get muscle spasms.

## Mind/Body

*Relaxation*
Using progressive relaxation (see Chapter 18) to release tension in your muscles reduces pain. It also relieves the depression, anxiety, and feelings of helplessness you may feel as you try to cope with daily joint pain.

*Tai chi*
Tai chi is a traditional Chinese martial art that combines deep breathing with slow, gentle movements and good postures. It is also a weight-bearing exercise, so it has the potential advantage of stimulating the bones and strengthening connective tissues, which may be helpful for RA. It is often prescribed for arthritis sufferers in China. Recent research has shown tai chi to be safe for people who have RA.

## Exercise

While it's important to rest, especially during periods of flares, the days of no exercise for RA patients are long gone. Lack of exercise results in weak muscles and loss of joint mobility, only causing more problems. You can use the same exercises I recommend in the osteoarthritis section. However, avoid active exercise as well as range-of-motion work when your joints are acutely inflamed.

## Seeking Help from Complementary Practitioners

*Acupuncture*
By encouraging your body to release endorphins, acupuncture helps relieve pain.

*Massage with healing oils*
Swedish massage involves stroking or kneading the muscles, using lotion or oil. Nature's Chemist, a topical pain reliever, works well. So do essential herbal oils, such as eucalyptus, rose, lavender (a good stress reducer), rose-

mary, tea tree, and St. John's wort. Many essential oils can irritate the skin in their unadulterated form, so it's best to dilute them in wheat germ, almond, or sunflower oil. Using a medicine dropper, mix five to ten drops of essential oil with one tablespoon of the "carrier" oil. Because arthritic joints are sensitive, be sure your therapist is familiar with the disease.

## Red Flags

Contact your doctor if you have a fever or develop spasms, weakness, or generalized fatigue.

# 6

—

# Your Spine, the Body's Backbone

## EILEEN'S STORY

Eileen was a forty-three-year-old woman who managed a busy party goods store in an affluent part of town. She was frustrated and unhappy because she had chronic back pain. "My first bout took me by surprise nineteen years ago, several months after my oldest son was born," she told me. Back then, she recalled, her family doctor simply suggested that she keep off her feet for a couple of days.

But her problem never really went away. When Eileen came in, her back had troubled her for years, although she described her pain as sporadic. When it flared up, she felt a sore, aching sensation and spasms in the small of her back. Her internist had treated her with nonsteroidal anti-inflammatory medications and told her "not to overdo it." When that didn't do the trick, she referred Eileen to me.

As we talked, I realized that Eileen was a dedicated and conscientious worker. She pitched in at the store, frequently bending and lifting heavy boxes of party favors, which didn't help her achy back. Neither did her worn-out shoes, which affected the way she walked, giving her, in medical parlance, an "altered gait pattern." Making matters worse, she had gained twenty pounds over the past couple of months, thanks to refrigerator raids driven by her pain and by the stress of her job.

After reviewing her medical records, completing a thorough physical examination, and personally viewing her X rays and MRI studies, I decided that Eileen's back pain did not come from a damaged disc. It was largely mechanical in nature, although it was exacerbated by the extra weight she was carrying. I recommended a program of complementary treatments that would address the mechanical, postural, and lifestyle factors that were causing her pain.

Because it is effective for both weight control and pain management, I suggested acupuncture as a logical starting point. Of course, different acupuncture techniques are used for each problem. Usually, we use auricular (ear) acupuncture points for weight management and traditional meridian points for pain control. For an added measure of help with food cravings, portion management, and weight loss, I referred her to a hypnotist colleague.

I also gave Eileen a personalized formula for pain relief. This included postural exercises as well as a specific regimen to strengthen and tone her abdominal muscles, which would help support her spine. To mobilize her endorphins, I suggested a program of regular aerobic exercise. She balked at first, but she eventually began to take brisk daily walks, using a new, comfortable pair of impact-absorbing walking shoes. At one visit, she told me that she now looked forward to her walks. The secret of her success? "What really did it, Dr. Young, was listening to Yanni, my favorite singer, while I walk," she confided. Eileen also started a yoga class; besides the physical benefits of strengthening her muscles and increasing spinal flexibility, it also helped her unwind after work.

Over time, Eileen appeared stronger—and thinner—at her periodic visits. And her mood improved as the back pain that had plagued her for nearly twenty years gradually got better.

## LOW BACK PAIN

### Description

We all live with aches and pains. But low back pain is another story—it's a daunting ailment that has been around for centuries. As many as 60 to 80 percent of Americans experience low back pain at some point in their lives, with as many as 50 percent suffering from it every year. The annual cost to society, including direct medical expenditures and indirect costs, such as lost time from work, is estimated at a staggering $60 billion.

The jury is still out as to whether women actually suffer low back pain more often than men at all ages. A study of more than a thousand patients enrolled in an HMO found that women experienced more low back pain than men at young ages, but that the frequency of back pain increased significantly in men as they got older. However, in another study, women older than sixty years of age more frequently reported spine pain, possibly due to the rising incidence of osteoporosis. Other research has produced mixed results.

It may be that differences in the occurrence of low back pain have more to do with occupation than with gender. Still, it does appear that hormonal distinctions play an important role. And women bear the brunt of the astronomical human costs of low back pain, which frequently leads to time away from daily responsibilities and pleasures—working, child-rearing, recreation, and sexual activity.

There are several times during your life when you are uniquely susceptible to developing low back pain or aggravating an already-existing problem.

- During pregnancy, the burden of the baby you're carrying shifts your center of gravity forward, which may result in back pain. You also weigh more and have added breast tissue, which exacerbates the problem. Loosening of ligaments due to the hormones relaxin, estrogen, and progesterone, as well as pelvic widening, a normal physiological preparation for delivery, can increase lumbar lordosis, or normal curvature of the spine. (Typically, your spine has a curve or concavity in the back. The curve may become exaggerated when you're pregnant, creating "hollow back," "saddle back," or "sway back.") This dramatically alters body mechanics and puts stress on the lower back. These physical changes can also soften and loosen the ligaments that stabilize the pelvis.
- When your monthly menstrual period rolls around, cramps, pelvic discomfort, and bloating may aggravate existing low back pain.
- During menopause and the ensuing postmenopausal years, you may develop osteoporosis of the spine, placing you at risk for painful spinal compression fractures.

All back pain is *not* created equal. Back pain can take on many faces and can be mild or very severe. Besides, we need to distinguish between acute and chronic back pain, two sides of the same coin. Unlike acute low back pain, which is short-lived and temporary, chronic pain of the low back is protracted. It lasts three months or more and often demands a more innovative approach to treatment.

When I treat women with chronic low back pain, I like to keep in mind these words from the famed twelfth-century physician and philosopher Maimonides, who extolled the value of a restrained, middle-of-the-road, compassionate approach to dealing with medical illness, including low back pain: "To recognize the frailty of the human body and to effect a gentle cure is virtuous." I believe that if Maimonides were around today, he'd embrace the therapeutic value of complementary medicine for managing low back pain.

John Sarno's book *Mind Over Back Pain: A Radical New Approach to the Diagnosis and Treatment of Back Pain* (Berkeley Publishing Group, 1999) offers an intriguing and innovative approach to back pain that many of my patients find helpful.

## Causes

To get a handle on the causes of back pain, a brief anatomy lesson about the spine, also known as the backbone, vertebral column, or spinal column, is in order. I tell my residents and medical students that the spine is a structural bulwark. It's composed of twenty-four "building blocks" or individual bones called vertebrae. These include seven in the neck or cervical area, twelve in the chest or thoracic area, and five in the low back or lumbar area. In addition, there are five sacral bones fused together to form the sacrum, the large triangle-shaped bone at the top of the pelvis, and three smaller coccyx bones at the base of the spine. Other key elements of the spine include muscles and ligaments, which play a structural and supportive role.

The spinal cord is a critically important cablelike structure that sends and receives electrical impulses between the brain and the nerves. It passes through the vertebrae by means of the spinal canal, a tubelike passageway made up of a series of interconnected holes located within each vertebra. The spinal cord terminates in the upper lumbar spine and sends nerve projections to the sacral regions.

The causes of low back pain in women are many and diverse. Some are more severe than others. The mind-boggling list includes degenerative, inflammatory, infectious, and metabolic ailments; cancer and traumatic injury; and developmental, musculoskeletal, vascular, psychological, organ-based (e.g., kidney pain), and postoperative conditions. In addition, there are many external factors that contribute to back pain, including postural problems, obesity, menstrual and pelvic disorders, and improper lifting techniques.

For the convenience of classification and simplicity, I divide back pain into three very broad categories: muscular and soft tissue, structural, and organic.

## Muscular and Soft-Tissue Causes

The most common source of back pain lies in soft tissue structures — muscles, tendons, and ligaments. This pain is often mechanical in nature; in other words, it is nondisc pain that is relieved by rest and worsened by activity. Typically, it occurs because you put too much stress on your back's supporting structures when you improperly bend, twist, or lift.

In your lower back, there are several major groups of muscles that stabilize, protect, support, and aid movement. Sometimes referred to as the paraspinous muscles, these key spine muscle groups include the erector spinae (from the Latin for spine extenders, they span the entire length of the vertebral column), the semispinalis muscles, the multifidus muscles, and the interspinales muscles.

Besides the spine muscles, other muscle groups including the psoas, or limb muscles, and the quadratus lumborum play an important role in buttressing and moving the spine. In addition, the abdominal muscles provide support from the front.

Many different things can go wrong with these spinal muscles, including sprain, strain, and outright injury. Back strain can develop over time from faulty posture, or it can happen suddenly. You know this if, for example, you have ever twisted the wrong way and felt it immediately. Back strain can also result from automobile accidents or other trauma.

Spasm of the spinal muscles can lead to stiffness and aching in the low back and difficulty bending. After pregnancy and childbirth, slack belly muscles can contribute to back strain. And tight hip flexor muscles (the psoas) tilt your pelvis backward, placing added strain on the back.

### Myofascial pain

This is back pain caused by inflammation and irritation of muscles and their supportive tissue, or fascial, lining. Myofascial pain, often an important component of the myofascial pain syndrome (MPS), can lead to pain in a specific region on one side of the back. MPS is often confused with fibromyalgia syndrome because of the presence of "tender pointlike areas" called trigger points, but it is *not* associated with fatigue, stiffness, or generalized aching. I organized a symposium at Johns Hopkins University Medical School in 1992 with the late Dr. Janet Travell (JFK's physician). She explained myofascial pain this way: "acute strain to the back muscles can result in localized tissue and muscle (myofascial) damage." This may injure the body's calcium storehouse (called the sarcoplasmic reticulim) and lead to muscle contraction and fatigue. Together with other metabolic changes, this causes amplified pain in the muscles of the back. (See Chapter 12 for information on fibromyalgia and MPS.)

*Fibromyalgia*

This syndrome is the most frequent rheumatic cause of chronic widespread pain and it is certainly a leading cause of back pain. More than 75 percent of people with fibromyalgia are women. Symptoms include fatigue, sleep disturbances, and stiffness. It also causes generalized aching with multiple tender points, as opposed to myofascial pain syndrome, which results only in localized lower back pain. Tender points occurring in fibromyalgia and myofascial conditions can be treated with local injections as well as myofascial "spray and stretch." This technique uses a prescription-only vapo-coolant spray, called ethyl chloride or fluori-methane, to chill the muscle before and during stretching.

## Structural Causes

Back pain caused by abnormalities in bone and disc structures comprise this category.

*Herniated disc*

The intervertebral disc (disc located between vertebra) is a jellylike protective shock absorber that cushions adjoining spinal vertebrae. If the inner core of the disc (the nucleus pulposus) moves or "herniates" out of its tough, fibrous outer envelope (the annulus fibrosus) it may place pressure on neighboring nerves and/or spinal structures. There are several variations of this ailment. Ranging from the mildest to the most severe, they are:

- Disc bulge—a slight dislocation or abutment of the disc associated with weakening of the annulus.
- Disc protrusion—migration of the disc, along with partial tearing of the annulus.
- Disc extrusion—the disc pushes through or tears the full thickness of the annulus. This may even result in a "free fragment," where a part of the nucleus pulposus completely separates or is dislodged from the disc.

Disc rupture is the general term used to signify a severe form of herniation.

Many factors contribute to disc damage, including bone degeneration, poor posture, weak muscles, obesity, and stretched ligaments. Because of the burden of the added weight on the lumbar (lower) spine, pregnancy increases the risk.

A herniated disc often leads to numbness and tingling as well as shooting pain down the leg or in the buttocks or back. It may also cause pinching of neighboring nerve structures (radiculopathy) or squeezing of the sciatic nerve, the body's thickest and possibly most painful nerve.

### Sciatica

This dreadful condition often results from pressure on the sciatic nerve from a herniated disc or other lumbar abnormalities, such as spinal stenosis (see below). It causes sharp, shooting pains down the thigh and leg that get worse when you walk, run, cough, sneeze, or even laugh. Because of its enormous size and its location, the sciatic nerve is especially susceptible to pressure from the growing uterus during pregnancy. If you have referred pain down your leg (pain whose source is elsewhere in your body) it does not necessarily mean you have sciatica. It could be referral from myofascial trigger points, or sacroiliac or facet dysfunction. There are also other nerves that run from the spine down the leg that can elicit similar symptoms.

### Compression fractures

With age, and particularly after menopause, you may lose key bone minerals, including calcium and magnesium. This decreases bone density and places the spine at risk for fracture (see page 137). As the spine becomes less dense and more fragile, portions of the vertebrae may disintegrate and collapse onto one another. On an X ray this looks like a wedge. Loss of height, pain, stiffness, spasm, and a deformity known as dowager's hump are often the result.

### Spinal stenosis-lumbar

Although it is sometimes the result of a birth defect, this condition, common in older women, more often occurs when the spinal canal and/or existing nerve roots become narrowed from degenerative arthritis or trauma (often superimposed on a congenitally narrowed spinal canal). If you have X rays or other imaging studies your doctor will probably see evidence of an enlarged disc, bone spurs, or thickened ligaments. Symptoms include pseudo-claudication, or cramping in the legs and feet, weakness, numbness, and pain radiating down the leg. Your doctor will need to differentiate this pain from hardening of the arteries in your leg.

*Spondylolisthesis*
Sometimes, a malfunction of the spinal stabilizing ligaments causes slippage of one vertebra over a neighboring one, resulting in spinal instability. A small fracture, a prior trauma history, a birth defect, or another abnormality of the bones may be associated with this ailment. While most cases of spondylolisthesis are inconsequential, severe slippage (more than 50 percent) can threaten the spinal cord or nerves.

*Spondylosis*
This is a common condition that does not necessarily produce symptoms. It is caused by degenerative joint disease (osteoarthritis) and loss of flexibility of the spine. As a result, you may feel stiff and sore.

*Scoliosis, kyphosis, or exaggerated lordosis*
These are different types of abnormal curvature of the spine. They may be present at birth and worsen with age or they may occur during adulthood.

*Other causes*
Other structural causes of low back pain include rheumatoid arthritis and ankylosing spondylitis, or AS, a genetic condition where the vertebral bones fuse to one another. (AS is three times more common in men than in women.) It's not unusual to have these conditions along with osteoarthritis of the spine. (For more information on arthritis, see Chapter 5.)

Occasionally, a combination of mechanical and structural problems may cause back pain. Examples include an imbalanced or rotated pelvic bone (pelvic obliquity), ligament abnormality, facet joint arthritis, or myofascial pain.

## Organic Causes of Low Back Pain

Low back pain is sometimes the result of infection or disease. Some of the more common causes are: infections of bone or disc; kidney stones or infections; gynecological, intestinal, or pancreatic diseases; cancer that originates in (myeloma or leukemias) or spreads to the spine (breast, lung, prostate, and colon cancers); and aneurysms.

## Signs and Symptoms

These vary, depending on the specific problem. However, common symptoms include:

- Stiffness
- Pain
- Muscle spasms
- Pain shooting down to the buttocks or legs
- Numbness or tingling in the buttock or groin
- Numbness or tingling in the feet, legs, or toes

## Conventional Treatments

Because there are so many possible causes for back pain, it is important for a medical professional to sort through them and diagnose your pain. Physiatrists, medical doctors who specialize in physical medicine and rehabilitation, are specially trained in this area. They are the best medical doctors to evaluate and treat acute and chronic back and neck pain without surgery. If you consult a physiatrist, you can expect to undergo a thorough physical examination that focuses on your neurological and musculoskeletal systems, in addition to other important organ systems. Your functional status (how well you walk, work, and perform basic activities of living) will be evaluated. It may be necessary for your doctor to order additional diagnostic testing including X rays, MRI, or electrodiagnosis (nerve conduction studies and electromyography to pinpoint nerve injury). The physiatrist will carefully assess your body mechanics and suggest a customized, conservative (i.e., nonsurgical) strategy for dealing with your back pain, depending on its cause. If necessary, she will refer you to a physical therapist for a customized home exercise regimen or she will provide one herself.

Several classes of medications are used for back pain:

*Analgesics*
Pain relievers are a first line of treatment. These include everything from Tylenol (good for pain relief but not for battling inflammation) and other over-the-counter drugs (e.g., aspirin, Motrin, Aleve) to prescription nonsteroidal anti-inflammatory drugs (NSAIDS), Cox-2 selective inhibitor NSAIDS (Vioxx and Celebrex), and narcotics, such as codeine. Bear in mind that narcotics can cause constipation, breathing difficulty (in large doses), sedation or drowsiness, or addiction. Tramadol (Ultram), another type of analgesic, acts on your central nervous system and may act as a weak opioidlike drug. However, this drug can lower your seizure threshold. Also, use caution if you take St. John's wort or 5-HTP. (See page 304.)

*Topical pain relievers*
Recent developments include topical forms of nonsteroidals. Because they can be applied locally, topicals do not cause stomach upset or other forms of organ damage that may be associated with NSAIDS in pill form. As I travel all over the world for visiting lectureships and scientific symposia, I marvel at these rub-on prescription pain relievers that are readily available in other countries, and I regret that they are not available in the United States. Over-the-counter topical creams that can help include Arthromax, Ben Gay, Icey heat, and similar formulations.

There is some good news, however. Complementary topical pain relievers, such as Nature's Chemist and Joint-Ritis, are starting to appear in the American marketplace. They've proven to be effective for many of my patients (see page 96).

*Other medications*
If you suffer from muscle spasms, your doctor may prescribe muscle relaxers, such as Valium, baclofen, Flexeril, Skelaxin, and Robaxin. For severe conditions, to improve your mood and help you sleep, she may suggest Elavil or another antidepressant, an antianxiety drug, such as Valium or Xanax, or sleeping pills, like Ambien or Sonata.

When you see your physiatrist or musculoskeletal physician, she will determine forms of treatment best suited for your particular situation. If your pain comes from compression fractures due to osteoporosis, improving your bone stock is a priority, and calcitonin or Fosamax may help.

*Injections or nerve blocks*
Depending on the cause of your pain, your doctor may recommend the following:

- Fibromyalgia and myofascial pain frequently involve trigger points or tender points in individual muscles. Lidocaine injections or a lidoderm patch may help.
- If you have an extremely severe case of structural pain, and your doctor determines that true nerve root irritation is the cause, a spinal block (epidural injection) may be indicated. Other types of blocks include facet joint blocks and paravertebral blocks.
- Prolotherapy, or injections of concentrated sugar water and alcohol, stimulate the body to produce connective tissue. This can strengthen ligaments and tendons, thus stabilizing the spine or pelvic joints.

## TENS

Applied over the painful site, a transcutaneous electrical nerve stimulator (TENS) unit uses electrical impulses to help block the pain signals before they enter your spine.

## Mechanical strategies

Your doctor may recommend a back brace, lumbar supports, switching to a comfortable mattress, using new shoes, getting shoe orthotics, or correcting a leg length discrepancy.

## Hydrotherapy

Swimming is an excellent choice since it improves flexibility of the spine and extremities in a low impact, soothing environment. Other types of hydrotherapy include the whirlpool or Jacuzzi.

## Supplements

### Melatonin

This is a natural hormone that modulates sleep. If you have trouble sleeping take 1 or 2 mg, thirty minutes before bed.

### SAMe (S-adenosyl methionine)

This nutritional supplement is composed of two amino acids. It is useful in many types of pain syndromes, including back and neck pain. Studies of SAMe in patients with osteoarthritis have found that it is as effective as NSAIDS. SAMe is also an antidepressant. Dose is from 200 mg twice a day up to 400 mg three times a day, if you can tolerate it. Large doses may upset your stomach. Do not take SAMe if you take levodopa for Parkinson's disease. This nutrient may trigger manic episodes in people with bipolar disease.

## Herbs

### White willow bark (Salix alba)

Used in China for centuries as a treatment for pain and fever, white willow bark has become a popular mode of treating back pain. A study published in *Rheumatology Diseases of North America* demonstrated its benefits and, best of all, found that it caused minimal gastrointestinal discomfort, an advantage over other anti-inflammatory drugs. Do not take willow concurrently with aspirin or NSAIDS. Use caution if you take blood thinners, diuretics, or blood pressure medications. Recommended dose is 60 to 120 mg a day.

*Valerian* (Valeriana officinalis)
Since sleep may be difficult for you when you are experiencing back pain, you may be able to catch some "Zs" with the help of valerian, a plant that is on the FDA's list of herbs generally recognized as safe (GRAS). It's best taken as a tea, one cup before bedtime. Some people complain of the odor, so if you prefer a tincture, the recommended dose is 1/2 to 1 teaspoon (1–3 ml).

*Chamomile* (Chamaemelum nobile *or* Matricaria recutita)
This sweet-smelling herb helps fight inflammation and promotes relaxation. To help you sleep, make a double-strength tea by using two tea bags or steeping 2 teaspoons of dried flowers in one cup of boiling water. Avoid contact with your eyes; chamomile may cause irritation. It may also cause an allergic reaction.

**Herbal Creams and Ointments.**

*Nature's Chemist* (See page 96)

*Joint-Ritis* (See page 96)

*Dimethyl sulfoxide* (DMSO)
DMSO is an industrial solvent that has been a subject of great controversy. It has not been approved by the FDA despite its popularity as a remedy for musculoskeletal pain, arthritis, and neck and low back pain. However, I believe the gel may have value. In a recent double-blind placebo-controlled study, using it led to a 25 percent reduction in pain. Rubbing it on twice daily is enough.

*Arnica*
Rub Arnica cream or ointment into the affected area. Don't use this herb on broken skin.

*Capsaicin cream* (0.025–0.075 percent) (See page 96)

## Spine Injections and Interventional Procedures

Some physiatrists, orthopedists, and anesthesiologists perform interventional pain procedures, including epidural blocks, paravertebral blocks, facet blocks, and others. These may decrease your pain.

## Do-It-Yourself

*Everyday things*
- Back pain is linked to smoking, so here's one more reason to stop if you haven't already.
- Avoid sleeping on your stomach. Instead, curl up on your side with a pillow between your knees, or sleep on your back. And stay away from soft, sagging mattresses.
- If you have to lift something from a height above your shoulders, stand on a sturdy, steady ladder or stool to bring your shoulders above the object. Test the weight of the object by pushing against it before picking it up; if it's too heavy for you, ask for help.
- When lifting heavy objects, start with your legs bent and your feet apart. Take a deep breath and tighten your stomach muscles to support your back. Lift with your legs; as you straighten your legs and return to a vertical position, hold the object close to your body. Bend your legs to set the object back down.

*Acupressure (See page 353)*
This is a convenient way to use your fingers to exert pressure over acupoints, which stimulates the flow of *qi* through the key bladder and gallbladder meridians.
1. With your knees bent, lie on your side.
2. Take the pulpy surface of your thumb and place it on your sacrum (tailbone).
3. While applying firm pressure, glide your fingers upward along your spine until you can reach the topmost reachable vertebra.
4. Repeat this process 5 times.
5. After the fifth time, take the pulpy surface of your thumb and place it on the top of your spine, near your neck.
6. Using your other hand, follow the contour of your ribs, applying pressure in an outward direction.
7. Repeat this process, following the path of your ribs.
8. Turn over and repeat for the opposite side.

*Reflexology*
Several potent reflexology points can reduce discomfort in your back.

- *Bl-60 (Bladder 60)* is located around the outer ankle bone and is a good point for severe lumbar and neck pain. CAUTION: Avoid if you are pregnant.
- *SP-3 (Spleen-3)* is located at the inner arch near the front of the foot, at the very end of the first foot bone, this point fortifies the spine.
- *KI-1 (Kidney 1)* Pressing on this point, situated on the sole of the foot, between the second and third foot bones (metatarsal bones), relieves low back pain.

If you are in public and don't want to remove your shoes and socks, try some of these points instead:

- *GV-26 (Governor Vessel 26)* To strengthen the spine, try this point, which lies within the vertical depression in the midline under the nose.
- *SI-3 (Small Intestine 3)* For back pain, apply pressure to the outer edge of the knuckle below the little finger (pinky).
- *SI-4 (Small Intestine 4)* For back pain, try the point near the wrist, at the base (bottom) of the pinky.

## Mind/Body

*Yoga*
Cat Pose, Cobra, and Spinal Twist will help increase strength and flexibility in the spine. (See pages 344–351.)

## Exercise

*Strengthening Exercises*
Try the Pelvic Tilt, Half Sit-up, and Leg Raises. (See pages 331–338 for exercises.)

*Flexibility Exercises*
Try the Seated Low Back Stretch, Knee to Chest Raise, and the Lower Back Piriformis Stretch. (See pages 331–338.)

## Seeking Help from Complementary Practitioners

*Acupuncture*

The value of acupuncture in treating back pain was recognized as far back as the late 1800s by the legendary Sir William Osler of Johns Hopkins Hospital. More than a hundred years later, study after study has provided contemporary corroboration for his early insight, culminating in an endorsement from the Consensus Group of the National Institutes of Health. Although no one knows for sure how acupuncture works, we believe it promotes the release of endorphins, thereby curbing pain and spasms and reducing anxiety.

*Chiropractic and osteopathic manipulation*

A substantial body of research supports the use of spinal manipulation for relief of low back pain, including several large analyses of studies that show it to be at least as effective as most standard medical treatments. Besides, in 1994, the federal Agency for Health Care Policy and Research, after reviewing thousands of studies on low back pain, concluded that spinal manipulation does provide relief. Chiropractic is more effective for acute, rather than chronic, back pain.

*Massage therapy*

There's plenty of anecdotal evidence for the effectiveness of massage therapy for low back pain, but until recently there haven't been many solid studies. However, an article published last year in the *Canadian Medical Association Journal* is convincing. The study compared the effectiveness of comprehensive massage therapy and a "sham" laser therapy placebo for low back pain lasting between one week and eight months. The comprehensive massage therapy group had significantly improved function and less pain. One month later, 63 percent of the people in the massage therapy group were still reporting no pain.

## Red Flags

Call your doctor if you experience:

- Pain shooting down to your legs or buttocks
- Loss of control of your bladder or bowels
- Numbness or tingling in your buttocks, groin, feet, legs, or toes
- Muscle weakness in your legs or feet

- Inability to raise your foot or big toe
- Protracted night pain, when you are lying still
- Night sweats, loss of significant weight over time

## LOW BACK PAIN IN PREGNANCY

### Description

You are not alone if you have back pain during pregnancy. More than half of pregnant women suffer from this problem. It occurs most frequently after the sixth month of pregnancy and often lasts well after the baby is born. If you have had other episodes of back pain or if you have given birth before, you are more likely to have back pain.

### Causes

When you are pregnant, a number of factors change your body mechanics, leaving you vulnerable to back pain. Obviously, you're carrying a lot of extra weight, which shifts your center of gravity forward. As your abdominal muscles stretch to accommodate your growing belly, they provide less support to your back. Your body significantly ups its production of hormones, especially relaxin, which increases tenfold. This hormonal adaptation, courtesy of Mother Nature, allows your pelvis to widen in preparation for delivery by loosening key pelvic joints, including the sacroiliac joint and the pubic symphysis (the slightly movable joint at the front of the pelvis). Rising relaxin levels also affect the anterior and posterior longitudinal ligaments, which normally act as critical guide wires for the spine. As they loosen, it significantly weakens the spine's ability to resist stress, strains, and shear forces. You may experience pain from the discs as well as other important mobile disc structures, like the facet joints.

### Signs and Symptoms

- Spasms or other pain, especially in the lower back
- Tenderness
- Feeling achy
- Stiffness
- Pain that shoots down your legs

## Conventional Treatments

If you suffer from lower back pain while you're pregnant, it's likely your obstetrician will recommend Tylenol and hot packs. However, be careful about bathing in hot tubs; hot water raises your body temperature, which can injure the developing fetus.

## Do-It-Yourself

### Cold

Applying ice bags, rubber or plastic gloves filled with ice, or frozen gel packs can numb sore areas, slowing transmission of pain signals. Keep a thin towel between your skin and the cold pack; apply for twenty minutes at a time.

### Massage

Here are two easy techniques that may help. First, have your partner apply as much pressure as you can tolerate to the center of the middle of your back. Or if you prefer, try effleurage: Have your partner use a "feather touch," a very soft, tender application of the fingers to your back.

### A sacroiliac corset

This maternity corset surrounds the pelvis, helping you to maintain proper position and preventing structural damage.

### Bra

Be sure to wear a good, comfortable bra, preferably with nonelastic straps. This will stabilize and support your breasts and decrease low back and neck pain.

### Everyday things

- Avoid strain and injury by learning and using good body mechanics. Simple movements to avoid include sitting for long periods, bending from the waist, and lifting and carrying heavy objects far away from your body's center of gravity.
- Maintain a neutral spine position. Prevent excessive curvature of the spine (lordosis) or excessive reversal of lordosis by avoiding shoes with high heels.
- To improve your comfort while standing, avoid bringing your shoulders back too far, since this increases lordosis. You can decrease strain on your lumbar spine and paraspinal muscles by putting your foot on a

chair; this relaxes the iliopsoas muscle and tilts your pelvis forward. Take frequent sitting breaks so you don't stand for long periods of time.

• Rest one foot on a chair when you are sitting.

## Mind/Body

*Relax*
Put on some soothing music and take a warm aromatherapy bath using a few drops of essential oil made from citrus (mandarin, orange blossom) or flowers (rose, lavender, jasmine, or geranium). Just make sure the water isn't too hot.

*Breathe*
Deep breathing with or without progressive muscle relaxation (see Chapter 18).

*Meditation (See Chapter 18)*

## Exercise

As long as you don't overdo it, physical activity and exercise throughout pregnancy will help keep your back muscles in shape. Walking briskly, yoga, dancing, and even running are options. I find swimming to be an excellent exercise for my pregnant patients, since it dramatically reduces the effects of gravity and relieves pressure on the back. Check with your physician before starting any new exercise program.

In addition, you can do the Pelvic Tilt (see page 331) to strengthen abdominal and low back muscles. However, do it very cautiously after the third month of pregnancy.

## Seeking Help from Complementary Practitioners

*Chiropractic*
Chiropractic is an effective method for dealing with low back pain, and it is safe to use during pregnancy. Two manipulative techniques in particular may be helpful: the "shotgun," which eliminates asymmetry in the pubic symphysis and the "pelvic rock," for relief of lower back pain.

*Acupuncture*
According to an expert panel convened by the National Institutes of Health, acupuncture is an effective treatment for low back pain. More to the point,

a recent study supported the value of acupuncture for low back and pelvic pain in pregnancy. However, you should still exercise caution and discuss your condition with your acupuncturist. Certain acupuncture points are off limits during this time of your life.

### Massage

Professional massage is safe during pregnancy as long as it is done gently, avoiding pressure on your belly and uterus. If possible, look for a masseuse who has had special training in pregnancy massage.

## Red Flags

Call your doctor if you experience bleeding, sustained pains, or contractions, fever, or discharge.

## NECK PAIN

### Description

The neck performs three major functions: it provides stability and a base of support for the head, it protects the spinal cord and nerve roots, and it permits you to move your head in all directions. Of the many areas of the spine, the neck (also known as the cervical part of the spine) is the most mobile. It is also relatively fragile, given that the head is a heavy load. These factors combine to make the neck especially vulnerable to strain or injury.

Throughout history, cervical neck pain and dysfunction have been recognized as major medical concerns. In ancient Greece, the philosopher-physician Hippocrates pioneered the use of cervical traction; he was also the first to recognize the relationship between neck injury and paralysis. And a bit later, in the second century, the Roman emperor Marcus Aurelius was cared for by the celebrated physician Galen, who also proudly served as a "neck surgeon" to injured gladiators.

Today, neck pain and dysfunction are common problems. About one-third of us experience neck pain at some point in our lives, with the problem even more frequent among physical laborers. Neck pain without associated arm pain is more common in women than men.

## Causes

To better understand the causes and types of neck pain, we need to digress for a brief anatomy lesson. Your neck is made up of a series of seven bones (numbered C1 through C7, with the C standing for cervical), or vertebrae, which can be conveniently divided into two sections, the upper neck and the lower neck.

### The upper neck bones

The top two bones in the upper portion of the neck are unique in appearance and are called the Atlas (C1), an appropriate name because this ring-like bone holds up the weight of the head, and the Axis (C2). These two bones have a special relationship; they are connected by a structure called the odontoid process, which is bound by a transverse ligament. If disease, such as rheumatoid arthritis, or trauma disrupt this joint, the neck may become unstable. The Atlas and Axis permit flexion and extension (nodding) and rotation (saying no).

### The lower neck bones

All of the lower neck bones (C3 through C7) are similar in dimension and function. They are suited for flexion, extension, and sideways flexion.

### Soft tissue structures of the neck

Sandwiched between each of the cervical vertebra, except the Atlas and Axis, is an intervertebral disc. These discs facilitate motion; they are also shock absorbers that protect the spine. Degenerative changes or herniation in these discs can cause nerve root damage or even spinal cord injury.

Attached to the cervical vertebrae are a series of ligaments that lend stability and strength to the neck. In addition, the neck muscles help facilitate movement and give additional support to the cervical spine and head. The muscles in the front of the spine are flexors; they bring the head forward. Those in the back are extensors, which move the head backward.

Some of the same muscles in the lumbar spine (see page 113) are also present in the neck. Deep beneath them are the rotator muscles. Certain shoulder muscles—the trapezius, rhomboid, and levator scapulae—are attached to the cervical spine, so some shoulder injuries may cause neck pain.

The causes of neck pain are as diverse as they are numerous. Frequently it's a simple, correctable habit, such as:

· An uncomfortable sleeping position, especially if you have neck pain in the morning

- Poor posture or sitting in the same position for long periods
- Cradling a phone between your ear and shoulder
- If you already have a neck injury, leaning your head back over a sink for a shampoo in a hair salon can aggravate it
- Emotional stress

But your distress may be more than a simple "pain in the neck." Causes of neck pain include this mind-boggling list: degenerative, inflammatory, infectious, and metabolic ailments, cancer and traumatic injury; as well as developmental, musculoskeletal, vascular, psychological, organ-based (e.g., kidney pain), and postoperative conditions. I like to distill these causes into three broad categories: muscular and soft tissue, structural, and organic.

## Muscular/Soft-Tissue Causes

Whiplash, which affects a million Americans every year, is the most common type of neck injury in this country. It is the result of sprain or strain injuries to the muscles, tendons, or ligaments of the neck. The most common scenario for whiplash is an overextension injury. For example, your car is rear-ended, and you first flex and then hyperextend your neck. It's not surprising, then, that epidemiological studies have shown that whiplash is far more common in major cities, where there are more cars. Women have a higher incidence of this ailment than men. About one-third of whiplash victims develop pain within twenty-four hours.

## Structural Causes

### Herniated disc

The disc is a jellylike protective shock absorber that cushions adjoining spinal vertebrae. If the inner core of the disc (the nucleus pulposus) moves or "herniates" out of its tough, fibrous outer envelope (the annulus fibrosis) it may place pressure on neighboring nerves and/or spinal structures. There are several variations of this ailment. (See page 115.)

Many factors contribute to disc damage, including bone degeneration, poor posture, weak muscles, obesity, and stretched ligaments. A herniated disc in the neck often leads to shooting pain as well as numbness and tingling that extends down to the fingers (radiculopathy). It may also cause painful pinching of neighboring nerve structures. Depending on which nerve roots are affected, you may also get numbness in your thumb and second finger or in your ring finger and pinky.

*Cervical spondylosis*
This condition is caused by degenerative joint disease (osteoarthritis) of the spine, which causes it to lose its flexibility. As a result, you feel stiff and sore.

*Cervical stenosis*
Although it is sometimes the result of a birth defect, this condition, common in older women, more often occurs when the spinal canal and/or existing nerve roots become narrowed from degenerative arthritis or trauma. (A congenitally narrowed canal often predisposes you to narrowing from other causes.) If you have X rays or other imaging studies, your doctor will probably see evidence of an enlarged disc, bone spurs, or thickened ligaments.

### Organic Causes

Neck pain is sometimes the result of infection or other disease. Rheumatological conditions that may cause neck pain include ankylosing spondylitis, psoriatic arthritis, degenerative arthritis, and polymyalgia rheumatica (PMR). Infectious diseases, such as meningitis, influenza, German measles, mononucleosis, osteomyelitis, discitis, Lyme disease, and herpes zoster may also cause neck pain. Neurological causes of neck pain include cervical dystonias, which are involuntary, spasmodic contractions of neck muscles that lead to abnormal neck and head positioning and pain. Finally, neck pain may result from endocrinological and metabolic disorders, such as osteoporosis, osteomalacia, Paget's disease, parathyroid gland abnormalities, and pituitary tumors.

## Signs and Symptoms

- Pain, spasm, or deep ache in the neck, shoulder, or arm
- Limited range of motion
- Stiffness of the neck and shoulder muscles
- Headache

Neck pain is often a temporary condition. However, you may need medical diagnosis and treatment if it persists or is associated with shooting pains, numbness, tingling, loss in strength, or abnormal reflexes.

## Conventional Treatments

Analgesics, or pain relievers, are a first line of treatment. These include everything from Tylenol (good for pain relief but not for battling inflammation) and other over-the-counter drugs (e.g., aspirin, Motrin, Aleve) to prescription nonsteroidal anti-inflammatory drugs (NSAIDS) and Cox-2 selective inhibitor NSAIDS (Celebrex and Vioxx). Narcotics, such as codeine, are sometimes prescribed but they can cause constipation, breathing difficulty (in large doses), sedation or drowsiness, or addiction. Tramadol (Ultram), another type of analgesic, acts on the central nervous system and may act as a weak opioidlike drug. This drug, however, can lower your seizure threshold. Also, use caution if you take St. John's wort.

Recent developments include topical (rub-on) forms of nonsteroidals, available abroad but not yet in the United States. Because they can be applied locally, they do not cause stomach upset or other forms of organ damage that may be associated with NSAIDS in pill form.

If you suffer from muscle spasms, your doctor may prescribe muscle relaxers, such as Valium, baclofen, Flexeril, Skelaxin, and Robaxin. For severe conditions, to improve your mood and help you sleep, she may suggest Elavil or another antidepressant, an antianxiety drug, such as Valium or Xanax, or sleeping pills, like Ambien or Sonata. Be sure to ask your doctor about side effects; some of these drugs may be addictive.

If there is significant evidence of tender points or trigger points on examination, injections can be helpful. Occasionally, spinal interventional procedures are useful.

If you have neck pain emanating from cervical dystonia, injection with Myobloc (botulism toxin), along with oral medication and exercise may be the answer.

In some instances, your doctor may recommend a soft collar. This won't immobilize your neck, but it will provide cushioned comfort and remind you to keep your neck straight. The Philadelphia collar and other more rigid forms of immobilization may also be used.

## Supplements

Take calcium carbonate to slow down osteoporosis. The accepted dose range is 1,300 to 2,500 mg a day.

### Vitamin E
This is a potent antioxidant that may reduce muscle damage from free radical activity. The dose range is 15 to 1,000 mg a day.

## Vitamin C
To promote tissue healing and cut down on soreness, take from 90 to 2,000 mg a day. Combining your vitamin C with pantothenic acid may improve the strength of healing tissue.

## SAMe
A nutritional supplement composed of two amino acids, SAMe is useful in many types of pain syndromes, including back and neck pain. In some studies, it's been as effective as NSAIDS. SAMe is also an antidepressant. Dose is from 200 mg twice daily up to 400 mg three times a day, if you can tolerate it. Be aware, however, that in large doses it can upset your stomach. Do not take SAMe if you take levodopa for Parkinson's disease. This nutrient may trigger manic episodes in people with bipolar disease.

## Herbs

### Meadowsweet (Filipendula ulmaria)
This herb contains flavonoids and salicylates and has anti-inflammatory properties. Use caution with this herb if you are sensitive to aspirin. Meadowsweet may also cause diarrhea. Herbalists suggest that you make an infusion by steeping 1 or 2 teaspoons of dried herb in one cup of boiling water for 10 minutes. Drink up to 3 cups a day.

### Kava kava (Piper methysticum)
If neck pain is making you anxious, try kava kava, a widely used natural solution. Although its effects are not always immediate, this herb's key chemical, kavalactone, has calming, sedative, and pain-relieving properties. In some cases it may also alleviate spasms. Kava kava's mechanism of action seems to be similar to that of the conventional drugs Xanax and Valium. A six-month double-blind study of a hundred people found that kava kava reduced general anxiety levels significantly more than a placebo. The recommended dose is 70 mg three times a day.

### White willow bark (Salix alba)
Long used by Native Americans for pain and fever, white willow bark is now a popular mode of treating back pain. A double-blind, randomized, controlled study published in the *American Journal of Medicine* in 2000 showed that 39 percent of treated patients were pain-free after five days, compared with 6 percent in the nontreated group. Do not take this herb with aspirin or NSAIDS. Use caution if you are on blood pressure medi-

cations, blood thinners, or diuretics. The recommended dose is 60 to 120 mg a day.

## Do-It-Yourself

There are many effective techniques you can use to prevent and relieve neck and shoulder pain.

### For Prevention

- Practice good posture. Keep your head up and your chin somewhat tucked in. Your ear, shoulder, and hip should be in a straight line when sitting, standing, or lying down. Don't hunch your shoulders.
- Sleep on a firm surface using a thin pillow, a specially contoured foam cervical pillow, a rolled-up towel, or no pillow at all.
- Do not cradle the telephone between your neck and shoulder. Use a headset.
- Avoid sleeping on your stomach—this can twist your neck.
- When carrying a heavy shoulder bag or luggage, try to carry the weight equally on both sides. If you can't, use a backpack.
- Move your seat up or use pillows when you're driving to help you maintain good posture. Do not drive leaning forward.
- Try not to tip your head back.

### For Pain Relief

Improvement is slow and may take several weeks. Be patient.

#### Cold

For neck pain and most musculoskeletal problems, it's best to apply cold during the first twenty-four hours. This helps decrease inflammation and cramping. Apply ice, a cold pack, or a bag of frozen vegetables for ten to fifteen minutes every few hours.

#### Heat

After the first twenty-four hours, switch to heat. To relieve spasms and pain, take hot showers or apply hot compresses or a heating pad for fifteen to twenty minutes every few hours.

### Herbal rubs

- Rub arnica tincture or ointment into the affected area to ease any bruising. This is especially effective if your neck pain develops after a car accident.
- Wintergreen liniment, ointment, or cream contain methyl salicylate (aspirin), which helps mask pain because of its analgesic, counterirritant effects. Use cautiously if you are pregnant, breast-feeding, or taking anticoagulants.

### Posture

For acute pain relief, try:

1. Lie on your back with your head on a soft feather pillow and a small towel, rolled up and propped under your neck. Keep your knees bent and supported by large pillows.
2. Lie on your side with a soft feather pillow and a small towel rolled under your neck.
3. When sitting, use pillows so you can rest your head back comfortably, with pillows propping up and supporting your arms.

### Reflexology

Apply pressure to these points:

- GB-20 (Feng Chi point), above the hairline on the nape of the neck. There are two, one on each side.
- Bl-10 (celestial pillar), at the hairline, two finger widths outside of the spine.
- LI-4 (Large Intestine-4), (He GU), on the back of your hand in the web space between the thumb and first finger. This is one of the four most potent acupressure/acupuncture points in the body.

### Massage

1. Take your arm and wrap it around your neck from the front.
2. Place your fingers on the back of your opposite shoulder and squeeze and knead the muscles.
3. Work your way toward the spine and up and down.
4. Using both hands, grasp the back of the neck on each side and squeeze in a circular motion.
5. Move up the back of your neck and skull.

*Pressure*

Use a tennis ball to apply pressure to "hot points." Hold a tennis ball cupped in your palm. With your head and neck on a pillow, apply it to the following spots:

1. Just under the skull on the upper neck.
2. Above the shoulder blade, 4 to 5 inches from the spine or the base of the neck.
3. At the back of the shoulder, 2 to 3 inches above the crease of the arm against the body.
4. In the deltoid muscle area, 1 to 2 inches below and to the side of the top of the shoulder.

## Mind/Body

*Relaxation (See Chapter 18)*

Because tension and stress often lodge in your neck and shoulders, relaxation techniques are particularly useful.

*Tai chi and yoga*

With their emphasis on gentle stretching, good posture, and deep breathing and relaxation, these techniques are excellent for neck and back pain.

## Exercise

Gently stretching the neck loosens stiff muscles and relieves tension. Stop these exercises if the pain increases or moves to your arms. Try Side Stretches and Chin Tucks. (See pages 331–338.)

## Seeking Help from Complementary Practitioners

*Acupuncture*

A three- to four-week course of acupuncture may reduce your pain and help you cut back on pain medications.

*Body manipulation*

A variety of techniques, including massage, will speed your recovery, reduce pain, release spasms, and promote circulation.

## Red Flags

Call your doctor if:

- Your pain is associated with fever and headache, or your neck is too stiff to touch your chin to your chest; these symptoms are associated with meningitis.
- The pain travels down your arm, or you have numbness or tingling.
- You have painful or swollen glands in your neck that persist for several days.

## OSTEOPOROSIS

### Description

Osteoporosis is the most common metabolic bone disease, and one of the most important age-associated disorders in Western societies. In the United States it affects more than 25 million people, 80 percent of whom are women.

This skeletal disease causes reduced bone mass and deterioration of bone leading to weakness, brittleness, and an increased tendency to fracture. Typically occurring during the first or second decade after menopause, osteoporosis is the leading cause of fractures in postmenopausal women. In fact, half of all women develop osteoporosis-related fractures. The most common fracture sites are the spine, hip, and forearm. Osteoporosis can also lead to changes in posture and spinal deformities, such as the "dowager's hump," or hunchback. It is potentially a disabling disease.

### Causes

Contrary to what most people believe, bones are not dead; we are constantly making and losing bone. Depending upon the type of bone involved, we replace anywhere from 5 to 25 percent each year. This normal bone metabolism depends on heredity, nutrition, lifestyle, hormones, and liver and kidney function. In childhood, we build far more bone than we lose, so our bone mass increases steadily. And during our young adult years, total bone mass is relatively stable.

But after about age thirty, both men and women start to lose bone. Until women reach menopause, the pace at which this occurs is about the same for both sexes because female reproductive hormones, especially estrogen, play a major role in maintaining the density and integrity of bone.

As your estrogen levels drop, however, you go through a period of accelerated bone loss, and your skeleton begins to deteriorate. Your bones may become more "porotic" as you age—they have more holes and are thinner and weaker. You are at a higher risk of dropping below an imaginary line called the fracture threshold, which means that you are more prone to fractures from even relatively normal behaviors. Men reach this threshold, too, but not until they are significantly older.

A number of factors increase your chances of developing osteoporosis. Some of them can't be changed; unfortunately, you're stuck with them:

- Being a woman
- Age (postmenopausal women are at highest risk)
- Caucasian race
- Heredity—both a maternal history of hip fracture and a family history of osteoporosis
- Previous vertebral fracture
- Early menopause—either naturally occurring before age forty-five or surgical- or drug-induced
- Erratic periods
- Late onset of menstruation
- Absence of ovulation
- A history of anorexia nervosa, diabetes mellitus, Cushing's disease, hyperthyroidism, or hyperparathyroidism (an overactive parathyroid)
- Medications, such as glucocorticoids (steroids), water pills, anticonvulsants, and heparin, which increase bone loss

The good news is that there's a lot you can do to lower your risk.

## Signs and Symptoms

Unfortunately, the first symptom of osteoporosis is frequently a bone fracture. You may also experience:

- Loss of height
- Spinal deformity (neck hump)
- Severe bone pain

## Conventional Treatments

Since prevention is the best treatment, it's important to identify your risk factors early. In addition to recommending that you exercise, take calcium and vitamin D, stop smoking, and avoid heavy alcohol use, your doctor may want to assess your calcium metabolism and bone density to help guide treatment.

A variety of drugs may be prescribed for osteoporosis:

### Estrogen

Alone or in combination with progestin, estrogen is used for prevention and treatment. It slows bone loss and preserves and increases bone density. In one study, women taking estrogen increased calcium in their bones by 7 percent; they also had 50 percent fewer fractures. However, estrogens are associated with a slightly increased incidence of breast and uterine cancer; if you've had breast cancer, they are not recommended. Combining estrogen with progestin greatly reduces the risk of uterine cancer. You'll need to discuss this complicated decision with your doctor and carefully weigh the risks and benefits.

### Tamoxifen (Nolvadex)

This was the first hormone-blocking drug. If you're postmenopausal it helps you maintain bone mass, but it has an estrogenlike effect on the endometrium (the lining of the uterus) and therefore raises the risk for endometrial cancer.

### Selective estrogen receptor modulators

SERMs are a relatively new class of drugs that produce estrogenlike effects on select tissues without affecting the breasts or uterine lining. An example is raloxifene (Evista), which decreases bone resorption (breakdown) and increases bone mineral density but does not stimulate other tissues.

### Bisphosphonates

These are nonhormonal inhibitors of bone breakdown. The first of these drugs is called aldendronate (Fosamax). Although it slows bone resorption and increases bone mineral density, it may cause gastrointestinal irritation. To prevent problems, you must follow the instructions carefully by taking it on an empty stomach with 8 ounces of water and then remain upright for thirty minutes. A newer bisphosphonate is risedronate (Actonel).

### Calcitonin

Another conventional treatment is calcitonin, a naturally occurring hormone found in salmon that inhibits bone resorption and results in a slight increase in bone mineral density. It is administered by injection or in a nasal spray. However, it may cause nausea, flushing, or diarrhea.

*Fluoride*

Not just for teeth anymore. When combined with calcium, it appears to promote bone growth, increase spinal bone density, and reduce the occurrence of spinal fractures.

## Dietary Strategies (See Chapter 14 for food sources of specified nutrients)

*Soy foods*

A study published in the January 2001 issue of *Obstetrics and Gynecology* reported that a group of postmenopausal Japanese women who ate a diet high in isoflavones, plant-derived estrogens found especially in soy foods, including miso and tofu, had increased bone mass. Asians eat significantly more isoflavones, which might explain why osteoporosis-related fractures are far less common in Asia than in the West.

*Vitamin D*

Vitamin D is essential for healthy bones.

*Calcium*

This is especially important if you have breast-fed your babies. The body regulates serum calcium levels very carefully and stores extra calcium in the bones. If levels get too low, the body will rob calcium from the skeleton. The daily requirement for calcium is 1,000 mg a day before and 1,500 mg a day after menopause. The average adult in this country consumes between 500 and 700 mg a day, so you may have to take supplements to achieve this level (see page 143).

*Silicon*

We now think this trace mineral is important for bone formation in animals.

R E C I P E S

BROWN RICE WITH TOFU AND MUSHROOM SAUCE

This dish emphasizes soy, which is linked to increased bone mass.

> 2 tablespoons olive oil
> 1 onion, chopped

*2 cloves garlic, minced*
*1 cup mushrooms, thinly sliced*
*2 tablespoons chopped parsley*
*1 cup diced firm tofu*
*¼ cup unbleached white flour*
*2 tablespoons Spectrum Spread*
*1 cup water*
*¾ cup soy or rice milk*
*¼ teaspoon each pepper and salt*
*4 cups cooked brown rice*

1. Add olive oil to a saucepan and sauté the onion, garlic, mushrooms, and parsley for 3 minutes. Add the tofu and sauté for 3 more minutes.
2. Stir in the flour and Spectrum Spread. Mix in the water and milk, salt and pepper and stir until the flour is dissolved and the liquid is smooth.
3. Place the rice into a round serving dish and pour the tofu mushroom sauce over it.

SERVES 4

## SALMON BURGERS

Canned salmon, with its thin, white bones, is a concentrated source of calcium. It is also high in omega-3 essential fatty acids. This recipe is a tasty way to get these vital nutrients. A salmon burger, served on a whole-grain bun with green lettuce and tomato, makes a bone-building, powerhouse sandwich.

*2 14-ounce cans, Red Sockeye Salmon*
*5 egg whites, beaten*
*½ cup bread crumbs*
*½ cup sweet onion, finely chopped*
*¼ cup carrot, finely grated*
*2 teaspoons garlic powder*

1. Preheat oven to 375 degrees.
2. Mash the salmon—*with* its fine white bones—in a mixing bowl, discarding the large central bones and skin.
3. Add the rest of the ingredients to the bowl and mix well.
4. Spread olive oil on the bottom of a nonstick baking pan or cookie sheet with a basting brush.

5. Form six patties with the salmon mixture and place on the pan. Bake for 20 minutes, turn once, and bake for 10 more minutes.
6. Serve hot or cold.

SERVES 6

## ROOT VEGETABLE CASSEROLE

Root vegetables contain silicon, which is linked to the formation of healthy bones.

>1 butternut squash, cut into chunks (1 to 2 cups)
>1 parsnip, diced
>2 potatoes, cut into chunks
>1 cup large lima beans
>2 tablespoons Spectrum Spread
>1 tablespoon flour
>1½ cups soy or rice milk
>½ teaspoon nutmeg
>Salt and pepper, to taste

>TOPPING
>1 cup fresh whole-grain bread crumbs
>½ cup cashew nuts, chopped
>¼ cup almonds, ground

1. Preheat oven to 350 degrees.
2. Cook the squash, parsnip, potatoes, and lima beans in a pot of boiling water for 10 minutes. Drain and place the vegetables and beans in an oblong baking dish.
3. Melt Spectrum Spread in a pan over low heat. Stir in flour, mixing until smooth.
4. Slowly stir in the milk, remove from heat, and mix in the nutmeg, pepper, and salt.
5. Pour the sauce over the vegetables.
6. Mix together the topping ingredients and sprinkle them over the vegetables and sauce.
7. Bake for 30 to 35 minutes until top is golden brown.

SERVES 4

*Nutritional "No-Nos"*
- Limit your alcohol consumption. Drinking alcohol promotes bone loss and, through its effects on estrogen, increases your risk of fractures. (Along with a colleague, I published research in the *New England Journal of Medicine* in 1988 that documented a link between alcohol consumption and bone fractures in men, as well.)
- Cut back on salt and salted, processed foods. Although a definitive link hasn't yet been made, salt increases the amount of calcium you lose in your urine and may lead to bone loss over time.
- Reduce your intake of caffeine, which also increases urinary loss of calcium and has been linked to fractures of the hip. In addition, if your calcium intake is less than 800 mg a day, two to three cups of coffee per day may speed bone loss.

## Supplements

*Calcium*
You can take calcium supplements to make up the difference between what you get from your diet and the recommended daily intake (between 1,300 and 2,500 mg a day). This is likely to be between 500 and 700 mg a day. The FDA advises limiting calcium supplements made from dolomite or bone meal because of potentially high levels of lead.

*Vitamin D*
If you don't get out into the sun and don't eat many dairy products or fish, you may want to take a multivitamin that includes vitamin D. The accepted range is 15 to 50 mcg a day.

*Magnesium*
This mineral is essential for parathyroid function and release, which is in turn critical for activating vitamin D. In addition, magnesium depletion stops bone growth. The dose range is 320 to 350 mg a day.

*Manganese*
Deficiency of this mineral reduces calcium in your bones, leading to an increased risk of fracture. Recommended dose range is 1.8 to 11 mg a day.

*Boron*
A trace mineral, boron limits how much calcium and magnesium you lose in your urine. The upper limit is 20 mg. The RDA has not been established.

### Zinc

This mineral is essential for normal bone formation. It also enhances vitamin D activity. Recommended dose range is 8 to 40 mg a day.

### Copper

A deficiency of this mineral has been linked to abnormal bone growth in growing children. It has also been shown to inhibit bone breakdown. The accepted dose range is 900 mcg to 10 mg a day.

### Folic acid

This nutrient is involved in the breakdown of homocysteine, an amino acid that builds up to harmful levels in some individuals. Increased levels of homocysteine may promote osteoporosis. Recommended dose range is 400 to 1,000 mcg a day.

### Vitamin B6

This vitamin also plays a role in the metabolism of homocysteine. In addition, in animal studies, a deficiency of B6 has been linked to increased fracture healing time, impaired cartilage growth, defective bone formation, and more rapid development of osteoporosis.

The recommended dose is 2 to 100 mg a day.

### Vitamin C

This important nutrient promotes formation and cross-linking of protein structures in bone. In animal research, vitamin C deficiency causes osteoporosis. The accepted dose is 90 to 2,000 mg a day.

## Herbs

### Phytoestrogens

Although technically not herbs, these compounds originate in plants or are derived by your body's metabolism from precursors found in plants. The most important class, phenolics, includes isoflavones and lignans. You have two choices:

- Isoflavones found in soybean protein, while not as effective as estrogen, do produce positive effects. The two forms of phytoestrogen isoflavones with the strongest scientific support are genistein and daidzein. The recommended dose is 25 to 60 mg a day.
- Ipriflavone is a synthetic derivative of isoflavones. It inhibits the activity

of osteoclasts, cells that break down bone. The recommended dose is 200 mg, three times a day.

### High-mineral herbs

Nettles, oat straw, red raspberry leaves, chamomile, and dandelion greens have a high mineral content, so they are a good way to build your mineral stores. I suggest that you purchase commercially prepared teas which have these ingredients. (Dr. Stuart's and Traditional Medicinals are two brands that are readily available.)

### Black cohosh (Cimicifuga racemosa)

Although not yet studied for this purpose in humans, this popular women's herb, used for many hormonal ailments, does improve bone mineral density in animals. The recommended dose is 1 or 2 pills a day of a standardized extract.

### Alfalfa (Medicago sativa)

A member of the pea family, this herb contains isoflavones with weak estrogenic effects. The recommended dose is 1 or 2 ml of tincture three times a day.

## Do-It-Yourself

- Stop smoking. Smokers have lower bone mass and lose bone more rapidly.
- Get out in the sun, since it's the best natural source for vitamin D.
- Talk to your doctor about your risk factors.
- If you're older, make your home safer to reduce your risk of falls. Install handrails for stairs, bathtubs, showers, and toilets. Put nonskid suction mats in your tub and showers and on slippery bathroom floors. Remove loose throw rugs and keep your rooms and hallways well lit.
- Don't be a couch potato—get some exercise.
- Try homeopathy. The remedies don't reverse bone loss but they may be helpful for aching bones and for preventing and healing fractures. Besides, they ensure that your body uses minerals and other nutrients efficiently. Follow instructions on the package.
  - Calcarea carbonica is helpful if you are easily fatigued, feel anxious and stressed, and experience cravings for eggs and sweets.
  - Calcarea phosphorica is useful for stiffness, soreness, and weakness of your bones and joints.

- Phosphorus is indicated for spinal weakness and burning pain between your shoulders. If you are easily tired, weak, and crave refreshing foods (such as ice cream) and cold or carbonated drinks, this remedy may be for you.
- Silicea (silica) may be helpful if you are often chilly or nervous, tire easily, or if you have night sweats, injuries that are slow to heal, and a low resistance to infection.
- Comfrey (*Symphytum officinale*) strengthens and heals bones, so you can use it to ease the pain from earlier fractures.

## Mind/Body

A steady, long-term yoga practice is a wise choice if you have or are at risk for osteoporosis. Yoga not only reduces stress, but it also includes weight-bearing postures for your lower *and* upper body and spine. This is important because spinal fractures are a major cause of disability in women with osteoporosis.

For an excellent all-around pose, try Downward Facing Dog. (See pages 344–351 for postures.)

## Exercise

Perhaps more than any other part of the body, bone gives meaning to the phrase "use it or lose it." That's because bone cells, when stressed, respond by building more bone. The more you use your bones, the larger and stronger they get; bones literally alter their architecture in response to mechanical loading or weight-bearing.

But the opposite is also true; decreased stress, or not using bones, leads to profound and rapid bone loss. For example, after six months of immobilization from prolonged bed rest, you can lose as much as 50 to 55 percent of your bone mass. Studies of astronauts are enlightening in this respect, because the no-gravity atmosphere of space replicates the effects of not using bone. After five months on MIR, Russian cosmonauts typically lost around 40 percent of their bone mass. And once lost, bone is very hard to replace.

If you exercise regularly, you are more likely to have a greater peak bone mass, maintain bone mass as you age, and have a significantly lower risk of fractures. Weight-bearing exercises—those that work against gravity—increase muscle mass and bone formation. After consulting with your physician, develop this or a similar regular exercise program:

- Begin slowly
- Warm up for five minutes before each session and stretch for five to ten minutes afterward.
- Train with weights, with particular emphasis on your hip, spinal, and scapular (shoulder) muscles, every other day for six weeks.
- Add an aerobic exercise component. I recommend at least thirty minutes of weight-bearing activities on most days of the week. You want to stress your bones. In addition to weight-training, good activities include brisk walking, jogging or running, gymnastics, and basketball.

## Red Flags

Call your doctor if you develop:

- Pain in a bone that is severe and/or getting worse; you may have a fracture.
- Any visible deformity in a bone.
- Sudden pain in your back that wraps around in a bandlike fashion. You may have an osteoporotic compression fracture.

# 7

—

# Are You Well-Connected?

Your musculoskeletal system is a complex array of structures that provide movement, support, and protection. In Chapters 5 and 6, I described painful ailments that affect the "stars" of your musculoskeletal system—the bones, joints, muscles, and spine. In this chapter I will go into problems of the supporting actors—the tendons, ligaments, bursae, and menisci. These structures play a yeoman's role in stabilizing and aligning the movement of the body's bony framework.

## BURSITIS

### Description

Bursitis is an inflammation of the bursa (plural is bursae), which is a small, fluid-filled sac that allows friction-free motion of muscles and tendons over bones. The bursal sac is lined with a membrane that, much like the synovial lining of the joints, produces a lubricating fluid.

There are eighty bursae on each side of the body. Each one has its own special protective role. You can develop the swelling and pain of bursitis in the upper or lower extremities, but it usually occurs in the bursae around the elbows, shoulders, hips, knees, and other large joints.

Bursitis is a very common ailment, affecting between 5 and 10 percent of people over age sixty-five. Women suffer more frequently than men from bursitis at most ages.

Common forms of bursitis include:

## Upper Extremities

### Subacromial bursitis

Shoulder pain is one of the most common musculoskeletal complaints for people over age forty. Your shoulder is a complex ball and socket joint that facilitates arm movement in all directions. Normally, many types of structures, including muscles, bones, ligaments, and tendons, effortlessly come together at the shoulder, allowing it to function properly and coordinating pain-free motion. The bursae protect these structures and facilitate frictionless movement.

Several "sister" bursae in the shoulder are potential pain culprits, but the most common type of shoulder bursitis is subacromial bursitis, which is often associated with another condition — rotator cuff tendinitis, also known as impingement syndrome (see page 161).

Subacromial bursitis causes pain and aching in the front or side of the shoulder. If it's severe enough, the shoulder may also swell or feel warm. Because it hurts when you lift or rotate your arm, or raise it above your head, your shoulder's range of motion may be limited. Subacromial bursitis is sometimes the result of repetitive shoulder motion, such as overhead lifting. Arthritic conditions can also contribute to this ailment.

### Olecranon bursitis

Because it often results from chronic and prolonged pressure on the elbow, such as leaning on a table or desk for long periods of time, this ailment is sometimes called "student's elbow." It may also occur after a blow or other sudden injury.

Inflammatory conditions such as gout, pseudo-gout, or rheumatoid arthritis may play a role in the development of student's elbow. Less frequently, it may be the result of infection (septic bursitis) or it may develop if you are undergoing kidney dialysis.

Whatever the cause, the elbow reddens, feels warm, or becomes tender. You may also develop a fluid-filled sac around the joint.

## Lower Extremities

### Prepatellar bursitis

Also known as "housemaid's knee," this ailment can result from prolonged kneeling on a hard surface. It causes redness, swelling, and pain around the front of the lower portion of the kneecap. It is especially painful if you apply pressure to the knee.

### Infrapatellar bursitis

A relative of prepatellar bursitis, this condition involves the bursa right below the kneecap, between the patellar ligament and the shinbone.

### Pes anserine bursitis

Pes anserine bursitis is a common ailment in obese middle-aged or elderly women. If you take your fingers and place them on the medial, or inner, portion of your knee about 2 inches below the kneecap and press, prepare to yelp! Walking up steps can also be painful.

### Ischial bursitis

The ischial bursa is strategically located on top of the "sitting bone," the ischial tuberosity, and below the gluteus maximus, the large muscle in your buttock. Ischial bursitis may be caused by trauma, but it is more often the result of sitting on a hard surface for long periods of time. This accounts for its common name, "Weaver's bottom."

The pain of ischial bursitis can be excruciating. And because this bursa is situated so close to the gluteus maximus, you may also experience "referred" pain (pain not precisely at the site of injury) throughout the back of your buttock and thigh.

In addition to the standard conventional and complementary treatments (see below), you may get relief from sitting on a special gel-filled cushion.

### Trochanteric bursitis

The trochanter is a large, flat, expansive portion of the thigh bone, or femur. Since it is an anchor for many hip muscles, the trochanter is especially susceptible to injury.

More common in middle-aged and older people and in women, trochanteric bursitis causes aching pain and tenderness in the upper, outer part of the hip and the outer thigh. A good way to confirm this ailment is to apply deep pressure to the trochanteric area (over the side of your hip) and see if it hurts. You may also feel multiple tender points throughout the outer thigh muscle. It typically hurts more when you move your hip outward with your knee flexed at 90 degrees.

Besides traumatic and overuse injuries, rheumatoid arthritis, lumbar spine disease, leg-length discrepancy, and scoliosis may cause this problem. Your risk of developing trochanteric bursitis rises if you spend a lot of time on your feet, putting pressure on your hips, or if you are bedridden for long periods because of illness.

*Iliopectineal/iliopsoas bursitis*
Inflammation in the bursa located between your iliopsoas muscle and the inguinal ligament in the groin may cause tenderness and pain in that area. You may feel it when you bring your hip back (extension). Don't be surprised if you notice that your stride length is shorter; that's because you may be unconsciously taking smaller steps to avoid triggering pain when you extend your hip.

## Bursitis of the Feet (See Chapter 11 for more foot ailments)

*Retrocalcaneal bursitis*
This condition causes pain at the back of the heel, behind the Achilles tendon and in front of your calcaneus, or heel bone. It hurts most when you bring your foot and toes up (dorsiflexion). Common causes include bad shoes, walking too much, and trauma to your foot. In addition, certain diseases such as arthritis, gout, spondylitis, and Reiter's syndrome can contribute to its development.

*Achilles bursitis*
Also known as "pump bumps," this condition is all too common in women, thanks to tight, foot-damaging, high-heeled shoes. It occurs in a bursa located next to the lower portion of your Achilles tendon, right above the spot where your tendon attaches to the back of your heel bone. Sometimes, Achilles bursitis is the result of inflammatory diseases like gout, arthritis, and ankylosing spondylitis. (However, ankylosing spondylitis, or AS, is three times more common in men than in women.)

## Causes

In addition to the specific causes I described above, infection, injury, overuse, and prolonged pressure may all lead to inflammation and increased fluid in your bursae. Rheumatic disease or calcium buildup on the tendons connected to your joints may also contribute to the problem.

## Signs and Symptoms

- Loss of motion due to swelling
- Dull pain and tenderness
- Fluid accumulation

## Conventional Treatments

P.R.I.C.E.M.M is a handy mnemonic I teach my residents to remember for standard bursitis treatment:

Protection—Place a foam pad, pillow, or other cushioning over the inflamed bursa to prevent outside pressure or trauma that will worsen the pain.

Rest—To help inflamed tissues heal, limit weight-bearing on the joint, and avoid aggravating activities or anything that stresses neighboring bursae.

Ice—Apply ice to the area for fifteen to twenty minutes at least once a day, or as often as necessary, until the swelling goes down. I tell my patients to put the ice in a plastic sandwich bag, cover it with a cloth, and apply it to the inflamed area.

Compress—Put on an elastic bandage to limit motion and reduce swelling. If you prefer, you can wrap the area a few times, add an ice bag, and wrap it in place.

Elevate—Reduce the swelling by using pillows, a sofa back, or a chair to elevate the affected area, making sure it is higher than the joint above it. For example, if your elbow is inflamed, keep it higher than your shoulder.

Medication—You can use a variety of pain relievers, including acetaminophen, aspirin, and over-the-counter or prescription nonsteroidal anti-inflammatory drugs (NSAIDS), such as ibuprofen or Mobic. The new drugs, called Cox-2 inhibitors, may be a bit easier on your gastrointestinal tract. NSAIDS work particularly well since they have analgesic as well as anti-inflammatory properties. Topical application of aspirin-containing creams or rubs is another option.

Modalities—Use ice at first, when you are in the acute stage and the bursa is hot, tender, and inflamed. Once it has cooled down and swelling, tenderness, and inflammation have subsided, you've entered the chronic phase, when it's okay to use heat or ultrasound.

Gentle stretching exercises can help restore range of motion. You can follow them with strengthening exercises.

If these conventional treatments fail, your doctor may recommend a steroid injection, which will provide immediate relief. However, it can cause local trauma, bleeding, or black-and-blue marks. I discourage repeated (more than three times a year) injections with steroids, since they can damage surrounding tendon structures.

Should the inflamed area become infected, your doctor may need to prescribe antibiotics and drain the fluid.

## Dietary Strategies (See Chapter 14 for food sources of specified nutrients)

In general, it's important to stick with a well-balanced diet that emphasizes whole grains, fruits, and vegetables. Use sugar, alcohol, and salt only in moderation.

As I mentioned in Chapter 5, there are several emerging, scientifically proven nutritional and dietary strategies that reduce inflammation, curb pain, and decrease the swelling of arthritis. Since bursitis and tendinitis share some common inflammatory features with arthritis, some of the strategies mentioned earlier will help here as well. They include:

*Bromelain (See page 324)*

*Avocados and soybeans*
In 1998 French researchers focused on the potential value of an avocado/soybean oil combination. People in their study had less pain and used fewer pain relievers. There are many ways to eat soy. You can eat raw soybeans or try commercial brands that are lightly dried and toasted to enhance the taste. You can even sample soy chocolate bars. Some of these tasty items provide a whopping 12 grams of soy protein.

*Vitamin B3*
A 1996 study by Wayne Jonas, M.D., the former chief of the National Institutes of Health Office of Alternative Medicine, demonstrated in double-blind placebo-controlled fashion that taking niacinamide can improve joint flexibility and reduce inflammation. It also helped osteoarthritis patients use smaller doses of pain relievers.

*Vitamin E and selenium*
These nutrients may relieve pain.

*Fish oils*
Eating cold-water fish containing the essential oils known as omega-3 fatty acids blocks inflammation.

*Vitamin C*
A powerful antioxidant, this vitamin speeds repair of damaged tissue by fortifying collagen, an important biological protein within tendon, cartilage, and connective tissue. There are advantages to getting vitamin C from your food because it is bundled with carotenes, bioflavonoids, and other nutrients.

*Beta-carotene*
Another nutrient that speeds healing.

RECIPE

## PINEAPPLE SMOOTHIE

Besides bromelain, pineapple contains small amounts of vitamin C and fiber. Bromelain helps digest protein, so it's beneficial to eat it after consuming a heavy meat meal.

> 1 cup orange juice
> 1 cup frozen berries (strawberries, blueberries)
> 2 kiwis
> 1 fresh, ripe pineapple

1. Pour the orange juice into a powerful blender and add the berries.
2. Peel the kiwis and add them to the blender.
3. Trim the top and bottom off the pineapple and cut it into quarters lengthwise. Remove the peel, cut the pineapple quarters into chunks, and add to the blender.
4. Blend on high for 2 minutes or until well blended.
5. Drink immediately and enjoy!

SERVES 1

## Supplements

*Calcium*
Calcium builds bones, thereby fortifying neighboring bursae and other supportive structures. The accepted dose range is 1,300 to 2,500 mg a day.

*Magnesium*
Magnesium balances calcium and promotes muscular function. The accepted dose range is 320 to 350 mg a day.

*Vitamin A*
Vitamin A is an antioxidant that protects the body against damage from free radicals. The accepted dose range is 900 to 3,000 mcg a day.

### Vitamin C
Vitamin C, another powerful antioxidant, plays a role in reducing inflammation and promoting tissue healing. The accepted dose range is 90 to 2,000 mg a day.

### Vitamin E
Vitamin E is a worthwhile antioxidant with anti-inflammatory properties. The recommended dose range is between 15 and 1,000 mg a day.

### Vitamin B
Vitamin B complex is important for cellular repair. Take 1 tablet daily.

### Glucosamine sulfate
This is a nutritional supplement that comes from seashells or seafood. It is an important building block for the manufacture and repair of cartilage and the formation of connective tissue. Although its main use is for osteoarthritis, you can also use it for bursitis, since it improves joint motion and decreases pain and swelling. Take 500 mg three times a day.

### Methylsulfonylmethane (MSM)
This is a chemical compound that contains sulfur. It is found naturally in vegetables, fruits, milk, and meat. Early evidence from a study of people with osteoarthritis indicates that it reduces pain. Use as directed on the package label.

## Herbs

### Meadowsweet (Filipendula ulmaria)
This flowering plant of the meadow acts as an anti-inflammatory and contains flavonoids as well as salicylates (the active ingredient in aspirin). The recommended dose is up to three cups a day. Avoid meadowsweet if you are allergic to aspirin.

### White willow bark (Salix alba)
The bark of willow trees contains an anti-inflammatory compound similar to aspirin. You can use it to reduce your need for pain relievers. Unlike other anti-inflammatory drugs, willow may be less likely to upset your stomach because it is converted into its active ingredient (salicylic acid) after it is absorbed by your gut. The recommended dose is one cup of infusion, 3 to 5 times a day. Do not use this herb if you are allergic to aspirin or other

NSAIDS, when pregnant or breast-feeding. Use caution if you take blood-thinning medications.

### Devil's claw (Harpagophytum procumbens)

Despite its scary name, Devil's claw, which comes from the underground tuber of a South African plant, stood up as an effective herbal anti-inflammatory in a randomized, double-blind, multicenter study in France. Researchers compared the herb to a standard, slow-acting drug used to treat osteoarthritis. The two drugs relieved pain similarly, but the people in the group using Devil's claw used fewer NSAIDS and other analgesics and had significantly fewer side effects. Recommended use of Devil's claw is as an infusion, up to 3 times a day. Do not use Devil's claw if you are pregnant. Because it may aggravate your stomach, avoid it if you have gastritis or ulcers.

## Herbal Creams and Ointments

### Slippery elm (Ulmus fulva) and chamomile (Chamaemelum nobile or Matricaria recutita) poultice

Slippery elm, from the inner bark of a tree, and chamomile, a small, daisy-like flower, are both useful for fighting local inflammation. Mix 1 table-spoon of dried slippery elm with an equal amount of dried chamomile, and add hot water to make a paste. Spread it on a piece of clean cotton and apply to the affected area for forty-five minutes. You can do this three times a day.

### Comfrey (Symphytum officinale) liniment

Also known as knitbone or boneset, this common wild plant has large bristly leaves and purple flowers. It promotes healing because it contains allantoin, which assists in repairing damaged tissue, and rosmarinic acid, an anti-inflammatory. Because comfrey also contains pyrrolizidines, chemicals that are potentially toxic to the liver, it is best used externally.

### Aloe (Aloe vera)

A common house plant, aloe cools, soothes, and relieves inflammation. Creams are readily available; be sure to buy one with a high aloe content (it should appear as one of the first listed ingredients). To make your own medicated oil: Slice up the leaves of an aloe vera plant and put them in a glass jar. Cover with vegetable oil. Let the mixture steep for sixty days. Strain and store in a dark-colored container. Spread the oil on sore joints as necessary. If skin irritation occurs, discontinue.

*Joint-Ritis*

This commercially available pain reliever containing menthol, eucalyptus, copaiba oil, glucosamine, and chondroitin (the latter are skin emollients) is unique because of its composition, as well as its roll-on applicator. You can conveniently use it when bursitis flares up.

## Do-It-Yourself

*Baths*

Add cider vinegar or ginger (mix ½ teaspoon of ginger powder and 1 cup of hot water) to a bath or foot bath to fight inflammation.

*Compresses*

Hot or cold compresses can reduce swelling. Use cold initially, when the bursa is warm, red, and tender. Once this has subsided, you can use heat.

*Self-massage for the knee*

1. Sit on the floor or in a chair.
2. Put one hand on your thigh above your knee and the other hand on the side of your leg.
3. Move the hand on top of your leg in a circular motion that goes over the knee, along the side of the knee, and back to the starting position.
4. Make a similar motion with the other hand.
5. Continue to massage with alternating hands for 10 to 15 minutes.

*Aromatherapy*
- Juniper oil (*Juniperus communis*)—Add 3 to 4 drops of oil to the water for a cold compress. Do not use while pregnant, or if you have kidney disease.
- Soothing bath—Add 3 drops of lavender oil, 3 drops of chamomile oil, and 2 drops of neroli oil (made from bitter orange blossoms) to a warm bath.
- Pain relief massage—Add the preceding mixture to 3 teaspoons of grapeseed or sweet almond oil and use it to massage the sore spots.
- Rosemary (*Rosmarinus officinalis*)—To fight inflammation and relieve pain, add a few drops of rosemary oil to the water for a compress. Or add it to a neutral oil or lotion and use it to massage the sore area.

You might also enjoy this after-sport shower formula: Add 2 drops of rosemary oil, 2 drops of pine oil, and 4 drops of lemon oil to a small dollop of unscented shower gel. Work it into a lather with a sponge and use it in the shower.

Avoid rosemary if you're pregnant or if you have epilepsy or high blood pressure.

*Homeopathy*
There are many homeopathic remedies for specific symptoms of bursitis. A good all-purpose homeopathic ointment is Traumeel, which contains twelve ingredients, including: *Calendula officinalis* (marigold), *Arnica montana*, *Hamamelis virginiana* (witch hazel), Millefolium (milifoil), Belladonna (nightshade), *Aconitum napellus* (monkshood), Chamomilla, *Symphytum officinale* (comfrey), *Bellis perennis* (daisy), *Echinacea angustifolia* (coneflower), and *Hypericum perforatum* (St. John's wort).

*Reflexology (See page 353 for techniques)*
Try these points:

- Shoulder and Neck
    - SI-3 (Small Intestine-3), "Black Ravine"—along the outer side of the fifth metacarpophalangeal joint base of the pinky.
    - SI-9 (Jian Zhen), "True Shoulder"—at the border of the scapular (the bone at the back of the shoulder) and the deltoid muscle.
    - SI-11 "Celestial Gathering"—on the scapular, just below the infraspinatus muscle, right in the middle of the spine.
- Forearm and Wrist
    - On the outer side (ulnar side) of the base of the pinky.
- Elbow or Knee
    - On the outer foot, approximately mid-foot, behind the bony prominence (toward the heel).
- Hip
    - On the foot, at the base of the padded part of the heel.

## Mind/Body

*Yoga*
Try Sankatasana (Contracted Posture) and Garudasana (Eagle Posture). (See pages 344–351 for postures.)

## Exercise

Use gentle, controlled movements to feel better and maintain mobility.

PENDULUM FOR SHOULDER INJURIES AND TO KEEP THE
SHOULDER MOBILE
1. Stand or sit in a chair.
2. Bend slightly at the waist toward your injured side, and reach out with
   your arm a few inches from your body.
3. Slowly make small circles, forward and then backward, 5 times each
   way.
4. Do this for 5 minutes, twice a day.

SCAPULAR RANGE OF MOTION
FOR SHOULDER BURSITIS
1. Shrug your shoulders up and hold 5 seconds, then release.
2. Squeeze your shoulder blades together, hold 5 seconds, then release.
3. Relax for 5 seconds.
4. Repeat 10 times.

WAND EXERCISE
FOR SHOULDER BURSITIS
1. Hold a stick or a lightweight broom in both hands.
2. Keep your arms straight and lift them up over your head. If you feel
   pain, lower your arms slightly. Hold 5 seconds.
3. Lower your arms completely.
4. Repeat 10 times.

HIP STRETCH
FOR TROCHANTERIC BURSITIS
1. Stand sideways, one arm-length away from a wall, with your injured hip
   toward the wall.
2. Rest your hand on the wall, with your arm straight out.
3. Push your hip toward the wall.
4. Repeat 5 times.

## Seeking Help from Complementary Practitioners

*Massage (See page 326)*
Avoid direct massage for areas that are acutely inflamed.

## Red Flags

Call your doctor if you experience:

- Repeated pain or discomfort in a joint
- Fever, increased swelling, oozing, or other signs of infection
- Sweating

### TINA'S STORY

Tina is a successful thirty-two-year-old account executive for a dot-com start-up. Her job calls for a great deal of traveling, since she represents her company at national trade shows throughout the United States. Today, she is trim and fit, and she enjoys playing tennis whenever she has the time.

When I first met her, though, her tennis game was in serious trouble. Over the course of three months she had developed a dull, aching pain in her elbow and forearm. The pain was annoying at best, and it really flared up when she was whacking forehands on the court. "I take Advil, which provides some relief, but it only lasts for a little while," she said. Tina's boyfriend, a third-year medical student, suggested that it might be tennis elbow, and sent her to see me.

I had already noticed that Tina winced when I gently shook her hand and introduced myself. I wasn't surprised; when you have tennis elbow, movements that extend your wrist irritate an already sore, inflamed outer elbow. As I examined her, I noted that she had pain and tenderness in her elbow and throughout her forearm. In spite of her elbow pain, however, her neck and back were fine. Nor did she have any loss in strength or changes in her reflexes or sensations.

Recognizing the important impact of mechanical stressors on her pain, I described for Tina the biomechanics of her arm and elbow, and how she might be exacerbating her pain with her tennis game. I could see the disappointment in her eyes when I advised her to ease off for a while: "I was afraid you were going to say that. Tennis is the one thing I do to stay fit and keep my weight down," she said. I suggested she start a swimming program at the local Y, at least for the short term.

I had also noticed another nonmedical problem during the course of our visit. When I took Tina's history, she joked that her computer was her lifeline: "I'm tethered to it, Doctor; I carry a briefcase with a fully equipped laptop wherever I go." Since traveling without her computer was out of the question, I suggested that she buy a backpack-style carrier for it.

To ease her pain, I prescribed a tennis elbow splint and started her on acupuncture. And for home benefit, I provided her with a diagram of acupressure points as well as a technique for self-massage, and a sample of a topical rub, called Joint-Ritis.

Although Tina loved her job, the constant traveling and presentations were stressful. And stress makes pain worse, so I taught her an easy-to-use relaxation and meditation technique.

Several weeks later, Tina came back for a follow-up. Her pain wasn't entirely gone, but it had improved significantly. She had found a stylish backpack for her laptop and was doing relaxation exercises while enduring the inevitable delays at airports: "It makes the waits bearable and it keeps me away from the fast-food stands," she said. And she was staying only at hotels that had swimming pools. "Swimming isn't so bad, after all," she confessed. Then, she laughed: "But when can I get back to tennis?"

## TENDINITIS

### Description

Tendons are fibrous, cordlike structures that attach the muscles to the bones. They are strong, but not particularly elastic. Overuse or sudden, abrupt movement may inflame tendons, causing tendinitis. More common in women than in men, tendinitis can happen in many areas of the body. The most common types of tendinitis are:

#### Upper Extremities

*Rotator cuff tendinitis (also called supraspinatus tendinitis or impingement syndrome)*
This ailment, clearly the most frequent cause of shoulder pain in both women and men, can be extremely painful. In its chronic form, it causes dull, aching pain on the side of the shoulder, over the rotator cuff muscles. Typically, you suffer most when you raise your arm to the side (abduction) between 60 and 120 degrees, and when you lower it. So putting on your blouse or brassiere becomes a grueling exercise. In severe cases, all shoulder motion is painful.

Acute rotator cuff tendinitis is more frequent in younger women. It can cause sudden, sharp pain in the shoulder. Usually, this is the result of calcium deposits that form in the supraspinatus tendon. Again, it really hurts to reach over your head or behind your back. And your pain may be worse at night. Sometimes subacromial bursitis (see page 149) exacerbates rotator cuff tendinitis pain.

Rotator cuff tendinitis may develop for many reasons. Excessive overhead shoulder and arm motions such as lifting a baby over your head to play, clearing the top shelves of the pantry, or loading and unloading bookshelves are frequently a source of the problem. Sometimes, trauma or a blow to the shoulder is the offender. Chronic diseases like rheumatoid or osteoarthritis can play a role. So can getting old; as you age, bony outgrowths called osteophytes may form under your acromioclavicular joint, the hinge between the collarbone and the shoulder blade, and they can cause tendinitis.

### Bicipital tendinitis
This ailment causes pain in the front of the shoulder, right where the biceps tendon originates. Sometimes, the pain radiates down to the forearm. Bicipital tendinitis commonly occurs when the acromion—the outer, upper edge of the shoulder blade—pinches its neighboring biceps tendon. In medical lingo, the symptoms get worse when you "supinate your forearm against resistance." In plain English, it hurts to use a screwdriver to turn a tight screw or twist a corkscrew to open a bottle of wine.

### Lateral epicondylitis
This overuse injury, commonly known as "tennis elbow," affects not only tennis players but also anyone who repeatedly performs activities that involve bending the wrist up against resistance (forcible wrist extension). You'll notice pain and tenderness on the outside of the elbow and sharp pain when you grip something or twist your hand and forearm. Bending your wrist up often makes the pain worse. Even simple actions, such as lifting a tote bag or portfolio, shaking hands or gardening, can make you wince (see Chapter 10 for more information).

### Medial epicondylitis
Tenderness on the inside of the arm is the hallmark of this type of tendinitis, which is also called "golfer's elbow." It's especially painful when you flex your wrist (bend it down) against resistance (see Chapter 10 for more information).

### Tenosynovitis
This is an inflammation of a tendon that extends to the synovium, or joint lining. It usually occurs in the hands, feet, and other areas that have many small joints.

- De Quervain's tenosynovitis — Repetitive tasks using thumb and wrist motions cause this ailment, which involves pain, swelling, and tenderness along the thumb. It also affects the tip of the radius bone, which goes from the wrist to the elbow. De Quervain's tenosynovitis is common in pregnant women. If you're a new mom, you may find that lifting your baby up, diapering her, or closing safety pins makes it hurt more. You can confirm that you have this problem by gently folding your thumb into your palm, wrapping your fingers around it, and deviating your wrist downward, to the ulnar, or outer side.
- Flexor tenosynovitis — Rest is usually sufficient treatment for this complaint, which causes pain in the palm of the hand that worsens when you move your fingers.

## Lower Extremities

For more about foot and ankle ailments, see Chapters 10 and 11.

### Patellar tendinitis

"Jumper's knee" causes pain, tenderness, and swelling of the tendon that connects the kneecap and the leg. Repetitive jumping, running, volleyball, basketball, and high-impact aerobics are likely to make your symptoms worse. Kickboxers and cheerleaders beware!

### Achilles tendinitis

A common complaint among runners, Achilles tendinitis causes inflammation and pain in the tendon that connects the heel bone and the calf muscle (see Chapter 10 for more information). Discomfort and swelling can also occur over the spot where the tendon attaches. Overuse, tight calf muscles, uphill running, or a too rapid or sudden increase in sports activities can lead to Achilles tendinitis. It is often worsened by diseases like gout, rheumatoid arthritis, and Reiter's syndrome.

## Causes

Although its possible causes are numerous, tendinitis is usually the result of overuse or overtraining. It develops when repeated motions cause tiny tears, inflammation, and thickening in the tendon.

## Signs and Symptoms

- Sharp or dull pain, which is worse when you use the tendon
- Limitation of motion

- Tenderness
- Swelling

## Conventional Treatments

P.R.I.C.E.M.M is the mnemonic I teach my residents to remember for standard tendinitis treatment. Refer to page 152 for specifics.

Your doctor may refer you for shoe supports, orthotics, or other shoe corrections. If you have Achilles tendinitis, a heel cup, a cushioned orthotic made of rubberized material that you insert into your shoe, may be helpful. It absorbs impact, relieves heel pain, and may reduce the load on your Achilles tendon.

Speaking of shoes, you should probably take a skeptical look at yours. Often, the wrong types of shoes or poor-fitting shoes can exacerbate tendinitis.

If these conventional treatments fail, your doctor may recommend a steroid injection. It will provide immediate relief but it can cause local trauma, bleeding, or black-and-blue marks. I discourage repeated (more than three times a year) injections with steroids, since they can cause damage to surrounding tendon structures.

## Dietary Strategies (See Chapter 14 for food sources of specified nutrients)

*Vitamin C*
A powerful antioxidant, this vitamin prevents free radical damage and is a critical player in the manufacture of collagen, which is an important biological protein found within tendon, cartilage, and connective tissue. Getting your vitamin C from citrus carries a bonus because it's also rich in quercetin and other bioflavonoids that appear to play a role in wound healing and tendon recovery after injury. One study of forty collegiate football players showed that taking vitamin C and citrus bioflavonoids before competition can reduce athletic injuries.

*Vitamin E and selenium*
For pain relief.

*Beta-carotene*

*Bromelain (See page 324)*

*Turmeric (Curcuma longa)*
An integral part of Indian cooking, this spice has anti-inflammatory properties. Do not use turmeric if you have hepatitis or if you are pregnant or trying to conceive.

## RECIPE

### COUSCOUS WITH TURMERIC

*4 cups water*
*2 cups couscous*
*3 teaspoons olive oil*
*¼ teaspoon cinnamon*
*¼ teaspoon saffron*
*¼ teaspoon cumin*
*1 teaspoon turmeric*
*½ cup chopped green pepper*
*1 cup grated carrots*
*1 teaspoon pure maple syrup*
*2 cloves garlic, minced*
*1 can chickpeas, rinsed and drained*

1. Bring the water to a boil.
2. Add all the ingredients, reduce heat and simmer, covered, for 10 minutes.
3. Remove from heat and let stand for 5 minutes.
4. Fluff with a fork.

SERVES 6

## Supplements

*Vitamin C*
This vitamin speeds healing. The acceptable daily dose range is 90 to 2,000 mg. It's best to break up the dose throughout the day. Excessive amounts may cause kidney stones, gout, cramps, or diarrhea.

*Vitamin E*
The recommended dose range for this antioxidant is between 15 and 1,000 mg a day.

## Zinc

Zinc is a nutrient that encourages healing. The acceptable range is 8 to 40 mg a day.

## Selenium

Selenium is a trace element and antioxidant. The acceptable range is 60 to 400 mcg a day.

## Vitamin B

Vitamin B complex is important for cellular repair. Take one pill a day.

## Calcium

Calcium helps to build bones and fortify joints and connective tissue. You can take between 1,300 and 2,500 mg a day.

## Magnesium

Magnesium balances calcium and promotes muscular function. The recommended dose range is between 320 and 350 mg a day.

## Vitamin A

Vitamin A is an antioxidant that prevents free radical damage to tissue. The recommended dose range is between 900 and 3,000 mcg a day.

## SAMe (S-adenosyl methionine)

This compound occurs naturally in the body and is a key player in many biochemical reactions. SAMe has proven itself a helpful supplement for arthritis pain relief. It also helps tendinitis pain. Multiple scientific studies and many of my patients vouch for its effectiveness, with some reporting that it is as effective as NSAIDS. The starting dose is 200 mg twice daily. In large doses, SAMe can upset the stomach. Do not take SAMe if you take levodopa for Parkinson's disease. This nutrient may trigger manic episodes in people with bipolar disease.

## Glucosamine sulfate and chondroitin

Used to bolster bones and cartilage, these can fortify the joints, potentially making them less susceptible to bursitis and tendinitis. Take 500 mg of each, three times a day.

## Creatine and HMB

Although creatine and HMB (beta-hydroxy-beta-methylbutyric acid) have been touted as a possible remedy for tendinitis, I don't recommend these supplements since there is insufficient scientific evidence to back up their use.

## Herbs

*White willow bark* (Salix alba)
If you want to reduce your dependence on pain relievers, try white willow. This tree's bark contains an anti-inflammatory compound much like aspirin. And willow is less likely than other anti-inflammatory drugs to upset your stomach because it is converted into its active ingredient (salicylic acid) after it is absorbed by your gut. The recommended dose is one cup of infusion, three to five times a day. Do not use willow if you are allergic to aspirin or other NSAIDS, when pregnant or breast-feeding. Use caution if you take blood-thinning medications.

*Horse chestnut*
Classically used to treat varicose veins and swelling, horse chestnut may cut down swelling from tendinitis. It's too soon for me to make a recommendation, but this is one I'm following; future research will tell the full story.

*Grapeseed oil, pine bark, and bilberry*
These all contain OPCs (oligomeric proanthocyanidins), which help to decrease inflammation and nourish elastin and collagen. OPCs are safe and nontoxic but can interact with blood thinners. Follow package instructions for dosing.

## Herbal Creams and Ointments

*Capsaicin cream* (0.025–0.075 percent) (See page 96)

*Arnica* (Arnica montana)
Easy-to-find ointments made from this well-known herb are useful for tendinitis, bursitis, joint problems, swelling, and bruising.

*Joint-Ritis* (See page 96)

*Turmeric infused oil*
Apply a turmeric-infused oil externally to fight inflammation around sore areas.

## Do-It-Yourself

*Compress and wrap*
- Apply a vinegar compress to reduce inflammation.
- Wrap a wet plantain leaf around the affected area to reduce swelling and stiffness and encourage healing.

*Aromatherapy*
- Lavender (*Lavandula angustifolia*)—This herb calms and soothes your spirits and reduces pain. Add four drops of the essential oil to a bath or the water for a cold compress. Or try adding three drops of lavender oil, three drops of chamomile oil, and two drops of neroli oil to a warm bath. If you prefer, you can add this mixture to 3 teaspoons of grapeseed or sweet almond oil and use it for a massage. Be careful with lavender if you have hay fever or asthma; it could cause an allergic reaction.
- Rosemary (*Rosmarinus officinalis*)—To fight inflammation and relieve pain, add a few drops of rosemary oil to the water for a compress, or put it in a neutral oil or lotion and use it to massage the sore area.
- Chamomile (*Chamaemelum nobile* or *Matricaria recutita*)—Make a soothing compress by adding four or five drops of chamomile oil to a bowl of ice cold water. Soak a cloth in the bowl, wring it out, and apply to the painful area. Avoid contact with your eyes; it may cause irritation. Do not use chamomile oil during the first three months of pregnancy.

*Reflexology (see Bursitis, page 158)*

## Seeking Help from Complementary Practitioners

*Acupuncture*
I use acupuncture frequently for my patients with tendinitis. My personal experience is buttressed by reports issued by both the World Health Organization and the National Institutes of Health Consensus Panel, which support acupuncture's effectiveness for this ailment.

## Red Flags

Call your doctor if you experience:

- Prolonged pain
- Persistent swelling
- Fever

- Loss of muscle strength
- Numbness or tingling

## INJURIES OF THE LIGAMENTS AND MENISCI

Joints are formed where bones come together. To keep joints stable, their connecting surfaces must be firmly reinforced. Two key structures perform this role. Ligaments serve as guide wires that allow the joints to move in a particular direction without deviating. They actually connect bone to bone. Menisci are made of fibrous cartilage; they protect the connecting bones. When you injure menisci or ligaments, you may also harm your joint.

Unlike injuries to the tendons and bursae, injuries of the ligaments and menisci, especially tears, are frequently severe enough to require surgery. And they also cause major-league pain.

There are many joints that benefit from the structural support of ligaments and menisci, but these injuries usually involve the knee and ankle. (For more information on treating specific ligament injuries, see Chapter 10.)

### The Knee

The knee is vulnerable, especially if you run or play contact sports. Ligament injuries are common and problematic, since they can trigger additional damage to other structures of the knee joint, including the menisci. The knee may start to wobble or buckle, making it difficult to walk. And you may also become predisposed to early degenerative arthritis.

Four ligaments are most frequently affected. The lateral and medial collateral ligaments, located on each side of the knee, connect the upper outer portion of the lower leg bone (fibula) to the bottom portion of the thigh bone (the femur) and stabilize the knee. They also prevent the knee from moving side to side. In addition, you have two ligaments inside the knee — the anterior cruciate and posterior cruciate ligaments. They also provide stability and prevent the knee from overextending or rotating too much.

### Meniscal injuries

A meniscus is a tough, rubberlike piece of cartilage in the knee that acts as a shock absorber. It cushions and protects the joint surface. In each knee, you have a medial meniscus and a lateral meniscus. The most common injury is a meniscal tear. You'll need a positive MRI to clinch the diagnosis, but symptoms may include one or more of the following:

- You cannot flex the knee or extend it beyond resting position.
- The knee is locked in full extension.
- You have tenderness along the joint line.

The first line of treatment for meniscal injury is to apply ice to the knee for twenty to thirty minutes every three or four hours for two or three days. You can use an elastic bandage around the knee to keep down the swelling; it also helps to elevate your knee with a pillow beneath it for support. You may need to use crutches to relieve pressure on the joint and anti-inflammatory drugs for the pain.

## The Ankle

The ankle is also prone to ligament injuries. Sprains often happen after a sudden twisting or turning motion that stretches or tears the ligament. Running, wearing improper shoes, or walking on uneven terrain can result in a sprained ankle.

# 8

—

# You've Got Nerve

Pain—that unpleasant sensory feeling that signals damage to your body or a perceived threat to your existence—could not be possible without an elaborate communication infrastructure, known as the nervous system. Here's a brief primer on how it works.

Neurons (nerve cells) are the basic building block of the nervous system. There are an estimated 100 billion throughout the human body and each is composed of a cell body, an axon for sending messages, and a receiving device known as a dendrite. Neurons interconnect with each other in complex ways to form nerves. Faster than the highest-speed modem, almost too fast to comprehend, nerves transmit messages in the form of electrical signals from the axon of one neuron to a neighboring neuron's dendrite.

Each axon is surrounded by myelin, an insulation material that enables efficient nerve transmission. As they travel, the electrical impulses encounter synapses, strategically positioned between the neurons, which release neurotransmitters. These specialized chemicals, such as serotonin and dopamine, help facilitate message delivery.

Nerves are essential for detecting pain. Throughout your body, you have specialized pain receptors that convey messages along the nerves to the spinal cord and then to the brain.

Two components, the central nervous system and the peripheral nervous system, comprise the nervous system. The central nervous system includes the brain and spinal cord.

The peripheral nervous system is made up of all the nerves outside of the central nervous system. This includes the cranial nerves, which connect the nose, eyes, and ears to the brain, and the many nerves that link the spinal cord to the arms, legs, and torso.

The peripheral nervous system serves as an "electronic bridge" between the central nervous system and the rest of the body. There are thirty-one pairs of spinal nerves that come off of the spinal cord. Each pair has one in the front (motor nerve), which transmits information from the spinal cord to the muscles, and one in the back (sensory nerve), which moves sensory information to the spinal cord. The spinal nerves form "plexuses," or networks, in the neck, shoulders, and pelvis. These networks divide, forming peripheral nerves that supply the outer reaches of the body.

Made of bundles of nerve fibers, peripheral nerves vary in diameter, depending on the type of information they carry. They are insulated by multiple layers of a fatty material called myelin, which facilitates the transfer of impulses. The smaller fibers carry sensory information, such as temperature and pain, from the body to the spine, whereas larger fibers transmit motor information from the spine outward to power the muscles. Larger fibers also carry some information on touch and position.

Many very painful conditions derive from nerve dysfunction, especially in women. The first part of this chapter deals with three ailments caused by nerve compression: carpal tunnel syndrome, cubital tunnel syndrome, and thoracic outlet syndrome. I use the same dietary strategies, supplements, and herbal treatments for all three, so I'm putting those recommendations right up front. You'll find other, specific information on each of these conditions in the sections that follow.

The remainder of the chapter covers two long-term, chronic nerve problems — reflex sympathetic dystrophy and peripheral neuropathy — and briefly touches on shingles (herpes zoster) and trigeminal neuralgia (tic douloureux), an excruciating ailment that affects the trigeminal nerve in the face.

## Dietary Strategies (See Chapter 14 for food sources of specified nutrients)

- Cut back on salt, since it increases water retention that may aggravate swelling.
- Eat pineapple, which contains bromelain (see page 324).
- Cook with turmeric or ginger, which may enhance bromelain's anti-inflammatory effects.
- Green tea contains a number of chemical constituents with anti-inflammatory properties, including polyphenols and apigenin. Besides the great reputation that green tea has earned for its overall health benefits, it may also protect against osteoporosis, cancer, and heart disease. According to the U.S. Department of Agriculture Phytochemical Database, green tea contains many phytonutrients that may help prevent ulcers. If you frequently take NSAIDS, green tea may give your GI tract some extra protection. Try to drink three to four cups a day.

- Vitamin B2 (riboflavin) enhances the effectiveness of B6.
- Vitamin B6 plays a role in the production of neurotransmitters, specialized chemicals that transport signals between nerve cells. It may be of help for all types of nerve pain conditions.

R E C I P E

## SAVORY SPINACH BARLEY

2 tablespoons olive oil
2 cloves garlic, minced
1 onion, chopped
¼ cup chopped fresh parsley
8 ounces frozen chopped spinach, thawed and drained
2 cups water
1 cup barley

1. In a saucepan, sauté in the olive oil the garlic, onion, parsley, and spinach for 3 minutes.
2. Add water and bring to a boil.
3. Stir in the barley, lower heat, cover pot, and simmer on low heat for 35 minutes.

SERVES 4

## Supplements

*Vitamin B6*

Although you may have to wait several months to see the effects, this vitamin may ease nerve-related symptoms. Start with 50 mg a day and gradually increase the dose. Or you can take a B complex that contains B6.

If your symptoms get worse, stop taking the vitamin and consult your physician. Excessive, long-term, daily doses of vitamin B6 can cause nerve damage. Do not use vitamin B6 if you are taking anticonvulsants for epilepsy or levodopa for Parkinson's disease. You may need to take more if you are taking: isoniazid, penicillamine, theophylline, MAO inhibitors, or hydralazine. The acceptable range for this vitamin is 2 to 100 mg a day.

### Vitamin B2 (Riboflavin)

To increase the effects of B6, the acceptable dose is 1.1 mg a day. The upper limit has not been determined. You can also take it as part of a B complex.

### Bromelain

This also helps to supplement the effects of vitamin B6 and turmeric (see below). Bromelain is best consumed in its natural form — pineapple. Still, if you wish to supplement, a dose of 40 mg, taken two to three times a day, has been used in several studies. Do not take bromelain if you are on anticoagulant medications.

### Green tea

Green tea may help reduce your pain. If you prefer pills to tea, take 100 to 150 mg of green tea extract, three times a day.

## Herbs

### Ginger (Zingibar officinale)

To enhance the effects of bromelain (see above), the suggested dose is 100 to 300 mg of this anti-inflammatory herb three times a day. Even better, use it to spice up your meals. Other options include ginger tea and ginger candy. Ginger may cause mild heartburn; avoid it if you have gallstones.

### Chamomile (Chamaemelum nobile or Matricaria recutita)

Dating back to biblical times, chamomile is a mild stress reducer and re-laxant. It also helps fight inflammation. To make chamomile tea, pour 150 ml of boiling water over 3 grams of chamomile, cover for ten to fifteen minutes and strain. (Note: one teaspoon equals one gram.) Drink three cups a day.

### Turmeric (Curuma longa)

Turmeric helps reduce the inflammation associated with nerve compression syndromes. It is available in capsules, tablets, and liquid extracts. Be sure any product you buy contains at least 95 percent curcumin, the active ingredient. The recommended dose is 400 to 600 mg of curcumin, three times a day. Avoid turmeric or check with your doctor if you have gallstones or blood clotting or fertility problems. Prolonged use or higher doses may cause stomach upset or ulcers.

*Passionflower* (Passiflora incarnata)
If your symptoms get worse at night, try this herb, which helps you relax and improves sleep patterns. The recommended dose is one cup of tea twice a day. Use caution if you take sedative medications. This herb is on the Food and Drug Administration's list of herbs "generally recognized as safe" (GRAS).

## Herbal Creams and Ointments

*Traumeel ointment (See page 158)*

*Capsaicin cream (0.025–0.075 percent) (See page 96)*

*Arnica cream*
The German Commission E has approved arnica as a topical agent with anti-inflammatory, analgesic, and antibacterial properties. It reduces pain, numbness, and tingling.

*Joint-Ritis (See page 96)*

*Sports gel*
You can rub on this homeopathic gel, made from *Bellis perennis* (daisy), *Hypericum perforatum* (St. John's wort), *Rhus toxicodendron* (poison ivy), and *Ruta graveolens* (rue), up to four times a day.

*Nature's Chemist (See page 96)*

# CARPAL TUNNEL SYNDROME (CTS)

## Description

The carpal tunnel is a narrow passageway in the wrist through which the median nerve travels. This is the major peripheral nerve supplying the thumb side of the hand. When it is compressed, carpal tunnel syndrome, a common, painful disorder of the wrist and hand, is the result.

The pain of carpal tunnel syndrome ranges from minor and tolerable to truly miserable. My patients describe it in many ways—"electriclike," dull and aching, lacerating, burning. Particularly bothersome is the numbness, tingling, and pain in the first three fingers of the hand. At night, in certain sleeping positions, it may hurt more; you may even find yourself waking up to shake your hands out. As the syndrome advances, the hand muscles may weaken and atrophy (thin).

This annoying ailment seems to favor women; in one study, three times as many women as men suffered from CTS. Why this is so is the subject of several theories:

- Anatomical—women are simply made differently from men. Because they have smaller wrists, their median nerve must travel through a narrower space.
- Vocational—women are more frequently employed in jobs that require repetitive movements of the hands and wrists.
- Recreational—many women are involved in recreational pursuits like gardening, ceramic work, and needlecrafts that also involve repetitive motion and take a toll on the wrist.
- Hormonal—CTS is sometimes associated with hormonal changes due to the menstrual cycle, birth control pills, pregnancy, and menopause.

CTS is often job-related. It is well known as an ailment of people who do data entry or other jobs with heavy use of computers. But it can affect anyone who performs repetitive hand motions—illustrators, carpenters, assembly-line workers, knitting workers, and guitar players, for example. People with rheumatoid arthritis, diabetes, and hypothyroidism are also prone to developing CTS. This condition usually occurs between forty and sixty years of age.

## Causes

A large percentage of CTS cases are idiopathic, meaning that we don't know the cause. When we can figure out why CTS has occurred, it's usually due to one of two reasons. Sometimes the ligaments and tendons passing through the carpal tunnel have gotten bigger because of swelling, caused by repetitive motion. Or, the tunnel has gotten narrower, thanks to fluid retention, fat deposition, carpal synovitis, tenosynovitis, a fracture, arthritic spurs, or tumor. Either way, the net result is the same: compression of the median nerve, pain, and discomfort.

## Signs and Symptoms

Carpal tunnel syndrome usually strikes the dominant hand, but it may occur in either or both. Symptoms include:

- Tingling and numbness in the thumb, index finger, middle finger, and half of the ring finger
- Numbness, tingling, and/or burning in the wrist, palm, and forearm
- More pain when you bend your wrist
- Loss of strength in the affected hand(s)
- Clumsiness and inability to hold or feel objects
- Symptoms are often worse at night
- Shaking or rubbing your hand(s) provides relief

## Conventional Treatments

Your doctor may recommend a special test, called a nerve conduction velocity study/electromyography examination, to electrically troubleshoot the median nerve. Usually, a physiatrist or a neurologist performs this assessment.

If you have carpal tunnel syndrome, you'll want to avoid activities that overuse the affected hand. You can also support your wrist by wearing a splint when sleeping or during physical activity.

Depending on your job, one of the key treatments may be making changes in your work habits. An occupational therapist can help you figure out how to modify your regular tasks to prevent carpal tunnel syndrome or reduce the likelihood of a recurrence. It's important to pay attention to proper ergonomics. If you work at a computer, repositioning your workstation to better support your arm and wrist is at the top of the list. Adjust the height of your chair so that your arms and wrists are in a straight line with your elbows at a 90-degree angle. And when you type, your arm, wrist, and thumb should be in a straight line, with your fingers lower than your wrist. Do not rest your hand on the keyboard or mouse pad and take frequent breaks, as often as every hour.

NSAIDS, such as ibuprofen or naproxen, are the first line of treatment for pain and inflammation. You can also try topical analgesics. Neuropathic pain agents (drugs that act on nerves), like Neurontin, are sometimes used. If these treatments don't help, your doctor may recommend corticosteroid injections. I believe a steroid injection into the carpal tunnel can sometimes help, but it should not be done repeatedly. If conservative treatments fail and your pain continues to worsen, or you develop muscle atrophy and hand weakness, you may need surgery.

## Do-It-Yourself

*Ice*

When your symptoms are acute, apply a flexible ice pack (or a bag of frozen peas) to your wrist for ten minutes every hour. Cold constricts blood vessels and will reduce swelling.

*Every day*

Use these simple techniques to take care of your wrists:

- Elevate your arm with pillows when you lie down.
- Avoid resting your wrists on hard or ridged surfaces for prolonged periods.
- Take regular breaks from repetitive motion. At least once an hour, flex your fingers and shake your hands.
- Try to keep your wrists straight. Flexing or twisting stresses the carpal tunnel.
- To reduce strain on your wrists, use both hands to lift objects.

*Magnet therapy*

Although I haven't seen solid research, there is anecdotal evidence that magnet therapy provides relief for some people with CTS. The idea is that the magnets create a mild electric current that stimulates nerve endings and blocks pain sensation. To try this treatment, buy magnets that have at least 250–500 gauss (the unit for magnet strength); button-sized magnets are best for this ailment. Position the magnets above and below the wrist crease and hold them in place with adhesive tape. You can also buy wristbands with magnets.

*Acupressure (See page 353 for technique)*

This treatment may lessen swelling and numbness. To decrease pain, promote relaxation, and reduce stress associated with carpal tunnel and other disorders, try:

- LI4 (Large Intestine 4), located at the top of the web space between the thumb and second finger. Do not use it when you are pregnant.

## Mind/Body

*Yoga*

I recommend yoga to my carpal tunnel syndrome patients because it is an effective treatment for this condition, in addition to its general health benefits. According to a study published in the *Journal of the American Medical Association*, patients who did yoga twice a week for eight weeks had less pain and more flexibility and strength than those using a splint, a conventional treatment for CTS. Try Overhead Arm Extension and Trunk Extension. (See pages 344–351 for postures.)

## Exercise

Doing gentle exercise every day may relieve your pain and improve function. It will also prevent further injury.

THERAPEUTIC EXERCISES
Try these simple exercises three to four times a day.

- Lift your arms above your head, and rotate them inward and outward.
- Extend your arms straight out in front. Move your hands in a circle, using your wrists. Repeat in the opposite direction.
- Hold your hands out in front of you with palms up. Close your fingers into your palms and open slowly until you feel a pull in the muscles. Close your hands and repeat.
- With your palms together, press your fingertips against each other. Hold, release, and repeat.
- Wrap a rubber band around all of your fingers. Spread your fingers, hold, and release.

ACTIVE RANGE OF MOTION
- Flexion: Gently bend your wrist forward. Hold 5 seconds. Relax. Repeat 10 times.
- Extension: Gently bend your wrist backward. Hold 5 seconds. Relax. Repeat 10 times.
- Side to side: Gently move your wrist from side to side (a handshake motion). Hold 5 seconds at each end. Relax. Repeat 10 times.
- Stretching: With your uninjured hand, bend your injured wrist down by pressing the back of your hand. Hold for 15 to 30 seconds. Relax. Then, stretch your injured hand back by pressing the fingers in a backward direction. Hold 15 to 30 seconds. Relax. Repeat.

- Tendon glides: Extend the fingers of your injured hand. Gently press down on the middle joints of your fingers, toward your palm. Hold 5 seconds. Relax. Repeat 10 times.
- Wrist flexion: Hold a full soda can or the handle of a hammer, with your palm facing up. Bend your wrist upward. Hold 5 seconds. Relax. Repeat 10 times. Gradually increase the weight you are holding.
- Wrist extension: With your palm down, hold a full soda can or similar object. Bend your wrist up. Hold 5 seconds. Relax. Repeat 10 times.
- Grip strengthening: Squeeze a rubber ball and hold 5 seconds. Relax. Repeat 10 times.

## Seeking Help from Complementary Practitioners

### Acupuncture

In one recent study, thirty-five of thirty-six patients had symptomatic relief from acupuncture, and two-thirds of the individuals reported long-term results—from 2.5 to 8.5 years of pain relief. The Consensus Panel of the National Institutes of Health has endorsed acupuncture as a treatment for CTS, and I've found it to be successful with many of my patients.

## Red Flags

- Development of muscle wasting or weakness that limits function
- Numbness or tingling that persists or worsens

## CUBITAL TUNNEL SYNDROME (ULNAR NEUROPATHY)

### Description

The cubital tunnel is found below the "funny bone" (medial epicondyle), on the inside of the elbow. It is the passageway through which the ulnar nerve passes as it goes from the upper arm to the forearm and hand. This nerve is the culprit responsible for the odd sensation you feel when you hit your funny bone.

Cubital tunnel syndrome is a compression of the ulnar nerve at the elbow. It leads to numbness, tingling, or "pins and needles" in the ring finger and pinky. If damage to the ulnar nerve is severe enough, you can develop muscle atrophy and a claw-hand deformity.

Cubital tunnel syndrome is not as common as carpal tunnel syndrome. What's more, the extra padding women tend to have may, in this instance, be advantageous. Why? Because more fat around the elbow protects the cubital tunnel from damage.

## Causes

Direct trauma to the cubital tunnel may damage the ulnar nerve. More commonly, though, this ailment is the result of overuse. When you repeatedly bend and straighten your elbow, your ulnar nerve may become irritated and inflamed. This may happen if you lean on your elbow frequently or for long periods of time, or if you do a great deal of typing, data entry, or assembly-line work.

Sometimes the nerve actually shifts position and rubs against the funny bone, snapping every time it passes over the bone. This repeated snapping further stretches and irritates the nerve.

Arthritis, diabetes, and thyroid problems raise your risk for developing nerve compressions, as does consuming large amounts of alcohol.

## Signs and Symptoms

- Weakness of the ring and little fingers
- Pain in the elbow
- Weakness when pinching the thumb and index finger together
- Numbness on the inside of the hand
- Loss of hand strength, so you drop things or have difficulty opening jars
- The hand and arm become cold or numb when gripping the top of a steering wheel or other objects
- The symptoms worsen when you hold a telephone, rest your head on your hand, or cross your arms over your chest
- Pain may be worse at night

## Conventional Treatments

If you have cubital tunnel syndrome, you'll want to avoid or modify activities that cause irritation. You can do this by cutting back on tasks that require repeated bending and straightening of the elbow.

Depending on your job, a key treatment may be making changes in your work habits. It's important to pay attention to proper ergonomics. If you work at a computer, repositioning your workstation to better support your arm and wrist is at the top of the list. Adjust your chair and desk so that your elbow is flexed no more than 30 degrees, and your wrist is in a neutral position. For more extensive help, your doctor may refer you to an occupational therapist, who can help you figure out how to modify your regular tasks to prevent cubital tunnel syndrome, or reduce the likelihood of a recurrence.

NSAIDS, such as ibuprofen or naproxen, help decrease pain and inflammation. Because they are easier on your stomach and GI tract, the Cox-2 inhibitor NSAIDS, Celebrex or Vioxx, are safer for long-term use.

Your doctor may want to use immobilizing therapies, such as splints, wraps, or casts to protect and allow inflamed tissue to heal. To increase circulation and soothe muscles, she may also recommend hydrotherapy and electrotherapy. Finally, physical therapy may also be an option.

### Do-It-Yourself

- When your symptoms are acute, apply a flexible ice pack (or a bag of frozen peas) to your elbow for ten minutes every hour. Cold constricts the blood vessels and will reduce swelling.
- Aromatherapy: Add a couple of drops of lavender oil to your bath. It will curb any spasms and help you relax.
- Take frequent breaks—five minutes every half-hour—from repetitive activities.
- If your pain worsens at night, wrap your elbow with a towel or thin pillow to keep it straight.
- Avoid crossing your arms across your chest.

### Exercise

To relieve pain, improve function, and prevent further injury, try this gentle exercise:

FINGER SQUEEZE
One by one, squeeze a sponge or pen between the individual fingers of your hand. Hold for 10 seconds, relax, and repeat 5 times for each finger.

### Mind/Body

I recommend yoga to my patients. (See carpal tunnel syndrome, page 175, for specifics.)

## Seeking Help from Complementary Practitioners

Acupuncture relieves the pain of cubital tunnel syndrome by triggering a massive outpouring of endorphins. I've found it to be a successful treatment.

## Red Flags

- Development of muscle wasting or weakness that limits function
- Numbness or tingling that persists or worsens

# THORACIC OUTLET SYNDROME
# (NECK, SHOULDER, ARM, AND HAND PAIN)

## Description

The thoracic outlet is a passageway located at the top of the rib cage, in the area between the base of the neck and the armpit. Thoracic outlet syndrome (TOS) can affect the neck, shoulder, arm, and hand.

Although we don't always know its cause, TOS is often related to a compression of the nerves and arteries that pass through the thoracic outlet. Sometimes, because of overcrowding, blood vessels or nerves get crunched between a rib and an overlying muscle. The result is pain, numbness, and tingling. Less oxygen may get to the hands, shoulders, and arms, causing them to swell or turn blue.

Thoracic outlet syndrome is more common in women than in men. It usually strikes between the ages of thirty-five and fifty-five. You may be especially prone to developing this condition during pregnancy because of the significant postural changes that occur. An increased thoracic curve, with rounded shoulders and a head-forward position, tightness in your middle and anterior scalene muscles, and a tendency for the clavicles (collarbone) to depress into the first ribs, may all contribute to thoracic outlet syndrome.

If you have TOS symptoms, try the ADSONS test: Take a deep breath and hold it in, while tipping your head back and turning it toward the other side. If your pulse slows down during this maneuver, you may indeed have TOS. Of course, you should see your doctor to confirm the diagnosis.

## Causes

Sometimes it's not possible to figure out why you have thoracic outlet syndrome. But the usual causes are:

- Repetitive activities that require you to hold your arms overhead or extended forward. Weight lifting or loading and unloading shelves are examples.
- TOC may be associated with poor posture and rounded shoulders, large, pendulous breasts, and regular use of heavy handbags.
- Any condition that leads to swelling or movement of the tissues of, or near, the thoracic outlet. This includes muscle enlargement, injuries, and, in rare cases, tumors at the top of the lung.
- Some people are born with an extra rib in the neck (cervical rib) that can cause problems in the thoracic outlet.

## Signs and Symptoms

- Pain, weakness, numbness and tingling, swelling, fatigue, or coldness in the arm and hand
- Discoloration caused by impaired circulation

## Conventional Treatments

For relief of pain, your doctor may suggest a trial of NSAIDS or neuropathic agents (drugs that act on nerves). Seeing a physical therapist for postural exercises may help relieve pain. It's also important to take frequent breaks during any activities that aggravate your condition. If you get no relief, surgery may be necessary.

## Do-It-Yourself

*Every day*
- Limit how long you stretch your arms out or overhead.
- Avoid lifting or carrying heavy objects.
- Decrease the tension on the shoulder straps of your seat belt.
- Take frequent breaks during any activities that aggravate your pain.
- Carry your purse or briefcase with the unaffected arm.
- Avoid sleeping on your stomach with your arms above your head. Instead, sleep on your side or back with your arms below chest level.

- If you have to lift a heavy object from anything over shoulder height, use a step stool.
- Heavy breasts can cause strain on your shoulders; be sure to wear a supportive brassiere. (In some cases, breast reduction may be in order.)

*Aromatherapy*
- Lavender (*Lavandula angustifolia*)—This herb is a strengthening tonic for your nervous system. Use it by boiling 100 grams of lavender with 2 liters of water and then adding it to your bath. Otherwise, you can buy a commercial preparation.
- Rosemary (*Rosmarinus officinalis*)—This herb may decrease pain and regional muscle spasms associated with thoracic outlet syndrome. To prepare a bath, add 50 grams of herb to 1 liter of hot water and add to your bath. Alternatively, use several drops of a commercial preparation. Do not use rosemary during pregnancy.

## Mind/Body

Tai chi, a twelve-hundred-year-old, gentle form of martial arts, has gained a tremendous amount of popularity throughout China. It involves deep breathing, accompanied by slow, fluid movements through a series of body postures. The aim is to achieve balance between mind and body, and to focus *chi*, or vital energy. Although there isn't a great deal of literature on the subject, I believe tai chi enhances balance and coordination. Because it also improves poor posture, which is sometimes associated with thoracic outlet syndrome, it may be an effective treatment.

## Red Flags

Call your doctor if you develop:

- Muscle weakness or wasting that limits function
- Persistent numbness or tingling
- Swollen or blue hands, shoulders, or arms

## REFLEX SYMPATHETIC DYSTROPHY (RSD)

Also known as reflex sympathetic dystrophy syndrome (RSDS) or complex regional pain syndrome.

## CAROL'S STORY

Carol, a woman in her thirties, had been a gardener until an awful accident with a lawn mower mangled her entire leg. That was two years before she came to see me. The obvious injuries had long since healed, but she was still in excruciating pain. She couldn't put any weight on her leg and needed a cane to walk. She described herself as "trapped in a prison of pain," unable to sleep, work, or even socialize with friends. And she was in a state of constant anxiety.

After I examined her and reviewed the necessary testing, I explained that she was suffering from complex regional pain syndrome, more commonly known as reflex sympathetic dystrophy (RSD), a painful disorder that can occur after a nerve injury or other trauma to an extremity. The pain is intense, chronic, and unremitting. But that's only the first stage; RSD is a progressive disorder. I told Carol that, without treatment, her leg would eventually become red, inflamed, swollen, and begin to lose its hair. When she responded: "Then let's get going. We have to take care of it before it gets worse," I knew I had a motivated patient on my hands.

In the office, Carol responded minimally to conventional modes of treatment. She did get an added measure of relief from nerve blocks. But she benefited more from complementary strategies, including electrical stimulation and hypnosis. I also used acupuncture, accessing what's called the "Valium point" of the ear to reduce her anxiety. Many of our most effective interventions were techniques she could use on her own at home. Carol learned to elevate and compress her leg to fight the swelling, and to use contrast baths—alternating cold and hot water—to address some of the blood vessel changes that occur in RSD. She was particularly successful with guided visual imagery. By learning to couple an unpleasant stimulus (her pain) with a pleasant thought, she was able to relax. "I think about a beach on Maui and the pain and anxiety just disappear," she laughed.

In time, Carol was able to give up her cane. She has started to go out again and has gone back to work. Today she swears by these treatments and even appeared in a local television news story about acupuncture. "I have my life back," she says.

### Description

Reflex sympathetic dystrophy (RSD), known in academic circles as complex regional pain syndrome, is a potentially devastating disorder thought to be driven by the sympathetic nervous system. Among other things, this network of nerves controls the opening and closing of blood vessels and sweat glands.

RSD evolves in phases. The pain, typically accompanied by blood flow and soft tissue changes, swelling, and sweating, is intense, and has an awful, burning quality. Because the disease also leads to muscle weakness and wasting, you may suffer dystrophy, or weakness, in the affected area, in addition to severe pain. Your joints may become stiff from disuse and your skin, muscles, and bone may atrophy.

This ailment may occur as a result of injury, or from damage to nerves. It most often affects the hands, arms, feet, or legs but it may involve the knee, hip, shoulder, or other sites.

RSD occurs most frequently in women over age fifty. It is difficult to treat. Still, your chances of success are best if you start aggressive treatment early—within the first three months.

## Causes

Unfortunately, in nearly a third of RSD cases, the cause is unknown. However, it often follows a sprain, fracture, or injury to nerves or blood vessels, particularly in upper or lower extremities. It can also occur after surgery.

## Signs and Symptoms

You may experience the following in the area affected by RSD:

- Severe pain and burning
- Pallor (paleness) or redness
- Shiny red skin that turns bluish
- Increased or decreased sweating
- Swelling
- Skin atrophy or tightening of the skin
- Hypersensitivity to touch
- Muscle spasms
- Changes in skin temperature
- Difficulty moving
- Loss of hair in the involved extremity

## Conventional Treatments

This condition is a real challenge. Almost 60 percent of patients don't respond well to conventional treatments. Medications, such as corticosteroids, which are potent anti-inflammatories; vasodilators, which open blood vessels and enable blood flow to the extremity; and alpha- or beta-adrenergic blocking compounds, which affect the sympathetic nervous system, are commonly used. Your doctor may also inject you with a local anesthetic, such as lidocaine or bupivacaine, which provides a temporary respite from pain. Somewhat longer lasting relief may come from a nerve block. In this procedure, the doctor injects a substance, usually alcohol, near the involved nerves to block transmission of pain signals.

Physical therapy may help you regain some range of motion and motor control, as well as strengthen the limb. Your PT may also do "spray and stretch," where she stretches your muscles after applying a vapocoolant spray.

A physical therapist or an occupational therapist can also do desensitization. RSD causes hypersensitivity to touch and allodynia, a condition where normally neutral or even pleasant things, such as clothing, wind, cold or a light touch to the skin, cause pain. The goal of desensitization is to help your painful skin gradually adjust to rougher textures. It will help you tolerate the touch of clothing, bed sheets, and towels, for example. To do it, your skin will be rubbed with different materials, beginning with soft, light textures and proceeding to rough, irritating surfaces.

Your doctor may suggest that you try TENS (transcutaneous electrical nerve stimulation). To utilize this therapy, you carry a small, box-shaped device that sends brief electrical impulses through electrodes into nerve endings under your skin. The pulses of electricity interfere with your body's pain signals.

If all else fails, surgery is the last resort. This involves cutting nerves; so while it may stop your pain, it may also affect other sensations.

## Dietary Strategies

In one study, taking 500 mg of vitamin C for fifty days prevented the development of RSD in people who had sustained wrist fractures. Further research on this treatment is needed, although I can see no harm in trying it. In the meantime, I also recommend that you emphasize foods rich in vitamin C. (See Chapter 14.)

## Herbs

*St. John's wort* (Hypericum perforatum)
This well-studied herb is a sedative, antidepressant, and pain reliever. Suggested dose is one cup of infusion, three times a day. Do not take this herb with any other antidepressants.

*Valerian root* (Valeriana officinalis)
Since pain-related anxiety and tension are so often a component of RSD, you can use valerian to calm your nervous system. Herbalists suggest that you drink two to three cups of infusion a day.

*Passionflower* (Passiflora incarnata)
The intense, unremitting pain of RSD can cause great anxiety. This herbal tranquilizer will calm you down and ease nerve pain. The recommended dose is 1 to 4 ml of tincture or one cup of infusion, twice a day. An interesting note: This herb has been patented for use in a chewing gum in Romania.

## Herbal Creams and Ointments

*Traumeel ointment* (See page 158)

*Arnica cream*
The German Commission E has approved arnica as a topical agent. It reduces pain, numbness, and tingling.

## Do-It-Yourself

*Contrast baths*
Inflammation and swelling decrease blood supply to the affected area. Because contrast baths boost circulation, they increase the supply of nutrients from the blood, help to eliminate waste, and reduce pain. Immerse the limb in hot water for three minutes, then in cold water for thirty seconds. Repeat this process three to five times.

*Homeopathy (use dosage on the package)*
  • Sulfur, a mineral found in rocks around hot springs and volcanoes, can soothe red, hot, burning skin.

*Aromatherapy*
- Mix a few drops each of lavender oil, sandalwood oil, and calendula oil into a neutral lotion or oil, and massage the area.
- Add one cup of vinegar to a hot bath to help balance your skin.
- Apply a compress soaked in verbena or thyme tea to soothe and cool the area.
- To relax, take a bath with valerian. Mix 100 mg of herb in 2 liters of hot water and add it to your bathwater.

## Mind/Body

*Yoga*

PASCHIMOTTANASANA (POSTERIOR-STRETCH POSTURE)
This helps relieve skin diseases. (See pages 344–351 for postures.)

*Qi Gong*
This ancient Chinese exercise combines deep breathing with movement, and helps to circulate internal *chi*, or vital energy. In some studies, it has helped people with RSD by reducing pain and anxiety.

*Imagery (See page 341 for technique)*
Using imagery is an effective way to control pain.

## Seeking Help from Complementary Practitioners

*Acupuncture*
I've found that this therapy provides relief for some patients.

*Biofeedback (See page 341 for technique)*

## Red Flags

Call your doctor if you have:

- Persisting pain
- Fever
- Elevated white count
- Inflammation
- Redness that gets worse

## PERIPHERAL NEUROPATHY

### Description

The peripheral nerves are part of a network that connects the central nervous system (brain and spinal cord) to the muscles, skin, and internal organs. Peripheral neuropathy is a malfunction of these nerves. When it affects a single nerve, it is called a mononeuropathy. In contrast, a polyneuropathy affects many different nerves simultaneously.

Symptoms of peripheral neuropathy include pain, numbness, tingling, muscle wasting, and loss of strength. Also, loss of sensation may cause ulcers, cuts, small burns, and other injuries to go unnoticed, raising the risk of infection or other damage.

Since many peripheral nerves lie close to the surface of the body, they are particularly vulnerable to compression. Entrapment neuropathy, a common type of peripheral neuropathy, can occur because of physical injury to a nerve, or compression of a nerve by neighboring structures. Some types of entrapment neuropathy are:

- Median nerve peripheral nerve injury and entrapment. Better known as carpal tunnel syndrome, this is the result of repeated compression of the median nerve in the narrow carpal tunnel at the wrist (see page 175). Women are especially prone to this condition.
- Ulnar nerve peripheral nerve injury and entrapment. The ulnar nerve lies close to the surface of the elbow, so it is easily damaged. Symptoms range from numbness and tingling to muscle weakness in the hand and a claw-hand deformity (see cubital tunnel syndrome, page 180).
- Radial nerve peripheral nerve injury and entrapment, also known as Saturday-night palsy. This condition results in a wrist drop, where the wrist assumes a bent position with the fingers flexed.
- Peroneal nerve peripheral nerve injury and entrapment. This causes weakening of the muscles that lift the foot.

Peripheral neuropathy is especially common among people over the age of fifty-five, afflicting as many as 3 to 4 percent of those in this age group. It usually strikes the nerves of the limbs, especially the feet. Women, especially during pregnancy, postpartum, and breast-feeding, may be more vulnerable to some types of peripheral neuropathy:

- Bell's palsy, which affects the facial nerve and causes paralysis and weakness of the forehead and lower face, is three times more frequent in women during pregnancy. It usually occurs in the third trimester or during the first two weeks after birth.

- Meralgia paraesthetica is one-sided or bilateral entrapment of the lateral femoral cutaneous nerve of the thigh, when it passes under the inguinal ligament. While it's sometimes the result of trauma, this painful condition is also associated with obesity and/or the weight gain of pregnancy. It usually occurs during the third trimester and improves within three months after birth.
- Carpal tunnel syndrome, involving entrapment of a nerve in the wrist, occurs in 20 to 40 percent of pregnant women because of fluid retention (see above).
- Breast-feeding-related neuropathies
  - Pressure on the nerves under the arm (axilla) may occur when the breasts get engorged with milk. You may feel numbness and tingling in your forearm, especially on the outer, or ulnar, side. The symptoms may improve as the baby suckles.
  - If you use a hand-operated breast pump, you may experience pain and tingling when you bend your elbow.
- Postpartum foot drop can happen when the fetal head presses against the lumbosacral spine, or if there is compression of the peroneal nerve by leg braces during delivery. What happens is that you are unable to extend your ankle upward, so your foot slaps down when you walk. This injury is common in small women who deliver large infants.

## Causes

Peripheral polyneuropathy may be associated with a number of factors, including infection, autoimmune disease, toxic agents, cancer, and nutritional deficiency. Here are the major causes:

- Illnesses, including: AIDS, diabetes (a very common cause), kidney failure, and syphilis.
- Nutritional deficiencies, such as low levels of vitamin B12 and folate.
- Medications, including: AIDS drugs, antibiotics (metronidazole, an antibiotic used for Crohn's disease, and isoniazid, a tuberculosis treatment), chemotherapy drugs (such as vincristine), and gold compounds (used for rheumatoid arthritis).
- Exposure to chemicals, including: arsenic, lead, mercury, and pesticides made from organophosphates.

## Signs and Symptoms

You may feel any or all of the following in your affected limb(s):

- Decreased feeling or sensation distributed like a "glove and stocking"
- Weakness
- Loss of reflexes
- Numbness or insensitivity to pain or temperature
- Tingling, burning, or prickling
- Sharp pains or cramps
- Extreme sensitivity to touch, even light touch (wearing clothes, walking, or other activity may feel unbearable)
- Loss of balance and coordination
- Symptoms may get worse at night

## Conventional Treatments

The pain of peripheral neuropathy is often a challenging problem. Both analgesics and neuropathic pain agents (drugs that act on nerves) are used as a first line of attack. Tricyclic antidepressant drugs, like amitriptyline and nortriptyline, are also sometimes prescribed for pain and depression. Their side effects include urinary retention and low blood pressure. Trazodone is another drug that can be substituted if you cannot tolerate them. A second tier of drugs sometimes used for pain include anticonvulsants, such as gabapentin (Neurontin), carbamazapine (Tegretol), and phenytoin (Dilantin).

There is also a topical pain medication. Lidocaine, a short-acting anesthetic, is now available in patch form (Lidoderm).

Preventive treatment for peripheral neuropathy often depends largely on the cause. For example, if your problem is caused by diabetes, your physician will focus on controlling your blood sugar; vitamin therapies will be used if you're found to have a nutritional deficiency.

## Dietary Strategies (See Chapter 14 for food sources of specified nutrients)

*Fats*
Not all fat is unhealthy. Substitute good oils for bad. Called "essential fatty acids" (EFAs), omega-3 and omega-6 oils are used by the body to make EPA and DHA, which are critical for healthy cell membranes. This is true for every cell in the body, and it's especially important in the nervous system

and brain. Tragically, the American diet has traditionally relied on saturated fats or oils lacking the correct balance of omega-3 and omega-6 fatty acids.

Make sure that you avoid saturated and trans fats and consume foods and oils that have plenty of omega-6 and omega-3 fatty acids.

In general, don't burn oil and don't allow it to get rancid. Keep it in the refrigerator.

- Drink plenty of water. Season it with lemon or citrus.
- Vitamin B6 is involved in producing neurotransmitters. If you are lacking in this nutrient, muscle twitches and weakness, numbness, and tingling may be the result.
- Vitamin B5 (pantothenic acid) is important for cellular metabolism.
- Vitamin E is an antioxidant that can prevent nerve damage.
- Vitamin B1 (thiamine) occupies a site on the nerve cell membranes and improves their functioning.
- Zinc protects the body from chemical damage.
- Chromium is a trace mineral that acts as a helper to insulin. It unlocks the cell membrane door, allowing glucose to enter. Considerable research exists on its ability to help diabetics, even women with pregnancy-induced diabetes, control blood sugar. Since peripheral neuropathy is associated with diabetes, anything that helps you manage your glucose level is worth doing.

## Supplements

*Vitamin B6*
A deficiency of B6 can cause muscle twitching, muscle weakness, numbness, and tingling. The accepted dose range is 2 to 100 mg a day.

*Vitamin E*
The accepted dose range is 15 to 1,000 mg a day.

*Vitamin B1*
Enhances nerve cell functions. The accepted dose range is 1.4 to 50 mg a day.

*Zinc*
The accepted dose range is 8 to 40 mg a day.

*Chromium*
As described above, this important trace mineral helps maintain the body's blood glucose level. The lower limit for chromium is 25 mcg; no safe upper limit has been established.

*Gamma-linolenic acids (GLAs)*
Found in black currant seed oil, borage oil, and evening primrose oil, GLAs have been shown to help the symptoms of some types of neuropathy, including diabetic neuropathy. I prefer that you use it in its natural form (i.e., in food); however, if you want to take supplements, the dose is 1,500 mg a day.

*Lipoic acid*
This supplement is used extensively in Germany to treat diabetic complications like peripheral neuropathy as well as diabetic autonomic neuropathy (neuropathy affecting the nerves that supply the digestive tract and the heart). Although there isn't a huge body of literature yet, there is some evidence that supports its use, especially when combined with GLA. Doses used for treating diabetic complications are usually 300 to 600 mg daily; people in a recent study used 800 mg. Up to 1,800 mg daily of lipoic acid appears to be safe, but more is not necessarily better.

**Herbal Creams and Ointments**

*Capsaicin cream (0.025–0.075 percent) (See page 96)*
This is a "hot" botanical remedy harvested from red peppers, or cayenne. It can be a potent analgesic for peripheral neuropathy. A 1992 study of 277 diabetics with peripheral neuropathy demonstrated a significant improvement in pain when they applied capsaicin to their extremities.

**Do-It-Yourself**

- Examine your ailing limb(s) every day. Injuries must be treated early to prevent infection. Lacking sensation, you are especially prone to breaks in the skin, so vigilance is the watchword.
- Eat a nutritious diet.
- If your neuropathy is diabetes-related, strict control of your sugar is helpful.
- Exercise regularly.
- Abstain from excessive alcohol consumption.

## Exercise

If you can, keep up your aerobic exercise. Swimming is particularly beneficial. Without any pain from impact, it strengthens the muscles and tones
the body.

## Seeking Help from Complementary Practitioners

*Acupuncture*
Some of my patients benefit from this therapy.

*Biofeedback (See page 341 for technique)*

## Red Flags

Call your doctor if you experience:

- Numbness or tingling in your extremities
- Chronic weakness or heaviness in your muscles, which may be accompanied by cramping
- Prickling, burning, stabbing or any other uncomfortable and sponta-
  neous sensation on your skin

# TRIGEMINAL NEURALGIA

## Description

This excruciating condition leads to brief, recurrent bursts of severe, knifelike pain in the face that follows the distribution of the trigeminal nerve.
There are two trigeminal nerves, one on each side of the face. Often, the
pain happens instantaneously and without provocation. It can also be triggered by chewing, speaking, or swallowing or by stimulation as mild as a
touch to the area or a breeze. Typically, the pain is felt in the cheek near
the nose, or in the mouth or jaw.

Trigeminal neuralgia affects twice as many women as men. It does not
usually strike people under age fifty, although it may be associated with
multiple sclerosis in younger individuals.

## Causes

We don't know what causes this ailment. It usually occurs spontaneously, with no precipitating event or disease, although it does occasionally happen after a dental procedure.

## Symptoms

- Blinding facial pain, lasting from a few seconds to one to two minutes.
- Tic douloureux—A facial muscle tic caused by repeated wincing after each paroxysm of pain.

## Conventional Treatments

With facial pain, a dental evaluation is usually in order. If you do indeed have trigeminal neuralgia, your physician will probably prescribe seizure medications, such as carbamazepine (Tegretol), and antidepressants. She may also prescribe baclofen, a drug that acts on the central nervous system to help relax muscles and relieve spasms.

## Dietary Strategies

*Celery (Apium graveolans)*
In ancient times, Hippocrates believed that celery was able to calm nerves. Today we also know that celery has anti-inflammatory properties. You can drink celery juice or celery tea. In addition, you can make a celery tonic by steeping 2 tablespoons of bruised celery seeds in a pint of brandy. Then, two or three times a day, drink 2 tablespoons of water mixed with 1 tablespoon of infused brandy.

## Supplements

*Vitamin B2*
To help growth and repair of the skin, the accepted daily dose range is 1.6 to 50 mg a day.

*Vitamin E*
An antioxidant that may prevent nerve damage. The accepted daily dose range is 15 to 1,000 mg a day.

## Do-It Yourself

- Apply warm compresses steeped in cider vinegar or chamomile tea to the painful area.
- Using organic fruit, cut a lemon in half and rub it on the painful spot.
- Rub peppermint onto the affected area.

## Seeking Help from Complementary Practitioners

Acupuncture or deep tissue massage may be helpful.

## Red Flags

Call your doctor if you experience:

- Persisting pain
- Fever
- Generalized aches and pain

## HERPES ZOSTER (SHINGLES)

Shingles is an infection characterized by intensely painful blisters that follow the path of a nerve. It begins with a feeling of weakness, fever, tingling, or pain on one side of the body. In a few days, along a line that follows the affected nerve, a rash appears. As the rash develops, it turns into small, fluid-filled blisters that are initially highly tender and painful. It may even hurt when your clothing touches the lesions. After a couple of weeks, the blisters begin to heal, becoming itchy scabs. Herpes zoster usually occurs on the chest, abdomen, back, face, or neck.

After the initial infection subsides, some people develop deep pain, known as postherpetic neuralgia.

### Causes

Shingles is a reactivation of the herpes zoster virus, which also causes chickenpox. The virus can remain dormant in the body for many years. We don't know what brings about the recurrence of infection; it may be triggered by stress.

## Conventional Treatments

In addition to pain relievers (analgesics), your doctor may prescribe antiviral medications, such as valacyclovir (Valtrex) or acyclovir (Zovirax). Check with your doctor before taking these drugs if you may become pregnant. You may also be given corticosteroids. For longer-lasting pain, she may prescribe tricyclic antidepressants. And if any of the blisters become infected, antibiotics may be in order.

## Supplements

- Vitamin E prevents damage to tissue. The accepted daily dose range is 15 to 1,000 mg a day.
- Vitamin C speeds healing. The accepted daily dose range is 90 to 2,000 mg a day.

## Herbal Creams and Ointments

*Capsaicin cream (0.025–0.075 percent) (See page 96)*

## Do-It-Yourself

*Aloe vera*
The best way to use aloe is to buy a plant, break off a leaf, and apply directly to the rash the sticky gel that oozes out.

*Calamine lotion*
It may be an old standby, but it still works.

*Cold*
Ice relieves pain and reduces inflammation. To protect your skin from direct contact with the ice, I recommend putting it in a plastic sandwich bag, covering it with a cloth, and applying it to the inflamed area.

*Aromatherapy*
Make a compress using essential oil of lemon balm (*Melissa officinalis*) mixed with water and apply it to the lesions.

*Colloidal oatmeal powder (Aveeno)*
Add a few drops of water to the powder, make a paste, then apply it to your rash.

## Red Flags

Call your doctor if you have:

- Persisting pain
- Fever
- Your lesions appear infected (signs include redness, warmth, swelling, and tenderness)

# 9

—

# When It Really *Is* All in Your Head

Headache is one of the top ten reasons for visits to the doctor. While there are many types, migraine or tension headaches are the most common. Although the pain they cause can be frighteningly severe, headaches are rarely the sign of a serious disorder. Nonetheless, you should take them seriously.

Depending on the type of headache you have, you may feel the pain all over your head or in only one spot—your forehead or the side or back of your head. Sometimes the pain moves from one place to another during the course of your headache. It may be dull and throbbing, or excruciatingly sharp and piercing.

With the exception of cluster headaches, which occur less frequently than migraines or tension headaches, women are more likely than men to experience most recurrent headache disorders. In surveys of the general population, women also suffer more headache-related emotional distress and disability, such as anxiety and depression.

It's not always possible to identify the culprit causing your headache, but the most common triggers are psychological stress, sleep difficulties, irregular eating habits or responses to specific foods, and hormonal shifts. Working in a noisy or stuffy office, exposure to chemicals, cigarette smoke, or fluorescent lights, and other environmental factors may also play a role.

## MIGRAINE HEADACHES

### Description

Migraines, from the Greek word *hemikrania*, which means "half the head," affect more than 25 million Americans. Whether it comes on suddenly or with a warning aura, the intense throbbing or pounding of a migraine may last for hours or even days. You may also experience nausea, vomiting, and sensitivity to light and sound. Migraines can be so debilitating that 35 percent of people polled say they have wished they were dead during an attack! In addition, new research has revealed that people with migraines report lower levels of mental, physical, and social well-being than people who do not experience headaches, and they are also more likely to suffer from depression.

Almost one in five women—three times as many as men—suffer from migraine headaches. They are most common between the ages of twenty-five and forty-five. Not only do women experience migraines more frequently, they are also more severely disabled by them. Nearly 52 percent of women, compared to 38 percent of men, miss at least six workdays per year because of this painful disorder. Women also cancel normal activities and report disruptions in their family or social relationships more often.

Because there is no cure for migraines, you'll need to focus on preventing the attacks and treating their symptoms.

## Causes

Migraines used to be considered an emotional problem. Thankfully, that idea has now been dismissed. Still, we don't really know what causes them. They do run in families; if both of your parents suffer from migraines, your chance of developing them is a whopping 75 percent. We now believe that some sequence of events causes blood vessels in the brain to tighten and then relax, a process that irritates the nerves surrounding those blood vessels. The nerve endings then transmit sensations of pain, resulting in the throbbing misery of a migraine. This sickening process is caused by certain migraine triggers, which activate parts of the brain and cause the release of neurotransmitters, or brain chemicals, such as serotonin and dopamine, which carry nerve impulses between brain cells. Triggers include:

- Foods and/or alcohol
- Emotional stress
- Environmental factors—perfume or other odors, loud noises, cigarette smoke, household cleaners and chemicals, insufficient ventilation, bright lights or glare, or changes in humidity or temperature
- Lifestyle—sleeping too little or too much, missed meals, lack of exercise or an irregular exercise routine, getting too much sun, or air travel
- Certain types of medications

Hormones, especially estrogen, have a powerful, though as yet unexplained, impact on migraines. The headaches often begin during puberty, when hormone levels are fluctuating. Do your migraines occur just before or during your menstrual period? This may be due to sustained high levels of estrogen, followed by a sudden drop, that comes about during the normal course of your menstrual cycle. Migraines frequently diminish with menopause, although in some cases they worsen. Pregnant women usually report an improvement in migraines, probably because they have consistently high levels of estrogen. But about 4 to 8 percent of women experience worse headaches during pregnancy. And estrogen-containing medications, such as birth control pills and hormone replacement therapy, are also associated with increased headaches.

## Signs and Symptoms

### Prodrome
You may notice symptoms such as hunger, water retention, mood changes, and irritability many hours before your migraine begins.

### Aura
Most migraines occur without any warning. But about 20 percent of women experience an aura, which is a visual, motor, or sensory occurrence that goes on for about ten to thirty minutes before the actual headache starts. This is different from the aura of a seizure, which lasts only a couple of seconds before the seizure. Symptoms of an aura may include flashing lights, dancing spots or blindness, auditory hallucinations, as well as dizziness or numbness.

### Pain
You may feel pounding, tapping, or severe throbbing on one or both sides of the head. Noise, light, and movement—especially bending over—intensify the pain.

### Nausea and vomiting

### Weakness or numbness in parts of your body

### Cold, blue feet and hands

Women tend to report more severe, more frequent, and longer-lasting headaches than men. They also suffer more nausea, vomiting, numbness, and tingling. But they experience visual auras far less frequently than men.

**Conventional Treatments**

Conventional pain relief includes both prescription and over-the-counter medications. Nonprescription analgesics (pain relievers) include Tylenol, aspirin, and nonsteroidal anti-inflammatory drugs (NSAIDS), such as ibuprofen. Your doctor may prescribe a Cox-2 inhibitor, a drug in the new category of NSAIDS. There are also some pain medications available in oral, nasal spray and injection form (Zomig, Maxalt, Imitrex).

Other conventional techniques for pain relief include cold compresses for your forehead and eyes, complete rest, and minimizing light, noise, and smells.

Standard prevention strategies for migraines include avoiding food (see below) and other triggers. Wearing polarized sunglasses whenever you are outside in the sun can help tame a common trigger—bright light or intense glare. If you suffer frequent or particularly severe migraines, or if pain relief medicines don't help, your doctor may prescribe any of a wide range of preventive medications. These include beta-blockers, calcium channel blockers, serotonin antagonists or agonists, tricyclic antidepressants, serotonin reuptake inhibitors, anticonvulsants, or alpha-adrenergic blockers. Like any powerful medications, these all have significant side effects (see Chapter 13 for details).

**Keeping a Headache Diary**

Do a little detective work to find out what triggers your migraines by keeping the headache diary on page 205. Pay close attention to recurring trends. Do your headaches come at a particular point in your menstrual cycle? Do they occur after eating particular foods or when you haven't had enough sleep? Note when you start nutritional supplements or other treatments, and see if your pattern improves.

**Dietary Strategies (See Chapter 14 for food sources of specified nutrients)**

*Food triggers*
One of your most important strategies for managing migraine headaches is avoiding food triggers. Check your headache diary to see if your headaches occur after eating certain foods. If you notice a connection between your headaches and a particular food, try avoiding it for two weeks and then

## Sample Migraine Diary

| Date | Possible Triggers | Point in Menstrual Cycle | Warning Signs | Time Headache Began and Ended | Other Symptoms | Location and Type of Pain (throbbing, dull; left, right, both sides) | Pain Intensity (mild, moderate, severe) | Treatments Used |
|---|---|---|---|---|---|---|---|---|
| | | | | | | | | |
| | | | | | | | | |
| | | | | | | | | |
| | | | | | | | | |
| | | | | | | | | |
| | | | | | | | | |
| | | | | | | | | |
| | | | | | | | | |
| | | | | | | | | |
| | | | | | | | | |
| | | | | | | | | |
| | | | | | | | | |
| | | | | | | | | |
| | | | | | | | | |

reintroduce it, noting your response. This is called an elimination/challenge. If the reintroduced food does trigger a headache, remove it from your diet for at least six months.

Common food triggers and allergens include:

- Frankfurters and other processed meats containing nitrates
- Foods containing MSG, aspartame, preservatives, colorings, and other additives
- Chocolate
- Cheese, especially those that are aged or strongly flavored
- Shellfish
- Alcohol, especially red wine
- Citrus
- Wheat
- Eggs
- Fermented, cured, pickled, or marinated foods
- Cow's milk and milk products
- Caffeine
- Nuts

### Riboflavin (vitamin B2), omega-3 oils, and magnesium

These have been shown to decrease the intensity and frequency of migraines. Aim to include more of these nutrients in your diet.

### Water

Be sure to drink enough water. Insufficient consumption can lead to dehydration and exacerbate headaches. Aim for at least six 12-ounce glasses a day. Substituting water for soda or coffee is especially effective; not only will you feel refreshed, but you'll eliminate any caffeine-related headaches. I tell my patients to make regular water drinking more pleasurable by using filtered water or bottled water "seasoned" with a few drops of freshly squeezed organic lemon.

### Caffeine

If caffeine does not trigger your headaches, you can try it as a treatment—caffeine constricts blood vessels in the head. Drink one or two cups of strong coffee at the start of an attack and lie down in a dark, quiet room.

### Salt

Eliminating salt may be helpful.

### Protein

You may have success in reducing migraine attacks with a low-protein diet. This is because protein-rich foods are high in tryptophan, an amino acid that the body converts to serotonin, and serotonin may worsen some migraines.

**Migraine Meals**

These recipes include many of the key nutrients that prevent and treat migraines—omega-3 fatty acids (fish oil), calcium, magnesium, and riboflavin. They are also rich in zinc, folic acid and other B vitamins, and vitamins A and E—nutrients that are essential for a strong immune system, good circulation, proper cellular functioning, and a healthy nervous system. My recipe for treating a migraine is to start with one of these migraine meals, follow it with a therapeutic lavender oil bath and contrast compresses, and finish your day or evening with a soothing herbal tea to help you get to sleep.

R E C I P E

## BAKED SALMON WITH CHICKPEA SALAD

SALMON
*1 pound of salmon fillet*
*½ fresh lemon*
*Dill*
*Onion powder*
*Garlic powder*

CHICKPEA SALAD
*1 can chickpeas, rinsed and drained*
*1 red onion, chopped*
*4 Roma tomatoes, chopped*
*1 red pepper, chopped*
*1 cucumber, diced*
*4 ounces green lettuce, leaves separated*
*1 teaspoon coriander*
*1 teaspoon garlic powder, or one clove fresh garlic crushed*
*½ teaspoon black pepper*

1. *To prepare fish*: Heat oven to 400 degrees. Place fish in ovenproof baking dish and squeeze lemon over fish. Sprinkle dill, onion powder, and garlic powder over fish and bake in oven for 40 minutes.
2. *While the fish is baking, prepare the chickpea salad*: Place all the ingredients for the chickpea salad into a bowl and toss well.

3. *To serve*: Cut the baked salmon into cubes. Place chickpea salad on individual plates and arrange salmon cubes on top of the salad.

SERVES 2–3

## Supplements

### Riboflavin (vitamin B2)

In a study published in *Neurology* in February 1998, patients taking riboflavin reported 37 percent fewer migraines than those taking a placebo; their headaches went away faster, too. The dose used in the study was 400 mg, which is more than the RDA. If you want to try this dose, you will need a doctor's prescription. It may take about a month before the vitamin's protective benefits kick in.

### Essential fatty acids (EFAs)

Essential fatty acids play a role as precursors to prostaglandins, hormonelike substances that are part of the body's anti-inflammatory responses. They may also affect the widening and narrowing of blood vessels that cause migraines. You can try supplementing with refrigerated flaxseed, 1,500 to 3,000 mg a day.

### SAMe (S-adenosyl methionine)

SAMe is an important biological agent that is involved in more than forty different biochemical reactions in the body. It functions as a neurotransmitter and an antioxidant. It's widely used in Europe to treat depression and inflammatory and pain syndromes, such as osteoarthritis. There's preliminary evidence that SAMe also relieves migraines. Recommended daily dosage is 800 mg. Be aware, however, that in large doses it can upset the stomach. Do not take SAMe if you take levodopa for Parkinson's disease. This nutrient may trigger manic episodes in people with bipolar disease.

### Magnesium

Magnesium relaxes the muscles and calms excited nerves. Although we don't yet understand the role it plays in migraines, it's clearly important: Decreased blood levels of magnesium have been reported in patients with migraines, and intravenous injection of magnesium can stop a migraine within minutes. More important, though, two double-blind studies suggest that daily supplements of magnesium may reduce the frequency of headaches. The acceptable daily dose range is 320 to 350 mg. Excess magnesium may cause diarrhea; it goes away when you stop taking the supplement.

*Calcium and vitamin D*
Daily supplements of calcium and vitamin D may reduce the frequency and duration of headaches. The acceptable range for calcium is 1,300 to 2,500 mg a day; for vitamin D, it's 15 to 50 mcg. (You may want to try taking vitamins and minerals in effervescent form, in which you mix the vitamin into water. That way, you're also helping to keep yourself hydrated.)

## Herbs

*Feverfew* (Tanacetum parthenium)
This is the herb of choice for migraines. Its active ingredient is parthenolide, a spasm-reducing chemical that relaxes blood vessels in the head by making the smooth muscle inside them less reactive to possible constrictors. It also helps prevent migraines or makes them less severe by neutralizing vasoconstrictors such as serotonin, prostaglandins, and norepinephrine.

Feverfew has been used for centuries in European folk medicine for the treatment and prevention of migraines. But its worth has also been substantiated by a wealth of scientific studies. In one, patients using feverfew had fewer migraines as well as a significant reduction in nausea and vomiting. In an article published in 1998 in *Cephalgia*, a prestigious headache journal, the authors systematically examined the evidence for and against feverfew. Their conclusion? The majority of studies examined favored feverfew use over placebo.

Feverfew is best used preventively, so you need to take it every day. It may take a month or two to take effect. This herb comes in many formulations, so you can harness its potent ability to reduce inflammation and relieve pain by using it as a tea, a decoction, or in tablet form. Simply follow directions on the package. Be sure that any feverfew product you buy is standardized to contain at least 0.4 percent parthenolide.

Do not take feverfew if you are pregnant or breast-feeding. If you take blood-thinning drugs such as aspirin or warfarin, use feverfew with the supervision of your physician.

*Ginger* (Zingiber officinale)
Ginger is particularly useful in treating nausea. The usual dose is 250 mg to 1 gram several times a day. My preference is that you get as much as you can from your diet.

*Teas*
Both chamomile (*Chamaemelum nobile* or *Matricaria recutita*) and elderberry (*Sambucus nigra*) teas have a calming, sedating effect. If your head-

aches are related to stress, these infusions may help relieve anxiety. You may use commercially available tea bags or, if you prefer, steep 1 teaspoon of dried herb in a cup of hot water.

## Herbal Creams and Ointments

*Nature's Chemist*
This product contains menthol and a copaiba extract, harvested from the Amazon. It's a counterirritant—that is, a chemical that promotes the release of the body's natural pain relievers. Use it during your headache by rubbing small amounts onto your neck muscles and forehead.

## Do-It-Yourself

*Acupressure massage (See page 353 for technique)*
Because it is unobtrusive, you can use acupressure on the subway, during a meeting, or whenever you feel a headache coming on. It is also an effective technique to use while in the throes of a migraine. Press one or more of the points listed here, depending on where your headache is, for two to five minutes each. Repeat the process for at least twenty to forty minutes.

- LI4 (Large Intestine-4) is the point on the back of the hand in the web between the thumb and index finger. Press here for general pain in the front of the head.
- GB20 (Gallbladder-20) is found in the hollow between the front and back neck muscles, behind the bony prominence behind the ears (there are two GB-20 points). Use this spot if you have general pain at the side and back of your head.
- For headache, toothache, and earache, try TH23 (Triple Heater-23), the "Silk Bamboo Hole," located at the outer edge of the eyebrow where the brow departs from the bone.

*Scented bath*
Lavender oil is traditionally used to relieve anxiety and nervousness. Since migraines may be associated with stress, soaking in a bath to which you've added several drops of lavender oil is a good strategy when you feel a headache coming on.

*Contrast compresses*
Alternate cool and warm compresses for five minutes each, with a two-minute break in between. Apply the compresses to your forehead or, if the back of your head aches, to your neck.

*Peppermint oil* (Mentha piperita) compress
Peppermint is an effective tension-reliever. Soothe your headache by applying to your forehead a washcloth saturated with cool water to which you've added two drops of peppermint oil.

Try a commercial compress, like the ones sold by Johnson and Johnson. The effectiveness of these convenient heated compresses is supported by clinical studies.

## Mind/Body

*Biofeedback (See page 341 for technique)*

*Relaxation and imagery (See pages 340-341)*

## Exercise

Aerobic exercise promotes the release of the body's natural painkillers or endorphins (sometimes called a "runner's high"). But this fact is often neglected when it comes to migraines. Still, exercise can help prevent *and* treat headache-related pain.

Regular aerobic exercise at least three times a week can reduce both the frequency and intensity of your migraines. And if you can bear it, try exercising when you feel a headache coming on. Avoid isometric or other exercises that produce abrupt variations in blood pressure. Instead, aim for activity that uses the large muscle groups, such as bike riding or swimming.

## Seeking Help from Complementary Practitioners

*Acupuncture*
In a 1997 report, the National Institutes of Health approved acupuncture as an effective treatment for headaches. It reduces headache frequency and severity with no side effects. In some cases, patients receiving acupuncture can reduce their medications by as much as 50 percent.

*Massage*

Classical Swedish massage affects the interaction between the muscles and the nervous system. The muscles are stimulated by nerve cells to contract and relax. The stroking and deep kneading of a Swedish massage softens "knots" in the muscles and relieves migraines by releasing chronic neck and shoulder tension, and maintaining an even blood flow to the head. In addition, as the muscles relax, the body releases endorphins, which relieve pain and enhance feelings of well-being.

## Red Flags: When to Call Your Doctor

Call your doctor if:

- Your migraine persists longer than usual, or after several days.
- You experience prolonged visual changes or neurological symptoms, such as motor loss, numbness, weakness, or tingling; slurred speech, a change in balance; or memory loss.
- The headache started after you injured your head or were knocked out.
- Along with the headache, you have fever, vomiting, and a stiff neck.

# TENSION (MUSCLE CONTRACTION) HEADACHE

## SARAH'S SAGA

Sarah's woes began shortly after she and her boyfriend of seven years decided to split up because she was moving to another city. Young, enthusiastic, and eager to make it professionally after graduating college with a degree in education, Sarah had decided to take a job as a "big city" schoolteacher. She soon learned that the pressure of her job was intense. Each day she faced twenty screaming, unruly children. For hours, she sat scrunched at a small desk. At lunchtime, she often grabbed a candy bar and a cup of coffee rather than a square meal; she preferred to use her time to prepare her afternoon lessons. Unfortunately, her stressed-out colleagues and supervisors offered little support or camaraderie.

Sarah came to me for help while she was in Baltimore during her holiday break. She was hurting, and extremely anxious about it. Although she had always experienced headaches, her pain had been getting progressively more ferocious since she started the new job. "It begins every morning and worsens as the day goes on. By late afternoon, I feel like I've been hit by a Mack Truck," she sighed. After a comprehensive examination and workup, I concluded that she was suffering from tension headaches.

Recognizing the value of a multipronged approach toward this problem, I sat down with Sarah and reviewed her lifestyle, especially diet and exercise. Then we talked about medications, relaxation, and other treatments.

That day I started Sarah on an acupuncture regimen. Since she was going back home after her break, I taught her some simple reflexology and acupressure techniques she could do on her own. She could even do some of them while in class, without attracting the attention of her students. Because I could sense her anxiety and tension, I provided her with several self-hypnosis tapes and strategies for meditating.

I suggested that she exercise before work and make some changes in her diet. Especially important were cutting back caffeine and drinking more water. I recommended that she continue to use Tylenol or other nonprescription pain relievers, but also told her that once her lifestyle changes and self-help "tools" kicked in, she might no longer need medication.

A couple of weeks later, Sarah called with the kind of news I love to get from patients—she was feeling better.

## Description

Nearly 90 percent of headaches are tension headaches, which occur when muscle spasms irritate the nerves and cause tension or tightness in the head, face, and neck. When tension headaches occur more than fifteen times a month, they are considered chronic. Episodic tension headaches happen less than once or twice a week, but still often enough to make you miserable.

Although no one has yet figured out why, disabling chronic tension headaches occur in 5 percent of women compared to only 2 percent of men. And when women get tension headaches, they report higher levels of tenderness in all the muscles surrounding the skull. Among women, the frequency of this debilitating disorder rises at around age forty-five and peaks between the ages of fifty and fifty-nine. Although the gender disparity isn't as large, women also have more episodic tension headaches.

## Causes

The most common triggers of tension headaches are:

- Stress
- Unbalanced diet
- Inadequate sleep
- Hormone changes
- Depression
- Poor posture that causes tension in neck, scalp, or facial muscles

## Signs and Symptoms

Tension headaches may last for as little as thirty minutes or for as long as several days. They may occur once or twice a month or nearly daily, and they may be mild or severe. With a tension headache, you're likely to experience:

- A gradual onset of steady, dull aching
- Pressure on your head (sometimes described as feeling as if your head is in a vise)
- Tightness and discomfort in your back, shoulders, face, or neck
- Tenderness in the muscles surrounding your skull

## Conventional Treatments

If you avoid your known triggers, such as staying up too late or skipping meals, you may be able to prevent tension headaches. If stress is the trigger, try to figure out what is causing it and either remove the problem or deal with it more effectively by learning relaxation or other stress management techniques.

Once your headache begins, the usual treatment includes painkillers, such as aspirin, ibuprofen, or acetaminophen. For severe cases, muscle relaxants or prescription pain relievers may be necessary.

## Dietary Strategies

- Aim for at least six 12-ounce glasses of water a day. Not drinking enough fluids can leave you dehydrated and will worsen your headaches. I tell my patients to make regular water drinking more pleasurable by using filtered water or bottled water "seasoned" with a few drops of freshly squeezed organic lemon.
- Curb your caffeine consumption.
- Don't skip meals; eat regularly.

- Cut down on sugary, sweet foods; these cause a sudden surge and then a dip in blood glucose levels, which can lead to a headache.
- Drink invigorating carrot juice.

## Supplements

*Melatonin*
Melatonin is a hormone manufactured by the pineal gland, an organ that controls your wake/sleep cycle. Taken as a supplement, it can help improve your sleep patterns. Follow dosing on the bottle.

## Herbs

*Valerian root* (Valeriana officinalis)
Herbalists suggest this herb to relieve anxiety and stress. Follow package instructions for dosing.

*Chamomile* (Chamaemelum nobile *or* Matricaria recutita)
This sweet-smelling herb fights anxiety and helps you relax. To help you sleep, make a double-strength tea before bedtime by steeping two tea bags or 2 teaspoons of dried flowers in one cup of boiling water. Avoid contact with your eyes; it may cause irritation. Chamomile may cause an allergic reaction.

*Stress reducer tea*
Mix three parts chamomile, two parts sage, and one part basil with one cup of boiling water. Drink it twice a day. Or look for Tension Tamer, a commercially available herbal tea.

## Do-It-Yourself

*Every day*
- Keep your neck muscles relaxed when working or exercising and try to maintain good posture, paying special attention to slumping shoulders.
- Try to identify and avoid situations that cause tension or stress.
- When you feel a headache coming on, rest in a quiet, dark room.
- For simple but effective pain relief, apply a cold pack to your forehead, eyes, and neck or take a hot shower.
- To relax your muscles and relieve dull, steady pain, make a ginger compress. Cut and peel one fresh gingerroot; boil it in three cups of

water until the water turns cloudy. Soak a washcloth in the mixture and apply it to the back of your neck.

### Aromatherapy

Try aromatherapy for pain relief. Soak for twenty to thirty minutes in a bath to which has been added two or three drops of lavender (reduces nervousness; useful for all types of headaches) or peppermint (its calming, cooling scent relieves headache pain). Do not use these oils for long periods of time or during pregnancy.

### Massage

Give yourself a massage in one of these tension-laden areas:

For the neck: Sit in a chair and tip your head back slightly to relax your muscles. Grab the back of your neck lightly and squeeze. Start at the bottom of your skull and work down. After five squeezes, increase the pressure and repeat.

For the shoulder: Use your right hand to grasp your left shoulder. Knead toward your neck, using increasing pressure. Repeat on the other side using your left hand to grasp your right shoulder. Find the most sensitive places and press up to one minute or until the pain eases.

### Acupressure

Try these acupressure points (see page 353 for technique).

- GV-16 (Governing Vessel 16), on the back of the head at the base of the skull. This relieves a stiff neck and pain in the eyes, ears, and nose.
- GB-20 (Gallbladder 20), on the back of the head at the base of the skull, on either side of the large vertical muscle that helps control movement of the head. Use this if you have a stiff neck.
- Bl-2 (Bladder 2), in the upper hollows of the eye sockets, where the eyebrow meets the bridge of the nose. Try this for frontal headaches, eyestrain, and tension.
- GB-41 (Gallbladder 41), on the top of the foot, one inch up from the web connection between the fourth and fifth toes. Use this point for tension and muscle pain.
- To improve blood circulation in the head, brush your hair and scalp using firm, downward strokes. Then, starting at your left temple, make tiny circles over your ear and down the back of your head to your neck; repeat on the right side.

## Mind/Body

If you suffer from frequent tension headaches, one of the best things you can do is learn how to manage stress. Try the relaxation and meditation techniques described in Chapter 18.

*Yoga*
Try Siddhasan (Perfect Posture), on page 349.

## Exercise

Regular exercise helps to relieve tension. Particularly useful in this regard is aerobic exercise. I recommend twenty to thirty minutes of biking, swimming, walking, dancing, tennis, or aerobics at least three times a week.

## Seeking Help from Complementary Practitioners

*Hypnotherapy*
If you can discover what they are, hypnotic suggestion may help to eliminate your headache triggers.

*Chiropractic treatments*
These may help tension headaches.

## Red Flags

Call your doctor if:

- Self-help strategies don't work after three days.
- You experience prolonged visual changes or neurological symptoms, such as motor loss, numbness, weakness, or tingling; slurred speech; a change in balance; or memory loss.
- The headache started after you injured your head or were knocked out.
- Along with the headache, you have fever, vomiting, and a stiff neck.
- Your headaches are unusually severe or recur frequently.

# TEMPOROMANDIBULAR DISORDERS

## Description

Temporomandibular disorder (TMD) is the name for a collection of medical and dental conditions that affect the hingelike joint that attaches the lower jaw to the skull, as well as its surrounding muscles and tissues. Pain and dysfunction in this joint can be frightening, since you use it for speaking, chewing, and swallowing.

For a long time, many authorities doubted the existence of TMD because it involved such a broad array of symptoms, ranging from mild to very severe. Perhaps the fact that it predominantly affects women—as many as seven times more women than men—also had something to do with their dismissive attitude. Today, however, TMD is recognized as a legitimate ailment, although there is still controversy over its causes and proper treatment. This is unfortunate because TMD is very common; about one in four young women suffer from this painful problem.

If you have TMD, you may get frequent headaches. They occur when muscles around the joint go into spasm, causing facial pain, primarily in the jaw, mouth, and around the ear. As pressure builds on other parts of the skull, you may also get pain that is similar to a tension headache.

### Causes

There is no one clearly identifiable cause for TMD. But we do know that these factors can lead to problems:

- Jaw misalignment
- Clenching or grinding your teeth
- Dental problems (tooth decay, impacted wisdom teeth, gum disease, infection, crooked teeth)
- Degenerative arthritis or trauma to the jaw
- Poor posture
- There is some evidence that TMD is linked to fibromyalgia, another predominantly female ailment (see Chapter 12)

I'm intrigued by evidence that reproductive hormones play a role in this ailment. I've already mentioned how much more common TMD is in women. In addition, using oral contraceptives or estrogen replacement therapy raises your risk for TMD. And pain from TMD ebbs and flows across the menstrual cycle. You may notice that your pain is worse just before or during your period. Finally, there seems to be a link between premenstrual syndrome (PMS) and TMD. Women with PMS are more likely to report TMD; likewise, a recent study suggests that women with TMD have more PMS symptoms.

## Signs and Symptoms

The range of aches and pains associated with TMD can be bewildering. Your symptoms may be so mild that they have little impact on your daily life. Or they may be persistent and seriously debilitating. You may experience:

- Headaches, similar to tension headaches (see page 212)
- Pressure on top of your head
- A clicking or popping sound from your jaw
- A tendency to chew on one side
- Earache
- Neck, head, face, and shoulder pain
- Tenderness around your jaw
- Dizziness
- Difficulty opening or closing your mouth
- Pain when you chew, yawn, or open your mouth wide
- Disturbances in sleep or mood

## Conventional Treatments

Conventional treatments for TMD range from simple stretching exercises to surgery, depending on the severity of the problem. Nonsteroidal anti-inflammatory drugs are used for pain; if muscle spasms are involved, your doctor may prescribe muscle relaxants. Physical therapy, electrical stimulation, moist heat, and ultrasound are all possible therapies. Spray and stretch, a technique where the muscles around the jaw are sprayed with a coolant spray and then stretched, may be recommended. You may also be referred for laser treatments, which can increase blood flow to the affected area, or for a mouth guard, a device that keeps your upper and lower teeth apart and helps your jaw muscles relax. If your joint is seriously deteriorated, your doctor may suggest arthroscopic surgery or joint replacement.

## Supplements

### Melatonin
Melatonin is a hormone manufactured by the pineal gland, an organ that controls your wake/sleep/wake cycle. Taken as a supplement, it can help improve your sleep patterns. Follow dosing on the bottle.

## Herbs

*Valerian root* (Valeriana officinalis)
This herb may relieve anxiety and stress. Follow package instructions for dosing.

## Do-It-Yourself

*Visit your dentist*
Correcting crooked or misaligned teeth and fixing any damaged fillings or crowns may alleviate your headaches.

*Stress*
Avoid activities that put stress on your teeth and jaw:

- Excessive yawning
- Chewing gum, candy, ice, and hard candies
- Resting your chin on your hand
- Cradling the telephone between your jaw and shoulder
- Clenching your teeth
- Nail biting
- Eating hard foods

*Massage*
Try some of these:

- Use your fingers to locate sore spots around your eyes. Press these spots with your finger and hold for ten seconds.
- Grab your ears and gently pull them down and away from your head.
- Rub your ears between your forefinger and thumb.
- Press the areas where your neck and skull meet and hold 10 seconds.
- Finally, using your thumb, find tender points along your jaw and apply pressure for 10 seconds.

*Acupressure (see page 353 for technique)*
- GB-14 (Gallbladder 14), one finger width above each eyebrow, for jaw pain.
- LI-4 (Large Intestine-4) is the point on the back of the hand in the web between the thumb and index finger. Press here for general pain in the front of the head.

• ST-7 (Stomach 7), place your middle finger one thumb width in front of your ear. Find the indentation on your upper jaw and press for one minute.

*Ice*

If your jaw is swollen, apply ice for twenty to thirty minutes. You can do this frequently, but take one-half hour breaks in between treatments.

*Warmth*

To reduce pain, apply a warm compress or a hot-water bottle to your jaw for twenty minutes.

## Exercise

Here's a simple jaw exercise:

1. Open your mouth 1 inch wide.
2. Make a fist and put it in front of your chin.
3. Using your lower jaw, push your chin into your fist.
4. Then, put your fist on one side of your jaw and push your jaw toward it.
5. Repeat on the other side
6. Repeat 6 times. Do this exercise twice a day.

## Seeking Help from Complementary Practitioners

Hypnotherapy and biofeedback may give some symptomatic relief.

## Red Flags

Call your doctor if you have persistent pain or swelling, or if your jaw is misaligned.

## SINUS HEADACHE

## Description

The sinuses are hollow areas under the bones of the face that connect the nose and throat. When they get irritated or inflamed, they cause a throbbing headache that is centered in the face. True sinus headaches are rare; they account for only 2 percent of all headaches. Instead, most "sinus headaches" are actually tension or cluster headaches, mild migraines, or headaches due to allergies.

## Causes

Most sinus headaches are caused by an inflammation or infection of the sinuses. They may be aggravated if you have noncancerous growths, called nasal polyps, or anatomic abnormalities, such as a deviated septum or deformities in the sinus ducts that inhibit normal drainage.

## Signs and Symptoms

- Dull, aching pain in your face, especially your forehead, cheeks, across your nose and behind your eyes
- Pressure between your eyebrows and above or below your eyes
- A runny or stuffed nose
- Postnasal drip
- Watery eyes
- Feeling worse as the day progresses
- More pain when you bend your head forward

## Conventional Treatments

Treatment depends on the cause. If you have a sinus infection, your doctor may prescribe antibiotics to clear it up. (Because antibiotics may cause yeast infection, be sure to take an acidophilus supplement or eat yogurt that contains live cultures every day.)

Likewise, if allergies are the culprit, antihistamines may provide some relief. You may also use nasal sprays or decongestants to unclog your sinuses; I find that sprays usually work better than pills. Carefully follow the directions and warnings on the labels of over-the-counter products.

The usual treatments for temporary pain relief include aspirin, ibuprofen, or acetaminophen.

## Herbs

*Echinacea* (Echinacea angustifolia, Echinacea purpurea)
This popular remedy, made from purple coneflowers, has been proven in well-constructed, double-blind, placebo-controlled research to reduce the symptoms, frequency, and duration of colds. Laboratory studies have proven

that it can increase antibody production and bolster cellular immune function. The recommended dose is 1 cup of tea or 1 teaspoon of tincture three times a day.

## Do-It-Yourself

*Every day*
- Stop smoking and avoid other people's smoke, as well as other airborne irritants.
- Use oral or nasal decongestants before flying, travel to high altitudes, or swimming in deep water, especially if you have a cold.
- Use a humidifier if the air in your home is dry.
- When you have a sinus headache, avoid leaning over. In bed, keep your head elevated to relieve pressure.
- Try these treatments to relieve congestion and pain:

Salt water nasal douche: Salt water shrinks swollen tissues and blood vessels. Add 1 tablespoon of sea salt to 1 cup of warm water; lean your head back and apply one eyedropper-full into each nostril. Repeat two to three times a day until the swelling is gone.

Warm herbal compress: Boil 3 cups of water and pour it over 1 tablespoon of dried lavender and 1 tablespoon of dried chamomile. Steep for twenty minutes. Soak a cloth in this mixture, wring it out and apply it to the back of your neck or your forehead.

*Acupressure*
Try these acupressure points (see page 353 for technique).

- GV-26 (Governing Vessel 26), located directly under the middle of the nose, is a useful point for anything to do with the head or sinuses.
- LI-20 (Large Intestine 20) helps many nasal problems, including sinusitis and allergic rhinitis. To find these points, smile. They are in the creases in the face, near the nose.

*Aromatherapy*
Lavender reduces pain and is an anti-inflammatory. Add two to three drops to a hot bath and soak for twenty to thirty minutes.

*Sinus massage*
Using a circular motion, massage the bridge of your nose with your index finger and thumb for thirty seconds. Then press your thumb into your brow-

line—the spot where your nose meets your forehead, between your eyebrows. Apply pressure there for thirty seconds. Move up your forehead, halfway between your browline and the middle of your forehead and massage in a circular motion for thirty seconds.

## Exercise

Perform these cranial stretch exercises at least twice a week.

FRONTAL SINUS RELEASE
1. Hold your nose with one hand and your hair above your forehead with the other.
2. Pull your nose down and your hair up.
3. Hold 15 to 60 seconds.

MAXILLA SINUS RELEASE
1. Place your right thumb on the roof of your mouth on the left side and your left thumb on the roof of your mouth on the right side.
2. At the same time, hold your hands out in front of your face in a prayer position.
3. Press your thumbs into the roof of your mouth.
4. Hold 15 to 60 seconds.

## Red Flags

Call your doctor if:

- Your symptoms don't go away in three to five days.
- Your temperature is higher than 102 degrees.
- You experience nosebleeds, blurred or double vision, or balance problems.

## EYESTRAIN HEADACHE

### Description

Steady pain and pressure behind the eyes and on the forehead and face is often a sign of eyestrain. When you overwork your eye muscles by squinting, straining, prolonged close work, or blinking this type of headache may be the result.

## Causes

- Reading or staring at a computer monitor for long periods of time
- Reading or working with insufficient lighting
- Incorrect eyeglass or contact lens prescription
- Wearing contact lenses for too long, or wearing ill-fitting contact lenses
- Trouble seeing things close-up (presbyopia)
- Blurred vision or an inability to see objects clearly (refractive disorders)
- Irregular curvature of the eye, resulting in blurred vision (astigmatism)

## Signs and Symptoms

If your headaches are caused by eyestrain, you're likely to experience:

- Steady frontal pain, often behind your eyes
- Pain in your forehead and face, and sometimes in the back of your head and neck
- Pressure around or on top of your head
- Symptoms that often occur when your read or focus on objects that are close to you

## Conventional Treatments

In addition to pain relievers, the usual treatments for headaches caused by eyestrain include getting glasses (or new glasses) and eye exercises. Your doctor will also remind you to rest your eyes and avoid excessive computer use.

## Dietary Strategies (See Chapter 14 for food source of specified nutrients)

*Vitamin A*
Improves vision and helps relieve chronic eyestrain.

*Vitamin B12*
This, too, helps relieve eyestrain.

## Supplements

*Vitamin A*
To improve vision and relieve eyestrain, take between 900 and 3,000 mcg a day. Do not take vitamin A supplements if you are pregnant; they may cause birth defects.

## Do-It-Yourself

*Every day*
- Get regular eye exams with an optometrist or ophthalmologist.
- Clean your contact lenses daily. Use an enzymatic or heat cleaner once a week to remove protein buildup.
- Look up from close work and change your focus every fifteen minutes.
- Make sure your work and reading areas are well-lit.
- Wear sunglasses and a hat when you're out in bright sunlight.
- To reduce inflammation, roast an apple. Lie down for half an hour and put slices of the pulp on your eyes. You can do the same with slices of cucumber.

*Acupressure*
Use this acupressure point for eyestrain headaches:

- Bl-2 (Bladder 2), in the upper hollows of the eye sockets, where the eyebrows meet the bridge of the nose, relieves frontal headache, eyestrain, and tension.

*Aromatherapy*
- Add a few drops of fennel, chamomile, rosemary, or parsley oil to cool water. Soak a cloth in the mixture and wring it out. Lie in a dark room and apply the compress to puffy, swollen eyes.
- Mix 1 drop of lemon or rose oil and 2 tablespoons of a neutral carrier oil, such as wheat germ, almond oil, or sunflower oil, and massage it into your temples and the bony areas around the eyes.

*Palming*
This will relax your eyes. Try it!
1. If you wear contact lenses, take them out.
2. Turn down the lights and sit or lie down.
3. Place your hands over your eyes, palms down to block out light.
4. Keep your eyes open and stare into the darkness for 30 to 60 seconds.
5. Close your eyes and remove your hands.
6. Slowly open your eyes.

## Exercise

To relieve eyestrain, relax your mind, strengthen your eyes, and prevent future vision problems, do this eyeball stretch:

EYEBALL STRETCH
1. Sit comfortably in a chair.
2. Without moving your head, move your eyes up toward the ceiling and down toward the floor.
3. Move your eyes from left to right.
4. Move your eyes diagonally from the upper left to the lower right, and then from the lower left to the upper right.
5. Rotate your eyes clockwise, then counterclockwise.
6. Repeat these steps 10 times.
7. Rub your hands together until they feel warm. Cup them over your eyes; do not press. Allow the warmth to relax your eyes.

## Mind/Body

To relax and relieve your eyes, try relaxation, imagery, or meditation (see Chapter 18).

## Red Flags

Call your doctor if:

- Self-help strategies don't work.
- You experience prolonged visual changes or neurological symptoms, such as motor loss, numbness, weakness, or tingling; slurred speech; a change in balance; or memory loss.
- The headache started after you injured your head or were knocked out.
- Along with the headache, you have fever, vomiting, and a stiff neck.
- Your headaches are unusually severe or recur frequently.

# CLUSTER HEADACHES

## Description

With pain so intense they are sometimes described as "suicide" headaches, cluster headaches are a daunting ailment. Cluster headaches rarely affect women; 90 percent of them occur in men.

The excruciating pain is caused by abnormal contraction and expansion of blood vessels. Why are they called "cluster" headaches? Unfortunately it's because they occur in a series that can last for weeks or even months, followed by a remission for some period of time. Episodic cluster headaches strike from one to six times a day for several weeks; the chronic form brings almost daily headaches with no relief for six months or more. Thankfully, they usually last only about an hour.

## Causes

We don't yet know why cluster headaches occur. Some of the likely causes are:

- Problems with the hypothalamus gland, which controls normal body cycles such as sleep, appetite, and hormone secretion.
- Hormones or hormone imbalance are always a possible suspect whenever an ailment strikes one sex more than the other. One study found that men's testosterone levels were lower during an active cluster cycle than during a remission.
- Digestive disorders, such as peptic ulcers, constipation, hypoglycemia (low blood sugar), and food allergies increase your risk for cluster headaches. It may be that your body is thrown off balance if you don't absorb nutrients normally.
- Swelling and inflammation of the nerves behind your eye may play a role.
- Alcohol consumption can trigger a cluster headache; it also increases your risk of developing this disorder to begin with.
- Smoking tends to increase your chances of having cluster headaches; it also worsens attacks.
- Bright or glaring lights.
- Lack of sleep.

## Signs and Symptoms

Cluster headaches often occur early in the morning and may wake you from sleep. Symptoms include:

- Localized, intense pain, usually on one side of your head or around or behind one eye. The throbbing, knifelike pain comes in frequent, stabbing bursts.
- Pain may also occur in your forehead, cheek, nose, ear, or chin and jaw area
- Sweating on your forehead and abdomen
- Watery eyes
- Flushed face

## Conventional Treatments

The best treatment for cluster headaches is prevention; in other words, avoid any triggers you're aware of.

Aspirin, ibuprofen, and acetaminophen don't usually work because the headache disappears before they take effect. Prescription medications, such as quick-acting inhalants or sprays, are a better choice for pain relief.

## Dietary Strategies

Raw honey may help prevent a cluster headache. Take 1 tablespoon at the first sign of a headache, followed by another tablespoon in half an hour if symptoms develop.

## Do-It-Yourself

*Breathing exercises*
These techniques bring more oxygen into your blood and may help prevent cluster headaches.

DEEP INHALATION
1. Lie flat on the floor, a couch, or your bed. Inhale deeply, dividing your breath into three parts: First raise your stomach, then fill your lungs, and finally fill your chest.
2. Hold your breath for 3 seconds.
3. Slowly exhale.
4. Repeat 5 times.

WU BREATHING
This is a Chinese breathing technique for headache relief.
1. Lie down with your arms by your sides, and your feet hip width apart.
2. Put the tip of your tongue on the roof of your mouth, behind your teeth.
3. Breathe in through your nose.
4. Imagine your breath coming through the nose, to the top of the head, and down to your belly.
5. Continue breathing in this way for 20 to 30 minutes.
6. Do every day, in the morning and at night.

## Seeking Help from Complementary Practitioners

Acupuncture is sometimes effective for cluster headaches.

## Red Flags

See your doctor if you have pain around your eyes. This may be an indication of glaucoma.

## TREATMENTS USEFUL FOR ALL TYPES OF HEADACHES

### Dietary Strategies

Coriander (*Coriandrum sativum*), an herb known as cilantro in its fresh form, provides pain relief for headaches. Try sprinkling it on your food or using it in salsa.

### Do-It-Yourself

*Acupressure (See page 353 for technique)*
For headache pain, in general:

- SI-1 (Small Intestine 1), on the outside of the pinky finger, next to the nail.
- LI-4 (Large Intestine 4), in the web between the thumb and forefinger.

For face and head pain:

- BL-1 (Bladder 1), in the inner corners of the eyes.

For eye pain:

- ST-1 (Stomach 1), on the cheekbones, directly below the pupils.
- BL-1 (Bladder 1), in the depression above the inner corner of the eye.
- GB-1 (Gallbladder 1), at the outer corner of the eye.

For toothache:

- SI-19 (Small Intestine 19), in the depression next to the ears when your mouth is open.

*Aromatherapy*
A combination of eucalyptus (*Eucalyptus globulus*) and peppermint (*Mentha piperita*) relieves headache pain. Use it in a diffuser or sprinkle a few drops into your bath.

## Seeking Help from Complementary Practitioners

*Acupuncture*
A recent review of the use of acupuncture for headaches asked this question: Does acupuncture have any value in the management of patients with headaches? After reviewing twenty-seven studies over the last twenty years, the authors answered yes: Acupuncture has clear potential, and should be one of the first approaches to consider when dealing with headaches.

# 10

—

# Are You a Good Sport?

It's enormously gratifying when my women patients tell me how good they feel after they exercise or participate in sports or fitness programs. There is no doubt in my mind that physical activity helps you stay trim and fit and keeps your pain in check. It boosts your spirits and can leave you downright exhilarated. My patients' anecdotes are bolstered by the scientific literature, which again and again substantiates the many benefits of regular exercise. Unfortunately, exercise also has a down side—the risk of musculoskeletal injury—and that's the subject of this chapter.

One question I frequently hear is: Are women more prone to sports injury and pain? Although this issue is still debated in scientific journals, we do know that women are at greater risk for getting hurt from certain activities and sports. Women playing sports that involve pivoting, such as soccer, volleyball, and basketball, have the highest injury rates—higher than men who play these sports and higher than women in other sports. Women are especially prone to certain types of problems, particularly knee injuries, which they suffer between two and eight times as frequently as men, and stress fractures.

You may be more susceptible to pain and injury in certain parts of your body because of innate sex-linked differences in anatomy, hormonal makeup, and the elasticity of your ligaments. During pregnancy, as well as other times during your menstrual cycle when your hormones are fluctuating, joint dislocations are more common, and they may be exacerbated by sporting activity.

Some of the anatomical factors that predispose you to suffer more sports injuries than your male partner or friends include:

- Leg alignment, or how the femur (the thigh bone) and the tibia and fibula (lower leg bones) are connected to one another.

- Increased knee valgus—the knees point out to a greater degree. Combined with the wider pelvis, this means that the stresses and strains placed on certain structures, especially the knee, are different. Women's knees are more unstable, and because they bear such high forces, they are particularly susceptible to injury.
- More joint laxity, leading to a greater risk of sprain, strain, and dislocation.
- The hormonal cycle may also cause greater laxity of the ligaments, soft tissue, and support structures.

Fitness level also influences whether you are likely to be injured. Are women less fit than men? A recent study of 861 army recruits enrolled in an eight-week basic training course found that woman were *twice* as likely as men to experience exercise-related injury because they had a general lower level of fitness. This distressing finding is consistent with the U.S. Surgeon General's recent report that 60 percent of adult women in our country don't get enough physical activity. In fact, according to both the Centers for Disease Control and the Surgeon General, women are consistently less physically active than men.

These appalling statistics persist, despite landmark legislation that encourages female participation in sports. For example, as a result of Title IX, which prohibits sex discrimination in schools, women's involvement in high school athletics jumped from 300,000 when the law was passed in 1972, to 2.7 million in 1999. And today, women are actively involved in the U.S. Olympic Team; 37 percent of American Olympians are women.

But we can't all be Olympians. Whatever you do, I can't emphasize too strongly how important it is to get out there and move.

In this chapter, I'll start by providing general how-to advice for all types of sports injuries. Many of the dietary strategies and home remedies listed here will enhance your sports performance and fitness, as well as minimize pain should you suffer an injury. In later sections, you'll find more particulars about specific problems.

## Prevention

- Get a medical check-up before you start any exercise program.
- Choose an activity that is appropriate for you. For example, if you have bad knees, swimming or cycling is more appropriate than running.
- Start slowly, especially if you are not used to strenuous exercise. Injuries frequently occur when you push your body too fast or too hard. You

can add more activities, or increase the intensity or duration of your workout, as your body becomes accustomed to more activity.

· Use proper form. Any exercise can be unsafe if you don't do it correctly. Get advice from a certified exercise leader or personal trainer.

· Warm up for five to ten minutes before exercising. For instance, if you are a jogger, walk for the first five minutes of your run.

· Cool down for five to ten minutes after your activity and then stretch. This will help loosen muscles that have become tight and contracted while you exercised.

· The key to staying injury-free is daily activity. An estimated 20 million "weekend warriors" suffer sports-related injuries leading to permanent or temporary disabilities. I recommend that you do *at least* thirty minutes of moderate exercise *at least* three times a week. You don't have to join a gym. Moderate exercise includes vacuuming and cleaning your house, washing your car by hand, going for a 2-mile walk, gardening, or taking a couple of brisk laps around the mall. I also suggest doing strength training (with weights) once or twice a week.

· "No pain, no gain" is a damaging myth. Exercise may be tiring, but it should not be painful. If it hurts, stop! Remember, pain is a warning; along with swelling, tenderness, or redness of your skin it is often the first sign of injury.

· Old, worn-out shoes can lead to hip, knee, ankle, and foot injuries. These areas of the lower body account for 90 percent of all sports injuries. Wear supportive, cushioned footwear appropriate for your activity. There are shoes designed for aerobics, running, and tennis, as well as cross trainers if you do several different sports.

· Wear appropriate clothing. Lightweight, breathable clothes are important in hot weather; when it's cold, wear warm, protective clothing. Clothes that are too tight restrict movement and circulation.

· Use safety equipment designed for the type of exercise you do—a bicycle helmet if you bike, a safety helmet and guards for wrists, elbows, and knees if you Rollerblade.

· In one study, 71 percent of women complained of breast discomfort after exercise. This led to the development of ergonomically designed sports bras that provide comfortable support and limit movement of the breasts during exercise. The American Council on Exercise (ACE) suggests that you consider these pointers when you buy a sports bra:

    · Sports bras work in one of two ways, through compression or encapsulation. Compression bras, which are better if you are small-breasted, push your breasts against your chest. Harness-type sports bras, appropriate if you have larger breasts, encapsulate and provide support for each breast.

- Select a bra based on comfort, not on size.
- Bras that provide adequate ventilation prevent chaffing and minimize friction caused by sweating.
- Pay attention to the clasps or straps on the bra and make sure they don't dig into your skin.
- Before making the purchase, try the bra on and mimic the movements of your activities to ensure that it fits comfortably.

## Conventional Treatments

Sports injuries happen, even if you are super careful. Don't ignore them. Some injuries can take a long time to heal.

The standard treatment for sports injuries is known by the acronym R.I.C.E, which stands for:

*Rest*
Avoid activities that cause pain or swelling. Don't resume until your exercise is pain free. Exercising before your injury has healed may make it worse; it can also increase your chance of reinjury.

*Ice*
Ice is a pain reliever, slows blood flow to the injury, and reduces swelling. It also limits tissue damage and speeds repair. Apply it as soon as possible and continue for ten to thirty minutes at a time, intermittently for two to three days. Do not apply ice for more than thirty minutes. To protect your skin from direct contact with the ice, I recommend putting it in a plastic sandwich bag, covering it with a cloth, and applying it to the inflamed area.

*Compression*
Apply a compression bandage, such as an ACE wrap, to reduce swelling and limit motion. Do not make the bandage too tight—you don't want to impair blood flow to the injured area.

*Elevation*
To reduce swelling, elevate the injured limb above the level of your heart using pillows, a sofa back, or a chair.

For relief of pain and inflammation, take ibuprofen or aspirin.

## Dietary Strategies (See Chapter 14 for food sources of specified nutrients)

### Calcium

Since more than 99 percent of the calcium in the body is warehoused in the bones, you can imagine how important calcium is for sports competition. It's also critical for preventing osteoporosis. Calcium is most effective when combined with vitamin D, which helps ensure its adequate absorption.

### Vitamin E

A potent antioxidant, this vitamin can increase your immune response and may offer protection against the formation of free radicals during heavy exercise. Because free radicals can cause tissue damage leading to muscle soreness, vitamin E can help curb pain. It may also be helpful during weight training, since lifting weights also induces muscle fiber damage.

### Vitamin C

This vitamin helps your body make collagen, which is an important protein found in cartilage, tendon, and connective tissue. These structures "play overtime" when you exercise. Researchers have studied vitamin C and sports injuries for decades. In one study, done in 1960, vitamin C and bioflavonoids decreased athletic injury potential in football players. There's also evidence that vitamin C relieves muscle soreness, reduces the frequency of cold and upper respiratory symptoms in marathon runners, and limits bruising tendencies for people who play contact sports. And a recent study, published in the journal *Pain*, showed that vitamin C intake reduced exercise-related soreness. Unlike animals, humans cannot manufacture ascorbic acid, so you must get it from food or supplements.

### Other antioxidants

Your muscles may hurt if you overexert yourself during heavy-duty exercise. Since muscle soreness and pain may be caused or exacerbated when free radicals damage tissue, it is helpful to use antioxidants, which quench or neutralize them. Besides vitamins C and E, other helpful nutrients are selenium and beta-carotene.

### OPCs (Oligomeric Proanthcyanidins)

This is a tongue-twisting fancy name for a class of compounds originally discovered in a French maritime pine tree. Most commercially available supplements are made from grapeseed or pine bark.

Few studies have directly examined the effects of OPCs on women's sports injuries; however, in some research they've been shown to decrease swelling, strengthen tissue, and fortify blood vessels. I'm impressed by scientific evidence showing that OPCs strengthen and protect elastin and collagen, some of the building blocks for muscles, tendons, and cartilage.

OPCs are present in a wide variety of everyday foods, such as blueberries, bilberries, red wine, onions, green and black tea, legumes, and parsley. If you're a normal, healthy woman, I believe that eating OPC-laden foods is sufficient. You can beef up your consumption of OPCs by cooking with grapeseed oil. Unlike flaxseed or other healthy oils, grapeseed oil has an extremely high boiling point, making it ideal for cooking.

## B complex vitamins

These serve a multitude of purposes. I'd emphasize these:

- B1, or thiamine, is important for the processing of carbohydrates, fats, and proteins. Your cells need this vitamin to manufacture ATP (adenosine triphosphate), a critical energy-transporting chemical, which is obviously valuable for athletics.
- B2, or riboflavin, is also needed for the production of ATP. It aids processing of fats and amino acids and helps to activate folate and vitamin B6.
- B3, or niacin, enables more than fifty of the body's enzyme reactions. It helps to manufacture energy and fat from carbohydrates and sex hormones. There are several forms of vitamin B3, including nicotinic acid, niacinamide, and inositol hexaniacinate. The latter improves walking distance in people with intermittent claudication. (This painful condition is a result of hardening of the arteries in the leg; it can be a real problem for older people who want to exercise.)
- B6, or pyridoxine, is an extremely versatile vitamin that helps manufacture neurotransmitters, hormones, and proteins. Although deficiencies of this vitamin are scarce, certain drugs can accelerate its depletion. These include penicillamine (used for arthritis), hydralazine (blood pressure), isoniazid (TB), and MAO inhibitors (depression).
- B12, or cobalamine, helps your body produce SAMe, a potent pain reliever. B12 is also needed for nerve cell activity and to prevent anemia. Since adequate stomach acidity is needed to absorb B12, if you are on acid-reducing drugs like Prilosec (omeprazole), Zantac (ranitidine), or one of the others, you are likely to need supplemental B12. This vitamin is a perfect illustration of one of my mottos: "for every force, there is a counterforce." Acid-reducing drugs are frequently pre-

scribed for people who take nonsteroidal anti-inflammatory drugs for pain. The irony is that one of their side effects is to diminish production of SAMe, a natural pain reliever. Other drugs that hinder B12 absorption are AZT (for AIDS), phenformin and Metformin (for diabetes), nitrous oxide, and colchinine (for gout).

- Get plenty of water. Be sure to drink an 8-ounce glass before you start and after you finish exercising. If you're out there for a long time, especially in hot weather, take frequent water breaks. To get all that water to go down the hatch more easily, you can spice it up with a few drops of orange, lemon, or grapefruit juice.

R E C I P E

## WILD RICE SALAD WITH CITRUS DRESSING

This delicious dish contains B vitamins, vitamins C and E, and OPCs.

> 4 cups cooked wild and brown rice
> 1 red pepper, chopped
> 1 small red onion, chopped
> 2 bok choy stalks including leaves, chopped
> 1 carrot, diced or thinly sliced
> ½ cup cashews or pecans
>
> DRESSING
> ¼ cup orange juice
> ¼ cup lemon juice
> 1 clove garlic, minced
> ¼ cup olive oil
> 1 tablespoon rice syrup

1. In a large bowl combine the rice, red pepper, onion, bok choy, carrots, and nuts.
2. In a separate small bowl, whisk together the dressing ingredients, and then mix it into the rice mixture.
3. May be served warm or cold.

SERVES 6

## Supplements

### Coenzyme Q10

Since muscle soreness and pain after exercise may be caused or exacerbated when free radicals damage tissue, it's helpful to use antioxidants, which quench or neutralize them. CoQ 10 is a powerful antioxidant, but it's hard to get a therapeutic dose from food. I recommend supplements. The U.S. Dietary Reference Intake has not been established for CoQ 10. The typical dose range suggested in the literature ranges from 30 to 300 mg divided into three doses daily.

### Minerals

Minerals, including magnesium, zinc, chromium, and copper, are important for many of the body's enzymatic functions. You can get them from a daily multivitamin and mineral supplement.

### Sports drinks

Another source of minerals is a good sports beverage, containing water, minerals, electrolytes (potassium, sodium, chloride), and carbohydrates. The water prevents dehydration during or after an intense sports workout. The carbohydrates give the body fuel for energy production, preventing the breakdown of muscular stores of glycogen.

### Vitamin B

As discussed earlier, you need B vitamins. Take a B-complex vitamin that includes vitamins B1, B2, B3, B6, and B12. It's best to take a complex rather than individual B vitamins because they work as a team and you want to get the correct ratio.

### Creatine

Found naturally in the body, creatine is converted to phosphocreatine, which helps produce energy. As a nutritional supplement, it's been touted as a great way to enhance athletic performance. It's been shown to help in high-intensity, short-duration exercises like swimming, soccer, and volleyball. Men may benefit more from creatine than women, possibly because women's muscles contain more creatine to begin with. I'm waiting for more scientific proof before I wholeheartedly endorse this supplement for all sporting activity. If you want to try it, follow dosing instructions on the package.

*HMB (Beta-hydroxy-beta-methylbutyric acid)*
This is another chemical that occurs naturally in the body; it is related to leucine, an amino acid. Based on two small but well-designed studies of women, it looks like HMB supplements have no effect on body mass and strength if you are sedentary. But if you do weight training, it may improve your response. It might also keep you from developing muscle damage during a heavy workout. In addition, HMB may prevent muscle damage and pain during exercise. I'm waiting for more research before I recommend it conclusively.

*Ergogenic aids*
You may hear about these products or see them in your health food store. They are said to build muscle or enhance athletic performance (and as a consequence may reduce pain), but there is insufficient evidence for me to recommend them. As far as I'm concerned, their value still needs to be scientifically proven. They include:

- Conjugated linoleic acid
- Amino acids
- Phosphatedidylserine
- Branched chain amino acids (leucine, isoleucine, valine)
- Carnitine
- Phosphate
- Pyruvate
- Stimulants, such as ephedra (Ma Huang)
- Caffeine (tea, coffee, guarana)
- Ribose
- NADH (Nicotinamide Adenine Dinucleotide)

## Herbs

*Ginseng*
Ginseng is sometimes used as a sports supplement, and there is some evidence that it can significantly improve aerobic capacity. There are three species: American ginseng (*Panax quinquefolius*), Asian ginseng, Korean ginseng (*Panax ginseng*), and Siberian ginseng (*Eleutherococcus senticosus*).

Most of the positive research that I have seen utilized *Panax ginseng*. The usual dose is 200 mg of an extract. Ginseng can interfere with drug metabolism, so check with your doctor if you regularly take any medications. It can also cause breast tenderness, menstrual abnormalities, insomnia, and tachycardia (rapid heartbeat).

*White willow bark* (Salix alba)

The bark of willow trees contains an anti-inflammatory compound similar to aspirin. It's appropriate for exercise-related musculoskeletal pain. Unlike other anti-inflammatory drugs, willow is less likely to upset your stomach because it is converted into its active ingredient (salicylic acid) after it is absorbed by your gut. The recommended dose is one cup of infusion, three to five times a day. Do not use willow if you are allergic to aspirin or other NSAIDS, or when pregnant or breast-feeding. Use caution if you take blood-thinning medications.

*Meadowsweet* (Filipendula ulmaria)

This flowering plant of the meadows acts as an anti-inflammatory because it contains salicylates, the active ingredient in aspirin. It is helpful for exercise-related musculoskeletal pain. Use 1 to 2 teaspoons of dried herb per cup of hot water for a tea. The recommended dose is up to three cups a day. Avoid meadowsweet if you are allergic to aspirin.

## Herbal Creams and Ointments

*Aloe vera*

A common house plant, aloe cools, soothes, and relieves inflammation. Creams are readily available. Be sure to buy one with a high aloe content; it should appear as one of the first listed ingredients.

*Joint-Ritis (See page 96)*

*Sports Gel*

Made from *Bellis perennis* (daisy), *Hypericum perforatum* (St. John's wort), *Rhus toxicodendron* (poison ivy), and *Ruta graveolens* (rue), you can rub this homeopathic gel into sore, aching muscles, tendons, or joints up to four times a day.

## Do-It-Yourself

*Every day*

- Apply a vinegar compress to reduce inflammation.
- Wrap a wet plantain leaf around the affected area to reduce swelling and stiffness and encourage healing.
- Give yourself an herbal massage to ease muscle pain and stiffness. Make a muscle rub by combining 2 drops of coriander oil, 4 drops of juniper

oil, 4 drops of black pepper oil, and 4 teaspoons of grapeseed oil. Use the oil to massage the painful spot.

### Aromatherapy

- Rosemary (*Rosmarinus officinalis*): To fight inflammation and relieve pain, add a few drops of rosemary oil to water for a compress. You can also add it to a neutral oil or lotion and use it to massage the sore area.
- After-Sport Shower Formula: You might also enjoy this. Add two drops of rosemary oil, two drops of pine oil, and four drops of lemon oil to a small dollop of unscented shower gel. Work it into a lather with a sponge or washcloth and use it in the shower. Avoid rosemary during pregnancy or if you have epilepsy or high blood pressure.

## Mind/Body

### Yoga

Try Tree Pose, Chair Pose, and Standing Yoga Mudra. (See pages 344–351 for postures.)

## Red Flags

Call your doctor if you have:

- Any injury that doesn't improve after ten days of home care and rest.
- Pain that lasts for more than an hour or wakes you at night.
- Any injury where a joint "pops" and immediately becomes difficult to use.

## SPRAINS AND STRAINS

### Description

Sprains and strains are the most common sports-related injuries. A sprain is an injury to the ligaments around a joint that results in an excessive stretch or a tear. Ligaments are bands of tissue that bind joints together; they also support many internal organs.

Sprains may occur around any joint, but they usually affect the back, fingers, knees, wrists, and, especially when it comes to sports injuries, the ankles. Day in and day out, the ankles support the body's entire weight. Making matters worse, when you run or jump they absorb forces three times your body weight. Small wonder, then, that the ankle is your most vulnerable joint.

The ankles are prone to many sports-related injuries, including fractures and dislocations, but sprains are the most common. They may be more of an issue for women than men—in at least one study, women suffered mild ankle sprains 25 percent more frequently. If you play basketball or tennis, or do aerobics or other activities that involve jumping, quick starting, and stopping, watch out.

Sprains may be mild, moderate, or severe. Depending on their severity, they are graded from I to III:

- Grade I (mild): The ligament stretches but does not tear and there is no looseness of the joint. You still have full range of motion with only mild pain. Treatment includes ice with physical therapy, and the prognosis for recovery is excellent.
- Grade II (moderate): The ligament is partially torn and there may be some looseness of the joint. You have pain, bruising, and swelling and it may hurt to walk. Treatment includes ice, bracing, and/or a cast. The prognosis is good.
- Grade III (severe): The ligament is completely torn and the joint is loose and unstable. Your pain is severe and you also have swelling, bruising, and occasional bleeding under the skin. In addition to ice and a splint, treatment involves surgery. The prognosis for recovery is variable.

A strain is an injury, without a tear, of a muscle. Muscle strains are also called pulled muscles.

## Causes

Strains are caused by overuse, overstretching, or overloading the muscles in a particular area. This causes inflammation and fluid buildup.

Sudden or unexpected twisting is the most frequent cause of sprains. Improper footwear or poor athletic form can also cause problems.

## Signs and Symptoms

- Swelling
- Immediate pain, mild to severe
- Burning or popping

- Because there may be bleeding into the injured area, it may appear swollen or bruised
- In the case of a sprained ankle, it hurts when you move the ankle or try to put weight on it

## Conventional Treatments

Your doctor will do a physical exam and may order an MRI (magnetic resonance imaging) to evaluate the damage. R.I.C.E. and anti-inflammatory medications are standard treatments for strains and sprains. Physical therapy is sometimes recommended, too. Depending on how severe the sprain is, your other options include braces, crutches, and surgery.

## Supplements

In addition to the dietary strategies mentioned at the beginning of this chapter, I recommend these nutrients to hasten healing:

*Vitamin C*
The acceptable daily dose range is 90 to 2,500 mg. Try to spread your intake over the course of the day. Large amounts of vitamin C may cause kidney stones or gout, or cramps and diarrhea.

*Vitamin E*
The acceptable dose range is 15 to 1,000 mg a day.

*Vitamin A*
The acceptable dose range is 900 to 3,000 mcg a day.

*Zinc*
The acceptable dose range is 8 to 40 mg a day.

*Selenium*
The acceptable dose range is 60 to 400 mcg a day.

## Herbs

*Ginger* (Zingibar officinale)
Ginger is a natural anti-inflammatory. Herbalists suggest adding five to twenty drops of tincture to your favorite herbal tea once a day. Use caution if you take blood-thinning medication.

*Chamomile* (Chamaemelum nobile *or* Matricaria recutita)
This sweet-smelling herb helps fight inflammation, promotes relaxation, and decreases spasms. To help you sleep, make a double-strength tea by using two tea bags or steeping 2 teaspoons of dried flowers in a cup of boiling water. Avoid contact with your eyes; it may cause irritation. Chamomile may cause an allergic reaction.

## Herbal Creams and Ointments

*Arnica* (Arnica montana)
Also called leopard's bane, mountain tobacco, and sneezewort, arnica is helpful for sprains, strains, and bruising. Use an arnica cream, or add several drops of a tincture to a cold compress and apply hourly for the first eight hours to reduce swelling. Do not use on open wounds.

*Capsaicin cream (0.025–0.075 percent) (See page 96)*

*Traumeel ointment (See page 158)*

*Triflora Arthritis Gel*
You can use this homeopathic ointment to relieve minor muscle aches and stiffness that result from overexercising or sports injuries.

## Do-It-Yourself

*Prevent ankle injuries*
- Wear quality athletic shoes with good ankle support. Be sure they are specific for your activity.
- Consider high-top shoes, which provide extra ankle support.
- If your ankle is weak, tape it or wear a brace.

*Injuries*
When you get a strain or a sprain, elevate the area and apply a cold compress as soon as possible. Continue with the cold compresses until you've reduced the swelling. While a compress using plain old cold water is fine, here are some options that will promote quicker healing:

- Add cider vinegar to your compress to relieve pain and swelling.
- Mix ½ teaspoon of ginger powder and 1 cup of boiling water; let it cool and use it on your compress.
- Pour boiling water into a bowl containing a handful of chamomile

flowers and stir until it turns into paste. Let it cool, spread it on a cotton wrap, and apply it to the affected area for at least fifteen minutes.

### Aromatherapy

- Lavender: This herb calms and soothes your spirits as it reduces pain. Add 3 drops of lavender oil to a foot bath or cold compress. Or try adding 3 drops of lavender oil, 3 drops of chamomile oil, and 2 drops of neroli (made from bitter orange blossoms) to a warm bath. You can also add this mixture to 3 teaspoons of grapeseed or sweet almond oil and use it for a massage. Be careful with lavender if you have hay fever or asthma since it may cause an allergic reaction.
- Rub in a small amount of peppermint oil onto the injured area to numb it.
- Add a few drops of sweet marjoram oil and rosemary oil to a compress to encourage healing and reduce inflammation.

### Homeopathy

Use these remedies one at a time, following the dosages listed on the package labels:

- Arnica (*Arnica montana*, leopard's bane, mountain tobacco, sneezewort) stimulates healing of damaged tissue.
- *Ruta graveolens* (rue, bitter herb, herb of grace) is used primarily for bruising and ligament strains.

### Acupressure (see Chapter 19 for instructions)

To cut pain, use ST 44 (Stomach-44), on the top of the foot, in the web space between the second and third toe.

## Exercise

If you have a sprained ankle, it's important to stop exercising until the pain and swelling resolves and your ankle has healed. Still, it's important to do gentle stretches and range-of-motion exercises to preserve movement in the joint.

### First phase

- Ankle pumping: With your knee fully extended, bring your toes and foot up and then down, repetitively in sequence. Repeat five times.
- Sit comfortably and write the alphabet in the air with your big toe. Move only the foot and ankle, not the leg.

· Stretch the gastrocnemius-soleus, a major muscle in the calf, by standing 30 inches from a wall, placing your palms on the wall and leaning into the wall until you feel a stretch in the back of your leg.

### Second phase

When you are able to bear weight on your ankle, you can balance on your leg for twenty to sixty seconds. If it hurts, put a foam cushion under your foot.

### Third phase

You can strengthen the major muscles of your foot and ankle by using elastic tubing to move your foot up, down, in and out.

## Seeking Help from Complementary Practitioners

A massage may be helpful.

## Red Flags

Call your doctor if you experience:

· Pain, stiffness, or swelling that lasts longer than two to three days
· Inability to bear weight on or move the joint
· Popping when you move a sprained joint
· Poor alignment or crooked bones

## COMMON SPORTS-RELATED KNEE INJURIES

Your knee is a critically important joint that flexes and extends the leg. The collateral ligaments, one on each side, connect the upper bone, or femur, to the bones of the lower leg, the tibia and fibula. These ligaments also prevent the knee from moving from side to side. Within the knee itself are the anterior cruciate and posterior cruciate ligaments. They provide stability and serve as guide wires, stopping the knee from overextending or rotating too much.

Whether you're a young runner who leads an active lifestyle or an older woman suffering from arthritis, your knees are particularly vulnerable to pain and injury. Far more than men, women are prone to get runner's knee and other knee ailments. Women have a relative risk of injuring the anterior cruciate ligament, the patellofemoral (knee cap) joint, and the meniscal cartilage (the knee's shock absorber) that is respectively 3.5, 2.3, and 2.1 times higher than in men.

## RUNNER'S KNEE

### Description

Also called chondromalacia patella, patellofemoral disorder, or patellar malalignment, runner's knee is an overuse injury. Besides running, it's associated with walking, jumping, or bicycling and can also occur if you ski, play soccer, or do high-impact aerobics. Sometimes, when you repeatedly bend and straighten the knee, you irritate the inside surface of the kneecap, which then grinds against the thigh bone, or femur. This causes the cartilage behind the knee, which usually helps absorb shock, to break down. The result is pain.

### Causes

- Imbalanced muscle strength or flexibility
- Unequal leg lengths
- Alignment problems—turned-in thighbones, wide hips, underdeveloped thigh muscles, or knock-knees
- Flat feet (overpronation), where the feet roll inward, the arches collapse, and the mid-feet flatten out more than normal when you walk or run

### Signs and Symptoms

- Dull, aching pain under, behind, or around the kneecap
- Snapping, popping, or grinding in the knee
- Swelling
- Pain when you walk, run, or sit for a long time
- Going down stairs or hills is particularly painful

### Conventional Treatments

Standard care for this and many other sports injuries includes R.I.C.E. (see page 235) and anti-inflammatory medication. To take pressure off the knee, switch to a nonweight-bearing exercise, such as swimming or rowing, until you are better. You may need a knee sleeve or brace to support the knee.

It's wise to have your muscle strength, gait pattern, and flexibility assessed by a physiatrist, orthopedist, or sports medicine physician. You can be fitted for semirigid orthotics if it turns out that you overpronate. In addition, your doctor or a physical therapist may recommend exercises, specifically a quadriceps strengthening program.

## Do-It-Yourself

To prevent runner's knee, I recommend these tips:

- Avoid running straight down a hill; instead, walk down or run in a zigzag fashion
- Don't do deep knee bends
- Stay away from shoes with cleats or high heels
- Buy shoes made for running with arch support and cushioning (see page 262 for details about how to choose proper shoes)
- Replace your running shoes every three hundred to five hundred miles

## Exercise

Try the Hamstring Stretch, Quadriceps Set, and Straight Leg Raises to gently strengthen and stretch your injured knee. (See pages 331–338 for exercises.)

## Red Flags

Call your doctor if you have:

- Pain, stiffness, or swelling that lasts more than two to three days
- Inability to bear weight on or move the joint
- Popping sounds
- Poor alignment or crooked bones

## COLLATERAL LIGAMENT INJURY

### Description

The collateral ligaments are found on both sides of the knee. They connect the femur, or thigh bone, with the bones of the lower leg, the tibia and fibula. Collateral ligaments prevent the knee from moving from side to side.

Bending or twisting can sprain or tear them (also see "Sprains and Strains," page 242).

## Causes

Collateral ligament injuries are common in activities such as running, jumping, and contact sports. Like other knee injuries, they are also more likely to happen if you are overweight.

## Signs and Symptoms

- Poor alignment of the knee joint
- Pain on the outer side of the knee
- Swelling and tenderness
- The knee feels as if it's going to give way
- An audible pop or snap at the time of injury

## Conventional Treatments

Standard care for this and many other sports injuries includes R.I.C.E. (see page 235) and anti-inflammatory medication. Until you get better, switch to a nonweight-bearing exercise such as swimming or rowing. If the damage is severe, you may need to use crutches, a knee immobilizer, or a knee brace to prevent further injury.

To prevent further problems, have your muscle strength, gait pattern, and flexibility assessed by a physiatrist, orthopedist, or sports medicine doctor. If you overpronate, you can be fitted for semirigid orthotics. Also, your doctor or a physical therapist may recommend a quadriceps strengthening program or other exercises.

## Do-It-Yourself

To prevent collateral ligament injuries, I recommend these steps:

- Be sure to warm up before exercising
- Wear proper shoes and use appropriate knee protection for the sport
- Learn weight-lifting techniques to build the muscles that support and strengthen the knee

## Exercise

Do not return to sports until you are fully recovered and have been cleared by your doctor. I suggest that you meet these conditions before you start exercising again:

- You can bend and straighten the injured knee without pain.
- The swelling has improved.
- You have regained normal strength in the knee and leg.
- You can bear weight enough to resume.

In the meantime, do these rehabilitation exercises for your knee: Heel Slide, Prone Knee Flexion, Straight Leg Raise, and Wall Squat. However, do the Wall Squat only after your pain has lessened. (See pages 331–338 for exercises.)

## Red Flags

Call your doctor if you have:

- Pain, stiffness, or swelling that lasts more than two or three days
- Inability to bear weight on or move the joint
- Popping noises when you move your knee
- Poor alignment or crooked bones

## PATELLAR TENDONITIS (JUMPER'S KNEE)

### Description

If you exercise too much or train too hard, you may develop pain in the patellar tendon. This strip of fibrous, cordlike tissue connects the kneecap to the shin. Patellar tendinitis is a risk if you run, walk, bike, or do sports that involve jumping. (*Note*: There is more information on treatments for tendinitis in Chapter 7.)

### Causes

In addition to overuse, several kinds of movements can damage the patellar tendon. These include twisting with your feet in a fixed position, rapid squatting, or sharply extending your knee. In severe instances, you can tear the tendon.

## Signs and Symptoms

- Pain, swelling, and tenderness around the patellar tendon
- Swelling of the knee joint
- Pain with jumping, running, or walking
- Pain when you bend or straighten the knee
- Tenderness behind the knee

## Conventional Treatments

It's likely that your physician will simply recommend ice and compression, along with anti-inflammatory medication for the pain. She may also suggest that you use a knee brace or immobilizer to support the knee. Sometimes, shoe orthotics can be helpful.

## Do-It-Yourself

- To prevent injury, add shock-absorbing insoles to your shoes to reduce the impact of activity on your knee.
- Try an ice massage for the pain.
    1. Freeze water in a Styrofoam cup.
    2. Peel the top of the cup away to expose the ice and hold on to the bottom of the cup.
    3. Rub the ice into your leg for five to ten minutes.

## Exercise

Until you are fully recovered, switch to a sport that is less stressful for your knee, such as swimming. Meanwhile, you can do the Hamstring Stretch and Patellar Mobility Exercise to promote strengthening and healing. (See pages 331–338 for exercises.)

Once the pain in your knee has lessened, try Quadricep Sets, Quadriceps Stretches, and Straight Leg Raises, which strengthen the muscles that support and stabilize your knee. (See pages 331–338.)

**Red Flags**

Call your doctor if you have:

- Pain, stiffness, or swelling that lasts more than two or three days
- Inability to bear weight on or move the joint
- Popping when you move the joint
- Poor alignment or crooked bones

## ANTERIOR CRUCIATE LIGAMENT (ACL) TEARS

This ailment has begun to receive national attention, thanks in part to the terrible spectacle of women NCAA basketball players in agony after tearing their ACLs on live television. It's estimated that a female athlete will tear this ligament once out of every three hundred times she participates in practice or games.

We don't know why women are so vulnerable to ACL injuries, but apparently certain female anatomical characteristics tend to put you more at risk. As a woman, you have a wider pelvis and more flexible hips so the ACL, located inside the knee, is under more strain than a man's. Over the past couple of years, medical researchers have found that women's knee muscles don't provide as much protection as do their male counterparts, even when they use the same strengthening and conditioning programs. They suggest that innovative strengthening exercises, designed especially for women, may need to be developed.

The bottom line is that women suffer more injuries from noncontact sports, including basketball, soccer, gymnastics, snow skiing, and handball. If you participate in sports where you pivot or jump and land on one foot, you are particularly susceptible to ACL tears. These injuries can be very painful. What's more, because the ACL gives your knee most of its ability to rotate, you lose stability when you make lateral and twisting motions.

ACL tears are usually diagnosed by MRI (magnetic resonance imaging). Immobilization of the knee and, depending on the severity of the ACL tear, surgery to reconstruct the knee is often required.

**Signs and Symptoms**

- Loud audible pop, signifying a tear
- Difficulty standing on the injured leg

- Swelling of the leg and knee (hemorrhage)
- Intense pain

## Red Flags

Pain, swelling, and loss of motion in the knee are signals for you to call your doctor.

## OTHER SPORT-RELATED INJURIES

### ANDREA'S STORY

Andrea, a thirty-four-year-old caterer, appeared to be in great shape. This was not surprising, given her exercise habits. "Twice a week I take aerobic dance at the local community center and I run two to three miles a day," she told me.

Andrea had come to see me shortly after a midwinter vacation. She had decided to surprise her husband and their seven-year-old son and four-year-old daughter with a weeklong stay at a Miami Beach resort. While enjoying the sun, the sand, the surf, and the "early-bird specials," she made it a point to keep up her exercise. "I did my daily run on the beach, finishing up on the boardwalk," she explained.

Unfortunately she was now in exquisite pain. "It started toward the end of my vacation—this awful pain and discomfort in my shins," she said. I already had an inkling of what her problem was; then, she mentioned the kicker: "I keep thinking it's getting better; then, when I start to run, it starts up again."

Andrea had shin splints, a common condition that is sometimes caused by running on an uneven surface. Those otherwise-glorious runs on the beach in Miami were the reason for her misery.

I told her to ease off on high-impact sports, like running and aerobics, and substitute swimming, in-line skating, or biking until her sore, damaged muscles felt better. To speed up the process, I suggested a diet loaded in antioxidants, such as vitamins C and E, selenium and beta-carotene, which encourage healing. In addition to the Arnica cream she was already using on her legs, I suggested that she whirlpool her legs twice a day and gave her instructions for an easy-to-make herbal rub she could use to massage away muscle pain and stiffness. Finally, I gave her a series of stretches to do every day.

As she was getting ready to leave, I asked Andrea when she had last bought running shoes. "Gosh, I can't even remember," she replied. Because worn-out running shoes can cause or aggravate shin splints, new shoes were added to her list of "prescriptions."

A month later, I ran into Andrea at our local sporting goods store. She was buying new running shoes, which I took as a good sign. She flashed me a big smile and a thumbs-up. "Cured!" she said.

## SHIN SPLINTS (SHIN PAIN)

### Description

If you're a runner, shin splints can stop you dead in your tracks. This ailment comes in two varieties: anterolateral and posteromedial. The anterolateral, as its name implies, affects the muscles and causes pain in the front and outer part of the lower leg. You're prone to this type of shin splints because of the normal imbalance between the muscles in the front of the shin (tibialis anterior, whose job is to raise the foot up), and the overpowering calf muscle (gastrocnemius muscle) in the back. When the calf muscle is significantly stronger, it can cause damage to the front shin muscles.

Posteromedial shin splints affect the muscles in the back, inner part of the leg. It hurts along the inner leg above the ankle, and gets worse when you lift up on your toes or move your ankle inward. Often, these shin splints are provoked by running on uneven roads or a banked track, or if your feet deviate inward without the support of a good pair of running shoes.

Although runners are especially susceptible to shin splints, other athletes get them, too. You can develop inflammation of the shin bone (tibia), or the muscles and tendons that attach to it, if you run or jump on hard surfaces or exercise too much, too fast, or too soon. The tibia is where the muscles that raise the arch of the foot are attached, so shin pain can also occur if you have tight calf muscles or wear worn-out shoes.

### Causes

Overuse is the usual cause of shin splints. They often occur when you increase your mileage or pick up your pace. If you participate in aerobics, basketball, volleyball, or other activities that involve repetitive pounding, you may also develop this problem. And your shins may object if you switch your exercise routine to a hard surface, like asphalt or the hard wooden floor of a gym.

If your arches collapse when you walk or run—your foot flattens out more than normal—you are at greater risk for shin splints. This condition, called overpronation, puts more stress on the leg muscles.

## Signs and Symptoms

- Pain is in the front, outer part or the back, inner part of your lower leg. Your shin bone or the muscles on either side of it may hurt.
- Tender and/or swollen shins.
- Generally, it hurts most during exercise and feels better when you rest. You may, however, have pain at rest.
- Usually, but not always, shin splints affect both legs.

## Conventional Treatments

R.I.C.E. (see page 235) and rehabilitation exercises are standard treatments for shin splints. You may use ibuprofen or aspirin for pain relief and inflammation. You can get prescription, custom-made arch supports (orthotics) to correct overpronation, if that's part of the problem.

## Do-It-Yourself

*To prevent shin splints*
- Wear well-cushioned, stable running shoes.
- Run on soft surfaces (grass or dirt) and do aerobics on an exercise mat.
- Increase the intensity of your workout gradually.
- Include calf stretches in your warm-up and cooldown (see exercise section below).
- Check with a podiatrist about getting orthotic inserts for your shoes.
- If you are a runner who's had recurrent shin splints, examine your running style and correct improper form. Get help from a trainer if necessary.

*Ice massage for pain*
1. Freeze water in a Styrofoam cup.
2. Peel the top of the cup away to expose the ice and hold on to the bottom of the cup.
3. Rub the ice into your leg for five to ten minutes.

*Hydrotherapy*
Submerging your legs in a whirlpool can be helpful.

## Exercise

My patients with shin splints often ask me when they can return to their activity. Although I know it's frustrating to hear this, my answer is: "It depends." My general rule of thumb is that the longer you have symptoms before you start treatment, the longer it will take to get better. Still, everyone recovers from injury at a different rate. Remember though, if you start too soon you may worsen your problem or even cause permanent damage. You can return to your normal activity when you have complete range of motion and full strength in both legs, you can jog or sprint straight ahead without pain or limping, and you can jump on either or both legs without pain. Until then, to tide you over and help you stay in shape, substitute swimming or another low-impact activity.

When it's time to go back to your regular routine, start slowly. If it hurts, stop and resume your treatment.

In the meantime, you can do therapeutic exercises, including Calf Stretch with Towel, Standing Calf Stretch, Active Range-of-Motion of the Ankle, Heel Raises, and Sitting and Standing Toe Raises. (See pages 331–338 for exercises.)

## Seeking Help from Complementary Practitioners

*Massage*
Deep massage of sore muscles can help relieve soreness and pain.

*Acupuncture*
I've found this therapy to be very helpful for my patients with shin splints.

## Red Flags

If you develop tightness, numbness, or tingling in the lower leg while you work out, or shin pain that doesn't subside with rest, see your doctor. You may have **compartment syndrome**. Your lower leg muscles are separated into compartments by membrane walls. When you overindulge in your favorite sport, your muscles may get too big for their compartments, putting pressure on nearby nerves and blood vessels. Symptoms may clear up when you stop exercising; however, it may take several hours to a few days for them to clear up. Compartment syndrome is a serious problem that may require surgery. Left untreated, it can become a surgical emergency.

## STRESS FRACTURE

### Description

Stress fractures are hairline cracks in bone that can cause severe pain. They are serious injuries; if left untreated, stress fractures may get worse, or even lead to complete fractures. The most common sites for them are the bones of the mid-foot (metatarsals), shin bone (tibia), outer lower leg bone (fibula), thigh bone (femur), and back bones (vertebrae).

### Causes

Stress fractures are the result of repeated or prolonged activity, which is why they're common in long-distance runners and ballet dancers. Suddenly increasing your workout time or intensity can also cause a stress fracture. They occur more often in women, especially women with thinner bones, so if you're a postmenopausal woman with osteoporosis, watch out and be sure to take calcium.

Discrepancy in leg length, high arches, and using shoes with poor shock absorption may also predispose you to stress fractures.

### Signs and Symptoms

- Pain at the site of the fracture, triggered by a workout. Unlike shin splints (see page 255), this is not muscle pain. The fractured bone is what hurts.
- Site is tender and sore to touch.
- Activity makes the pain worse.
- Pain gradually becomes more intense over time.

An X ray doesn't always reveal a stress fracture during the early stage. When the bone heals and callus tissue develops around it, an X ray is more helpful. A bone scan can pick up a stress fracture earlier than an X ray.

### Conventional Treatments

If you have shin pain, apply ice packs for twenty to thirty minutes every three to four hours for two or three days until the pain subsides. You can also take anti-inflammatory drugs. If the pain doesn't diminish, you will need an X ray or bone scan to see if you have a stress fracture. If you do, the most important treatment is rest; you'll have to stop exercising for a while. In addition, you may need to wear a cast for three to six weeks while the bone heals.

## Seeking Help from Complementary Practitioners

### Hypnosis
One interesting study suggests that hypnosis that focuses on the healing process, including the stages of fracture healing, and on speeding up the process, may reduce your recovery time and promote faster healing.

## Red Flags

Call your doctor if you experience pain, swelling, or immobility around a bone.

## TENNIS ELBOW

### Description

Tendons attach the muscles to the bones. Tennis elbow, also known as lateral epicondylitis, is a type of tendinitis, or inflammation of the tendons. Tennis elbow affects not only the tendons but also the epicondyle, the bony point where they are anchored. (For more information on conventional and complementary treatments for tendinitis, see Chapter 7.)

### Causes

Tendons are strong and fibrous but not especially flexible, so overuse or sudden, abrupt movement may irritate or inflame them. Tennis elbow is frequently the result of improper form. For example, if you turn your wrist during a serve or hit a stroke poorly, you may be jarring or putting extra stress on your muscles and tendons. Obviously, this ailment affects tennis players, but it can also be a problem if you play golf or do other activities where you repeatedly bend your wrist up against resistance.

### Signs and Symptoms

Pain and tenderness on the outside of your elbow and sharp pain when you grip something or twist your hand and forearm are the hallmarks of tennis elbow. Simple actions that involve bending your wrist up may make the pain worse; it may hurt just to carry your briefcase or shake hands with a friend.

## Exercises

Try Wrist Range-of-Motion, Forearm Range-of-Motion, and Elbow Range-of-Motion. (See pages 331–338 for exercises.)

## Red Flags

Call your doctor if you:

- Have excessive pain
- Can't fully move your elbow
- Have swelling, numbness, or tingling around your elbow

## GOLFER'S ELBOW

### Description

Tendons attach muscles to bones. Golfer's elbow, also known as medial epicondylitis, is an inflammation of the tendons, known as tendinitis. It causes pain and tenderness on the bony bump located on the inner side of the elbow. (For more information on conventional and complementary treatments for tendinitis, see Chapter 7.)

### Causes

Overuse may irritate and inflame the tendons because they are strong and fibrous but not especially flexible. Repeated bending of the wrist and fingers is the usual suspect in golfer's elbow. Besides golf, you can get this injury if you play baseball or racquet sports, as well as from carpentry, typing, and other occupations.

### Signs and Symptoms

- Pain in your elbow, at the side closest to your body
- Bending your wrist causes pain along the inner side of your forearm
- It hurts to make a fist
- Pain worsens when you flex your wrist (bend it down) against resistance

## Exercises

Try Wrist Range-of-Motion, Forearm Range-of-Motion, and Elbow Range-of-Motion. In addition, wrist strengthening exercises include Wrist Flexion, Wrist Extension, Wrist Radial Deviation Strengthening, and Pronation and Supination Strengthening. (See pages 331–338.)

## Red Flags

Call your doctor if you:

- Have excessive pain
- Can't fully move your elbow
- Have swelling, numbness or tingling around your elbow

## ACHILLES TENDINITIS

### Description

This ailment, common among runners, is an inflammation of the thick tendon that attaches the calf muscles to the heel. If you love basketball or other sports that involve jumping, or if you play racquetball and other activities that use frequent stop-and-go movements, you are putting considerable stress on your Achilles tendon. You can prevent Achilles tendinitis with good shoes, proper training, and stretching. (For more information on conventional and complementary treatments for tendinitis, see Chapter 7.)

### Causes

There are many causes of Achilles tendinitis:

- Poor conditioning
- Frequent uphill running
- Running on your toes
- Doing too much too soon or increasing your activity too quickly
- Tight calf muscles
- Wearing worn-out shoes
- Insufficient stretching
- Anatomical factors, such as bowlegs, having one leg shorter than the other, or high arches

## Signs and Symptoms

You'll feel pain and tenderness along the cordlike tendon at the back of your heel and calf.

## Exercises

Start out with the Calf Stretch with Towel and then move on to the Standing Calf Stretch and the Stair Stretch. When the pain has let up, you can try Toe and Heel Raises and the One-Leg Balance.
   (See pages 331–338 for exercises.)

## LOW BACK PAIN (SEE CHAPTER 6)

## HOW TO BUY ATHLETIC SHOES

I find it perplexing that people continue exercising in poor-fitting, worn-out shoes. It's relatively inexpensive to keep yourself well-shod, athletically speaking. And it can help prevent so many injuries. Here are some tips for getting the right shoes for you:

- Determine your correct shoe width by placing your bare foot on a white piece of paper and tracing it. Compare the width of this tracing with the width of your shoe. If your shoe is less than one-quarter of an inch of the maximum tracing width it is too narrow. Shoes that are too narrow can aggravate bunions and toe deformities.
- Feet normally swell as the day goes on. To get the right size, shop for shoes late in the day when your feet are their largest.
- When you buy shoes, wear the same socks you use when you exercise.
- If your feet are wide, look for shoes with a wide toe box; be sure you can easily wiggle your toes.
- You probably have one foot that is larger than the other; most people do. Always size your shoe to your bigger foot.
- Do not buy snug-fitting shoes assuming they'll be okay after you break them in. They should be comfortable as soon as you try them on.
- Don't be surprised if your feet get longer and wider as you age and after pregnancies.

## THE FEMALE ATHLETE TRIAD

Certain sports ailments are related specifically to the menstrual cycle. Amenorrhea, or lack of periods, occurs in nearly 20 percent of vigorously exercising women. Some girl and female athletes suffer from a complex interplay of menstrual irregularity, eating disorders, and premature osteoporosis—a syndrome called the Female Athlete Triad. The pressure many young women feel to achieve or maintain unrealistically low body weight only makes the problem worse.

Not only does this syndrome diminish your physical performance, it is a serious risk to your long-term health. If you have any component of the Triad, you are at risk and should be screened for the others. Keep accurate records of your menstrual cycle; if it begins to diverge from its normal pattern, take note and follow it carefully. Mention it to your physician. She may want to evaluate your bone mass and make recommendations for preventing osteoporosis. It may be necessary for you to train less intensely and increase your total calories and calcium intake. It may also be wise to begin a program of resistance training to increase your muscle strength and mass (see Chapter 6 for more information about osteoporosis).

# 11

—

# Oh, My Aching Feet

At some point in their lives, three-quarters of Americans have foot problems. When you think about it, that's not surprising. Just by standing, we put a force on our feet that is 50 percent greater than our body weight. Nor did Mother Nature have concrete sidewalks or high-heeled shoes in mind when our feet and upright stance evolved. Our long life spans don't help either; as we age, our feet widen and get flatter, and the protective padding of fat on the soles wears down.

Women are at higher risk than men for most kinds of severe foot pain. This has a lot to do with high-heeled shoes, which are responsible for most women's foot deformities and problems. Think about it: Are you, like Cinderella's sisters, forcing your feet into shoes that are too tight? In a 1992 survey done by the American Podiatric Medical Association, 44 percent of women said they wear shoes that look good but don't fit well.

Ironically, the same design features that make your shoes fashionable—narrow width, pointed toes, and high heels—are deadly for your feet. Two-inch heels increase the pressure on the front half of your foot by 57 percent; in 3-inch heels, that pressure rises to an astounding 76 percent. And because high heels cause your feet to slide forward in your shoes, your toes are also under duress. In fact, most foot problems can be prevented or successfully treated by wearing proper footwear.

Pregnancy may also make your feet more vulnerable to foot trouble. Enlargement of the belly, breasts, and thighs, along with swelling of the feet and ankles, leads to changes in posture, movement, joint stability, and weight distribution. This has a dramatic effect on your feet and the way you walk. Also, you widen your base of support—the amount of distance between your feet—to compensate as your center of gravity migrates up and forward, and to give yourself greater stability. The net effect is greater pressure on different parts of your feet. In addition, you release hormones that relax ligaments, further weakening your feet and ankles.

Other risk factors for foot problems include:

- Being overweight
- High-impact sports, such as tennis, jogging, or racquetball
- Heavy lifting
- Extensive walking
- Diabetes

In this chapter, I'll start by providing several all-purpose, do-it-yourself treatments for painful foot ailments, such as heel spurs, diabetic feet, ingrown toenails, athlete's foot, and warts. Following that, you'll find more particulars about other specific problems. One note: For information about Achilles tendinitis and ankle injuries, please go to Chapter 10.

## Prevention

You can prevent many foot ailments simply by wearing well-fitting, comfortable shoes. The ideal shoe is roomy and has low heels, a thick sole, and arch support. Here are some tips for buying shoes:

- Your feet swell as the day goes on; they also change shape and size, depending on whether you are walking, sitting, or standing. Shop for shoes in the evening, when your shoe size is biggest. Be sure the shoe fits the widest part of your foot.
- Foot size changes with age and after pregnancy, so have your feet checked every few years and after each baby.
- Soft glove leather allows breathing room and stretches to accommodate your feet. Avoid synthetics and patent leather.
- Get shoes with enough room for you to wiggle your toes. Avoid pointy-toed styles and allow one-half inch between the end of your longest toe and the shoe.
- Be sure that the heel fits snugly and doesn't slip. Shoes with laces, straps, or buckles can be helpful.
- Avoid shoes with stitching around bunions or other sensitive areas.
- Wear high-quality athletic shoes that have good ankle support and are made specifically for your activity (for tips on buying athletic shoes, see Chapter 10).

## Do-It-Yourself

*Self-massage for your feet*

WATER MASSAGE
1. Fill a bathtub or basin ankle deep with cool water.
2. In tandem, rhythmically move your feet back and forth, allowing the water to gently caress them, for 2 minutes.
3. Raise your feet completely out of the water after each stroke.

For added pleasure, you can add a few drops of a pleasant-scented herbal essential oil, like lavender or rosemary. If athlete's foot is a concern, try adding several drops of tea tree oil, which has documented antibacterial and antifungal effects.

BALL ROLL
1. Sit on a chair and place a tennis ball or another small rubber ball under the arch of your foot.
2. Roll your foot backward and forward for 1 minute.
3. Repeat with the other foot.

*Reflexology*
1. Use your thumb and index finger to rotate your toes in a circular motion.
2. Then, make a fist and rotate it around the bottom of your foot.
3. Finally, twist your foot as if you're wringing wet clothes, moving the top and bottom in opposite directions.

*Contrast baths to ease aching feet*
Soak your feet in cool water, then in warm water, alternating every few minutes for about fifteen minutes.

## Exercises

Try Sitting and Standing Toe Raises and Head and Foot Bounces. (See pages 331–338 for exercises.)

## Mind/Body

*Yoga for your feet*
Try Guptasana (Concealed Posture), Utkatasana (Squatting Posture), and Kneeling Foot Stretch. (See pages 344–351.)

## METATARSALGIA

### GILDA'S STORY

Gilda is a seventy-year-old woman who works as a candy striper in our local hospital, where she delivers newspapers and magazines to the patients. She is on her feet a great deal.

I've known Gilda a long time, ever since she came to me for rehabilitation after suffering a stroke about seven years ago. When I ran into her one day in the elevator, she told me she had developed a sore, aching pain in the balls of her feet. "It gets worse when my husband and I go out on the town, and I wear my high heels," she explained. Gilda and her husband loved ballroom dancing, and this pain was putting a cramp in their style. "I'm afraid I may have to give it up," she said, wistfully. I watched the way she walked down the hall, and noticed that she tended to shift her weight abnormally.

The next time I saw her, I offered to take a quick look at her feet. When she stopped by my office, I noted that the skin over her metatarsal bones was thinned out, which is common in women of her age. But I also noticed that the shoes she was wearing looked "tired" and lacked cushioning. "I know they're worn," she confessed. "But I just love these shoes. I won them in a dance contest a couple of summers ago, when I was vacationing at a bungalow colony."

Gilda had metatarsalgia, a painful condition that is common among middle-aged and older women. I suggested that she try herbal foot soaks, as well as a new pair of cushioned sneakers for everyday use. I also gave her the name of a podiatrist colleague who could fashion a metatarsal bar, or some other form of metatarsal support for her feet. Finally, I gave her some exercises that she could do while she watched TV at night. With these tips, Gilda's pain improved. The next time I saw her, she said: "My feet hurt so much less. In fact, we're going out dancing tonight."

### Description

Metatarsalgia, or pain in the metatarsal bones, is probably the most common cause of foot pain among middle-aged women. The metatarsal bones are the long bones of the foot; they lie in the mid-foot area. These bones connect with the tarsal bones and heel bones (calcaneus) in the rear, and the phalanges (toe bones) in the front. The agonizing pain of metatarsalgia feels like a bruise, or a dull aching pain in the ball of the foot (on the underside of the forefoot, underneath the metatarsal heads). Occasionally, the pain radiates to other areas. Metatarsalgia generally occurs because you abnormally distribute weight on your forefoot when you walk, and this leads to inflammation. You can sometimes get relief by walking or standing on the outside of your foot, since this removes pressure from the ball of the foot.

## Causes

You can develop metatarsalgia for many reasons. The aging process causes thinning of the fat pad in the foot, making you more vulnerable to metatarsal forces. Other common causes include:

- Wearing narrow pointy shoes, with high heels and a narrow toe box
- Being overweight or obese
- Repeated, forceful pounding of your foot when walking or running or doing too much of a weight-bearing activity, such as jumping
- High arches or foot abnormalities that flatten the front of your foot
- Arthritis
- Trauma

## Signs and Symptoms

- Pain on the bottom of the middle of the foot, made worse when you stand or bear weight.
- Tenderness over the bony surfaces of your feet.

## Conventional Treatments

Treatments for metatarsalgia focus on relieving pressure on the bottom of the foot. More comfortable shoes are certainly in order. If you are currently using shoes that give you pain in your metatarsal area, it may be time for a shoe "checkup":

- Make sure your shoes are not worn out—that the tread on the bottom is intact and the wear pattern is even.
- If your foot has a tendency to pronate, or migrate inward, you might benefit from a shoe that provides greater restraint.
- Look for a shoe with forefoot cushioning.

If you are a do-it-yourselfer, you can create your own padded shoe inserts simply by fabricating a circular shoe insert, made of moleskin, that you can place under your metatarsals. This will provide some cushioning and give you some relief.

If that doesn't help, a podiatrist can fit you for custom-made arch supports (orthotics), or work with you to devise other mechanical methods to relieve the pain in the mid-foot. These include redistributing weight-bearing pressure and force behind the metatarsal head.

- Internal: An orthotic, known as a "cookie" or metatarsal pad, can be conveniently placed inside your shoe, right in back of metatarsal heads 2, 3, and 4. The orthotics should fit snugly between the inner border of the big toe and the outer side of the small toe.
- External: A metatarsal bar is a ¼-inch piece of tapered durable plastic that is placed on the sole of the shoe.

You may need to take anti-inflammatory medications for pain or change your choice of athletic activity, if that's what's causing the problem.

## Do-It-Yourself

*Every day*
- Put your feet up to get relief, whenever possible.
- Watch your weight, staying at the appropriate level for your height and build.
- Avoid high-heeled shoes or narrow, pointy footwear. Instead, wear comfortable shoes with a small heel and plenty of room for your feet.
- Soak your feet in Epsom salts nightly for twenty minutes.
- Use ice. You can make a convenient ice applicator by freezing water in a 12-ounce paper cup. Then, remove the icicle and place it in a plastic bag before applying it to your foot.
- Massage your feet:
    1. While sitting comfortably in a chair, cross your right foot over your left leg.
    2. Sprinkle several drops of massage oil (or lavender oil) on your left hand.
    3. Using your thumb, gently stroke the bottom of your foot in a circular fashion, beginning with the outer circumference and working your way toward the center.
    4. Do this for three minutes. Then, switch to your other foot. CAUTION: Never massage cracked, blistered, or broken skin, especially if you are diabetic.

*Herbal foot bath*

Add five to eight drops of lavender, rosemary, or juniper oil to a basin of warm water and allow your feet to soak for thirty minutes. Allow them to air dry.

## Exercise

To condition the small muscles of your feet and keep them in good shape, try the following exercise:

1. Obtain a set of marbles.
2. Set them out on the floor.
3. One by one, pick up the marbles with your toes and deposit them into a 16-inch Styrofoam cup.

## Seeking Help from Complementary Practitioners

*Acupuncture*

Your acupuncturist can help relieve the pain of metatarsalgia.

*Massage*

A professional foot massage can work wonders.

## Red Flags

Call your doctor if:

- Your pain significantly limits how far you can walk
- You have a fever or your foot looks red (you may have an infection)
- The pain lasts more than seven days

## MORTON'S NEUROMA

### Description

A neuroma is a benign (noncancerous) tumor of nerve tissue. But benign is a strange word to use for this ailment, which can cause horrible, shooting pain, as well as numbness and tingling. Often confused with metatarsalgia, because the pain is found in the metatarsalgia area, Morton's neuroma is not, technically speaking, a true neuroma. It is actually a fibrosis, or tissue thickening, around the nerves that supply the toes. It strikes the nerve that passes between the base of two toes, most commonly between the bones of your third and fourth toes, or those of your second and third toes. This ailment causes the nerve to thicken and become inflamed and very painful. Usually, it's a result of repetitive irritation that occurs when the bones of your toes rub together. Like so many of the foot ailments I've described in this chapter, it's often connected to constrictive shoes—the sure giveaway being that it affects five times as many women as men.

## Causes

Although it may develop for no reason, Morton's neuroma is commonly caused by:

- Wearing shoes that are too tight
- Running or walking too much
- Running on hard surfaces

## Signs and Symptoms

- Burning pain, often worse when your toes are pointed up or when your toes are squeezed together
- Numbness or tingling
- Tenderness and pain on the bottom of the foot, between the bones of the third and fourth toes, or the second and third toes
- Pain travels from the outer side of one toe to the inner side of the adjoining toe
- Tight and/or high-heeled shoes make the pain worse
- Walking barefoot relieves the pain

## Conventional Treatments

To ease the sharp pain of a neuroma, the best thing you can do is to allow your toes plenty of room by wearing properly fitting shoes with a wide toe box. A metatarsal pad worn in the shoes will help spread your toes and take pressure off the inflamed nerve. Custom-made arch supports (orthotics) sometimes serve the same purpose.

If the pain is bothering you and ibuprofen and aspirin don't provide relief, your doctor may suggest using a whirlpool with cold water, or ultrasound. Or she may recommend Xylocaine or cortisone injections. Should all else fail, surgery may be required.

## Herbs

*Ginger* (Zingibar officinale)
Ginger is a natural anti-inflammatory. Herbalists suggest adding five to twenty drops of tincture to your favorite herbal tea once a day. Use caution if you take blood-thinning medication.

## Herbal Creams and Ointments

*Triflora cream*
This is a homeopathic gel; its ingredients include comfrey (*Symphytum officinale*), poison ivy (*Rhus toxicodendron*), and marsh tea (*Ledum palustre*).

## Do-It-Yourself

- Herbal foot bath: Add five to eight drops of lavender or rosemary oil to a basin of warm water. Soak your feet for thirty minutes. Allow them to air dry.
- Regularly treat yourself to a barefoot walk on the beach. Walking on hard surfaces provokes pain, so the beach can be quite a relief. CAUTION: If you are diabetic, do not walk barefooted.
- Stop any activity that makes the condition worse.
- Use ice to massage the top of your foot. Cold can physiologically slow down the trapped nerve transmission, relieving the tingling, burning pain. Fill a 12-ounce paper cup with water and freeze. Then, remove the icicle and put it in a plastic bag before applying it to your foot.
- Avoid high-heeled shoes or narrow, pointy footwear. Instead, wear comfortable shoes with a low heel and plenty of room for your toes.
- In your shoe, use a foam rubber pad under the sole of your foot to keep your toes spread apart and decrease pressure on the nerve.
- Remove your shoes frequently and massage your feet.

## Exercise

To condition the small muscles of your feet and keep them in good shape, try this exercise: Stand with your feet parallel. Bend your toes up into the air. Hold for a couple of seconds, then release.

## Red Flags

Call your doctor if:

- You develop loss of sensation or worsening tingling
- Your pain significantly limits how far you can walk
- Your pain gets progressively worse
- The pain lasts more than seven days

# BUNIONS

## Description

Also known as hallux valgus, a bunion is a painful, bony lump that forms on the joint at the base of the big toe (the metatarsophalangeal, or MTP joint). This occurs when the bone or tissue that make up the big toe migrates out of place, usually because the toe is squeezed inward. In addition to the bump, the joint swells and the toe turns in. Because this part of the foot bears much of the weight when you walk, bunions can really hurt. A "mini bunion," or a bunionette is a similar deformity that develops beside your little toe.

Bunions are common only in shoe-wearing societies. What's more, they occur ten times more frequently in women than in men. It's likely that their major cause is—you guessed it—women's high-heeled shoes.

## Causes

Bunions form when the big toe is forced inward, putting pressure on the joint at its base. This is usually the result of a lifetime of abnormal forces and pressure on the joints and tendons during normal walking. It happens for a variety of reasons:

- Genetic predisposition—you may be born with a foot type whose mechanics, or distribution of forces, is vulnerable to bunion formation
- Flat feet or low arches—a normal arch is one inch or more above the ground
- Frequently wearing high-heeled shoes, especially those that squeeze the toes together
- Foot injuries
- Tight Achilles tendon

- Arthritis
- Inflammatory joint disease
- Neuromuscular disorders
- Congenital deformities
- Being a ballet dancer or having another occupation that stresses the feet

## Signs and Symptoms

- A bony bump at the base of the big toe, which may be accentuated when you put weight on your foot
- Swelling, redness, and soreness of the big toe joint
- Thickening, irritation, or blistering of the skin on the bunion
- Restricted movement of the big toe
- Pain, especially caused by pressure when wearing shoes

## Conventional Treatments

Bunions don't go away unless you have them surgically removed. But non-surgical treatments can reduce pain and stop them from getting worse. To relieve pressure on the bunion, wear shoes with flat heels and a wide toe box. Avoid any shoes with heels more than 2 inches high.

You can cover the bunion with commercially available pads to prevent irritation and shield the bone from external pressure. There are also special inserts you can wear between your first and second toes to correct their alignment. A podiatrist can apply padding and taping to further reduce stress and pain.

If the bunion is swollen, apply ice packs several times a day. Anti-inflammatory medications can relieve pain. Traction or corticosteroids can also relieve severe pain.

For severe pain, hydrotherapy and ultrasound can offer an additional measure of relief.

I believe surgery to correct bunions should be a last resort, to be used only when the deformity has advanced, more conservative measures have failed, and you still have significant pain. Any surgery is risky, but in the case of bunions it may result in a decrease in the range of motion of your great toe, a particular problem if you are a dancer or an athlete.

## Herbal Creams and Ointments

*Marshmallow* (Althaea officinalis)
You can use a paste made from this wild, light pink–flowered plant to relieve inflammation and swelling. Use enough root powder to cover the affected area and add cold water to make a paste. Apply a thick layer to your bunion and let it dry. Reapply as often as necessary, every two to three hours if needed. Do not apply to any open areas.

*Comfrey* (Symphytum officinale)
If you have an open abrasion on the skin overlying your bunion, you can apply a comfrey compress to help heal the wound. Comfrey contains an oil that forms a protective, soothing film over the area that will help speed healing. Please note that you should never take comfrey for internal use.

## Do-It-Yourself

- Give your feet a rest and go barefoot every now and then.
- Switch shoes frequently.
- Switch to a flat-heeled shoe instead of high heels. High heels put extra pressure on your toes and joints. Also, be sure your shoes have plenty of room for your toes.
- Soak your feet in warm water and massage them.
- Aromatherapy: Add a drop of the essential oil of lemon balm (*Melissa officinalis*) or chamomile to a massage oil and rub it into the area.

## Exercise

Because bunions may be caused by tight Achilles tendons, try the Stair Stretch. (See pages 331–338.)

## Red Flags

- Worsening deformity that prevents walking
- Excessive pain

## CORNS

### Description

Corns are tough, thickened skin on your feet, caused by pressure or friction. They are harder than calluses and may be quite painful.

### Causes

Anything that causes prolonged pressure or rubs on the skin of your foot, especially in an area covering a bony prominence, can result in a corn. Common culprits are:

- New, tight, or poor-fitting shoes
- Wearing sandals or shoes without socks
- High-heeled shoes
- High arches, which may put added pressure on your toes when you walk
- Any physical deformity that distributes your weight unevenly when you walk
- Protruding bones or not enough flesh to cushion the bones of your feet.

### Signs and Symptoms

- A hard, tough area of thickened skin. It is usually yellow, but it may become red when irritated or inflamed.
- Tenderness or pain under the skin
- Sensitivity to pressure

### Conventional Treatments

Standard care for a corn involves removing the source of friction or pressure on the area. Change to more comfortable, foot-friendly shoes and use a special shoe insole for added cushioning. You can also apply a special sock or protective sheath over the corn.

Corns are made of keratin, thickened skin that forms as a protective padding in response to outside pressure. You can dissolve the keratin layer by covering it with salicylic acid paste and applying a foam pad to protect it from friction. You can also use a pumice stone after bathing to debride it. If you prefer, a podiatrist can shave the corn down with a scalpel.

## Dietary Strategies (See Chapter 14 for food sources of specified nutrients)

*Vitamins A and E*
These vitamins encourage healthy skin.

*Vitamin C*
This vitamin encourages healing.

## Supplements

To encourage healing you can take:

- Vitamin A—the acceptable daily dose range is 900 to 3,000 mcg.
- Vitamin E—the acceptable daily dose range is 15 to 1,000 mg.

## Herbal Creams and Ointments

*Tea tree* (Maleluca alternifolia) *mix*
Mix 4 drops of tea tree oil, 3 drops bergamot oil, 3 drops lavender oil, and 2 teaspoons of jojoba oil. Dab onto the affected area. This helps provide pain relief while softening up your corn and preventing infection.

*Goldenseal* (Hydrastis canadensis) *cream*
This herb has astringent, anti-inflammatory properties. Used topically, it can prevent infection and speed healing.

## Do-It-Yourself

- Always wear loose comfortable shoes with a wide toe box.
- Use a file or pumice stone to rub down a corn. This works best if you first take a bath or soak your foot in water. You can also use fresh lemon juice or vinegar to soften the skin. Repeat this process daily until the corn disappears. Use a pad or a piece of moleskin, available at any drugstore, to cover the area and prevent another corn from forming.

## Red Flags

Call your doctor if you see any signs of infection, including:

- Redness
- Swelling
- Fever
- Discharge

## HAMMERTOE

### Description

Hammertoe usually involves the second toe, which bends under, and takes on a cramped, hammer, or clawlike appearance. As the toe bends, it may rub against the top of your shoe, causing painful, hard corns to develop.

### Causes

Hammertoe is often a congenital condition, but other contributing factors include:

- Wearing shoes that are too tight or too narrow. This causes the second toe to buckle
- A flat front arch
- A bunion, which may cause the big toe to slide under the second toe
- Muscle and nerve damage from diabetes or other diseases

### Signs and Symptoms

- A toe that bends under
- A callus or hard corn on top of the toe
- Redness and inflammation
- Pain at the tip of the toe, where it hits your shoe

### Conventional Treatments

It's especially important to wear shoes that don't cramp your toes. You can also tape the affected toe to an adjacent toe to maintain their proper alignment. A lambswool insert or a splint can also keep your toes in position.

Hammertoe is not especially painful, but you can take ibuprofen, acetaminophen, or aspirin to relieve pain or inflammation, if necessary. Available in pharmacies are small, doughnut-shaped pads you can wear on top of the toe to reduce friction and irritation.

In extreme cases, surgery may be needed to straighten the toe or remove any bony prominence that develops on top of it.

## Do-It-Yourself

- Be sure your shoes are roomy, with a wide toe box
- Take an evening foot bath
- Stretch out your toe
- Try taping the affected toe to an adjacent toe
- Consider wearing sneakers or running shoes as often as possible

## Exercise

Exercises that stretch your toes may provide some relief. For example:

PICK UP MARBLES
1. Obtain a set of marbles and set them out on the floor.
2. One by one, pick up the marbles with your toes and deposit them into a 16-inch Styrofoam cup.

TOWEL PICKUP
Lay a towel flat on the floor and, keeping your heel in the air, use just your toes to move it toward you and crumple it up. When it becomes too easy, put a book or some other weight on the towel.

## Red Flags

- Worsening deformity
- A wound or open abrasion from pressure on the toe
- Difficulty walking

## PLANTAR FASCIITIS AND ARCH PAIN

## Description

The plantar fascia is a broad band of connective tissue that runs along the bottom of the foot, from the ball to the heel. It helps to maintain the arch of the foot. If you overstretch it, small painful tears and inflammation may develop.

Runners and other athletes are particularly prone to plantar fasciitis, which is one of the most common causes of painful feet I see in my practice. It frequently strikes people over fifty, developing twice as often in women as in men.

Sometimes, plantar fasciitis becomes chronic and severe, even disabling. About half the time, bone spurs develop near the front of the heel, causing a related ailment known as heel spur syndrome.

Plantar fasciitis is also the most common cause of arch pain (sometimes called arch strain). What happens is the tissue pulls away from the heel, causing pain, inflammation, and a burning sensation at the arch of the foot. Arch pain may also develop if you have a structural abnormality such as flat feet.

## Causes

While overuse is the usual cause of plantar fasciitis, there are others:

- Flat feet or overpronation
- Suddenly increasing how much you run, especially up and down hills
- High arches
- Bowlegs
- Knock-knees
- Differences in leg length
- Poor running shoes

## Signs and Symptoms

- Pain and tenderness, especially in the front of your heel and your arch
- Local swelling in the affected area
- More pain in the morning, just after you get up, or after periods of rest
- Pain increases when you walk, run, or do anything else that puts pressure on your feet

## Conventional Treatments

You can take anti-inflammatory medications, such as aspirin or ibuprofen, for the pain and swelling. Acetaminophen relieves pain but not inflammation. If you get no relief, your doctor may recommend a steroid injection, which will provide immediate relief. But there are side effects, including local trauma, bleeding, or black-and-blue marks. I discourage repeated (more than three times a year) injections with steroids.

Your doctor may also recommend that you be fitted for arch supports or orthotics to treat flat feet.

If this ailment becomes severe or chronic, you may require surgery.

## Do-It-Yourself

- Wear comfortable shoes with thick soles.
- Put cushioned heel lifts or heel cups in your shoes; this shifts your weight forward and cushions the sore spot; a shoe with a *slightly* elevated heel—½ to 1 inch—will do the same thing.
- Use arch supports, which will limit the movement of your plantar fascia and allow it to heal.
- Roll an old-fashioned glass soda bottle, a rolling pin, or a foot roller back and forth with the sole of your bare foot.

## Exercise

- Take a break from any activity that involves pounding. Switch to swimming, biking, or another sport that is kind to your feet.
- Once pain has subsided, resume your regular exercise slowly. If you feel any pain, stop.
- Meanwhile, to speed healing, try these exercises: Plantar Fascia Stretch, Gastroc Stretch, Soleus Stretch, and Bicycle Stretch. (See pages 331–338.)

## Red Flags

- Worsening pain
- Inability to walk

## MISCELLANEOUS FOOT AILMENTS AND HELPFUL REMEDIES

- Horsechestnut (*Aesculus hippocastanum*), used both externally and internally, helps leg swelling and circulatory disorders. Used as a lotion, it helps to heal leg ulcers. The seed coating can be toxic, so peel them if you are making remedies yourself.
- Tea tree oil, oil of bitter orange, peppermint oil, and garlic are useful treatments for athlete's foot.

# 12

## Unending Pain

Pain is aptly labeled the most vicious of all evils. I was intimately acquainted with the terrific torment of chronic pain when, several years ago, my mother was stricken with terminal cancer during the prime of her life. Like many advanced cancer patients, Mom endured the torture and indignity of excruciating pain with a delicate blend of stoicism, melancholy, cautious optimism, and a strong will to overcome.

As each day brought her a fresh onslaught of demonic pain, I came to realize the power of complementary medical approaches. My mother received world-class care from her doctors. Yet, when I reflect back, I see that their conventional approaches to managing her pain included little creativity or innovation. Notwithstanding their stalwart and compassionate pleas to us to rely exclusively on narcotic painkillers to do the trick, I knew better. Traditional painkillers were okay in small measure, but they were by no means a sole solution.

My philosophy was shaped by my conviction that chronic pain, especially cancer pain, demands a holistic approach incorporating the best in nutrition, mind-body techniques, acupuncture, and other complementary strategies. These therapies fortify your spirit and give you the strength and resolve to endure.

Recognizing the critical yet intangible link between environment and healing, my wife, Marlene, insisted that we move my mom to our house. A budding clinical nutritionist and biologist with a flare for creative, healthful cooking, Marlene developed several customized therapeutic recipes, based on a thorough review of the literature. Motivated by the work of the acclaimed scientist Dr. Judah Folkman, the father of the angiogenesis theory of cancer — which posits that starving cancer cells of their blood supply helps wage the war against cancer — my wife used many soy products in her prescriptives. Soy products contain genistein, which may act by inhibiting endothelial growth (the inner cell lining) of capillaries. This stops the development of blood vessels to aid tumor tissue.

We found music therapy to be a wonderful way of maintaining my mother's spirits during the painful and dark days she endured while undergoing chemotherapy and radiation. Although she was still in pain, it gradually diminished in intensity, and her days became more pleasant. We also used exercise, acupuncture, and "grandchildren therapy." I observed firsthand the power of mind over body: snug in our family's nest, my mother kept herself alive for several months so she could welcome the birth of her youngest grandchild.

Cancer pain is but one of many types of unending pain. Although it's often impossible to cure chronic pain, there's a lot you can do to ease your misery, discouragement, and frustration. Taking something positive from a very challenging time in the life of my family, I now use complementary therapies as an adjunct to conventional modes of treatment to help empower my chronic pain patients. And I should add that many patients are well ahead of their doctors on this issue; more than 50 percent of cancer patients use complementary therapies, and a U.S telephone survey found that cancer was one of the top five reasons for using alternative medicine.

## CANCER PAIN

Cancer is a chronic illness that can occur anywhere in the body. Up until ten or twenty years ago, a cancer cell was a black box. Today, scientists know a great deal about carcinogenesis—the development of cancer. Still, the antidote to cancer pain remains a mystery.

Today's researchers, using the techniques of cellular and molecular biology, look at the fundamental mechanisms that underlie cancer. The target of research is DNA, which makes up the genetic material, or building blocks, of the body's cells. In each cell, genes encode the proteins necessary to perform all body functions. For some reason—spontaneously, as a result of environmental damage, or even because of viral infection—genetic changes, or mutations, occur in a normal cell. There may be many varieties of cancer, but in all cases, something that is supposed to limit a cell's growth has broken down. Instead of growing and replicating normally, the cell becomes malignant. Your body has "fail-safe" mechanisms to destroy these abnormal cells, but they don't always work. So malignant cells may begin to accumulate. At some point, they reach a critical mass that is identified clinically as a tumor growth. Finally, the cancerous cells become invasive, entering the bloodstream to metastasize at other sites in the body. Pain is not far behind. The pain associated with cancer can be ravaging, and if left untreated, can become all-consuming.

Despite three decades and billions of dollars spent on research, the war on cancer has not produced a "cure." That's because cancer has many forms; it is not a single virus, like polio. Yet, many types are curable, if detected and treated early.

## Causes

When you consider cancer pain, it's important to recall the old adage: an ounce of prevention is worth a pound of cure. Preventing cancer by considering its causes and modifying your risk factors is an ideal way to avert the disaster of cancer pain. There is no one cause of cancer, or the pain that derives from it.

## Signs and Symptoms

Although these depend largely on where the cancer is located, common symptoms include:

- A lump or thickening
- A wound that doesn't heal
- Unexplained weight loss
- Night sweats or unremitting fevers
- Pain that is present at night and when at rest

## Conventional Treatments

There are three major conventional treatments for cancer. These invasive and difficult-to-endure approaches are intended to shrink tumor bulk, thereby decreasing pain and minimizing functional impairment. They may be used on their own or in combination:

*Surgery to remove abnormal cells*
In addition to traditional surgery, your doctor may use cryosurgery, where liquid nitrogen is applied to freeze tumors. This technique is used especially for skin cancer. With laser surgery, the doctor uses a high-intensity light beam to destroy cancer cells.

*Radiation to shrink and destroy tumors*
Radiation may be used by itself or in addition to surgery. Treatment involves regular exposure, every day or every couple of days, for several weeks. You

may be treated with a machine that emits radiation or with an internal radiation source that is implanted in the body. Often, shrinkage of a tumor leads to a considerable reduction in pain, especially if the tumor is pressing on the spinal cord and neighboring roots.

### Chemotherapy, or drugs that kill cancer cells

You may undergo chemotherapy by taking pills or injections, or having the chemicals infused intravenously. Chemotherapy usually goes on for two to twelve months. Then your body is given time to recover from the often-severe side effects, the most common of which are nausea and hair loss.

The following complementary approaches are meant to be used in conjunction with conventional treatments, not instead of them. Whenever you use complementary treatments, it's important to keep your doctor informed.

## Dietary Strategies (See Chapter 14 for food sources of specified nutrients)

It's been estimated by some experts that diet alone accounts for 60 percent of cancers in American women. To help prevent cancer:

- Eat at least five servings of fruits and vegetables every day, especially those with antioxidants, such as beta-carotene and vitamin C. Antioxidants help to counter the effects of free radicals, by-products of normal bodily processes that cause cell damage.
- The cruciferous (cabbage family) vegetables, including broccoli, cauliflower, cabbage, and brussels sprouts, also contain anticancer substances called indoles.
- A high-fiber diet speeds food through the intestines and contributes to regular bowel movements, thereby allowing the body to get rid of cancer-causing substances more rapidly. Fiber also appears to lower blood estrogen levels.
- Consuming flaxseeds or flaxseed oil is helpful, since it may have an antiestrogenlike effect.
- Cut back on animal fat from meat and dairy, which has been linked to higher rates of colorectal cancer. Instead, emphasize foods of plant origin. In addition to high levels of vitamins, minerals, and fibers, these foods contain phytonutrients that play a protective role in many cancers.
- You can also substitute fish for meat. A growing body of evidence shows that fish oils slow tumor growth.
- Eat foods containing vitamin E, which is an antioxidant that boosts your immune system and may prevent some cancers.

- Lycopene, found in tomatoes and pink grapefruits, may reduce your risk of cancer.
- Landmark research at the Johns Hopkins Hospital has shown the benefit of broccoli as an anticancer food.
- Soy can reduce the risk of hormone-related cancers. Soybeans contain estrogenlike compounds, called isoflavones (genistein and daidzein), which bind to estrogen sites and prevent your body's natural estrogen from attaching to these sites. In so doing, they may prevent stimulation and growth of cancer cells.
- Tart cherries have potential value in fighting cancer and cancer-associated pain because of their high concentrations of anthocyanins and bioflavonoids. These two potent antioxidants inhibit cyclooxygenase 1 and 2 in a way that is similar to aspirin, Naprosyn, and other NSAIDS. So promising is the potential therapeutic value of tart cherries that the National Institutes of Health (NIH) has awarded an $8 million grant to Johns Hopkins University to study the effects of tart cherries and soy on cancer pain.
- Eat berries—blueberries, blackberries, strawberries, and cherries are full of flavonoids and antioxidants.
- Eat pomegranate. This fruit is very rich in antioxidants and it appears to have enormous medicinal properties. Several universities are conducting clinical trials to evaluate its cancer-fighting potential. Interestingly, the healing power of the pomegranate is thought to be related to its stature as a sacred fruit in several major religions, including Judaism, Christianity, Buddhism, and Islam. In Judaism, the number of commandments—613—corresponds to the number of seeds in a pomegranate. And the ancient Greeks hailed it as a form of life and regeneration.

## RECIPES

### BERRY SMOOTHIE

Use organic fruits if possible.

*1 cup frozen blueberries*
*1 cup frozen strawberries*
*1 banana*
*1 mango, peeled and pitted*

*1 cup orange juice*
*1 cup tangerine juice*

Place all ingredients in a blender and mix thoroughly.

SERVES 6

## POMEGRANATE-TANGERINE JUICE

Peel 4 pomegranates. Peel and pit 5 tangerines. Press the fruit in a citrus press.

SERVES 2

## BRAN MUFFINS

*3 cups raisin bran cereal*
*1 cup sugar*
*2½ cups unbleached white flour*
*2½ teaspoons baking soda*
*1 teaspoon salt*
*4 egg whites*
*⅓ cup orange juice*
*⅓ cup olive oil*
*1¾ cup soy milk*
*¼ cup rolled oats*

1. Preheat oven to 375 degrees.
2. Lightly grease a muffin pan or line it with paper baking cups.
3. In a large mixing bowl combine cereal, sugar, flour, baking soda, and salt.
4. In a separate bowl, slightly beat the egg whites. Beat in the orange juice, oil, and soy milk. Stir in the dry ingredients and mix well.
5. Fill muffin pans ¾ full, and sprinkle the tops with rolled oats.
6. Bake at 375 degrees for 25 minutes.

MAKES ABOUT 12 MUFFINS

## Dietary Supplements

To help prevent and fight cancer, try these supplements:

### Selenium

In a double-blind study, half of the patients were given 200 mcg of selenium and followed for six years. They had a 50 percent reduction in overall cancer mortality, including significantly less lung, colon, and prostate cancer. The acceptable daily dose range is 60 to 400 mcg.

### Vitamin C

Vitamin C (ascorbic acid), a powerful antioxidant, boosts your immune system and helps you fight cancer. In addition, a deficiency in vitamin C has been linked to certain types of tumors. The acceptable dose range is 90 to 2,000 mg a day. Spread it out over the course of the day for best results. This vitamin may cause diarrhea or cramps at high doses.

### Zinc

Zinc facilitates more than three hundred enzymatic reactions in the body. A deficiency may lead to decreased immunity and impaired healing. The acceptable dose range is 8 to 40 mg a day.

### Vitamin E

Another antioxidant that boosts your immune system, reduces fatigue, and accelerates healing, we also think vitamin E may prevent certain types of cancer. The acceptable daily dose range is 15 to 1,000 mg.

### Folate

Research has shown that this nutrient, also known as folic acid, helps to prevent certain types of cancer. The acceptable dose ranges from 400 to 1,000 mcg a day.

## Herbs

### Garlic (Allium sativum)

Garlic has shown promising ability to inhibit or reverse growth of certain tumor cells. For example, one large observational study of nurses found that garlic consumption led to a 30 percent reduction in colon cancer. Garlic also reduces blood pressure and lowers cholesterol. Take garlic tablets, following the dose on the package. Or you can chop garlic and mix it with an equal amount of honey and take 1 teaspoon, three to six times a day.

### Green tea (Camellia sinensis)

Polyphenols, the active ingredient in green tea, may detoxify carcinogens, so drinking this beverage can protect you against stomach, breast, lung, esophageal, pancreatic, colon, and duodenal cancers. Drink three cups a day.

## Do-It-Yourself

*Health habits*
Prevent cancer with healthy habits:

- Quit smoking and/or avoid secondhand smoke
- Abstain from alcohol, or use it only in moderation
- Avoid overexposure to the sun; wear sunscreen
- Do monthly breast self-exams and regular mammograms
- Have regular gynecologic exams
- Drink plenty of water

*Aromatherapy*
Do not use essential oils as a massage immediately before or after chemotherapy because this can encourage the spread of cancer cells through the body. In the early stages of cancer, use oils only in a bath or diffuser.

- Rosemary (*Rosmarinus officinalis*) — for fatigue: Avoid this oil during pregnancy or if you have epilepsy or high blood pressure.
- Fennel (*Foeniculum vulgare*) — for nausea: Do not use fennel during pregnancy or if you have epilepsy.
- Geranium (*Pelargonium graveolens*) — for depression: Do not use during the first three months of pregnancy; if you have a history of miscarriage, do not use at all.

*TENS (transcutaneous electrical nerve stimulation)*
This therapy helps you manage pain by applying brief pulses of electricity that block pain messages to the brain. I've found it very helpful for my patients; studies show that it provides relief for 30 to 50 percent of people with chronic pain. Although this is often a conventional treatment, performed in a physician's or physical therapist's office, home units are available.

*Seek support*
I always refer my cancer patients to support groups. Those who go feel less overwhelmed by depression and hopelessness. Studies show that people in support groups experience psychological improvement, and tend to live longer than those who try to deal with cancer on their own. I believe that

the positive change in outlook and mood helps bolster the immune system. Other forms of support include psychotherapy and creative arts therapy, especially music and painting.

## Mind/Body

*Meditation (See page 340)*

*Imagery (See page 341)*

*Yoga*
Siddhasan (Perfect Posture), Kagasana (Crow Posture), and Shavasana (Corpse Posture) can ease muscles that may be tense from pain. They will also calm you, helping you fight depression, restlessness, and insomnia. (See pages 344–351 for postures.)

*Autogenic training (see page 341)*

*Music therapy*
My colleague Professor Mathew Lee, chairman of physical medicine and rehabilitation at New York University's prestigious Rusk Institute, has co-authored a book called *On Music for Health.* Dr. Lee, himself a cancer survivor, states that "Music is a joyful expression of life. We have witnessed the power of music. We have watched how music can lift our fallen spirits, enrich our busy minds and heal our battered bodies." I saw this in a direct and powerful way, as I watched my mother benefit from the beauty of Brahms during the painful throes of her struggle with terminal illness. My recommendation is that you listen to music that you love; music that penetrates your soul, whether it's songs from your childhood, Sondheim, or Schubert. If you're a musician, making music counts, too.

## Exercise

My esteemed colleague and mentor, the late professor emeritus Heinz Lippman of the Albert Einstein College of Medicine in New York, used to joke that exercise allowed his old age to outlive his cancer. There is no doubt about the power and vitality of exercise. Even in the face of life-threatening illness, exercise helps you feel good. For example, in a ten-week randomized study of twenty-four breast cancer survivors, the women who did aerobic exercise four days a week had significantly less depression and anxiety over time compared to women in a control group.

You may not feel up to such a rigorous regimen. But I still recommend that you do as much light aerobic exercise as you can tolerate. For physical and spiritual healing, many of my patients enjoy light gardening or taking time to walk around, appreciate nature, and smell the roses.

## Seeking Help from Complementary Practitioners

*Hypnotherapy*
In studies of breast and other cancers, self-hypnosis reduced pain and suffering more effectively than therapy groups and other supportive treatments. Once you learn how, you can use this technique on your own.

*Acupuncture*
Acupuncture is a scientifically validated method for relieving the nausea of chemotherapy.

## Red Flags

See your doctor if you have:

- Persisting fevers
- Weakness
- Malaise
- Intractable nausea and vomiting

## CHRONIC FATIGUE SYNDROME (CFS)

### Description

The subject of controversy for a long time, chronic fatigue syndrome used to be dismissed as "psychosomatic" or imaginary. Since the late 1980s, when the Centers for Disease Control first acknowledged it, CFS has gained acceptance as a legitimate diagnosis. Women with CFS outnumber men by two to one, and it is especially common among women between the ages of eighteen and thirty-five.

CFS is a collection of many clinical features. Symptoms linger for months and sometimes never go away completely. Instead, they periodically come and go with no apparent reason. One of the most salient hallmarks of CFS is pain. This is a miserable illness that causes unexplained, persistent, or relapsing pain. It is not due to overexertion; nor is it relieved by rest. But it is usually so bad that it forces you to reduce your activity level.

According to a small, recently published study, if you have chronic fatigue syndrome, you may be at higher risk of developing other health problems, including fibromyalgia (CFS shares some features with fibromyalgia; see page 296), irritable bowel syndrome, chronic pelvic pain, and temporomandibular disorder (see Chapter 9). CFS sufferers bear other costs as well—high unemployment and disability rates, and large health care expenses.

We make a diagnosis of CFS if someone has at least four of the following:

- Muscle pain
- Pain in many joints, but without inflammation or infection
- Headache
- Sore throat
- Tender lymph nodes in your neck or armpit
- Poor sleep pattern
- Generalized weakness, caused by physical exertion, that lasts more than twenty-four hours
- Problems with memory or concentration

## Causes

The roots of CFS are still being debated. It seems, however, to be a complex interaction of biological, psychological, and environmental factors. Researchers are investigating possible viral infections, including herpes, polio, and Epstein-Barr. Some experts think it may stem from damage to the immune system, while others believe it is a psychological or neurological disorder.

## Signs and Symptoms

- Extreme fatigue
- Fever
- Headache
- Nausea
- Dizziness
- Muscle and joint pain
- Sleeping problems
- Depression

- Memory loss
- Sore throat
- Tender lymph nodes

## Conventional Treatments

Many physicians find CFS baffling and difficult to deal with. Drugs are the usual conventional answer. Your doctor will probably recommend traditional pain medications including NSAIDS, such as ibuprofen or naproxen. If you have allergy-type symptoms, you'll be given antihistamines and decongestants. And to improve your energy and mood, your physician may prescribe Prozac, Zoloft, amitriptyline, or other antidepressants.

## Dietary Strategies (See Chapter 14 for food sources of specified nutrients)

*Elimination/challenge diet*
Sometimes food allergies cause or contribute to CFS. The most common allergies are dairy products and wheat. Try avoiding all dairy products for two weeks and then reintroduce them, noting your response. This is called an elimination/challenge. Keep a diary and see if your symptoms improve while you are off dairy products; then watch what happens when you start eating them again. You can repeat the same process with wheat and/or with any other foods that appear to aggravate your symptoms.

*Bromelain (See page 324)*

*Vitamin B6*
This nutrient increases the brain's production of a chemical that helps control pain.

*Astragalus (Astragalus membranaceus)*
This perennial plant in the pea family strengthens the immune system. To make an immune-enhancing broth that you can use as a stock for vegetable soup or for cooking brown rice, simmer 1 ounce (25 grams) of chopped astragalus root in a pint of water. Drink one cup every day.

*Mustard (Synapse arvensis)*
As an herb, mustard is useful for relieving depression and melancholy. I prefer you use it in its nutritional form, in recipes or as a condiment.

*Olive (Olea europea) and olive oil*
These small, evergreen fruits are the source of olive oil. They help fight extreme fatigue and exhaustion.

## Supplements

*B-complex vitamins*
For a healthy nervous system and more energy, take one pill a day.

*Evening primrose oil (EPO) (Oenothera biennis)*
This is a type of essential fatty acid that is available as capsules or as an oil. Take 500 mg a day.

*Acidophilus (Lactobacillus acidophilus)*
Because chronic yeast infections may have a connection to CFS, it's a good idea to take these "friendly" bacteria, often found in high-quality yogurt, that help to prevent yeast overgrowth in your body. Acidophilus is also available in tablets, and it's safe and nontoxic. Follow dosage on the package.

*NADH (nicotinamide adenine dinucleotide)*
This is a natural chemical that helps the cells produce energy. Some research has shown an improvement in symptoms after patients took 10 mg a day for four weeks. However, the research is not yet strong enough for me to endorse its use.

*Carnitine*
This is another substance that occurs naturally in the body. It converts fatty acids into energy. Some researchers have found that supplements relieve CFS symptoms. I have not seen enough solid research to recommend it.

## Herbs

*Echinacea (Echinacea angustifolia, Echinacea purpurea)*
This popular remedy, made from purple coneflowers, has been proven, in well-constructed, double-blind, placebo-controlled research, to reduce the symptoms, frequency, and duration of colds. Because its effects are attributed to stimulation of the immune system, it has been touted as a treatment for CFS. Laboratory studies have proven that it can increase antibody production and bolster cellular immune function. Recommended dose is 1 cup of tea or 1 teaspoon of tincture three times a day.

*Ginseng root* (Panax ginseng, Eleutherococcus senticosus)
This tonic herb increases energy and strengthens the immune system. Herbalists suggest 3 cups of tea a day. Do not take ginseng during pregnancy, or if you have high blood pressure.

*Gingko* (Gingko biloba)
This herb, which is actually leaves from the maidenhair tree, improves blood flow, boosts energy, and acts as an anti-inflammatory. Recommended dose is 3 cups of tea a day. Tablets are also available; follow dosing listed on the package.

*Licorice* (Glycyrrhiza glabra)
No, it's not just a candy. This healing root stimulates white blood cell formation and helps the body heal itself. It also, however, raises blood pressure, so avoid regular use if you have hypertension. Recommended dose is 3 cups of tea a day if your symptoms are acute; use half that dose for chronic ailments.

## Exercise

A study in the *British Medical Journal* found that patients who were put on a program of mild-to-moderate aerobic activity (walking, cycling, or swimming) for thirty minutes, five days a week reported less fatigue. I suggest that you do thirty minutes of brisk walking or bike riding at least three times weekly.

## Do-It-Yourself

*Aromatherapy*
Here are three choices of essential oils, and several methods for using them:

- Neroli (Orange Blossom, *Citrus aurantium var. amara*), a blossom from the bitter orange tree, and bergamot (*Citrus aurantium bergamia*), the oil from the fruit of a bergamot tree, will help to lift your spirits.
- Tea Tree (*Maleluca alternifolia*) works against infection and strengthens the immune system.

Methods:

- Add five to ten drops of the oil to your bath.
- Steam inhalation: add three to four drops of oil to a pot of boiling

water, cover your head with a towel, bend over the pot, and breathe deeply for a few minutes.

- Add six to eight drops of oil to the water in a vaporizer.
- Make a massage blend (for neroli only): Add 3 drops of neroli, 3 drops of celery, and 4 drops of rose to 5 teaspoons of grapeseed or vegetable oil. Use it to massage sore, aching parts of your body.

## Mind/Body

*Yoga*
Siddhasan (Perfect Posture), Vajrasana (Adamantine Posture), and Virasana (Hero's Posture) ease pain, encourage relaxation, and fight depression. (See pages 344–351 for postures.)

*Meditation (See Chapter 18)*

## Red Flags

Call your doctor if you have:

- Fever
- Malaise
- Depression
- Weight loss

## FIBROMYALGIA

### NATALIE'S STORY

Natalie, a woman in her late thirties, came to see me late one November afternoon. "I have fibromyalgia and I'm in constant pain—in my muscles, in my back, all over," she confessed. I could see the distress in her eyes as she peppered me with questions: "My family doctor told me it's all in my mind. Do you agree? I toss and turn all night—I feel like a rotisserie chicken—and I'm exhausted all the time. Is there anything I can do? Am I just going to feel lousy forever? I'm stressed out. I'm so morose all the time, my friends barely want to see me. Should I take antidepressants?"

It was clear after a few minutes that I was another stop on Natalie's doctor merry-go-round. For months she'd been going from one specialist to another, looking for answers. But she still hadn't found what she wanted—advice on taking charge of her pain.

On examination, it was obvious that Natalie did indeed have pain in multiple tender points—a clear case of fibromyalgia. She was also overweight, which put additional stress on her back. Although she had considerable chronic back and shoulder pain, that didn't mean she needed surgery, as one doctor had suggested. I told her that complementary strategies might be the answer to her problems.

We started by talking about proper nutrition and the role it plays in weight loss. In addition, some research suggests that nutrients like magnesium, 5-HTP (5-hydroxytryptophan), vitamin B1, vitamin E, SAMe, and malic acid might lessen the chronic fatigue, sleep disturbances, and muscle pain of fibromyalgia. Because a healthy diet rich in vegetables, fruits, and other whole foods contains many of these nutrients, a well-planned diet can actually decrease pain.

I also explained to her that vitamins C and E play a healing role by promoting the vitality and longevity of collagen and soft tissues. In addition, calcium, along with vitamin D and the amino acid lysine, improves the durability of bony structures. I reminded Natalie that drinking plenty of water (with a squeeze or two of lemon to enhance taste) helps to fend off dehydration, and promotes important chemical reactions in the body. And I recommended that she try soy foods, since cutting-edge research done at Johns Hopkins suggests that soy protein may promote pain relief.

Next, we discussed body mechanics. "Every step you take places stress on your joints and spine, and the problem is exacerbated if you are overweight," I told her. Natalie might benefit from shoe orthotics, which would act as shock absorbers, protecting her back from repeated strain.

I asked Natalie whether and how much she exercised. "I haven't exercised in months because I'm afraid it will hurt too much," she revealed. I urged her to take up swimming, which would help her lose weight. And far from making things worse, once she got started, the exercise would actually help her feel better. Releasing and mobilizing endorphins through exercise is a time-tested, surefire way to relieve pain.

Exercise also lessens anxiety and relieves depression. As I told Natalie, rock-solid research on the mind-body connection has shown that a more positive outlook reduces pain. Besides, I told her: "Starting and then sticking with an exercise regimen will make you feel better about yourself. When your self-esteem is restored, you'll be surprised how your pain takes less of a toll."

Regular exercise would also help Natalie in another way. Like many women with fibromyalgia, she had trouble sleeping. "I often have to take strong medications to get to sleep, and I hate the way they make me feel in the morning," she confided. I described how she could use meditation and visual imagery to relax, and recommended regular infusions of chamomile tea, an effective and gentle aid to sleep.

After a few months, Natalie came back, looking much better. She had lost 12 pounds. She told me: "I swim every other day and I've been watching my diet. I'm practicing meditation, too. I'm sleeping like a baby again and I can't believe how much better I feel. Best of all, I'm in charge of my own destiny."

## Description

This poorly understood and often misdiagnosed disease occurs nine times more often in women than in men. If you have fibromyalgia, you're part of a large sorority—3.4 percent of women suffer from this malady, and the figure rises to 7 percent for women between sixty and seventy-nine.

Fibromyalgia is characterized by widespread, long-term, musculoskeletal pain. Typically, people with fibromyalgia "ache all over." Long dismissed as psychosomatic, it is now accepted as a bona fide disease. The American College of Rheumatology has established criteria for its diagnosis. These include widespread pain on both sides of the body for at least three months in eleven of eighteen "tender points." Tender points are located in the muscles of the upper neck, back, shoulders, and hips. According to these criteria, fibromyalgia is the second most common diagnosis in rheumatology clinics, right after osteoarthritis.

## Causes

There are some fascinating clues, but no answer, to the question: What causes fibromyalgia? It does not appear to be an inflammatory disease or a degenerative disorder. Nor has a virus been clearly implicated. Many fibromyalgia patients have had other ailments, such as chronic fatigue syndrome (see page 291), chronic headaches, irritable bowel syndrome, or depression. They also have intriguing physical abnormalities—some patients have changes in nervous system chemicals, such as substance P or peptides that are related to pain. Others report that they had physical or emotional trauma, or an infection, such as Lyme disease, before they developed fibro-myalgia. Still, the mystery remains.

## Signs and Symptoms

Pain is just part of the fibromyalgia picture. The full range of symptoms includes:

- Mild aches to incapacitating pain
- Chronic, stiff, aching muscles
- Chronic headaches
- Depression
- Sleep disturbances
- Fatigue
- Morning stiffness
- Co-existing conditions, including chronic fatigue syndrome (see page 291), irritable bowel syndrome, depression, and other forms of arthritis
- Stress, inappropriate exercise, and weather can worsen the symptoms

## Conventional Treatments

Fibromyalgia is a perplexing ailment that conventional physicians treat with medications and, sometimes, psychological counseling. Your doctor will probably recommend traditional pain medications including NSAIDS, such as ibuprofen or naproxen. To improve energy and mood and help you sleep, your physician may also prescribe Prozac, Zoloft, amitriptyline, or other antidepressants. Sleeping pills, antianxiety medications, and muscle relaxants are other possible treatments.

Trigger point injections—injections of a local anesthetic directly into painful spots—may help.

## Dietary Strategies (See Chapter 14 for food sources of specified nutrients)

- Eat a healthy diet, emphasizing fruits, vegetables, and whole grains. These foods contain nutrients that can promote healing and reduce pain.
- Eat foods containing vitamins C and E, which boost healing.
- For strong bones, be sure to get enough calcium and vitamin D.
- Limit caffeine and alcohol, which interfere with sleep.
- Eat apples and drink their juice. Apples are high in malic acid, a sub-

stance that has been shown in some preliminary studies to be helpful for fibromyalgia.

· Include soy foods in your diet. Preliminary research has shown that soy protein may help relieve pain.

## Supplements

*SAMe (S-adenosyl methionine)*
SAMe is a natural substance produced from methionine, an amino acid, and adenosine triphosphate (ATP), a metabolic chemical associated with energy production. It can reduce pain and fatigue as well as morning stiffness. SAMe is also an antidepressant. The dose is 400 to 800 mg a day. Be aware, however, that in large doses, it can upset the stomach. Do not take SAMe if you take levodopa for Parkinson's disease. This nutrient may trigger manic episodes in people with bipolar disease.

*5-HTP (5-hydroxytryptophan)*
This supplement has been shown to decrease the number of tender points and improve sleep patterns, morning stiffness, and fatigue. The dose is 100 to 300 mg a day. Do not take this with antidepressants.

## Herbs

*St. John's wort* (Hypericum perforatum)
For depression and increased tolerance to pain the recommended dose is 300 mg three times a day.

## Do-It-Yourself

*Aromatherapy (See Chronic Fatigue Syndrome, page 291)*

## Mind/Body

*Yoga*
Siddhasan (Perfect Posture) and Virasana (Hero's Posture) ease pain, encourage relaxation, and fight depression. (See pages 344–351 for postures.)

*Meditation (See Chapter 18)*

## Exercise

If you have fibromyalgia, it's easy to get caught in a vicious cycle. You're in pain, so you don't exercise. But not exercising weakens your muscles, and unused muscles are more likely to be vulnerable to pain. It's important to keep your muscles moving, so I recommend low-impact aerobic conditioning exercises, such as swimming or using a stationary bike. Gentle stretching exercises, like the ones below, will improve your general flexibility.

ELBOW CIRCLE
1. With your elbows bent, slowly lift your arms up.
2. On both sides, bring your fingertips up to the tops of your shoulders and point your elbows straight out to the sides.
3. Move your elbows in circles. Begin with small movements and progress to large circles.

HIP ROTISSERIE
1. With feet spread apart, place your hands on your hips, with your thumbs in front.
2. Slowly move your hips from side to side four times.
3. Then, move your hips forward and backward four times.

## Seeking Help from Complementary Practitioners

*Acupuncture*
I've found this therapy to be extremely helpful with my fibromyalgia patients. The massive outpouring of endorphins triggered by needling reduces the pain.

*Massage therapy*
A good massage can ease stiffness in your muscles and deactivate tender points. In addition, it will help you relax, which will make it easier to get to sleep.

**Red Flags**

- Persisting pains
- Fever
- Weight loss

## MYOFASCIAL PAIN SYNDROME (MPS)

**Description**

MPS is sometimes confused with fibromyalgia, and indeed, they are similar. Both are characterized by chronic pain in the muscle tissues. But the pain of MPS is localized, not widespread, as it is in fibromyalgia. And MPS affects men and women equally.

Myofascial pain syndrome is a neuromuscular condition that involves inflammation and irritation of the muscles and their supportive tissue, or fascial, lining. The myofascial tissues become thickened and lose elasticity, and you develop trigger points. These sensitive, sore areas in the muscle or the junction of the muscle and fascia are tender and painful to the touch. They also cause referred pain; in other words, when pressure is applied, you feel pain at that point *and* elsewhere in your body. This is in contrast to the "tender points" of fibromyalgia, which cause local discomfort only.

**Causes**

You may develop or be predisposed to MPS for a variety of reasons:

- Sudden trauma to musculoskeletal tissues (muscles, ligaments, tendons, bursae)
- Injury to an intervertebral disc
- Poor posture that results in muscle overload or spasm
- Generalized fatigue
- Repetitive motions, excessive exercise, or muscle strain due to over-activity
- Systemic conditions, such as gallbladder inflammation, heart attack, appendicitis, or stomach irritation
- Underlying metabolic or endocrine problems, such as thyroid disease
- Inactivity—for example, having a broken arm in a sling
- Nutritional deficiencies, including anemia
- Hormonal changes—you may develop trigger points during PMS or menopause

- Nervous tension or stress
- Getting a chill somewhere on your body—for example, sitting under an air-conditioning duct or sleeping in front of an air conditioner
- Sleep deprivation
- Medications, including narcotics

## Signs and Symptoms

The major symptom of MPS is localized and referred pain from trigger points. Here's a look at the differences between MPS and fibromyalgia:

| Symptoms | FMS | MPS |
|---|---|---|
| Pain | Diffuse | Local |
| Fatigue | Common | Uncommon |
| Morning stiffness | Common | Uncommon |
| Tender points | X | |
| Trigger points | | X |
| Prognosis | Chronic | Resolves with treatment |

## Conventional Treatments

You may be given anti-inflammatory medications and/or tricyclic antidepressants, such as amitryptyline, for the pain. Otherwise, physical therapy and other conventional treatments for MPS focus directly on the trigger points. One option is trigger point therapy, also known as myofascial release therapy, myotherapy, or massotherapy, a form of medical massage therapy done by a physiatrist or other medical doctor. A physical therapist or physiatrist may do spray and stretch. She will start by applying a vapocoolant spray to your trigger points to reduce the pain; then she will stretch the affected muscles.

Some treatments mechanically disrupt the trigger point. Trigger point injections involve injecting a local anesthetic, such as lidocaine, directly into the trigger points. Dry needling does the same thing but without injecting any substances. The use of lidocaine is no more effective, but it does reduce the soreness after the injections.

## Dietary Strategies (See Chapter 14 for food sources of specific nutrients)

- Vitamin B6 increases the brain's production of a chemical that helps control pain.
- Be sure to eat plenty of fruits and vegetables to prevent nutritional deficiencies.
- Drink at least eight 8-ounce glasses of water a day.

## Supplements

### 5-HTP (5-hydroxytryptophan)
This supplement may decrease trigger point discomfort. The dose is 100 to 300 mg a day. Do not take this with antidepressants or serotonin-acting medications, like Ultram (tramadol) or Ambien (zolpidem tartrate).

### SAMe (S-adenosyl methionine)
A natural substance produced from methionine, an amino acid, and adenosine triphosphate (ATP), SAMe is a metabolic chemical associated with energy production. It can reduce pain and fatigue as well as morning stiffness. SAMe is also an antidepressant. The dose is 400 to 800 mg a day. Be aware, however, that in large doses it can upset your stomach. Do not take SAMe if you take levodopa for Parkinson's disease. This nutrient may trigger manic episodes if you have bipolar disease.

## Herbs

### Gingko (Gingko biloba)
This herb, the leaves of the maidenhair tree, improves blood flow, boosts energy, and has anti-inflammatory properties. The recommended dose is 3 cups of tea a day. Tablets are also available; follow dosing on the package.

### Valerian (Valeriana officinalis)
This herb helps calm the nervous system, relieving insomnia and anxiety. Herbalists suggest 2 or 3 cups of tea a day.

### St. John's wort (Hypericum perforatum)
For depression and increased tolerance to pain, the recommended dose is 300 mg three times a day.

## Do-It-Yourself

*Aromatherapy*
- Neroli (Orange Blossom, *Citrus aurantium var. amara*), a blossom from the bitter orange tree, and bergamot (*Citrus aurantium bergamia*), the oil from the fruit of a bergamot tree, will help to lift your spirits.
Methods:
  - Add five to ten drops of the oil to your bath.
  - Steam inhalation: add three to four drops of oil to a pot of boiling water, cover your head with a towel, bend over the pot, and breathe deeply for a few minutes.
  - Add six to eight drops of oil to the water in a vaporizer.
  - Make a massage blend (for neroli only): Add 3 drops of neroli, 3 drops of celery, and 4 drops of rose to 5 teaspoons of grapeseed or vegetable oil and use it to massage sore, aching parts of your body.
- Rosemary (*Rosmarinus officinalis*) helps prevent fatigue. Use this oil on a compress or to massage tender spots. Avoid during pregnancy, or if you have epilepsy or high blood pressure.
- Geranium (*Pelargonium graveolens*), for depression. Use geranium in a bath or a diffuser. Do not use it during the first three months of pregnancy, and do not use it at all if you are pregnant and have a history of miscarriage.
- Shower rub—To make an invigorating shower rub, add two drops of rosemary oil, two drops of pine oil, and four drops of lemon oil to a small dollop of unscented shower gel. Work it into a lather with a sponge and use on your sore, aching muscles.

## Mind/Body

*Meditation (See Chapter 18)*

*Yoga*
Try Kagasana (Crow Posture), Boat Pose, and Bow Pose. (See pages 344–351 for postures.)

## Seeking Help from Complementary Practitioners

- Massage and chiropractic may help relax muscle tissues and relieve pain
- Acupuncture is also helpful for pain relief

**Red Flags**

Call your doctor if you experience:

- Persisting sleep disturbances
- Weight loss
- Night sweats
- Fever
- Worsening depression

## CHRONIC PAIN

Chronic pain, or pain that continues for six months or more, is more common than you might think. In a recent survey, one in five Americans reported suffering from chronic pain, and seven in ten said the pain interfered with their daily life. Women suffer somewhat more frequently from chronic pain, and they are more likely to become depressed as a result.

Chronic pain ranges from mild to disabling, and it can last from six months to many years. It may be the result of an injury or disease, but it is sometimes difficult to find its cause. Whatever its source, chronic pain often becomes a problem in and of itself, one that overwhelms other symptoms you may have. If you are in constant, long-term pain, you run the risk of falling into what we call the "terrible triad" of suffering, sleeplessness, and sadness. Your appetite falls off and physical activity seems impossible. You may become preoccupied with your pain, depressed, and irritable. Because of your inability to control it, chronic pain can cause low self-esteem and a sense of helplessness. Trouble sleeping aggravates an already miserable situation. And on top of this, you may have side effects from medications, mounting medical expenses, problems getting to work, and strains in your closest personal relationships.

**Causes**

There are countless reasons why you may develop chronic pain, and sometimes we can't pinpoint any source. Common causes include:

- Improperly treated acute pain
- Chronic diseases or syndromes, such as arthritis, endometriosis, headaches, fibromyalgia, cancer, and interstitial cystitis
- Gastrointestinal diseases and disorders, such as irritable bowel syndrome

- Failed joint or back surgeries
- Back or neck pain from nerve damage, joint problems, muscle loss, osteoporosis, herniated disk, or other sources
- Overuse injuries, often in your hands and wrists, from computer use or other repetitive motions
- Chronic nerve syndromes. These include complex regional pain syndrome, an intense, long-lasting nerve injury with pain, typically in an arm or leg; peripheral neuropathy, which causes tingling, numbness, and pain in your hands and feet; and postherpetic neuralgia, which is nerve damage resulting from a viral infection.
- Dental, nerve, or joint problems may cause mouth, jaw, and facial pain.

## Conventional Treatments

Of course, treatment depends on the cause of the pain. A thorough, holistic medical assessment of a chronic pain condition is best performed by a physiatrist (a physical medicine and rehabilitation specialist), who can oversee your comprehensive pain management program.

Analgesics, including aspirin, acetaminophen (Tylenol), and NSAIDS, are a first line of defense. Your doctor may also prescribe other, more potent painkillers. Physical or occupational therapy may be options. TENS, a treatment that uses electrical charges to block pain messages, may also be of some help.

Occasionally, when more conservative measures have failed, your doctor may propose another intervention to temporarily blockade the pain generator. Options include an epidural block, a facet joint block, or a peripheral nerve block. Be aware, though, that loss of all sensation—not just pain—in that part of your body as well as other complications can result.

When all else has failed, your doctor may want you to consider surgery. Yet surgery is risky business, especially when there are no new objective neurologic findings to justify it. Besides the risks attendant with any surgery, there can be additional complications, like scar tissue, infection, or even a worsening of pain. Besides, relief is not always permanent; your pain may return six months or a year later.

## Dietary Strategies

### Soy foods

Recent studies in Israel and at Johns Hopkins suggest that consuming soy protein may help reduce pain.

*Turmeric* (Curcuma longa) *and ginger* (Zingibar officinale)
Turmeric is a spice used in Ayurvedic (Indian) and Chinese medicine, both as a seasoning and as a tea, because of its potent anti-inflammatory properties. A study with arthritis patients convincingly demonstrated its effectiveness in helping to relieve pain. And gingerroot has been found to have five known inhibitors of prostaglandin synthesis. In plain English, that means that it's capable of fighting inflammation in a fashion that is similar to aspirin and other anti-inflammatory medications.

*Pineapple*
Eat pineapple and drink its juice; it contains bromelain. (See page 324.)

## Supplements

*SAMe*
There is mounting scientific evidence for SAMe's ability to relieve osteoarthritis, chronic fatigue syndrome, fibromyalgia, and other forms of chronic, long-term pain. It also has a well-documented antidepressant effect. Take 200 mg twice a day. Do not take SAMe if you take levodopa for Parkinson's disease. This nutrient may trigger manic episodes if you have bipolar disease.

*Vitamin E*
This nutrient speeds healing, reduces fatigue, and boosts your immune system. The acceptable daily dose range is 15 to 1,000 mg.

*Multivitamin with antioxidants*
A good daily multivitamin supplement can help counter the effects of free radicals, which have been implicated in the development of many forms of chronic disease. Follow the dosing on the package.

## Do-It-Yourself

*Alexander technique (See page 310)*

*Aromatherapy*
Aromatherapy is beginning to be recognized as part of an integrated, multidisciplinary approach to chronic pain management. It's thought to encourage deep relaxation, so it changes your perception of pain.

In several clinical studies, lavender oil has significantly reduced pain and discomfort. In one study, patients in a critical care population had a 50 percent reduction in pain perception when they received a lavender oil massage. In another, conducted in a hospice population, researchers hypothesized that this volatile oil reduced pain by limiting the effects of external emotional stimuli on a particular part of the brain, called the amygdala. Other research shows that lavender, applied topically, relieves pain and can enhance the effects of conventional pain medications.

I suggest that you take a warm bath and add several drops of lavender oil (*Lavandula angustifolia*). Other oils that may provide relief are eucalyptus (*Eucalyptus globulus*) and mandarin (*Citrus reticulata*).

## Mind/Body

*Relaxation techniques and meditation (See Chapter 18)*

*Imagery (See Chapter 18)*
Imagery has proven to be an effective way to control and ease pain.

*Biofeedback (See page 341)*

*Music therapy*
In addition to my own personal experiences with patients, there is solid research supporting the effectiveness of music therapy in reducing suffering and the physical sensation of pain. Both listening to music and making music are helpful.

*Yoga*
Try these postures to relax, ease pain and depression, and help you sleep: Shavasana (Corpse Pose), Vajrasana (Adamantine Posture), and Child's Pose. (See pages 344–351.)

## Exercise

If you're in constant pain, you may be afraid to start exercising because you're afraid it will increase your pain. But this is a self-defeating proposition. The body releases pain-killing endorphins during aerobic exercise. And exercise fights depression. By depriving yourself of exercise, you may be making things worse. Instead, make it your goal to maintain as much normal activity as possible, including going to work and your responsibilities around the house. Start your exercise program slowly and increase gradually until you can work out for thirty to forty-five minutes, three to five times a week. Duration is more important than intensity. An ideal way to get started is swimming three times a week, which can make an enormous difference in the way you feel.

## Seeking Help from Complementary Practitioners

*Acupuncture*
I find this treatment very useful as a complement to conventional methods for treating long-term, chronic pain. It is especially helpful for musculoskeletal conditions, fibromyalgia, chronic fatigue syndrome, arthritis, and other forms of long-term pain.

*Biofeedback (See page 341)*

*The Alexander technique*
This is a method of reeducating your body with movement patterns. The goal is to learn how to minimize tension in the muscles that support your skeleton. It's an ideal way of improving your posture and battling chronic pain. Once you've learned it, you can do it on your own.

*Hypnosis*
Studies suggest that hypnosis is an effective way to reduce pain. You'll need some training from a hypnotist, but your ultimate goal is to do it yourself.

## Red Flags

Let your doctor know if you experience:

- An abrupt change in the severity or intensity of your pain
- Evidence of weakness in your muscles
- Increasing or worsening fatigue
- Loss of appetite
- Fever

## REFLEX SYMPATHETIC DYSTROPHY (RSD) (SEE CHAPTER 8)

## PERIPHERAL NEUROPATHY (SEE CHAPTER 8)

# YOUR

# PAIN

# PRESCRIPTIONS

# 13

## The Traditional Medicine Cabinet

I consider myself a practitioner of integrative medicine, which combines the best of conventional and complementary care. When we treat something as terrible as pain, we have to use all the tools in the arsenal.

I recognize that conventional treatments can be ineffective, or fraught with side effects or unintended consequences. And because pain is so complex, it doesn't fit as neatly into the "one bug, one drug" model. Despite my emphasis on complementary strategies, however, I still firmly believe that modern medicine and technology can do wonders, and that there is an important place for them in the treatment of pain.

### NSAIDS

Nonsteroidal anti-inflammatory drugs, or NSAIDS, are the largest class of pain relievers.

### Aspirin

Aspirin, or acetylsalicylic acid, works by inhibiting production of cyclooxygenase (COX), an enzyme in the body, which prevents formation of inflammatory chemicals, known as prostaglandins. Aspirin relieves pain *and* inflammation. However, aspirin may: harm your stomach and gastrointestinal tract; irreversibly affect platelets (blood cells that promote clotting) and cause you to bleed; cause tinnitis, or ringing in your ears and dizziness; worsen asthma and/or cause nasal polyps.

## Traditional NSAIDS

There are more than thirty brands of NSAIDS available. Some you can buy over the counter, like ibuprofen (Motrin, Nuprin, or Advil), naproxen (Aleve and Naprosyn), and ketoprofen (Orudis). Prescription NSAIDS are stronger and they may have a longer duration of action. Examples include Mobic (meloxicam), Lodine XL (etodolac), Relafen (nabumetone), Daypro (oxaprozin), Voltaren (diclofenac), Anaprox (naproxen), and Toradol (ketorolac).

A popular NSAID "combo agent" is Arthrotec. It combines diclofenac sodium with misoprostol, a prostaglandin E chemical that protects your gastrointestinal tract. Avoid it if you are of childbearing age because misoprostol can cause abortion or birth defects.

All NSAIDS provide pain relief and reduce redness, swelling, and tenderness. As a result, they can improve your range of motion. Like aspirin, they also reduce fever. NSAIDS don't affect your central nervous system, or cause physical dependence or tolerance, like opioids (narcotics).

However, NSAIDS also have many side effects, including some that are quite serious. Common side effects are stomach pain, nausea, vomiting, and diarrhea. Less frequent side effects include anemia, blood or protein in the urine from kidney damage, hypertension, headache or drowsiness, liver, stomach, and gastrointestinal damage, and abnormal blood platelet function. Prolonged use may cause gastrointestinal ulcers. In some cases, NSAIDS may take weeks or months before there is noticeable improvement in your pain. NSAIDS and other non-narcotic analgesics often have a "ceiling effect." This means that when you increase the dosage above a certain point, it may not improve analgesia.

If you take other medications, or if you are pregnant or breast-feeding, check with your physician or pharmacist.

## Cox-2 Inhibitors: The New NSAIDS

Now, a new and exciting generation of NSAIDS has been developed. Rather than inhibiting both Cox-1 (which plays a protective role for your stomach and gastrointestinal tract, kidneys and blood clotting functions), and Cox-2 enzymes, they selectively inhibit only Cox-2 enzymes. Their analgesic effectiveness is comparable to conventional NSAIDS. But because they do not interfere with Cox-1 enzymes, they cause a much lower incidence of ulcers. They result in less than half as many GI complications as the older NSAIDS. In addition, they are better tolerated, causing less nausea and abdominal pain. And preliminary research shows that Cox-2 inhibitors may reduce your risk of colorectal cancer.

There are only two on the market right now — celecoxib (Celebrex) and rofecoxib (Vioxx) — but others are in development. Although Vioxx has been approved by the FDA as a treatment for menstrual pain and other types of acute pain, Celebrex is also often used successfully for these purposes. Vioxx is currently indicated only for osteoarthritis, and studies are in progress to support its use in rheumatoid arthritis. Celebrex is indicated for both rheumatoid arthritis and osteoarthritis. Both of these drugs are available only by prescription.

The Cox-2 inhibitors do have some disadvantages. They may interact with certain drugs, such as beta-blockers, anti-arrhythmic medications, and tricyclic antidepressants. And unlike aspirin, they do not have antiplatelet effects, so they won't help prevent heart attack. Since its chemical structure includes a sulfa molecule, you should not take Celebrex if you are allergic to sulfa. Vioxx does not contain sulfa.

## Other Non-Narcotic Pain Relievers

*Acetaminophen (Tylenol)* is an effective over-the-counter analgesic that relieves both acute and chronic pain. It also reduces fever. Acetaminophen does not, however, reduce inflammation, which is a major disadvantage in treating many ailments. It is the safest of all analgesics. However, large doses can cause liver damage.

*Tramadol (Ultram)* is used for moderate to moderately severe pain. Available by prescription only, it is approved for low back pain, osteoarthritis, peripheral neuropathy, and postoperative and orthopedic pain. Your body absorbs Tramadol rapidly, so you may feel relief within an hour. Its primary side effects are nausea, vomiting, and dizziness. It should not be used with opioid drugs or if you are pregnant.

## Narcotics

Also known as "painkillers," narcotics are an extremely powerful class of drugs. Morphine is the prototype, upon which all others are based. Because of their addictive potential, narcotics are known as "controlled drugs," and are strictly regulated. They are sometimes called opiates or opioid drugs because they are synthetic drugs that behave like opium. Examples of narcotics include: propoxyphene (Darvocet), pentazocine (Talwin), hydrocodone (Lorcet), dihydrocodeine (Panlor), oxycodone (Percocet, Percodan), methadone, hydromorphone (Dilaudid), meperidine (Demerol), and morphine. Longer acting oral narcotics (Oxcontin and MS Contin) are available, as well as long-acting patches (Duragesic patch).

Narcotics are effective for severe acute or chronic pain. Unfortunately, narcotics have many potential side effects. Because they are available by prescription only, you will need to thoroughly discuss these drugs with your physician.

### Antidepressants

Depression can amplify pain and limit your ability to deal with discomfort and anxiety. By relieving depression and anxiety, antidepressants can help reduce pain.

There are three major classes of antidepressants. All are prescription-only. Selective serotonin reuptake inhibitors (SSRIs) are the newest. Prozac, Paxil, and Zoloft are among the most well known. Because they have fewer side effects than older drugs—and they still have plenty—most doctors prescribe these SSRIs first.

If SSRIs are ineffective, the next course of action is often a tricyclic antidepressant. These include imipramine (Tofranil), amitriptyline (Elavil), clomipramine (Anafranil), doxepin (Sinequan), or trimipramine (Surmontil).

Phenelzine (Nardil) and other monoamine oxidase (MAO) inhibitors are usually the last choice of treatment for depression, used when other types of antidepressants have been ineffective.

Finally, there are several new antidepressants that don't fit into these three categories. They include Bupropion (Wellbutrin), Venlafaxine (Effexor), Mirtazapine (Remeron), and Trazodone (Desyrel).

## MUSCLE RELAXANTS AND TRANQUILIZERS

Muscle spasms can exacerbate your pain. Adequately addressing these spasms can give you significant relief. Muscle relaxants step up to the plate by helping to curb tension and decrease spasms associated with low back and neck pain. Among the most commonly used muscle relaxants are: diazepam (Valium), cyclobenzaprine (Flexeril), methocarbamol (Robaxin), metaxalone (Skelaxin), baclofen (Lioresal), dantrolene (Dantrium), orphenadrine (Norflex), and tizidium (Zanaflex).

## ANTICONVULSANT DRUGS

In addition to controlling seizures, these medications are "membrane stabilizing agents," which can relieve certain types of pain. Chronic pain syndromes, such as diabetic peripheral neuropathy, neuropathic pain, complex regional pain syndrome (RSD), migraines, and post-herpetic neuralgia, respond best to this treatment. The anticonvulsants most frequently prescribed for pain are: gabapentin (Neurontin), carbamazepine (Tegretol), phenytoin (Dilantin), and mexiletine (Mexitil).

## HYPNOTICS

Often, when you're in pain, you get trapped in an endless cycle. You can't sleep because of your pain; then you're so exhausted that everything hurts even more. Hypnotics break this cycle by allowing you to sleep. If your pain is keeping you awake, you may want to consider zolpidem (Ambien) or zaleplon (Sonata).

## NERVE AND MUSCLE BLOCKS

### Traditional Nerve Blocks

When other pain therapies don't work, it's sometimes necessary to resort to more heavy-duty options. One possibility is a nerve block. Just as its name implies, this intervention blocks the transmission of pain signals through your nerves. A traditional nerve block can relieve pain for several days to weeks and, in some cases, months to years. However, you may experience numbness, tingling, muscle paralysis, or loss of feeling in the area affected by the nerve. You'll also need injections several times a year.

### Other Nerve Blocks

*Stellate ganglion block*
We do this procedure most frequently when we suspect that a patient has Reflex Sympathetic Dystrophy (RSD) (see Chapter 8). It is both diagnostic and therapeutic. The stellate ganglion is a junction point for your sympathetic nerves, which control some of the involuntary functions of your body, such as opening and narrowing blood vessels. When we block this "circuit box," it can suppress pain and other symptoms. However, a stellate ganglion

block is a technically difficult procedure that is fraught with side effects and complications.

### SI joint block

It's been estimated that in as many as one in six cases of chronic low back problems, the pain actually comes from the sacroiliac (SI) joint, but it masquerades as back pain. An SI joint block can differentiate between the two problems, and ensure an accurate diagnosis. It is therapeutic as well as diagnostic.

### Sarapin blocks

Nerve blocks traditionally use conventional injection chemicals, such as lidocaine, procaine, phenol, and steroids. However, Sarapin, a botanical chemical harvested from the pitcher plant (*Sarraceniaceae*), is also listed in the *Physicians' Desk Reference* as a useful injection medium. I believe that we need more research to prove its effectiveness.

## Muscle Blocks

Blocks can also be performed on muscles. These procedures are especially helpful for treating dystonias, which are painful neurological ailments that cause slow, sustained contractions of muscles that commonly cause twisting movements and abnormal posturing. They are frequently painful and can disturb your sleep.

The latest treatment for dystonias is somewhat surprising: botulism toxin, once only known as a horrifying poison. In an FDA-approved preparation called Myobloc, botulism toxin is now extolled for its therapeutic value in cervical (neck) dystonias. Botox, another botulism preparation, is also available.

Unlike nerve blocks, which interrupt pain transmission in your nerves, Myobloc works by interrupting the transmissions between your nerve and the affected muscle, so the treated muscle relaxes. We can decrease the pain, without the risk of sensory complications. And the effects are sustained. There are risks, however, including skin bruising and inadvertent paralysis of muscles.

## Trigger Point and Tender Point Injection and Deactivation

The late Dr. Janet Travell, JFK's physician, along with Dr. David Simons, discovered that the hallmark clinical feature of the myofascial pain syndrome (see Chapter 12) is something she named the "trigger point." Dr.

Travell spent many years mapping out the anatomical locations for trigger points throughout the body. She published her work in a now-famous textbook. The term trigger point has long since achieved widespread acceptance. In recent years, Dr. Andrew Fisher has furthered our understanding of trigger points through his novel anatomical observations.

Trigger points are discrete, tender spots located in a muscle. When pressed, they cause a sudden triggering of pain throughout the muscle's zone of reference, which follows the trajectory of the muscle's fibers. Injecting a solution of an anesthetic called lidocaine into these trigger points helps deactivate them.

Dr. Travell also advocated using a vapocoolant ethyl chloride and florimethane spray to help stretch muscles, a technique we call "spray and stretch." The spray, produced by the Gebauer family in Cleveland, relaxes the muscle so it stretches more easily. Another technique pioneered by this impressive woman is ischemic compression, which is somewhat akin to acupressure. By pressing on the trigger point for sixty seconds, we can relieve the pain.

As part of a multidisciplinary pain program, these techniques are important strategies for treating MPS, fibromyalgia, and other painful conditions.

## Spinal Interventional Procedures and Surgery

When conservative measures have failed to lessen pain in your spine, it might be time to consider a variety of spinal interventional procedures, or surgery. However, these are beyond the scope of this book.

# 14

# Foods That Heal

A diet that includes certain nutrients can speed healing, prevent or slow down the development of painful ailments, and reduce pain and inflammation. Here's a brief summary of important pain-related nutrients and their food sources.

## Fat

Cholesterol, saturated, monounsaturated, and polyunsaturated are the four types of dietary fats. It's important to reduce your total fat intake to 30 percent or less of your calories and to limit your saturated fat intake to 10 percent of your diet. But it is *critical* to avoid trans-fatty acids and hydrogenated or partially hydrogenated oils, which are found in margarines, mayonnaise, salad dressings, chocolate bars, and snack foods. Besides raising LDL cholesterol (so-called bad cholesterol) levels, these fats lead to the premature oxidation of cell membranes and to the development of chronic illnesses, such as arthritis, diabetes, cardiovascular disease, and degenerative nerve and muscular diseases.

On the other hand, olive oil, which is the basis of the Mediterranean diet, has been linked to lower risk for heart disease and other chronic illnesses.

## Essential Fatty Acids

Omega-3 (linolenic acid) and omega-6 (linoleic acid) fatty acids, which are types of polyunsaturated fats, are called "essential fatty acids (EFAs)" because our bodies can't produce them; we have to get them from food.

EFAs are very important when we think about pain. Omega-3 fats help fight inflammation, while omega-6 fats contribute to inflammatory processes. More than the absolute amount of each of these fatty acids in your diet, what's important is the *ratio* between the two. To reduce pain and inflammation, increase your intake of omega-3s. Dietary sources are:

- Coldwater fish, such as mackerel, salmon, bluefish, flounder, herring, sardines, halibut, striped bass, sable fish (black cod), anchovies, and tuna. Strive to eat fish at least three times a week.
- Wild game, walnuts, wheat germ, and flaxseeds.
- Canola, grapeseed, walnut, hemp, and flaxseed oils. These oils are highly unstable. To prevent them from turning rancid, buy them in dark containers, if possible, and keep them in the refrigerator. Because heating these oils destroys the omega-3s, put them on salads, or add them to foods after cooking. Grapeseed oil is your best choice for frying; its omega-3s are less likely to be destroyed since it has a higher boiling point than the others.

To fight pain, it's equally important to cut back on linoleic acid, gamma-linolenic acid, and arachidonic acid, all members of the omega-6 family. Your body uses them to produce substances called prostaglandins and leukotrienes, which contribute significantly to inflammation and pain. Foods high in linoleic acid are cottonseed, corn, and other types of vegetable oils, except for canola, safflower, soybean, and olive oils. Meat is high in arachidonic acid. Duck and pork are the worst culprits, while beef and lamb contain smaller amounts.

## Protein

Proteins, which build and repair body tissue, are made of amino acids. Specific amino acids, and even certain types of protein-rich foods, have an influence on pain. Tryptophan, for example, reduces sensitivity to pain. Your body uses it to produce 5-hydroxytryptophan (5-HTP), which is used in the manufacture of the neurotransmitter serotonin. The important part serotonin plays in pain and inflammation is just now unfolding. For example, people with fibromyalgia often have low serotonin levels in their blood.

Increasing your intake of tryptophan, and therefore your serotonin levels, may help reduce chronic pain. To do this, you must reduce the total amount of protein in your diet *and* focus on carbohydrates and foods that contain high levels of tryptophan, including salmon, tuna, soy flour, bulgur, garbanzo beans, meat, turkey, bananas, pineapple, yogurt, and dairy products.

Phenylalanine, another amino acid, seems to influence certain chemicals in the brain that relate to pain sensation. It has been useful in treating chronic pain conditions, such as osteoarthritis and rheumatoid arthritis. The richest food sources are seaweed, kelp, dairy products, pumpkin, sunflower seeds, poultry, fish, eggs, and collard greens.

In addition, soy may reduce pain. A groundbreaking study at Johns Hopkins University demonstrated that rats on a soy-based diet had decreased pain sensitivity. It's certainly worth a try, especially given soy's many other benefits. Soy may help prevent the development of breast, stomach, and skin tumors. It also may relieve the hot flashes of menopause and prevent osteoporosis. Besides soybeans, you can get soy milk, ice cream, and protein. Other soy products are miso, tofu, and tempeh.

## Vitamins

Vitamins are organic nutrients necessary to regulate many of your body's chemical processes. Many vitamins help reduce pain and inflammation.

**Vitamin A** improves your body's ability to heal. It acts as a major antioxidant, and promotes cell differentiation, which helps maintain cell membranes, tissues, and the skin. This nutrient also promotes good vision and supports your immune system and healthy bones. There are two forms of vitamin A. Retinol is found in cod liver oil, liver, kidneys, eggs, and dairy. Beta-carotene is an orange pigment and a vitamin A precursor, found in plants. Good sources are yellow-orange fruits and vegetables, such as carrots, sweet potatoes, pumpkin, cantaloupe, apricots, and peaches as well as dark leafy greens, including collards, mustard, and spinach.

**Vitamin C** blocks the effects of inflammatory substances and is involved in wound healing. It is also a powerful antioxidant that protects cells and cell membranes from free radical damage. You use vitamin C to make collagen, which strengthens muscles, blood vessels, bones, teeth, gums, skin, tendons, ligaments, and joints. Food sources of this nutrient are rosehips, black currants, broccoli, cauliflower, oranges, green and red bell peppers, tangerines and other citrus fruits, strawberries, kale, kiwi fruit, papaya, mangoes, brussels sprouts, cabbage, potatoes, and tomatoes.

Foods high in vitamin C tend to contain **bioflavonoids,** such as rutin, hesperidin, quercitin, and genistein. They are not vitamins, but they have anti-inflammatory properties.

**Vitamin E** is a powerful antioxidant. It protects white and red blood cells, lipids, vitamin A, and other components of cells and their membranes from destruction. Research involving patients with rheumatoid arthritis suggests that vitamin E also reduces pain. Food sources include avocado, fresh wheat germ, and safflower oil, broccoli, leafy greens, peanuts, soybeans, whole grains, nuts, and seeds.

**Vitamin B1 (Thiamin) and Vitamin B2 (Riboflavin)** are both involved in your cells' energy production, and in nerve function. Food sources include low-fat dairy products, lean meat, leafy green vegetables, sea vegetables, whole grain breads and cereals, legumes, spinach, broccoli, acorn squash, watermelon, and sunflower seeds.

**Vitamin B3 (Niacin)** is essential for energy metabolism. It also supports normal vision, maintains healthy skin, and is key to a smoothly functioning nervous and digestive system. It's found in milk, eggs, meat, fish, legumes, poultry, spinach, avocado, and sweet potatoes.

**Pantothenic acid (Vitamin B5)** synthesizes neurotransmitters, steroid hormones, and hemoglobin. It's also involved in metabolizing glucose and fatty acids. Best sources are whole grains, breads, cereals, nuts, and beans.

**Pyridoxine (B6)** reduces muscle spasms, cramps, and skin inflammation. It also is essential for the production of serotonin. Low levels of this neurotransmitter are linked to pain and inflammation. Vitamin B6 is found in meat, fish, milk, eggs, whole grains, fresh vegetables, dried yeast, bananas, nuts, and potatoes.

**Folic acid (B9)** is a natural anti-inflammatory. Food sources include leafy greens, wheat germ, whole grains, nuts, eggs, bananas, oranges, legumes, and organ meats.

**Vitamin B12** is involved in the breakdown of fatty and amino acids and the synthesis of new cells. It maintains the sheath that surrounds and protects nerve fibers, and it may help prevent muscle weakness and neurological conditions, such as peripheral neuropathies. Best food sources are meat, fish, shellfish, poultry, dairy products, eggs, sea vegetables, and soy products.

**Biotin** works with the B vitamins to reduce muscle aches and pains. It's found in nuts, fruit, beef liver, egg yolks, milk, kidneys, brewer's yeast, and cauliflower.

**Vitamin D** is essential for metabolizing calcium. Dietary sources include vitamin D–fortified milk, sardines, fresh mackerel, herring, salmon, and shrimp.

## Minerals and Trace Elements

These inorganic chemical substances are also necessary for various body processes.

**Calcium** is essential for strong, dense bones. Adequate intake and absorption prevents the bone loss associated with osteoporosis. Calcium is also helpful if you have leg cramps. Food sources include low-fat dairy products, leafy greens, salmon, eggs, beans, nuts, tofu, and canned sardines.

**Magnesium** repairs and maintains your body cells. Good food sources are brown rice, millet, oats, soybeans, leafy greens, nuts, brewer's yeast, whole wheat flour, legumes, and milk.

**Zinc** is essential for wound healing, and for a healthy immune system. Zinc-rich foods include seafood, turkey, yogurt, lentils, tofu, green peas, green beans, ricotta cheese, lean meat, sunflower seeds, and garbanzo beans.

**Copper** can help reduce pain and inflammation. It also helps prevent free radical formation. The best source for this trace element is oysters; you can also get it from liver, shellfish, nuts, fruit, kidney, legumes, seeds, cereal, and potatoes.

**Selenium** works in concert with vitamin E to protect you against free radicals. Brazil nuts are the best source of selenium (one nut gives you all you need for the day); other sources are seafood, meat, and whole grains.

**Cobalt** promotes a healthy nervous system and maintains the sheath that surrounds your nerves, which can affect how pain is transmitted. Food sources include fresh leafy greens, meat, liver, milk, oysters, and clams.

**Chromium** acts as a helper to insulin. Considerable research exists on its ability to help diabetes, which is linked to many painful ailments. Food sources of chromium include legumes, soybeans, lima beans, pinto beans, miso, tofu, cooked greens, mushrooms, pumpkin seeds, red meat, and fish.

**Silicon,** important for bone formation in animals, is found in whole grain breads and cereals and root vegetables.

## Bromelain

This enzyme is an all-purpose anti-inflammatory. Promoted extensively throughout Europe for many forms of musculoskeletal injury, arthritis, menstrual cramps, and for use after surgery, it's also listed in the German E Monographs as an agent helpful in reducing post-traumatic swelling.

I suggest taking it in its natural form, rather than in supplements. The best source is pineapple juice. Try drinking one twelve-ounce glass of juice three times daily, or make yourself the delicious Pineapple Smoothie found on page 154. Bromelain may interact with blood-thinning medications, sedatives, and antibiotics.

## Fiber

Adequate fiber prevents and controls diabetes, helps lower cholesterol, prevents diverticulosis and hemorrhoids, and helps you maintain a healthy weight. The best sources are whole grains, raw vegetables and fruits, and legumes. You can also drink fresh vegetable juices (without added sugar).

# 15

## Manual Muscle Strategies

Practitioners of manual healing methods rely primarily on their hands to gather information, diagnose, and treat you. Using physical touch, pressure, and movement, they manipulate soft tissues, realign your body, promote endorphin release, and improve circulation. In so doing, they aim to bring localized areas of your body back to optimum health, and restore your body's overall equilibrium and well-being.

### Chiropractic

Spinal ailments—low back and neck pain—account for most chiropractic visits. Unfortunately, there isn't sufficient scientific data to prove the safety and effectiveness of chiropractic for *all* types of chronic pain and other ailments. I'm most likely to refer my patients to chiropractors for low back pain; that's the area where the research is strongest.

Currently, a number of major studies supported by the National Center for Complementary and Alternative Medicine of the National Institutes of Health are investigating the use of chiropractic for pain syndromes and other problems, so we should know more in the near future.

Most chiropractic visits involve adjustment or manipulation of your spine. There are (remote) risks associated with chiropractic care. For the most part, they are direct complications of spinal manipulation, such as ruptured discs, increased pain, paralysis, stroke, or other neurological problems. If you have fractures, cancer that has metastasized, or a structural anomaly of your spine, chiropractic is not a good idea.

## Osteopathy

Historically, osteopaths differed from conventional doctors because of their reliance on manipulation, nutrition, and lifestyle. Today, though, osteopathy is a separate but equal branch of conventional medicine; a growing number of osteopaths gravitate toward physiatry because of its focus on conservative management of the musculoskeletal system.

Osteopathic manipulation is used primarily for low back, neck, or joint pain, headaches, sports injuries, sciatica, and other musculoskeletal ailments. It can involve anything from gentle manipulation of your joints and spine, to light pressure on your muscles or other soft tissues, to high-velocity thrusts on your joints.

Other than a bit of soreness for a day or two, osteopathic manipulation has no side effects. However, if you have bone or joint disease, including cancer, infection, or osteoporosis, manipulation is probably not a good idea. The same is true if you've had spinal fusion, or have disk problems.

## Massage Therapy

Massage doesn't just feel good; it's an effective way to fight pain. When you're hurt, one of your natural defenses is to stiffen your muscles and joints. Massage relaxes tense muscles, so it relieves the pain. It also enhances mobility, improves your range of motion, and increases serotonin and endorphins, your body's natural painkillers. And by helping you relax, therapeutic massage also alleviates the psychological and emotional toll of pain.

Scientific research has shown massage therapy to be effective for back pain, cancer pain, anxiety, PMS, chronic fatigue syndrome, fibromyalgia, and headaches. In addition, massage can be helpful during pregnancy, labor, and childbirth.

Massage is not a good idea when you have a skin infection, fever, open wounds, or burns, or if performed directly over a tumor. If you have a low blood platelet count, massage may cause bruising.

## Shiatsu

Shiatsu (Japanese for "finger pressure") is based on the theory that illness is caused by a disturbance in vital energy (*qi* in Chinese and *ki* in Japanese). Shiatsu practitioners use their fingers, thumbs, palms, elbows, knees, and feet to massage and apply pressure to these points to unblock *ki*. Although there is little science to explain shiatsu's effects, one theory is that it may release endorphins, or reduce levels of adrenaline and other stress hormones.

## Rolfing

Rolfing is a form of deep tissue manipulation and rigorous massage, used to strengthen and realign your body. It focuses on your fascia, sheets of connective tissue that bind muscle fiber together, attach muscles and bones, shape and support your body, and cover your organs, nerves, and blood vessels, holding everything in place. Injury, emotional trauma, or poor posture can damage your fascia, throw your skeleton out of alignment, and cause pain. Rolfers attempt to stretch the distorted fascias back to normal, realigning your bones and muscles, and allowing your body to return to equilibrium.

# 16

—

# Nature's Remedies

Although they are very different, homeopathy and herbal medicine both rely on remedies derived from natural substances. Both are highly popular methods of self-care for painful conditions.

## Herbal Medicine

Herbal medicines are integral to complementary care. A growing number of scientific studies are being conducted to validate the effectiveness of specific herbs and some of the results are very encouraging. Herbs are used by a variety of practitioners; in addition, many people treat themselves. However, I strongly recommend consulting with your doctor before you try any herbal remedy. Many herbs can interact with medications and cause serious side effects. This is especially important if you are pregnant or breast-feeding, taking prescription medication, or undergoing chemotherapy or radiation therapy. And if you are going to have surgery, inform the surgeon and anesthesiologist about *all* medicines—including herbals—that you take.

Herbs aren't used only to treat disease. Many products support your body's ability to withstand disease and some of the stressors that might be precursors to illness.

Still, herbal remedies can be tricky. You can't assume that something is safe just because it's natural. Since passage of the Dietary Supplement Health and Education Act (DSHEA) in 1994, herbal products are not regulated by the Food and Drug Administration (FDA), except as dietary supplements. Therefore, they have not been tested in this country for therapeutic effectiveness or safety. As a result, herbal preparations vary widely in content, purity, and potency.

If you're thinking of giving herbal medicines a try, see your doctor first, so you don't delay receiving a proven treatment. Besides, certain ailments are best treated conventionally. For example, bacterial infections usually clear up rapidly when remedied with antibiotics. And herbal medicines are not meant as solo treatments for serious conditions.

The two most scientifically respected sources of herbal information are: *The Complete German Commission E Monographs: Therapeutic Guide to Herbal Medicines*, edited by Mark Blumenthal, and *PDR for Herbal Medicines*, edited by Georg Gruenwald et al.

## Homeopathy

Many homeopathic medicines are derived from herbal extracts, but homeopathy is not a form of herbalism. By the time any substance is a homeopathic remedy, it has been diluted to such a point that it no longer has any resemblance to the plant from which it came. And some homeopathic remedies are based on animal and mineral substances.

Homeopathic medicines, which are regulated by the FDA, aim to stimulate your body's innate ability to heal itself in a safe, gentle way, without using strong medications that have toxic side effects. You can buy many of them over the counter. Those used to treat serious conditions have to be dispensed under the care of a licensed practitioner.

Solid research about the effectiveness of homeopathy is hard to find, and skepticism about its validity is rampant. You can use homeopathy as an adjunct to conventional therapy.

# 17

# Exercise for Relief and Prevention

The healing power of exercise never ceases to amaze me. The general health benefits of exercise are well known. But every day in my practice, I see that exercise also effectively relieves pain. And, by reducing your risk of injuries, exercise can prevent pain from occurring in the first place.

Researchers have done laboratory experiments to show that exercise does indeed reduce pain. More impressive, though, are the clinical studies. A sampling of recent research from credible medical journals shows that patients with chronic pain syndromes, including low back pain, temporomandibular disorders (TMD), complex regional pain syndromes, tension-type headache, and irritable bowel syndrome, all benefited from aerobic exercise. In addition, aerobic exercise relieved the symptoms of fibromyalgia, and rheumatoid and osteoarthritis. And isometric strength training helped reduce neck and shoulder pain among women industrial workers who had work-related pain.

In addition, exercise may break a vicious cycle I often see with my patients: When you live with pain, particularly chronic pain, you're much more likely to suffer from depression. Then, when you're depressed and anxious, you are less able to tolerate pain. That's why your doctor may suggest that you take antidepressant medication for pain.

Instead of popping another pill, however, you may prevent yourself from spiraling into depression and more pain with regular exercise. Researchers have been studying the role of exercise in improving mental well-being for more than twenty years, and there is substantial evidence that exercise reduces depression. That's why exercise is sometimes called "Nature's Prozac."

It's never too late to start exercising. However, it's important to check with your physician before starting a new routine. If you have painful or debilitating ailments, your doctor can help you find a program that matches your level of fitness and physical condition.

I recommend that you develop a varied regimen that includes aerobic exercise, stretching or flexibility training, and strength or resistance training. Each of these major types of exercise provides different, worthwhile benefits. Besides, playing the "fitness field" can help prevent injuries and keep you from getting bored with your routine.

Aerobic exercise strengthens your heart and lungs, and improves your overall fitness by increasing your body's ability to use oxygen. Brisk walking, swimming, aerobic dancing, bicycling, running, dancing, jumping rope, cross-country skiing, and playing tennis are all aerobic exercise.

Stretching improves physical performance, increases the supply of blood and nutrients to your joints, reduces soreness, improves posture and balance, expands your range of motion, and decreases the risk of low back pain, torn ligaments, and muscle strain.

Strength training helps you avert injuries. Stronger muscles are less vulnerable. In addition, they better support weak joints, helping to prevent sore hips, knees, and shoulders. By stressing your muscles, you also stimulate bone growth, which can prevent osteoporosis. And resistance training is the best exercise for controlling or losing weight. Remember, if you're overweight, you're more vulnerable to injury and disease.

## Specific Exercises

THE PELVIC TILT
1. Lie flat on your back, with your knees bent and your feet flat on the floor.
2. Tighten your buttock and belly muscles.
3. Push your lower back and pelvis down against the floor, as if you were trying to squash a pea.
4. Hold the position for 3 seconds (count 1-2-3).
5. Begin with 5 repetitions and, as you get stronger, slowly increase the number of reps in intervals of 5.
6. As a variation, raise both arms over your head while you are in the pelvic tilt. Be sure to keep your lower back flat.

HALF SIT-UP
1. Lie on your back, with your knees slightly bent.
2. Cross your arms on your chest.

3. Slowly lift your head and shoulders off the floor, to about 45 degrees. Be sure to keep your lower back firmly on the floor.
4. Hold for a slow count to 6 and then lower.
5. Repeat 10 times.


LEG RAISES
1. Lie on the floor with your right knee bent and the right foot flat.
2. Slowly raise your left leg until it is perpendicular. Point your toes to the ceiling.
3. As you exhale, keep your leg straight and lower it to the floor. Be sure to keep your lower back on the floor.
4. Repeat, 5 times on each side.


SEATED LOW BACK STRETCH
1. Sit in a chair with your knees apart. Your feet should reach the floor.
2. Bend forward toward the floor. Don't bend so far that it hurts, but you should feel a comfortable stretch in your lower back.
3. Hold for 15 to 20 seconds.


KNEE TO CHEST RAISE
1. Lie on your back on the floor, with both knees bent and your feet flat.
2. Grasp your right leg below the knee and pull it toward your right shoulder.
3. Hold for 5 seconds. You should feel the stretch in your lower back or buttock area.
4. Repeat this exercise 3 times with each leg.


LOWER BACK-PIRIFORMIS STRETCH
1. Lie on your back on the floor, with your legs outstretched.
2. Grasp one knee from behind and pull it toward your chest.
3. Using your hands, pull the knee toward the opposite hip.
4. As you move your knee, slowly straighten the leg, pointing your toes toward the floor.
5. Hold for 10 seconds, then relax.
6. Repeat this exercise 3 times with each leg.


SIDE STRETCHES
1. Sit or stand in a comfortable position.
2. Bend your head slowly to one side, bringing the ear close to the shoulder.
3. Relax and hold for 5 to 10 seconds.

4. Return your head to center.
5. Repeat on the other side.


## CHIN TUCK

1. Sit or stand comfortably. Pinch your shoulder blades together.
2. Bring your chin in line with your right shoulder and hip.
3. Look straight ahead, not up or down.
4. Relax and hold for 5 to 20 seconds; then, return your head to center.
5. Repeat on the left side.


## HAMSTRING STRETCH

1. Stand up, with the heel of your injured leg resting on a stool or chair that is about 15 inches off the ground. Your knee should be straight.
2. Bend forward from your hips until you feel a stretch in the back of your thigh. Do not twist, round your shoulders, or bring your head toward your toe. Your aim is to stretch your hamstrings, not your low back.
3. Hold 30 to 60 seconds.
4. Repeat 3 times.


## PATELLAR MOBILITY EXERCISE

Do not attempt this if it's painful to move your kneecap.
1. Sit with your injured leg straight out in front of you. Keep the muscles in your thigh relaxed.
2. With your index finger and thumb, gently press your kneecap down toward your foot.
3. Hold 10 seconds and return to starting position.
4. Pull your kneecap toward your waist.
5. Hold 10 seconds and return to starting position.
6. Try to gently push your kneecap in, toward your other leg.
7. Hold 10 seconds.
8. Repeat these steps 5 times.


## QUADRICEPS STRETCH

1. Stand an arm's length away from a wall, with your uninjured side facing the wall. Brace yourself on the wall with your hand.
2. With your other hand, grab the ankle of your injured leg and pull your heel toward your buttocks. Don't arch or twist.
3. Hold 30 seconds.
4. Repeat 3 times.

## QUADRICEPS SET

1. Lie on a firm flat surface, with your legs straight out.
2. Tense your left extended knee and push down the kneecap.
3. Maintain this pressure for 10 seconds and then release.
4. Repeat with right leg.
5. Repeat 10 times with each leg. Do it 4 times a day.

## LEG LIFTS

1. Sit comfortably in a chair.
2. Straighten your right knee (extension) and raise your leg as high as the seat of your chair.
3. Hold in this position for 10 seconds and then lower your leg.
4. Repeat with left leg.
5. Do 5 times with each leg.

## STRAIGHT LEG RAISE

1. Sit on the floor with your injured leg straight out. Keep your other leg bent, with the foot flat on the floor.
2. Flex the toes of your injured leg toward you as far as you can.
3. Raise your leg 6 to 8 inches off the floor.
4. Hold 3 to 5 seconds and slowly lower your leg.
5. Do 3 sets of 10.

## HEEL SLIDE

1. Sit on the floor with your legs straight out in front of you.
2. Bend your knee, slowly sliding the heel of your injured leg toward your buttocks.
3. Straighten your leg and repeat 20 times.

## PRONE KNEE FLEXION

1. Lie on your stomach with a rolled-up towel under your injured thigh, just above the knee.
2. Slowly, bend your injured knee and try to touch your heel to your buttock.
3. Return your leg to the starting position.
4. Repeat 10 times.
5. As this becomes easier, you can add 3 to 5 pound weights.

## WALL SQUAT

1. Stand with your back, shoulders, and head against a wall. Your feet should be one foot away from the wall, about shoulder-width apart. Try to keep your shoulders relaxed.

2. Keep your head against the wall and slowly squat. You should be almost in a sitting position, but your thighs will not be quite parallel to the floor.
3. Hold for 10 seconds.
4. Slide back up.
5. Repeat 10 times.

CALF STRETCH WITH TOWEL
1. Sit on a firm surface, with your injured leg straight out in front of you.
2. Loop a towel around the ball of your foot.
3. Pull the towel toward you.
4. Hold 30 seconds, then relax.
5. Repeat 3 times.

STANDING CALF STRETCH
1. Face the wall, with both hands at about eye level on the wall.
2. With your uninjured leg forward, put the injured leg back about 12 to 18 inches. Keep your leg straight with your heel on the floor.
3. Bend the knee of the forward leg and lean into the wall until you feel a stretch in your calf muscle.
4. Hold 30 to 60 seconds, then relax.
5. Repeat 3 times.

ACTIVE RANGE-OF-MOTION OF THE ANKLE
1. Sit or lie down with your legs straight out.
2. Bend your ankle to move the foot up and down, in and out, and in circles. Do not bend your knee. Push hard in all directions.
3. Repeat 20 times in each direction.

HEEL RAISES
1. Stand with your hands on a counter, table, or chair for balance.
2. Raise yourself up onto your toes, then slowly lower.
3. Do 2 sets of 10.

SITTING TOE RAISES
1. Sit with your feet flat on the floor.
2. Keep your heel on the floor and raise the toes off the floor.
3. Do 3 sets of 10.
4. When you can do this with ease, progress to standing toe raises (see below).

STANDING TOE RAISES
1. Stand with your feet flat on the floor.
2. Rock back onto your heels and lift your toes off the floor.
3. Hold 5 seconds.
4. Do 3 sets of 10.

WRIST RANGE-OF-MOTION
1. Bend your wrist forward and backward as far as you can.
2. Repeat 10 times.
3. Do 3 sets of 10.

FOREARM RANGE-OF-MOTION
1. With your arm at your side, bend your elbow 90 degrees.
2. Face your palm upward and hold 5 seconds.
3. Slowly turn your palm facedown and hold 5 seconds.
4. Do 3 sets of 10.

ELBOW RANGE-OF-MOTION
1. With your arm by your side, palm up, bring your hand up toward your shoulder. In other words, flex your elbow.
2. Straighten out, or extend, your elbow as far as you can.
3. Do 3 sets of 10.

WRIST STRENGTHENING EXERCISES
Start these exercises by holding a soup can or hammer handle. As you get stronger, you can increase the weight.
Wrist flexion:
1. Hold the weight with your palm up.
2. Slowly bend your wrist up.
3. Slowly lower the weight and return to the starting position.
4. Do 3 sets of 10.
Wrist extension:
1. Hold the weight with your palm facing down.
2. Gently bend your wrist up.
3. Slowly lower the weight and return to the starting position.
4. Do 3 sets of 10.
Wrist radial deviation strengthening:
1. Hold the weight with your wrist sideways and your thumb up.
2. Gently bend your wrist up with your thumb reaching toward the ceiling.

3. Slowly lower to the starting position.
4. Do not move your forearm throughout this exercise.
5. Do 3 sets of 10.

Pronation and supination strengthening:
1. Hold the weight with your elbow bent 90 degrees.
2. Slowly rotate your hand, first palm up and then palm down.
3. Do 3 sets of 10.

## STAIR STRETCH

1. Stand with the ball of your injured foot on a stair.
2. Slowly lower your heel toward the step below until you feel a good stretch in the arch of your foot.
3. Hold 30 seconds, then relax.
4. Repeat 3 times.

## ONE LEG BALANCE

1. Stand with both feet together. Take a couple of deep breaths, in and out.
2. Bending it at the knee, lift your uninjured leg and try to balance on the injured side.
3. Hold for 30 seconds.
4. When you can do that, try closing your eyes and balancing.
5. Repeat 3 times.

## HEEL BOUNCE

1. While standing, raise and lower your heels, one at a time.
2. Keep your toes on the ground at all times.
3. Do this 20 times.

## FOOT BOUNCE

1. Sit down with your feet flat.
2. Keep your heels on the ground and raise your feet, one at a time.
3. Repeat 20 times.

## PLANTAR FASCIA STRETCH

1. Put your hands on a wall and lean on them, with your uninjured foot on the floor in front of you and your injured foot placed behind you so that the heel is not touching the floor.
2. Gently bounce or bob up and down.

GASTROC STRETCH
1. Stand on the edge of a step.
2. Rise up on your toes and lower yourself slowly as far as you can until you feel a stretch in your calf.
3. Hold one or two seconds.
4. Repeat 10 to 20 times.

SOLEUS STRETCH
Same as above, except with knees bent.

BICYCLE STRETCH
1. Lie on your side with your top leg straight.
2. Bend your knee up toward your nose until you feel a stretch in your hamstring (in back of your thigh).
3. With your top leg, start pedaling as if you were on a bicycle.
4. Repeat 10 to 30 times with each leg.

# 18

---

# Mind-Body Therapies

Your mind and your body are inseparable. Your experience of pain, and the meaning you give to it, depends to a great extent on your emotional state. The therapies in this chapter take that all-important fact as their starting point.

### Relaxation and Meditation Techniques

Tense muscles and anxiety make pain worse. With some ailments, such as headaches or low back pain, tension may even be the root of the problem. Relaxation, meditation, and imaging help you reduce pain by altering your mental state, and reducing tension. They are also particularly useful if your pain comes from cancer or another disease that makes you fearful.

### Belly Breathing

I recommend that you try this simple exercise once or twice a day for ten or twenty minutes. You'll find that it reduces stress and brings you a sense of inner peace.

1. Find a comfortable position. You can lie on your back with your knees bent, or sit cross-legged with your back straight.
2. Put one hand on your belly, just below your navel, and the other on your chest. As you breathe in through your nose, your belly—and nothing else—should move. Do not push your belly out; this is a small, gentle movement.
3. As you exhale, your belly should contract. Imagine pain and stress leaving your body with each breath.

## Relaxation

With Progressive Muscle Relaxation, you systematically focus on reducing muscle tension in all of your major muscle groups by first tensing and then relaxing them.

1. Set up a relaxing environment by putting on soft music, dimming the lights, lighting a candle, or doing anything else you find calming.
2. Lie on a flat surface—the floor, a couch, or a bed. Be sure to wear comfortable clothes and take your shoes off.
3. Starting at your feet and working up, gradually tighten and relax all the muscles in your body. Don't forget your neck, face, and head.
4. Lie, completely relaxed, until you are ready to get up.

## Meditation

There are many forms of meditation. In addition to seated forms, there are moving types of meditation, such as tai chi, the walking meditation of Zen Buddhism, and yoga.

Whatever type of meditation you choose, your goal is to quiet the hubbub of your mind, to achieve a state of relaxed but alert awareness. This brings profound psychological and physical benefits. Research-documented effects of relaxation and meditation include reduced pain, anxiety, depression, and use of pain medications in patients with chronic diseases, as well as lower blood pressure and stress relief.

It takes a while to learn this powerful therapy. You'll probably have more success if you make it a habit and do it at the same time every day.

1. Wear comfortable clothing that is not restrictive. (No tight jeans or compressive bra.)
2. Sit somewhere quiet, warm, and well ventilated. Assume an erect sitting position that helps you relax but keeps you awake. Keep your back straight and your shoulders relaxed. Use a pillow for support, if you need it. Rest your hands in your lap or on your knees, whichever is more comfortable.
3. Close your eyes. Breathe deeply, in and out through your nose.
4. Slowly and consciously, begin to relax your body—your shoulders, arms, hands, fingers, toes, feet, legs, neck, and face.
5. Begin to focus on one word or phrase.
6. If other thoughts come into your head, take notice of them and let them go. Don't get upset if you can't stop thinking; no one can. After some practice, repeating your phrase will help keep other thoughts at bay.

7. Continue to meditate for fifteen minutes to one-half hour.
8. When you are ready to stop, take a deep breath in, exhale, gently stretch your limbs, and open your eyes.

## Autogenic Training

By directing your mind to physical sensations, this technique promotes release of stress and pain. It's best done three times a day, after each meal.

Get into a relaxed state. Then, in your mind's eye, put yourself in a peaceful environment. Focus on one of the following: easy, natural breathing; warmth in your arms and legs; a sensation of heaviness throughout your body; coolness on your forehead; or the steady beat of your heart.

## Imagery

With imagery, often referred to as visualization, you use the power of your imagination to help you change your physical or emotional state. You can do this with audiotapes, music, or meditation. The idea is to encourage your mind to focus on pictures that represent changes you want to occur in your body. What's key is that you come up with images that are personal and meaningful for you.

Imagery has been used successfully for pain control, especially for cancer and other chronic pain, tension and migraine headaches, and neck and back pain. It helps reduce anxiety and depression, and can relieve the side effects of surgery, radiation, and chemotherapy.

Here's a simple way to start doing imagery on your own. First, get into a relaxed, meditative state (see above). Then:

- Turn your pain into an image. For example, if you have burning pain, imagine it as a fire. Then picture yourself fighting the pain. In this example, call in the fire brigade to quench the fire with lots of cold water.
- Picture a place where you feel happy—see it, smell the air, feel the breeze, listen to the sounds around you. Then put yourself into the picture as a pain-free woman.

## Biofeedback

This is a method for learning how to become aware of and control what are usually involuntary, or autonomic, body processes. Autonomic pain responses include skin temperature, muscle tension, pulse, blood pressure, and heart rate. It's probably best to start with a course of biofeedback training. However, once you master this technique, you should be able to do it on your own.

Biofeedback is often used for stress-related illnesses or for ailments related to muscle tension. A recent study found that biofeedback was a successful treatment for neuropathic, or nerve-related, pain. Here's an example of a simple "low tech" biofeedback exercise:

1. In a quiet place, stretch out and get into a relaxed state by progressively and consciously working your way through all of your muscles, from your toes to your head. If it helps you relax, you can listen to music as you do this exercise.
2. Be sure you are breathing deeply; in other words, that your belly, not your chest, is moving up and down.
3. Once you are relaxed, focus on bringing the blood to your hands. You'll know you are successful when your hands start to feel warm.

## Hypnosis

Hypnosis, once dismissed as the mumbo jumbo of magic shows, can help you harness the power of your mind to reduce pain. By entering a state of deep relaxation and eliminating all distractions, you allow your subconscious mind to take over. Because you are better able to concentrate, and because your subconscious is more receptive to suggestion, you can direct your brain to meet your needs, whether it's coping with pain or reducing anxiety.

In 1995, the National Institutes of Health, in a Technology Assessment Conference Statement, endorsed the use of hypnosis as an adjunct to conventional treatment in alleviating cancer pain. In research published in 1998, approximately one-third of patients with chronic pain syndromes, including low back pain, fibromyalgia syndrome, temporomandibular disorders, complex regional pain syndromes, tension-type headaches, and irritable bowel syndrome, got some benefit from hypnosis. And hypnosis reduces anxiety and depression, which helps you sleep, increases energy, and makes pain more bearable.

## Aromatherapy

Fragrances stimulate a part of your brain that affects emotion, blood pressure, heart rate, and breathing. Aromatherapy, which means "treatment using scents," is a branch of herbal medicine that uses concentrated plant oils, called essential oils, to heal. Aromatherapy can relax your mind and body, relieve pain, and restore balance, although it may take several weeks of treatment before you see results.

## Music Therapy

Music therapy consists of listening to music, making music, or creating music. Chanting, an integral part of the Hasidic, Tibetan, Buddhist, Native American, and other traditions, is also associated with healing. During my acupuncture treatments, I routinely play traditional Chinese "Five Element Music."

Music can reduce anxiety and fear, which both aggravate pain, and it helps relieve fatigue and depression. In addition to these indirect effects, music decreases pain response. For example, a study of women in labor found that music diverted their attention from their pain. Similarly, music can significantly decrease hospitalized cancer patients' awareness of pain. When music is played in operating rooms, patients have fewer postsurgical complications and less pain. And there's also evidence that the use of music during postoperative care can reduce pain reactions and requests for pain medication.

## Humor Therapy

Research shows that laughter has physiological effects. It may reduce pain, lower levels of stress hormones, boost immune function, trigger endorphin release, and decrease blood pressure.

We can't say conclusively that laughing speeds healing. But it can distract you from your pain. Besides, it's free, and it has no side effects!

## Yoga

The goal of a yoga practice is to prevent illness by maintaining balance within your mind and body. Like many complementary therapies, there isn't a lot of solid research about yoga and pain, but studies have shown that yoga may lower the incidence and severity of migraine headaches, reduces chronic neck and shoulder pain, and helps relieve symptoms of carpal tunnel syndrome and osteoarthritis. Yoga may also help if you have lower back pain, other nerve disorders, menstrual problems, joint pain, and chronic pain.

If you're interested in yoga, mention it to your doctor, especially if you have high blood pressure, arthritis, or spinal disc injuries. Begin by taking lessons from an experienced teacher. Performing postures incorrectly can cause muscle strain or tears.

## Yoga Postures

ALTERNATING LEG LIFTS
1. Lie down on your back.
2. Press the small of your back onto the floor. This activates your abdominal muscles.
3. Take a deep breath in; at the same time, slowly and smoothly raise your left leg.
4. Keep your leg steady.
5. Maintain your back flat on the floor while keeping your body relaxed. Hold the position for a few breaths.
6. Gradually, lower your leg and exhale.
7. Repeat with the right leg.
8. Repeat the exercise 10 times, alternating legs.

BOAT POSE
1. Lie on your stomach, with your arms stretched out in front of you and your forehead on the floor.
2. Breathe in and lift your arms, legs, and head.
3. Hold for 3 seconds, then breathe out and relax.
4. Repeat 1 to 3 times.

As you get stronger, try these two variations:
1. Get into Boat Pose. On an exhale, sweep your arms out sideways. Hold for 3 seconds, then return to Boat Pose. Exhale again and relax.
2. Get into Boat Pose. On an exhale, sweep your arms behind you, clasping your hands. Hold for 3 seconds, then return to Boat Pose. Exhale and relax.

BOW POSE
1. Lie on your stomach with forehead on the floor and your arms at your sides.
2. On an exhalation, bend your knees, bringing your feet up toward your buttocks.

3. Reach back with your arms and take hold of your left ankle with your left hand and your right ankle with the right hand. Flex your feet.
4. Inhale deeply. As you exhale, raise your head, chest and legs. Try to get your thighs off the floor. Your ribs and pelvis should be lifted so your belly bears the full weight of your body. Hold for a few breaths and release.

CAT POSE
1. Get onto your hands and knees, with your hands under your shoulders and your knees under your hips.
2. As you inhale, curl your toes into the floor, lift your head, and drop your belly, gently arching your back.
3. As you exhale, flatten your toes, drop your head, and round your back, pushing it up toward the ceiling.
4. Repeat this sequence 10 times.

CHAIR POSE
1. Stand upright, feet together, hands at sides. Imagine your head stretching up toward the ceiling.
2. As you exhale, bend your knees until your thighs are perpendicular to your shins.
3. Bend your torso forward, as if you were going to sit in a chair.
4. Raise your arms up over your head, keeping them apart with your palms facing.
5. Continue breathing, and hold, working up to 30 seconds.

CHILD'S POSE
1. Sit on your knees, with your buttocks resting on your feet. Your knees should be together and your feet slightly apart.
2. Inhale deeply and lift your head toward the ceiling, elongating your spine.
3. Bend at your hips, moving your torso forward until your forehead rests on the floor. Tuck your chin into your chest to lengthen your neck.
4. Place your hands alongside your torso, palms up.
5. Allow gravity to absorb the weight of your body. Relax and breathe deeply, feeling your back expand with every breath.

COBRA
Stop this pose if you experience any low back pain.
1. Lie on your belly with your forehead touching the floor. Bend your

elbows and place your hands flat on the floor, underneath your shoulders. Keep your elbows tucked into your side.

2. Press your pelvis into the floor and bring your shoulder blades together.

3. Inhale and roll your head back, slowly raising your forehead, nose, and chin. Continuing to inhale, raise your shoulders and upper back off the floor. Roll your neck back and look up. Keep your pelvis and legs pressing into the floor. Use your hands only for balance. Breathe in and out a few times.

4. If you can, on your next inhalation, use your arms to push yourself up higher, but keep your belly button on the floor.

5. On an exhalation, slowly unroll—first your belly, then your upper body, then your chin, nose, and forehead—back to the floor.

## DOWNWARD-FACING DOG

1. This traditional pose is excellent for strengthening bones in your upper and lower body. Get onto all fours on the floor, with your hands directly under your shoulders and your knees directly under your hips.

2. Point your fingers forward and spread them apart.

3. Curl your toes under, and gradually straighten your legs, raising your buttocks into the air. Stop before your legs are completely straight.

4. With your knees still slightly bent, push your buttocks toward the wall in back of you. Slowly straighten your legs until your body forms a "V," and your heels approach the floor (they may not reach).

5. Let your head and neck hang loosely. Keep pressing your buttocks toward the ceiling and at the same time, bring your chest between your arms.

6. Hold the pose for 10 to 15 seconds, pressing your hands into the floor.

7. Release on an exhalation, returning to all fours.

8. As you get stronger, hold the pose longer.

## GARUDASANA (EAGLE POSTURE)

1. Stand upright with your feet together.

2. Bend your left knee and wrap it around your right calf with your toes curled around your calf.

3. Wrap your left arm around the right arm in a similar fashion.

4. Join the hands together, raise them and point them outward like a beak.

5. Repeat with the opposite side.

GUPTASANA (CONCEALED POSTURE)
1. Sit on the floor, legs outstretched, with your heels and toes touching.
2. Bend your left leg in until you are sitting on your foot.
3. Using your hands to raise yourself up, bring in your right leg and sit on your right foot. So you are now sitting on your feet, in a cross-legged position.
4. Rest with your hands palms up on your knees.
5. Look straight ahead.

HEAD TO KNEE POSE
1. Sit straight with your legs straight in front of you.
2. Inhale, and bring both arms up, shoulders next to your ears. Stretch your head up toward the ceiling.
3. Exhale and lean forward from your hips. Keeping your back and legs straight, reach forward and grab your shins, ankles, or feet, depending on your flexibility. Your goal is to bring your chest as close to your knees as possible.
4. Hold for 30 seconds.
5. Inhale and bring up your head and shoulders, still holding on to your feet.
6. Exhale and go back down. Hold 30 seconds.
7. Inhale and bring your arms back up next to your ears. Slowly come up as you press your buttocks and legs into the floor. If you have back problems, just slide your hands up your legs as you come back to sitting.

KAGASANA (CROW POSTURE)
1. Squat on the ground by bending your legs and resting your rear on your heels.
2. Cup your hands over your knees, keeping your neck straight.
3. Gaze forward and hold.

KNEELING FOOT STRETCH
1. Begin on your hands and knees. Your legs and feet should be together, with the tops of your feet and your ankles on the floor.
2. Exhale and walk your hands back, placing them on your knees.
3. Sit back on your heels.
4. Using your hands if necessary, curl your toes into the floor.
5. Allow the weight of your body to settle onto your toes. Go slowly and stop if you feel any pain.
6. Hold for 1 or 2 breaths.

LOCUST POSE

If you have low back problems, consult your doctor before trying this.

1. Lie flat on your stomach on a mat or blanket on the floor.
2. Make your hands into fists and put them under your body, inside your hips and near your ovaries.
3. Keep your chin and upper body on the floor and, exhaling, raise your legs as high as you can without hurting yourself. Keep your feet together and your legs straight.
4. Breathe deeply through your nose. Hold for as long as you can, working up to 1 to 3 minutes.
5. Then, while exhaling, lower your legs, make a pillow out of your hands, rest your head and relax, breathing deeply. Allow yourself to melt into the floor.

MODIFIED BRIDGE POSE

1. Lie on your back on a mat or blanket on the floor.
2. Bend your knees and put your feet on the floor close to your buttocks, keeping them parallel and about hip width apart.
3. With your arms beside you, palms down, exhale and press your feet firmly into the floor as you slowly raise your hips and back off the floor.
4. Hold, making sure that your knees are pointing forward.
5. Meanwhile, squeeze your pelvic floor muscles tight and hold while you slowly breathe in and out 3 times.
6. When you're ready to release, slowly roll down, one vertebra at a time.

OVERHEAD ARM EXTENSION (URDHVA HASTASANA)

1. Stand straight with your feet parallel and your arms at your sides. This promotes blood flow to the hands.
2. Raise your arms out in front of you with your elbows and fingers straight and your palms facing the floor.
3. Slowly raise your arms above your head, inhaling through your nose.
4. Keep your throat and shoulders relaxed.
5. Hold 15 to 30 seconds. Continue to breathe through your nose.
6. As you exhale, slowly lower your arms to your sides.

PASCHIMOTTANASANA (POSTERIOR-STRETCH POSTURE)

Do not attempt this posture if you have backache, cervical spondylitis, or sciatica.

1. Sit on the floor with your legs together, stretched out in front of you.
2. Raise both arms above your head and take a deep breath.

3. Exhale as you bend over and reach for your ankles. If possible, try for your toes.
4. Continuing to bend forward as far as possible, try to touch your forehead to your knees.

SANKATASANA (CONTRACTED POSTURE)
1. Stand with your feet together and your arms at your sides with palms facing in.
2. Shift your weight to your right foot and twist your left leg over your right one.
3. Raise your arms, interlock your fingers, and twist your hands so that your knuckles face the front and back, rather than the sides, of your body.
4. Hold for 15 to 30 seconds.
5. Repeat with the other side.

SHAVASANA (CORPSE POSTURE)
1. Lie on your back with your legs stretched out, about a foot apart, so your hips are relaxed.
2. Put your arms at your sides, a few inches away from your body. Your palms may be up or down, whichever is more comfortable.
3. Close your eyes and relax.

SIDDHASAN (PERFECT POSTURE)
1. Sit on the floor with your legs stretched out and apart.
2. Bring the heel of your left foot in, toward your groin.
3. Bring in your right foot and wedge the toes of each foot between your thighs and calves.
4. Place your hands on your knees, palms up, and gaze straight ahead.
5. Inhale and exhale deeply and hold as long as you comfortably can.

SPINAL TWIST
1. Sit up tall in a comfortable cross-legged position, with your hands on your knees.
2. Put your left hand in back of you, fingers facing back.
3. Inhale. Then, on the exhale, slowly twist, moving your right hand to your left knee. Turn your entire body to the left, including your head. Gaze back and to the left.
4. With each inhalation, stretch up through your spine. On each exhalation, see if you can extend the twist.

5. Return to the front on an exhale.
6. Repeat on the opposite side.

## STANDING FORWARD BEND
1. Stand upright; lift your arms over your head with your palms facing forward and stretch upwards.
2. Take a couple of deep breaths. On an exhalation, bend slowly forward.
3. Rest your fingertips or palms on either side of your feet and inhale. If you have lower back problems, keep your knees slightly bent.
4. Continue to breathe, sinking down a bit further on each exhalation. Hold, allowing gravity to lengthen your spine.
5. On an inhalation, press your feet into the floor and slowly roll back up.

## STANDING YOGA MUDRA
1. Stand with your legs apart and your arms at your sides.
2. Inhale and raise your arms in front of you.
3. Exhale and sweep your arms around in back of you, squeezing your shoulder blades. Interlace your fingers and begin to raise your arms up as far as you can.
4. Pushing your chest forward, gradually bend forward from the hips. Push your buttocks back and continue moving down from the hips, extending your torso forward and then down, bringing your head toward the floor. At the same time, you continue to raise your arms away from your buttocks. You can bend your knees to relieve any pressure on your lower back.
5. Hold for 10 to 20 seconds.
6. Pushing your feet into the floor, slowly roll up, bringing your arms down as you do. Allow your head to come up last.
7. Unclasp your hands and slowly return your arms to your sides.

## TREE POSE
1. Stand with your feet together and your arms at your sides.
2. Shift your weight to your right foot and, using your hands, place your left foot on your right ankle, calf, or thigh (whichever you can reach).
3. Find a point of focus on the floor or wall in front of you.
4. Place your palms together in front of your heart and raise them overhead, with elbows straight.
5. Balance evenly on the inner and outer edges of your right foot.
6. Slowly push your raised leg more to the side and back, opening your hip.

7. For better balance, tighten your abdominal muscles.
8. Hold for 15 to 30 seconds.
9. Repeat with the other side.

## TRUNK EXTENSION (DANDASANA)

1. Sit in a chair.
2. With arms at your sides, press the palms of your hands into your seat. Do not tense your shoulders or neck.
3. Press your shoulders back and down.
4. Hold for 30 seconds.
5. Breathe through your nose.
6. Relax and repeat.

## UTKATASANA (SQUATTING POSTURE)

1. Squat on the ground, balanced on your feet, with your elbows resting on your knees.
2. Intertwine your fingers and rest your chin on them.
3. Shift weight completely to your toes.
4. Hold for 30 to 45 seconds.

## VAJRASANA (ADAMANTINE POSTURE)

1. Sit on your knees.
2. Keep your back straight and place your hands on your knees.
3. Look straight ahead.
4. Hold 20 to 60 seconds, then release.

## VIRASANA (HERO'S POSTURE)

1. Kneel on the floor with your knees together and your feet about 18 inches apart.
2. Rest your buttocks on the floor. If you can't reach the floor, use a small pillow or rolled-up towel under your buttocks. Do not put any weight on your feet. Your feet should be on the sides of your thighs, with the inner side of each calf touching the outer side of its respective thigh.
3. Keep your toes pointing back and touching the floor.
4. Put your hands on your knees palms facing up. With each hand, form a circle with your thumb and index finger and keep your other fingers extended.
5. Hold the position, breathing deeply, as long as you can.

# 19

## Acupuncture and Reflexology

### Acupuncture

Since I completed my training in medical acupuncture, I have incorporated this indispensable art into my everyday practice, with fantastic results. I believe it is one of the safest, most effective tools in the pain relief arsenal. Its lack of side effects is another big advantage. Still, like most complementary therapies, I see it as an adjunct to medical care, not a substitute.

A variety of techniques fall under the rubric of acupuncture. What they have in common is that they all stimulate locations on the skin called acupuncture points. These points are the gateways to your meridians, through which your *qi*, or vital energy, flows. There are points connecting to every part of the body and to every organ. The continuous flow of *qi* is vital to your health. Pain is also the result of congested *qi*. By getting the *qi* moving again, acupuncture reduces swelling, relieves pain, and promotes healing.

Of all the complementary medical practices, acupuncture may just be the most thoroughly researched and well documented. When master acupuncturist Dr. Joseph Helms conducted a comprehensive, worldwide literature survey of all human clinical research studies relating to acupuncture, he found that 25 percent of all studies focused on pain-related disorders, with as many as 65 percent of them related to musculoskeletal disease. In short, acupuncture and pain is a well-studied area.

Two highly respected groups—the World Health Organization and a Consensus Panel convened by the National Institutes of Health—have endorsed the use of acupuncture, either alone or in combination with other treatments, for a variety of ailments. It's appropriate for many painful conditions, including sinusitis, neck, myofascial, and low back pain, headaches, tennis elbow, tendinitis, sciatica, osteoarthritis, postoperative dental pain, menstrual cramps, fibromyalgia, and carpal tunnel syndrome.

Using acupuncture also reduces the need for conventional painkilling drugs so it reduces the risk of their side effects, too. By combining painkillers and acupuncture we can bring complete pain relief to some patients. Acupuncture also helps people relax, reduces anxiety, and relieves spasms.

### Acupressure

Acupressure, a needle-less form of treatment, is another part of the system of traditional Chinese medicine. Acupressure is also thought to release blocked vital energy, or *qi*, allowing your body to heal itself. However, because it does not involve penetration of the skin, acupressure is not as potent or precise. Still, it has one big advantage: you can do it yourself. Here is what I teach my patients to do:

Use your index finger or fingers, your thumb or your whole hand. Gently explore the specific acupressure point until you find a slight indentation. (Points on your hands and feet are under thicker skin, so you may need to probe a bit more to find them.) Press the point firmly and steadily for about 30 seconds until you feel a dull ache, or a tingling that spreads around the area. Strong pressure that causes pain is not necessary or helpful. You can use direct pressure, a circular massaging motion, or both. Maintain the pressure for another 30 to 60 seconds; you may feel the tension under your fingers relax. Then, release. The dull ache may continue for a few minutes. Meanwhile, move on to the other points you wish to massage.

If a point feels extremely sensitive, don't work on it for very long. It may take several sessions for it to release. For chronic ailments, try five minutes twice a day. For acute problems, such as migraines, you can work for a minute or two on each point; then stop. If necessary, you can go back to those points after a few minutes.

Avoid acupressure points on your legs, belly, and in the web between your thumb and first finger during pregnancy. You should also avoid working points on your legs if you have varicose veins or phlebitis.

### Reflexology

Although there are similarities, reflexology is not the same as acupressure. This form of regional massage focuses on specific points only on your ears, hands, and feet. Still, the locations of reflex points and acupuncture points overlap considerably. And both techniques share the idea that applying pressure to these points will ease pain or promote healing in other areas of your body.

The jury is still out when it comes to solid scientific evidence for the effectiveness of reflexology in treating specific disorders. But because pain is so intimately interwoven with tension and anxiety, I recommend reflexology to my patients as a nonpharmaceutical, noninvasive means of reducing pain through relaxation.

Reflexology is a complementary therapy; it's not a substitute for medical treatment. If you're in pain, see your medical doctor first to be sure you don't have a condition that needs conventional treatment. And although reflexology is quite safe, discuss it with your doctor if you have a foot injury, clots, phlebitis, or other vascular problems in your legs.

The technique I prefer for applying pressure to reflex points was imparted to me by an experienced reflexology master, Beryl Crane:

- The Rotating Knuckle, Finger, Thumb Pressure Technique:
    1. Explore the area to find the indentation where the point lies.
    2. Take the pad of your thumb, finger, or knuckle and gently apply it to the reflex point. Avoid any fingernail contact with point.
    3. Maintaining constant pressure, firmly press the point. You may feel a dull ache.
    4. Simultaneously rotate around the point in a clockwise direction.
    5. Continue pressure for another 30 to 60 seconds, then release.
    6. Move on to the next point.

Other techniques you can use include:

- Rubbing or friction—Use your thumb and forefinger to pincer the point (i.e., put the thumb on one side and the forefinger on the other) and rub. If you're working the edges of your foot, use your palms.
- Kneading—This technique works well for your heels, or other thick-skinned areas. Make a fist and use your knuckles in a circular motion on the point. Or knead the area like dough.
- Walking—When you want to apply gentle pressure to a large area, such as the top of your hand or foot, put your thumb on one side of your hand or foot and two or three fingers on the other. Start at the toes or fingers and "finger-walk" along your hand or foot, ending at your ankle or wrist.

# The Future of Pain Management for Women

In writing this book, I seek to validate what you probably already know—that there are pain issues unique to you, as a woman. I also hope that the book will serve as an inspiration to my esteemed colleagues in medicine to keep an open mind, to continue to recognize the importance of mind *and* body in pain management, and to recognize the diversity of human experience. Men and women are fundamentally different, and they require a customized, individualized approach to pain management.

Medical care has changed enormously over the last few decades. Scientists have made astounding leaps in comprehending the basic mechanisms of illness and pain. And treatments such as organ transplants and genetic therapy—once only possible in the realm of science fiction—are now an everyday reality.

To a great extent, though, pain is still a black box. Still, the newborn field of gender-based research has begun to bear fruit. Perhaps nowhere else in contemporary medical science are the results so likely to alleviate human suffering. If we put our hearts and minds into advancing gender medicine, the future will be bold, exciting, and rewarding. I believe that we must press forward on many fronts.

Gender is a basic human variable that we have to take into account when designing and analyzing the results of all pharmaceutical, biomedical, and health research. No longer should men be considered "the norm." We need basic research to study the fundamental anatomical, physiological, and genetic differences between men and women. We must also develop a more nuanced understanding of the neurobiology of pain. Do our pain responses vary during childhood or adolescence? When do our differences begin to manifest themselves and how do they affect aging? And how do genetic differences, hormones, and/or past experiences shape our reactions to pain?

Clinical research also requires a healthy infusion of gender awareness, even if it's expensive or complicated to do so. There are many questions to answer: Why do some illnesses disproportionately affect men or women? And why, even when they have the same disease, do men and women have different symptoms?

We must also consider gender when it comes to treatment. Already, we know that certain types of pain receptors, known as Kappa receptors, are more closely linked to analgesia in women than in men. Now we need to apply that knowledge as we develop better pain medications. As a pain researcher and doctor, I believe that failure to take advantage of gender differences to improve palliative care is tantamount to a cardinal sin.

I'm also excited by advances we are making in understanding and quantifying pain. Pain assessment has always been bedeviled by the lack of objectivity. To a great extent, pain is "in the eye of the beholder." But better means for measuring pain are slowly emerging. For example, functional MRIs and other imaging studies help us see what's actually going on in the brain when someone is in pain.

Advances in molecular biology are allowing us to study pain at the level of the gene. Pain researchers are working to define which of our genes are involved in transmitting and controlling pain messages and whether specific mutations are associated with pain conditions. We are also learning about the mechanisms of pain, both our "pain wiring" and the chemical pain mediators, such as serotonin, substance P, and nerve growth factor, that affect how we feel, transmit, and respond to pain. This work is crucially important because it will help us develop innovative therapies, such as "designer drugs," tailored to our individual needs.

Meanwhile, our conventional arsenal for pain relief is growing rapidly. The new Cox-2 inhibitor medications relieve pain without the side effects of older non-steroidal anti-inflammatory drugs (NSAIDS). We are just beginning to see that these drugs may also decrease the risk of colorectal cancer. More powerful Cox-2 drugs are in the pipeline. And we've also learned how to use other drugs, such as antidepressants and anticonvulsants, to treat severe chronic pain.

But the new, exciting paradigm of pain management that is on the horizon encompasses far more than state-of-the-art pharmaceuticals and biomedical technology. It also pays homage to the richness and bounty of ancient healing traditions and respects the profound benefits we can reap from complementary medicine.

Spearheaded by the National Center for Complementary and Alternative Medicine, we will learn how complementary therapies work. Are central and peripheral nervous system receptors activated during acupuncture and acupressure? Is magnet therapy a useful treatment or is it bogus? What role does prayer and spirituality play in pain treatment? Through basic science, we will begin to unlock the tangled relationship between mind and body. Just what happens during hypnosis and biofeedback, or when you breathe in the essential oil of, say, lavender? Perhaps we will learn to harness the power of one of the great medical mysteries—the placebo effect.

Even without understanding their mechanisms, we are amassing a substantial body of literature about when, and for what ailments, complementary therapies work. Already, growing numbers of academic medical centers and hospitals have embraced some complementary treatments. I am confident that in the near future, nutrition will also be recognized as a critical component of pain modulation. Throughout this book, I've tried to include some of the latest thinking on how vitamins, minerals, and other nutrients influence pain and inflammation.

I also believe that major pharmaceutical houses will, more and more, look toward botanicals to find treatments for pain. This will be driven not only by public demand and a burgeoning interest in going back to the basics, but because these natural compounds work. At the same time, the manufacture of herbal medicines will change from a cottage industry to a more advanced quasi-pharmaceutical enterprise. My hope is that an increasing level of scrutiny from federal authorities and improved industry standards of purity and composition will bring herbal remedies into the legitimate limelight in this country, as they are in much of Europe.

But why not get the best of both worlds? When we combine new medical technologies with complementary approaches, such as mind-body research, we can develop therapies that positively leap into the future. For example, psychologists are exploring clinical applications for virtual reality (VR), or interactive artificial worlds created by computers. This astounding treatment is already being used to treat agonizing pain, phobias, posttraumatic stress disorder, and eating disorders.

As we begin the twenty-first century, I am enormously excited and optimistic about the revolution in pain management. Ironically, though, to take full advantage of these new frontiers, we have to pay much more attention to something that goes back to the beginning of time—the difference between men and women.

# REFERENCES

(A complete list of references, by chapter, can be found on Womenandpain.com)

Armitage, K. J., Schneiderman, L. J., Bass, R. A. 1979. *JAMA* 241(20), May 18: 2186–2187.

Bendelow, Gillian. 2000. *Pain and Gender.* Prentice Hall Publishers.

Bendich, A., and Deckelbaum, R. J. 2000. *Nutrition: Primary and Secondary Prevention.* Humana Press.

Berkley, Karen J. 1997. "Sex Differences in Pain." *Behavioral and Brain Sciences* 20(3): 371–380.

Berman, B. M., and Swyers, J. P. 1997. "Establishing a Research Agenda for Investigating Alternative Medical Interventions for Chronic Pain." *Primary Care* 24: 4, 743–758.

Blumenthal, M., et al. 1998. *The Complete German Commission E Monographs: Therapeutic Guide to Herbal Medicines.* Integrative Medicine Communications.

Braddom, R. L. 2000. *Physical Medicine and Rehabilitation,* 2nd ed. W. B. Saunders Company.

Calderone, Karen L. 1990. "The Influence of Gender on the Frequency of Pain and Sedative Medication Administered to Postoperative Patients." *Sex Roles* 23: 11–12.

Campbell, J. N. 2001. "Women and Treatment of Pain." *Journal of Women's Health & Gender-Based Medicine* 10, No. 4, May.

Cleeland, C. S., Gonin, R., Hatfield, A. K., Edmondson, J. H., Blum, R. H., et al. 1994. "Pain and Its Treatment in Outpatients with Metastatic Cancer." *New England Journal of Medicine* 330: 592–596.

DeLisa, J. A., Gans, B. A., and Bockenek, W. *Rehabilitation Medicine: Principles and Practice*. Lippincott, Williams & Wilkins.

Eisenberg, D. M., et al. 1998. "Trends in Alternative Medicine Use in the USA." *JAMA* 280(18), November 11: 1569–1575.

"Exploring the Biological Contributions to Human Health: Does Sex Matter?" Institute of Medicine Report, 2001.

"FDA Approval Process Still Not Catching Risks of Prescription Drugs to Women." 2001. Reuters Health, February 8.

Feine, Jocelyne S., et al. 1991. "Sex Differences in the Perception of Noxious Heat Stimuli." *Pain* 44: 255–262.

Fillingim, Roger B. *Sex, Gender, and Pain: Progress in Pain Research and Management*, Volume 17. International Association for the Study of Pain (IASP Press).

Fishbain, David A., et al. 1986. "Male and Female Chronic Pain Patients Categorized by DSM-III Psychiatric Diagnostic Criteria." *Pain* 26: 181–197.

Gear, R. W., Miaskowski, C., Gordon, N. C., et al. 1996. "Kappa-opioids Produce Significantly Greater Analgesia in Woman Than Men." *Nature Medicine* 2: 1248–1250.

——. 1999. "The Kappa-opioid Nalbuphine Produces Gender and Dose Dependent Analgesia and Antianalgesia in Patients with Postoperative Pain." *Pain* 83(2): 339–345.

Giamberardino, M. A., and Berkley, K. J. 1997. "Pain Threshold Variations." *Pain* 71: 187–197.

Gnatz, S. M., and Childers, M. 2000. "Acute Pain." In *Physical Medicine & Rehabilitation* by Grabois M., Garrison, et al. Blackwell Science, pp. 1001–1015.

Greeberger, P. 2001. "Women, Men, and Pain." *Journal of Women's Health & Gender-Based Medicine* 10, May 4.

Gruenwald, J., Brendler, T., and Jaenicke, C. 2001. *PDR for Herbal Medicines* 2001. Medical Economics Company.

Haythornthwaite, J. A., Menefee, I. A., Heinberg, I. J., and Clark, M. R. 1998. "Pain Coping Strategies Predict Perceived Control Over Pain." *Pain* 771(1): 33–39.

Helms, J. M. 1997. *Acupuncture Energetics: A Clinical Approach for Physicians*. Medical Acupuncture Publishers.

Hohmann, A. A. 1989. "Gender Bias in Psychotropic Drug Prescribing in Primary Care." *Med Care* 27(5), May: 478–490.

Komisaruk, B. R., and Whipple, B. 1995. "The Suppression of Pain by Genital Stimulation in Females." *Annals of Review of Sexual Research* 6: 151–186.

Lamberg, Lynne. 1998. "Venus Orbits Closer to Pain Than Mars, Rx for One Sex May Not Benefit the Other." [Medical News & Perspectives] *JAMA* 280(2), July 8: 120–124.

LaResche, L. 1995. "Gender Differences in Pain: Epidemiological Perspectives." *Pain Forum* 4: 228–230.

Legato, M. J. 2000. "Is There a Role for Gender Specific Medicine in Today's Health Care System?" *Journal of Gender-Specific Medicine* 3, Issue 3, April: 12–21.

Loeser, ed. *Bonica's Management of Pain*, 3rd ed. 2001. Lippincott, Williams, & Wilkins.

McDonald, D. 1994. "Gender and Ethnic Stereotyping and Narcotic Analgesic Administration." *Research in Nursing & Health* 17: 45–49.

McDonald, D., and Bridge, R. G. 1991. "Gender Stereotyping and Nursing Care." *Research in Nursing & Health* 14: 373–378.

Melzack, R., and Wall, P. D. 1965. "Pain Mechanisms: A New Theory." *Science* 150(699), November 19: 971–979.

Merkatz, R. B., Temple, R., Subel, S., Fieden, K., Kessler, D. A. 1993. "Women in Clinical Trials of New Drugs: The Working Group of Women in Trials." *New England Journal of Medicine* 329: 292–296.

Miaskowski, C. 1997. "Women and Pain." *Critical Care Nursing Clinics of North America* 9(4): 453–458.

Miaskowski, C., Levine, J. D. 1999. "Does Opioid Analgesia Show a Gender Preference for Females?" *Pain Forum* 8(1): 34–44.

Mogil, J. S., Yu, L., Basbaum, A. J. 2000. "Pain Genes?: Natural Variations and Transgenic Mutants." *Annu Rev Neurosci* 23: 777–811.

Myles, P. S., McLeod, A. D., Hunt, J. O., Fletcher, H. 2001. "Sex Differences in Speed of Emergence and Quality of Recovery after Anaesthesia: Cohort Study." *BMJ* 322(7288), March 24: 710–711.

National Institute of Health Conference/NIH Pain Research Consortium. 1998. "Gender and Pain: A Focus on How Pain Impacts Women Differently Than Men." Bethesda, Maryland, April 7–8.

"Nociceptors and Pain." 1995. *Brain Briefings*. Society for Neuroscience, Winter.

O'Young, B. J., Young, M. A., Stiens, S. A. 1995. *PM&R Secrets*, 1st ed. Hanley & Belfus Publishers.

Pardue, M. I., and Magasanik, B. 2001. "Exploring the Biological Contributions to Human Health: Does Sex Matter?" Institute of Medicine Report Preface.

Pasternak, G. W. 1993. "Pharmacological Mechanisms of Opioid Analgesics." *Clinical Neuropharmacology* 16: 1–18.

Patil, J., Guarino, A., and Staats, P. 2001. "Chronic Pain." In *PM&R Secrets*, 2nd ed., ed. O'Young, B. J., Young, M. A., Stiens, S. A. Hanley & Belfus Publishers.

Pear, Robert. 2000. "Research Neglects Women, Studies Find; Reports Say Health Trials Often Disregard Differences in the Sexes." *New York Times*, April 29.

——. 2001. "Sex Differences Called Key in Medical Studies." *New York Times*, April 25.

Peyron, J. G., Altman, R. D. 1992. "The Epidemiology of Osteoarthritis." In Moskowitz, R. W., Howell, D. S., et al., eds. *Osteoarthritis, Diagnosis and Medical/ Surgical Management*, 2nd ed. W. B. Saunders, Inc., pp. 15–37.

Reisine, T., Pasternak, G. 1996. "Opioid Analgesics and Antagonists." In Hardman, J. G., Limbard, L. E., eds., Goodman and Gilman's *The Pharmacological Basis of Therapeutics*, 9th ed. McGraw-Hill, pp. 521–555.

Rubin, Rita. 2001. "Researchers Urged to Consider Gender." *USA Today*, April 25.

Ruda, M. A. 1993. "Gender and Pain." *Pain* 53: 1–2.

Sarton, E., Olofsen, E., Romberg, R., den Hartigh, J., Kest, B., Nieuwenhuijs, D., Burm, A., Teppema, L., Dahan, A. 2000. "Sex Differences in Morphine Analgesia: An Experimental Study in Healthy Volunteers." *Anesthesiology* 93(5), November: 1245–1254.

Sheiner, E. K., Sheiner, E., Shoham-Vardi, J., Mazor, M., Katz, M. 1999. "Ethnic Differences Influence Care Giver's Estimates of Pain During Labour." *Pain* 81(3), June: 299–305.

Simoni-Wastila, L. 1998. "Gender and Psychotropic Drug Use." *Med Care* 36(1), January: 88–94.

Stretcher, R. M. 1975. "Heberden's Nodes: A Clinical Description of Osteoarthritis of the Finger Joint." *Annals of Rheumatic Disease* 34: 379–387.

Turk, D. C., and Okifuzi, A. 1998. "Does Sex Make a Difference in Chronic Pain?" *Pain* 82: 127–138.

Unruh, A. M. 1996. "Gender Variations in Clinical Pain Experience." *Pain* 65: 123–167.

Walker, J. S., and Carmody, J. J. 1998. "Experimental Pain in Healthy Human Subjects: Gender Differences in Nociception and in Response to Ibuprofen." *Anesth Analg* 86(6), June: 1257–1262.

Wesselman, U. 1998. "Gender Differences in Chronic Pain Syndromes of the Reproductive Organs." National Institute of Health Gender and Pain Conference, April.

Young, M. A. 2001. "Acupuncture in Headache: A Critical Review." *The Integrative Medicine Consult*, April.

Young, M. A., and Lavin, R. 1995a. *Conservative Care and Spinal Rehabilitation.* Hanley and Belfus Publishers.

———. 1995b. *Spinal Rehabilitation: State of the Art Review.* Hanley and Belfus Publishers.

Zborowski, M. 1969. *People in Pain.* Jossey-Bass.

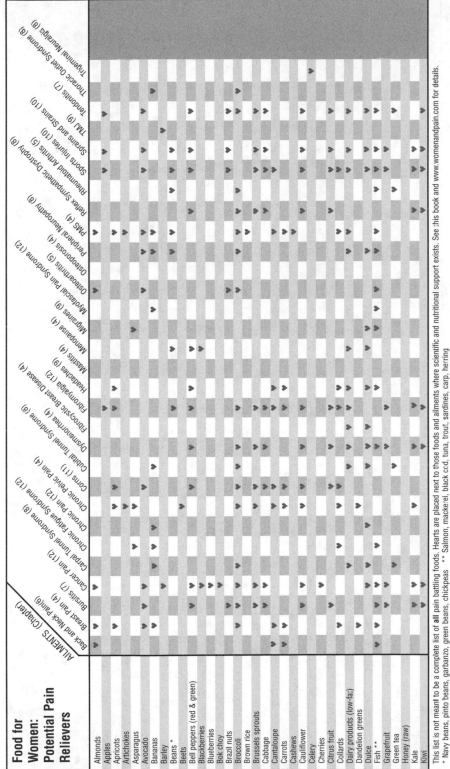

# Food for Women: Potential Pain Relievers

**AILMENTS (Chapter):**

- Back and Neck Pain(?)
- Breast Pain (4)
- Bursitis (7)
- Cancer Pain (12)
- Carpal Tunnel Syndrome (8)
- Chronic Fatigue Syndrome (8)
- Chronic Pain (12)
- Chronic Pelvic Pain (4)
- Corns (11)
- Cubital Tunnel Syndrome (8)
- Dysmenorrhea (4)
- Fibrocystic Breast Disease (4)
- Fibromyalgia (12)
- Headaches (9)
- Mastitis (4)
- Menopause (4)
- Migraines (9)
- Myofascial Pain Syndrome (12)
- Osteoarthritis (5)
- Osteoporosis (4)
- Peripheral Neuropathy (8)
- PMS (4)
- Reflex Sympathetic Dystrophy (8)
- Rheumatoid Arthritis (5)
- Sports Injuries (10)
- Sprains and Strains (10)
- TMJ (9)
- Tendonitis (7)
- Thoracic Outlet Syndrome (8)
- Trigeminal Neuralgia (8)

**Foods:**

Almonds, Apples, Apricots, Artichokes, Asparagus, Avocado, Bananas, Barley, Beans *, Beets, Bell peppers (red & green), Blackberries, Blueberries, Bok choy, Brazil nuts, Broccoli, Brown rice, Brussels sprouts, Cabbage, Cantaloupe, Carrots, Cashews, Cauliflower, Celery, Cherries, Citrus fruit, Collards, Dairy products (low-fat), Dandelion greens, Dulse, Fish **, Grapefruit, Green tea, Honey (raw), Kale, Kiwi

This list is not meant to be a complete list of **all** pain battling foods. Hearts are placed next to those foods and ailments where scientific and nutritional support exists. See this book and www.womenandpain.com for details.

* Navy beans, pinto beans, garbanzo, green beans, chickpeas    ** Salmon, mackerel, black cod, tuna, trout, sardines, carp, herring

# Food for Women: Potential Pain Relievers (cont'd)

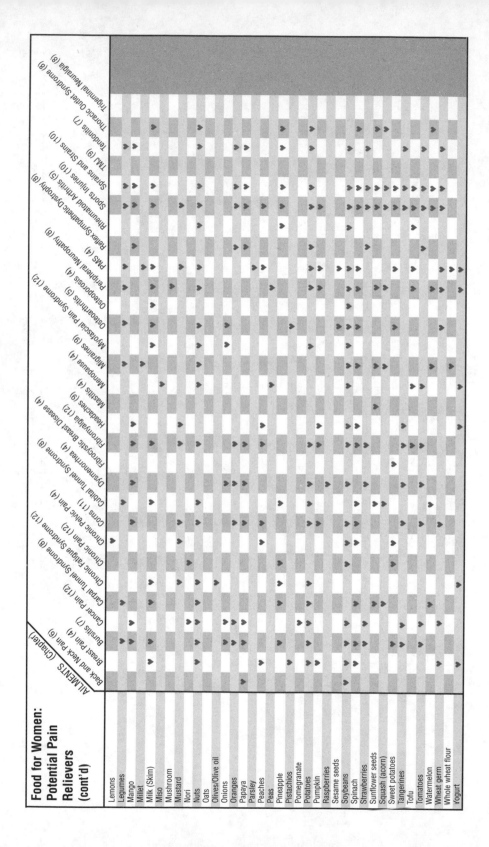

**AILMENTS (Chapter):** Back and Neck Pain (6); Breast Pain (6); Bursitis (7); Cancer Pain (12); Carpal Tunnel Syndrome (8); Chronic Fatigue Syndrome (8); Chronic Pain (12); Chronic Pelvic Pain (4); Corns (11); Cubital Tunnel Syndrome (8); Dysmenorrhea (4); Fibrocystic Breast Disease (4); Fibromyalgia (12); Headaches (9); Mastitis (4); Menopause (4); Migraines (9); Myofascial Pain Syndrome (12); Osteoarthritis (5); Osteoporosis (4); Peripheral Neuropathy (8); PMS (4); Reflex Sympathetic Dystrophy (8); Rheumatoid Arthritis (5); Sports Injuries (10); Sprains and Strains (10); TMJ (9); Tendonitis (7); Thoracic Outlet Syndrome (8); Trigeminal Neuralgia (9)

Foods listed: Lemons, Legumes, Mango, Millet, Milk (Skim), Miso, Mushroom, Mustard, Nori, Nuts, Oats, Olives/Olive oil, Onions, Oranges, Papaya, Parsley, Peaches, Peas, Pineapple, Pistachios, Pomegranate, Potatoes, Pumpkin, Raspberries, Sesame seeds, Soybeans, Spinach, Strawberries, Sunflower seeds, Squash (acorn), Sweet potatoes, Tangerines, Tofu, Tomatoes, Watermelon, Wheat germ, Whole wheat flour, Yogurt

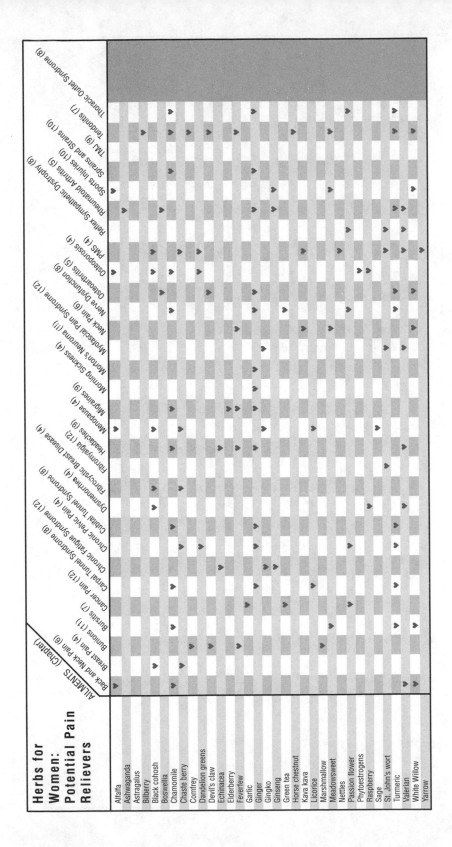

# Herbs for Women: Potential Pain Relievers

# Vitamins, Minerals and Supplements for Women: Potential Pain Relievers

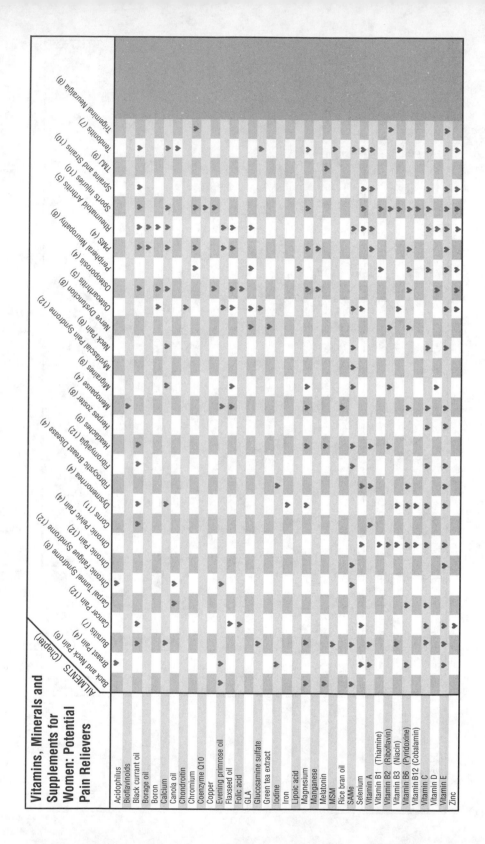